# WORLD RELIGIONS

## EASTERN TRADITIONS



EDITED BY
WILLARD G. OXTO

OXFORD UNIVERSITY PRESS
TORONTO NEW YORK OXFORD

Oxford University Press
70 Wynford Drive, Don Mills, Ontario M3C 1J9

Oxford New York
Athens Auckland Bangkok Bombay
Calcutta Cape Town Dar es Salaam Delhi
Florence Hong Kong Istanbul Karachi
Kuala Lumpur Madras Madrid Melbourne
Mexico City Nairobi Paris Singapore
Taipei Tokyo Toronto

and associated companies in
Berlin Ibadan



**Canadian Cataloguing in Publication Data**

Main entry under title:

World religions: eastern traditions

Includes bibliographical references and index.
ISBN 0-19-540750-4

1. Religions. I. Oxtoby, Willard G. (Willard Gurdon), 1933– .

BL80.2.W67 1996 291 C95-933183-2

Editor: Valerie Ahwee

Designer: Brett Miller

Maps: Visutronx



4 5 6 — 00 99 98 97

This book is printed on permanent (acid-free) paper ∞

Printed in Canada

# Contents

# List of Photographs

# List of Figures

# A Personal Invitation

Willard G. Oxtoby

Once upon a time, many in the West regarded religion as a kind of cultural fossil. Aesthetically rich, anthropologically intriguing? Yes. But relevant to today's hard-nosed world of business and politics? Hardly at all. When I said that I studied religion, I used to be asked why I was wasting my life on something that had so little to do with where today's action is.

Nobody has asked me that question since 1979. In that year, the Shah of Iran was deposed in an Islamic revolution. A nation of 40 million people was apparently ready to make phenomenal sacrifices, putting people's lives and livelihoods on the line, to defend the values voiced by their religious leaders. Such values seemed utterly alien to those of development economists and politico-military strategists in the West. And not only in Iran but elsewhere, Muslims were saying no to the modern West. In increasing numbers, men from Algeria to Zanzibar started to wear turbans and grow beards, and more Muslim women on several continents began to wear head scarves.

To understand the modern world, we now realize, we need to take into account the meanings that its traditional religions have for their adherents.

Another breathtaking year was 1989, when the communist order of eastern Europe and the Soviet Union began to crumble. That year there were high hopes for democracy, peace, and progress. But experience soon showed that when the restraints of the socialist order were loosened, old passions and identities resurfaced—passions that one might have expected to die out. Feuds and divisions of populations in the Balkans, the Caucasus, and Central Asia erupted into bitter conflict. As often as not, these struggles had old religio-ethnic roots.

In the secular intellectual climate of the modern world, some philosophers and even theologians have asserted that God is dead. In the practical ethno-political climate of the modern world, however, religion is very much alive.

# THE INVITATION

We invite you to share our fascination with religion. We do not see our mandate as making you either more religious or less religious. Rather, we want you to be better informed *about* religion—regardless of your own investment in any of its particular forms.

Evaluations of religion range all the way from enthusiastic praise to bitter condemnation. Religion has been considered by some as the loftiest, most profound expression of the human spirit. By others, it has been termed a blight on civilization, responsible for superstition, ignorance, hatred, repression, even genocide. There is a selection of evidence to support either extreme, since the history of religion displays a mix of spectacular success and abject failure.

Many who support a positive view of religion regard all or most of the religious traditions as having more or less equal value. Religions promote ideas of order and purpose in the universe, and motivations for order and benevolence in society. Some who hold a largely positive view of religion would go further and assert that the religious traditions are actually saying the same essential thing. If you find such a view tempting, we invite you to become more fully informed about the actual detail of the world's religious traditions, in their diversity and variety, so that you can advocate your position in a sophisticated rather than a naïve fashion.

Many in the modern world are disinclined to identify with any traditional religion. Some do so because they regard their own attitudes towards purpose and value in the universe as a private matter; they find no circle or group congenial for the expression of such an outlook in ritualized and traditional form. Others are appalled at the actions of human societies that consider themselves religious while perpetuating misery, plundering, and butchering in the name of God.

The positive and the negative assessments of religion we have just sketched are both characteristically modern. Both types have come to the fore in Western civilization in the last 300 years. Both types take humanity as the common denominator of the various religions—as a measure of their achievement and sometimes also as an explanation of their nature and function.

But prior to the modern era, another kind of view was dominant in the West: one that differentiated between the positive and the negative in religion by distinguishing between one's own and others'. People over the centuries have seen their own way as truth and others' as error. A powerful influence of that type of view continues today, especially among religiously committed people. For very many, some aspects of religion, namely the faith and practice commanded by one's own tradition, are desirable, while the faith and practice of others is at best a waste of time and possibly downright damaging.

Comparisons are odious, we are told, and comparison of religions may be among the more odious of activities. Yet it is an irresistible human impulse to compare. Are there any guidelines?

One thing our observations may bear out is that evaluations of religions need to have a uniform standard. Achievements should be compared with achievements, and ideals compared with ideals. Religion's critics have concentrated on its poor achievement record. Its enthusiasts have often seen only its ideals. Apologists for particular religions have often praised their own tradition's ideals while denouncing others' poor achievement.

We tend to notice what we were looking for in the first place. Those who seek contentiousness in religion will find it in ample measure; and those who seek generosity of spirit may well for their part be pleasantly surprised at how much of it can be seen.

## Insider and Outsider

One of the abiding issues in the academic study of religion is the conscious role of the observer. Being 'objective' is a value we are taught early in schools. Theorists today tell us that objectivity as a goal is in principle impossible. Some even say that there is no such thing as objective truth; there are only people's status-related and class-determined interests.

We should recognize that every attempt at a historical account is a selection of material, and in that sense is an interpretation. Even if it were theoretically possible to describe something 'objectively', the choice to describe that thing and not something else can hardly be justified as objective.

The study of religion wrestles perpetually with the contrast of 'insider' and 'outsider' perspectives.

The religious participant can presumably speak from first-hand experience. One of the most famous formulations of a view of this type was stated by the German theologian and philosopher of religion Rudolf Otto, in the opening of his 1917 book known in English as *The Idea of the Holy*:

> The reader is invited to direct his mind to a moment of deeply-felt religious experience, as little as possible qualified by other forms of consciousness. Whoever cannot do this, whoever knows no such moments in his experience, is requested to read no farther; for it is not easy to discuss questions of religious psychology with one who can recollect the emotions of his adolescence, the discomforts of indigestion, or, say, social feelings, but cannot recall any intrinsically religious feelings (Otto 1923:8).

For more than two generations since Otto wrote those words, the argument has often been made that there is no substitute in religion for the faith of the adherent. Often, however, the discussion has confused information and analysis. Testimony is one thing, and cross-examination is another. A participant may, but also may not, be able to identify the assumptions on which a tradition rests, or the major transitions it has undergone. A participant may, but also may not, be able to describe fairly a variety of interpretations of the tradition offered by different sectors of the community.

At an opposite pole from Otto is the view that the only hope for scholarly credibility is to be found in the outsider's 'objective' detachment from religion and its claims. Stated in the extreme, one has lost that credibility if one even says a kind word about religion. Indeed, among scholars of religion are quite a few who have become profoundly alienated from the faith communities in which they were raised. And in the study of the major traditions of Asia, many significant findings have been achieved by outsiders—Westerners—some of whose pioneer figures did not even set foot in the lands about which they wrote. An outsider may not, but also may, have something important and useful to say about a religious tradition.

The insider-outsider question can be framed in terms of individual scholars' and students' attitudes, but we can also situate it in the context of institutional accountability. In the Middle Ages, theology was the 'queen of the sciences' in European universities, many of which had Christian church connections. In eighteenth- and nineteenth-century North America, a link with some ecclesiastical body continued to be characteristic of many colleges and universities.

The secularization of older institutions and the founding of new secular ones has meant an emerging distinction throughout the Western world between religiously sponsored and secularly sponsored efforts. Often what religious groups support in the study of their own traditions is now referred to as 'theological' activity, and the work of publicly funded institutions is termed 'scientific' study. But, in fact, there is a considerable overlap of scholarly findings among persons working in these two types of institutions, and scholars have worked in both types, sometimes simultaneously.

As a result, 'religious' versus 'secular' study of religion is a distinction that is much easier to draw when one compares institutions and their support than it is when one considers what individual authorities have to say. Many of us, particularly in historical studies, have become semispectators of our own traditions at the same time as we continue to identify with and participate in them. The contact of religions and the comparison of religions has resulted in our adopting a perspective of disciplined description—science?—towards our own tradition that is like what we use to handle others'. At the same time, we have come to extend towards the traditions of others some of the sympathy or empathy—theology?—that religiously committed people have classically claimed for their own.

In this text, our authors speak in some sense for their identities. Vasudha

Narayanan is Hindu, Roy Amore identifies as a Buddhist, and Julia Ching's Chinese family has numbered Confucians, Buddhists, Muslims, Christians, and Marxists among its members. None of the book's team is a Sikh, a Jain, or a follower of Shinto. But we hope that in all our descriptions we have been able to walk the tightrope of disciplined empathy without falling into the abyss—of advocacy on the one side, and of debunking on the other.

## East and West

If one is to separate an Eastern group of religious traditions from a Western one, where and how does one draw the line? Borderlines, arbitrary or otherwise, produce borderline cases. To use the pigeonholes we create, we have to cut some birds in half.

Our list puts Islam with Christianity and Judaism as a 'Western' religion. The Hindu, Jain, Buddhist, Chinese, and Japanese traditions, by contrast, make up the 'Eastern' roster. This leaves the Sikhs (whom we treat in the Eastern volume) and the Zoroastrians (discussed in the Western) very appropriately perched as fence-sitters along our provisional cultural boundary.

As a concept, 'the East' makes sense at least to Europeans. Well into the twentieth century, the East was everything to the east of Europe. The Orient began where the Orient Express ran: Istanbul. For some purposes, it even included North Africa and began with Morocco.

A century ago, Islam was thought to be an Eastern religion, and Westerners who studied it were called orientalists. To us today, calling Islam Eastern seems misleading if not absurd. Islam shares its historical and theological roots with Judaism and Christianity, and developed virtually all its classic structures in the Mediterranean and Persian-speaking world. Scholars today regard Islam a religion of the West, even though the numerical majority of Muslims today live east of that world: in the Indian subcontinent, Malaysia, and Indonesia. When it comes to these lands, the boundary between East and West is blurred at best.

Some have contended that the Western religions are united by the notion of prophetic and scriptural revelation from their one God, while the Eastern religions share a focus on the achievement of reflective human insight by a wise teacher or sage.

Prophecy is a kind of religious communication where someone claims (or is claimed) to transmit a message from a divine source. The message is the word of God, whether dictated verbatim by the deity or formulated in language by the human prophet. The prophet proclaims, 'thus says the Lord'. This characterizes much of the most important insight in the religious traditions that have prevailed in our Western group.

Meanwhile, in the case of wisdom, insight is achieved by an individual through his or her own reflection. What is apprehended may be presented as an eternal or cosmic divine truth, but the sage's testimony is, 'I have meditated and reflected, and this insight has come to me.'

Such a classification has been used by a landmark work in the field. The Oxford scholar R.C. Zaehner (1913–74) employed it in 1959 when editing *The Concise Encyclopedia of Living Faiths*—actually not an alphabetically arranged reference work, as its title would suggest, but an advanced introductory survey. His two major divisions within the volume were 'Prophecy' and 'Wisdom'.

There are enough grains of truth in the prophecy-wisdom contrast to make it a useful topic for comparison and review *after* one has studied the individual traditions in the specific detail of their development and teachings, but it can be misleading if adopted beforehand and allowed to structure one's observations. For there are wisdom traditions in the West mixed in with the prophetic ones, and there are notions of revelation and scriptural authority here and there in the East.

We can speak in a fairly coherent fashion about the West and its role in the world. Since the end of the fifteenth century, European (subsequently Euro-American) civilization has achieved world dominance. This civilization's science and technology have spread worldwide, as have its political and philosophical traditions. Its dominant religion, Christianity, has been carried to the 'four corners' of the globe. And with Christianity's influence have gone particular notions of what 'religion' is in relation to other spheres of life such as the 'secular', notions not necessarily shared by the indigenous cultures of those lands.

But the East, for its part, is a hugely diverse region, with an inventory of cultural differences between southern and eastern Asia that could fill volumes. At the level of daily custom is the fact, for instance, that a billion people in China take their baths in the evening, while nearly a billion in India bathe in the morning. Or again, Japanese are Buddhists, but the Buddha as a historical individual who lived and taught in an Indian environment figures surprisingly little in their understanding and practice of Buddhism.

Does any common thread unify the East? We could even go so far as to suggest that 'the East' is a Western construct, existing as a coherent entity only in the mind of the West. The ancient Chinese, for instance, termed theirs the 'Middle' kingdom, not the Eastern one. In that, they were not unlike Westerners, who named a sea Mediterranean to imply that it was at the middle of their world.

For identifying the Eastern religions as a cohesive family, history and geography offer us a more useful foundation than do contrasts of outlook with the West. Buddhism is probably our best candidate for a common thread, in the following fashion. In India, the aggregate indigenous heritage, which we in modern times term Hinduism, was the milieu in which Buddhism arose and with which Buddhism shares some (but by no means all) of its own outlooks and practices. Carried then to East Asia, Buddhism interacted with the indigenous traditions

**Figure Intro.1**

**DISTRIBUTION OF INDIGENOUS RELIGIONS OF THE INDIAN SUBCONTINENT TODAY: Hindus, Buddhists, Jains, Sikhs**

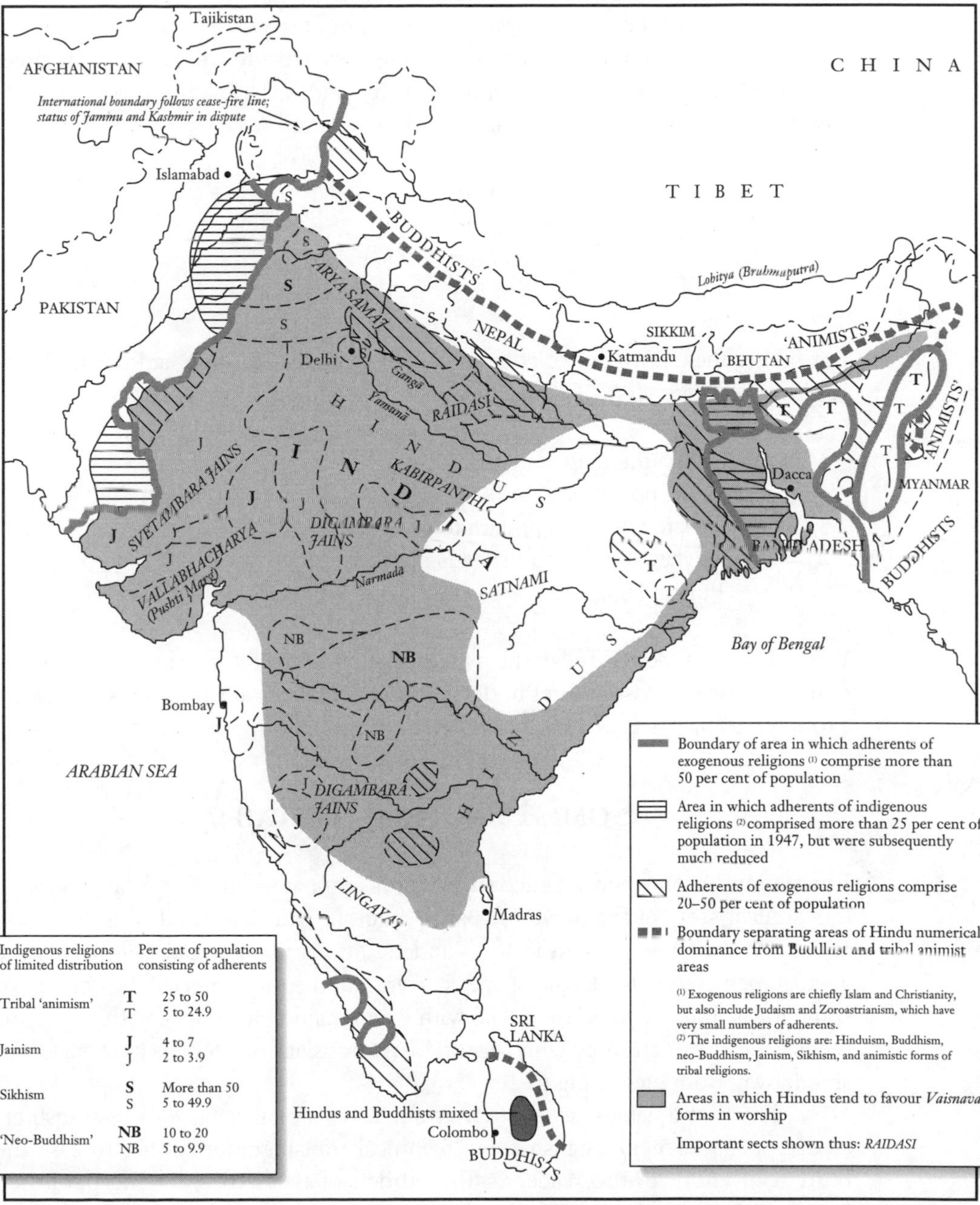


*Source:* I. R. al Fārūqī and D.E. Sopher, eds, *Historical Atlas of the Religions of the World* (New York: Macmillan, 1974):86.

there, which we identify in China as Confucianism and Taoism and in Japan as Shinto. With this perspective, a historical case can be made for seeing the principal Eastern religious traditions as a coherent package.

If we think that any contrast between East and West is overdrawn, we can point to challenges in life that human beings face worldwide. People sometimes quote the 1889 'Ballad of East and West' by Rudyard Kipling (1865–1936) to assert, or to excuse, Westerners' failure to understand Asia:

> Oh, East is East, and West is West
> and never the twain shall meet
> Till Earth and Sky stand presently
> at God's great Judgment Seat.

But taking these lines out of context can reverse what Kipling had in mind. For Kipling continues:

> But there is neither East nor West,
> border, nor breed, nor birth,
> When two strong men stand face to face,
> tho' they come from the ends of the earth!
> (Kipling 1892:75)

If Kipling were active today, he would doubtless call for a human common denominator in cross-cultural understanding. What distant traditions express in exotic vocabularies is often a universal appeal to human experience.

## SOME PRACTICAL DETAILS

Frustration sets in when we encounter words and names in strange languages, as the biblical story of the Tower of Babel suggests. The rich fund of information about religions is expressed in texts and traditions in more languages than the average person can list, let alone speak. Translation equivalents can be chosen for some ideas, but one must soon deal with exotic names, as well as with key terms whose meanings are inevitably distorted in translation. Our authors have not shied away from presenting these.

Terms and names not written in our Latin alphabet have to be transliterated. Some writers in English avoid technical transliteration, either to ease the burden of effort for the reader or the burden of typesetting for the publisher. Some books compromise by burying diacritical marks in indexes, glossaries, and notes, leaving them out of the main text. Non-technical spellings may offer an initial advantage, but they can hinder the reader who wants to move on to a more advanced level. We have therefore chosen to use standard transliterations throughout the text to help the reader become accustomed to their use.

There have been changes in fashion regarding which transliteration system to use, and there will doubtless continue to be changes. We can take as a current benchmark, however, the usage in the sixteen-volume *Encyclopedia of Religion* (Eliade 1987), one of the principal reference resources to which the reader may be inclined to turn. For the languages that are the principal sources of world religions terminology—Arabic, Sanskrit, Chinese, and Japanese—we use the same transliteration systems as the *Encyclopedia of Religion*.

Like the *Encyclopedia*, we have had to take sides on what is the most divisive current transliteration question affecting our material. It regards Chinese in particular. It is the choice between an earlier twentieth-century translation system, known after its originators as the Wade-Giles system, and another, introduced since mid-century, known as Pinyin. A page illustrating the operation of each of these appears in the appendix.

Wade-Giles is used by scholars in humanistic and literary studies and in Chinese-English contacts in Taiwan and Singapore. Pinyin is official in mainland China; consequently, it has been adopted by newspapers covering China as well as by many social scientists. Each of these systems, as we explain, has features that are counterintuitive to native speakers of English. We opt for the Wade-Giles only partly because it provides more direct access to the *Encyclopedia of Religion*. More importantly, it approximates the transliteration system used by the Library of Congress, and therefore provides access to many research materials not likely to be recatalogued in the foreseeable future. But at the first occurrence of a name or term in the Wade-Giles transliteration, we also provide its equivalent in Pinyin if the difference is at all significant.

The reader will find diacritics on foreign terms, which are given as words in lower-case italics. Premodern foreign personal names and a few place names bear diacritics; since they are proper names, they are not italicized, nor are the proper names for holidays. If something is both italicized and capitalized, it is generally the title of a book.

Capitalization poses some problems in its own right. Remember that the distinction between capital and lower-case letters inheres in our alphabet, and not in the scripts of Arabic, Sanskrit, Chinese, or Japanese. Context in these languages may tell you whether something is a word or a name, but not necessarily and not always. Therefore, capitalization is a signal sent by the writer or editor in English, not by the material in a source language.

In the pages of this book, we have tried to use capitalization in a novel way to draw one important distinction in particular. We say 'the Buddha' (roman type, capitalized) when referring to one particular enlightened being, Siddhārtha, also titled Śākyamuni, who lived in India about 2,500 years ago. We say 'the *buddha*' (italics, not capitalized) when referring by role to any one of the myriad celestial figures that various schools of Buddhism believe to manifest enlightenment in past and also future ages. This usage is our own, to avoid ambiguity about which *buddha* figure is being talked about; it should not be understood as a convention endorsed or practised widely by writers on Buddhism.

Italics (or their equivalent, underlining, if one is writing by hand or on equipment where italics are unavailable) make possible a conventional distinction, but one that in this work we have tried to dodge. That is the discrimination, long established in English usage, between scripture and other books. One uses italics, for instance, to give ordinary book titles, for instance, Homer's *Iliad*—but not the Bible nor, conventionally, any part of the Bible. Given this convention, to name a text in English is to be involved in every instance in a forced decision as to whether it is or is not scripture.

Confident that the scripture-versus-other-literature distinction could easily be generalized to the religious literatures of Asia, earlier writers in English have applied it wholesale. Did not the major Asian traditions themselves distinguish between more authoritative and less authoritative texts, between older works and later commentaries on them? Yes and no; the idea of a strictly limited canon hardly works for Taoism, for instance, and Shinto's narratives of Japanese origins are not agreed on as 'scripture' by everybody. And how helpful is it to decide that the Hindu Vedas are canonical, and therefore in roman type, while the *Bhagavad Gītā* is less so, and therefore to be written in italics? Hence, to avoid the arbitrariness of dividing the world's religious literature somewhere down the middle, we have elected to italicize the name of practically every scriptural text simply as a book, rather than privileging with roman type certain texts, including even the *Qur'ān* and individual biblical books.

We do not use the abbreviations BC and AD with calendar dates, however acceptable these may remain in fields outside religion. The expressions BC ('before Christ') and AD (Latin *anno Domini*, 'in the year of our Lord') are taken by some to imply special status and privilege for Christianity. Instead, writers on religion often use BCE and CE (referring to the 'common', not the 'Christian', era). The theological division of history around the birth of Jesus, it can be argued, is a move that belongs to the participant mode of religious discourse and not the mode of the observer.

Likewise problematical but less conventionalized is the handling of religious traditions' revelational, mythological, and hagiographical narratives. Christians assert that Jesus achieved miraculous things, and Buddhists report Śākyamuni's accomplishments—in both cases as historical events, in the past tense. Does the observer 'bracket' every faith-narrative with an expression like 'according to tradition' or 'some Hindus hold'? Scrupulous following of the observer's stance in this fashion can become both cumbersome and intrusive.

The solution we have tried to apply consistently is to use the present tense for reporting all faith-narratives. It is a convention often practised in describing the plot lines of imaginative literature; it is also commonly employed by philosophers to write about the views of particular authors and the structure of their arguments. In both cases, the present tense permits one to enter into the content and spirit of what is being reported without being so immediately distracted by questions of its historical verifiability. Our editorial experience is that present-tense usage renders traditional narratives vivid and accessible simultaneously in the participant mode and the observer mode. We retain the past tense, on the other hand, to describe the changes over time within a tradition that any historian would describe as developments.

Of many other things, large and small, we could speak editorially, but more words of welcome will only delay the use of this book to which all are now invited. As we start, it remains only to render thanks—to the spiritual powers and devoted followers we are to meet, and also to the numerous colleagues and students whose responses and reactions have assisted in this work's preparation.

W.G.O.
Thanksgiving, 1995

## REFERENCES

Eliade, M., ed. 1987. *The Encyclopedia of Religion*. New York: Macmillan.

Kipling, R. 1892. 'The Ballad of East and West'. In *Barrack-room Ballads and Other Verses*, 75–83. London: Methuen.

Otto, R. 1923. *The Idea of the Holy*. London: Oxford University Press.

# Key Dates

| | |
|---|---|
| c. 2700 BCE | Evidence of Indus Valley civilization |
| c. 1500 BCE | Aryan invasion of northern India |
| c. 800 BCE | Collection of oral *Vedas* |
| c. 600 BCE | Production of *Upaniṣads* |
| 326 BCE | Greek armies in India under Alexander |
| c. 272 BCE | Accession of King Aśoka |
| c. 100 BCE | Composition of *Bhagavad Gītā* |
| c. 200 CE | Compilation of *Laws of Manu* completed |
| c. 500 | Beginnings of tantric tradition |
| c. 700 | Āḻvars, Tamil *bhakti* poets |
| c. 800 | Śaṅkara's Advaita Vedānta |
| d. 1137 | Rāmānuja, Vaiṣṇava theistic philosopher |
| 1206 | Mughal sultanate established in Delhi |
| d. 1518 | Kabīr, North Indian *bhakti* poet |
| 1556 | Accession of the emperor Akbar |
| d. 1583 | Caitanya, Bengali Vaiṣṇava *bhakti* leader |
| d. 1623 | Tulsīdās, North Indian *bhakti* poet |
| 1757 | British rule established in Calcutta |
| 1828 | Ram Mohan Roy founds Brāhmo Samāj |
| 1875 | Dayānanda Sarasvatī founds Ārya Samāj |
| 1878 | Theosophist Helena Blavatsky settles in Madras |
| 1893 | Vivekananda at World's Parliament of Religions, Chicago |
| 1914 | Aurobindo founds ashram in Pondicherry |
| 1948 | Assassination of Mohandas Gandhi |
| 1992 | Hindu militants demolish a mosque at Ayodhya |

CHAPTER ONE

# THE HINDU TRADITION

VASUDHA NARAYANAN

## INTRODUCTION

The earliest compositions considered 'revealed' within the Hindu tradition are called *śruti* ('that which was heard'), but those who transmitted the sacred words were called *ṛṣis* ('seers'). This dual emphasis on hearing and seeing what is holy characterizes the Hindu tradition; the sacred is experienced through sound and vision. When Hindus go on a pilgrimage or visit a temple, they go to have a *darśana*. *Darśana* is to see with piety, to behold with faith, and to be seen by the deity or holy teacher (and the Hindu tradition recognizes thousands of deities).

But the Hindus also believe in the importance of uttering or reciting prayers aloud. Chanting from Sanskrit texts in the temple, or recounting in Hindi the story of the god Rāma, or singing the devotional songs of the sixteenth-century woman poet Mīrā, or chanting Sanskrit and vernacular prayers, or meditating on a holy mantra—these are just some of the ways in which people enjoy and experience the sacred words of the Hindu tradition. Through sight and sound the Hindu seeks the sacred and experiences the divine.

It is hard to identify a common denominator in Hinduism. While some texts and some deities are accepted by many, there is no single text, single deity, or single teacher that all Hindus would deem authoritative or supreme. There is a corpus of holy works, and many people hold some of those texts to be revealed and of transhuman origin; but other, non-literate, Hindus may not even have heard of these compositions. Similarly, there are many local deities with local names who may or may not be identified with the more recognizable pan-Indian gods. Hundreds of communities and sectarian movements make up the Hindu tradition, and each community has its own hallowed canon, its own sacred place to which its members make a pilgrimage, and its own deity whom it holds to be absolutely supreme.

## 'Hinduism', a Problematical Term

The absence of a single authoritative text or divine identity can be understood if one keeps in mind that the people of the Indian subcontinent have not considered 'Hinduism' a single entity. The people we call Hindu (about 80 per cent of the people in India, together with their kindred communities overseas) do not have one consistent name for their faith. Although their religion is commonly referred to as 'Hinduism', the term is not a word most Hindus have used for themselves in the past or use with any enthusiasm even now, although the term *Hindutva* ('Hinduness') has received political currency in recent years. Hindus generally describe themselves by their particular caste or community and seldom refer to themselves as 'Hindu'. As an alternative that designates a comprehensive tradition, the term *sanātana dharma* ('eternal faith') has gained some currency in recent centuries. However, that term remains élitist and is applied more to philosophical interpretations of the religion than to the colourful local manifestations of the faith. In many contexts, including this chapter, we use the term 'Hinduism', which makes up in convenience for what it lacks in precision.

### *'Hinduism'*

The term 'Hinduism' is largely a Western construct, a name given by outsiders to the majority religious heritage of the people of the Indian subcontinent. It was given prominence by the British, who became the dominant colonial power in India in the eighteenth and nineteenth centuries. To them, 'Hinduism' meant the religion of the Indian population, except for the Muslims. (A few smaller groups, such as the Jains, Parsis, Christians, Jews, and sometimes the Sikhs, possessed sufficiently recognizable identities that their faith likewise often escaped being swept up into the category of 'Hinduism'.) As a term for religious identity, the term 'Hinduism' caught on during the nineteenth century. The student who wishes to look for the term in books printed earlier is unlikely to find it.

### *'Hindu'*

Behind the history of 'Hinduism' as a name for a religious faith lies the history of 'Hindu' as the name for a people. This term, too, derives from an outsider's perspective—in this case, the medieval Muslims. This usage, which the British encountered on arrival in India, had been established among the North Indian Muslim ruling élites. These rulers came to India mainly from Iran and contributed a sizeable inventory of Persian words to the North Indian vernacular we know as Hindi. For them, 'Hindu' meant 'Indian'. After the fourteenth century, it also meant 'non-Muslim'. As late as the nineteenth century, this part of the subcontinent was accordingly known as Hindustan, meaning 'the land of the Indians' in Persian and related languages. So over time, people in the Indian subcontinent—of various faiths—were called Hindu.

**Figure 1.1**
**HINDUISM**

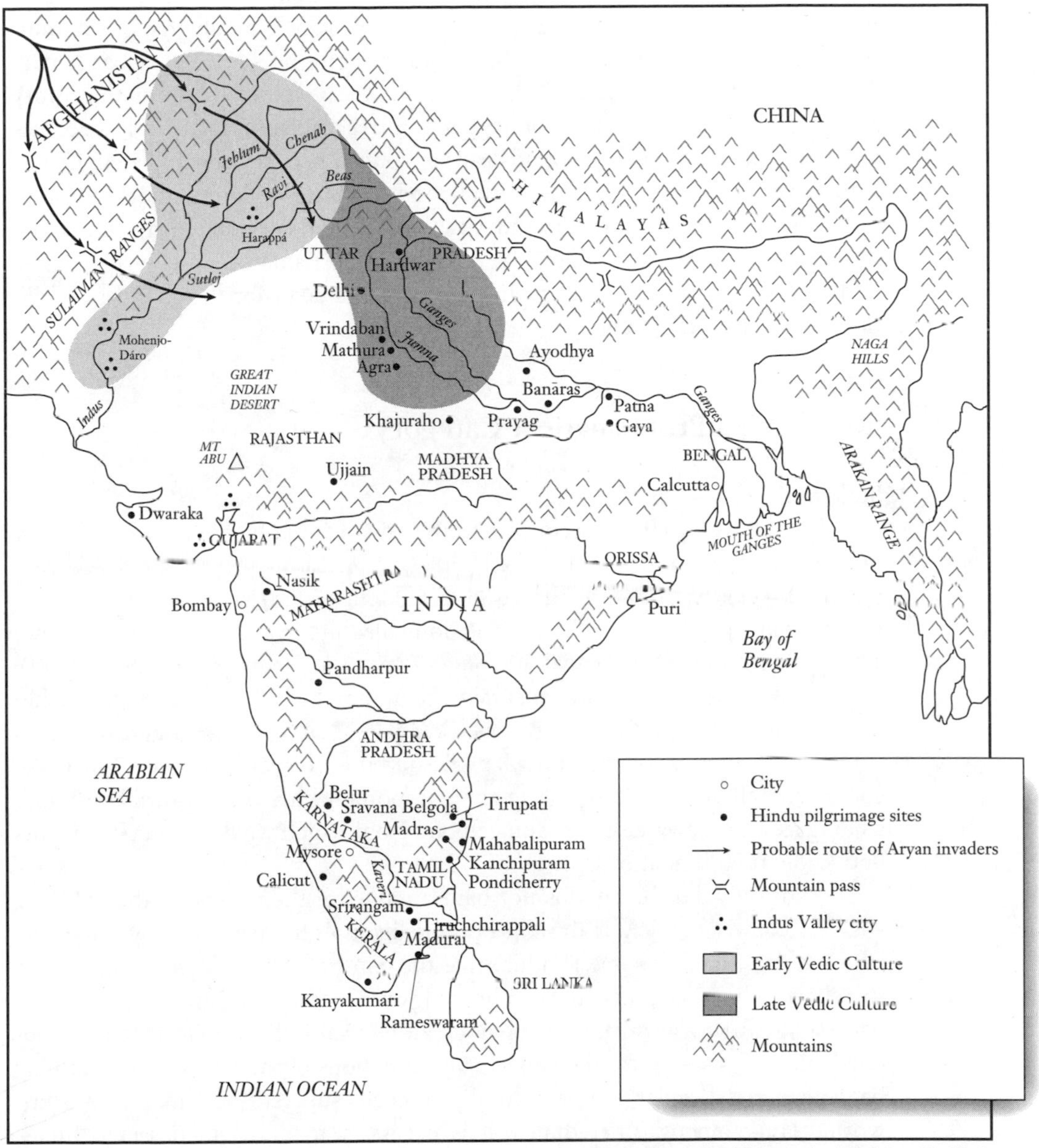


*Source*: Adapted from N.C. Nielsen et al., eds, *Religions of the World*, 3rd ed. (New York: St Martin's Press, 1993):85.

### *'India'*

'India' as the name for an entire subcontinent was also the contribution of outsiders. In this case, it was the Greeks before Islam who generalized 'Sind', the name for the region of the river Sindhu (Indus) in the northwest of the subcontinent, into the name that comes to us as India.

What the Greeks did was to name the larger region by the local name of the part of it where they first arrived. (A similar example is 'Canada', originally the name of a region along the St Lawrence River, but eventually that of a dominion extending 'from sea to sea', as the Canadian motto puts it.) The Achaemenian Persians' territorial conquests extended to Sind in the middle of the sixth century BCE. In their texts, by a process of linguistic correspondence, the initial *s* becomes *h*: Hind. (This same shift of sounds can be noticed between *soma*, the elixir consumed by priests in the Vedic ritual, and its Iranian counterpart *haoma* in Zoroastrianism.) Then, as Alexander with his Greek-speaking army conquered the Persian Empire in the fourth century BCE, the name of Hind turned up as 'India' in Greek, which, lacking an alphabetic character for the sound of *h*, did not in this case preserve it.

## 'Religion', a Problematical Category

### *'Religion'*

The definition of a Hindu according to the law of India highlights the difficulty of determining who is a Hindu. The Hindu Family Act says that it applies to anyone who belongs to one of the Hindu 'denominations', such as Vīra Śaiva or Brāhmo Samāj and 'to any other person domiciled in the territories to which [the] act extends who is *not a Muslim, Christian, Parsi or Jew by religion*' (italics added).

Just as the law does, we must take account of the lack of fundamental cohesion and recognize that there is no overriding single holy book, dogma, religious leader, or authority for the entire Hindu tradition. Nevertheless, we can make some generalizations and delineate some important lines of historical continuity as long as we are aware of the vantage point from which we make our statements and know their limitations.

Not only did the Hindus not have a name for their religion; they did not even have a word to denote the concept of religion. It has been held by some outside scholars (and by some Hindus) that the Sanskrit word *dharma* comes close to 'religion', but this holds only in a limited way. *Dharma* for Hindus means righteousness, justice, faith, duty, a religious and social obligation, but it does not cover all that is sacred for the Hindu. Hindu notions of sacrality cover what may be considered 'secular', 'supernatural', or even 'superstitious' in the Western world. Thus, among other things, it is necessary to understand sacred times, places, omens, architecture, music, trees, and plants in the Hindu tradition.

Subjects such as astronomy and astrology, phonetics, and studies on poetic metre are traditionally considered *vedāṅga* or ancillary to the study of scripture. These subjects would also come under the purview of 'religion'. While it would be impossible to do justice to all these areas that fall under the rubric of sacred texts and sacrality for the Hindus, our discussion of the Hindu tradition in this chapter will include features not covered by the word 'religion' in the Western world.

## HINDU ORIGINS

Historically, Hindu traditions have grown from a fusion of the indigenous religions that existed in the Indian subcontinent with the faith of the Indo-European people (the Aryans), who migrated there possibly between 1750 and 1500 BCE. Some scholars have held that our knowledge of Hinduism begins only with the coming of the Indo-European people because the earliest religious compositions go back to that era, but historical reconstruction is not based on texts alone. Looking at archaeological evidence, one can speculate on the religious practices that existed prior to the invasion of Indo-European migrants.

### The Harappa Culture

In 1926, the excavations of Sir John Marshall (1876–1958) revealed the existence of large towns on the banks of the Indus River. Two of these towns are known today as Mohenjo Daro ('Mound of the Dead') and Harappa. They are over 480 km (300 mi.) apart, but there is a certain uniformity in the civilization that existed in that entire area, stretching from the northwest part of India to Kalibagan in Rajasthan and Lothal in Gujarat. From this homogeneity—the prevalence of many similar objects in towns several hundred miles away—we may conclude that there was continuous travel and communication among them. Because the towns were already quite mature, we do not know exactly when people began to settle in that area. From excavations and some radiocarbon testing, it is believed that the towns existed around 2750 BCE, but some historians tend to push the dates back even earlier. Still popularly known as the Indus Valley civilization, it is now referred to by scholars as the Harappa culture because it covers a much larger area than the Indus basin.

The people of this civilization knew the art of writing; we have found inscriptions on their carved seals, but we have not yet been able to decipher the script with any assurance. Both a Danish and a Russian team working on the script have produced concordances, but there is still considerable doubt whether symbols like U and E mean a boat and a comb or something completely different. Current scholarship also focuses on the connections between this language and later ones in India. It is generally believed that the language is closer to Dravidian ones of southern India than to any other and that the script relied upon homophones, i.e., different words having the same pronunciation. Until we decipher the script, most of our statements on their culture will have to be tentative and based on archaeological evidence.

The people of the Harappa civilization were impressive builders and lived in what appear to have been planned cities. The cities were divided into a citadel-like area, which seems to be the centre for civic and religious activities, and a large residential area. Streets often run parallel, and houses are situated at right angles to the streets and accessed through lanes perpendicular to the streets. In the citadel mound at Mohenjo Daro, there is a huge swimming-pool-like structure that archaeologists call 'the Great Bath'. It is built of brick, and the bottom of the pool is of bricks set with gypsum mortar. Its measures 12 x 7 m and is about 3 m deep (39 x 23 x 10 ft). The whole structure is surrounded by porticos and rooms. Two flights of stairs lead into the pool. There is an elaborate system for filling the pool from an adjacent well and draining it. The care with which the complex was built has led scholars to believe that it served more than a civic function: that it was meant for religious rituals of some sort.

The houses at Mohenjo Daro range from one-room tenements to large ones with a dozen rooms and a courtyard. Almost all of the larger houses had a well attached to them. A remarkable drainage and sewer system existed in the houses. This feature alone seems to give the Harappa culture a distinctive character. There were bathrooms even on the second floor, and the household drain system was connected with the street. The presence of these connected drains indicates some township authority that probably planned and supervised these functions.

Apart from the many houses, there are a number of other buildings both in the citadel area of Mohenjo Daro and in the lower town that have tentatively been identified as worship houses. In a recently excavated citadel mound in Kalibagan, there is a series of raised brick platforms and fire altars. Nearby, lined with bricks, are pits containing ashes and animal bones. There are also bathing places near a well. The whole complex seems to be a religious ritual centre. From this centre we can hypothesize that there existed a form of fire ritual, ablutions with water, and animal sacrifices. Some of the houses also seem to have a room with a fire altar, suggesting a domestic fire ritual.

From the buildings that have tentatively been identified as worship halls, some stone sculptures, which probably served as icons, have been excavated. From the large numbers of terracotta figurines unearthed in the excavations, scholars surmise that some were used as icons in worship.

These include statuettes of what seems to be a mother goddess. This female figure wears only a short skirt, but has abundant jewellery and a fan-shaped head-dress with two cups on either side. These little cups have smoke stains in them, leading us to believe that they were used for fire or incense offerings by the worshipper. Because images of this figure were common in this civilization and it is similar to figures found in other excavations, Marshall, who made the initial study, says that they may be earlier forms of the goddesses known as Pārvatī and Kālī. Although some Western scholars believe that goddess worship in a society indicates a high status for women, we have no hard evidence in the Harappan civilization to support this thesis. Indeed, as we shall see, though goddesses were worshipped in the later Hindu tradition, not all women were held in high esteem.

About 2,000 flat square or rectangular seals and many amulets have been found in the excavations around the Indus River. Some of the seals most likely were protective like the amulets; the purpose of the others is not yet clear. A few seals represent a man seated in what may be called a yogalike posture on a low throne with animals near him. The man appears to have three faces. The animals near him include deer, antelope, a rhinoceros, an elephant, and a buffalo. On his head is a hat with two horns, with a plantlike object protruding between them. Marshall points out that this kind of head-dress was worn only by divine beings and kings in Sumer in the Ancient Near East.

The suggestion is that because of both the head-dress and the animals around him, this god may be a prototype of the one known as Śiva in later years. Except for a set of bangles and some jewellery, there is no clothing on this being. The male deity in the Indus Valley is seated with his feet drawn up beneath him, toes turned down, heels touching each other, and hands extended above the knees—a position that was typical of yoga in later years. Although they have no evident direct link with this deity, several stones that seem to have a phallic significance have also been found in the excavations. This find is intriguing because the god Śiva is generally depicted by a *liṅga*, a conical stone considered to be a phallic symbol, which for Hindus represents the beginnings of creation.

Another recurrent theme in the seals is that of a spirit emerging from a *pīpal* tree and worshippers standing in front of it with little plants. The *pīpal* tree is still important in the Hindu tradition, and we know that it has been so for about 2,500 years. If it indeed had religious significance during the Indus Valley period, we can say that this has been one of the more enduring features of the religious tradition. In some seals, we see a horned person coming from the *pīpal* tree and a row of seven figures with long braids standing in front of it. The notion of seven beings is important in later Hindu mythology. These figures have been identified both as the seven holy men (*ṛṣis* or seers) and as the seven mothers of later Hindu myths.

Many animals are represented on the seals. The religious nature of some of these is still unclear, although scholars have attributed a religious function to the seals with bulls and cows. But there is general agreement that the representations with half human and half animal forms and mythological animals like the unicorn were considered divine. Some seals show a half human, half tiger form. Others show a composite animal with parts of a bull and an elephant, or a combination of a ram, an elephant, and a bull. Many of these, including the lion-elephant animal, seem very similar to mythical beasts that became popular in later Hinduism. Other abstract symbols like variations on the swastika, and designs that resemble threshold rice-powder drawings, seem popular in the seals.

Scholars are not yet sure how the people in these cities disposed of their dead. Since the manner of disposal frequently reveals religious convictions, this is an important lacuna in our information on the religion of this culture. No large cemeteries have been found, but possibly some of these lie under alluvial soil and have not yet been discovered. The small number of graves that have been found are on a north-south axis. A few of them have objects buried with the bodies, and sometimes we find more than one body in a grave. Perhaps people believed that the dead might need the materials buried with them for an afterlife.

Multiple burial in one grave is more problematic. It is not known whether a spouse or attendants were buried along with the dead. We bear in mind the later practice of *satī*, the culturally expected suicide of a widow, who throws herself onto her husband's funeral pyre. In that connection, the fragmentary evidence of multiple burials in the Indus Valley gives rise to a new set of speculations. It is supposed that most bodies were generally cremated around the river-bank. Some pots hold collections of bones; it is possible that there was partial burial of these.

There is no consensus on the likely cause for the end of the Indus Valley civilization. Some scholars have held that the growing invasions of the Indo-European people from Central Asia, starting around 1750 BCE, eventually destroyed the Harappa culture. Others believe that the Indus River may have changed its course drastically and flooded the region, but the theory of flooding as a single cause of destruction is generally discounted now. An epidemic may have wiped out the population. Possibly a combination of these factors may have contributed to the eventual decline of the civilization.

Although these cities died, the indigenous religious traditions of the subcontinent of which they were a part continued in many ways, even through the early centuries of Indo-European cultural domination. From the fragmentary evidence and clues that we find in the Indus Valley, as well as in other regions of India, we can tentatively say that some features of the Hindu religion as practised today go back before 1750 BCE to Mohenjo Daro and Harappa.

Our knowledge of the civilization in other parts of the subcontinent is even less than that of the Indus Valley, but scholars have observed a curious fact in some sites of archaeological importance. They have noticed an intriguing correspondence between places frequented by people about 4,000 years ago and sites that are of religious significance today. For example, some places that were inhabited and popular 4,000 years ago, like the Gudiyam caves near Madras, are seen as the abode of the divine. While there is some debate over whether there has been a continuous belief in the sacrality of a particular place such as Gudiyam for the last four millennia, this pattern is repeated in so many sites that it is considered significant. The Hindu tradition as we know it historically has many features that cannot be traced to Indo-European sources. It is probable that at least some of these elements have been part of the religious culture of the subcontinent for the last 4,000 to 5,000 years.

## The Indo-Europeans

Between 2000 BCE and 1500 BCE, thousands of people who lived in Central Asia began migrating to widely distant regions. Some of these people settled in western and northern Europe, all the way from Ireland to the Scandinavian countries. Others went south or east and settled near Iran; these people referred to themselves as Aryans. One branch of the Aryans migrated into Iran, where they came to constitute the majority of the population. That branch gave their name to the region; etymologically, the name 'Iran' is part of the geographical expression meaning 'homeland of the Aryans'. The other branch, the subject of this chapter, migrated into India from the northwest, where it seems they destroyed the Indus Valley civilization and became rulers of a sizeable indigenous population. In the case of this branch, the name Aryans took on a social class connotation. Applied to the people who were the conquering overlords, it came to mean 'noble ones'.

Although it is widely held that the Indo-Europeans migrated from Central Asia around 2000 BCE, some scholars think that the emigration began around 6000 BCE. The work of these archaeologists, anthropologists, and linguists suggests that it was a peaceful migration undertaken because of the farming interests of the population. Further, some of these scholars posit that the people were not from Central Asia but the region around modern Turkey.

The Aryans spoke a language from which we get the ancient language of Sanskrit. The word 'Aryan' is also used as a synonym for Indo-European languages. Some of the members of the Indo-European family of languages are Sanskrit, Persian, Russian, Greek, Latin, German, and English. Similar features of vocabulary are recognized in many of these languages. For example, the Sanskrit word *jñāna* is a cognate of the English word '*knowledge*'; 'lack of knowledge' is *ajñāna* in Sanskrit and '*ignorance*' in English. There are hundreds of words like this, including the words for 'father' and 'mother'. And besides their stock of vocabulary, the Indo-European languages have many grammatical structures in common.

The Indo-European immigrants settled down near the river Sindhu (Indus) and later migrated near the river Ganga (Ganges). These early settlers composed many poems and eventually manuals on rituals and philosophy. For a long time none of these were written down; the act of writing them was tabooed as defiling. These traditions were committed to memory in an elaborate and disciplined process, and passed from generation to generation by word of mouth to students, who would likewise memorize them by rote. Many mnemonic devices were utilized to ensure accurate pronunciation, rhythm, and utterance.

## The *Vedas*

The earliest compositions we have from the Indo-European people are called *Veda* or 'knowledge'. (The Sanskrit root of this word, *vid*, is related to the English word 'wit'.) Collectively, they are called *śruti* ('that which was heard'). Something a Hindu child may learn from school history texts—but most probably *not* from home—is that the four *Vedas* were composed between 1500 BCE and about 600 BCE. As in many cultures, there is a tendency for piety to exaggerate the antiquity of sacred texts. Nonetheless, it is evident that the *Vedas* are India's earliest surviving compositions.

There are four Vedic collections, each divided into four sections. The four collections or *Vedas* are known as *Ṛg*, *Sāma*, *Yajur*, and *Atharva*. The sections in each of these collections are *saṃhitās* or hymnic compositions; *brāhmaṇas* or ritual treatises; *Āraṇyakas* or 'compositions for the forest'; and *Upaniṣads*, 'sitting near [the teacher]'.

The earliest compositions are hymns in the *saṃhitās* of the *Ṛg Veda*. The hymns were used in sacrificial rituals, and some of the instructions on conducting rituals are contained in the *Yajur Veda* and the *brāhmaṇas*. Later philosophical speculation is found in the sections called *Āraṇyakas* and *Upaniṣads*.

The earliest section of the *Ṛg Veda* has 1,028 hymns. These are contained in ten *maṇḍalas* or sections. The hymns of the *Sāma Veda* and *Yajur Veda* are largely borrowed from the *Ṛg*, but the *Sāma Veda* was meant to be sung in a specific manner. The *Yajur Veda* also contains many hymns from the *Ṛg Veda*, but in addition to them has information pertaining to Vedic sacrifice.

Each *Veda* has its own *Upaniṣads*, philosophical works composed around 600 BCE. Thus the famous *Chāndogya Upaniṣad* belongs to the *Sāma Veda*, the *Bṛhadāraṇyaka* and *Taittirīya Upaniṣads* are affixed to the *Yajur Veda*, and the *Aitreya* to the *Ṛg Veda*.

The *Atharva Veda* is different from the other three *Vedas*, in that it includes material scholars consider non-Aryan. It contains incantations and remedies to ward off illness and evil spirits. Unlike the hymns of the other *Vedas*, these chants were not used for sacrificial purposes but for situations that called for medical or other actions. It has chants calling for harm to befall one's enemies, such as 5.29: 'pierce his eyes, pierce his heart, break his tongue'. A verse (7.38) uses healing herbs to make a lover return, and another (7.50) requests luck in gambling.

The term *Veda* has been used in the Hindu tradition to denote the whole corpus, starting with the hymns, continuing through the ritual treatises, and concluding with the texts of a more philosophical character. Orientalists and Western Indologists, however, have often used the term *Veda* to apply only to the hymns, the *saṃhitā* portion of each collection. This narrower sense of the term is generally not accepted by Hindus.

## The Status of the *Vedas*

While almost all educated Hindus may point to the *Vedas* as their most sacred texts, they would be hard pressed to know their contents. Although considered to be extremely important by all orthodox philosophers and theological treatises, the *Vedas* are not books kept in people's houses. Rather, they are ritual texts understood by Hindus as eternal sound, eternal words passed on through the generations without change. A few hymns from them are known and recited regularly at temple and home liturgies, and the philosophical sections have been translated and commented upon frequently, but the rest of the *Vedas* are known only to a handful of ritual specialists and to Sanskritists familiar with the early Vedic form of the language.

The *Vedas* are particularly significant to the brahmins, the class of society that has historically considered itself as the 'highest'. From a brahminical standpoint, for many centuries, acceptance of the *Vedas* determined whether one was an orthodox member of the society we call Hindu. As custodians of the *Vedas*, the brahmins reserved to themselves the authority to study and teach these holy words. While members of two other classes were technically 'allowed' to study the *Vedas*, in time this privilege was lost and, in some cases, abandoned.

The *Vedas* have been considered to be 'revealed', though not necessarily by a deity. The *Vedas* were considered by the brahmin commentators in medieval times to represent 'eternal truth' and 'eternal sound', coeval with God. All schools of medieval thought agreed that the *Vedas* have a transcendental aspect and an authoritative nature. They differed, however, on what was meant by the status of their composition as transhuman (*apauruṣeya*, literally, superhuman; not of the authorship of man; of divine origin). The followers of Nyāya ('logic'), one school of philosophy, believed that God was the author of the *Vedas* and that, since God is perfect, the *Vedas* are infallible.

Many of the other Hindu schools did not subscribe to this view. Two of them that have been influential till today, the Mīmāṃsā and Vedānta, say that the *Vedas* are transhuman—eternal and authorless. The Vedic seers (*ṛṣis*) 'see' the mantras and transmit them; they do not invent or compose them. The words have a fixed order that has to be maintained by a tradition of recitation. The Vedic seers transmitted the words to their disciples, starting an oral tradition that has come down to the present.

Not being composed by human beings, the *Vedas* are considered faultless, the perfect and supreme source of knowledge. From them we can learn about the supreme being, and their authority grants credibility to particular doctrines. But the Mīmāṃsakas do not assume the role of God or any other being in their authorship. Except for the Nyāya school, orthodox Hindus have not necessarily derived the perfection of the *Vedas* from a claim of divine composition.

The Vedic collections have functioned as revelation, with a notion of their unchanging, immutable, eternal sound. They have also served as manuals of ritual for the many strands of the Hindu tradition, with some sections of the texts recited and acted on without major changes for at least the last 2,000 years.

But there has been a pattern of dynamic interpretation as well, in which the perceived meaning of the *Vedas* has been made accessible and adaptable to different places and changing times. The *Vedas* themselves, as well as many of the later commentators on the texts, assert the force of a 'unifying' truth underlying the hymns and the philosophical speculation. But the process of understanding and decoding the *Vedas* has not been static. In any given generation, their perceived message has been interpreted in a manner fitting and applicable to that generation. The process of making the message relevant has been at the heart of Vedic hermeneutics.

Despite the composition of several works that have been more popular than the Vedic revelation among the masses, the theoretical, ritual, and epistemological significance of the *Vedas* has been unquestioned. Thus the highest honour given to a religious text that was important to any Hindu tradition was to call that work the 'fifth *Veda*'.

In the last 2,000 years this title has been accorded to several such texts. The *Mahābhārata*, one of the two major Hindu epics, was consistently called the 'fifth *Veda*'. Similar claims were made for other Sanskrit *Purāṇas*, compositions that will be discussed later. Bharata's *Nāṭya śāstra*, an important treatise on dance and performance composed around the beginning of the Common Era, was also hailed as the fifth *Veda*. Vernacular compositions in the south, especially the *Tiruvāymoḻi* ('sacred utterance') of Nammāḻvār in the ninth century and the *Periya Purāṇam*, a hagiography of saints who were devotees of Śiva, were also considered to be equivalent to the *Vedas*.

These texts did not make even a cursory attempt to imitate the *Vedas* self-consciously or reproduce them in any way, nor were they commentaries on the Vedic texts. Their claim to the title *Veda* is that the people who venerated these works thought of them as containing the wisdom embodied in the original Sanskrit *Vedas*. Any fifth *Veda* was regarded as making the eternal wisdom and truth of the other four relevant to the adherent's own particular place and time.

## The Vedic Hymns

The earliest hymns of the *Vedas* are addressed to many gods. There are allusions to battles between the warrior gods like Indra and other cosmic powers, but these stories are generally not known by Hindus today. (It is generally accepted that at any given time span, a god like Indra or Varuṇa was considered to be the most important but would eventually be replaced by another deity.)

## THE CREATION HYMN, *ṚG VEDA* 10.129

There was neither non-existence nor existence then; there was neither the realm of space nor the sky which is beyond. What stirred? Where? In whose protection? Was there water, bottomlessly deep?

There was neither death nor immortality then. There was no distinguishing sign of night nor of day. That one breathed, windless, by its own impulse. Other than that there was nothing beyond.

Darkness was hidden by darkness in the beginning; with no distinguishing sign, all this was water. The life force that was covered with emptiness, that one arose through the power of heat.

Desire came upon that one in the beginning; that was the first seed of mind. Poets seeking in their heart with wisdom found the bond of existence in non-existence.

Their cord was extended across. Was there below? Was there above? There were seed-placers; there were powers. There was impulse beneath; there was giving-forth above.

Who really knows? Who will here proclaim it? Whence was it produced? Whence is this creation? The gods came afterwards, with the creation of this universe. Who then knows whence it has arisen?

Whence this creation has arisen—perhaps it formed itself, or perhaps it did not—the one who looks down on it, in the highest heaven, only he knows—or perhaps he does not know (Doniger O'Flaherty 1981:25–6).

Agni, the god of fire, is seen as a messenger between human beings and the deities because offerings were placed in the fire to be carried to other worlds. Soma, also addressed in the hymns, is identified as the moon and, frequently, as an elixir that some modern scholars believe was derived from a hallucinogenic mushroom.

A goddess known as Sarasvatī is also spoken of, sometimes as a river, sometimes as representing learning. In the *Ṛg Veda*, Sarasvatī is described as the inspirer of noble thoughts, one who gives rise to truthful words, one who is beautiful and fortunate, the best of rivers filled with dynamic vitality. In later literature—the ritualistic sections called the *Brāhmaṇas*—Sarasvatī is identified with the goddess Vāc ('speech'), who has an individual identity in the early verses of the *Ṛg Veda*. Vāc was perceived to be the consort of the creator Prajāpati. The stories and attributes associated with her become superimposed on Sarasvatī. As Vāc, she is speech incarnate, the power of the word, the mother of the *Vedas*.

When identified with speech in some texts, Sarasvatī is also known as Gāyatrī ('singer') and Sāvitrī ('sun') and is associated with the formula that is given to young boys in a ceremony when they are invested with a sacred thread.

## THE HYMN TO PURUṢA, THE COSMIC PERSON, *ṚG VEDA* 10.90

The Man has a thousand heads, a thousand eyes, a thousand feet. He pervaded the earth on all sides and extended beyond it as far as ten fingers.

It is the Man who is all this, whatever has been and whatever is to be. He is the ruler of immortality, when he grows beyond everything through food.

Such is his greatness, and the Man is yet more than this. All creatures are a quarter of him; three quarters are what is immortal in heaven.

With three quarters the Man rose upwards, and one quarter of him still remains here. From this he spread out in all directions, into that which eats and that which does not eat.

From him Virāj [the female creative principle] was born, and from Virāj came the Man. When he was born, he ranged beyond the earth behind and before.

When the gods spread the sacrifice with the Man as the offering, spring was the clarified butter, summer the fuel, autumn the oblation.

They anointed the Man, the sacrifice born at the beginning, upon the sacred grass. With him the gods, Sādhyas, and sages sacrificed.

From that sacrifice in which everything was offered, the melted fat was collected, and he made it into those beasts who live in the air, in the forest, and in villages.

The *Gāyatrī*, dedicated to the sun, becomes the mantra that marks the initiation of a young boy into his life as a student. The important deities of later Hinduism are mentioned a few times in these earliest hymns. It is only in the later Vedic literature that goddesses like Śrī (Lakṣmī) or gods like Nārāyaṇa (Viṣṇu) are addressed directly in hymns.

Some of the hymns were written by women poets. Their names, Ghoṣā, Apālā, and Lopamudrā, appear in the early *saṃhitās*. While the hymns are composed for divine beings (Ghoṣā addresses the Aśvins, the celestial physicians, and Apālā talks to Indra), these songs are similar to those composed by male poets in that they do not contain pleas for salvation or eternal bliss.

In fact, there are not very many references to the afterlife in these hymns. Most of the petitions are for a good and happy life on this earth: Agni is asked to protect those who praise him, Indra is asked to crush the enemies of the worshipper, and Indu is said to give cattle, children, horses, and food. A *ṛṣi* called Sobhari simply asks the divine physicians for 'all good things', but Ghoṣā specifically asks them to cure her of her white-tinted skin, so that she may get married and live happily with her husband. Apālā, who apparently does not have any hair growing on her head or body, asks Indra for lush growth on her father's balding head, her own head, and the growth of crops in her father's barren fields.

From that sacrifice in which everything was offered, the verses and chants were born, the metres were born from it, and from it the formulas were born.

Horses were born from it, and those other animals that have two rows of teeth; cows were born from it, and from it goats and sheep were born.

When they divided the Man, into how many parts did they apportion him? What do they call his mouth, his two arms and thighs and feet?

His mouth became the Brahmin; his arms were made into the Warrior, his thighs the People, and from his feet the Servants were born.

The moon was born from his mind; from his eye the sun was born ... and from his vital breath the Wind was born.

From his navel the middle realm of space arose; from his head the sky evolved. From his two feet came the earth, and the quarters of the sky from his ear. Thus they set the worlds in order.

There were seven enclosing-sticks for him, and thrice seven fuel-sticks, when the gods, spreading the sacrifice, bound the Man as the sacrificial beast.

With the sacrifice the gods sacrificed to the sacrifice. these were the first ritual laws. These very powers reached the dome of the sky where dwell the Sādhyas, the ancient gods (Doniger O'Flaherty 1981: 30–1).

One of the dominant features of Vedic religious life was the ritual sacrifice (*yajña*). Both domestic and community rituals ranging from the simple to the extremely complicated were usually performed with a fire. Ritual specialists and priests conducted these sacrifices and supervised the making of altars, sacrifice of animals, and the recitation of the hymns. Many sacrifices involved the making, offering, and consuming of *soma* juice from plants.

In the hymns composed by around 1000 BCE, there is speculation on the origins of the universe and a description of a cosmic sacrifice through which creation begins. In the *Hymn of Origins*, there is initially wonder at the creation of the universe from nothing. The hymn ends with the statement that perhaps no one knew how it all came to be.

A delicate connection was seen between the rituals and the prevalence of cosmic and earthly order, *ṛta*. *Ṛta* is truth and justice, the rightness of things. It makes harmony and peace possible in the earth and the heavens. Although it is an impersonal cosmic principle, Vedic gods like Varuṇa were considered its upholders.

In one key hymn, the 'Hymn to the Supreme Person' (*Puruṣa Sūkta*), the universe itself is said to have come out of a cosmic sacrifice in which the primeval man (Puruṣa) was offered. The hymn is important even today in domestic and temple ritual for the Hindus and has figured continuously in the tradition for about 3,000 years. In it, the composer strains to capture infinity in words and uses the notion of a 'thousand' to denote all that cannot be measured or perhaps even conceptualized:

(1) The cosmic person has a thousand heads
a thousand eyes and feet
It covers the earth on all sides
and extends ten finger-lengths beyond
(2) The cosmic person is everything
all that has been and will be …

Various elements of the universe are said to arise from this sacrifice:

(13) From his mind came the moon
from his eye, the sun
Indra and Agni from his mouth
the wind came from his breath.
(14) From his navel came space
from his head, the sky
from his feet, earth;
from his ears, the four directions
thus the worlds were created.

### *The Four Classes*

In this context a concept is introduced that is to change forever the religious and social countenance of the Hindu tradition:

(12) From his mouth came the priestly class
from his arms, the rulers.
the producers came from his legs;
from his feet came the servant class.

It is said that the four classes (*varṇas*, literally 'colours') of society came from this initial cosmic sacrifice. While the origins of what eventually came to be called the caste system are generally seen to lie in these verses from the *Ṛg Veda*, it is probable that long before its composition, the stratification of society had already taken place. It is widely held that when the Indo-Europeans conquered the people of the subcontinent, they considered the indigenous people as socially inferior. The conquerors divided themselves loosely into the priestly, ruling, and mercantile classes. Eventually the others were looked upon as servants. We will discuss the caste system later, but for now simply note that the first mention of the concept in literature is in the *Vedas*.

## The *Upaniṣads*

The sacrificial worldview of the early Vedic age gave way to philosophical inquiry and discussion in the *Āraṇyakas* and the *Upaniṣads*. The *Āraṇyakas* and the *Upaniṣads* were composed at a time of intellectual ferment and philosophical speculation. They were composed a little before and perhaps during the times of Gautama Buddha and the Jain teacher Mahāvīra. The mood of critical thinking was characteristic of the seventh and sixth centuries BCE. It was a time of questioning and rejecting authoritarian structures: the religious leadership of the priestly class (the brahmins), the caste system itself, and the revealed or 'transhuman' status of the *Vedas*.

The *Upaniṣads*, however, do not totally reject the early hymns and sacrificial rituals. Rather, they contain a reformulation and a rethinking of the earlier materials. Thus rituals are sometimes interpreted allegorically, and the symbolic structures of the sacrifices are analysed in some detail. The *Upaniṣads* do show some continuity with the earlier hymns and rituals. The *Bṛhadāraṇyaka Upaniṣad*, for example, gives instructions with exquisite details on how one may beget a learned daughter or a heroic son.

The *Upaniṣads* are usually conversations between a teacher and a student, between a husband and wife, or between fellow philosophers. In the beginning of one study session a teacher exclaims: 'May he protect us; may he be pleased with us. May we work with vigour; may our study illumine us both. May there be no discord between us. *Oṃ*. Let there be peace, peace, peace' (*Taittirīya Upaniṣad* II.1.1).

After years of *Veda* instruction, a departing student receives moving advice from his *guru* or teacher:

> Speak the truth. Practice virtue. Do not neglect to study every day. Do not neglect truth, virtue, studying or teaching ... Be one to whom your mother is a god, your father is a god, your teacher is a god, a guest is like a god ... Give with faith ... give liberally, give with modesty ... give with sympathy ... This is the command. This is the teaching. This is the secret of the *Veda* ... (*Taittirīya Upaniṣad* I.11.1–6).

### *Karma and Saṃsāra*

In these books we find the first mention of the concept of *karma*. *Karma* literally means 'action', especially ritual action, but eventually in the *Upaniṣads* comes to

## *BṚHADĀRAṆYAKA UPANIṢAD* 3.8

Then Vācaknavī said, 'Venerable Brāhmaṇas, I shall ask him two questions. If he answers me these, none of you can defeat him in arguments about Brahman.' 'Ask, Gārgī' [said he].

She said, 'As a warrior son of the Kāśis or the Videhas might rise up against you, having strung his unstrung bow and having taken in his hand two pointed foe-piercing arrows, even so, O Yājñavalkya, do I face you with two questions. Answer me these.' 'Ask, Gārgī'.

She said, 'That, O Yājñavalkya, of which they say, it is above the heaven, it is beneath the earth, that which is between these two, the heaven and the earth, that which the people call the past, the present and the future, across what is that woven, like warp and woof?'

He said, 'That which is above the heaven, that which is beneath the earth, that which is between these two, heaven and earth, that which the people call the past, the present, and the future, across space is that woven, like warp and woof.'

She said, 'Adoration to you, Yājñavalkya, who have answered this question for me. Prepare yourself for the other.' 'Ask, Gārgī.'

She said, 'That, O Yājñavalkya, of which they say, it is above the heaven, it is beneath the earth, that which is between these two, the heaven and the earth, that which the people call the past, the present, and the future, across what is that woven like warp and woof?'

He said, 'That which is above the sky, that which is beneath the earth, that which is between these two, sky and earth, that which the people call the past, the present, and the future, across space is that woven like warp and woof.'

He said, 'That, O Gārgī, the knowers of Brahman call the Imperishable. It is neither gross nor fine, neither short nor long, neither glowing red (like fire) nor adhesive (like water). (It is) neither shadow nor darkness, neither air nor space, unat-

mean the system of rewards and punishments attached to various actions. Thus it refers to a system of cause and effect that may span several lifetimes. That is, human beings get rewarded or punished according to the merits and demerits of their behaviour. The theory of *karma* also implies continuing rebirths (*saṃsāra*). Liberation from them (*mokṣa*), according to the *Upaniṣads*, comes from a supreme, experiential, transforming wisdom.

When one gets this transforming knowledge, one is never reborn and never dies; one attains immortality. The word for 'immortal' in Sanskrit is *a-mṛta* ('without death'). Rebirth or reincarnation and its connection with *karma*—notions that are central to the later Hindu tradition—are articulated clearly in the *Upaniṣads*. So also is the ultimate goal, liberation from the cycle of birth and death.

tached, without taste, without smell, without eyes, without ears, without voice, without mind, without radiance, without breath, without a mouth, without measure, having no within and no without. It eats nothing and no one eats it.'

'Verily, at the command of that Imperishable, O Gārgī, the sun and the moon stand in their respective positions. At the command of that Imperishable, O Gārgī, heaven and earth stand in their respective positions. At the command of the Imperishable, O Gārgī, what are called moments, hours, days and nights, half-months, months, seasons, years stand in their respective positions. At the command of that Imperishable, O Gārgī, some rivers flow to the east from the white (snowy) mountains, others to the west in whatever direction each flows. By the command of that Imperishable, O Gārgī, men praise those who give, the gods (are desirous of) the sacrificer and the fathers are desirous of the *darvī* offering.'

'Whosoever, O Gārgī, in this world, without knowing this Imperishable performs sacrifices, worships, performs austerities for a thousand years, his work will have an end; whosoever, O Gārgī, without knowing this Imperishable departs from this world, is pitiable. But, O Gārgī, he who knowing the Imperishable departs from this world is a Brāhmaṇa (a knower of Brahman).

'Verily, that Imperishable, O Gārgī, is unseen but is the seer, is unheard but is the hearer, unthought but is the thinker, unknown but is the knower. There is no other seer but this, there is no other hearer but this, there is no other thinker but this, there is no other knower but this. By this Imperishable, O Gārgī, is space woven like warp and woof.'

She said, 'Venerable Brāhmaṇa, you may think it a great thing if you get off from him though bowing to him. Not one of you will defeat him in arguments about Brahman.' Thereupon [Gārgī] Vācaknavī kept silent (Radhakrishnan 1953:230–4).

The quest for a unifying truth is a distinctive feature of the *Upaniṣads*, and recurs in Hindu philosophical traditions of later centuries. In the *Muṇḍaka Upaniṣad* (1.1.3), the one who seeks the truth phrases his question, 'What is it that being known, all else becomes known?'

Unifying truth comes with enlightenment, which may be related to but quite distinct from book learning. The *Bṛhadāraṇyaka Upaniṣad* of the *Yajur Veda* has some lines reflecting the quest for wisdom that characterizes the *Upaniṣads*:

*Om asato mā sad gamaya*
*tamaso mā jyotir gamaya*
*mṛtyor mā amṛtām gamaya*
*Om śāntiḥ, śāntiḥ, śāntiḥ.*

### *Chāndogya Upaniṣad* 6.11

'Bring hither a fruit of that *nyagrodha* tree.' 'Here it is, Venerable Sir.' 'Break it.' 'It is broken, Venerable Sir.' 'What do you see there?' 'These extremely fine seeds, Venerable Sir.' 'Of these, please break one.' 'It is broken, Venerable Sir.' 'What do you see there?' 'Nothing at all, Venerable Sir.'

Then he said to him, 'My dear, that subtle essence which you do not perceive, verily, my dear, from that very essence this great *nyagrodha* tree exists. Believe me, my dear.'

That which is the subtle essence, this whole world has for its self. That is the true. That is the self. That art thou, Śvetaketu. 'Please, Venerable Sir, instruct me still further.' 'So be it, my dear,' said he (Radhakrishnan 1953:462).

Lead me from the unreal to reality
Lead me from darkness to light
Lead me from death to immortality
Om, let there be peace, peace, peace.

The *Upaniṣads* distinguish 'lower' knowledge, or that which can be conceptualized and articulated, from the 'higher' knowledge of true wisdom. Significantly enough, in later centuries the 'higher wisdom' is divorced from Vedic or any book learning or conceptual knowledge. One is freed from the birth-and-death cycle by an enlightenment experience.

#### *Ātman and Brahman*

This higher wisdom comes from experientially knowing the relationship between the human soul (Ātman) and the Supreme Being (Brahman). Brahman pervades and yet transcends the universe as well as human thought. Ultimately, Brahman cannot be described. The sage Yājñavalkya, who is interrogated on this matter by a woman philosopher, Gārgī Vācaknavī, finally says that one can only come close to describing Brahman by stating what it is not. To describe is to curtail and confine; Yājñavalkya does not fall into the trap of trying to contain infinity.

To know Brahman is to enter a new state of consciousness; to know Brahman is to reach the Supreme. This state cannot be described. With our lower conceptual knowledge, we cannot put in words what is ultimately ineffable. The *Taittirīya Upaniṣad* says that Brahman is existence or truth (*satya*), knowledge (*jñāna*), and infinity (*ananta*). Beyond that, the only words saying anything about Brahman are that it is existence (*sat*), consciousness (*cit*), and bliss (*ānanda*). The

## *TAITTIRĪYA UPANIṢAD* 1.2

Having taught the Veda, the teacher instructs the pupil thus: Speak the truth, practice righteousness, do not neglect your daily reading … Do not neglect truth, do not ignore righteousness, do not neglect what is the happiness of all, do not neglect prosperity, do not neglect study and teaching …

Be one to whom the mother is a god, a father is a god, a teacher is god, a guest is god. Practice what is not reprehensible; avoid evil deeds. Adopt the good practices that you see amidst us, not others.

… Give with faith … give generously, give with modesty, give with fear, give with sympathy …

This is the command; this the teaching, this is the teaching of the Veda. This is the instruction. This is the manner of worship.

relationship between Ātman and Brahman is discussed in many conversations, but invariably they suggest rather than declare the connection between or the identity of the two. In one famous conversation between Uddālaka Āruṇi and his son Śvetaketu, in the *Chāndogya Upaniṣad*, the father asks the son to dissolve salt in water and says that Brahman and Ātman are united in a similar manner. The father ends his teaching with the famous dictum: *tat tvam asi* ('you are that'). In this statement, the 'that' refers to Brahman and the 'you' to Ātman.

Philosophers who interpreted this passage more than 1,000 years afterwards elicited different messages from it. Śaṅkara (eighth century) thinks that 'you are that' refers to an identity between Brahman and Ātman. On the other hand, Rāmānuja (eleventh century) says that while it means that Brahman and Ātman are inseparably united, they are not identical.

In some passages in the *Upaniṣads*, as in the lengthy conversation between Yājñavalkya and his wife Maitreyī, and later in a philosophical contest in which Yājñavalkya is being quizzed by the woman philosopher Gārgī Vācaknavī, we learn more of the relationship between Brahman and Ātman. In some passages, Yājñavalkya refers to Brahman as the hidden, inner controller of the human soul; in others, as the frame of the universe. In the last analogy mentioned, the reference is to a weaving loom: the universe is said to be woven over Brahman.

The *Upaniṣads* are also referred to as the *Vedānta* ('end of the *Vedas*'), although the term is more often used for a system of thought in which the *Upaniṣads* play an important but not exclusive role. The *Upaniṣads* form the beginnings of Hindu philosophical thought and, according to some Hindus in the last 2,000 years, also reflect the best discussions in Hindu speculation. The quest

The medieval philosopher *Rāmānuja is carried in a palanquin in a painting at Sriperumbudur.* (V. Narayanan)

for a unifying knowledge or higher wisdom is continued in various systems of Hindu philosophical reasoning and has preoccupied thinkers till this century.

***Women in the Upanishadic Age***

Women participated in the quest for ultimate truth and sought salvific knowledge both in domestic and public forums. Gārgī Vācaknavī questions the sage Yājñavalkya in a royal court, and when he does not answer to her satisfaction, she presses the question. Eventually, she pronounces a judgement about him to the company of fellow philosophers and says that he is indeed wise. Obviously, women like Gārgī and Maitreyī were honoured and respected for their wisdom, as were dozens of other women whose names are mentioned.

These women were among the various teachers through whom the sacred teaching was transmitted. While in some lists of teachers the father's name is mentioned (*Bṛhadāraṇyaka Upaniṣad* II.6.3; IV.6.1), in others (*Bṛhadāraṇyaka Upaniṣad* VI.5.1) the teachers are identified as sons of particular women. Here, instead of the usual father's name, more than forty-five male teachers are listed with their mothers' names. This list is particularly interesting because sometimes fathers' and other times mothers' names are given, and the lineage goes back to a creator god Brahmā. So, while it is clear that a male spiritual lineage is generally accepted (after all, it is the male teachers who are being named), it may be possible to interpret this passage by saying that in some cases the teachers received spiritual instruction from their mothers.

# CLASSICAL HINDUISM

## The Epics

The *Vedas*, considered absolutely transhuman by the many Hindu traditions, are termed *śruti* ('that which was heard'). However, the literature that was composed after their period, starting approximately around 500 BCE, was acknowledged as human and loosely called *smṛti* ('that which is remembered').

Though of human authorship, the material called *smṛti* was nonetheless considered inspired. And while this literature has been theoretically of lesser authority than the *Vedas*, it has played a far more important role in the lives of the Hindus for the last 2,500 years. Sometimes this category is divided into the epics (*itihāsas*), ancient stories (*purāṇas*), and codes of law and ethics (*dharmaśāstras*). The term *smṛti* can also mean the codes alone.

The two epics, the *Rāmāyaṇa* (Story of Rāma) and the *Mahābhārata* (Great Epic of India or, alternatively, the Great Sons of Bharata), have been the best-known works within the Hindu tradition. Children hear these stories from their grandparents or parents. Almost any child can tell you the story of Rāma, the young prince who is the hero of the *Rāmāyaṇa*, and many households have printed copies of it. Invariably the narration of the epics is their first and most lasting encounter with Hindu scripture. In fact, for many Hindus, the phrase 'sacred books' connotes these epics in particular.

In some houses one will find copies of the *Bhagavad Gītā* (The Song of the Blessed One). The *Gītā* is an episode of eighteen chapters from the much longer epic, the *Mahābhārata*. With approximately 100,000 verses, the *Mahābhārata* has the dubious honour of being the longest poem in the world. The complete *Mahābhārata* is not a book one would find in a typical home, but the *Gītā*'s presentation of the hero Arjuna and the lord Kṛṣṇa is a widely copied portion of the *Mahābhārata*.

### *The Rāmāyaṇa*

The *Rāmāyaṇa* has been memorized, recited, sung, danced, enjoyed, and experienced emotionally, intellectually, and spiritually for the last 2,500 years. It has been a source of inspiration for generations of devotees in India and in many parts of the world. When the *Rāmāyaṇa* and *Mahābhārata* were broadcast over sixty weeks on Sunday morning television, the show drew the largest audience in the history of Indian television and turned Sunday morning from inexpensive into prime advertising time. The epic is danced and acted in places of Hindu (and Buddhist) cultural influence in Southeast Asia. Its characters are very well known as far away as Thailand and Indonesia.

The story of the *Rāmāyaṇa* focuses on the young prince Rāma, who is born in Ayodhya, the capital of the Kosala kingdom. He has three half-brothers named

*The Rāmāyaṇa is popular throughout the culture of Southeast Asia in societies that are now Buddhist or Muslim.* (V.R. Rajagopalan)

Lakṣmaṇa, Bharata, and Śatrughuna. On the eve of his coronation, his father Daśaratha exiles him. Daśaratha is heartbroken about his action, but is forced into this decision because of a promise he made previously to one of his wives. Rāma accepts his father's decision cheerfully and leaves for the forest. He is accompanied by his wife Sītā and his brother Lakṣmaṇa, who both refuse to be separated from him. Daśaratha dies of grief. Bharata, the brother who has now been designated to be king, returns from a trip to find his father dead and his brother in exile. Because of his love for Rāma, he hastily follows his brother and begs him to return and rule Ayodhya, but Rāma refuses because he feels he has to honour his commitment to his father. He asks Bharata to rule as his regent in Ayodhya.

While in the forest, Sītā, the beautiful wife of Rāma, is captured by Rāvaṇa, the demon king of Laṅkā. She refuses to marry him, and Rāvaṇa keeps her captive in a grove. Rāma, full of sorrow at being separated from his wife, searches for her with his brother. They are helped by a group of monkeys. Hanumān, a monkey with divine ancestry, is particularly helpful and on a search mission finds Sītā. He reports her whereabouts to Rāma. Rāma, aided by the monkeys, goes to war with Rāvaṇa. After a protracted battle, Rāma kills Rāvaṇa and is reunited with Sītā. They eventually return to Ayodhya and are crowned. Rāma is held to be a just king; the phrase *Rām rājya* ('kingdom or rule of Rāma') has become the Hindu political ideal.

Both Rāma and Sītā have become idealized figures in the Hindu tradition; the story is said to reflect many paradigmatic relationships. Rāma is the ideal son and husband, at least in most of the story. In a sequel to the *Rāmāyaṇa*, Rāma banishes Sītā because his subjects are suspicious about her virtue, citing that she has been held captive in Rāvaṇa's grove. Because there is no way of proving her innocence, and he does not want to set this up as a legal precedent, Rāma banishes his own wife. Rāma comes to this painful decision after learning about a washerman who does not want to take back his unfaithful wife, but the wife retorts that if Rāma can take back Sītā after she spent several weeks in Rāvaṇa's house, surely she can return to the washerman's house. The pregnant Sītā is thus banished and gives birth to twins. Several years later, the twins accost Rāma in battle, and it is then that Sītā tells them that he is their father. There is a brief reunion. Rāma asks Sītā to prove her innocence in public by undergoing some ordeal. Sītā refuses and asks Mother Earth to take her back. Sītā is then swallowed by the ground.

While many Hindus have traditionally seen Sītā as the ideal wife who follows her husband to the forest, others see her as a model of strength and virtue. She complies with her husband as he does with her; their love is one worthy of emulation. Yet, she is also a woman who stands her ground when asked by her husband to prove her virtue on at least two different occasions. Once in Laṅkā she acquiesces, but the second time, she gently but firmly refuses and so rules out any possibility of a reunion. There have been other versions of this tale called *Sītāyana*, telling the story from Sītā's viewpoint. Even traditional interpreters agree with the comment, *Sītāyās caritaṃ mahat* ('the deeds of Sītā are indeed great').

There have been many vernacular versions of the *Rāmāyaṇa*, and the story has been interpreted theologically in many ways. In one thirteenth-century interpretation, Sītā voluntarily undergoes captivity and suffering to save other human beings and the world from evil. Another interpretation is allegorical: Sītā is the soul, captured by the material body. The ten heads of Rāvaṇa represent the five sense organs and five motor organs. Rāma will vanquish the earthly body and rescue the human soul from the clutches of the sense organs.

Whatever the interpretation, the story of Rāma, Sītā, and their devotee Hanumān has endured through the centuries in simple and complex forms, engaging the piety and adoration of generations of Hindus. In later centuries Rāma was considered to be an incarnation of the lord Viṣṇu. He is a paragon of human virtue; temples to Rāma and Sītā, his wife, are found all over India. According to a traditional statement, the story of Rāma and Sītā will be told as long as the rivers flow on earth and as long as human beings live.

### *The Mahābhārata*

The *Mahābhārata* is the story of the great (*mahā*) struggle among the descendants of a king called Bharata, the modern name for India. The main part of the story deals with a war between the Pāṇḍavas and the Kauravas. They are cousins, but the Kauravas try to cheat the Pāṇḍavas out of their share of the kingdom and will not accept peace. After all peace initiatives are repudiated by the Kauravas, a battle ensues in which all the major kingdoms are forced to take sides. Kṛṣṇa, by this time considered to be the ninth incarnation of the god Viṣṇu, is on the side of the Pāṇḍavas. Refusing to wield arms, he nevertheless accepts being Arjuna's charioteer, a role that is interpreted allegorically in later centuries.

Just as the war is about to begin, Arjuna, who has hitherto been portrayed as a hero emerging victorious from several battles, becomes distressed at the thought of having to fight against his cousins, uncles, and other relatives. Putting down his bow, he asks Kṛṣṇa whether it is correct to fight a war in which many lives, especially of one's own kin, are to be lost. Kṛṣṇa replies in the affirmative; it is correct if we fight for what is right. One must fight for righteousness (*dharma*) after trying peaceful means. The conversation that Arjuna and Kṛṣṇa have on the battlefield takes about eighteen chapters. These are the chapters called *Bhagavad Gītā*.

### *The Gītā*

The *Bhagavad Gītā* is held in high esteem as one of the holiest books in the Hindu tradition. The political leader Mohandas K. Gandhi (1869–1948), for instance, referred to the *Gītā* as his spiritual mother. The *Gītā* speaks of loving devotion to the lord and the importance of selfless action. The *Bhagavad Gītā* was probably written around 200 BCE or during the following three centuries and added to the epic *Mahābhārata*. It is frequently printed separately, and many people have a copy of this sacred text. People learned it by heart for centuries. In the *Gītā*, Kṛṣṇa instructs his cousin Arjuna (who is generally understood to be any human soul who seeks spiritual guidance) on the nature of the human soul, God, and how one can reach liberation.

In verses that are still recited at a Hindu's funeral, Kṛṣṇa describes the human soul as being beyond the reach of human senses and thought; it is not affected by the sense organs or physical nature and is removed from it. Just as a human being casts off old clothes and wears new ones, so too does a soul discard bodies and assume new ones. Thus the soul inhabits bodies that are born and that die. This continues through the ages until the soul is finally liberated from the cycle of births and death. The soul does not die when the body dies; it is never born and never killed.

Thus Arjuna is told that he is not to grieve at what is to happen; however, he is also warned that if he does not do his duty (*dharma*) and fight for righteousness, he is guilty of moral cowardice. If he fails in his duty, he has to face the consequences of quitting when it is time to wage a just war and protect the people.

Kṛṣṇa also makes several statements about himself that reveal a new shift in Hindu theology. In the *Upaniṣads*, the sages were reluctant to describe Brahman; but in the *Bhagavad Gītā*, Kṛṣṇa reveals himself. He is the ultimate deity, a personal, caring one, filled with love for human beings, and one who incarnates himself periodically to protect them.

> Whenever righteousness diminishes and evil arises ….
> I send myself forth …

## FROM THE *BHAGAVAD GĪTĀ*

*On the immortality of the soul:*

Our bodies are known to end,
but the embodied self is enduring,
indestructible, and immeasurable;
therefore, Arjuna, fight the battle!

He who thinks this self a killer
and he who thinks it killed,
both fail to understand
it does not kill, nor is it killed.

It is not born,
it does not die;
having been,
it will never not be;
unborn, enduring,
constant, and primordial,
it is not killed
when the body is killed ...

As a man discards
worn-out clothes
to put on new
and different ones,
so the embodied self
discards
its worn-out bodies
to take on other new ones.

Weapons do not cut it,
fire does not burn it,
waters do not wet it,
wind does not wither it.
It cannot be cut or burned;
it cannot be wet or withered;
it is enduring, all-pervasive,
fixed, immovable, and timeless ...

*On the way of action:*

Be intent on action,
not on the fruits of action;
avoid attraction to the fruits
and attachment to inaction!

Perform actions, firm in discipline,
relinquishing attachment;
be impartial to failure and success—
this equanimity is called discipline ...

Wise men disciplined by understanding
relinquish the fruit born of action;
freed from these bonds of rebirth,
they reach a place beyond decay ...

When suffering does not disturb his mind,
when his craving for pleasures has
vanished,
when attraction, fear, and anger are gone,
he is called a sage whose thought is sure.

When he shows no preference
in fortune or misfortune
and neither exults nor hates,
his insight is sure ...

*On the mystery and purpose of incarnation:*

Though myself unborn, undying,
the lord of creatures, I fashion nature,
which is mine, and I come into being
through my own magic.

Whenever sacred duty decays
and chaos prevails,

then, I create
myself, Arjuna.

To protect men of virtue
and destroy men who do evil
to set the standard of sacred duty,
I appear in age after age ...

*On the nature of God and the way of devotion:*

Always glorifying me,
striving, firm in their vows,
paying me homage with devotion,
they worship me, always disciplined ...

I am the universal father,
mother, granter of all, grandfather,
object of knowledge, purifier,
holy syllable OM, threefold sacred love.

I am the way, sustainer, lord,
witness, shelter, refuge, friend,
source, dissolution, stability,
treasure, and unchanging seed.

I am heat that withholds
and sends down the rains;
I am immortality and death;
both being and nonbeing am I ...

Men who worship me,
thinking solely of me,
always disciplined,
win the reward I secure.

When devoted men sacrifice
to other deities with faith,
they sacrifice to me, Arjuna,
however aberrant the rites.

I am the enjoyer
and the lord of all sacrifices;
they do not know me in reality,
and so they fail ...

The leaf or flower or fruit or water
that he offers with devotion,
I take from the man of self-restraint
in response to his devotion.

Whatever you do—what you take,
what you offer, what you give,
what penances you perform—
do as an offering to me, Arjuna!

You will be freed from the bonds of action,
from the fruit of fortune and misfortune;
armed with the discipline of renunciation
your self liberated, you will join me ...

If he is devoted solely to me,
even a violent criminal
must be deemed a man of virtue,
for his resolve is right ...

Keep me in your mind and devotion,
sacrifice to me, bow to me,
discipline your self toward me,
and you will reach me!
(Miller 1986:32–87)

To protect the good people and to destroy the evil ones
To establish righteousness, I incarnate myself age after age.
(*Bhagavad Gītā* 4:7–8)

There has been a clear move from what is sometimes called the absolutism or the monistic trends of the *Upaniṣads*, where the Supreme Being was beyond any human conceptualization, to the loving, gracious deity of the *Bhagavad Gītā*. Kṛṣṇa describes himself as the goal, supporter, lord, witness, refuge, sanctuary, and friend of the human being. He is the origin, dissolution, and maintenance of the universe. Many of the traditions within Hinduism have retained this overtly theistic flavour from the time of the *Bhagavad Gītā* till today, at least in terms of domestic and public worship. When Arjuna is not quite clear about Kṛṣṇa's claim to be God incarnate, Kṛṣṇa reveals his own cosmic form, which is only visible to Arjuna's divine eye. Arjuna quakes at this vision and is filled with love and awe. Trembling, he seeks forgiveness of Kṛṣṇa and implores him to resume his normal form.

## The Three Hindu Ways

In the course of the *Bhagavad Gītā*, Kṛṣṇa describes three ways to liberation (or as some Hindus believe, three aspects of one way to liberation) from the cycle of births and death: (1) the way of action, (2) the way of knowledge, and (3) the way of devotion. Each way (*mārga*) is spoken of also as a discipline (*yoga*).

The way of action (*karma yoga*) entails the path of unselfish action; one must do one's duty, but it should not be done either for fear of punishment or hope of reward. The right action should be done without expectation of praise or blame. For example, one is to study or do good acts because it is correct to do so—because it is one's duty (*dharma*) to do so, not because other people will reward and praise one for it.

Acting with the expectation of future reward leads to bondage and unhappiness. On one level, such actions instigate further action and thus further *karma* is incurred, for one is never satisfied when one reaches a goal. One may long for a promotion, more money, or to be loved by a particular person, and when one acts with these goals in mind, one may meet with disappointment and react with anger or grief. Even if one is temporarily successful, the goal that has been reached is replaced with another. Thus the thirst for material success is never quenched. Instead, one succeeds only in accumulating more *karma*, which leads to further rebirth.

Indeed, on one level (according to other books of the time), even the *karma* one gets from performing good deeds is ultimately bad and causes bondage because to enjoy the good *karma*, one has to be reborn. A later Hindu philosopher calls good *karma* 'golden handcuffs'. Therefore, one is to act according to one's *dharma*. Kṛṣṇa urges Arjuna to act without any attachment to the consequences. Then evil will not touch such a person, just as water does not stick to a lotus leaf. All actions are to be offered to Kṛṣṇa. By discarding the fruits of one's action, one attains abiding peace.

Kṛṣṇa also talks of the way of knowledge (*jñāna yoga*): through the means of attaining scriptural knowledge, one may achieve a transforming wisdom that destroys one's past *karma*. True knowledge is an insight into the real nature of the universe, divine power, and the human soul. Later philosophers say that when one hears scripture, asks questions, clarifies doubts, and eventually meditates on this knowledge, one achieves liberation. Kṛṣṇa tells Arjuna that just as fire reduces firewood to ashes, so, too, does the fire of knowledge reduce all *karma* (actions) to ashes.

The third way is the most emphasized throughout the *Bhagavad Gītā*: the way of devotion (*bhakti yoga*). If there is a general amnesty program offered to those who sin, those who have a karmic overload, it is through the way of devotion:

> Even if a sinful person adores me with exclusive devotion
> He must be regarded as righteous ...
> quickly his soul becomes righteous and
> he gets eternal peace ...
> My devotee is never lost.
> (*Bhagavad Gītā* 9:30–1)

Ultimately, Kṛṣṇa makes his promise to Arjuna; if one were to surrender to the lord, he will forgive the human being all sins:

> Letting go all dharma, take refuge in me alone;
> I shall deliver you from all sins; do not grieve.
> (*Bhagavad Gītā* 18:66)

These are held to be almost the 'last words' of the *Bhagavad Gītā*, and thus the ultimate teaching of this work.

## The Deities of Classical Hinduism

Hinduism flourished in the Gupta era (c. 320–540). The rise of the Gupta Empire in the fifth century ushered in a time of great cultural and scholarly activity in India. Advances in mathematics were noteworthy; the use of zero and the decimal system is seen in inscriptions. Around 499 Āryabhaṭṭa calculated that the value of $\pi$ is 3.1416 and that the solar year is 365.3586 days. He also stated that the earth is spherical and rotates on its axis. In commerce, there was increased contact with Greek and Roman trade missions from the Mediterranean. Coastal towns flourished, particularly in southern India.

The Gupta period saw a renewed surge in religious and literary activity. Temple building was encouraged, pilgrimages were undertaken, and playwrights used religious themes in their dramas. Hindus, Jains, and Buddhists composed poems and dramas from which we can learn a great deal about the religion of the time. Temple architecture, literature, astronomy, and astrology received royal patronage.

During the previous seven centuries, under the Mauryan dynasty, the Kushan invasion, and a number of other regimes, the Hindu tradition was by no means dormant; the *Bhagavad Gītā*, to take only one example, comes from those years. But what we know in retrospect as Hindu tradition had coexisted with the ascendancy and patronage of Buddhist teachings and institutions in India. Now, under the Guptas, Buddhism receded, while the Hindu tradition came to dominate. Siddhārtha Gautama, the Buddha, eventually was assimilated in some Hindu texts as one of the incarnations of Viṣṇu.

It would be impossible to locate the transition at a single time or in a single text, but from the Gupta era onward, we observe an increasing prominence of Viṣṇu and Śiva among Hinduism's myriad manifestations of the deity. In the allegiance of both Indian élites and Indian masses, one or other of these gods often (but by no means always) emerges as supreme. Devotees who give primacy to Viṣṇu are termed Vaiṣṇavas, those who focus on Śiva are termed Śaivas, and the followers of the Goddess are called Śāktas.

Starting around 300 BCE and continuing until a little after 1000 CE, books known as the *Purāṇas* were composed. The word *purāṇa* means 'old' in Sanskrit; the *Purāṇas* dealt with old tales. These devotional books, whose use was not limited to the priestly caste, are well known. The *Purāṇas* praised deities that became important in the Hindu pantheon. Older Vedic gods and goddesses were ignored.

No being, no concept is really discarded in the Hindu tradition. Things are just piled up, and older notions or gods are ignored till eventually they are discovered afresh by someone. Instead of Indra, the Aśvins, or Varuṇa, the chief deities of the *Purāṇas* are Viṣṇu, Śiva, and the goddess Pārvatī (also known as Devī) in their many manifestations. Both Viṣṇu and Śiva were mentioned in Vedic literature, but they did not attain any fame. We have seen that there was a prototype of the god Śiva in the ancient Harappa culture.

As these deities emerged in the epics and *Purāṇas*, the Hindu tradition as we know it today crystallized. We observe in the *Purāṇas* an amalgamation of Vedic culture and autochthonous structures. The Puranic literature brings together and makes explicit notions that were implicit in the epics and in the *Bhagavad Gītā*.

### *Viṣṇu*

Viṣṇu ('the all-pervasive one') is portrayed as having several incarnations (*avatāras*); he comes down to earth aeon after aeon in animal and human form to rid it of evil and establish *dharma* or righteousness.

One of Viṣṇu's incarnations is as a fish, to save Manu, the primeval man, from the flood. This story was originally seen in the Vedic literature, but is expanded now in the *Purāṇas*. It focuses on Manu, the progenitor of all human beings. While bathing in a lake, he finds a small fish in his hand. The fish speaks to him and asks him to take it home and put it in a jar. The next day, it has expanded to fill the jar, and Manu is asked to put it in a lake, and eventually when it outgrows it overnight, into a river and then the ocean. The fish, who is really Viṣṇu, then tells him that he is to build a boat, put his family in it, along with the seven sages and 'the seeds of all the animals'. Manu does as he is told. When the floods sweep the earth, the fish asks him to harness the boat to its horn and they ride the waves. Thus he and those on the ship survive the flood. This story is reminiscent of some of the flood myths in other religions.

Eventually, Viṣṇu has ten incarnations in this aeon. Nine of these are said to have already happened. Of them, the fish is the first. The seventh incarnation is as Rāma, the hero of the epic. In some narratives his ninth incarnation is as the Buddha, who, according to some interpreters, diverted people from Hindu teachings, but according to others gave an important place to non-violence as an ethic. The tenth incarnation is to come at the end of this cycle of creation of the universe.

Viṣṇu's ninth incarnation in some texts is as Kṛṣṇa, whom we have already met in the *Bhagavad Gītā*. The *Purāṇas'* stories also deal with the life of Kṛṣṇa, but here we do not see the mature adviser of the *Gītā* or the peacemaker of the *Mahābhārata*. Rather, we meet the infant and child who has been the delight of Hindu devotion for centuries. We see a mischievous toddler who loves butter and steals it from the houses of the cowherd girls. We see a divine youngster who miraculously kills the demons sent out to kill him. We encounter an adolescent Kṛṣṇa who steals the hearts of teenaged girls, a youth who mercilessly teases them and who dances away moonlit nights in their company.

Some of the later *Purāṇas* glorify the love of Kṛṣṇa and his girlfriend Rādhā. In many of the incarnations that Viṣṇu takes, he is said to be accompanied by Śrī or Lakṣmī, his consort. In some traditions that worship Kṛṣṇa, Rādhā is identified with Śrī. In other communities, Kṛṣṇa's wife Rukmiṇī is seen as the incarnation of Śrī. As on most issues, there is no agreement among the Hindu traditions on the details.

Viṣṇu reclining on his serpent called Ananta ('infinity') is always attended by Lakṣmī or Śrī. In the *Purāṇas*, Śrī is worshipped as the goddess of good fortune, who bestows grace in this world and in the next. She embodies all

*Stone carving of Śiva with Pārvatī in the temple at Belur.*
(V. Narayanan)

auspiciousness and blesses her worshippers with wealth and eventually with liberation.

### *Śiva*

Like Viṣṇu, Śiva emerged as a great god in the post-Upanishadic era, but unlike Viṣṇu, he did not become the important focus of a doctrine of consecutive incarnations. Instead, the manifold aspects of Śiva's power were expressed in simultaneous and often mutually contradictory roles: as threatening but benevolent, creator but destroyer, exuberant dancer but austere yogi. As we shall discuss in more detail, in union with a divine consort (often with Pārvatī) Śiva's creative energy is symbolized or manifested, sometimes more abstractly and sometimes more explicitly, in sexual terms. The wedding portrait of Śiva and Pārvatī is one of the dominant images in the tradition of Śiva.

### *The Goddess*

The worship of the great Goddess also became prominent in the Hindu tradition. Pārvatī is her benevolent image, but in fury, she can emerge as Durgā, the warrior goddess, or as Kālī, with wild hair and a garland of skulls. Pārvatī and Durgā are worshipped all over India today at temples and in homes.

While there were many goddesses worshipped in the *Vedas*, none of them was all-powerful. Likewise, the epics and the early *Purāṇas* describe and worship many consort goddesses, but no supreme goddess. From the time of the *Purāṇas*, we see explicit goddess worship.

It may have been in the first millennium CE that the full-fledged worship of a female deity finally developed. In a few *Purāṇas* she is seen to be the Supreme Being who takes many forms. The distinctive characteristic of this Goddess worship is that she was seen to be the ultimate power, the creator of the universe, the redeemer of human beings, and not just an appendage to a male deity. She was sometimes considered to be the *śakti* or power of Śiva, but frequently her independence from the male deity was stressed.

The Goddess, sometimes called Devī in Sanskrit literary tradition, was usually seen as a manifestation of Pārvatī, the wife of Śiva. Western scholars see clear distinctions among the many manifestations of this goddess, talking of Durgā and Kālī as separate entities, but for many Hindus, the lines between these manifestations are blurred.

In her beneficent aspect, she is frequently called Amba or Ambika ('little mother'). As a warrior goddess, she is Durgā, represented in iconography with a smiling countenance but a handful of weapons. As Kālī she is a dark, dishevelled figure with a garland of skulls. Even in this manifestation, she is called 'mother' by her devotees. In rural areas, local goddesses with distinctive names and histories are identified as a manifestation of the Sanskritized, pan-Hindu Devī.

Festivals like the autumn celebration of Navarātri ('nine nights') were dedicated to her. Devotional songs and prayers to her are offered with great fervour by millions of Hindus. The continuing importance of the Goddess is a distinctive characteristic of the Hindu tradition.

### *Sarasvatī*

In the time of the *Purāṇas* the Vedic goddess Sarasvatī becomes the goddess of learning. She is depicted as the consort of Brahmā, the creator god, but though he plays a role in the creation process, he is not one to whom entire *Purāṇas* are dedicated. Nor is their relationship emphasized in iconography or painting, as are the unions of Viṣṇu and Lakṣmī or Śiva and Pārvatī.

Sarasvatī seems to enjoy a certain iconographic and pictorial autonomy. Portraits usually depict her alone, not as a consort or appendage to a male god. She is a beautiful young woman with a white *sāri* and a golden crown over flowing hair, radiant with beauty and wisdom, sitting gracefully on a rock beside a river. She has four hands; two of them hold the *vīṇā*, which is a stringed musical instrument, another holds a string of beads, and another holds a manuscript. The *vīṇā* sings about her being the patron goddess of music; the manuscript shows she is a goddess of learning.

Writing was not considered favourably in India till possibly well into the Common Era, yet Sarasvatī is now seen with a manuscript that conveys to the devotee her knowledge and mastery of writing and books. In fact, around the twelfth or thirteenth century a library was called *Sarasvatī bhāṇḍāram*, or 'the storehouse of Sarasvatī'. Her prayer beads signify counting and the recitation of holy names, leading to transformative knowledge or wisdom. In some literature, Sarasvatī is also portrayed as the one who gave rise to the *devanāgarī* script used for writing the Sanskrit language. In later Hindu tradition, all these themes coalesce, yielding the composite picture of Sarasvatī as a patron goddess of arts and education, music and letters.

*Stone carving of Gaṇeśa, the elephant-headed deity.*
(V.R. Rajagopalan)

### *Other Deities*

Devotion to Gaṇeśa, Murukaṉ, and Hanumān is very popular. Gaṇeśa, the elephant-headed son of Śiva and Pārvatī, is probably the most popular god in all of Hinduism. He is seen as a remover of all obstacles and hindrances, and no new project or venture begins without propitiating him with a coconut or at least a prayer. Murukaṉ, another son of Śiva and Pārvatī, is popular in the Tamil region of South India. And the monkey god Hanumān, also known as Māruti, son of the wind god and the paradigmatic devotee of Rāma and Sītā, is everyone's protector.

In South India, Viṣṇu, Śiva, and Devī are frequently known by local names. Thus, temples devoted to them are seldom referred to as Viṣṇu or Śiva temples. The presiding deity of the Tirupati hills and Srirangam is Viṣṇu, but he is known as Venkatesvara ('lord of the Vēṅkaṭa hill') and as Raṅganātha ('lord of the stage' or *raṅga*) in these places. Each manifestation has a unique personality, a unique history that links it with a place. These myths are recorded in books called *sthala purāṇas* ('*purāṇas* about the place'). Local manifestation is an extremely important feature of Hinduism. Every village has its own deity, and it is sometimes only after considerable effort that one can even identify it (if one absolutely has to) with a pan-Indian god or goddess.

***Popular Expectations of the Deities***

Gods and goddesses in the Hindu pantheon intervene on behalf of human beings. We see this in the story of the gracious Pārvatī, who comes down as a princess and begins a new Pāṇḍyan dynasty, thus nurturing her subjects. We see this faith when one prays to Gaṇeśa to help one find lost keys or get out of a difficult situation.

Śrī or Lakṣmī is called the mother of all creation, who bestows wisdom and salvation and is grace incarnate. Many teachers have composed hymns celebrating her compassion and wisdom. Vedānta Deśika (1268–1369) states her importance thus:

> She fulfils all [our] desires. She is noble, she gives prosperity,
> she is filled with good thoughts; she gives righteousness,
> pleasure, attainment and liberation (*dharma kāmārtha mokṣa dā*).
> She gives the highest state (*parinirvāṇa*) ... she helps one cross
> the ocean of life and death ...

Śrī is considered to be a mediator between all human beings and God in the matter of salvation, but at least one community is split on the issue of her equality to God. Vedānta Deśika holds she is equal and coeval with Viṣṇu, and capable of saving human beings on her own instead of just interceding on behalf of human beings. Others, following the teachings of Piḷḷai Lōkācārya (1264–1369) believe she is an elevated soul, not equal to or coeval with Viṣṇu, and therefore incapable of salvific power.

## The Hindu 'Trinity'

The notion of the *trimūrti* ('three forms') seems to be quite old within the Hindu tradition. It is discussed by the time of the poet-playwright Kālidāsa around the fourth century.

In the symbolism of *trimūrti*, the gods Brahmā, Viṣṇu, and Śiva coalesce into one form with three faces. The concept is sometimes interpreted to imply a polytheism of the Hindu people, with a belief in Brahmā as creator, Viṣṇu as preserver, and Śiva as destroyer. This interpretation has a grain of truth, for the concept does try to bring together the three great functions of a supreme god and divide them up among known deities. However, in two ways the notion misleads more than it informs.

First, *trimūrti* is taken to imply that Hindus give equal importance to all three gods. In practice, however, the *sectarian* Hindu worshipper frequently adores only one. This may be Śiva, Viṣṇu, the Goddess in one of her multiple forms, or one of the local deities who may not be necessarily recognized in another part of India. The other deities are recognized as important, but secondary to the focus of one's worship. And although Viṣṇu and Śiva are certainly popular, Brahmā has not been a focus of worship in modern Hinduism. While portrayed in mythology as the creator god, he is himself created by another god; he is the agent of either Viṣṇu, Śiva, or the Goddess, creating at the pleasure of the supreme deity.

Second, *trimūrti* suggests that creation, preservation, and destruction are separate functions. But followers of Viṣṇu or Śiva commonly understand that the god they hold supreme is responsible for an integrated creation, preservation, and destruction of the world. In this context, destruction is not forever and not unplanned; it is in the cosmic nature of evolution and devolution of the universe. All of creation temporarily enters or becomes one with the body of Viṣṇu or Śiva until a new cycle of creation begins again. These cycles will go on forever for all the souls still caught up in the wheel of life and death. Thus, the devotee of Śiva, Viṣṇu, or the Goddess would say that the supreme deity he or she worships is the creator, maintainer, and destroyer of the universe.

## Ages of Time

The *Purāṇas* speak about cycles of creation and destruction of the cosmos. These cycles are known as the days and nights of the creator god (a minor deity) called Brahmā. During a day (which is called a *kalpa*) there are secondary cycles of creation and destruction. Each *kalpa* is approximately 4,320 million earthly years. (There are distinctions between earthly years and the much longer years of the gods.) The nights of Brahmā are of equal length. The total of 360 such days and nights makes a year of Brahmā, and Brahmā lives for 100 years. This cycle therefore is 311,040,000 million years. After this, the entire cosmos is drawn into the body of Viṣṇu or Śiva (depending on which *Purāṇa* one is reading), and remains there until another Brahmā is evolved.

During each of his days, the creator god brings out the universe periodically and withdraws it into himself. A day in the life of Brahmā is divided into fourteen *mānavāntaras*, and each lasts 306,720,000 years. During the long intervals between *mānavāntaras*, the world is recreated and a new Manu or primeval man appears and begins the human race.

Each *mānavāntara* contains seventy-one great aeons (*mahā yugas*), each of which is divided into four aeons (*yugas*). A single one of these aeons is the basic cycle. The golden age (*kṛta yuga*) lasts 4,800 divine years (1,728,000 human or earthly years). During this time, *dharma* is on firm footing. To use traditional animal imagery, the bull of *dharma* or righteousness stands on all four legs. The Treta age is shorter, lasting 3,600 god years, that is, 1,296,000 earthly years; *dharma* is then on three legs. The Dvāpara age lasts half as long as the golden or *kṛta* age; it is 2,400 god years long (864,000 earthly years) and *dharma* is now hopping on two legs. During the *kali yuga*, the worst of all possible ages, *dharma* is on one leg and things get progressively worse. This age lasts for 1,200 god years (432,000 earthly years). We live in this degenerate *kali yuga*, which, according to traditional Hindu reckoning, began around 3102 BCE.

There is a steady decline through the *yugas* in morality, righteousness, life span, and human satisfaction. At the end of the *kali yuga*—obviously still a long time off—there will be no righteousness, no virtue, no trace of justice. When the world ends, seven scorching suns will dry up the oceans, there will be wondrously shaped clouds, torrential rains will fall, and eventually the cosmos will be absorbed into Viṣṇu. The *Purāṇas* deal with astronomical units of time; the age of the earth and of the human being is infinitesimally small in relation to the aeons of time the universe goes through. Note that while according to many Hindu systems of thought, it is entirely possible for a human being to end his or her cycle of birth and death through transforming wisdom and/or through devotion, the cycles of creation and destruction of the universe are independent of the human being's attaining *mokṣa* or liberation.

## Caste and the *Laws of Manu*

'Caste' is used as a shorthand term to refer to thousands of stratified and boundaried social communities that have multiplied through the centuries. We referred to the beginnings of the caste system in the 'Hymn to the Supreme Person' in the *Ṛg Veda*, with its enumeration of priestly, ruling, mercantile, and servant classes.

From the simple fourfold structure eventually arose a plethora of endogamous social and occupational divisions. There are more than 1,000 *jātis* ('birth groups') in India. People regularly identify themselves by their *jāti*. An underlying idea in the hierarchical system is that people are born with different spiritual propensities as a result of their past *karma*. Ritual practices, dietary rules, and sometimes dialects differ between the castes. Deviation from caste practices in past centuries sometimes resulted in one's being excluded from the caste.

The word 'caste' comes from the Portuguese, who used '*casta*' to refer to the various sections of Hindu society. The modern word 'caste' signifies both the four broad *varṇas* and the minutely divided *jātis*, although Western scholars sometimes translate *varṇa* as class and *jāti* as caste.

By the first centuries of the Common Era, many treatises on the nature of righteousness, moral duty, and law were written. These are called the *dharmaśāstras* and form the basis for later Hindu laws. The most famous of these is the *Mānava Dharmaśāstra*, or the *Laws of Manu*, named after the figure we encountered in the story of Viṣṇu's incarnation as a fish. These were probably codified around the first century and reflect the social norms of the time. We see the caste system firmly in place. Women have slipped to an inferior position from the relatively high status that they had in the *Vedas*.

When reading Manu, we have to understand that the prescriptive behaviour he records was seldom followed strictly. Thus, while a twice-born man—that is, a man of the upper three classes of society—was said to undergo four stages of life, he seldom did so. In a similar vein, we have to take his pronouncements on women with some grains of salt. Historical evidence tells us that Manu was probably not taken too seriously by most classes of society.

The upper classes were generally called 'twice born'. The expression referred to the initiatory rite whereby the males of these social groups were spiritually reborn, this time from their religious teachers. This rite, the *upanayana*, described later in this chapter, initiated one into life's first stage, that of a student.

In time, this rite was practised usually by the brahmins, the priestly class of society, who retained the authority to teach and learn the *Vedas*; no others were given this right. The term 'priestly' is used in a loose manner; not all members of this community were priests. Frequently, they were in the business of teaching and counselling. Even when not engaged in religious pursuits, they held the power and prestige generally associated with spiritual learning. The monopoly that the brahmins exercised in teaching the *Vedas* orally was jealously guarded, and for centuries these hymns were not supposed to be written down.

The *rājanya* ('royal') class was the one from which kings and rulers emerged. Eventually the term *rājanya* was replaced with the better known word *kṣatriya*. The men from this community were allowed to learn but not teach the *Vedas*; their *dharma* was to protect the people and the country. Arjuna, the hero of the *Bhagavad Gītā*, is from this class. When Kṛṣṇa urges him to do his *dharma*, he is reminding Arjuna of the duties incumbent on him by virtue of his birth. The *kṣatriyas* generally traced their ancestry either to the lineage of the sun (*sūrya vaṃśa*) or the lineage of the moon (*candra vaṃśa*), both going back to the primeval progenitors of humanity. We see here classic instances of the ruling class seeking legitimacy by invoking divine antecedents; even usurpers of thrones eventually began to trace their ancestries thus. In the Hindu tradition, both then and now, lines of claimed biological descent are all-important. The *kṣatriya* families held the power of rulership and governance, and rituals of later Hinduism explicitly emphasized their connection with divine beings.

The *Laws of Manu* describe in detail the duties of a king. He is asked to strive to conquer his senses, for only the person who has conquered his own senses can lead or control his subjects. The king is asked to shun the vices of pleasure, such as hunting, gambling, drinking, and obsession with women. He must also shun the vices that arise from wrath, such as violence, envy, slander, unjust seizure of property, and assault.

The mercantile class (*vaiśyas*) was in charge of most commercial transactions. According to the codes of law, they, like the ruling class, had the authority to study but not teach the *Vedas*. They were to rear cattle, trade, and deal with agricultural work. The power of wealth and economic decisions lay with this community.

## FROM THE *LAWS OF MANU*

(2.6) The root of religion is the entire *Veda*, and (then) the tradition and customs of those who know (the Veda), and the conduct of virtuous people, and what is satisfactory to oneself.

(2.7) Whatever duty Manu proclaimed for whatever person, all of that was declared in the Veda, for it contains all knowledge.

(2.10) The Veda should be known as the revealed canon, and the teachings of religion as the tradition. These two are indisputable in all matters, for religion arose out of the two of them.

(2.11) Any twice-born man who disregards these two roots [of religion] because he relies on the teachings of logic should be excommunicated by virtuous people as an atheist and a reviler of the Veda.

(2.145) The teacher is more important than ten instructors, and the father more than a hundred teachers, but the mother more than a thousand fathers.

(5.5) Garlic, scallions, onions, and mushrooms, and the things that grow from what is impure, are not to be eaten by twice-born men.

(5.7) And do not eat ... meat that has not been consecrated ...

(5.8) or the milk of a cow within ten days of calving, or the milk of a camel or of any animal with a whole, solid hoof, or of a ewe, or of a cow in heat or a cow whose calf has been taken from her.

(5.11) Do not eat carnivorous birds or any birds that live in villages, or any whole-hoofed animals that have not been specially permitted; or little finches.

(5.147) A girl, a young woman, or even an old woman should not do anything independently, even in (her own) house.

(5.148) In childhood a woman should be under her father's control, in youth under her husband's, and when her husband is dead, under her sons'. She should not have independence.

The last class mentioned formally in the *dharmaśāstra* is the *śūdras*, a term that has generally been translated as 'servants'. In the original social scheme, this group is thought to have been called *dāsa* or 'servant' and to have consisted of the population conquered by the Indo-European invaders. The *dharmaśāstras* say that the duty of a *śūdra* is to serve the other classes, especially the brahmins. *Śūdras* who desire to obtain good *karma* are advised to know their duty, to commit no sin, and to imitate the practice of virtuous men without reciting sacred texts. The *śūdra* was not allowed to accumulate wealth, even if he was able to do so. There was no area of power that the *śūdra* could tap into; a *śūdra* could be respected because of his or her old age and not for any other reason. As the *Laws of Manu* put it, 'The seniority of brahmins comes from sacred knowledge, that of *kṣatriyas* from valour, *vaiśyas* from wealth, and *śūdras*, only from old age.'

(2.213) It is the very nature of women to corrupt men here on earth; for that reason, circumspect men do not get careless and wanton among wanton women.

(9.95) A husband takes his wife as a gift from the gods, not by his own wish; he should always support a virtuous woman, thus pleasing the gods.

(9.96) Women were created to bear children, and men to carry on the line; that is why the revealed canon prescribes a joint duty (for a man) together with his wife.

(9.101) 'Let there be mutual absence of infidelity until death'; this should be known as the supreme duty of a man and a woman, in a nutshell.

(5.154) A virtuous wife should constantly serve her husband like a god, even if he behaves badly, freely indulges his lust, and is devoid of good qualities.

(2.67) The ritual of marriage is traditionally known as the Vedic transformative ritual for women; serving her husband is [the equivalent of] living with a guru, and household chores are the rites of the fire.

(2.210) The guru's wives who belong to the same class should be revered like the guru, but those who do not belong to the same class should be revered by rising to greet them.

(2.21) The country between the Himalayas and the Vindhya mountains, to the east of the 'Disappearance' and to the west of Prayāga, is known as the Middle Country.

(2.22) From the eastern sea to the western sea, the area in between the two mountains is what wise men call the Land of the Aryans.

(2.23) Where the black antelope ranges by nature, that should be known as the country fit for sacrifices; and beyond it is the country of the barbarians.

(2.24) The twice-born should make every effort to settle in these countries; but a servant may live in any country at all if he is starved for a livelihood (Doniger and Smith 1991:17–209).

Manu's injunctions were apparently not followed in many parts of India. The caste system is far more complex and flexible than the *dharmaśāstra* descriptions. The Veḷḷālas, for instance, were considered a *śūdra* caste technically, but wielded considerable economic and political power in the south. They were a wealthy caste of landowners, and the *dharmaśāstra* prohibitions do not seem to have had any effect on their fortunes.

The *Laws of Manu*, as well the *Bhagavad Gītā*, tell us that it is better for a person to do one's own *dharma* imperfectly than to do another's well. However, the law books acknowledge that in times of adversity, one may do other tasks, and list these in order of preference for each class. While these codes of law emphasize the importance of marrying within one's own class, they recognize that mixed marriages take place quite often, and so go on to list the kind of subcastes that emerge from various permutations. A marriage is generally acceptable if the male partner is of a higher caste. However, if a woman is higher, the offspring is considered of a lower caste than either parent.

The Indian caste system is not a feature of the Hindu tradition alone. It is such a strong social force that non-Hindu communities such as the Christians, Jains, and Sikhs have absorbed parts of it. Nadar Christians from the south, for instance, will only marry people of the same heritage, and one may draw similar parallels all over India.

Eventually, various groups of outcastes emerged. These came either from mixed marriages or more often from association with professions deemed inferior. Such occupations included working with animal hides and dealing with corpses, as dead animal or human flesh is considered polluting. The word 'pariah', for instance, is of Tamil origin, meaning 'drummer'. Since drums were made with animal hides stretched taut over a frame, the drummer dealt with polluting material and thus belonged to an outcaste community. From that comes the English meaning of 'pariah' as a social outcaste.

The code of Manu also contains prescriptions of criminal law, where the punishment frequently depended on the caste of the offender and the caste of the victim. The lower castes faced harsher punishments for the same crime than the higher ones according to this text, but one is not sure whether these prescriptions were followed. Scholars have shown that the *Laws of Manu* had limited import: that in fact the law was mitigated by learned people, and each case was decided with reference to the immediate circumstances.

It was only in the nineteenth century, after the establishment of British rule, that the *Laws of Manu* and other texts received more attention than they had commanded in the previous centuries. The British assumed that these laws were binding, when in fact they had been only one factor among the many considerations in the judicial process and in society itself. A reassessment of the importance of these religio-legal texts in the last 2,000 years is necessary before we make any final statement on their authority.

## The Stages and Goals of Life

The texts of law recognized four stages of life, called the four *āśramas*, for males of the upper three classes of society. First, a young boy was initiated with the *upanayana* ceremony into the stage of a student when he was to remain celibate and concentrate on learning. Education was to be provided for all those who desired it. Families were to support a student. While in the earlier Vedic literature there is some evidence that girls could also become students, it is probable that by the time of Manu in the first century, this right was withdrawn.

After being a student, a young man was to get married and repay his debt to society, his forefathers, and his spiritual debt to the gods. He earned a living to support his family and other students. Whereas it was a student's *dharma* not to work for a living and to remain celibate, a householder's *dharma* was to be employed and lead a conjugal life with his partner in *dharma* (*saha-dharmacāriṇī*). It is probable that most men never went beyond these two stages, and even the first may have been of a cursory nature to some.

The *Laws of Manu*, however, give details of two more stages: those of a forest dweller and an ascetic. When a man sees his skin wrinkled and his hair grey, says Manu, when he sees his grandchildren (that is, when his children are now in the householder stage and the economic pillars of society), he may retire to the forest with his wife, lead a simple life, and spend the time in reciting the *Vedas* and in quietude. The final stage, *saṃnyāsin*, was entered by very few: a man apparently staged his own social death and became an ascetic. His old personality was now dead; the ascetic owned nothing, living off the food given as alms and eating but once a day. He was to spend his time pursuing salvific knowledge and cultivating detachment from life. With the increasing popularity of the *Bhagavad Gītā*, which stresses detached action, the need to enter formally into the life of a renunciant was diminished considerably within the Hindu tradition.

The epics and classical texts of the period just before the beginning of the Common Era also recognized that there were certain aims that human beings strive for. These are not good or bad in themselves, but the intensity with which one is preoccupied with them as well as the stage of life when one pursues them make them appropriate or immoral. The aims are: *dharma*, the discharging of one's duties; *artha*, wealth and power in all forms; *kāma*, sensual pleasure of many types including, but not limited to, sexual pleasure and the appreciation of beauty; and finally, *mokṣa*, or liberation from the cycle of birth and death. The last category was sometimes seen as being on a different plane, but the *Bhagavad Gītā* and similar texts make it clear that if one acts without attachment, one may strive for liberation even through the performance of daily work.

# DEVELOPMENTS OVER THE CENTURIES

## Hindu Philosophical Schools

Six traditional or orthodox systems of philosophy are recognized within the Hindu tradition. The word translated as 'philosophy' is literally *darśana* or 'vision'. One may call these schools viewpoints or visions of reality. Some of the schools go back to about 500 BCE. The development of Vedānta, on the other hand, continued through the twentieth century. Of the six schools only the last two survive. The fifth school, Mīmāṃsā, focuses on the performance of rituals. The sixth school, Vedānta, is of considerable speculative significance in the intellectual history of the Hindu tradition. We shall focus on its development below.

Sāṃkhya was probably one of the earliest philosophical schools. It predates the *Bhagavad Gītā* and is explicitly dualistic in its conceptual framework. Innumerable souls are seen to be enmeshed in matter. Matter is composed of three strands, which also colour human attributes. These are *sattva* ('purity'), *rajas* ('passion'), and *tamas* ('sloth'). Liberation of the soul is through its extrication from primordial matter. In its liberated state, the soul is blissful in its splendid isolation. In later compositions like the *Bhagavad Gītā* (200 BCE–100 BCE), the worldview of Sāṃkhya yoga is integrated into a theistic worldview. Elements of the Sāṃkhya worldview were also integrated into Buddhism and Jainism.

Yoga, the second school, was tied up with Sāṃkhya in its philosophical framework. Yoga in its theoretical aspects is theistic in outlook, differing from Sāṃkhya philosophy, which does not focus on a deity.

Nyāya, the third school, focused on epistemology; that is, on philosophical discussion of the conditions for knowing anything. Vaiśeṣika, the fourth school, dealt with nine categories of irreducible principles constituting the universe. Pūrva Mīṃāṃsā, the fifth school, spoke of the eternal and transhuman nature of the *Veda*s and the centrality of ritual in religious life.

Vedānta (end of the *Veda*s) is the sixth school of philosophy and has been significant over the last 1,000 years. While yoga gave way to *bhakti* in importance, the intellectual and spiritual interpretation of Vedānta philosophy has preoccupied and continues to engage many Hindu thinkers. Traditionally the term *Vedānta* was used to denote the *Upaniṣads*, the final part of the Vedic corpus.

But the term has more popularly been used to denote systems of thought based on a coherent interpretation of three works, the *Upaniṣad*s, the *Bhagavad Gītā*, and a text called the *Brahma sūtras*. The *Brahma sūtras* (also known as the *Vedānta sūtra*) was composed possibly after the first century; some scholars give an even later date for it. It consisted of approximately 500 aphorisms. These aphorisms did not generally have any obvious meaning; they had to be interpreted with passages from the *Upaniṣad*s and the *Gītā*.

The word *sūtra* means 'thread'. It may have denoted the string used to bind palm leaf manuscripts together like a Venetian blind. Others say this thread was one on which gems of wisdom could be strung. In Buddhist literature, *sūtra* came to mean a holy book, specifically one purporting to be a discourse given by Gautama Buddha.

In Hindu usage, however, *sūtra* simply means a book, and the *Brahma sūtras* are 'a book on Brahman'. It was meant to be a mnemonic aid, summarizing the teachings of the other two texts. Since many phrases did not have an obvious meaning, Vedantic philosophers wrote extensive commentaries on this text. The school of Vedānta is still alive. Whereas earlier philosophers wrote the commentaries on the *Brahma sūtras* in Sanskrit, modern writers do it in English and also give oral discourses to the public, explaining particular viewpoints.

Śaṅkara, who lived around 800, was a prominent interpreter of Vedānta.

He portrayed this earth and life cycle as having limited reality; once the soul realizes that it is and always has been Brahman, 'this life passes away like a dream'.

For Śaṅkara, reality is non-dual (*advaita*). There is only one reality, Brahman, and this Brahman is indescribable and without any attributes. Brahman and Ātman (the human soul) are identical; he interprets the Upanishadic phrase 'you are that' in a literal way and upholds the unity of what appear to people as two distinct entities. It is because of *māyā*, an illusory power that ultimately defies definition, that one believes one is different from Brahman. When this *māyā* is cut through, the soul is liberated through the realization of its true nature. Liberation, therefore, is removing ignorance and dispelling illusion through the power of transforming knowledge. This can be attained in this life itself. Human beings can have liberation while still embodied (*jīvanmukti*); final release will come after the death of the body. Those liberated in this life act without binding desire, and having crossed over, help others to achieve liberation.

Śaṅkara also posits three levels of reality. He recognizes that human beings believe they are different from each other and that life is real. He agrees with this estimate, but points out that when we sleep and have dreams, we believe the dream situation is real. It is only when we wake up from the dream that we discover that it was not real. So, too, is this cycle of life and death. We live, die, and are reborn, believing that all this is real. And it is—until we are liberated and wake up to the truth about our identity. One may argue that while the dream seems true only to the individual, this phenomenal world seems true to millions of people who all seem to share the same reality. The school of Śaṅkara would argue that this is simply one's perception, that ignorance and illusion hold good for everyone. Through transforming knowledge, the higher knowledge that is spoken of in the *Upaniṣads*, one realizes that one is really Brahman and is liberated from the cycle of life and death. But the cycle of life and death would go on for the other souls still caught in the snares of *māyā*.

Śaṅkara's philosophy has been criticized by later Vedānta philosophers like Rāmānuja (traditionally 1017–1137) and Madhva (c. 1199–1278). One of their principal objections is connected with the status of *māyā*. If *māya* is real, the critics argue, then there are two realities: Brahman and *māyā*. But Śaṅkara insists that there is only one reality. If *māyā* is unreal, argue these later philosophers, then it seems absurd to believe that an unreal entity like *māyā* can cause cosmic bondage of the proportion claimed for it. It seems hardly possible, they say, that a non-existent *māyā* could delude millions of souls into believing that they are different from Brahman. Śaṅkara tries to avoid these charges by saying that *māyā* is indescribable, that it is neither real nor unreal, but the critics are left unconvinced. The followers of Śaṅkara would also say that criticisms such as these are not valid in the ultimate state of liberation, which is totally ineffable. At that time questions that arise from a limited human intellect will fade away as inconsequential.

Rāmānuja was the most significant interpreter of theistic Vedānta for the

Śrīvaiṣṇava community of South India. The name 'Śrīvaiṣṇava' is given to the community that worships Viṣṇu and his consorts Śrī (Lakṣmī) and Bhū (the goddess Earth). In his commentaries on the *Brahma sūtras* and the *Bhagavad Gītā*, as well as in his independent treatises, Rāmānuja proclaims the supremacy of Viṣṇu-Nārāyaṇa and emphasizes that devotion to Viṣṇu will lead to ultimate liberation. He challenges Śaṅkara's interpretation of scripture, especially the concept of *māyā*, and the belief that the supreme reality (Brahman) is without attributes. For Rāmānuja, Viṣṇu (whose name literally means 'all-pervasive') is immanent in the entire universe, pervading all souls and material substances, but also transcending them. His personal form is pleasing to human beings, and he is replete with all auspicious attributes such as compassion and grace.

Thus, from a certain viewpoint, there is only one reality, Brahman, but from another, one may say that Brahman is qualified by souls and matter. Since the human soul is the body (*śarīra*) and the servant (*śeṣa*) of the supreme being, liberation is not portrayed as the realization of identity between the two. Rather, it is the intuitive, total, and joyful realization of the soul's relationship with the lord. It surpasses a lesser goal called *kaivalya*, where the soul is freed from the cycle of *saṃsāra*, but is aware of bliss in an isolated state. While technically *kaivalya* is also liberation, one is warned not to be trapped by it because communion with the deity is said to transcend the rapture of isolation.

The philosopher Madhva is unique in the Hindu tradition in classifying some souls as eternally bound. For him, even in liberation there are different grades of enjoyment and bliss. He is also one of the explicitly dualistic Vedānta philosophers, holding that the human soul and Brahman are ultimately separate and not identical in any way.

## The Sacred Syllable *Oṃ*

The word *oṃ* is recited at the beginning and end of all Hindu and Jain prayers and recitations of scripture, and is used by Buddhists also, particularly in Tibetan Vajrayāna. The word is understood to have three sounds, *a–u–m*; when *a* and *u* come together, they produce the sound of *o*. The sound of the word begins deep within the body and ends at the lips; it is claimed to be auspicious. *Oṃ*'s history in the Hindu tradition is ancient; the *Māṇḍūkya Upaniṣad* discusses its meaning and power. Hindu philosophers and sectarian communities all agree that *oṃ* is the most sacred sound.

However, almost every Hindu community has speculated about the meaning of *oṃ*, and the speculations vary widely. *Oṃ* is said to represent the supreme reality or Brahman. Many Hindu philosophers have held this word to be at the beginning of the manifest universe and also to contain the essence of true knowledge. Some say that its three sounds represent the three worlds: earth, atmosphere, and heaven. Others say that it represents the essence of the three *Vedas*:

*Rg, Yajur*, and *Sāma*. Some derive the word from the Sanskrit verbal root *av-*, to mean 'that which protects'.

According to followers of the philosopher Śaṅkara, that is, non-dualist interpreters of Vedānta, the three sounds *a*, *u*, and *m* have the following experiential meanings:

- The sound of *a* stands for the world that we see when we are awake, the person who is experiencing it, and the waking experience.
- *U* stands for the dream world, the dreamer, and the dream experience.
- *M* represents the sleep world, the sleeper, and the sleep experience.
- These three states we experience on this earth. The fourth, the untold syllable, represents the state of liberation.

Some Vaiṣṇava devotees, on the other hand, say that *a* represents the lord Viṣṇu, *u* denotes the human being, and the meaning of *m* is the relationship between the two. Other Vaiṣṇavas say that they represent Viṣṇu, Śrī, and the devotee.

So, Hindus say that *oṃ* is the most sacred sound, but disagree regarding its meaning. Among the many Hindu traditions, the sound of *oṃ* is in a sense a whole greater than the sum of its parts, exceeding in significance the many meanings attributed to it.

## Yoga

Yoga entails physical and mental discipline by which one 'yokes' one's spirit to a god. It has been held in high regard in many Hindu texts, and has had many meanings in the history of the Hindu tradition. Its origins are obscure, but it is generally thought to have come from non-Aryan sources. Some scholars point out that seals from the Harappan culture portray a man sitting in a yogic position.

Many Hindus associate yoga with Patañjali, considering classical his text, the *Yoga sūtras*, composed of short, fragmentary, and aphoristic sentences. We do not know when Patañjali lived, but the material in the book may come from before the first century BCE even if his own dates were as late as the third century CE. Yoga was probably an important feature of religious life in India several centuries before the text was written. Patañjali acknowledges that he is only codifying and presenting an accurate version of what has already been known, not presenting a new philosophy.

Patañjali's yoga, as interpreted by commentators on his book, involves moral, mental, and physical discipline, and meditation concentrating on a physical or mental object as the 'single point' of focus. This form of yoga is described as having eight 'limbs' or disciplines, of which the first two are *yama*, consisting of restraints, and *niyama*, consisting of positive practices.

*Yama* is the avoidance of violence, falsehood, stealing, sexual activity, and avarice. Interestingly enough, these prohibitions are included in the 'right conduct' taught by the Jain tradition.

*Niyama* includes cleanliness, equanimity, asceticism, the theoretical study of yoga, and the effort to make God the focus of one's activities. Cleanliness includes internal and external purity; in some forms of yoga, this aspect receives considerable attention. The Sanskrit term Patañjali uses for asceticism is *tapas* or 'heat', a kind of energetic concentration.

In addition to *yama* and *niyama*, Patañjali recommends bodily postures and correct techniques of breathing. Proper bodily posture is one of the unique characteristics in the discipline of yoga. Detaching the mind from the domination of external sensory stimuli is also important in its practice.

Perfection in concentration (*dhāraṇā*) and meditation (*dhyāna*) lead one to *samādhi*, the final state of absorption into and union with the divine. In the many stages of *samādhi*, the ultimate stage is a complete emancipation from the cycle of life and death. The state is spoken of variously as a coming together, uniting, and transcending of polarities; the state is empty and full, it is neither life nor death, and it is both. In short, this final liberation cannot be adequately described in human language.

While Patañjali's yoga is considered the classical form of yoga by many scholars, there are many other variations as well. At the broadest level, the word has been used to designate any form of meditation or practice with ascetic tendencies. More generally, it is used to refer to any path that leads to final emancipation. Thus in the *Bhagavad Gītā* the way of action is called *karma yoga* and the way of devotion *bhakti yoga*. In some interpretations of *karma yoga* and *bhakti yoga* the eight 'limbs' or members of classical Patañjalian yoga are not present; *bhakti yoga* simply comes to mean *bhakti mārga*, the way of devotion. In this context yoga becomes a way of self-abnegation, and through passionate devotion the worshipper craves union with the Supreme Being. Some philosophers, such as the eleventh-century Rāmānuja, say that *bhakti yoga* includes elements of yoga taught by Patañjali, but many Hindus use the term 'yoga' in a much looser manner.

While the theoretical aspects of Patañjali's yoga have had considerable importance in particular times and traditions, its place in the religious life of Hindus in the past 1,000 to 2,000 years appears overemphasized by many interpreters. It simply has not enjoyed mass popularity over the years, nor has it been mentioned as a path to liberation by many of the religious teachers.

Nonetheless there has been an uninterrupted tradition of its practice by a small minority of Hindus, primarily males. Yoga schools have frequently been located in pilgrimage centres. In the twentieth century there has been a resurgence of interest in its physical techniques. This interest only sometimes extends to an interest also in yoga's underlying psychological and theoretical assumptions.

In the past century a distinction between two avenues of discipline has been drawn in the use of the term: *rāja yoga* and *haṭha yoga*. *Rāja yoga* deals with mental discipline; occasionally this term is used interchangeably with Patañjali's yoga. *Haṭha yoga* largely focuses on bodily posture and control over the body. The term *haṭha* is said to be derived from the words for sun (*ha*) and moon (*ṭhat*), referring to particular patterns of breath control. The human body is said to have 'suns' and 'moons' within it; final liberation can be attained only after one homologizes different centres in the body with the cosmos. This form of yoga is what has become very popular in Western countries.

## Tantra

The component of the Hindu tradition that is termed 'tantric' is hard to define, partly because it is portrayed differently by its advocates and detractors. Essentially it centres on a body of ritual practices that are otherwise socially unacceptable, and of texts interpreting them that appear independent of the brahminical ritual and the Vedic literature.

Tantra, which etymologically means 'loom', began to gain importance in the Hindu and Buddhist traditions around the fifth century. Some scholars see it as part of the indigenous pre-Aryan culture, surfacing at this time of Hindu history, more than a millennium after the Aryan conquest. Others see it as a later non-Vedic, but not an anti-Vedic, movement. Of course, no movement in the Hindu tradition could hope to succeed if it actually claimed to be against the *Vedas*; many doctrines were put forth as the implication or application of these hymns.

The tantric tradition influenced many sectarian Hindu movements; Śaiva and Vaiṣṇava temple liturgies, still practised, are in large measure derived from tantric usage. For example, when the images of the deities are installed in temples, large geometric drawings (*maṇḍalas*) representing the god or goddess and the cosmos are drawn on the floor and used as a tool for meditation and ritual.

The tantric tradition advocated its own form of yoga, known as *kuṇḍalinī yoga*. *Kuṇḍalinī* (literally, 'the one with earrings') refers to the *śakti* or power of the Goddess, which is said to lie coiled like a serpent at the base of one's spine. When awakened, this power rises through a channel passing through six *cakras* or 'wheels' to reach the final centre located under the skull. This centre is known as a thousand-petalled lotus.

The ultimate aim of this form of yoga is to awaken the power of the *kuṇḍalinī* and make it unite with Puruṣa, the male supreme being, who is in the thousand-petalled lotus. With this union, the practitioner is granted several visions and given psychic powers. The union leads eventually to final emancipation.

There are many ways of looking at tantric materials. The best-known division is between the *vāmācāra* (left-handed practice) and the right-handed or more conservative school. As the left hand is associated with the inauspicious in the Hindu tradition, 'left-handed' was applied to sectarian movements that did not meet with the approval of the other larger or more established schools. The left-handed schools' practices involved ritual performance of activities forbidden in everyday life, such as drinking liquor, eating fish and meat, and having sexual intercourse with a partner not one's spouse. These activities were disapproved of in many other Hindu circles, so that to a large extent left-handed tantrism remained esoteric.

One may also see divisions in tantra along the sectarian lines of Śaiva, Śakta, and Vaiṣṇava, each with its own canon of texts called *tantras*. The texts may also be classified into those that focus on temple worship and those that are about individual rites at home.

## Medicine

In the first millennium, the field of medicine made great progress in the Hindu world. One of the major systems of medicine was Āyurveda, the *veda* or knowledge of enhancing life. The physician is called *vaidya* ('one who is learned'), promoting both longevity and in the quality of life. The prototype is a deity called Dhanavantari, sometimes identified as an incarnation of Viṣṇu. Parallel to Āyurveda is Siddhā, the Tamil system developed in South India.

Folk medicine, as still practised by exorcists, snake-bite curers, and astrologers, presumes a largely supernatural causation of illness. Similarly, the Vedic *saṃhitās*, especially the *Atharva Veda*, attribute illness to the work of demons and prescribe various charms and rituals of exorcism to mitigate it.

At some time during the last three centuries BCE, writings in the developing tradition of Āyurveda were produced by the surgeon Suśruta and the physician Caraka. Each of their collections presented new theories, attributing their transmission to the human authors from the gods through inspired sages. The teachings themselves embodied an understanding of illness as a lack of balance among three elements: air, phlegm, and bile. Āyurveda thus had an analytic approach resembling in general Greek and Chinese medical theory of about the same period, but differing in detail; the Greeks saw health as a balance among four humours (blood, phlegm, choler, and black choler or melancholy) while the Chinese formulated a theory of balance in terms of two principles, *yin* and *yang*. For cures, Āyurveda used diet and an impressive repertory of medicinal plants, along with enemas, inhalation of substances, and bleeding. Minerals were and still are used in remedies; ingesting microscopic amounts of gold is supposed to increase strength.

Suśruta's opening remark in his work, the *Suśruta saṃhitā*, is that a physician's aim is 'to cure the diseases of the sick, to protect the healthy, to prolong life'. The work attributed to Caraka, *Caraka saṃhitā*, contains the following impressive statement on the ethics of a physician:

> The Physician should not betray patients for his own advantage, nor take advantage of women. He should dress modestly and avoid drink. He should be collected and self-controlled, measured in speech at all times. He should constantly strive to improve his knowledge and technical skill. He should refuse to treat the king's enemies, evil-doers, and loose women. In the home of a patient he should be courteous and modest and should direct all his attention to the patient's welfare. He should not divulge any knowledge he may acquire concerning the patient or his family (*Caraka saṃhitā* iii.8.13).

With the growth of tantra after about 500, ritualized magical techniques had an increased influence. This was reflected in Ayurvedic literature, with increasing attention to ritual techniques in healing, complementing treatment with medicines. Moreover, though Suśruta and Caraka did make some place for possession by demons as a cause for mental illness in their writings, the roster of demons held responsible more than doubled by the thirteenth century.

In today's India, Āyurveda bridges modern international medicine and traditional Indian religio-philosophical theories. In its clinical practice it parallels modern medicine, while its theory draws on elements of tantra and yoga. It shares their outlook on life and the world, but its emphasis is more on health than on spiritual attainment.

## South Indian *bhakti*

The standard portrait of Vedic and classical Hinduism is sketched from the compositions and culture that existed in the northern part of the Indian subcontinent. The culture of the south—that is, the area south of the Vindhya mountains and Gujarat—flourished at least from 500–400 BCE, and possibly even earlier. We now turn our attention to this part of the land. Here we find historically significant changes taking place in the structures of the Hindu tradition after 600. In medieval times the revolution of devotion (*bhakti*) began here and swept all over India.

A sophisticated body of literature in Tamil, one of the South Indian languages, existed 2,000 years ago. The earliest literature, usually referred to as *Caṅkam* (Academy) poems, was said to have been composed at the time of three great Tamil academies. These classical poems were secular and focused on the outer (*puṟam*) and inner (*akam*) worlds. The poems that dealt with the outer sphere were those concerned with kings, nobles, and warfare. These poems of chivalry, honour, and generosity were composed by bards who praised the valour of kings. The inner poems focused on love and romance: secret meetings between lovers, forbidden love, the anguish of separation, and the overwhelming joy of union.

The Tamil language had a long history of sophisticated poems, drama, and grammatical analysis. Even in the earliest extant Tamil composition (which is probably the original stratum of the *Tolkāppiyam*, a text dealing with the Tamil language as well as values) there are some undeniable similarities to Sanskrit literature. One may also note that the early poems of love and war have borrowed many words from Sanskrit. Tamil literature on the whole, however, is neither imitative of nor derived from early Sanskrit material.

The oldest collections of Tamil poems, known as the *Eṭṭutōkai* (Eight Anthologies) and the *Pattupāṭṭu* (Ten Songs) were probably composed between the first and the third centuries. The earliest sections of the *Eight Anthologies* and the *Ten Songs* deal primarily with the two themes of romantic love and heroic or war poetry. These poems had been lost for over 1,000 years and were rediscovered in the nineteenth century.

The Tamil poems that deal with love and war refer to five basic situations reflecting particular moods. These situations correspond to five landscape settings (*tiṇai*). The situations for *akam* are lovemaking, waiting for a beloved anxiously, separation, the patient waiting of a wife, and anger at the lover's infidelity. These are represented in poetry by mountain, seaside, arid, pastoral, and agricultural lands. Trees, flowers, birds, and even gods become part of a symbolic landscape in these poems, and each expresses a situation in love or war. A reference to the seashore, for example, means that there is a separation between lovers. The jasmine flower indicates a woman's patient waiting, and the mountains symbolize a rapturous union. The underlying meaning of the poem was understood by the audience that heard it being recited.

Religious literature began to flourish after the fifth century. The *Paripāṭal* is a work included in an anthology of early classical poetry, but is probably later than most other poems in that collection. Several poems in it are addressed to Viṣṇu, and other hymns are written in praise of Murukaṉ, the son of Śiva and Pārvatī. Murukaṉ was, and continues to be, a popular god in the south, and a considerable number of poems are dedicated to him.

The *bhakti* movement, which A.K. Ramanujan (1929–93) has aptly described as 'a great, many-sided shift that occurred in Hindu culture and sensibility', began in South India around the sixth century. Several saints travelled from temple to temple singing in praise of Viṣṇu or Śiva. The twelve canonized devotees of Viṣṇu were called the Ālvārs and the sixty-three devotees of Śiva were known as Nāyaṉmārs. For the first time in Hindu history, we have surviving literature expressing devotion in a mother tongue, a language tapping the roots of childhood and adolescence. Unlike Sanskrit, Tamil, the language of their poems, was a vernacular language associated with powerful emotions. The deity addressed here was as intimate as language fraught with the tender words used for beloved ones.

The twelve Ālvārs were poet-saints who lived during the seventh to ninth centuries and composed devotional hymns in Tamil, expressing their devotion to the lord Viṣṇu. The eleven men and one woman are considered to be paradigmatic devotees by the devotees of Viṣṇu and Śrī in the Tamil region, although some of the Ālvārs were from low castes. The Ālvārs sing about the many incarnations of Viṣṇu, but focus on his manifestations in the many temples of South India.

The songs of the Ālvārs were gathered in the eleventh century and called the *Nālāyira Divya Prabandham* or the *Sacred Collect of Four Thousand Verses*. Selections are recited daily by the Śrīvaiṣṇava community, which considers these Tamil poems equivalent to the Sanskrit *Vedas*. The poems are recited in temples and homes, and the entire collection is recited in annual cycles. The Ālvārs, especially a poet called Nammāḻvār and the woman saint Āṇṭāḷ, are enshrined in Śrīvaiṣṇava temples and venerated by the community.

The poems of the Ālvārs reflect the literary conventions of earlier Tamil poems. They draw freely from their Tamil heritage and incorporate the symbols of the *akam* and *puṟam* poems into their works. The lord is seen as a lover and a king, both accessible and remote, gracious and grand. Through their songs of devotion, the Ālvārs seek from Viṣṇu the embrace of the beloved and the protection of the king.

In contradistinction to the secular poems of love and war, the devotional hymns of the Ālvārs and the Nāyaṉmārs have been chanted, studied, enacted, and enjoyed by Viṣṇu and Śiva devotees in the Tamil area without interruption for the last thousand years. In the tenth century, the Tamil poems of the Ālvārs were introduced into temple liturgy and commented upon orally. Moreover, the Ālvārs, who were from different castes of society (one was apparently an outcaste), were held to be ideal devotees. These claims were made by brahmin theologians and were historically very significant. Vernacular lyrics introduced into the liturgy challenge the orthodox claim that Sanskrit is the exclusive vehicle for revelation and theological communication. The Ālvārs, venerated regardless of their sex or caste, call into question the hierarchical class system, which denied salvific knowledge to *śūdras* and women, and particularly the outcastes.

The Ālvārs refer to many incidents from the *Rāmāyaṇa*, the *Mahābhārata*, the *Purāṇas*, and also to stories not found in any of these sources. It is in the sustained and repeated recollection of the salvific actions and deeds of Viṣṇu and the various incidents associated with his incarnations that one can see the dimensions of their devotion. To them, the supremacy of Viṣṇu-Nārāyaṇa and his coming down as Rāma or Kṛṣṇa, or his presence in the temple proclaim his ability and desire to save all beings. They frequently long to see him and also identify him as the lord enshrined in the local temple. In the following verse, Kulacēkara Ālvār believes that Rāma is present in the temple at Tillai (the modern city Chidambaram) and expresses his longing to see him:

In the beautiful city of Ayodhyā, encircled by towers,
a flame that lit up all the worlds
appeared in the Solar race
and gave life to all the heavens.
This warrior, with dazzling eyes,
Rāma, dark as a cloud,
the First One, My Lord,
is in Chitrakuta, city of Tillai.
When is the day
when my eyes can behold him
and Rejoice?
(*Perumāḷ Tirumoḻi* 10.1)

Sometimes, the Ālvārs identify themselves as characters in the epics or the *Purāṇas* and sing with the voice of that person. They express their emotions through the voice of the Puranic character. Because the saints longed to see or be with the lord, the Ālvārs sing frequently from the viewpoint of one who is separated from Rāma or Kṛṣṇa. In the following verse, Kulacēkara ālvār, a royal devotee of Rāma, identifies himself as Daśaratha, the father of Rāma. Daśaratha has been filled with grief after banishing his son to the forest. Kulacēkara ālvār's words from around the eighth century echo this sorrow:

Without hearing him call me 'Father' with pride and with love,
Without clasping his chest adorned with gems to mine,
Without embracing him, without smoothing his forehead,
Without seeing his graceful gait, majestic like the elephant,
Without seeing his face [glowing] like the lotus,
I wretched one,
having lost my son, my lord,
Still live.
(*Perumāḷ Tirumoḻi* 9.6)

Apart from identifying themselves with Puranic characters, some poets speak in the voice of one of the characters found in the old secular Tamil poems of romance and chivalry.

Among the Ālvārs and Nāyaṉmārs were a few women. Āṇṭāḷ ('she who rules') was an eighth-century poet-saint, whose presence is powerfully felt through her words and images among the devotees of Viṣṇu in the Tamil region

She is enshrined and worshipped in many South Indian temples dedicated to Viṣṇu. Her passionate poetry is recited and sung not just by members of the community, but also broadcast over every radio station in Tamil Nadu and Karnataka in the month of December. Traditional hagiographies say that she refused to get married, and instead longed for union with Viṣṇu—a wish that was apparently fulfilled, according to these biographical accounts. Through her words and actions, Āṇṭāḷ presents an alternative lifestyle to what Manu perceived to be the role of women: she showed contempt for the idea of marrying a man and instead observed rites to marry Viṣṇu himself.

Rāmānuja is considered the chief teacher of the Śrīvaiṣṇava community. The Śrīvaiṣṇava community differs from other Hindu traditions as it considers not only Sanskrit texts like the *Vedas*, the *Bhagavad Gītā*, the epics, and the *Purāṇas* as sacred, but holds the Tamil compositions of the twelve poet-saints (Ālvārs) as revealed and on a par with the Sanskrit *Vedas*. Specifically, the *Tiruvāymoḷi* of Nammāḻvār is considered to be the *Tamil* (or *Dravida*) *Veda*. The Śrīvaiṣṇava community refers to its scriptural heritage as *ubhaya vedānta* or dual Vedic theology.

The Ālvārs are honoured in the Śrīvaiṣṇava temples. The community also considers the 108 temples that the Ālvārs glorified as heaven on earth. Worship in these Viṣṇu temples is conducted with selections from Sanskrit and Tamil scripture. In the Sanskrit devotional hymns of the Śrīvaiṣṇava community, following the Puranic literature, Viṣṇu is portrayed as reigning over *vaikuṇṭha* or heaven. The liberated human soul, after cleansing itself in the waters of the river Virāja, which encircles heaven, approaches Viṣṇu and his consort Śrī, renders loving service, and is never separated from them. The Śrīvaiṣṇava tradition reveres Rāmānuja as a saviour of the community; his images are found in many temples. While Rāmānuja held both devotional praxis (*bhakti yoga*) and surrender (*prapatti*) to Viṣṇu as ways to liberation, the community became divided over this issue in later generations.

Many of the Vaiṣṇava and Śaiva saints travelled extensively all over South India, and to some extent in the north, visiting temples in which the lord was enshrined. Temple worship and pilgrimage became an important feature of the Hindu tradition. Although they sang about Viṣṇu or Śiva, the deity in each place had an individual personality, and the place was glorified as much as the lord himself. Eventually, among the Tamil and Telugu devotees, 108 places in India came to be known as sacred places in which Viṣṇu abides, and the number was even more for the Śaiva tradition. There are even more sacred places if we include those of other communities.

Devotion to Śiva received royal patronage in the Tamil- and Kannada-speaking regions. Queens of the Chola dynasty in the Tamil region patronized Śiva temples in the tenth century and contributed liberally to build new ones and

## FROM THE *TIRUVĀYMOḺI*

Relinquish all;
having relinquished,
submit your life
to him who owns heaven. (1.2.1)

Think for a moment:
your bodies inhabited by your souls
last as long
as a lightning flash. (1.2.2)

Move to his side,
your bondage will loosen.
At the time your body falls,
think of him. (1.2.9)

Being
    poverty and wealth,
    hell and heaven
Being
    enmity and friendship,
    poison and ambrosia,
The great Lord, diffused everywhere
    is my ruler.
I saw him
    in the Sacred Celestial City,
a city of wealthy people. (6.3.1)

Being
    the joys and sorrows that we see,
    confusion and clarity,
Being
    punishment and grace,
    heat and shade,
The great one, rare to behold,
    is my ruler.
His is the Sacred Celestial City;
    a good city,
    surrounded by clear waters
    and waves. (6.3.2)

Being
    virtue and sin,
    union and separation,
    and all of these;
Being
    memory, being forgetfulness;
Being
    existence, being non-existence;
Being none of these,
The Lord resides
    in the Sacred Celestial City
    that is surrounded by lofty mansions.
See the sweet grace of Kaṇṇaṉ,
    [Can this be] false? (6.3.4)
    (Carman and Narayanan 1989: 202–23)

maintain old ones. In what is now the state of Karnataka, the Vīra Śaiva movement in the twelfth century gained popularity. The *vacanas*, or sayings of their saints, made explicit their contempt for the caste system. The Vīra Śaiva saints also rejected worship in a temple and instead preferred to show their adoration to a stylized manifestation of Śiva in the shape of a small *liṅga* that every devotee carried. Vīra Śaiva saints included the woman poet Akka Mahādevī of the twelfth century.

## Classical Carnatic Music

Worship in the Hindu tradition included music from the time of the *Vedas*. The mystical syllable *oṃ* was considered the beginning of sound in the universe and a manifestation of the supreme being. Knowledge of the proper nature of sound and its expressions was therefore considered to be religious knowledge. The *Vedas* specify the different kinds of pitch and tone by which the verses were to be recited. The exalted status of the *Sāma Veda* was in part derived from the melodious way in which it was to be sung.

Classical music was for the most part religious in nature. Treatises on music spoke of a divine line of teachers, frequently beginning with the deities Śiva and Pārvatī, and also offered worship to Sarasvatī as the patron goddess of the fine arts. Bharata's *Nātya śāstra*, a classical text on dance and mime, written possibly around the beginning of the Common Era, spoke of the performing arts as a spiritual path to liberation. Some later *Purāṇas* like the *Bṛhaddharma* say that Viṣṇu and Śrī are manifested as Nāda Brahman or the Supreme Being in the form of sound.

Sound, if properly controlled and articulated, could lead one to a mystical experience. Thus the sound of the music was considered as important as the lyrics themselves. *Nādopasana*, meditation through sound, became popular as one form of religious practice. The Āḷvārs envisaged their poems as being sung and danced. Many of the devotional poets and leaders addressed their songs to the deities.

Between the fifteenth and eighteenth centuries, classical music in South India evolved into its present distinctive form. The fifteenth-century musicians Purandaradāsa and Annamācarya composed songs in a new format, one that is continuous with the tradition today. As devotees of manifestations of Viṣṇu in particular sacred places (Pandharpur in Maharashtra and Tirupati in Andhra Pradesh), they sang his praises in many *rāgas* (musical modes based on specific scales) accompanied by particular rhythmic beats.

In the eighteenth century, three musicians, who were apparently born in the same village in Tamil Nadu at around the same time, but who never met one another, raised devotional music to new heights. Of these, Tyāgarāja (1767–1847) composed intensely moving songs in praise of Rāma, and Dīkṣitar wrote in praise of the goddess Pārvatī, especially in the form in which she is enshrined in the temples.

Tyāgarāja, whose songs and *bhakti* are celebrated through songfests every January, is the most renowned poet-musician of South India and is considered one of the greatest composers of the world. Tyāgarāja's father, Rāma Brahma, was well versed in the *Vedas* and had been initiated into a sacred phrase (mantra) that bore the name of Rāma. He was well known for his discourses on the *Rāmāyaṇa*, which must have influenced his son. According to legend, Tyāgarāja is said to have written 24,000 *kṛtis* or songs, parallel to the 24,000 verses of Vālmīki, the assumed author of the original Sanskrit *Rāmāyaṇa*. Tyāgarāja wrote about twenty-four songs in Sanskrit; the other 700 songs that are extant today are in the Telugu language. He also wrote two story poems. Tyāgarāja was taught the Rāma mantra by his father. He reportedly had visions of the lord Rāma after meditating on the mantra and his devotion increased. Rāma is regarded as the protector and companion of Tyāgarāja:

> Show pity and shower your mercy on me
> Rāma son of king Daśaratha …
> At the mere thought of you my skin
> just tingles all over, Rāma …
> When I long for you with love,
> the whole world becomes a straw.
> when you are near me—
> what, me worry? …
> Did you take the avatar
> of Rāma just for my sake?
> Did you walk this earth
> to save poor servants like me?
> … You are Tyāgarāja's
> sole companion Rāma
> show pity and shower your mercy on me,
> Rama, son of King Daśaratha.
> (Jackson 1991:188–9)

Tyāgarāja became an ascetic towards the end of his life. In his music, *bhakti* is a way to approach the lord. But in the end, the joy of the song and the devotion wherein the lord is present is the end in itself:

> Devotion steeped in the nectar
> of melodious tones and modes
> Is the celestial bliss,
> O my heart and soul
> (Jackson 1991:334).

Tyāgarāja died in 1847, but his music is played at wedding concerts, songfests, on radio and television broadcasts, and in many homes today.

## North Indian *bhakti*

The wave of devotion (*bhakti*) that began in the south was transmitted to western and northern India after the eleventh century, principally through the *Bhagavata purāṇa*, a work that translated some of the vernacular passion into Sanskrit. The devotion was also carried through the figure of Rāmānanda (1299?–1400), a charismatic saint, who is said to have influenced several devotees and religious leaders in the north.

Two features that contributed to the spread of *bhakti* are illustrated by key figures in western India. One was the use of vernacular languages: Jñāneśvar, a thirteenth-century poet, discussed the ideals of the *Bhagavad Gītā* in the *Jñāneśvari*, a treatise that bears his name. It is in Marathi, the language of Maharashtra. The other was its appeal across all social classes: by all odds, the most famous of the western Indian devotional poet-saints was Tukārām (1598–1649), a low-class *śūdra*. Despite his humble origins, his influence could cut across all levels of a highly stratified society, with a simplicity of devotion that appealed to the elite and to the masses alike. By contrast, Mīrā (1450?–1547) was a Rajput princess in Gujarat. She became a widow in her worldly life, but as a spiritual devotee wrote passionate poetry about her love for Kṛṣṇa. According to some legends, she merged with his icon in a temple.

In northern India, we can see clearly a third ramification of *bhakti*'s spread: its capacity to bridge the boundaries of religious communities. Bear in mind that 500 years ago, our idea of 'Hinduism' as a coherent, systematic entity did not yet exist; the Hindu community in itself was not a tightly delineated, boundaried group. However, a religion that had clear insider-outsider boundaries, namely Islam, was present, especially in northern India. Meat eating was one marker of such boundaries: Muslims avoided pork, but ate beef, and there are indications that Hindu avoidance of cattle slaughter and beef eating (which had evidently been practised in Vedic times) became intensified in the Muslim context. But both the social and the doctrinal boundaries of India's late medieval era under Islam could be transcended by devotional spirituality. Hindu *bhakti* had its counterpart in Islam's mystical tradition, Sufism. Where Hindus lived in contact with Muslims, the piety of each could be seen as having much in common with that of the other.

Among the most important virtuosi of North Indian devotional religion was the poet Kabīr (c. 1440–1518 or 1398–1494), a low-caste weaver from Banaras. His message is that God is beyond the particularities of either community.

> O servant, where dost thou seek Me?
> Lo! I am beside thee.
> I am neither in temple nor in mosque: I am neither in Kaaba nor in
> Kailash:
> Neither am I in rites and ceremonies, nor in Yoga and renunciation.
> If thou art a true seeker, thou shalt at once see Me: thou shalt meet Me
> in a moment of time.
> Kabīr says, 'O Sādhu! God is the breath of all breath'.
> (Tagore 1915:45)

**FROM KABĪR**

Go naked if you want,
Put on animal skins.
What does it matter till you see the inward Ram?

If the union yogis seek
Came from roaming about in the buff,
every deer in the forest would be saved ...

Pundit, how can you be so dumb?
You're going to drown, along with all your kin
unless you start speaking of Ram.

Vedas, Puranas—why read them?
It's like loading an ass with sandalwood!

Unless you catch on and learn how Ram's name goes,
how will you reach the end of the road?

You slaughter living beings and call it religion:
hey brother, what would irreligion be?
"Great Saint"—that's how you love to greet each other:
Who then would you call a murderer?

Your mind is blind. You've no knowledge of yourselves.
Tell me, brother, how can you teach anyone else?
Wisdom is a thing you sell for worldly gain,
so there goes your human birth—in vain.

(Hawley and Juergensmeyer 1988: 50–1)

Kabīr, a Hindu, had much in common with the Ṣūfī Muslim teacher Dādu (1544–1603), and with Nānak (1469–1538), revered by the Sikhs as their founding teacher. Each of these North Indian poet-saints came to have a circle of followers, termed a *panth* ('path'). The Kabīr *panth* and the Dādu *panth* were in time absorbed into the general body of Hindus and Muslims respectively, but Nānak's *panth* ultimately emerged as a separate boundaried community, the Sikhs, in ironic contrast to Nānak's unifying spiritual vision. Nānak's North Indian vernacular, Punjabi, became the language of Sikh literature and tradition.

In the vernacular *bhakti* literature, Viṣṇu (and his incarnations or temple manifestations) and Śiva are cast in several roles by the devotee. The devotee considers the lord to be a father or mother, lover, bridegroom, protector, innermost soul, and yet the relationships do not exhaust the emotion or the longing. Often the lord (or the goddess) is even portrayed as a young child, and the devotee sings with maternal love.

Sūrdās (c. 1483–1563), who settled just south of Delhi near Agra, was a blind singer and poet whose compositions are in a dialect of Hindi. In his

> **FROM MĪRĀBĀĪ**
>
> Sister, I had a dream that I wed
> the Lord of those who live in need:
> Five hundred sixty thousand people came
> and the Lord of Braj was the groom.
> In dream they set up a wedding arch;
> in dream he grasped my hand;
> in dream he led me around the wedding fire
> and I became unshakably his bride.
> Mira's been granted her mountain-lifting Lord:
> from living past lives, a prize.
> (*Caturvedi*, no. 27; Hawley and Juergensmeyer 1988:137)

*Sūrsāgar*, the youthful Kṛṣṇa is celebrated in lyrics valued by many Hindus. Kṛṣṇa is the mischievous butter thief, but also the seductive flute player, and the verses celebrate Rādhā's affection for him as a model of *bhakti*. Sūrdās's poetry addressed to the infant and adolescent Kṛṣṇa draws on elements of Puranic and Tamil devotion, but its own distinctiveness reinforced *Kṛṣṇa-bhakti* in northern India.

Another important exponent of *bhakti* was Tulsīdās (1543?–1623), who settled in Banaras. His *Lake of the Deeds of Rāma* was more than a recounting or translation of the ever-popular *Rāmāyaṇa*; its verses have their own beauty, inspiring hundreds of traditional storytellers and millions of Rāma devotees in the Hindi-speaking areas. People have learned large sections of it by heart: sidewalk vendors, shopkeepers, housewives, and learned people can all quote from it and enjoy it even today.

Puri, in Orissa to the east, is famous as the locale of the annual Jagannātha street procession featuring a massive float or wheeled cart (from which our word 'juggernaut' is derived). Likely associated with this cult was the poet Jayadeva, who may have lived in the second half of the twelfth century. He composed the *Gītā Govinda*, extolling the love of Rādhā and Kṛṣṇa, in Sanskrit. In subsequent centuries, however, eastern India saw exponents of Kṛṣṇa devotion who wrote in Bengali.

Important was Caitanya (1486–1583), from Muslim-ruled Bengal, who settled in Puri. At the age of thirty-four he took the religious name Kṛṣṇa-Caitanya, 'he whose consciousness is Kṛṣṇa'. Caitanya's views have an overtone of the faith-versus-works dialectic that Christians find in Paul and Luther and that Buddhists find in the Japanese Pure Land teachings of Shinran. That is, in the *kali yuga*, our present degenerate age, people have little capacity or likelihood to fulfil all the requirements of religious action and duty; a trusting devotion to the loving, gracious lord is the only way to *mokṣa*, liberation. Among the words attributed to Caitanya are these catechetical questions:

*Q.* What is counted wealth among human possessions?
*A.* He is immensely wealthy who has love for Rādhā-Kṛṣṇa.
*Q.* What is the heaviest of all sorrows?
*A.* There is no sorrow except separation from Kṛṣṇa.
*Q.* Among objects of meditation which should creatures meditate on?
*A.* The supreme meditation is on the lotus feet of Rādhā-Kṛṣṇa.
(Kennedy 1925:115–16)

For Caitanya, *mokṣa* itself is seen as the enjoyment of an intense, passionate, spiritual love of Kṛṣṇa, resembling the love that the cowherd girls felt for him. Being with Kṛṣṇa in the eternal paradise of Vṛndāvana is considered the ultimate goal one can reach. Caitanya is said to have led people through the streets, singing about the lord Kṛṣṇa. He urged people to engage in chanting Kṛṣṇa's names. Eventually many of his followers professed faith in Kṛṣṇa (and Rādhā) as present in Caitanya himself.

Towards the end of the nineteenth century, Caitanya's movement waned somewhat, but it was revived through the energies of a government official, Kedarnath Datta (1838–1914), who took the name Bhaktivinode Thakur. Datta's son, Bimalprasad Datta (1874–1937; religious name Bhaktisiddanta Sarasvatī), started monastic houses and publishing and missionary activity within India in an organized network.

The Hare Krishna movement has spread this lineage abroad. A pupil of the younger Datta, Abhaycaran De (1896–1977), who took the name A.C. Bhaktivedanta, launched the organization, known officially as the International Society for Krishna Consciousness, in New York in 1966. Directly traceable back to Caitanya are both its theology locating divine grace in Kṛṣṇa and its techniques of emotive, devotional chanting.

What has been the legacy of *bhakti*? With the spread of the *bhakti* movement all over India, the function of Sanskrit works as scripture was diminished. While some brahmins have learned and kept large sections of the Vedic tradition alive for centuries, other brahmins may know only a few of the hymns. However, although they may not be able to read them in Sanskrit, almost all the people have heard the stories from the epics and encounter Śiva, Viṣṇu, or Devī through the narrative tradition. Overwhelming numbers of Hindus can recite devotional verses written in vernacular languages by saints. Thus, the Hindi poems of Sūrdās on Kṛṣṇa, the songs of the woman saint Mīrā, the Tamil poems of Nammāḻvār or Āṇṭāḷ, may function as scripture for a particular community.

In this function the vernacular poems and songs guide, inspire, console, and offer hope and wisdom to the faithful, far more than the *Vedas* ever have. It is not that the vernacular literature is considered to be at variance with the message of the *Vedas*. Rather, in most communities, there is a belief that the saints gathered the truth from the incomprehensible *Vedas* and made it accessible to everyone. The saints' knowledge is said to quicken devotion in human beings and become the prelude to the shower of divine, salvific grace.

## Reform and Revival

Vasco da Gama (1469–1524), the Portuguese explorer, fulfilled Columbus's ambition and found a sea route to India from Europe. In 1498, he landed in Calicut, on the western coast of India, paving the way to the Indian subcontinent for a long line of traders, missionaries, and eventually rulers. The Dutch, English, and French also made their way to India and soon established settlements. Early European scholarship in Indian languages, especially Sanskrit, led to the historical reconstruction of the movements of the Indo-European people from Central Asia. Studies in comparative philology pioneered the theory of a common Indo-European ancestry. This was the first glimpse that Hindus received of their pre-Vedic historical antecedents.

In time the foreign powers became involved in local politics, and possession of territory became part of their agenda. The disintegration of the Mughal Empire led to many chieftains' seeking parcels of land. They tried to enlist English or French help in their enterprise. Eventually the domination of the East India Company and the British led to a loose unification of large parts of the Indian subcontinent under British control, bringing about reform in many areas. While most Hindu and Muslim forms of rule had generally accepted local autonomy, the British felt a moral and political obligation to govern the natives and have sweeping reforms in all parts of the land without particular sensitivity to local tradition or practice. Social and religious practices of the Hindus came in for severe scrutiny by many foreign missionaries, who were appalled by what they saw. Their criticisms were particularly severe regarding 'idolatry', the caste system, and some of the cruel practices applied to women. Ram Mohan Roy (1772–1833) was among the Hindu reformers.

### *The Brāhmo Samāj*

Roy was born in western Bengal into an orthodox brahmin family. His mother tongue was Bengali, and he learned Arabic, Persian, Sanskrit, and English. He served with the East India Company and retired early. He became familiar with Western social life and the Christian scriptures, and met members of the Unitarian movement. He wrote a book on the teachings of Jesus, considering him a compassionate human being rather than a son of God. He emphasized the moral teachings of Jesus in *The Precepts of Jesus* and felt that these were not at variance with the Hindu tradition.

He also read the *Upaniṣads* and the *dharmaśāstras* and came to the conclusion that what he objected to in Hindu practice was not part of classical Hinduism. He believed that if Hindus would read and understand their own scripture, they would discard some of their rituals and practices. He gave up going to temples and rejected the notion of reincarnation. In 1828, he set up a society to have discussions on the nature of Brahman as seen in the *Upaniṣads*. This organization came to be called the Brāhmo Samāj ('congregation of Brahman'). Rationalism, humanism, and social reform were the important features of this society. The considerable correspondence Roy had with American Unitarians helped him hone his message that one's beliefs had to be based on reason.

Roy translated some of the *Upaniṣads* and sections of the *Brahma sūtras* and distributed these free. In this Vedantic view of the universe, he was able to find the answers to combat missionary attacks on Hindu polytheism. Together with the Unitarians, he in turn accused the missionaries, who believed in the Christian Trinity, of straying away from monotheism. Roy rejected most of the epic and Puranic materials as myths that stood in the way of reason and social reform. A pioneer for education, he started new periodicals, established educational institutions, and fought to abolish the practice of *satī*.

Although the Brāhmo Samāj was never considered part of mainstream Hinduism (if one can even use that phrase), it vitalized the tradition at a critical time in its history by calling attention to inhumane practices and the need for education and reform.

### *The Ārya Samāj*

The Ārya Samāj was started by Dayānanda Sarasvatī (1824–83), a resident of Gujarat. Rejecting what he believed to be idolatry on the part of the Hindus, he spent his life as an ascetic in search of liberation. He left home when he was twenty-one to avoid marriage, and practised yoga for fifteen years. He also studied Sanskrit under a charismatic teacher, Virjānanda. Dayānanda promised Virjānanda that he would spread the true teaching of the *Vedas* to the Hindus.

Unlike the Brāhmo Samāj, which accepts the *Upaniṣads* as the source of inspiration, Dayānanda considers only the early hymns of the *Ṛg Veda* to be the true scripture. While the Brāhmo Samāj rejected the notion of revelation, Dayānanda holds the *Vedas* to be revealed by God. The fullness of life, the joy of living, and the concern shown for the individual, the family, and the community in the early hymns impress him. The hymns of the early *Ṛg Veda* were action-oriented, and Dayānanda advocates a life of vigorous work. He thinks that the best example of the perfect age is reflected in the Vedic hymns, and seeks to recapture that experience with his revivalistic stance. To revive the golden age, he started many educational institutions, instructing youth about their Vedic heritage.

Dayānanda believes that the *Vedas* contain eternal truths, that their messages are not at variance with science or reason, and that allusions to myth or supernatural phenomena urge one to act positively. He rejects the notion of a personal, loving, saviour god; in fact, he discards any anthropomorphic vision of

God. He believes that the human soul is in some way coeval with the deity. A radical feature of Dayānanda's teaching is that a total elimination of *karma* is almost impossible, and that therefore it is not possible to attain eternal liberation. His image of an ideal person is one who serves human beings and thus lives a full life, not one of renunciation. A good society is one in which people work to uplift humanity; this in itself leads to the welfare of a human soul and body.

### *The Ramakrishna Movement*

A Bengali, Gadadhar Chatterjee (1836–96) was raised in the Vaiṣṇava *bhakti* tradition, cultivating ecstatic trance experiences, and took the name Ramakrishna. In his early twenties he and his brother were employed as priests by a wealthy widow who was building a temple to the Goddess, the Divine Mother Kālī. From the age of twenty-five onward, he took instruction from tantric and also Vedantic ascetics.

By his account, he experienced the Divine Mother as an ocean of love, rescuing him from emotional turmoil. He pursued periods of Muslim and Christian meditation as well, arriving at visions of the common goal of all religions. Ramakrishna does not hold the view that all religions lead to the same formless Absolute. Rather, for him, all diverse manifestations of religion are experienced as true in their specific forms.

Ramakrishna's disciples in Calcutta formed the Ramakrishna Mission to spread his eclectic ideas. One of them, Swami Vivekananda (Narendranath Datta, 1862–1902), who had previously belonged to the Brāhmo Samāj, thought that Western science could help India make material progress, while Indian spirituality could enlighten the West. As a Hindu participant in the 1893 World's Parliament of Religions in Chicago, and subsequently lecturing in America and Europe, he attracted attention to Vedānta and spread an impression of it as the definitive or most representative form of Hinduism.

Under Vivekananda's leadership, the Ramakrishna movement gained momentum. The Ramakrishna Math (monastery) and Mission grew from it. Their teaching was neo-advaitin; that is, they spread a new interpretation of Śaṅkara's non-dualist (*advaita*) Vedānta. At the same time, the movement was eclectic, regarding all religions as true. It encouraged non-sectarian forms of worship.

The movement ignored caste distinctions. It opened hundreds of educational and medical institutions for the welfare of all. Its leadership was significant because until Ramakrishna came along, most of India's new medical and educational institutions were being run by Christian missionaries.

The monastic wing of the movement ordained monks and held that renunciation of the world promotes spiritual growth. Unlike other forms of monasticism, the Ramakrishna order believes in living in and for the world. Monks are not suppose to lead the life of an isolated ascetic but to give humanitarian service to others.

## Interpreting India Spiritually

### *The Aurobindo Ashram*

Nationalism and yoga come together in the contribution of Aurobindo Ghose (1872–1950), also from Calcutta. He was sent to England at the age of seven for education and returned to India only when he was twenty.

The maturing of Ghose's philosophy over the years is reflected in his writings. Early on, he became involved in Indian nationalism and focused his energies on the drive for Indian independence from Britain. At that stage of his religious career, he began to identify nationalism as a kind of religion. He saw human beings as instruments of God—whom he did not define—and nationalism as the work of God in India.

A Bengali, Aurobindo admired Ramakrishna, who came from the same region. He seems to have been influenced by Ramakrishna's devotion to the goddess Kālī. He considered Bhawani, a manifestation of the Goddess, as the infinite energy coming from what is eternal in the world and in human beings. This Goddess is the mother of the universe and the *śakti* or power of the supreme Brahman.

Aurobindo went further than most religious thinkers, however, identifying this personified *śakti* as India. He believed that the Absolute was the force working for the independence of India and that India was to be the teacher of all nations. True patriotism, said Aurobindo, is to see God as the Mother in India, as *śakti* in the Indians. The Motherland is divine and maternal power, and the fight for independence the way to spiritual liberation. In espousing these ideas, Aurobindo was more like some of the early Bengali freedom fighters than like Vedānta philosophers.

Subsequently, after spiritual yogic experiences, he said that he no longer called nationalism a creed, a religion, or a faith. Instead, he said, *sanātana dharma* ('the eternal faith') is nationalism. He termed the Hindu religion *sanātana dharma*, but said that this eternal religion is not circumscribed by geographic boundaries. Rather, the Hindu religion is the eternal religion because it is universal and embraces all others.

Aurobindo was imprisoned in 1908 on suspicion of sedition. He reports having had several mystical experiences while in prison, in one of them feeling the presence of the religious leader Vivekananda. In these experiences he came to the realization that the quest for Indian independence was of lesser value than the spread of Vedānta philosophy.

In 1910, responding to inner guidance, Aurobindo went to Pondicherry, then a French territory in southeastern India. He devoted his time to yogic practice and writing. Aurobindo reinterpreted the *Vedas*, claiming that most Western and Indian translators of the hymns were rather narrow and misguided in their interpretations. He believed that through his yogic experiences he had the key to their meaning and symbolism.

Though inspired by Ramakrishna's and Vivekananda's leadership, Aurobindo interpreted Vedānta differently from them. He saw the universe as ultimately real—not, as Vivekananda's version of Śaṅkara's *advaita* would have it, a manifestation of an illusory power termed *māyā*.

Aurobindo's philosophy, based on his own experiences and his understanding of the *Upaniṣads*, articulates the path of salvation as a two-way street. While human beings strive through yoga to ascend upwards, enlightenment descends from above. The meeting of these two in a human being creates what he calls a 'gnostic' individual. Supreme energy and bliss come down from above and meet the energy of a human being striving for wisdom. The meeting of the two creates the new spiritual human being. This enlightenment experience will lead a person to final liberation, and eventually everyone will be liberated.

Aurobindo was joined in 1914 by Mira Richard (1878–1973), a woman of French descent. In Pondicherry, they started a model spiritual centre with hundreds of followers. After Aurobindo's death, 'the Mother', as Mira Richard was known, was the leader of the Aurobindo Ashram (retreat centre, from the Sanskrit word for 'stage of life') until her death at the age of ninety-five.

### *The Theosophical Society*

At bottom, Theosophy is not a Hindu tradition but a European one that has made use of Hindu themes and has put down organizational roots in India. It shares the more general interpretation of theosophy as 'divine wisdom' that runs as a current from ancient Greek philosophers through Neoplatonism to mystical writers in medieval Europe. But it makes a more particular claim to discover such thought in Vedānta.

The Ukrainian Helena P. Blavatsky (born Helena Hahn; 1831–91) left her Russian aristocrat husband and travelled to North America, Europe, the Middle East, India, and Japan. Her claim to have spent seven years in Tibet under the guidance of Hindu *mahātmas*, great spiritual teachers, is not easily substantiated. At twenty-seven she was already promoting theosophical ideas, but it was in 1875, in her forties, that she organized the Theosophical Society in New York City in collaboration with the lawyer-journalist Henry S. Olcott (1832–1907) and the lawyer William Q. Judge (1851–96).

Blavatsky's views appear in her *Isis Unveiled* (1877) and *The Secret Doctrine* (1888) as a blend of Vedānta with Egyptian snake worship (which she attributes to Tibet), medieval European alchemy, and cosmological theories of nineteenth-century science. Written in English, these works circulated in spiritualist circles in the West and among some educated Indians.

Blavatsky and Olcott moved to India in 1878 and established the world headquarters of the Theosophical Society in a suburb of Madras, while Judge remained in New York to run the American branch. In India, leadership passed on Olcott's death to the Englishwoman Annie Besant (1847–1933). She thought her pupil Jiddu Krishnamurti (1895–1976) to be the messianic figure of the reincarnated Buddha, but he disavowed this identification in 1928. Krishnamurti, who engaged in discussions with scientists concerning cosmology, eventually settled in Ojai, California, forming the Krishnamurti Foundation in 1969.

Though it drew upon Vedānta for ideas, Theosophy has not been an authentically Hindu movement but an eclectic international one. Its significance for India is that it, too, has contributed to an overseas perception of Vedānta as the definitive form of Hinduism. And in certain circles both in India and abroad, it has perpetuated two misleading ideas: that India has the world's original, oldest, and most universal religious insight, and that India is a more spiritual place than anywhere else. One need only look at the strife among religio-communal factions in the twentieth century, aggravated by the appeals to group identity of even such respected figures as the nationalist Hindu politician M.K. Gandhi, to see that the Theosophical picture is a debatable one at best.

# HINDU RITUAL

## Temples

The Vedic literature does not indicate any trace of temple worship. In the Harappa culture, however, some buildings seem to have been set apart for worship, and some figures seem to have an iconic status. It is possible that by 500, worship in public shrines became popular. Temples are a common part of the Indian landscape now, but there are many regional variations in architecture and worship patterns.

The deity in a Hindu temple is treated like a king or queen and receives the hospitality given to royal guests. (The Tamil word for temple is *kōil*, 'house of the king'.) The deity is given a ritual bath, adorned, taken in procession, and given all royal honours. White canopies shelter the lord or the goddess; fans keep them cool, and music and dance entertain them. Wedding rituals between the god and goddess are celebrated, as are various other festivals. In the Srirangam temple, there are special festivities for 250 days a year. All this is done because, in most cases, the enshrined image is regarded as God. Devotees believe that the presence of God in the temple does not detract from his or her presence in heaven, immanence in the world, or presence in a human soul. The deity is always complete and whole, no matter how many manifestations take place.

Generally, within the many traditions of Hinduism, there is no congregational prayer in the style of the Sunday morning Christian worship or the Friday prayers for Muslims. Priests are ritual specialists more than counsellors or pastors; they offer prayers to the deity on behalf of the devotee. The priests offer fruit, flowers, or coconut to the lord and then give back some of the blessed objects to the devotee to take home. The food thus presented is considered ennobled

*The thirteenth-century temple at Somnathpur, just east of Mysore.* (V.R. Rajagopalan)

because it is now *prasāda* (literally 'clarity', but meaning 'divine favour'), a gift from the deity.

Because there are many philosophical and sectarian traditions within Hinduism, the meaning of temple images (*mūrtis*) varies among different devotees who come to worship. The term *mūrti* is variously translated as 'idol', 'icon', 'form', or 'object to be worshipped'. In Śaṅkara's non-dual Vedānta, discussed earlier, the supreme reality is not personified. Theoretically, Brahman is identical to the human soul Ātman, and it is transforming wisdom, not *bhakti*, that leads to liberation. Therefore Vedāntins should not have to worship in a temple. In practice, nevertheless, even they throng to worship at shrines, with a considerable manifestation of devotion.

Some people believe that the image in a temple is only a symbol of a higher reality. Some indeed, like the members of the recent Brāhmo Samāj and the Vīra

Śaiva movements, have been positively iconoclastic. The Śrīvaiṣṇava community, on the other hand, believes the image in the temple becomes God after its consecration. It is then the form of Viṣṇu, a piece of transcendental matter here on earth. It is not a symbol of God; God is present completely in image form because he wants to be accessible. The image in the temple then, is a direct analogue to the descent (*avatāra*) of Viṣṇu as Rāma or as Kṛṣṇa in times past.

Temple festivals mark events portrayed in the local myths in addition to the more generic observances that take place in many temples. For instance, in the Mīnākṣi-Sundareśvara temple at Madurai, one of the larger complexes in South India, Mīnākṣi is a goddess portrayed as a princess of the local Paṇḍyan dynasty, but she is also a manifestation of Pārvatī. After a military career in which she conquers the chiefs of all directions, she marries Sundareśvara, who is seen to be Śiva himself. The wedding of the god and goddess is celebrated with much pomp and joy every year in the temple, and pilgrims in the hundreds of thousands attend the festival.

Temples to Viṣṇu also have large shrines for the goddess Śrī or Lakṣmī. These apparently became popular after the twelfth century. Similarly, temples for a manifestation of Śiva or Pārvatī will usually have a shrine for the consort.

Śrī has a large separate shrine of her own in Śrīvaiṣṇava temples, and several festivals are celebrated for her exclusively. It is also worth noting that in the shrine of Viṣṇu, Śrī is always represented as lying on his chest. The processional image of Viṣṇu in the 'womb-house' is accompanied by his consorts, Śrī and Bhū, the goddess of the earth. However, in Śrī's shrine, she is represented alone, and is only occasionally accompanied by an image of Viṣṇu. In other words, while Viṣṇu can only be worshipped in conjunction with Śrī, Śrī may evidently be worshipped alone.

Temples to Murukaṉ, a son of Śiva and Pārvatī, are popular in the Tamil region of South India. Hanumān, who figures in the story of Rāma and Sītā, is venerated in temples and home shrines. Many temples also have representations of the nine planets. Malevolent forces from these planets may affect one adversely, so they have to be propitiated. Especially dreaded is Śani or Saturn, who is said to wreak havoc unless he is appeased by proper prayers or rites.

Generally there are few temples to the creator god Brahmā or his consort Sarasvatī. Sarasvatī, the goddess of learning, is worshipped in home shrines and in a famous temple at Sringeri, Karnataka, where she is known as Śāradā. The reason for Sarasvatī's not being worshipped in temples is usually associated with a myth about Brahmā. According to a Śaiva story, he lies about seeing the top or extent of Śiva in the form of a *liṅga* (an upright shaft, discussed later). For this, he is cursed and told that he will not be worshipped in any temple; the curse seems to include Sarasvatī. However, in a few places, there are temples to them; one such place is Karambanur or Uttamar koil near Srirangam in Tamil Nadu. Here, in one of the earliest syncretic temples of its type, there are separate shrines to Śiva, Pārvatī, Viṣṇu, Lakṣmī, Brahmā, and Sarasvatī. In this temple, Sarasvatī is worshipped regularly by a priest. Students frequent the shrine, especially on the eve of an examination. In domestic worship, devotion to Sarasvatī is more evident. Children recite prayers to her daily, and students carry little pictures of her to school.

Many of the temples in the southern part of India have been preserved well for centuries. We have examples of temple architecture from the seventh and eighth centuries. The temples in the north are much newer, as many were destroyed during Muslim rule and during various invasions. But architectural guides written after the fourth century specify the details of construction for temples and the icons, and at least some of these prescriptions have been followed.

The temple has a correlation to the universe itself and to the body of divine beings, and is therefore planned with care. In the Śrīvaiṣṇava community, the temple is said to be heaven on earth. An ideal temple has seven enclosures (*prākāras*). It is located near a body of water, which automatically becomes holy. This may be the sea, a river, a pond, a spring, or at least a tank (artificial pool). The devotees sometimes bathe in it before going into the temple if they are making a formal pilgrimage from a faraway place. In South Indian temples, the enclosures have gateways over which stand large towers (*gopuras*); the tallest one in the Srirangam temple is about 83 m (270 ft) high. The towers are an essential part of the religious landscape. In popular religion, even a vision of the temple tower is said to be enough to destroy one's sins.

At the centre of the temple is the *garbha gṛha*, 'the womb house', where the lord or the goddess is enshrined. The chamber is called a 'womb-house' because this is where a spiritual regeneration or rebirth is said to take place. On top of this womb-house is a smaller tower (*vimāna*). In the richer temples patronized in the past by royalty, these *vimānas* are gilded with gold. The emphasis is on seeing the deity; this is as important as hearing the sacred words of Hindu scripture. In South Indian temples, the devotee may go up only to the threshold of the womb-house. Only the priests and ritual specialists who have been specially initiated are permitted to go beyond the threshold. In many of the North Indian temples, devotees may go all the way into the inner shrine.

Devotees frequently walk around the temple inside one of the enclosures, thus circumambulating the deity; this is an essential feature of the temple visit. They may perform an *arcana* ('formal worship') in which the priest will recite the names of the deity, thus praising him or her. Devotees also bow down before the deity. Sometimes people go to the temple kitchen and receive or buy food or some token of the lord's grace called *prasāda*. Some temples give free food or *prasāda* from the monies received through the endowments made in the past by patrons. The patrons frequently earmark their donations for particular charitable deeds or functions in the temple, and their donations are inscribed on stone plaques on temple walls.

The inscriptions on the walls of the old temples are a wonderful record of transactions within the temple and give us considerable information on who

*The Horse Court sculptures outside the Hall of a Thousand Pillars, Srirangam temple, Tamil Nadu.* (V. Narayanan)

endowed the money. Through these we know of the many women who patronized temples and who generously donated money for pilgrims and festivals. The temples were and still are powerful economic institutions in which large amounts of money are endowed and where in return the devotee may receive some symbol of divine grace or tangible form of temple honour.

While some temples have minimal funds, others are endowed very well. An example is the Viṣṇu temple at Tiru Vēṅkaṭam (Tirupati hills in Andhra Pradesh). Viṣṇu here is known as Venkateswara, or 'lord of the Vēṅkaṭa hills'. (A branch of this temple in the United States is discussed at the end of this chapter.) The temple at Tiru Vēṅkaṭam has always been well known; Tamil texts of the fifth century refer to it, and the Ālvārs sang about it extensively. It also enjoyed royal patronage during the last thousand years, but only in the last hundred years has it attracted large numbers of pilgrims and substantial revenues. The popularity of the temple is said to have increased phenomenally after a major reconsecration in 1958.

The wealth of the temple is also frequently reported and commented upon by the media. In 1989, it had assets worth 1.5 billion rupees, reserves of about 1 billion rupees and an annual income—largely from the collection box or *hundi*—of about 800 million rupees. Cars and diamonds are collected, as are approximately 20 kg (640 troy ounces) of gold every month, from various pieces of jewellery deposited in the *hundi*. The temple is located on 28 $km^2$ (10.75 sq. mi.) of the Tirumala hills. Until 1965, when the government took them over, it owned more than 600 villages. The enormous funds of the temple are used for charitable purposes, universities, educational institutions, and hospitals.

## Sculptural and Pictorial Symbolism

### *Nāgas*

In addition to temples, there are other public places of worship. For instance, in many villages and in many quiet places in the cities, there are sacred trees that have a simple platform built around them. Under the trees may be many small stone images of intertwined snakes. These serpent images are venerated with red spots of *kum kum* powder that is used to adorn the forehead of women. Women come to these open-air shrines to worship at particular times of the year, or when they need a wish to be fulfilled. The serpents, called *nāgas*, may well be one of the earliest features of the Hindu tradition. They may predate the coming of the Indo-Europeans. We have very little evidence that their worship was prevalent in the Harappa culture, since only one seal possibly depicting the serpent has been found there, but they were probably venerated in other parts of the subcontinent.

### *The liṅga*

In temples, Śiva is usually portrayed as a *liṅga*, an upright shaft or stylized phallic image, often made of stone. The word *liṅga* means 'distinguishing symbol' and refers to the male procreative organ. It is placed in a receptacle called *yoni*, which is the female sexual organ. The union between the *yoni* and *liṅga* reminds one that male and female forces are united in generating the universe.

Although the term *liṅga* is translated as phallus and the *liṅga* sculpture is manifestly symbolic of the human genitals, Hindus do not normally interpret this as a physical object. Rather than reminding them of sexual connotations, it serves as a reference point to the spiritual potential in all of creation, and specifically to the positive energies of Śiva. Notice that although Śiva is stereotyped as the 'destroyer' in some literature, his creative role is what is represented in the temple.

The *liṅga* may be pre-Aryan in origin. Cylindrical pillars unearthed in the excavations at Harappa may be prototypes of the later Śiva *liṅga*. *Liṅgas* are made from many materials. Exact specifications of the ratio of height, width, and curvature are given in texts. *Liṅgas* are sometimes carved with faces, manifesting the different personalities of Śiva. In the temple, the *liṅga* and *yoni* are bathed, anointed, and worshipped.

### *The Dance of Śiva*

Iconographically, Śiva is portrayed in some temples as a cosmic dancer. In this form, he is also known as Naṭarāja or king of the dance. Śiva is the archetypal dancer and ascetic, symbolizing mastery over universal energy on the one hand, and inner absolute calm and tranquillity on the other.

In a classic Naṭarāja representation, we see Śiva with four hands. One of the right hands holds an hourglass-shaped drum, symbolizing sound—that is, speech and the divine truth heard through revelation. The other right hand shows a gesture granting fearlessness to the devotee. One of the left hands holds a flame, symbolizing the destruction of the world at the end of time. The feet grant salvation; one worships them to obtain union with Śiva. The left foot, representing the refuge of the devotee, is uplifted and thus denotes liberation. One of the left hands points to this foot.

As the cosmic dancer, Śiva dances through the creation and destruction of the universe. He is the master of both *tāṇḍava*, the fierce, violent dance that gives rise to energy, and *lasya*, the gentle, lyric dance representing tenderness and grace. The entire universe shakes when he dances; Kṛṣṇa sings for him, the snake around his neck sways, and drops of the Ganges River, which he holds in his hair, fall to the earth.

### *Erotic Sculpture*

Temple sculpture depicts deities in activities described in the *Purāṇas* and epics, correlating the imagery of text and art. Male and female figures in erotic postures are sometimes a theme of temple sculptures. Among the sites famous for such art are Khajuraho, in the state of Madhya Pradesh southeast of Delhi, and Konarak, in the eastern coastal state of Orissa. Many other temples also have erotic sculptures, although they are frequently in inconspicuous niches or corners. These sculptures have frequently shocked people from other cultures by their visual celebration of *kāma* or sensual love.

There are several meanings of *kāma*, ranging from sexual love to enjoyment through the senses. It has classically been considered a goal of human life. One perceived goal of a marriage is to fulfil the human need for *kāma*. A wife is her husband's partner in *kāma* as well as in *dharma*.

Some art historians see the sculptures as having aesthetic value, while others see them as educational. Recent scholarship sees the sculptures in Khajuraho as fitting the mythology of Śiva and the story of his wedding. They portray scenes that were enacted in various quarters and houses of the town as the wedding procession of Śiva wound its way through the streets. As in some other temples, these sculptures may be visual representations of passages from the *Purāṇas*, correlating the imagery of text and art.

### *Forehead Marks*

The deities' identities are reflected symbolically in the *tilaka*, or forehead mark, drawn in olden days with special earth, sandalwood, or coloured powder (usually red) by both men and women. The mark sometimes denotes sectarian affiliation, identifying the wearer as a devotee of Viṣṇu or of Śiva. Thus a white U- or Y-shaped mark with a red line in the middle indicates that the person is a devotee of Viṣṇu; the U or Y mark represents the feet of Viṣṇu, symbolizing his grace. The red line represents the goddess Śrī.

Followers of Śiva frequently place white horizontal marks on their foreheads. These lines are made of ash, the symbol of burning and destruction. They remind one that Śiva destroys all evil on the one hand and the devotees' attachments to worldly life that lead to further *karma* on the other.

## Domestic Worship

Rituals performed in the home are generally called *pūjā* ('worship'). Worship of the deity or a spiritual teacher at a home shrine is one of the most significant ways in which Hindus express their devotion. Many Hindu households set aside some space (a cabinet shelf or an entire room) at home where pictures or small images of the lord are enshrined. *Pūjā* may involve simple acts of daily devotion like the lighting of oil-lamps and incense sticks, recitation of prayers, or the offering of food to the deity. Usually all members of the family can participate in daily *pūjā*, but more elaborate or specialized rituals of worship, like the ones to

Satyanārāyaṇa (a manifestation of Viṣṇu) on full-moon days, may involve the participation of a priest or special personnel.

In home worship, simpler versions of some temple rituals take place. In daily worship family members, instead of an initiated priest, lead the rites. The concept of appropriate hospitality guides home worship. The image of the deity receives the hospitality accorded to an honoured guest in the home: ritual bathing, anointing with ghee (clarified butter), offerings of food and drink, lighted lamps, and garlands of flowers such as marigold or jasmine strung on a string.

There are some domestic rituals that do not involve prayers to a deity but to dead women. Strictly speaking, the prayers or petitions are addressed to women who died when their husbands were alive. That is, they died when they were *sumaṅgalīs* or 'auspicious women'. Such women, even in death, are said to have immense power to bring to fruition or to hinder the progress of any ritual. In some Hindu communities, principally in the south, before the occurrence of a major family celebration such as a wedding, the women may gather together to petition ritually the *sumaṅgalī* women ancestors to bless the oncoming event. Rituals such as these are found in certain geographic regions and in some communities, and may not be recognized by Hindus from other regions. Thus the veneration of a young virgin girl by other women (who believe she is a temporary manifestation of the Goddess) may take place in some northern communities, but may not even be heard of in the south.

More widespread are the 'auspiciousness' rituals that women conduct in many parts of India. They gather together on certain days of the year and celebrate the goddess by fasting and feasting, and then perform rites (*vratas*) for the happiness of the entire family.

In the home as well as in the temple, the worshipper participates in the mythic structures associated with the deity. When a prayer is enunciated or sung, the worshipper participates in the passion of the devotee who composed the hymn. Thus, in Śrīvaiṣṇava worship, when a devotee recites the woman poet Āṇṭāl's verses, to some extent he or she is participating in her devotion. Temple liturgies at home and in the temple are based on participation of the devotee in the myths of the many saints and the many acts of redemption that Viṣṇu, Śiva, or the goddess engaged in. The devotees participate in the passion and surrender of the saints whose verses they utter, and through this identification, link themselves with the devotional community extending through time. The passion of the saints and the composers of the prayers are appropriated by the devotee who recites or sings the songs.

## Significance of Food

The Hindu religious experience is centrally preoccupied with food: what is prepared, how and by whom it is prepared, to whom it is offered first, when it is eaten and not eaten, and to whom the leftovers are given. The fortnightly, monthly, and annual calendars have dates and lunar phases that involve fasting or feasting at appropriate times. There are technical distinctions among fasts; abstention from rice, or from all grain, or from all food will affect the results, as will the times of the fast and the intentions of the person fasting. According to some texts, observing the right kinds of fast can alone give one liberation from the cycle of life and death.

Contrary to Western expectations and stereotypes, most Hindus are not vegetarians. According to some estimates, fewer than 10 per cent are. Being vegetarian for Hindus does not mean abstaining from dairy products; milk and its products form a significant part of their meals. Generally, whether one is a vegetarian or not depends on one's community and caste. Brahmins in most places (except Bengal and Kashmir) are vegetarian.

The strictest vegetarians on a pan-Hindu level are the Vaiṣṇavas, devotees of Viṣṇu. In the West, these dietary regulations are best seen in the International Society for Krishna Consciousness (the Hare Krishna movement) where the devotees are not simply vegetarian but also avoid a whole battery of vegetables and spices, such as onions and garlic, thought to have negative propensities.

These dietary prohibitions and habits are based on the notion that food reflects the general *guṇas* or qualities of nature: purity (*sattva*), energy (*rajas*), and inertia (*tamas*). Food's properties include those that are intrinsic to it and those that are circumstantial. Pure or sattvic foods, like milk and dairy products and many vegetables, foster one's spiritual inclinations. Other foods, such as meat, poultry, onions, and garlic, are considered to have the quality of *rajas*, giving rise to passion and action. Food that is tamasic, such as liquor or stale food, makes one slothful and lazy. Thus, a strict vegetarian diet is prescribed for people who are to put paramount emphasis on cultivating spiritual tranquillity and avoiding passion, such as brahmins, Vaiṣṇavas, and widows.

Castes and communities, it is thought, have dominant inherent qualities, and food intake reinforces these qualities. Caste and class divisions impinge on what is pure and impure. The qualities of the cook are also supposed to enter the food by a kind of osmosis. Till the middle of this century, many orthoprax brahmins ate only food prepared by people of their own caste.

Food is also auspicious and inauspicious. Weddings, funerals, ancestral rites, and birthdays involve the use of auspicious or inauspicious lentils, spices, and vegetables. What one feeds the forefathers is different from what one feeds the gods and human beings; death and life-promoting rituals involve different kinds of food. Turmeric powder is auspicious, while sesame seed is inauspicious.

Many vegetables and spices were introduced in India only in the last few centuries. Potatoes and red pepper came from the New World, introduced according to one theory by French troops sent to Pondicherry, south of Madras, who had just finished a tour of duty in Mexico. Food prepared for ritual use in temple and death ceremonies is restricted to traditional ingredients, avoiding the newer spices and vegetables.

The permanent and lasting associations that most people have with religious holidays are with food. In the way a turkey is associated with Christmas and Thanksgiving in America and ham with Easter, each religious festival in India is connected with particular sweets and savouries, some prepared exclusively during those holidays.

Prominent in temple rituals is the offering of food to the deity, followed by serving the 'leftovers', now thought spiritually consumed by the deity, back to devotees. What the worshippers have brought and is now redistributed to them is termed *prasāda* ('favour'). From inscriptions on the walls of medieval temples, it is clear that most of the endowments were for food offerings. The inscriptions in Tirupati give a detailed description of the ingredients and the quantity to be used in each dish, as well as the details of the endowments that were to finance the making and distribution of each food item. Particular pilgrimage centres eventually became famous for particular kinds of *prasāda*. The cooking and distribution of *prasāda* is a multimillion-dollar industry in major centres such as Tirupati.

Beyond the experiential practicalities, food appears in Hindu thought as an important metaphor for spiritual experience. In a well-known story about the eighth-century poet-saint Nammāḷvār, the Supreme Being appears as the spiritual and physical nourisher of all human beings. Nammāḷvār, in a yogic trance under a tamarind tree, has not eaten nor spoken. When Nammāḷvār is sixteen, an old brahmin is guided to him by a vision of light. This man, Maturakavi āḷvār, sees Nammāḷvār meditating and asks him a question to test him: 'If a little thing is born out of the stomach of a dead thing, what will it eat and where will it lie?' As a question one might ask to ascertain enlightenment, this seems a trifle odd, but the answer is even more puzzling. Nammāḷvār, speaking for the first time in his life, replies, 'It eats that, and lies there.' Maturakavi ālvār is then convinced of Nammāḷvār's wisdom and becomes his disciple. The question is usually paraphrased by commentators as follows: if a human soul takes on a body (since flesh by itself is considered to be a 'dead' or inanimate substance), what will nourish it, and what is its support? Nammāḷvār's answer is interpreted to mean that the sustenance and support of the human soul is the Supreme Being, in this case the god Viṣṇu.

The mystical idea of the union between food and the person eating it matches the union between the sacrificer and the Supreme Being, Brahman, in the *Taittirīya Upaniṣad*, which belongs to the *Yajur Veda*. In this text, Brahman is spoken of as food and the concluding lines express the mystical rapture of the sacrificer:

Oh, wonderful! Oh, wonderful! Oh, wonderful!
I am food! I am food! I am food!
I am a food-eater! I am a food-eater! I am a food-eater!
(*Taittirīya Upaniṣad* III.10.5)

This verse is recited as part of the weekly temple liturgy in Viṣṇu temples all over the world. The Vedic sacrificer, after describing Brahman as food, identifies himself with Brahman both as food and as eater. As with other scriptural passages and ritual meals, theologians through the centuries have debated and interpreted this passage in varied terms of an experience of union between the sacrificer and Brahman, the supreme entity.

The medicinal value of many vegetables and herbs has also been discussed extensively. The principles derived from texts ancillary to the *Vedas* are implemented in diets recommended by Ayurvedic physicians. There are also many regional systems of medicine based on notions of 'cold' and 'heat' accumulated in the body.

## The Annual Festival Cycle

Almost every month there is a domestic or temple festival in the Hindu tradition. The birthdays of Rāma, Kṛṣṇa, and Gaṇeśa are the most popular. These festivals are marked in the lunar calendar, and many Hindus know whether these divine birthdays occur on the waxing or waning moon cycles. The lunar calendar is adjusted to the solar every few years, so the festivals fall within the same period every year.

Holī and Oṇam are examples of regional festivals. Holī, celebrated in some parts of northern India with bonfires and an abandoned throwing of coloured powder on crowds, commemorates an event in the life of Prahlāda, a devotee of Viṣṇu. To save Prahlāda, Viṣṇu takes his fourth incarnation, that of a man-lion. In the state of Kerala, Oṇam is celebrated in August-September; the fifth incarnation of Viṣṇu as a dwarf-brahmin is remembered in that festival.

Other festivals, like Navarātri and Dīpāvalī (colloquially known as Dīvālī in some areas) are more or less pan-Hindu festivals. A detailed discussion of Navarātri will give us an idea of the complexities involved in explaining the origins and the practice of the festivals within the many Hindu communities.

### *Navarātri*

The festival of Navarātri ('nine nights') lasts for nine nights and ten days, hence its name. It is celebrated all over India by Hindus, but in different ways and for different reasons. The festival begins on the new moon that occurs between 15

September and 14 October. The nine nights and ten days are dedicated to the goddesses Sarasvatī, Lakṣmī, and Pārvatī.

In the region of Tamil Nadu, Navarātri is largely a festival for women. A room is set apart and filled with exquisite dolls. Elaborate tableaux are set up depicting epic and Puranic scenes, similar to the nativity scenes that one sees in the West around Christmas. Usually in the centre there are large images or clay dolls of the goddesses. Every evening during this fall festival, women and children dressed in bright silks visit one another, admire the *kolu* or display of dolls, play musical instruments, and sing songs from the repertoire of classical music, usually in praise of one or another of the goddesses. Songs by the South Indian composers Tyāgarāja and Dīkṣitar are particular favourites. It is a joyous time of festivity, music, elegance, and beauty, and is a glorious celebration of womanhood. The last two days are dedicated to the goddesses Sarasvatī and Lakṣmī; these are special countrywide holidays. Large pictures of Lakṣmī and Sarasvatī, draped with garlands of fresh flowers, are kept in front of the display of dolls and worshipped.

Some Hindus believe that during these nine or ten days the goddess Durgā killed the buffalo demon Mahiṣa. Hindus in the state of West Bengal call this festival Durgā Pūjā. They make sumptuous statues of Durgā and worship her. After nine nights, they immerse the statues in water. For these ten days they believe that the spirit of the goddess is in the statue.

In the state of Gujarat during Navarātri, the nights are danced away in circular dances called *garbha*, in which a sacred lamp is kept in the centre as a manifestation of the goddess. *Dāṇḍiya*, a dance with sticks, reminiscent of the dance that Kṛṣṇa is said to have done with the cowherd girls, is also performed during the nights.

Some Hindus believe that during these nine nights and ten days Rāma fought against Rāvaṇa. In northern India, in Rāmnagar, a city near Varanasi (Banaras) on the river Ganga people act out the story of the *Rāmāyaṇa* and on the tenth day celebrate the victory of Rāma. This play is called *Rām līlā*. Little boys play the parts of Rāma and his brothers in what is considered to be the largest outdoor theatre, spanning several hectares or acres.

Some people believe that on the ninth day, Arjuna found the weapons that he hid a year before and paid respects to them before he started battle with his cousins. Because of this story, the last two days dedicated to Lakṣmī and Sarasvatī are called Āyudha Pūjā ('veneration of weapons and machines'). Hindus acknowledge the importance of all vehicles and many other instruments that day. Cars and buses in some regions of India are garlanded that day, and computers and typewriters are blessed with sacred powders and given the day off.

During Āyudha Pūjā, the ninth day is called Sarasvatī Pūjā. On that day the goddess Sarasvatī, the patron of all learning and music, is worshipped. One keeps all the musical instruments in the house, any writing device, and selected text-

*Young girls learn the garbha dance and the dāṇḍiya (or stick) dance, performed during Navarātri and before weddings.*
*(V. Narayayanan)*

books in front of her and the display of dolls, to be blessed by her for the rest of the year.

The next day is the victorious tenth day (Vijaya Daśamī), a day dedicated to Lakṣmī. People start new ventures, new account books, and new learning on that day after ritually writing *śrī* to begin the new scholarly year with an auspicious word. They learn new prayers and pieces of music, acquire new knowledge, and honour traditional teachers. On the last days of the Navarātri festival, the fortune of learning, the wealth of wisdom, and the joy of music are said to be given by the grace of the goddesses.

### Dīpāvalī

*Dīpa* is 'lamp', and *valī* means 'necklace' or 'row'. Thus Dīpāvalī means 'necklace of lights'. It is a Hindu festival of lights that occurs on the new moon between 15 October and 14 November. Seen as the beginning of a new year in some parts of India, it is celebrated by decorating houses with lights, setting off firecrackers, and wearing new clothes. As with Navarātri, Hindus celebrate Dīpāvalī for many reasons. In South India, it is believed that on that day at dawn, Kṛṣṇa killed

Narakāśura, the wicked demon from the nether world, thus insuring a victory of light over darkness. Fireworks, which resemble weapons, are used in celebrations all over India.

In North India the return of Rāma to Ayodhya and his coronation are celebrated on Dīpāvalī day. In Gujarat, it is the beginning of the new year. New account books for businesses are opened then.

In many parts of India people get up at four in the morning for a special ritual bath. It is said that the river Ganga itself is present in all the waters that day and that one is thus purified by the bath. The traditional greeting in some communities is 'Have you had a bath in the river Ganga?' In other areas, Dīpāvalī is the beginning of a new year and one is greeted with 'Happy New Year'. New clothes are worn, presents exchanged in some communities, and it is generally a time of feasting.

## Life-Cycle Rites

In every culture there are rites of passage: rituals marking an individual's transition from one stage of life to another. Some of the *dharmaśāstra* texts begin the discussion of the life-cycle sacraments with the birth of a child. Other texts begin with the sacrament of a wedding, for it is in this context, properly speaking, that the life of a new person will begin.

Two factors are important to note in discussing life-cycle rites. First, not all are pan-Hindu, and even those that are may have very little importance in some communities. Second, many of the important rites, especially those that are celebrated for girls or women, may not even be discussed in any classical text. This is possibly because many of the texts were written by men. Women were treated as partners to males, who were the main focus of the books. It may also be that some of these rites sprang up after the writing of these texts. We shall discuss first the normative *dharmaśāstra* sacraments, and then look at a few of the rites of passage that have more localized regional importance.

The English word 'auspiciousness' has been used as a shorthand term for a rather wide category of features in Hindu life. Certain kinds of people, animals, rituals, smells, sounds, and foods are considered auspicious. The Sanskrit words *kalyāṇa*, *maṅgala*, *śubha,* and *śrī* refer to it. Translating them as 'auspiciousness' indicates the expectation of power to bring about good fortune and a good quality of existence (*su asti*). A marriage is called 'the auspicious ceremony' in Tamil, and in some North Indian usage the word *śubha* ('auspicious') precedes the word *vivāha* ('marriage'). Auspicious times are chosen for the conduct of all sacraments; these times are in agreement with the person's horoscope, which is cast at one's birth.

The right hand is associated with auspicious activities, such as gift giving, eating, and wedding rituals. The left hand is associated with the inauspicious: insults, bodily hygiene, and funeral (including ancestral) rituals.

## Birth Rituals

A person's sacraments (*saṃskāras*; literally, 'perfecting') begin prenatally. The time at which a child is conceived, the rituals administered to a pregnant woman, and her behaviour during pregnancy are all supposed to condition the personality of the offspring. Thus, in traditional usage, there was a ritual for the proper conception of a child, and mantras were to be uttered before the man and woman came together. The *Upaniṣads* describe some rituals that one had to observe if one wanted a learned daughter or a heroic son; but in time, daughters were not sought. This sacrament for proper conception has largely been discarded now and is only observed by some communities as a part of rituals that accompany the consummation of a marriage.

According to some *dharmaśāstra* literature, the man has a veritable duty to approach his wife at particular times of the month to cohabit with her. While some texts mention this obligation, occasionally one will go so far as to say that if a man does not have sex with his wife when he is supposed to, he is guilty of the crime of abortion. Abortion has been generally considered sinful, but the texts apparently have not had much of an impact on practice in modern Hinduism because abortion is legal in India and practised quite widely.

Other prenatal rites called *puṃsavana* ('seeking a male offspring') and *sīmanta* ('hair parting') are followed by many communities in India. Although formerly performed in the fifth month of pregnancy, they are done much later now for the safe birth of a child, preferably a male.

After childbirth, a ceremony called *jātakarma* ('birth action') is performed. In earlier days this was supposed to be done before the umbilical cord was cut, but it is now done much later. The moment of birth was also noted, so that the exact horoscope of the child could be cast. The *jātakarma* rites included *medhjanana* ('birth of intelligence'), in which the father sought the intellectual well-being of the child, and *āyuṣya*, in which he prayed for longevity for himself and the child, saying, 'may we see a hundred autumns, may we hear a hundred autumns.' The ceremony finally ended with a seeking of physical well-being and strength for the infant.

## Initiation Rituals

The ritual that initiates a young brahmin boy into the study of the *Vedas* is called *upanayana* or *brahma upadeśa*. The word *upanayana* has two meanings; it may mean 'acquiring the extra eye of knowledge' or 'coming close to a teacher' to get knowledge. *Brahma upadeśa* means getting the sacred teaching (*upadeśa*) concerning the Supreme Being (Brahman).

The ritual of *upanayana* traditionally initiates a young boy at about age eight into the first stage of life, called *brahmacārya*. This word literally means 'travelling on the path that will disclose the Supreme Being', that is, studenthood. In this stage, the student was to concentrate on acquiring knowledge and not wealth. Therefore, he did not work for a living, but was supported by society. Frequently, the student lived in his teacher's house. As long as he was a student, it was society's duty to support and feed him. He begged for his food from some households and took the food home to his teacher's wife, who prepared it for him. Possibly before 600 BCE, women also underwent this ceremony, but that was discontinued.

The rituals for the *upanayana* ceremony take two days. On the first day, the ritual is called *udaga śānti* ('peace brought on the waters'). Sacred verses from the *Vedas* are recited by brahmin men. Rivers are life-giving; the essence of all the sacred and life-giving waters is invoked in a special silver pot, whose water is considered blessed. In a larger sense, the ritual seeks peace on the waters and lands of the earth. The verses end with the word *śānti* several times: peace for the individual, for the soul, the body, the divine beings, the family, the community, and the entire earth. When the waters have been blessed with sacred recitation, they are considered life-giving, and the young boy is bathed with them.

On the next day, before the actual rituals take place, the family priest seeks to insure that the sacrament will be valid. Its validity depends on a number of sacraments of childhood. These early sacraments include naming the child, feeding it its first solid food, ritually cutting its hair, and so on. Just in case these have not been performed properly, the priest repeats them all very quickly to be sure that they have all definitely been done. The father or the person who will be investing the young boy with the sacred thread will first wear a new sacred thread and then commence the childhood rituals.

The first part of the ritual is giving the young boy a sacred thread to wear over his left shoulder. The meaning of this cord is unclear. It may represent an upper garment the young student was to wear when he was fit to perform a sacrifice. Others who favour a symbolic meaning think it represents a spiritual umbilical cord to denote the young boy's rebirth through his spiritual parent (his teacher), who will now initiate him into the study of the sacred texts. The boy is now taught how to eat properly, thanking earth for his food and asking divine beings to bless it. He may then be given garlands that have been brought from various temples as a sign of divine blessing.

The next is the central part of the ritual: the actual *brahma upadeśa*, or imparting of the sacred teaching. As the boy sits with his father and the priest sit

*A father and brahmin priest prepare to give the sacred thread to a young boy in the* upanayana *ceremony.* (V.R. Rajagopalan)

under a silk cloth (symbolizing the spiritual womb, according to some), a sacred mantra, or sentence for chanting, is given to him. Three times a day, he is to repeat this mantra 108 times. The mantra is short: 'I meditate on the brilliance of the sun; may it illumine my mind.' This, the *Gāyatrī* or sun mantra, is considered the most important of all mantras. The boy is then taken outside and shown the sun, the source of light, knowledge, and immortality. He has to twine his fingers in a particular way to ward off the harmful rays while looking directly at the heart of the sun.

Finally, the young boy begs for his food for the day. Nowadays, of course, this is only symbolic. Since it is considered meritorious for women to feed brahmin boys, all the women attending the function (starting with the mother) line up to give three scoops of raw rice to the young initiate. The boy says, 'O generous lady, give me food' thrice, and three times the rice is placed on his plate.

In Vedic times and possibly even well into the first millennium of this era, the young boy began his Vedic studies at this stage and went to live with his new teacher for several years. The ceremony is now conducted with considerable social overtones in many communities. While traditionally male members of the upper three classes went through this ritual, it is now performed mainly by the brahminical sections of the Hindu community.

## Weddings

The auspicious marriage is a way to fulfil obligations to society. A man has an obligation in life to marry, raise children, and fulfil his debts to his community. According to codes of law and ethics (the *dharmaśāstra* literature), a man is born with debts to the sages, the gods, and the ancestors. A wife helps repay these debts. With the performance of correct domestic and social rituals with—and only with—his wife, a man pays his debt to the gods; by having children, the debt to the ancestors is discharged. A wife is a man's partner in fulfilling *dharma*, and without her a man cannot fully perform his religious obligations.

In Hindu scriptures, marriage and fidelity characterize the ideal for the woman. The myth of Sāvitrī and its enactment in ritual reinforce this point. In the narrative, the princess Sāvitrī chooses to marry Satyavān despite the prediction that he has just one more year to live. She repeats a prayer taught to her by Nārada, a divine minstrel, for the longevity of her husband. A year later, Yama, the god of death, comes to claim Satyavān. Sāvitrī follows them to the end of the earth. Touched by her devotion, Yama grants her three wishes, except the life of her husband. Sāvitrī's third wish is for a hundred sons, and since no Hindu wife (at that time) could properly have sons out of wedlock, Yama is eventually made to relinquish his grip on Satyavān's life. So, in rituals, Sāvitrī becomes the symbol of a faithful wife. In South India her triumph over death is marked by a domestic rite that women celebrate. In this rite, married women seek happiness with their husbands, and unmarried girls petition for a happy married life.

Wedding ceremonies vary greatly throughout India. Perhaps in no rite within the Hindu tradition is more regional variation found than in a wedding ceremony. In some communities in Kerala, the rite may take less than a half hour; in others, it may last five days.

Before a wedding is arranged, parents of the prospective bride seek a proper alliance through the help of the extended family and friends. A bridegroom from the same geographic region, speaking the same language, belonging to the same community and subcommunity, and in some cases belonging to a different *gotra* or clan, is sought. This person is to be compatible with the bride in education, looks, age, and outlook; the families are to be close in socio-economic status.

When such a person is finally found, the family then get the horoscope of the young man and match it with the horoscope of the bride. This reading, based on the positions of the astronomical bodies, is not only to allow for compatibility and character but also to balance the future lives of the partners. Thus, if the male is born under a particular star and planetary configuration, it is predicted by standard calculations that the good times and bad times of his life will occur during certain years. The bride's horoscope generally should balance these times so the couple do not go through times of acute adversity. Family astrologers are employed for this purpose, and their predictions are eagerly awaited.

To select the mate, parents sometimes take a stack of such horoscopes and do a first round of elimination based on the astrological data. While the search for such partners was largely made through informal networking in the past, formal marriage bureaus and non-profit organizations often do this work today. Sunday newspapers have three or four pages devoted to such matrimonial matters. Their advertisements carry details of caste and community, language, and dietary preferences for the partner sought. Since the 1980s, computers have been pressed into use for casting horoscopes when children are born and for the calculations necessary to match prospective partners according to the astrological configurations.

When the horoscopes match, the families of the prospective bride and bridegroom meet as a group. Later the young couple meet to decide whether they like each other. Sometimes the decision is based just on a brief look at each other; and both parties may opt out at this point. Sometimes the couple insists on getting to know each other a bit more. Obviously, arranged marriages were more common when women led sheltered lives. Today, with coeducational institutions more common and with men and women studying and working together, this kind of arrangement is short-circuited. A couple may simply decide to get married with or without the families' approval. Such marriages may be across caste lines or even across geographic, language, and community boundaries. Newer forms of eclectic rituals and lifestyles emerge from these unions.

If, with the parents' prodding, the young couple who have met in an arranged situation decide to get married, a betrothal ceremony is held after other arrangements are taken care of. These arrangements may involve transactions in cash. Euphemistically called a gift for the bride, the dowry may really involve a cash present to the bridegroom's parents by the bride's parents. There is no religious sanction for this practice; in fact, scriptural prescriptions speak of the cash transaction being given by the bridegroom's parents to the bride. While the practice is now also illegal, it is nevertheless quite common.

Apart from the several regional and community rites that accompany it, the sacrament of the marriage involves several basic features for it to be considered legal. These include the *kanyā dāna* (the gift of the virgin by the father), *pāni grahaṇa* (the clasping of hands), *sapta padī* (taking seven steps together around fire, which is the eternal witness), and *māṅgalya dhāraṇa* (the giving of 'auspiciousness' to the bride). In addition to these features, the bride and bridegroom exchange garlands.

Lavish exchange of presents to friends and extended family members, processions on horses or in antique cars, large feasts, entertainment, fireworks, and receptions may all be part of the wedding trappings. In a typical wedding, the atmosphere resembles that of a fair; there are splashes of colour, a high level of noise, and everyone has a good time. Not much attention is paid to the bride and bridegroom.

The ceremony itself lasts several hours and may involve several changes of elaborate clothing for the bride, who is decked with expensive jewellery. Often the couple sit on a platform with a fire nearby, to which offerings are made. The bride's parents have an active role to play, as do specific relatives (the bridegroom's sister, the bride's brother and maternal uncle) at particular moments in the ritual, but the hundreds of guests are free to come and go as they please. During the *kanyā dāna* or 'giving of the virgin', the father of the bride recites words from the epic *Rāmāyaṇa*. The words are those spoken by Janaka, the father of Sītā, when she is given in marriage to Rāma: 'This is Sītā, my daughter; she will be your partner in *dharma*.'

The bridegroom's family then presents the bride with 'the gift of auspiciousness'. The gift is a necklace or string, called the 'string of auspiciousness or happiness' (*maṅgala sūtra*). It may be a gold necklace, a string of black beads, a yellow thread, or anything else that the woman is to wear around her neck. The necklace is adorned with the insignia of the god the family worships. In a Vaiṣṇava family, the conch and discus, which are the emblems of Viṣṇu, may be inscribed on the necklace. In Śaiva families, the *liṅga*, a cylindrical shaft symbolizing Śiva, is marked on a pendant.

The South Indian bridegroom ties this string or places the necklace around the bride's neck as her symbol of marriage. It corresponds to a wedding ring in Western society. The married woman always wears it around her neck until death, or until her husband dies. There is no equivalent symbol for the bridegroom, but in the castes in which a man wears the sacred thread, a double thread is worn by married men.

In the central rite of the wedding, when the bride and the bridegroom take seven steps around the fire together, the groom says:

> Take the first step; Viṣṇu will follow you. You will not want for food for the rest of your life. Take the second step. Viṣṇu will guard your health. Take the third step; Viṣṇu will follow you and see that you may observe all religious rituals. Take the fourth step; Viṣṇu, following you, will grant you happiness. Take the fifth step; Viṣṇu will follow and grant you cattle and kine. Take the sixth step; let Viṣṇu follow you and let us enjoy the pleasures of the season. Take the seventh step; Viṣṇu will follow you. We shall worship together.

Then clasping the bride's hand (*pāṇi grahaṇa*), the groom says:

> You have taken seven steps with me; be my friend. We who have taken seven steps together have become companions. I have attained your friendship; I

shall not forsake that friendship. Do not discard our relationship.

Let us live together; let us think together. We have come to a right and fitting stage of our lives; let us be happy and prosperous, thinking good thoughts.

Let there be no difference in our hopes and efforts; let us attain our desires. And so we join ourselves (our lives). Let us be of one mind, let us act together and enjoy through all our senses, without any difference.

You are the song (*Sāma*), I am the lyric (*Rg*), I am Sāma, you are Ṛg. I am the sky, you are the earth. I am the seed; you shall bear my seed. I am thought; you are speech. I am the song, you are the lyric. Be conformable to me; O lady of sweet unsullied words, O gem of a woman, come with me; let us have children and attain prosperity together.

*Sapta padi: The bridegroom clasps the bride's hand and leads her around the fire seven times.* (V. Narayanan)

Many of these statements are from sections of the *Upaniṣads* and *Vedas* that prescribe ritual. The officiating priest utters the mantras, which the bride and bridegroom repeat after him. In the central ritual's references to Vedic literature, the wife is not considered a man's possession, chattel, or obedient servant. She is his partner in *dharma* and his companion and friend in love. Such passages predate the *dharmaśāstra* literature, parts of which took on a more misogynistic tone.

The central rituals are to take place only near a sacred fire. The importance of fire (*agni*) can be traced as far back as the coming of the Indo-European people to India around 1500 BCE. Fire was thought of as the master of the house. As the eternal witness to life and its sacraments, the sacred fire burns throughout the milestone moments of growth and aging. The path to old age begins in one's prenatal days. Oblations are made to the fire during prenatal rites, and also later when a child is one year old. Oblations are made during one's wedding, when a man is sixty, and later if he reaches eighty. Finally, when a person dies, his or her body is committed to fire. A wedding is valid only if the couple is married with a fire as the witness.

In another ritual, the bridegroom bends down and places the bride's foot on firm heavy stone. The act itself is significant in that the man touches the bride's feet. This is an unequivocal gesture of respect in Hindu culture, for the body represents a hierarchy. He then places rings on her toes, saying, 'Stand on this stone, be firm and steady as this stone. Stand conquering those who oppose you; be victorious over your enemies.' This rousing cry is hardly the speech of one who demands servitude or total compliance.

Later in the evening during the ritual called *Arundhatī darśana* ('the sighting of Arundhatī'), the newly married couple are taken to see the stars in the sky. The constellation of the Great Bear and the stars of Vasiṣṭha and Arundhatī are pointed out to the couple. In Indian astrology, the seven stars are the seven sages, and Vasiṣṭha is one of them. Arundhatī, his wife, is a symbol of fidelity on a pan-Indian basis. She is identified as a companion star to one of the seven that form the Seven Sages (Great Bear) constellation. Just as the companion stars remain close together through the years, the young couple is urged to stay together forever.

## Funeral Rites

As we have said, nothing is really discarded within the Hindu tradition. An interesting combination of beliefs from the *Vedas*, *Bhagavad Gītā*, and sectarian philosophy comes together in the funeral rites. Death causes a state of pollution for the family. This pollution is observed for a period that may last from twelve days to almost a year. Usually, the body is removed within a few hours. In most communities, cremation by fire is the final sacrament. In a few communities, and for people in certain stages of life (infant, ascetic), the body may be interred. Until the body is removed and the cremation fire is lit, no fire is to be lit or tended in the house where death occurred. Each religious community has its own list of scriptures to recite from. These include portions of the *Vedas* and the *Bhagavad Gītā*. The Śrīvaiṣṇava community recites *Tiruvāymoḷi*, a poem of Nammāḷvār in which the saint longs to be united with the lord.

Generally, the eldest son performs these rituals. The spirit of the person is a *preta* or ghost for the first few days. To quench its thirst, which comes from having gone through the fiery cremation, the spirit is offered water and balls of rice for a few days. Some of the rituals go back to the earliest Vedic beliefs. The dead were thought to live on the far side of the moon and thus to need food for their journey.

After a designated number of days, varying among different castes, there is an 'adoption of auspiciousness' when the injunctions relating to pollution are lifted. Every new-moon day the departed soul is offered food in the form of libations with sesame seeds and water. After a year, the anniversary of the death is marked with further ceremonies, and the family is then freed from all constraints.

## Women's Rituals

Women's rituals may be performed on a daily, recurring, or occasional schedule. While many of the well-known rituals are domestic and performed for the welfare of the family and earthly happiness, a few are performed for personal salvation or liberation. Many rituals, such as worship at home shrines or temples, pilgrimages, and the singing of devotional songs, are similar to patterns of worship practised by men, but some are unique to married women whose husbands are alive.

Underlying many of the rites is the notion that women are powerful and that rites performed by them have potency. While many rituals conducted by Hindu women share certain features, the differences among the many communities, castes, and regions are significant enough to caution against generalizations. Frequently, though not always, the rituals involve the worship of a goddess.

### *Early History*

There is a little evidence from the early *Vedas* from 1500 BCE onward, suggesting that girls, like boys of the upper classes of society, underwent a rite of initiation. Young girls were invested with a sacred thread and taught a mantra. This gave them the authority to study the *Vedas* for salvific knowledge, presumably at home or in a teacher's house. The epics tell of women lighting and tending the sacrificial fire to make ritual offerings to the gods. The epics (c. 400 BCE) also speak of women ascetics, who probably entered that stage of life after renunciatory rites.

By the time the *Laws of Manu* were composed (c. 100 BCE–100 CE), however, the rite of investing girls with the sacred thread seems to have been abandoned. Marriage is spoken of as the rite of initiation for girls. Serving the husband is equivalent to living in a teacher's house. And doing household work corresponds to tending the sacrificial fire (*Manu Smṛti* II.67). Asceticism and renunciation of family life were not allowed for women.

In southern India, a votive act called *nōmpu* was undertaken by girls. Ritually bathing themselves in a river or a pond during the Tamil month of Tai (January-February), they prayed to a regional manifestation of the goddess Pārvatī. In these rituals some petitioned for a human husband and others for a union with God. The intentions behind this rite seem to be typical of later women's rites where requests were made either for domestic happiness or otherworldly bliss.

### *Calendrical Rituals Today*

Besides the lighting of oil-lamps, daily rituals frequently include drawing designs on the threshold of a house and in front of a home shrine. The patterns are drawn with rice powder; coloured powder is used for important rituals. In some areas of India like Gujarat, this task is done by men, but in others, it is a daily ritual done by women. Personal prayers, using Sanskrit or vernacular verses drawn from religious texts, may be said daily at the home shrine. These conclude with ritual bowing before the pictures or images of the deities or one's spiritual teachers. While the rice patterns may be drawn both to beautify the house and keep away evil spirits, the prayers at the home shrine are usually for personal spiritual benefit.

Monthly rites are performed on particular days during specific lunar months. Many of these rituals are domestic in nature and observed for the welfare of one's husband, the entire extended family, or the community and are considered auspicious. The generic Sanskrit term *vrata* is used to denote a variety of these votive observances, in which only unmarried women or married women whose husbands are alive may participate. While Sanskrit manuals say that these rites enable a woman to get final liberation from the cycle of birth and death, most women who perform them pray to a goddess or a family god for marriage or a long life for their husbands.

After prayers to the family deity, the women may eat a meal together and distribute emblems of auspiciousness, which may include betel nut, betel leaves, bananas, coconuts, turmeric powder, and a red powder called *kum kum*, placed on one's forehead. The rituals may last anywhere between a few minutes and five days, with periods of fasting alternating with communal eating.

In some South Indian variations of these rituals, unmarried and married women tie a yellow thread around their necks on the first day of the Tamil month of Paṅkuṉi (14 March–13 April) in emulation of the mythic heroine Sāvitrī, who through her wisdom protects the life of her husband.

In Gujarat, the Gauri Pūjā is performed by prepubescent girls and involves a partial fasting in order to get a good husband. This ritual is usually done in June or July and lasts for five days, ending with the full moon night. The young girls eat only fruit and nuts and drink milk, abstaining from cooked food. In this rite, girls are also enjoined to sit on the ground for five days, rising as little as possible, so that their bodies are in touch and in harmony with the earth. Each girl is given a shallow container in which she grows seeds from a kind of millet, indicating the onset of her physical maturity and fertility, which will occur in the near future. A girl usually undertakes this ritual five times before puberty.

Women's rituals are celebrated by many communities and castes in many parts of South India during the month of Āṭi (15 July–14 August). Married women were traditionally enjoined to stay celibate during this month. Brahmin women pray to the goddess Lakṣmī for domestic happiness. Women of some non-brahminical castes carry special pots of water and other ritual items to temples of a local goddess and worship her for the benefit of the entire family. Others cook rice and milk dishes in the temples of the local goddesses and distribute the food. During this month, in the temple of Draupadi Ammaṉ, women and men may enter a trance and walk over hot coals in a ceremony called 'walking on flowers'.

In many parts of northern India during the autumn festival of Navarātri dedicated to the goddesses, women may invite seven prepubescent girls to a home. This is usually done on the eighth day after the new moon, and the girls are venerated as representatives of the goddess Durgā.

Many women's rites in northern India focus on the welfare of male relatives. During *rakṣa bandhan* ('tying of the amulet'), which generally occurs around August, girls tie a protective cord around the wrists of their brothers. In the lunar month that comes between 15 October and 14 November, women from the northern states undertake two fasts on the fourth and eighth days of the waning moon. This rite is performed for the well-being of their husbands. The fast on *hoi aṣṭami* is undertaken for the health of sons, and women break the fast only after looking at the stars.

Occasional rituals include the *sumaṅgalī prārtana* ('worship of married women') practised in South India and the *māta teḍya* ('respectfully inviting the mother goddess') in Gujarat. These rituals are done just before a major happy ritual in a family, like a wedding. In the *sumaṅgalī prārtana*, a family ancestor who died while her husband was still alive is propitiated and her blessings sought for the upcoming events.

In the *māta teḍya*, married women whose husbands are alive invoke the presence of the goddess Durgā into a little image or symbol kept on a plate in front of them and pray to her, seeking her blessings. Sometimes the goddess is represented by an image, or a small tiger as emblem of the goddess, or even bangles and a colourful *sari*. After the ritual, the goddess is borne on one's head and respectfully carried to the village shrine or temple. When the women carry the goddess, whose power and spirit now abide in her image, their feet are not supposed to touch the ground. A friend or relative usually precedes the women, spreading a piece of cloth in front of them, on which they walk all the way to the temple.

### *Women's Life-Cycle Rituals*

Life-cycle rituals for upper-caste women are similar to those performed for men and include those associated with naming a child, weddings, and funerals. Apart from these sacraments, there are many associated with women that have not received scriptural ratification. Some of these rites are region and community based.

In many communities there is celebration when a young girl gets her first menstrual period. She has now come of age; in many vernacular expressions, she has 'blossomed'. The first menstrual period is celebrated by the female members of the family, for now the girl is ready for procreation. The girl wears new clothing, has fresh flowers in her hair, sits on a specially decorated chair, and is fed special foods.

The intensity of celebrations varies from community to community. Some still put on a big show, to indicate to potential bridegrooms that they are a family of means, but in many other families, only a few simple rituals are conducted. Many communities celebrated this rite of passage in grand style prior to the 1950s; with increasing urbanization, these rituals have come to be regarded by young girls as shameful and vulgar. However, in many villages, the celebrations still take the form of a mini wedding, in which the girl is showered with money or clothing from the family.

In rituals that are conducted prior to a wedding in some communities in northern India, the bride's hands are ritually painted in intricate patterns with *mehendi* or henna, a bright red herbal paste. Much dancing, singing, and merriment occur on these occasions.

During pregnancy, especially the first, a woman may have special rituals. A popular women's rite in many communities in South India is called *vaḷa kāppu* ('bracelets and amulets'). This is accompanied by a ritual called *pūcūṭṭal* ('adorning with flowers'). The pregnant woman is dressed in heavy silk *saris*, and women of all ages slip bangles and bracelets onto her arm. A bangle seller used to be invited to the function in earlier days, and the pregnant woman's parents gave away glass bangles to all women who attended the ceremony. These bracelets were supposed to be like protective amulets, safeguarding the wearer from the effects of the evil eye and evil spirits.

The rite in which the hair is adorned with flowers is a gentle ritual of beautification. A woman is said to be radiant during her pregnancy, and the weaving of flowers into her hair is to enhance this time of beauty. It is also one of the last times in which the woman's hair will be completely woven with flowers like a bride, for she will be a mother soon. In the Hindu tradition, all married women wear flowers in their hair, but only a bride's hair is completely intertwined with flowers. This is repeated as a rite during the first pregnancy. After the young woman becomes a mother, she wears flowers in a simple way like all other women. Some of these rituals acknowledge the importance of a woman's body and celebrate its life-bearing potential.

## Hindu Roles for Women

On the whole, Hindu literature has maintained contradictory views on women. A woman is portrayed—often by the same author—as a servant and a goddess, a strumpet and a saint, a protected daughter and a powerful matriarch, a shunned widow and a worshipped wife. An understanding of what constitutes auspiciousness will help us sort out some of the conflicting views on women.

The *Laws of Manu* imply that society gave women a low status. Male commentators through the centuries have quoted approvingly some of Manu's statements: 'Though destitute of virtue, or seeking pleasure elsewhere, or devoid of good qualities, a husband must be constantly worshipped as a god by a faithful wife' (*Manu* 5.154).

However, Manu goes on to say that a wife is the goddess of fortune and auspiciousness (*Manu* 9.26), and that only if women are honoured will the gods be pleased and the religious rituals prove beneficial (*Manu* 3.56). On balance, however, the negative statements outweigh the positive ones. Perhaps the most famous of his lines are these, which deny a woman any independence:

> By a girl, by a young woman or even by an aged one, nothing must be done independently, even in her own house. In childhood a female must be subject to her father, in youth to her husband, when her lord is dead, to her sons; a woman must never be independent (*Manu* 5.147–8).

While the pronouncements of Manu have been influential in some areas of the Hindu tradition at certain times, they cannot be held either as prescriptive or normative. While later male commentators on Hindu law quote Manu approvingly and a study of these works has informed many Western notions of Hindu women, the dictates of Manu were not necessarily followed. Medieval women were more than dutiful wives. As we saw, in the Vedic age long before Manu, women composed hymns and took part in philosophical debates. After the eighth century, there were women who were poets, patrons of temple rituals, philosophers, and commentators on scripture. Women gave religious advice to people and wrote scholarly works. These women were not condemned or ostracized by society; they were respected, honoured, and in some cases even venerated. Thus, despite Manu and other male lawmakers, many women of the upper socio-economic groups enjoyed religious and financial independence and contributed considerably to literature and the fine arts.

Auspiciousness refers to prosperity in this life. It is seen in terms of wealth and progeny, along with the symbols and rituals connected with these. Cattle, elephants, kings, married women with a potential for bearing children, and rituals connected with birth and marriage are said to be auspicious. These are connected with the promotion of three human goals, *dharma* (duty), *artha* (prosperity), and *kāma* (sensual pleasure), recognized by classical scripture. There is also a second level of auspiciousness that is connected with the fourth and ultimate goal, *mokṣa* (liberation) and the path leading to it. The two levels of auspiciousness have been implicit in Hindu religious literature and rituals. In many contexts, women have auspiciousness in different degrees, which then determine the levels of their acceptance.

In the classical literature of the *dharmaśāstras* and in practice, it is auspicious to be married and fulfil one's dharmic obligations. A *sumaṅgalī* is the ideal woman with the ideal amount of auspiciousness, who can be a full partner in *dharma*, *artha*, and *kāma*, through whom children are born, and through whom wealth and religious merit are accumulated. Only a married woman bears the title Śrīmatī (the one with *śrī* or auspiciousness). She is called *gṛhalakṣmī*, the goddess Lakṣmī of the house. She is the most honoured woman in Hindu society, especially if she bears children, and is adorned in funeral rites.

A Hindu wife's *dharma* involved sexual fidelity as well as total obedience. The Hindu wife was to be monogamous, faithful to her husband in life and to his memory when he died. Some of these notions are still adhered to in Hindu life. A wife may occasionally be abandoned, but social pressures make it difficult if not almost impossible for a woman to leave her husband.

As late as the 1970s, these attitudes were reflected in literature and the media. For example, when *A Doll's House*, by the Norwegian playwright Henrik Ibsen (1828–1906), was adapted in the western Indian regional language of Marathi, the ending reflected Hindu cultural values rather than remaining faithful to the original story. In the English version, the heroine Nora becomes convinced that her husband is not worthy of her love and leaves him to build an independent life in her home town. The Marathi play *Kulawadhu* does not retain this key element of Ibsen's plot; the adapted version allows Nora no opportunity for unchaste behaviour. She does leave her husband, but goes to live with his parents and serve them dutifully.

In the *Purāṇas*, which reflect codes of conduct (*dharmaśāstras*) dating back to the beginnings of our era, the *dharma* of a faithful wife (*pativratā*) was to worship and serve her husband as god. A *pativratā* is one who is true to her husband. Her *dharma* is summed up in a line from the *Padma purāṇa* (written possibly after the eleventh century): she should ideally be like a slave in service, a harlot in love, a mother in offering food and nourishment to the husband, and a counsellor in times of need.

Conversely, however, but consistent with the Hindu value system, the faithful wife had almost limitless powers. This power was acquired through her total fidelity. Through her power a *pativratā* could supposedly burn the world and stop the motion of the sun and the moon. The *Purāṇas* and the oral tradition have many stories about the power that these women had to save people's lives and to perform miracles. In the first century, even Manu recognized the earlier notions of a faithful wife's powers:

> Where women are honoured, there the gods are pleased; but where they are not honoured, no sacred rite yields rewards. Where the female relations live in grief, the family soon perishes; but that family where they are not unhappy ever prospers. The houses on which female relations, not being duly hon-

oured, pronounce a curse, perish completely, as if destroyed by magic (*Manu* 3.56–8).

The virtuous dead as well as the living are credited with power. We see this in the rituals performed by *sumaṅgalīs* to seek blessings in honour of a dead *sumaṅgalī*. A *sumaṅgalī* who has died still wields power for the well-being of the family. When propitiated, she radiates auspiciousness; when offended, she has the power to curse. In this context she is held to be almost more powerful morally than the man; she is as worthy of worship as her husband.

## Courtesans and Prostitutes

In traditional Hindu society, courtesans often came from certain castes and families. In some communities, women are ritually dedicated to a temple or a god and married to that deity. Such a woman is known as a *devadāsī* ('servant of the god'). Since the deity is deathless, the woman is never widowed. She is continually 'wedded' through her sexual liaisons and therefore perceived as continually, eternally auspicious (*nitya sumaṅgalī*). Her presence anywhere, at any time, is supposed to be auspicious. However, such women have still been held in contempt as temple prostitutes and ostracized from mainstream society.

'Public' prostitutes were distinguished, at least in theory, from the sacred prostitutes. The public category, probably much older, was certainly established by the time of Cāṇakya's *Arthaśāstra* in the fourth century BCE. In a chapter called 'The Superintendent of Prostitutes', this manual clearly states the duties of and taxation procedures for the prostitutes. About eight centuries later, the *Kāma sūtra* also describes the intricacies of the art of being a woman about town. In these books, as well as the *Mahābhārata* and some *Purāṇas*, we find considerable detail.

The texts list these women's duties to a king, his guests, and retinue. The salary is 1,000 *panas* annually for the chief prostitute in a court. If a prostitute gets the money and then defaults, the fine is eight times the amount paid by her client. Her taxes are two days' wages per month. A prostitute who kills her lover is to be thrown to the dogs. A king must pay a monthly maintenance stipend to retired court prostitutes. Eligibility for a government stipend includes several categories, such as those who train the prostitutes in their art. Among the sixty-four listed arts of a refined prostitute are art, arithmetic, carpentry, logic, magic, mimicry, music, poetry, and swordplay. The texts mention ways, like spying and extracting information from other spies, in which a king could use a prostitute.

With a definite place and role in society, prostitutes had their own *dharma*. As in all of Hinduism, one who performed her *dharma* scrupulously was thought to acquire great powers. In one story, when the third-century BCE king Aśoka asks whether anyone can make the river Ganga flow upstream, a courtesan meets the challenge and succeeds. The king asks how she could accomplish this miracle. The prostitute says that she treats all her clients equally, regardless of caste. To serve them is her act of truth or *dharma*, and she is powerful because of that. Other stories, however, depict prostitutes in an unfavourable light. Women from the so-called higher classes were told never to go near them.

## Adulteresses

Even worse was the perception of women deemed unfaithful to their husbands. While courtesans were considered auspicious and some of them had ritual functions in the Hindu temples, an adulterous married woman's situation was different.

The fallen wife's position in Hindu society was not always low. In the epics and the *Arthaśāstra* prior to Manu, a woman's error was considered regrettable but not absolutely condemnable. She was allowed to resume a reasonably normal life after undergoing prescribed penances and rituals of purification; her menstrual cycle erased her lapses.

But from the time of Manu, about the first century onward, Hindu society no longer accepted adulteresses. Manu's condemnation of their behaviour is unmitigating in tone. His law code states: 'But for disloyalty to her husband, a wife is censured among men, and (in her next life) is born in the womb of a jackal and tormented by diseases, the punishment of her sin' (*Manu* 9.30 and 5.164).

In literature thereafter, one finds tales of married women unfaithful to their husbands, as in the medieval short-story collection *Vetālapañcaviṃśati*. Though these accounts enjoyed considerable popularity, their heroines are no longer remembered now. Leaving no mark on the collective consciousness, they have not been ratified as cultural archetypes.

The one difficult—and oft-quoted—counterexample on this issue is Rādhā's relationship with Kṛṣṇa. Rādhā, in some sacred texts, was a married woman, who later became the lover of Kṛṣṇa, but her position seems to be unique. Rādhā is sometimes portrayed as a paradigmatic human soul who will renounce everything to be with the lord. Her action is seen as a spiritual rather than social example in Hinduism.

## Widows

A widow has been considered inauspicious, a bad omen to anyone encountering her. In everyday situations in some Indian languages, the word for 'widow' is a word of abuse. Even in educated, reform-oriented circles, vestiges of this attitude remain. A widow's appearance distinguished her from society. Traditionally, the higher the widow's social caste, the greater the differentiation. South Indian brahmin widows underwent tonsure, a complete shaving of the head, till the middle of the twentieth century. In many communities, the widow removes the ornamental mark or *tilaka* from her forehead. The red dots or elaborate patterns, made of coloured powder, are worn by unmarried girls and women whose husbands are alive.

The status of a widow in recent years is summed up in *Toward Equality: Report of the Committee on the Status of Women in India*, an official publication of the government's Ministry of Education and Social Welfare (1974):

> The common blessing for a woman, 'May your husband live long' is self explanatory. Although the strict code of conduct prescribed for widows is no longer operative in its most restrictive and oppressive aspects, there are certain disabilities associated with widowhood. She is debarred from active participation in auspicious occasions. Besides the items of decoration associated with the married state, she is expected to discard colourful clothes, glass bangles, wearing of flowers, and attractive jewellery. Plain white colour is associated with widowhood, and by implication is forbidden traditionally for Sumangali, i.e., one whose husband is alive. The widows of Bengal, who abstain from fish, the Kammas and Reddy widows of Andhra Pradesh who give up meat are not yet extinct. Among the Brahmin and also among such non-Brahmin communities who do not have the custom of widow remarriage, there are a number of ways for restricting the life of a widow so that she gets little pleasure out of life and her natural desires are suppressed.

Significantly, the report concludes the above passage by stating, 'A distinct contrast between the status of a widow and a *sumaṅgalī* is characteristic of India as a whole.'

The status of widows, like that of adulteresses, was not too low in India prior to the beginning of the Common Era. In some cases, the widow was allowed to remarry; or if she was childless, a brother-in-law was appointed by the family to consort with her till a son was born. The fourth-century *Arthaśāstra* outlines a number of courses a widow can take, with special financial bonuses if she remains true to her husband's memory. But over time, the status of widows deteriorated. Inheritance rights were gradually denied to levirate (brothers-in-law's) sons. By the time of Manu, absolute chastity was recommended for the widow, and levirate practice was barely tolerated.

In southern India, the earliest literature depicts some dismal prospects for widows. Both tonsure and a form of widows' suicide are referred to in the poems. In secular poems of war composed around the first to third centuries, we hear of widows not wearing ornaments and sleeping on beds of stone. These circumstances may provide a clue as to why some widows committed suicide upon their husbands' death.

Suicide or *satī* (spelled 'suttee' by Western writers) was for some centuries a way that a woman ostensibly retained her honour and died a *sumaṅgalī*. She would immolate herself by throwing herself onto her husband's funeral pyre. This practice was outlawed as homicide by the British in 1829, although it has continued to occur from time to time. The *satī* of Roop Kanwar in 1987 received notoriety, as it was performed in front of hundreds of witnesses.

The so-called higher castes were considered the trend-setters regarding suicide and attitudes to widows in general. Brahmin women generally did not practise *satī*, but after the fourteenth century (especially in northern India), wives of warriors and kings thought it honourable to die with their husbands. While there were no injunctions for women in other castes to commit *satī*, or any practice of disfiguring widows, they did it to imitate the 'higher' classes. Thus, the humane attitudes and freedom theoretically accorded by tradition to women in the 'lower' castes were not always manifested in practice. In their eagerness to imitate the 'higher' castes' customs, the 'lower' castes also subjected their women to negative treatment.

Mothers, especially those with sons, were an important exception to the ill-treatment meted out to widows. We see this attitude reflected in scriptural texts. The *Skanda purāṇa* says, 'The widow is more inauspicious that all other inauspicious things; at the sight of a widow no success can be had in any undertaking.' But it adds a rider: 'excepting one's widowed mother, all widows are void of auspiciousness' (*Skanda purāṇa* III, ch. 7, 50–1). A mother, whatever her faults and even if she is an outcaste, should never be abandoned by her son. Even Manu, with his many negative opinions on women, says, 'The teacher is more important than ten teachers, the father is more important than a hundred teachers, but the mother a thousand times more than the father' (*Manu* II.145). However, Manu considers the spiritual teacher more important than one's biological parents.

The nineteenth and twentieth centuries have seen efforts to improve the lot of widows. These have aimed to keep pace with legal reforms, such as the 1829 proscription of *satī* and the 1856 legalization of widow remarriage. The efforts of Pandita Ramabai (1858–1922) and Mrs Subbulaksmi were noteworthy, as well as editorial exhortations in several leading newspapers. Pandita Ramabai's letters and books were acknowledged and quoted by leading Indologists like F. Max Müller (1823–1900), who wrote to the London *Times* in 1887 proposing a number of reforms for 'these waifs and strays of womanhood'. The legal age of marriage has been raised, lessening the number of child widows. Education for all women, especially for young widows, has been encouraged, but acceptance of reform is slow and painfully accomplished.

## Women and Pollution

In the Hindu tradition, menstruation is generally regarded as physically polluting. In the past this attitude was prevalent in almost all communities (except a few, notably the Vīra Śaiva) and involved total segregation of the menstruating woman from everyday life. In many households, especially those of the higher castes, the woman was not allowed in the same room or sometimes even the same house as the others. She was isolated in a little room with her own plate and mug to eat from. She could not go out or participate in daily prayers, nor could she cook, for her ritual pollution would contaminate the food. After the fourth day, she had a ritual bath to wash her hair and body thoroughly, and was reincorporated into the family. This segregation is still practised in many orthodox families and in villages. The belief is that a woman can have evil effects on growing things at this time and therefore should be careful not to plant any seeds or seedlings or to go near any young plants. Because her pollution is considered contagious, she is not permitted to go near anyone performing a religious ritual or attend any auspicious function, such as a wedding.

However, this strict segregation is no longer observed in many communities. Many of the barriers, especially in urban households, have to a large extent broken down, but vestiges remain in some families. Frequently, the menstruating woman (even in Vīra Śaiva households) is prohibited from cooking. In almost all cases, she cannot go near the home shrine, participate in any religious ritual, or go to a place of worship during her periods. Hindu women in India and overseas almost invariably have a purifying ritual bath on the fourth day and count their cycles from the day of the bath. Bathing becomes the euphemistic expression for having periods in many parts of India. In several South Indian communities, pregnancy is announced with the statement, 'She is not bathing.'

This sense of pollution extends to childbirth. The occasion of a childbirth is happy and auspicious. Nevertheless, it is ritually defiling and polluting to the entire family. For a certain number of days after a child is born, the family cannot go to a temple or celebrate an auspicious event. However, in many areas, it is only the mother who is considered defiled, sometimes for forty days. While the birth is a celebrated event, the mother, who bleeds for up to six weeks postpartum, is treated in a manner similar to a menstruating woman.

So the history of Hindu women has had many bleak periods. Wives have sometimes been repressed, sacred courtesans scorned, and widows abused. In spite of ill treatment, some women participated actively in many religious activities.

## Women as Poets, Patrons, and Philosophers

In the *Ṛg Veda* we encounter women like Ghoṣā, Apālā, and Lopamudrā, who composed hymns to various deities. In the *Upaniṣads*, Maitreyī, the wife of the philosopher Yājñavalkya, questions him in depth about the nature of reality. Gārgī Vācaknavī, a woman philosopher, challenges him with questions in a public debate. There were probably more women composers and philosophers, but they are not noted in the texts. In time, possibly because the *Vedas* were transmitted orally, many parts of the text, including verses composed by women, were lost. It is also possible that the women's compositions that came after the *Vedas* were suppressed when literature became more androcentric, but women continued to be involved with poetry and philosophy.

Starting with the eighth century, women poets like Āṇṭāl, Kāraikkāl Ammaiyār, Akka Mahādevī, and others rejected married life and dedicated passionate poetry to Viṣṇu and Śiva. These saints have been honoured and venerated in the Śrīvaiṣṇava, Śaiva, and Vīra Śaiva traditions.

Women, especially those from royal families, were also liberal benefactors of temples and other institutions. In the year 966, in Tiru Vēṅkaṭam (Tirupati) a woman called Sāmavai endowed money to celebrate some festivals and consecrate a processional image of the lord, a silver replica of the main deity. A record of her endowment is inscribed in stone; it concludes with the phrase *Śrīvaiṣṇava rakṣai* ('by the protection of the Śrīvaiṣṇavas'). The temple at Tirupati has the largest endowments and sources of revenue in India today. Within a short time Sāmavai endowed two different parcels of land, one of 4 ha (10 acres) and the other about 5.4 ha (13.3 acres) and ordered that the revenues derived from these were to be used for major festivals. She also gave a large number of jewels to the temple and asked that these be used to adorn the image of the lord.

This implies a certain independence of lifestyle and finances. Obviously, the record of such activities has to be integrated with our reading of scripture and hagiography to get a more complete vision of women's religious roles. Studies done by epigraphers and art historians show that Sāmavai was not an isolated example. We know, for instance, that queens of the Chola dynasty (c. 846–1279) were enthusiastic patrons of temples and religious causes for the Śaiva community of South India around the tenth century. At that time, a South Indian queen called Sembiyan Mahadevi gave major endowments to many Śiva temples.

While there were women philosophers in the *Upaniṣads*, their role in literature decreased for several subsequent centuries. But in the fourteenth or fifteenth centuries, a woman called Tiruk kōneri Dāsyai in South India wrote a commentary on a ninth-century poem, *Tiruvāymoḻi*. Using the words of the first verse of each poem to interpret the meanings of the later verses, Dāsyai teases out a new meaning and offers a different nuance, giving the reader a breathtaking kaleidoscope of linked images and pictures. It is possible that there were other women like her, and knowing more about them from inscriptions and literature will enhance our understanding of Hindu culture.

## HINDU EXPERIENCE TODAY

### Religious Leaders, *ācāryas*, and *gurus*

The Hindu tradition has venerated holy men and women for more than 2,000 years. In the *Taittirīya Upaniṣad*, a departing student is exhorted to consider his mother, father, and his teacher (*ācārya*) as God. The term *ācārya* is generally used for any formal head of a monastery, sect, or subcommunity, or for a teacher who initiates a disciple into a movement. Sometimes the term is simply used as a synonym for *guru*, which is a more generic term for any religious teacher.

In addition to these, there have been thousands of ascetics, women and men possessed by a god or spirit, mediums, storytellers, and *sādhus* ('holy men'), who have all participated in the religious leadership of the Hindu traditions. These leaders have commanded anything from veneration to absolute obedience. It would not be an exaggeration to say that for many Hindus, the primary religious experience is mediated by a leader who they believe is divine in some way.

Such leaders defy classification, and almost every one of them merits extensive study. In the twentieth century, Śrī Satya Sai Baba (Satya Narayan Raju, b. 1926), a charismatic and compassionate teacher, from Andhra Pradesh in the south, is believed to be an *avatāra* ('divine descent' or 'incarnation') by his followers.

Ānandamayī Mā (1896–1982), a woman from Bengal, was married but led a celibate life, and her husband became her devotee. After a number of spiritual experiences and practices, she heard an inner voice.

> One day I distinctly got the command: 'From today you are not to bow down to anybody.' I asked my invisible monitor, 'Who are you?' The reply came. 'Your Śakti (power).' I thought that there was a distinct Śakti residing in me and guiding me by issuing commands from time to time ... After some time I again heard the voice within myself which told me: 'Whom do you want to take obedience to? You are everything.' At once I realized that the universe was all my own manifestation. Partial knowledge then gave place to the integral, and I found myself face to face with the One that appears as many (Lipski 1977:10–11).

To many of her devotees, she appeared clearly as the Goddess. One of her disciples says that he saw her in the form of a beautiful goddess, illuminating the room like the sun at dawn. Another devotee saw her as the goddess Kālī.

The philosopher Śaṅkara in the eighth century is said to have established five monasteries around India. Their heads have borne the title *Śaṅkarācārya* ('master Śaṅkara'). The present abbots in these monasteries at Kanchipuram, Sringeri, and Puri exercise considerable leadership among the educated urban population. So also do intellectual Vedantic commentators such as Swami Chinmayananda, whose followers have been in the forefront of preserving traditional scriptural materials in print and electronic media. In their interpretation of the ancient scriptures and their mediation of traditional values, we see the dynamic and adaptable nature of the Hindu tradition.

*Guru-ma Jyotishanand Bharati, an ascetic, gives a discourse.*
(V. Narayanan)

In addition to these teachers, any charismatic leader may be known as *guru* ('teacher') or *swami* ('master') by his followers. Occasionally, a religious leader may have a title like *ṛṣi* ('seer') like the composers of the *Vedas*. This is seen in the case of the Transcendental Meditation movement, popularly known in the West as TM. Its founder, Mahesh (b. 1911), is known as Maharishi, or 'great seer'. Words like *swami* or *guru* are almost generic titles for any religious teacher in the Hindu tradition.

## Hindu-Muslim Encounters

The Mughals were Muslim rulers of a still largely Hindu population in northern India. The first Mughal emperor, Bābur (r. 1526–30), built a mosque, the Babri Masjid, in 1528 in Ayodhya, about 165 km (115 mi.) northwest of Banaras. In the late twentieth century, the mosque became a symbol for protest by Hindu militants, as its site is reported to be the actual birthplace of Rāma, one of the ten incarnations of lord Viṣṇu.

On 6 December 1992, a large group of Hindu demonstrators broke through the lines of police, paramilitary personnel, and government administrators attempting to protect the Babri Masjid. The militants swarmed over the structure and tore it apart, stone by stone and brick by brick, with little more than their bare hands.

The mainstream media decried the razing of the mosque. *India Today*, a magazine that self-consciously models itself on *Time*, called the event 'a nation's shame' and gave a detailed minute-by-minute commentary. *The Indian Express* called the event an 'outrage' in its editorial entitled 'A Nation Betrayed', and in a rare gesture published the editorial on the front page. It, too, ran a full narrative of the demolition, entitled 'Five Hours to Ram'. *The Hindu*, a leading newspaper in the south, spoke of 'Outrage in Ayodhya' and in its Sunday magazine added, 'We have met the enemy, and he is us.'

Communalism, that is, the political rivalry of religious communities, is a major problem for twentieth-century India. Tensions between Hindus and Muslims brought about the partition of India and Pakistan upon independence from Britain in 1947 and underlie the ongoing insurgency in Kashmir. Political and economic considerations have contributed to antagonistic and suspicious attitudes and to a widespread perception of perpetual and fundamental conflict between the two principal communities of the subcontinent.

While not minimizing the tragedy of these confrontations, we should not overlook the cordial relations between Hindus and Muslims that have also existed in many times and places. Encounter and integration characterize some devotional practices and also much of intellectual scholarship, architecture, and classical music. As with many other matters, the experiences of northern and southern India provide contrasts.

In South India, which has been free of major foreign invasions, the religious minorities are generally better integrated than in the north. The southern Muslims do not speak Urdu but the local languages and think of themselves as culturally different from the Muslims of the north. Tamil-speaking Muslims of Tamil Nadu and the Malayalam-speaking Muslims of Kerala say that they are descendants of seafarers who encountered Islam in their voyages and accepted it as converts. A Muslim group from Tamil Nadu, the Marakkayars, hold that their ancestors either came directly from Arabia or were reached by Muslim traders from the Middle East within a few years of the Prophet's death (or, by some accounts, during Muḥammad's lifetime), well before the Muslim conquest of northern India.

Partly because southern Indian Muslims do not see themselves as associated with military conquest, the Babri Masjid incident had a more limited impact in the south than in northern India. Besides illustrating regional differences in Indian Islam, it is instructive regarding regional forms of Hinduism. Communal and political tensions over Rāma's birthplace do not exist in the same measure in the south, where Rāma is one of the many deities, to be sure, but is not a main recipient of worship. In Andhra Pradesh, the Śiva temple at Srisailam and the Viṣṇu temple at Tirupati are the most popular places of worship. Indeed, the Tirupati temple, which is India's richest in income from offerings, is devoted not to a generic Viṣṇu but to one with a specific local identity, Venkateswara. In

Kerala, there is widespread worship of Kṛṣṇa, a different incarnation of Viṣṇu from Rāma. When the epic *Rāmāyaṇa* was telecast all over India, Kerala had the lowest number of viewers.

At Srirangam in Tamil Nadu, Viṣṇu is known as Raṅganātha. Among approximately sixty shrines in the 63-ha (155-acre) Srirangam temple complex is one for the deity's Muslim wife. Local legend tells of her as a Muslim princess who falls in love with the god Raṅganātha and goes there to be with him.

Several other Vaiṣṇava shrines have similar traditions. Popular in the state of Kerala is Ayyappaṉ or Śāstha, perceived to be an offspring of the Hindu gods Viṣṇu and Śiva. During the annual January pilgrimage, almost 2 million male pilgrims stop at a mosque that honours the Muslim friend of lord Ayyappaṉ and give their donations before embarking on the climb uphill to the Ayyappaṉ shrine.

Hindus in many regions of India have incorporated some Muslim saints and teachers into their pantheon, made pilgrimages to their tombs, and woven stories of Muslim devotees into the legends of their gods. Thus the tombs of many Muslim saints in Nagore in Tamil Nadu, and in Badaun in Uttar Pradesh, attract thousands of Hindu devotees. In the temple town of Kanchipuram in Tamil Nadu, *prasāda* or food offerings made to Viṣṇu is said to be regularly sent to the *darga* or tomb shrine of a Muslim *pīr* nearby.

During an annual February-March festival when Viṣṇu is taken in a procession from the small town of Sri Mushnam in Tamil Nadu, he makes a stop in the Muslim village of Killai. Apparently, a local king called Hazrat Rahamatullah Walliullah Suthari had his capital in the nearby village of Thaikal and endowed its temple with large tracts of land. Offerings are made in front of the ruler's tomb to the accompaniment of band music. A garland from Viṣṇu is placed on the tomb (called *samādhi*, like the burial place of Hindus) and camphor is lit. The *qāḍī* of the mosque recites from the *Qur'ān*, food offerings are made to the deity, and the *prasāda* is taken to the descendants of the *nawāb* (Muslim ruler). That night, Viṣṇu is taken in a flower-decked palanquin to the tomb, and Hindus and Muslims join in the fireworks show that follows.

Cordial relationships between Hindus and Muslims in many parts of India through the centuries have been fostered by affinities between Hindu *bhakti* and the Ṣufī devotional tradition in Islam. Kabir, who protested against blind ritualism in both religions and tried to extract the best of each, has been discussed earlier. Muslims have made important commitments to understanding aspects of the Hindu tradition. The Shaṭṭāri order of Indian Ṣūfīs practised yogic austerities. 'Abd al-Qādir Badā'ūnī (1540–c. 1615) translated the Hindu epics *Rāmāyaṇa* and *Mahābhārata* into Persian. Dārā Shikōh (1615–59), a son of the emperor Shah Jahan (r. 1628–57), translated the *Bhagavad Gītā* and the *Upaniṣads*. In southern India, there is a long tradition of Muslim scholarship on the ninth-century Tamil version of the *Rāmāyaṇa* produced by Kampan.

Perhaps the most fruitful areas of encounter over the centuries have been in architecture, painting, and music. Culturally, it is difficult to distinguish 'Indian' from 'Hindu' and 'Persian' from 'Islamic' when assigning credit for the contributions, as national and religious identifications overlap. For instance, the Tamil word for Muslim is 'Tulukka', which comes from 'Turushka' (i.e., Turk). And once the various styles became blended, forms of expression were hard to identify as distinctly Muslim or Hindu. The cities of northern India possess elegant examples of Mughal architecture such as the Taj Mahal, which is a mausoleum in Agra, south of Delhi. The palaces of Hindu rulers in Rajasthan, southwest of Delhi, show the adaptation of styles associated with Hindu (Indian) and Muslim (Persian and Central Asian) architecture. Integration of Persian and Indian styles is also evident in miniature painting from northern India.

North Indian (Hindustani) music shows a cross-fertilization of Indian and Persian traditions. Amir Khosrow (1253–1325), poet, historian, and musician, was proficient in both the Indian and Persian systems of music and is considered one of the pioneers of the modern system of Hindustani music. In the fourteenth century, after Malik Kafur's conquest of South India, several musicians were apparently taken to the north, with a considerable interchange ensuing. Music was also patronized by Mughal emperors such as Akbar (r. 1556–1605), Jehangir (r. 1605–27), and Shah Jahan (r. 1628–57). Following Amir Khosrow, Muslim musicians took an active part in the performance and development of Indian music forms. Many of these songs had devotional lyrics, which were modified in later years to be mutually compatible with both religious traditions. During Akbar's reign, legendary musicians like Tānsen and Swami Haridās flourished.

Performers of Carnatic music, classical South Indian classical music, adopted melodies perceived to be Muslim into their music's traditional *rāga* structure. The *rāgas* called Arabi, Husseini, and Paraz appear to have become popular around the seventeenth and eighteenth centuries, and some of the most famous *kīrtanas* of Tyāgarāja in praise of Rāma are in these *rāgas*. The dynamic participation of Hindus and Muslims in the preservation and perpetuation of Hindustani music, and to a lesser extent in Carnatic music, still continues. Although its rich devotional lyrics are addressed to Hindu deities, Carnatic music is practised as an art form by accomplished Muslim instrumentalists.

## Use of Modern Technology

A striking twentieth-century Hindu development is the acceptance of technological resources, notably in reproductive technology and the use of electronic devices for worship and ritual.

### *Reproduction*

Not only are the ethical issues surrounding reproductive technology still being debated, but some of their basic logic may at first seem to run contrary to the *smṛti* literature dealing with *dharma*.

Books on *dharma* written about 2,000 years ago by Manu and others emphasized the importance of married couples having children. Many Hindus today accept advances in reproductive technology, such as artificial insemination, as a means towards this goal. Since considerable importance is placed on biological descent, the husband is generally the only acceptable donor. Sperm banks as a source are rejected by 'higher' castes, who value the purity of their lineage. For similar reasons, adoption of an unknown child is unacceptable for many Hindus.

The Hindu epics and *Purāṇas* offer stories about supernatural or 'unnatural' means of conception and giving birth. In the *Mahābhārata*, 100 embryos are grown in separate containers by a queen called Gandharī. In other texts, an embryo is transplanted from one woman to another; Kṛṣṇa's brother Balarāma is transplanted into another womb when still in an embryonic stage. Divine potions are consumed and children born miraculously. And deities are invoked to 'fertilize' the woman if the husband cannot procreate. Even though these tales that legitimate the new reproductive technologies are generally not invoked, the technologies seem to have been accepted easily.

### *Abortion*

Society in ancient India was patrilineal and patriarchal. By having male children, one was fulfilling one's obligations to one's forefathers. In time, wedding gifts to a daughter became a significant financial burden. For this reason too, male children were more welcome in many Hindu families.

While abortions are done for a number of reasons, a growing recent trend appears related to sex selection. Sonograms and amniocentesis are performed to ascertain the sex of the unborn, and female foetuses are aborted. Statistics available from the state of Maharashtra, for instance, show that in recent years there has been a dramatic drop in the number of live births of girls.

According to the *dharmaśāstra* texts, the unborn foetus has life. And according to popular belief and stories from the *Purāṇas*, the foetus is even capable of hearing conversations that take place around it and learning from them. According to popular belief and the texts on *dharma*, the foetus is an entity. One would logically think that terminating its life would be ethically reprehensible. Clearly, the *dharmaśāstra* authors would not approve of killing a foetus. However, abortions are still conducted legally in India. Abortion is accepted without any strong dissent from religious leaders or prolonged editorial, legislative, or judicial debate.

Thus, despite the *dharma* texts' vehemence in condemning abortion, and despite notions of embryonic life, *karma*, and so on, decisions on abortions are less likely to be made on scriptural injunctions than on how much a child, particularly a female child, is wanted by the couple.

The religio-legal texts that condemn the wilful killing of a foetus have very limited bearing on daily life. Many Hindus are not even aware of the *dharmaśāstras*' pronouncements, and many who are apparently find it easy to ignore them. In other words, the *dharma* texts simply have not had the compelling authority that religious law has had in some other religious traditions.

Selectivity in implementing the prescriptions of *dharma* is not unique to birth technology. Hindus have been selective on other counts, too, in following the *dharmaśāstras*. For instance, despite Manu's law that *śūdras* should not own property, in South India the Veḷḷālas, a community of *śūdras*, were powerful and wealthy landlords. Also, as we have seen, many independent women (financially or otherwise) were patrons of temples. Historically then, it is easy to see that prescriptions from the books on *dharma* have often been ignored or flouted.

### *Audio Technology*

The recitation of the *Vedas* and singing of devotional songs, which traditionally took place within a temple or home, now reverberate through radio and cassettes.

The *Vedas* were considered to be *śruti* or 'that which is heard'. Vedic *ṛṣis* or 'seers' were believed to have 'seen' the sacred word, which they articulated. The *Vedas* in the Hindu tradition were the oral word, recited and transmitted unchanged through generations of male brahmins. The words were to be heard and experienced; the words themselves carried power. Both the *Vedas* and the later devotional songs were recited and sung in an atmosphere of piety, either in a domestic ritual or in the temples.

Devotional songs are now sung on the secular stage, which is an important transition in the history of the holy word in the Hindu tradition. Because the recitation and singing was traditionally done in front of the deity in a temple or home shrine, the audience listened to the sacred word and simultaneously had a vision of the lord.

The forum is now a music auditorium or recording studio rather than a temple or home shrine. Further, the devotional songs showcased in secular music festivals are made even more accessible by the production of audio cassettes. Cassettes of popular devotional songs are among the best-selling tapes on the market, and many stores sell only devotional music. Audio cassettes of 'do-it-yourself' rituals are also popular in the Indian marketplace for people who find it hard, if not impossible, to locate a priest to come and help with simple domestic rituals.

Brahmin priests are not counsellors or ministers; they simply attend to the ritual needs of their clientele. Each priest has a certain number of families traditionally under his care. The brahmin priests are not generalists. They attend to certain families of particular castes and communities and, in some cases, families who follow particular sections of the *Vedas*.

Given these limitations and the unavailability of priests in, for example, some rural areas in India or the suburbs of San Francisco, audio cassettes seem to be the logical alternative. These lead devotees through particular rituals. For instance, different cassettes are available to guide a man through the annual ritual of changing his sacred thread and putting on a new one. These cassettes are specific: some are targeted towards South Indian brahmin devotees of Śiva who follow the 'Black' *Yajur Veda*, a subsection of one of the *Vedas*. Some are directed towards followers of Viṣṇu who follow the *Yajur Veda*. There are cassettes for the followers of the *Ṛg Veda*, cassettes for particular communities in North India, and so on. At least a dozen cassettes give ritual instructions on how to perform monthly and annual ancestral rites. There are cassettes for the observation of particular *vratas* or votive rites for women, and scores of other area-specific, community-specific rituals.

This renewed interest in the *Vedas*, devotional songs, and rituals is regarded as a mixed blessing by some conservative Hindus. While the new-found interest and the popularity of the religious works is welcomed, some people are also apprehensive and occasionally alarmed about their electronic dissemination. Their objections seem startlingly similar to those voiced when some of these works were first printed, as the *Vedas* in particular were considered oral recitations and the exclusive purview of brahmin priests.

Some sceptics warn that the material may be misapprehended without a live teacher on hand to guide a student through it. Their wide availability can lead to casual attitudes in reading and listening. One should hear the sacred words with proper attention and veneration in the presence of the lord. Now one may pop a cassette into a portable player and listen to it while otherwise occupied; listening becomes secondary, and one's mind is focused on some other activity. Moreover, rendering the devotional songs in *rāgas* (particular scales of music) diverts the attention from the words to the music, and the sacred words may become mere entertainment.

Yet, one may argue, the dissemination of at least the devotional songs (if not the *Vedas*, which generally had restricted audiences) is indicative of the tradition's resilience throughout the centuries. The new renderings seem to appeal to the aesthetic taste of contemporary audiences. *Śruti* was always the perception and articulation of the sacred through words and sounds, considered an aural experience of reality. Now it is available through sixty- or ninety-minute cassettes.

### *Video Technology*

Similarly, visual technology brings new meaning to the notion of *darśan*. *Darśana* is to behold with faith, it is to be seen by a teacher or the deity, and it is the visual perception of the truth in the form of a god, goddess, or spiritual preceptor.

Television programs of the *Rāmāyaṇa* and the *Mahābhārata*, the life of Kṛṣṇa, and other shows now attract the largest audiences on national broadcasts. When the *Rāmāyaṇa* and *Mahābhārata* were broadcast over sixty weeks on Sunday morning television, the show drew the largest audience in the history of Indian television and turned Sunday morning from inexpensive into prime advertising time.

The publicity tape for the *Rāmāyaṇa* series has footage of people adorning television sets with garlands (traditional honour for a deity, a patron, or a guest) prior to the weekly segment of the show. In one case, people even wave a light in veneration of the television Rāma. Such acts of adoration may seem extreme, but one is prompted to rethink the concept of *darśan* in view of these television shows—which are known in Hindi as *dūr darśan* ('distant vision'). In some respects, the advent of religious television shows in India has had an impact comparable to the televangelists' programs in America.

Television also broadcasts rituals from sacred places all over India into one's house. With video cassettes, they can be recorded and played repeatedly. Thus one can experience vicariously the joys of a pilgrimage that someone else has taken. A video cassette series called 'Darshan' depicts the holy pilgrimage sites within India.

On a festival day when more than 400,000 pilgrims were expected in the Srirangam temple, the procession of the deity through the temple corridors was shown on closed circuit television screens for the pilgrims and then packaged in videotapes. Where once a priestly guide, and later a pamphlet, summarized for the eager pilgrim of the hierophany (manifestation of the sacred) that took place at a holy site, a videotape now gives the information in considerable detail.

Rituals were formerly passed on by verbal description and priestly tradition. Now they are videotaped for posterity. A new sense of history is emerging from the sacred sites. *Darśan* has never been easier or more accessible. One may not quite believe that viewing the tape confers the spiritual merit that comes with seeing a deity or holy person and being in a holy place, but one can confidently observe that sacred sites of Hinduism have never been more popular or understood more integrally than they are now.

## Hinduism in the Diaspora

India has numerous temples. When the early Śaiva brahmins crossed the seas in the fifth and sixth centuries to Cambodia and Indonesia, they continued their temple-building activity. The process of emigration has continued. In the last quarter of the twentieth century, some Hindu emigrants have been transforming their new home in America into a sacred place where the lord graciously abides.

While earlier places of worship were established in America, especially around New York, the first really ambitious Hindu temple that sought to reproduce the traditional architecture and recapture the flavour of a Vaiṣṇava sacred place was the Śrī Venkateswara temple in Penn Hills, a suburb east of Pittsburgh, Pennsylvania, built in 1976.

The Penn Hills temple enshrines a manifestation of Viṣṇu as Venkateswara, lord of the hill known as Vēṅkaṭa in South India. Venkateswara temples are now also in Malibu, California; Aurora, Illinois; and Atlanta, Georgia. The word *vēṅkaṭa* is interpreted as '[that] which can burn sins'. The American temple was built with the help, backing, and blessing of one of the most popular, richest, and oldest temples in India, the Venkateswara temple at Tiru Vēṅkaṭam in the Indian state of Andhra Pradesh.

Despite a desire to remain faithful to the code and sequence of rituals, there are some compromises and innovations. The sacred-time orientation of the Penn Hills temple is made to coincide, as far as the ritual almanac will allow, with American secular holidays. The reason for this time orientation is clear. The festivals are organized by people who do not necessarily live near the temple. Long weekends are often the only time available to many families for long-distance travelling. Thus, the ritual calendar is adapted to the secular working calendar of devotees in America.

But the land on which the temple is located is considered sacred like the land in India where Tiru Vēṅkaṭam is located. The devotees celebrate in song and literature the significance of having a temple on American soil. They proclaim the importance of having Venkateswara dwelling on Penn Hills with his consort Śrī, known locally as 'the lady of the lotus' or Padmāvatī. In a popular song that was sold as a cassette in 1986, the following verse is sung in Sanskrit:

> Victory to Govinda [Kṛṣṇa], who lives in America
> Victory to Govinda, who is united with Rādhā who lives on Penn Hills
> Victory to the Teacher, Victory to Kṛṣṇa.

The concept of sacred land is not just abstract for the devotees of the American temple. They see not only Penn Hills but the greater Pittsburgh area as geographically similar to the sacred land of India. The Penn Hills temple *bhakta* (devotee), drawing upon Puranic lore, recalls the importance of Prayāga, the sacred place in India where the rivers Ganga, Yamunā, and the underground Sarasvatī meet:

> Pittsburgh, endowed with hills and a multitude of trees as well as the confluence of the three rivers, namely, the Allegheny, the Monongahela, and the sub-terranean river (brought up via the 60 foot high fountain at downtown) to form the Ohio river is indeed a perfect choice for building the first and most authentic temple to house Lord Venkateswara. The evergrowing crowds that have been coming to *the city with the thriveni Sangama* of the three rivers

*Women devotees carry an image of the Goddess at their temple in Atlanta, Georgia. (V. Narayanan)*

> to worship at the Temple with the *three vimanas* reassure our belief that the venerable Gods chose this place and the emerald green hillock to reside in (Venkateswara Temple 1986).

Interestingly, the concept of sacred land is not unique to the Penn Hills devotee. Republicans from the Hindu community in the Dallas–Fort Worth area understand the notion of *karmabhūmi*, the land where actions bear fruit, in a far more general manner than Manu and his compatriots had intended. A document circulated by a small group of Hindu Republicans who took an active interest in the 1984 elections reinforces the importance many Hindus give to the sacrality of land. V.S. Naipaul (b. 1932), reporting on the Republican convention in Dallas, brings this passage to the attention of his readers. It deals with 'the Hindu-Interpretation of Americanism and Republicanism' as given in the 'Asian Indian Caucus Booklet' Naipaul says:

> Indians immigrated to the USA to pursue their 'DREAM' to achieve fully their potentials in this land of 'Opportunities'. They came in pursuit of their dreams, visions, happiness and to achieve excellence … During the last few years most of the people have changed from 'Green card holder' status to that of 'U.S. CITIZENS', thus enabling themselves to be full participants in socio-economic and political processes. They have chosen, by their free will, the U.S.A. as the 'KARMABHUMI'—the land of *karma* or action.

V.S. Naipaul's comment on this is equally fascinating:

> Texas as the theater of *karma*—what would Trammel Crow [Naipaul describes him as the 'real-estate king' of Texas] have made of that? But it was, really, no more than a Hindu version of ... fundamentalism, and in this Hindu version certain things could be seen fresh. To embrace one's economic opportunity and good fortune was more than a political act; it was also an act of religion (*The New York Review of Books*, 25 October 1984:5).

Texas and America interpreted as the *karmabhūmi*—the place where actions could produce merit or demerit—is a new idea in the topography of Hinduism. According to Manu and other lawmakers, the land of the Āryas where the black antelope roams freely was the only land that could be called *karmabhūmi*. Some Hindus in America—at least the Republicans near Fort Worth and Dallas—interpret it as referring to the big-sky rangeland where the deer and the antelope play.

### *Miracles and Temple Building*

Statues of Venkateswara and his consorts were carved in India, then brought to America, and the processes of vivification and consecration were done at Penn Hills. While the establishment of the temple is somewhat of a miracle in itself, given the enormous bureaucracy and red tape involved in such a collaborative venture, the temple does not have an origin myth, as some other temples in America do. An origin myth is a set of circumstances where someone has a dream or a vision, or 'discovers' the form of the lord in natural formations such as mountains or caves.

Generally these origin myths are seen in connection with Śaiva temples, especially if there is a strong connection with American devotees. Thus, the Light of Truth Universal Shrine temple at Yogaville, Virginia, became a reality after a vision seen by Swami Satchidānanda (b. 1919), of the Divine Life Mission. Overlooking the temple is the Kailas mountain, and on 27 March 1991 the deities were consecrated. The Iraivan/Kadavul temple on Kauai, Hawaii, was built in 1970 by Swami Shivaya Subramuniyaswami, who was born in America and initiated in Sri Lanka. In three of his visions in 1975, Śiva appears to him, seated and walking in the meadows near the Wailua River. Later, in 1987, a rare Śiva *liṅga*, a six-sided quartz crystal, is discovered and brought to Kauai from Arkansas, and a stone temple that they believe will last for 1,001 years is now being planned.

Perhaps the most unusual temple with mythic origins is the one at Wahiawa (Oahu), Hawaii, now completely run by Hindus from India. This temple is dedicated to Viśvanātha (which they translate as 'lord of the universe'), and the organization that is in charge of it is called the Lord of the Universe Society. The Śiva *liṅga* at the Wahiawa temple is said to be a healing stone. It is believed that this *liṅga* is the embodiment of the Hawaiian god Lono, the priest-healer of ancient times. According to another myth, this stone represents two sisters from Kauai who are turned into rocks. Classic hierophany (manifestation of the divine) is seen in this statement issued by the society:

> The Sacred Healing Stone has been discovered and rediscovered. Several people have experienced healings, visions, dreams and profound feeling of peace and well-being after coming into contact with the Healing Stone and its powers.
>
> More recently, in March 1988, some Indians were taken to the Healing Stone by their friends and they were awe-stricken by the resemblance of the Sacred Healing Stone to Lord Shiva in the form of a Shiva Lingam …
>
> In April 1988 a special Pooja was organized. It became apparent to those who attended the Pooja that this place was indeed special, sacred and holy (Sengupta n.d.).

Regular Hindu worship at the open-air temple on the north shore of Oahu is conducted and a permanent temple is being planned. The Hindus believe that the Hawaiian deity Lono is a manifestation of Śiva.

By undertaking to build a temple, overseas Hindu communities gain several things. They get a local place of worship where icons of the lord have been formally consecrated and where formal prayers can be offered by the priests on behalf of individuals. They get a place to conduct sacraments. They get a place where they can make offerings of devotion either in gratitude or as a petition for particular favours and receive a token of the lord's grace (*prasāda*) in return. They get an institution that has self-consciously undertaken the role of educating the younger American-born generation through weekly language and religion classes, frequent discourses, sponsorship of classical music and dances (which have a broad religious base in India), summer camps, and an outreach bulletin.

New temples are springing up all over the North American landscape. In many cases the community hall is being built even before the shrine. This is understandable in a situation where members of the Hindu tradition are trying to assert their identity in a larger society where they feel marginalized culturally and linguistically. The community hall is a place where different groups can meet to have language, music, and dance classes.

Significantly, tensions arise within the North American community over which deity is to be enshrined, and what mode of worship is to take place. Devotees of Viṣṇu, Śiva, the Goddess, Gaṇeśa, or those who worship Viṣṇu as Rāma or Kṛṣṇa want the temple to be primarily dedicated to that deity. A temple intended to unite the Hindu community in the diaspora frequently becomes the cause for division. The reason is clear: as we noted at the outset, Hinduism is not a unitary tradition. It is not a single identity and lacks a united community and central authority. Because of the many communities and traditions, a consensus is almost impossible. Lines are drawn on sectarian, caste, and regional lines, and the debates continue as they have throughout the history of the tradition.

### *The Outlook for Hinduism's Future*

As the communities in the diaspora face the challenge of raising a new generation in the faith, Hindus in many parts of the world are engaging in the process of self-definition. Many of the statements that are made in this context are questionable and possibly not historically true. Examples of these are statements such as 'Hinduism is not a religion, it is a way of life', or 'Hinduism is a tolerant religion.' Proving or disproving these claims only underscores the complexities of a religious tradition that has evolved through more than 3,000 years of recorded history—5,000 if one includes the Harappa culture.

The dynamism in the many traditions of Hinduism is unmistakable. Vedānta is continually being interpreted. People are possessed by known and unknown gods and spirits and continue to counsel their clientele. Temples are being built, consecrated, and preserved. The sacred words of the *Veda*s and the *smṛti* literature are being broadcast widely. Manuscripts are being restored, edited, and published, and new technologies are making literature more widely accessible; the tradition confining the sacred word to particular castes is gone forever. Radio waves are flooded with religious programs, horoscopes are cast and matched by computer, surgeries are scheduled for auspicious times. The Hindu tradition, or traditions, continues to retain and reinforce selective features of the scriptures and thus adapts itself to changing times and different lands.

## KEY TERMS

*ācārya*. Title for the leading teacher of a sect or head of a monastery.

**Advaita**. Śaṅkara's school of philosophy, which holds that there is only one ultimate reality, the indescribable Brahman, with which the *Ātman* or self is identical.

**Āḻvars**. Twelve devotional poets in South India whose contribution sparked the *bhakti* tradition.

*artha*. Wealth and power, as one of the three classical aims in life.

**Aryans**. Population that invaded northern India from the northwest in the second millennium BCE, becoming rulers over the indigenous Dravidian people.

*asramas*. Four stages in the life of an upper-class male: student, householder, forest dweller, and ascetic.

*Ātman*. The individual self, held by Upanishadic and Vedantin thought to be identical with Brahman, the world-soul.

*avatāra*. A 'descent' or incarnation of a deity in earthly form.

**Āyurveda**. A system of traditional medicine in India, understood as a teaching transmitted from the sages.

*bhakti*. Loving devotion to a deity, understanding the deity also as a gracious being who enters the world for the benefit of humans.

**Brahmā**. A creator god. But Brahman is the name for the world-soul, sometimes understood in impersonal terms, a brahmin is a member of the priestly class, and the *brāhmaṇas* are texts regarding ritual.

*darśana*. Seeing and being seen by the deity in the temple or by a holy teacher: the experience of beholding with faith.

*devanāgarī*. The alphabet used to write Sanskrit and northern Indian vernacular languages such as Hindi and Bengali.

*dharma*. One's religious and social duty, including both righteousness and faith.

**Dīpāvalī**. October-November festival when lamps are lit.

**Dravidians**. Population with roots in the Indian subcontinent prior to the Aryan invasion more than 3,000 years ago. Tamil is one of the Dravidian languages.

*guru*. One's teacher.

**Holī**. March festival when one splashes coloured powder or water on people one meets in the streets.

*jñāna*. Knowledge presented in the *Bhagavad Gītā* along with action and devotion as one of the three avenues to liberation.

*kāma*. Sensual (not merely sexual) pleasure, as one of the three classical aims of life.

*karma*. One's actions, whose cumulative result is held to have a determining effect on the quality of rebirth in future existences.

***kṣatriya***. A member of the warrior class in ancient Hindu society.

***liṅga***. A conical or cylindrical stone column, considered phallic, symbolic of the god Śiva.

***Mahābhārata***. A very long epic poem, containing the *Bhagavad Gītā* as one of its episodes.

**mantra**. An expression of one or more syllables, chanted repeatedly as a focus of concentration in devotion.

***mokṣa***. Liberation from the cycle of birth and death, listed as one of the three classical aims in life.

***mūrti***. A form or personification in which divinity is manifested.

**Navarātri**. A September-October festival of nine nights' duration.

***oṃ***. A syllable chanted in meditation, among whose varying interpretations are that it represents ultimate reality, or the universe, or the relationship of the devotee to the deity.

***prasāda***. A gift from the deity, especially food that has been placed in the presence of the god's temple image, blessed, and returned to the devotee.

***pūjā***. Ritual household worship of the deity, commonly involving oil-lamps, incense, prayers, and food offerings.

***Purāṇas***. 'Old tales', stories about deities that became important after the Vedic period.

***rājanya***. The royal class in early Indian society after the Aryan conquest, which subsequently became known as the *kṣatriya* class.

***Rāmāyaṇa***. An epic recounting the activity of Rāma, an incarnation of the god Viṣṇu.

***ṛṣi***. A seer. The composers of the ancient Vedic hymns are viewed as *ṛṣis*.

***sādhu***. A holy man.

***saṃnyāsin***. A religious ascetic, one who has reached the fourth of the classical stages of life for Hindu males after student, householder, and forest dweller.

***saṃsāra***. The continuing cycle of rebirths.

***satī***. The self-sacrificing devotion of a widow who throws herself onto her deceased husband's funeral pyre.

***smṛti***. 'What is remembered', a body of ancient Hindu literature including the epics, *Purāṇas*, and law codes formed after the *śruti* and passed down in written tradition.

***śruti***. 'What is heard', the sacred literature of the Vedic and Upanishadic period, recited orally by the brahmin priests for many centuries prior to being written down.

***śūdra***. A member of the lowest of the four major classes, with the status of 'servant' after the Aryan invasion of the Indian subcontinent, but in some cases enjoying prosperity in more recent centuries.

***tantra***. An emphasis apart from the Vedic and brahminical tradition, gaining momentum from the fifth century onward, with an esoteric lineage and involving ritual and sometimes sexual practices not universally accepted.

***tilaka***. A dot or mark on the forehead made with red or other coloured powder.

***trimūrti***. The combination of the gods Brahma, Viṣṇu, and Śiva into one concept with three faces or three aspects.

***upanayana***. The initiation of a young brahmin boy into ritual responsibility, in which he is given a cord to wear over his left shoulder and a mantra to recite and is sent to beg for food for the day.

***Upaniṣads***. Philosophical texts, in the form of reported conversations, composed around the sixth century BCE and reflecting on the theory of the Vedic ritual and the nature of knowledge.

***vaiśya***. In the ancient fourfold class structure of society, a member of the third or mercantile class.

***Vedas***. The four collections of hymns and ritual texts, constituting the oldest and most highly respected Hindu sacred literature. The hymns reflect the religion of the Aryans, who entered India from the northwest in the second millennium BCE.

**yoga**. A pattern of practice and discipline, which can involve a philosophical system and mental concentration as well as physical postures and exercises.

## FURTHER READING

Baird, R. 1993. *Religions and Law in Independent India*. New Delhi: Manohar.

Basham, A.L. 1954. *The Wonder That Was India*. London: Sidgwick & Jackson.

Beny, R., and A. Menen. 1969. *India*. London: Thames and Hudson.

Bhattacharji, S. 1970. *The Indian Theogony: A Comparative Study of Indian Mythology from the Vedas to the Puranas*. Cambridge: Cambridge University Press.

Blurton, T.R. 1992. *Hindu Art*. London: British Museum Press; Cambridge: Harvard University Press.

Brown, C.M. 1990. *The Triumph of the Goddess: The Canonical Models and Theological Visions of the Devi-Bhagavata Purana*. Albany: State University of New York Press.

Bumiller, E. 1990. *May You Be the Mother of a Hundred Sons*. New York: Random House.

Dimock, E., and D. Levertov, 1967. *In Praise of Krishna: Songs from the Bengali.* Garden City, NY: Doubleday.

Eck, D.L. 1981. *Darśan: Seeing the Divine Image in India*. Chambersburg: Anima Books.

Embree, A.T., ed. 1988. *Sources of Indian Tradition*, 2 vols. New York: Columbia University Press.

Erndl, K. 1993. *Victory to the Mother*. New York: Oxford University Press.

Felton, M. 1967. *A Child Widow's Story*. New York: Harcourt, Brace & World, Inc.

Findly, E. 'Gargi at the King's Court: Women and Philosophic Innovation in Ancient India'. In *Women, Religion, and Social Change*, edited by Y.Y. Haddad and E.B. Findly, 37–58. Albany: State University of New York Press.

Harlan, L., and P.B. Courtright. 1995. *From the Margins of Hindu Marriage: Essays on Gender, Religion, and Culture*. New York: Oxford University Press.

Hawley, J.S., and D.M. Wulff. 1982. *The Divine Consort: Radha and the Goddesses of India*. Berkeley: Berkeley Religious Studies Series.

______. 1996. *Devi: Goddesses of India*. Berkeley: University of California Press.

Hiriyanna, M. 1985. *The Essentials of Indian Philosophy*. London: Allen and Unwin.

Kinsley, D. 1986. *Hindu Goddesses: Visions of the Divine Feminine in the Hindu Religious Tradition*. Berkeley: University of California Press.

Leslie, J., ed. 1991. *Roles and Rituals for Hindu Women*. London: Pinter Publishers.

Marglin, F., and J. Carman, eds. 1985. *Purity and Auspiciousness in Indian Society*. Leiden: Brill.

Michell, G. 1989. *The Penguin Guide to the Monuments of India*, vol. 1. London: Penguin.

Miller, B.S. 1977. *Love Song of the Dark Lord*. New York: Columbia University Press.

Narayan, R.K. 1972. *Ramayana: A Shortened Modern Prose Version of the Indian Epic*. New York: Viking Press.

Radhakrishnan, S., and C.A. Moore, eds. 1957. *A Source Book in Indian Philosophy*. Princeton: Princeton University Press.

Rajagopalachari, C. 1953. *Mahabharata*. Bombay: Bharatiya Vidya Bhavan.

Ramanujan, A.K. 1981. *Hymns for the Drowning*. Princeton: Princeton University Press.

Renou, L. 1964. *Indian Literature*. New York: Walker.

Waghorne, J.P., N. Cutler, and V. Narayanan. 1985. *Gods of Flesh, Gods of Stone*. Chambersburg: Anima Publications.

Walker, B. 1968. *Hindu World: An Encyclopedic Survey of Hinduism*. 2 vols. London: Allen and Unwin.

Zimmer, H. 1946. *Myths and Symbols in Indian Art and Civilization*. New York: Pantheon.

## REFERENCES

Carman, J.B., and V. Narayanan, trans. 1989. *The Tamil Veda*. Chicago: University of Chicago Press.

Doniger, W., and B. Smith, trans, 1991. *The Laws of Manu*. London: Penguin Books.

Doniger O'Flaherty, W. 1981. *The Rig Veda: An Anthology*. Harmondsworth: Penguin Books.

Hawley, J.S., and M. Juergensmeyer, trans. 1988. *Songs of the Saints of India*. New York: Oxford University Press.

Jackson, W., trans. 1991. *Tyagaraja. Life and Lyrics*. Delhi: Oxford University Press.

Kennedy, M.T. 1925. *The Chaitanya Movement: A Study of the Vaishnavism of Bengal*. Calcutta: Association Press.

Lipski, A. 1977. *The Life and Teachings of Sri Anandamayi Ma*. Delhi: Motilal Banarsidass.

Miller, B.S., trans. 1986. *The Bhagavad Gita: Krishna's Counsel in Time of War*. New York: Columbia University Press.

Ministry of Education and Social Welfare. 1974. *Toward Equality: Report of the Status of Women in India*. New Delhi: Ministry of Education and Social Welfare.

Radhakrishnan, S. 1953. *The Principal Upanisads*. London: George Allen and Unwin.

Sengupta, D. n.d. 'The Historic Healing Stone—L.O.T.U.S.' Kauai: Lord of the Universe Society.

Tagore, R., trans. 1915. *One Hundred Poems of Kabir*. London: Macmillan.

Venkateswara Temple. 1986. 'Kavachas for the Deities'. Pittsburgh: Venkateswara Temple.

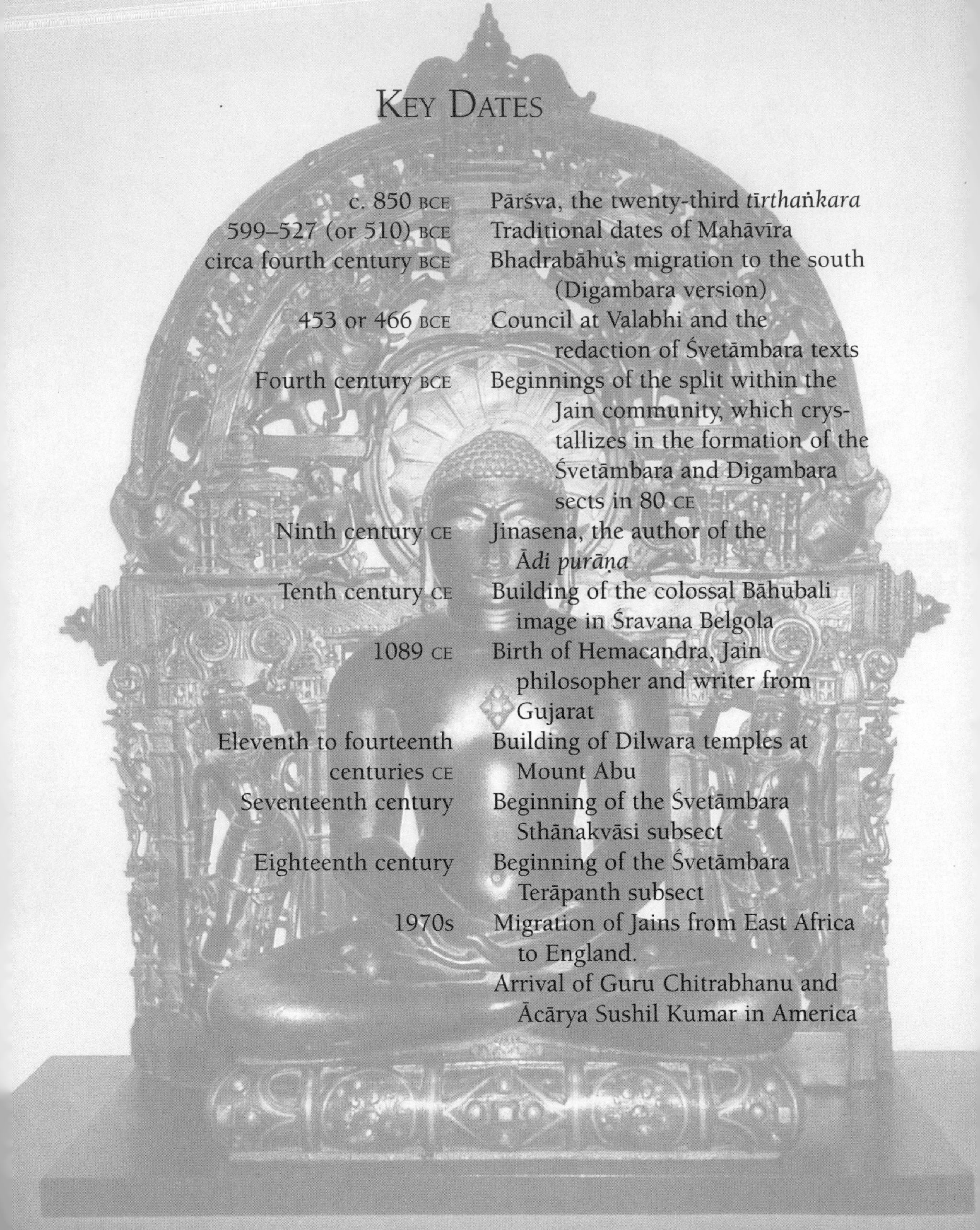

# Key Dates

| | |
|---|---|
| c. 850 BCE | Pārśva, the twenty-third *tīrthaṅkara* |
| 599–527 (or 510) BCE | Traditional dates of Mahāvīra |
| circa fourth century BCE | Bhadrabāhu's migration to the south (Digambara version) |
| 453 or 466 BCE | Council at Valabhi and the redaction of Śvetāmbara texts |
| Fourth century BCE | Beginnings of the split within the Jain community, which crystallizes in the formation of the Śvetāmbara and Digambara sects in 80 CE |
| Ninth century CE | Jinasena, the author of the Ādi *purāṇa* |
| Tenth century CE | Building of the colossal Bāhubali image in Śravana Belgola |
| 1089 CE | Birth of Hemacandra, Jain philosopher and writer from Gujarat |
| Eleventh to fourteenth centuries CE | Building of Dilwara temples at Mount Abu |
| Seventeenth century | Beginning of the Śvetāmbara Sthānakvāsi subsect |
| Eighteenth century | Beginning of the Śvetāmbara Terāpanth subsect |
| 1970s | Migration of Jains from East Africa to England. Arrival of Guru Chitrabhanu and Ācārya Sushil Kumar in America |

CHAPTER TWO

# THE JAIN TRADITION


## VASUDHA NARAYANAN


Popular pamphlets and brochures on the Jain tradition usually sum it up in the phrase: *Ahiṁsā paramo dharmaḥ* ('Non-violence is the highest form of religious conduct'). Commitment to this principle translates into the preservation of all forms of life on this earth, and ultimately the preservation of the earth itself. Jains today see this teaching of non-violence as relevant to individual spiritual well-being as well as to ecological and environmental issues and global peace.

Jain principles are seen as taught age after age by holy people who themselves transcend the suffering of life and attain enlightenment. In the series of the current age, the Jain community was established by—or, as many Jains and some scholars prefer to say, was reorganized by—Vardhamāna Mahāvīra, the final teacher in the series.

Born around 599 BCE and therefore a senior contemporary of Gautama Buddha, Mahāvīra is considered by the tradition to be the greatest religious leader in our historical age and is titled the *jina* ('victor'). His followers came to be called Jain(a)s or 'followers of the Victorious One'.

The Jain tradition has flourished in the Indian subcontinent since the sixth century BCE. Unlike the Buddhist tradition, which faded out in India, Jainism has maintained continuity as a religion in the subcontinent. Although numerically a tiny minority in India, the Jains have had considerable interaction with and influence on the Hindu tradition, while keeping their distinctive identity for about 2,500 years. Until its doctrines were succinctly presented to the World's Parliament of Religions at Chicago in 1893 by Virchand Gandhi, the Jain tradition was almost unknown to the Western world.

There are about 4 million Jains today in India, the United Kingdom, Canada, and the United States. There are now many Jain centres around the world. Through their members' activities and publications, they disseminate information about the tradition and encourage the preservation and transmission of the teachings of the *jinas* and the other teachers.

A Jain's diet, manner and times of eating, movements, travel, choice of career, mode of conducting business, and reflection on and confession of sins are all influenced by the doctrine of non-violence. The universe is seen to be pulsating with various forms of life. Violence to any of these through thought, word, or deed is said to stain one's soul. No other religion in the world has paid such close attention to the theory, discussion, practice, and propagation of non-violence as has the Jain tradition.

When one avoids hatred and all other forms of violence, whether intentional or not, and practises 'right conduct', then the translucent, luminous nature of one's soul is restored and one attains liberation from the cycle of life and death. Ultimately it is through one's spiritual practice—and not through the grace of a divine being—that one achieves liberation.

## THE ENLIGHTENED TEACHERS

### Mahāvīra

Who was Mahāvīra? According to the Jain tradition, he was the last of twenty-four teachers who were victorious over the afflictions of life. Jains believe many spiritual leaders have become perfected beings, victorious over the pain of rebirth. These great spiritual leaders come into being at special times. In the present span of time in this part of the universe, when happiness is in regression and conditions are becoming steadily worse, there have already been twenty-four such *jinas*. They are also titled *tīrthaṅkaras* ('bridge-builders'), a title that is given a double connotation. A classic sense of this term is that they have built a crossing over the sea of life and death to the other shore, to enlightenment. Jains also understand the title to signify that these figures bridge and integrate as *tīrthas* the four sections of their overall community—monks, nuns, laymen, and laywomen—providing the social structures needed for the pursuit of liberation.

There are differing accounts of Mahāvīra's life. The disagreements over biographical details run principally along sectarian lines. Around the fourth century BCE, 200 years after Mahāvīra, his followers began to split into two major branches, a split that crystallized several centuries later. These were the Śvetāmbaras ('white-clad' monks), who have been dominant in the more northerly regions such as Gujarat and Rajasthan, and the Digambaras ('sky-clad'), who are stronger in the south such as in Karnataka. We shall return to this division later, but mention it here since the two branches vary in their accounts of Mahāvīra.

*The image of Mahāvīra in a posture of meditation.*
(V. Narayanan)

According to some Jain texts, King Siddhārtha and his queen Triśalā, Mahāvīra's parents, were followers of the tradition of Pārśva. Other texts portray the royal couple as belonging to the *kṣatriya* ('warrior') class of society. Mahāvīra's given name is Vardhamāna ('one with increasing prosperity'); Mahāvīra ('great hero') is his title or epithet. He was born in Kundagrama, near the city of Patna, around 599 BCE. Scholars are in dispute about the dates of his life, some holding that his attainment of *nirvāṇa* should be placed closer to 350 BCE.

Although considered in many of the later biographies to be a human being, he is portrayed as almost divine. The reason for this is his previously accrued merit, ensuring rebirth as a *tīrthaṅkara*. In a pattern resembling birth stories of other spiritual teachers, Jain accounts depict his mother Triśalā as having fourteen wonderful and awe-inspiring dreams (or sixteen, depending on the text one reads) before the birth of her son. One story is well known in the Śvetāmbara tradition. According to it, Mahāvīra is conceived by a brahmin couple, and the embryo is later moved from the womb of Devānandā to the womb of Triśalā.

While the Śvetāmbara Jains accept this story as completely true, it may have emerged as an attempt to address a tension discernible in the values and beliefs among early Buddhists and Jains. Mahāvīra's early disciples all seem to be from the brahmin caste, which many took to be endowed with a potential for spiritual wisdom. At the same time, only a man of the *kṣatriya* class could be a world conqueror in either a military or spiritual sense. One may interpret this story as portraying the superiority of the *kṣatriya* class over the brahmins because he opts to be born in the warrior class.

In the Śvetāmbara narrative, Mahāvīra marries a woman called Yaśodā and has a daughter called Priyadarśanā. The account of the wedding is rejected by the other major Jain group, the Digambaras. He renounces secular life when he is thirty and at that point starts his quest for spiritual enlightenment. The event of his renunciation, like his birth, is attended by many celestial beings. He rides in a palanquin to a park. There, he becomes an ascetic after pulling out the hair of his head. Even today, Jains who become monks or nuns pull out the hair on their heads to show that they do not have a high regard for their own bodies. To some extent this action also shows that they are impervious to personal pain and comfort.

According to Digambara accounts, Mahāvīra gives up wearing clothes when he becomes a monk; according to the Śvetāmbaras, this happens at a later time. Digambaras consider wearing clothes to be indicative of an attachment to possessions, to a sense of selfhood, and to a sense of modesty or shame. It follows that by discarding clothes, one is renouncing all possessions. A true renouncer is not supposed to cling to anything.

Jain texts say that Mahāvīra achieves enlightenment after twelve years, at the age of forty-two, at the culmination of arduous and extreme ascetic practices.

## THE LIFE OF MAHĀVĪRA IN THE *KALPA SŪTRA*

*Mahāvīra's Birth*

[When] the Venerable Ascetic Mahāvīra was born, ... [there] rained down on the palace of King Siddhartha one great shower of silver, gold, diamonds, clothes, ornaments, leaves, flowers, ... sandal powder and riches.

...[His parents] prepared plenty of food, drink, spices, and sweetmeats, invited their friends, relations, kinsmen ... His three names have thus been recorded: by his parents he was called Vardhamāna; because he is devoid of love and hate, he is called Sramaṇa (i.e., Ascetic); because he stands fast in the midst of dangers and fears, patiently bears hardships and calamities, adheres to the chosen rules of penance, is wise, indifferent to pleasure and pain, rich in control ... the name Venerable Ascetic Mahāvīra has been given him by the gods.

*Enlightenment*

When the Venerable Ascetic Mahāvīra had become a Jina and Arhat, he was a Kevalin, omniscient and comprehending all objects; he knew and saw all conditions of the world, of gods, men, and demons: whence they came, whither they go, whether they are born as men or animals or become gods or hell beings ... he the Arhat for whom there is no secret, knew and saw all conditions of living beings in the world, what they thought, spoke or did at any moment.

*Mahāvīra's Physical Death*

In the fourth month of that rainy season ... in the town of Pāpā ... the Venerable Ascetic Mahāvīra died, went off, quitted the world, cut asunder the ties of birth, old age, and death; became a Siddha, a Buddha, a Mukta, a maker of the end (to all misery), finally liberated, freed from all pains ... [that night, the kings who had gathered there said]: 'since the light of intelligence is gone, let us make an illumination of material matter' (Jacobi 1884:251–2, 253–6, 263–4, 264–6).

For thirty years, he propagates his message, based on his enlightenment experience. Mahāvīra has eleven chief disciples, two of whom survive him.

> When the Venerable Ascetic Mahāvīra had become a Jina and Arhat, he was a Kevalin [liberated one], omniscient and comprehending all objects; he knew and saw all conditions of the world, of gods, men and demons: whence they come, whither they go, whether they are born as men or animals or become gods or hell-beings, the ideas, the thoughts of their minds, the food, doings, desires, the open and secret deeds of all the living beings in the whole world; he the Arhat, for whom there is no secret, knew and saw all

> conditions of all living beings in the world, what they thought, spoke, or did at any moment (*Kalpa sūtra* 121; Jacobi 1884:263–4).

After this momentous enlightenment experience, he comes to be called the *jina*. In the early texts, many religious leaders, including Gautama Buddha, were called *jinas*. The ascetic followers of Mahāvīra in particular were called Nirgaṇṭhas ('unattached ones'), but the Buddhists discarded the term *jina* as an epithet for their teacher. Hence when other sectarian movements waned, the Nirgaṇṭhas alone came to be called Jainas, the name that continues as 'Jains' today.

In many of the later biographies, especially those revered by the Digambara Jains, Mahavīra is portrayed as transhuman, especially after his enlightenment. There is a marked difference in the Śvetāmbara and Digambara descriptions of Mahāvīra from this point on. According to the Śvetāmbara version, Mahāvīra continues to live like other human beings and teaches; he eats, sleeps, speaks, and travels to places to propagate his message.

However, in Digambara sources, he is not engaged in any worldly activity. According to them, his body becomes like crystal, for he is free of all impurities; even the blood in his body is changed to a special substance. He occupies a wondrous hall termed *samavasaraṇa*, 'the refuge of all creatures' including celestial and human beings and animals. He does not speak; a sacred sound resembling *oṃ* emanates from him. His chief disciple, Indrabhūti, is given the power to decipher and interpret this sound, which he records as the sermons of the *jina*. The Śvetāmbara Jains say that Mahāvīra gave his first sermon on the importance of non-violence and that he spent several seasons travelling and spreading his message through northern India.

Five 'auspicious' events (*pañca kalyāṇaka*) in Mahāvīra's life are recognized by the Jain tradition as crucial to understanding the life of all *jinas*. These five events are portrayed in art and architecture, in rituals at temples and at home, in festivals, and in the performing arts. These are: the conception of Mahāvīra, his birth, renunciation, enlightenment, and final release from life.

These five events are sometimes enacted in rituals when images of Mahāvīra are enshrined in temples. The ceremonies connected with the installation of Mahāvīra's image are usually underwritten by patrons. The man and woman who sponsor these events usually assume the role of Śakra or Indra, and his wife Indrāṇī, the king and queen of the celestial beings. These celestial beings are said to rejoice at the birth of a potential *jina*. In the installation of Mahāvīra's image, the major events of his life are enacted. Sponsoring such activities is said to bring about an abundance of good *karma* for the patrons.

Mahāvīra 'dies', that is, attains liberation or *nirvāṇa*, at the age of seventy-two, possibly around 527 BCE. Within a few hours after the teacher's reaching *nirvāṇa*, his chief disciple, Indrabhūti, receives enlightenment. Jains celebrate Mahāvīra's attainment of *nirvāṇa* on the new moon that occurs between 15

October and 14 November. This is the same new moon that signals the Hindu festival of Dīvālī ('necklace of lights'), commemorating the victory of light over darkness and good over evil.

## The *tīrthaṅkaras*

Although Jains celebrate Mahāvīra as the teacher *par excellence*, they also venerate twenty-three other spiritual teachers preceding him. Ṛṣabha, the first *tīrthaṅkara*, is said to have lived in the Indian subcontinent, Jambūdvīpa, in the third stage of our regressive span of time. Before him, life was still enjoyable and conditions were not far removed from the golden age. The teachings of Ṛṣabha are held to be identical with those of Mahāvīra, the twenty-fourth and last in the sequence, because the Jains believe that truth is constant, discovered and proclaimed age after age.

Ṛṣabha establishes the world order with his son Bharata. Bharata is perceived to be the first emperor of India. Indeed, the subcontinent of India, which many Hindus and Jains call *Bharata varṣa*, is considered to be named after him. Ṛṣabha introduces social institutions such as marriage, the family, law, monarchy, agriculture, and asceticism in this world. In later texts, composed around the tenth century in South India, he starts the caste system in society.

According to Jain hagiography, Ṛṣabha eventually becomes a monk and after 600,000 years attains enlightenment, becoming the first *jina* of this age. His daughter Brahmi masters the art of writing (the script of many languages in India is said to be derived from one called *Brahmi lipī*). Jain scriptures present a picture of an ideal society that eventually becomes corrupt. When the decline of civilization begins, the first *tīrthaṅkara* and his family introduce the basic elements of the society, culture, and values that we know of today to bring order into a time of increasing chaos.

Other *tīrthaṅkaras* follow Ṛṣabha. One branch of the Jain tradition, the Śvetāmbaras, which we shall discuss later, holds that Malli, the nineteenth teacher, was female, but this is denied by the other branch of Jains, who believe that enlightenment is not possible for one who has the body of a woman.

Of the twenty-four acknowledged *tīrthaṅkaras*, great religious leaders of this present age, Nemi is the twenty-second. He reportedly lived in the Saurashtra peninsula in what is now Gujarat. Pārśva, who reportedly lived in Banaras, is the twenty-third. Other than Mahāvīra, the twenty-fourth, Pārśva is the only attested historical figure in the Jain lineage of teachers.

Pārśva is said to have preached the Jain tradition 250 years before Mahāvīra. His followers may have become part of Mahāvīra's entourage. Thus, within the Jain tradition, Mahāvīra is considered not a founder but a leader who gave new shape and impetus to an already existing religious tradition.

# Social and Sectarian Divisions

The Jain community or *tīrtha* is considered to have a natural fourfold division into monks, nuns, laymen, and lay-women. In later years there developed complex groupings based on lines of transmission, leadership, and caste issues.

Apart from the many sociological divisions within the Jain community, there are major lines drawn along differences of opinion on issues of philosophy and practice. Jain texts portray dissensions and splits within the tradition even during the time of Mahāvīra. One of his disciples, who went on to start his own sectarian movement, was Gosāla, the founder of the Ājīvika tradition. This sect was popular for a few centuries, but after the thirteenth century even the small remaining pockets of Ājīvikas in South India faded out.

## The Digambaras and the Śvetāmbaras

Despite many differences in interpretation, the major splits in the Jain tradition began only after several centuries. Approximately 200 years after Mahāvīra, the First Jain Council, held at the city of Pataliputra (today's Patna), tried to establish the official Jain platform.

According to the Digambara sect, it was soon after this time that Bhadrabāhu, a venerated leader, predicted a major famine and led many of the Jains to the area that is today Karnataka, in the south of India. According to some sources, he was accompanied by Candragupta (r. c. 324–302 BCE), the first emperor of the Mauryan dynasty. However, there is no inscription from that period to corroborate the account, the earliest datable inscription coming from twelve centuries later.

Digambara sources seem to indicate that Bhadrabāhu died before the group he led into the diaspora returned to northern India. When the southern emigrants returned to Pataliputra, it is said, they did not recognize some of the practices adopted by those who stayed behind.

A major issue divided the community: can one who has possessions, even if only simple clothing, ever be a true 'renouncer' and get liberation? The Digambaras denied that a monk can truly be thought of as one who has renounced everything (including the sense of 'I-hood' and a sense of shame) if he still wears clothes. The monks who stayed in northern India had apparently adopted the wearing of white clothes. The names Śvetāmbara ('white-clad') and Digambara ('sky-clad') reflect the northern and southern positions on this issue.

Upon their return, Bhadrabāhu's southern migrants also reacted to the new collection of texts now considered canonical. Many of the books in the new canon were not accepted by those who returned.

The Śvetāmbara account of all this is somewhat different. They do not believe that Bhadrabāhu emigrated south. According to their version, he spends some years in what is now Nepal. At any rate, the final split seems to have occurred before the first century.

On the whole, the two groups have agreed on many essential doctrinal positions in the Jain tradition, but they hold different opinions on many other subjects. Major differences in theory and practice focus on the issues of clothing for the ascetic, the attainment of liberation by women, the human nature of the *jina* after his enlightenment, and the content of the scriptural canon. There have been varying degrees of acrimony between them through the ages. The most bitter battles between the two movements have been fought over control of the temples, and legal disputes over temple sites continue.

In the temples of the 'white-clad' Śvetāmbaras, images of the *jinas* are covered with clothes and jewellery, while the 'sky-clad' Digambaras hold that clothed images are unsuitable for worship.

We have already noted that the two groups disagreed over the details of Mahāvīra's life. In addition to the biographical details, there are other differences on the nature of the enlightened being. The Digambaras hold that Mahāvīra—and indeed, all those who have reached the final state of liberation—do not become involved in human relationships and activities. They do not eat, drink, talk, or walk, but instead subsist on divine morsels of a supernatural sustenance. The Śvetāmbaras disagree on this and other details of Mahāvīra's life. They picture an earthly career for Mahāvīra and the other *jinas*, believing that he led a more or less 'normal' life.

There is considerable variation in scriptural canon between the two sects. Several Jain councils were held beginning at Mathura in the fourth century; more followed, possibly between 453 and 466, at Valabhi in what today is Gujarat. These councils, which were really a forum to hear the recitation of sacred texts, were almost exclusively Śvetāmbara. The Śvetāmbara movement crystallized with the fixing of a canon in the sixth century.

This editorial and redactional process and the resulting scriptural canon are rejected by the Digambaras. Believing that many of the ancient teachings were lost, they do not accept what the Śvetāmbaras hold as canonical. In time, the Digambaras wrote their own *Purāṇas*, which they hold in great respect. No subsequent agreement was reached between the Śvetāmbaras and the Digambaras, especially concerning a common canon.

While the initial schism resulted in the formation of the Śvetāmbara and Digambara movements, several subsects have emerged in the last 2,000 years. Śvetāmbaras who perform worship (*pūjā*) before images (*mūrti*) in temples are generally called Mūrtipūjaks. The Sthānakvāsi ('those who reside in halls', i.e., those who have no temples) and the reform group known as Terāpanth are considered to be Śvetāmbara sects. The Digambara movement has several subgroups, including the Taranapantha one called the Terāpantha. The Digambara

Terāpanths and the Śvetāmbara Terāpantha movements do not have any historical connection.

In addition to sectarian differences, regional variations also exist. Some Digambaras from northern India, for instance, do not use 'wet' items like water, flowers, leaves, or the perfumed paste made of sandalwood in their worship; rather, they use 'dry' items. Like much else in Jainism, this behaviour is based on the notion of *ahiṁsā* or non-violence; the plucking of flowers or the use of water is said to cause injury to the souls that live in them. The Digambaras from the south, on the other hand, make extensive use of many liquids in the rituals by which they bathe and anoint the images of the *jina*s and other spiritual leaders.

## Opportunities for Women

The Jain community is understood as made up of four *tīrtha*s or divisions: monks, nuns, laymen, and lay-women. The distinction between male and female is thus as fundamental as the distinction between ascetic and householder. And just as the tradition gives special respect to the renunciant compared with the householder, so it appears, like other ancient traditions, to confer special privilege on the male.

Can women achieve liberation? One of the Digambara arguments is that since it is wrong for women to discard clothing, but since clothing is an impediment to spiritual release, women logically cannot get liberation. A woman will have to be reborn as a man before reaching the final state of perfection. The Śvetāmbaras, on the other hand, believe that it is indeed possible for a woman not only to achieve liberation but to be a teacher (*jina*) as well. They consider the nineteenth *tīrthaṅkara*, Malli, to be a woman, while the Digambaras portray her as a man.

Mahāvīra apparently willingly ordained women as ascetics. Under the leadership of a holy woman called Candanā, thousands of women became nuns. Unlike in Theravāda Buddhism, where the institution of ordaining women died out, the practice of initiating women into the order continues in the Jain tradition and is quite prominent in the Śvetāmbara group. Mahāvīra's decision to initiate women came at a time when such was discouraged within the Hindu tradition. The *Kalpa sūtra* indicates that at the time of Mahāvīra's death, women ascetics outnumbered men by a ratio of 2.5 to 1.

Several Jain women were generous endowers of temples and pious builders of shelters, monasteries, and shrines. From stone inscriptions in the state of Karnataka, we learn of their involvement in religious activities as patrons of charitable works. Śantala Devi, a Jain queen of the Hoysala dynasty, was married to Biṭṭideva, who converted to become a Vaiṣṇava Hindu. She is considered the moving force behind the building of many Jain and Hindu temples and 'tanks' (pools) and gifts of land. Some women funded the copying and distribution of manuscripts. Also named are pious women who committed themselves to a holy fast unto death.

The question of whether a woman may get liberation was the focus of considerable debate in medieval Jain texts. Digambaras offer reasons why a woman cannot achieve liberation while in her present body. A woman's body, they say, is host to a number of micro-organisms, which live and die on her. In each menstrual cycle, over which she has no control, organisms are believed to be killed. She is consequently envisaged as inadvertently causing violence to life, resulting in further *karma* that prevents liberation.

The Digambara tradition also holds that only an ascetic can obtain liberation. This ascetic-monk should also give up wearing clothes, for as we saw earlier, the possession of clothes indicates attachment to material goods and a sense of shame. Both of these stand in the way of liberation. According to the Digambara sect, a woman should not discard her clothes and be naked; therefore, liberation is not possible for her. Further, a woman is thought to have only mediocre qualities, and to be therefore incapable of descending either to the worst hells or ascending to the highest state of liberation.

The Śvetāmbara tradition rejects these views of the Digambaras and holds that a woman may get liberation while possessing a female body. As we have indicated, they contend that Malli, one of the *tīrthaṅkaras*, was a woman. Further, they believe, the first person to get liberation in this cycle of time was Marudevī, the mother of the first *jina*, Ṛṣabha.

Within the Jain faith, women have had a choice of marrying or leading a religious life. Any woman not pregnant has been eligible to become a nun. A woman can become a nun if she has the strength to practise the difficult vows incumbent upon her. It is also important that by pursuing this vocation she is not causing hardship or grief to anyone in her family. The Jains understand that monks and nuns deprive their families of their participation and love, and that this may cause distress. In fact, some biographies of Mahāvīra say that he became a monk only after his parents' death because he did not want to cause them any anguish. A woman may become a nun, therefore, if her family will not suffer for it. In many Jain subsects, this rule also holds for a man.

There are fewer than a hundred Digambara nuns today. Strictly speaking, these nuns are considered not to be ascetics but householders of an elevated status. They accept that for many reasons, including their wearing of clothes, they will have to be reborn in the future as men to attain liberation. Among the Śvetāmbara community, the ordination of nuns takes place fairly frequently. These initiation ceremonies are sometimes advertised in the daily newspapers. All nuns, whatever their seniority, have to pay respect to monks, even to those who are very young and newly initiated.

*Shrine memorializing a twentieth-century Jain woman ascetic in Rajasthan.*
(L.A. Babb)

## Caste

Apart from sectarian divisions, there are many Jain social divisions drawn along caste lines. Although Mahāvīra did not accept the traditional caste system of the Hindus as a criterion for liberation, we see a strong awareness of it in Jain literature. Recall the story, mentioned earlier, in which Mahāvīra is conceived by a brahmin woman and the embryo is transferred to a *kṣatriya* or warrior-class woman. According to Jain hagiography, all the initial disciples of Mahāvīra seem to have been men from the brahmin class.

The Jain tradition has adopted parts of the Hindu caste system. Regionally, where parallel Hindu and Jain castes are found, caste divisions can override sectarian ones. Jains from higher castes prefer to marry members of parallel castes among Hindus than to marry a Jain perceived to be of a lower caste. In Rajasthan, for instance, the Śrimal and Oswal castes are considered above the Porwals and the Paliwals. While most Jains in this region marry within their own religion, sometimes marriages may be arranged between an Oswal (Śvetāmbara) Jain and an Oswal Hindu who is a Vaiṣṇava (a follower of the god Viṣṇu.) Since Vaiṣṇavas can be strict vegetarians like the Jains and also part of the trading community, the compatibility seems to outweigh other caste and sectarian concerns within the Jain tradition

# Jain Literature

According to the Digambaras, the earliest teaching of Mahāvīra was in the sound of a reverberating sacred syllable, echoing as '*oṃ*'. The earliest disciples, they say, deciphered this *oṅkāra* ('*oṃ*-expressing') sound and recorded the sermons that they heard in it. Śvetāmbara Jains, however, say that Mahāvīra spoke in a human language, which was recorded by the disciples.

Jain sacred texts are in a variety of languages. The earliest texts were composed in a Magadhan language called Ardhamāgadhi. Other texts were written in forms of Prakrit, and later on, in vernacular languages such as Tamil, Kannada, and Gujarati. Many medieval texts were also written in Sanskrit.

The Digambaras and Śvetāmbaras hold different books as sacred. Interestingly, books considered by the tradition to be canonical are not always important in the liturgy, while books that are popular in worship and ritual are not necessarily a part of either canon. Also noteworthy is that the issue of 'canon' itself is somewhat problematic in the Jain tradition. While in some traditions the idea of a scriptural canon connotes a fixed set of books considered sacred, in the Jain tradition that set tends to be fluid, without clearly fixed boundaries.

Both the Digambaras and the Śvetāmbaras hold that their earliest texts, the fourteen *pūrvas*, were lost long ago. They differ over how later texts might reflect or preserve what is supposed to have been in the *pūrvas*.

The Digambara tradition holds that two collections, the *aṅgas* ('limbs') and *aṅga bāhya* ('outside the *aṅgas*') were lost by the second century CE. But at about that time, Dharasena composed the *Ṣaṭkhaṇḍāgama*, which Digambaras say contains the essence of the *pūrvas*. The *Kaṣāyaprābhṛta*, by Guṇabhadra, is also held in reverence. Other texts, called the *prakaraṇas* (i.e., treatises), come from the beginning of the Common Era. The earliest of these treatises were by Vaṭṭakera (who wrote the *Mūlācāra*), Kundakunda, and Śivārya. The Digambaras also hold in esteem later texts such as the ninth-century *Ādi purāṇa* of Jinasena.

The principal sacred collection of the Śvetāmbaras, called the *āgama* ('tradition'), contains between thirty-two and forty-five treatises grouped into twelve *aṅgas*. Śvetāmbaras believe that the lost *pūrvas* were contained in their twelfth *aṅga*, which itself is lost now. They credit the editing of these texts to the early generation of Mahāvīra's disciples. The earliest sections of the *aṅgas* include the first two texts, the *Ācārāṅga sūtra* on Good Conduct and the *Sūtrakṛtaṅga*. The *Sūtrakṛtaṅga* describes the doctrines of the rival religious schools. Looking at the content of these texts, scholars believe they are the oldest surviving Jain compositions, going back to the fifth century BCE.

The Śvetāmbaras' *aṅga bāhya* or collection outside the *aṅgas* contains twelve *upāṅgas* ('ancillary limbs'), six *cheda sūtras* (books on monastic law), and other categories of literature. The editing of the *aṅga bāhya* material is credited to learned monks in times later than Mahāvīra's disciples.

Śvetāmbaras hold that the final redaction of their canon took place after recitation of the texts at the Council of Valabhi in the mid-sixth century. The basic distinction between *aṅga* and *aṅga bāhya* material was apparently being drawn by then, although literary evidence for its terminology comes only from the twelfth century. Also, the exact titles of the texts considered authoritative were not enumerated immediately. The list of forty-five sacred texts was finalized around the thirteenth century.

The classification of the *aṅga bāhya* into *upāṅgas*, *cheda sūtras*, and other material seems fairly late, but there are other, earlier forms of arranging the texts. One such grouping employs three categories: *āvaśyaka* (texts containing the six obligatory daily observances of all mendicants), *kāliya* (texts to be studied at particular times), and *ukkāliya* (books that can be read at any time). This is one of the better-known classification systems used by Śvetāmbaras, but there are also other arrangements.

Scripture is not just recited and studied; texts as such are also the focus of considerable veneration. *Āgam mandirs*, temples dedicated to holy texts, are located in the states of Gujarat and Maharashtra. In the town of Palitana (Gujarat), the main image has four faces. The names of four *jinas* are associated with it. There are also forty-five additional four-faced images to correspond to the forty-five sacred texts of the Śvetāmbara canon.

The Digambara sacred places also served as repositories of manuscripts. The temple at Mudbidri in Karnataka had the manuscripts of Dharasena's *Ṣatkhaṇḍāgama* and other texts. There, too, the sacred texts themselves serve as a focus for veneration and not just study.

The recitation of sacred texts is also a significant part of many rituals. As indicated, texts most popular in ritual do not belong to the *aṅgas* or even the *upāṅgas*. The *Kalpa sūtra*, dating possibly from the second century BCE, is one such text. It is actually the eighth chapter of the first text of the *cheda sūtras* (one of the subcategories of the *aṅga bāhya* texts). Two appendices are added to this chapter, and the whole anthology is called the *Kalpa sūtra*.

Just as in the Hindu tradition the *Bhagavad Gītā*, which is one section in the much larger *Mahābhārata* epic, is selected for special attention and printed separately as a book, the *Kalpa sūtra*, too, is printed separately and treated as an individual work, indeed as one of the most exalted works. This work, in its Prakrit text, Sanskrit and vernacular translations, and commentary, are all recited during the festival of Paryūṣaṇ in September. Various episodes in the life of the *jinas* are highlighted. Silver images are used as props on the fifth day during the enactment of Mahāvīra's conception and birth. During the recitation of the text on the eighth day, a young boy shows illustrations to the audience.

On the whole, study of the sacred texts by oneself, without active guidance and instructions from a teacher, is discouraged. The unqualified may misinterpret the sacred word, leading to mistaken ideas.

> By study [the soul] destroys the *karma* that obstructs right knowledge. By the recital of the sacred texts he obtains destruction of *karma* and contributes to preserve the sacred lore, whereby he acquires the Law of the *tīrtha*, which again leads him to the complete destruction of *karma* and to the final annihilation of worldly existence. By questioning the teacher he arrives at a correct comprehension of the *sūtra* and its meaning (*Uttarādhyayana* 29:18–20; Jacobi 1895:165).

A study of scripture by itself is also not commendable; to be efficacious in the quest for liberation, it should be accompanied by austerities.

A vast body of Jain literature, both Digambara and Śvetāmbara, has been composed over the last 2,000 years. Some texts are overtly religious, while others embed Jain morals in the context of narratives or poetry. Śvetāmbara teachers like Hemacandra in the eleventh and twelfth centuries compiled books containing prescriptions for the behaviour of an ideal layperson. These books, known as *śrāvakacāra* ('a layperson's conduct') have been very influential.

Jain literature in the Tamil language flourished as early as the fourth and fifth centuries. The two epics *Cilappatikāram* (The Story of the Anklet) and *Manimekalai* (The Jewelled Girdle) were composed by the Jain prince Iḷaṅkō Aṭikaḷ. The prince became a Jain monk. The character of a Jain nun who accompanies the main characters of the story is clearly delineated in *Cilappatikāram*. This story also shows quite clearly how a person's *karma* affects one's life immediately and also influences the quality of future lives. The authorship of the Tamil didactic work *Tirukkuraḷ* has been disputed, but the best-known commentary on it was composed by a Jain man, leading many to suppose that the author of the original work was also Jain.

The *Ādi purāṇa* of Jinasena, from about the ninth century, is a majestic poem narrating the lives of early *tīrthaṅkara*s and other important figures such as Ṛṣabha, Bāhubali, and Bharata. Ponna, a poet in the Karnataka region, wrote several works including the *Śānti purāṇa*. The *Yaśatilaka* of Somadeva is a complex story of many generations, with rebirth of the same entities in different forms. The suffering caused by thoughts and acts of violence, and the kinds of rebirth to which they lead, are articulated in this narrative.

Among other genres, Jains wrote works on medicine, including the dangers of eating meat. Commentaries on established and respected texts included the second-century *Tattvārtha sūtra* of Umāsvāti. The *Tattvārtha sūtra*, the first Jain work in Sanskrit, is accepted both by the Digambaras and Śvetāmbaras. *Stotra*s or hymns in praise of the *jina*s and other exalted beings are also an important part of the Jain compositions.

Biographical works on monks were also well known in Jain literature. Some of the better-known biographies include those on the monks Hemacandra, Siddhasena, and Bappabhaṭṭisūri. Another biography, the *Hīrasaubhāgya*, recounts the life of Hīravijaya and his connections with the Mughal court. Biographical works are explicitly didactic, urging the listener to avoid the mistakes narrated in the story and to model oneself after the exemplary characters portrayed in the work.

# JAIN TEACHINGS

## The Jain View of the Universe

### *Space*

Some interpreters discern in Jain literature a portrait of many other worlds. The structure of the universe has three principal realms, some with multiple subdivisions. The underworld, occupied by demons and demigods, consists of coloured layers with the darkest at the bottom. The earth's surface forms the middle world. Above the earth is the celestial world, with sixteen layers for beings born in the *kalpa* heavens without Jaina insight and fourteen layers for those born beyond the *kalpa* heavens with it. Atop all this, beyond the heavens, is the crescent-shaped apex of the universe, a region permanently occupied by souls who are already liberated. Jain texts go into great detail about the specific characteristics of various tiers in this unique physical arrangement of the universe.

In the middle or terrestrial layer, there are many worlds, only a few of which are conducive to human life. They are arranged in an infinite number of concentric rings, each separated from the others by water. The land in which Mahāvīra was born is called Bharata (the generally accepted classical name for India). It is located in the continent or island of the Jambū Tree (Jambūdvīpa). Jambūdvīpa and two of its adjacent worlds are the only places that may be called *karmabhūmi*, the land of action. Only in these worlds do human actions lead to merit and demerit, and only there may one reach the supreme goal of liberation.

***Time***

Like the Hindus, the Jains believe in cycles of time with units of progressive happiness or unhappiness, but the Jain system is unique to their tradition. For the Jains, each half-cycle of time consists of six stages when world civilization and individual happiness are either increasing or decreasing. Thus, according to Jain belief, this present half-cycle of declining values and happiness began millions of years ago, and we are now in the fifth stage of decline.

After tens of thousands of years, when civilization will have reached rock bottom, a half-cycle of six progressive stages will begin. That is, after the world has reached the worst possible stage, the quality of life will slowly begin to improve. Civilization will then progress through six stages, lasting millions of years. When the apogee of that prosperous time has been reached, decline will begin again. Twenty-four *tīrthaṅkaras* appear in each cycle of time. Mahāvīra is born and dies near the very end of the fourth stage in the descending cycle of time. The fifth stage, in which we currently are, and the sixth stage are said to last 21,000 years each.

There are worlds whose cycles of time may be quite different from ours. In some worlds the conditions are always similar to our third and fourth ages of time. Teachers or *jinas*, it is believed, can only be born in the third and fourth stages of time, when there is neither extreme unhappiness nor extreme happiness. So, no more teachers will appear in this world until there is an upward swing in civilization. But even now there may be *jinas* living in other worlds where the conditions are more felicitous than those on this earth.

## Physical Existence

With logical perseverance, Jains have pursued the issue of how one obtains and certifies information about the world we live in. Their remarkable system of knowledge is studied under two headings: *anekānta* ('many-sidedness') and *syādvāda* ('assertion with qualification').

According to the Jain tradition, when we observe an object, we can simultaneously be aware of its unchanging unified nature and its changing manifold modes. Anything that exists is said to have three aspects: substance, quality, and mode. Any substance (*dravya*) is the abode of inherent qualities (*guṇas*). Qualities constantly undergo changes, losing and acquiring modes (*paryāyas*).

For instance, when we look at a flower or a leaf, we can notice that it remains a flower or leaf continually over the minutes or even hours that we observe it; its fundamental unity is not changed. However, it is constantly changing, and in time, these changes show. One may observe the changes and the different aspects of the one leaf; it is this simultaneous recognition of the enduring entity and the changing variety of its being that is called *anekānta* (many-sidedness, or 'manifold aspects').

Describing a situation or object, Jains have persistently urged prudence in staying away from making absolute statements. Almost every statement can—indeed must—be qualified. Thus, one may say that the water is cold, but for a person coming in from the cold, it may seem warm. An object exists, but in the future it may not. Statements have to be qualified from the perspective of space and time from which one speaks. This adamant insistence on refraining from some absolute statements is known as *syādvāda*. The notion of qualification implies the unspoken phrase 'in some ways' as a preface to any statement one may make.

### *Categories of Reality*

Three basic categories of reality are recognized by Jain philosophers: matter (*pudgala*), sentient beings, and finally that which is neither material nor sentient. The last category consists of four subcategories: space, time, movement, and rest.

Matter is formed from atoms, which by themselves have no extension in space but begin to form shapes when combined with other atoms. Within the Jain tradition, *karma* also is material and forms the basis for bondage.

Jains do not believe that souls were originally pure and that they later became sullied. Rather, they believe that the souls have always been in some state of bondage, but that it is indeed possible to make them crystal-like and pure. Sentient beings or souls are said to have as many as four main qualities: consciousness, bliss, energy-potential, and perception. The soul itself is real and not illusory. The soul adapts to the dimensions of the body. While the soul in many ways is unchanging, its qualities do undergo change.

Many categories of souls populate the universe. These souls are constantly in a state of embodiment and transmigration. That is, they are born, they die, and they are born again into this universe. A soul may take one of four forms of existence: a celestial being or god, a human being, an inhabitant of an underworld, or a plant or animal.

The lowest birth is as an animal or plant. At the lowest level is the smallest, almost imperceptible creature called *nigoda*. *Nigodas* are born in clusters and die within milliseconds. They are said to be found in every part of the universe, including the bodies of human beings, plants, and animals. These *nigoda*s are said to have only one sense organ, that of touch. Then there are other souls, single-celled creatures, making up the basis of matter; they make up earth, water, fire, and air. Thus every time a lamp is lit and the flame is put out, fire bodies come into being and are extinguished. Plants, too, are considered to be creatures with only the sense of touch. Animals are categorized by the number of sense organs they are said to have, ranging from two to five. Animals are not considered much lower than human beings; Mahāvīra himself is said to have been a lion in one of his previous births. Embodiment occurs when a soul becomes entangled and entrenched in karmic matter.

### *Karma and Bondage*

The Jain tradition, like the Buddhist and Hindu, accepts the notion of *karma* as underlying the predicament of embodiment for the soul. *Karma*, literally 'action', generally means the fruits of one's action, especially as it impinges upon one's life.

Jain and Hindu views of *karma* differ in one important way: the Jains consider *karma* to be material in nature. It is said to exist as undifferentiated subtle matter particles. These particles become attracted to the soul when the being thinks, speaks, or acts in any way. Karmic matter seems to be specially attracted to souls that are 'moist' with desires; the drier, more dispassionate souls are not so easily polluted. Particles of karmic matter stick to the soul and keep it in a state of bondage. Over births, the souls become coloured with the type of *karma* they are polluted by; the darker the soul, the more soiled it is with negative *karma*. This is a far cry from the purity and crystalline nature of the liberated soul.

Jain texts divide *karma* into various categories. The major distinction is between *ghātiyā karma*, governing the nature of the soul, and *aghātiyā karma*, determining the conditions and circumstances of embodiment. As in the Hindu and Buddhist traditions, one's actions directly determine what happens to a person. For example, the law of *karma* decrees that if you take something that does not belong to you, in the future, someone may steal what is yours. But *karma* takes many years, sometimes many births, to bear fruit. One carries the baggage through the cycle of lives and deaths

One's intentions are as important as the action itself and determine the quality of *karma*. It makes a significant difference if a particular action is planned rather than accidental. The intention to hurt or harm a being is the most violent of *karma*s and the worst in the scheme of things. A tenth-century book, the *Yaśatilaka*, describes the harm that befalls a prince who sacrifices a rooster made of dough instead of a live bird. Although a live being was not killed, nevertheless, the intention to harm was present in the act. Such intentions darken the soul and prevent it from being liberated.

A well-known story depicts the precarious state of a soul falling into deeper layers of bondage. The story represents a soul as a human being who falls into a

## DHARMA

Dharma is the most important principle in the world. It is the main cause for all happiness. It comes from human beings and through it, human beings attain what is good (*Kalpa sūtra* 2).

well. He clutches the branch of a tree that is growing from the side of the well to save himself from falling deeper. As he hangs on, he sees two mice, one black and one white, gnawing at the branch. He realizes that when the mice chew through the wood, he will fall. Glancing at the pit under him, he sees poisonous serpents waiting for him. At this moment, a beehive on the tree above shakes a bit and drops of honey fall near the man. Forgetting his predicament, he reaches out for the honey and loses his grip on the branch just to have the fleeting sense of enjoyment.

The man in the well is the soul, which can at any moment fall into deeper trouble. The mice represent our lives; the white mouse symbolizes the days and the black mouse the nights. Time is eating away at our lives. And yet, instead of concentrating our energies in getting out of the problems that we find ourselves in, we try to experience a fleeting sense of enjoyment, even at the cost of our ultimate happiness. If one loses one's chance to get onto the right path, one is reborn again and yet again. But the situation of the man in the well is not entirely hopeless. He is not destined necessarily to revolve endlessly in the cycle of birth and death.

### *The Swastika*

The Sanskrit word *svastika* means 'well-being'. In the diagram of the swastika, Jains read not only the human predicament but the means for overcoming it. Its four spokes represent the four stages of this existence in the wheel of *saṃsāra*, the cycle of life and death.

The swastika appears frequently on temples and household doorways, and decorates Jain wedding invitations and greeting cards. The sacred symbol is the focus of considerable meditational practice among the members of the Jain laity as well as monks. Besides being in the presence of swastikas already drawn, the meditator may use grains of rice to draw the symbol on the floor or ground.

The swastika used in meditation is a special one, with additional marks. There are three dots above the swastika and a little crescent on top of all this, with a dot in the middle. The four arms represent the four realms of possible births: human, heavenly, infernal, plant, and animal. The crescent and dot symbolize the land of the perfected soul, which is described in cosmographical texts as being in the shape of an inverted umbrella. The three dots represent the hope for final

*The ancient Indian symbol of the swastika is used not only by Jains but by Hindus and Buddhists. It is seen here on the entrance to a Buddhist temple in Singapore.* (V. Narayanan)

emancipation; they represent the *ratna traya*, the three 'jewels' that one adopts and practises to escape from the cycle of life and death.

## Jain Practices

The three jewels are enumerated as right insight, viewpoint, or faith (*samyak darśana*), right knowledge (*samyak jñāna*), and right conduct (*samyak cāritra*). Right faith implies a moment of spiritual insight, a glimpse of the truth from a right viewpoint. This flash of insight is enough to start the soul on the path to eventual liberation. One is led on the long and arduous path by right knowledge and right conduct. Right conduct consists of five basic principles (*mahāvrata*) of practice for the layperson as well as for monks and nuns. These principles are non-violence, truthfulness, non-stealing, sexual purity, and non-possession.

## Five Practices

### *Non-violence*

Non-violence or not harming (*ahiṁsā*), the first of these, is the most important. Jains find both the thought and act of harming others abhorrent. This belief in non-violence is applied in all areas of life, but is perhaps most perceptible in dietary habits. Non-violence automatically means that all Jains are vegetarians:

> A Hasitāpasa: 'Every year we kill one big elephant with an arrow, and live upon it in order to spare the life of other animals.'
> Ārdraka: '… If a man kills every year but one animal, and lives in other respects as a *śramaṇa*, he is unworthy, and works his perdition. Such men will not become *kevalins*' (*Sūtrakṛtāṅga* ii.6.52–4; Jacobi 1884:418–19).

The taking of animal life is prohibited, and one must destroy plant life for food as sparingly as possible. Many periods of fasting are enjoined for Jain monks and laity. Many monks do not eat more than one meal a day. Digambara monks beg using their hands as a begging bowl and eat as sparingly as possible.

Jains mandate vegetarianism on general principles. Meat, fish, and fowl are always out of bounds. Jains prohibit certain specific kinds of other foods considered abundant with life forms and the potential for life. These include honey, alcohol, and eggplant. Root vegetables like potatoes, radishes, onions, and garlic are prohibited, to protect the millions of microorganisms thought to be living in them. Under extenuating medical circumstances, one may sometimes consume honey or some prohibited vegetables. And for many Jains, especially overseas, it is not practical to avoid all the prohibited vegetables, so they are frequently included in the diet today.

Another food restriction bans what has been touched by excrement or any other substance cast off from someone's body. Food that has been tasted by someone else, for instance, is deemed contaminated; the taster's saliva may be on the utensil dipped back into the cooking pot. Modern Jains interpret this prohibition (which is common to Hindus also) as reflecting a strong sense of personal hygiene. Intoxicants are prohibited, as are other materials considered to cause harm to one's body. Also banned are some fruits, in which many small insects are said to live.

## FROM THE *ĀCĀRĀṄGA SŪTRA* ON GOOD CONDUCT

He who injures these (earth bodies) does not comprehend and renounce the sinful acts; he who does not injure these, comprehends and renounces the sinful acts. Knowing them, a wise man should not act sinfully towards the earth, nor cause others to act so, nor allow others to act so. He who knows these causes of sin relating to earth, is called a reward-knowing sage. Thus I say (Jacobi 1884:10–11).

... the sage who walks the beaten track (to liberation), regards the world in a different way. 'Knowing thus (the nature of) acts in all regards, he does not kill,' he controls himself, he is not overbearing.

Comprehending that pleasure (and pain) are individual, advising kindness, he will not engage in any work in the whole world: keeping before him the one (great aim, liberation), and not turning aside, 'living humbly, unattached to any creature.' The rich in (control) who with a mind endowed with all penetration (recognises) that a bad deed should not be done, will not go after it. What you acknowledge as righteousness, that you acknowledge as sagedom ...; what you acknowledge as sagedom, that you acknowledge as righteousness. It is inconsistent with weak, sinning, sensual, ill-conducted house-inhabiting men. 'A sage, acquiring sagedom, should subdue his body.' 'The heroes who look at everything with indifference, use mean and rough (food, &c.)' Such a man is said to have crossed the flood (of life), to be a sage, to have passed over (the saṃsāra) to be liberated, to have ceased (from acts). Thus I say (Jacobi 1884:46–7).

Water is to be strained or boiled before drinking, so that one will not inadvertently consume any microorganism that might grow in it. In the past, evening meals were eaten before sunset. That was done to avoid lighting lamps for dinner; the flames in the lamps would attract insects and thus bring inadvertent violence against their souls.

Jain monks ritually sweep the ground before them as they sit down, to avoid harm to life forms. Monks and nuns of some subsects like the Śvetāmbara Terapanthis and Sthānakvāsis wear a small scarf or plastic screen around their mouths to avoid breathing in organisms and also to avoid causing harm to the creatures in the air with the hot air that they breathe out. Some Jain monks do not bathe; this is done to avoid harm to water bodies and to the organisms that may reside on one's body.

Careers that might give any harm to life are discouraged. Thus one should not be a butcher or fisherman; one must also not traffic in slaves, cut down trees, or burn fields. Although most rural and agricultural occupations entailed causing harm in some way, farming was something that Jains like others necessarily had to engage in. However, the practice of business was the career frequently enjoined for Jains, many of whom became merchants. Ironically, in a roundabout way, a choice of work motivated by altruistic concern for other beings had the effect of contributing to Jains' economic prosperity.

There were many Jain kings in medieval South India. A Jain king was allowed to fight in self-defence, but was forbidden to take an aggressive stance. This code of conduct was also prescribed for all Jain laymen who were called upon by their country or king to fight a war. They were to fight only in self-defence, responding to enemy attack. Soldiers who died in war were not promised any reward in heaven; in fact, anyone, soldier or civilian, who lived or died with hostility was considered condemned to a lesser form of life.

The Hindu socio-political leader Mahatma Gandhi (1869–1948) used non-violence as an instrument to fight the British and gain India its independence. There is no doubt whatever of Jain influence on this political leader.

### *Truthfulness*

Adherence to truth (*satya*) is also important for Jains. They are encouraged not to hide the truth and not to lie. The only exception is when by uttering the truth one may cause violence. The classic example involves a person witnessing a deer that runs in one's path. Moments later, a hunter stops the witness to ask which direction the deer ran. To be silent is as good as lying, for the witness is concealing the truth. However, this is preferable to telling the truth and being responsible for the death of the deer. In this case, the person may decline to tell the truth.

In daily life there can be a clash between the values of truth and non-violence. A roommate may ask if she looks attractive, or a friend may ask for one's opinion on an issue. An honest answer in these cases may cause hurt. One is enjoined to be silent rather than to cause harm. But apart from this exception, one is to speak the truth, the whole truth. One's actions are also to reflect this sense of truth. Thus, a shopkeeper is not to use false weights or make false assertions about his merchandise. Honesty is far more than expedient policy; it is crucial for the well-being of the soul.

### *Non-stealing*

Non-stealing in most circumstances means avoiding taking what does not belong to one; in many cases it is interpreted as not taking what was not voluntarily given.

### *Sexual Purity*

Sexual purity for laypeople involved fidelity to one's spouse or spouses in the Middle Ages. Till the nineteenth century, although monogamy was considered ideal, polygamy was accepted by the many religions of India, and the Jains lived in this milieu. Thus, one is exhorted to lead as celibate a life as one possibly can,

## 'KNOWLEDGE OF WOMEN'

As (men by baiting) with a piece of flesh a fearless single lion get him into a trap, so women may capture an ascetic though he be careful.

And then they make him do what they like, even as a wheelwright gradually turns the felly of a wheel. As an antelope caught in a snare, so he does not get out of it, however he struggles.

Afterwards he will feel remorse like one who has drunk milk mixed with poison; considering the consequences, a worthy monk should have no intercourse with women (*Sūtrakṛtāṅga* 1.4.1.8–10; Jacobi 1895:272–3).

When a monk breaks the law, dotes (on a woman), and is absorbed by that passion, she afterwards scolds him, lifts her foot, and tramples on his head ...

But when they have captured him, they send him on all sorts of errands ... (Bring) wood to cook the vegetables, or that we may light a fire at night; paint my feet, come and meanwhile rub my back! ... Give me the vessel (used in worshipping the gods), the water-pot. Friend, dig a privy. Fetch the bow for our son, ... the drum, and the ball of cloth for the boy (to play with) ...

This has been done by many men who for the sake of pleasures have stooped so low; they become the equals of slaves, animals, servants, beasts of burden—mere nobodies (*Sūtrakṛtāṅga* 1.4.2.2, 4, 5, 13, 18) (Jacobi 1895:275–8).

or at least limit one's activities to those that are socially permissible. A monk or a nun is asked to give up all thoughts of sexual activity.

***Non-possession***

Ideally, one is to renounce all possessions, and indeed, all craving for ownership. Human beings are said to have an unending desire to own and to possess, for it is indicative of one's power in life. These possessions distract one from the pursuit of knowledge and impel one to act in ways that may cause harm to others. One is asked to own as little as possible and give away what is not necessary. Laymen are asked to adopt fourteen principles of renunciation of external things. This renunciation includes abstaining from or limiting oneself in quantity of food, clothes, decorations, and the like. When one becomes a monk, one ceremoniously gives away all of one's belongings, in emulation of Mahāvīra.

## Ascetics and Householders

Like a layperson, an ascetic's code of conduct includes the practice of the six obligatory actions. All ordained monks and nuns are to practise equanimity, which is described as a tranquil meditative state of mind. They are also to sing a short hymn in praise of the *tīrthaṅkaras*. The third obligatory action is showing formal respect and reverence for one's teacher. The ascetic is also to show repentance (twice daily and on other formal occasions), after a thorough introspection of one's behaviour and faults. Fifth is standing motionless for long periods of time in a bodily position called *kātyosarga* ('abandonment of the body'). While standing, the ascetic meditates on his nature as a living being and recites a liturgical phrase. The sixth obligatory action concerns the intention to refrain from various acts of transgression and violence.

The householder affirms five ancillary or 'minor' vows (*aṇuvratas*), covering the five practices just enumerated: non-violence, truthfulness, non-stealing, self-control regarding sensuality (i.e., sexual purity), and non-possession. They match the list for the ascetic, but differ in degree.

For an ascetic, these practices are very rigorous and strict; the householder adopts a version that is more practical. In the case of sexual purity, for instance, an ascetic is to remain celibate and renounce all sexual activity. A householder, on the other hand, is enjoined to limit the relationship to one's spouse and within that exercise control over all sensual activities.

Non-possession is strongly advocated for Jain laypersons as well as monks. The degree and severity with which it is applied to the monk are again greater than to the layperson. While an ascetic is to give up all possessions, the householder is simply to restrict his or her buying to what is genuinely needed. The householder is to place a limit on accumulating real estate, gold, silver, jewellery, cash, cars and other vehicles, equipment, and all consumer goods. Austerity in every form is strongly encouraged.

## *Sallekhanā*, Fasting unto Death

A ritual unique among world religions is the Jain ideal of a holy fast unto death, while being in total control over one's mind and faculties and while having a meditative state of mind. This act is not recommended for everyone or even as a rule for holy people, but is to be undertaken only by a spiritually fit few. It is not considered a form of suicide; indeed, the taking of one's life by any other means is anathema for the Jain tradition. *Sallekhanā* is death with dignity and with dispassion.

> When a wise man, in whatever way, comes to know that the apportioned space of his life draws towards its end, he should in the meantime quickly learn the method of dying a religious death. As a tortoise draws its limbs into its own body, so a wise man should cover, as it were, his sins with his own meditation. He should draw in, as it were, his hands and feet, his mind and five organs of sense, the effect of his bad *karma*, and every bad use of language (*Sūtrakṛtāṅga* i.8.15–17; Jacobi 1895:299).

*Sallekhanā* has been undertaken by both ascetics and laypeople, and by men and women. It involves a state of equanimity and mindful meditation and there is a slow withdrawal from all forms of food. While in earlier days any Jain with the right disposition and the correct attitude could undertake this fast, by the beginning of this century it was only allowed with strict supervision. Ascetics do have the choice of embarking on this path on their own, but the act has been relatively rare in the last few centuries. The act of *sallekhanā* is usually in a public forum and done with the approval of the family and spiritual superiors.

Both men and women adopted *sallekhanā*. Many memorial stones in India bear testimony to their piety. In the Sravana Belgola region of Karnataka state alone, archaeologists have found almost 150 memorial stones and pavilions commemorating the deaths of men and women during the last fourteen centuries. Some of these were erected for those who adopted *sallekhanā*, others for those respected in this life who passed away without resorting to a ritual death. These memorials give us information of the person's name, his or her teacher, the spiritual group (*saṃgha*) that they belonged to, and other details. While these memorials seem to have come into vogue only after the seventh century, earlier incidents of death by *sallekhanā* are described in various textual sources.

While suicide by any other means is considered to be an act that involves passion and violence, and is therefore condemned, the voluntary abstention from food through *sallekhanā* is said to involve a restraint from all forms of violence to living beings. This is the ideal form of death and is considered to be a form of *paṇḍita-maraṇa* or the death of the wise. People who die in this way are considered to be only a few births removed from final liberation. In addition to death by *sallekhanā*, other forms of withdrawal from life, such as *sannyāsana maraṇa* (death through renunciation) and *samādhi maraṇa* (death through meditation) were also practised in conjunction with abstention from food.

While the adoption of *sallekhanā* is a momentous experience for the whole community, almost all Jains have regular periods of fasting and abstention from various kinds of food. Men and women fast regularly. It has been observed that women fast on more days and are frequently stricter about avoiding certain kinds of food perceived to entail violence to plant life.

## Images of the Revered *jinas*

Although the Jain tradition has frequently been represented as emphasizing asceticism and struggle as the only ways to get liberation, devotion and worship rituals have been an integral part of Jain piety. One may mentally worship and revere the *jinas* and other liberated beings, or one may worship them in the form of images. With the exception of the Terāpanthi and Sthānakvāsi sects of the Śvetāmbara movement, all Jains revere images (*mūrtis*) of Mahāvīra and other *jinas* in temples or home shrines. There is considerable variation in the rationale for revering these images, as well as in the size and type of images venerated.

Jains have had a tradition of worshipping *jinas* in the form of images. Textual sources describe the worship of images, but are often of late date, a thousand years after Mahāvīra. According to one story, which gained prominence only in the fifth century, a sandalwood image of Mahāvīra was made during his lifetime; this story is not accepted by many scholars. But from excavations and inscriptions, we may infer that reverence to the images of the *jinas* was a part of Jain piety possibly from the third century BCE, and it was certainly in place from the fifth century CE.

An inscription from the first century BCE in the Hathigumpha cave (near Bhubaneswar, in the state of Orissa) seems to suggest that an image of a *jina* was retrieved from a king of the Nanda dynasty around the fourth century BCE. Excavations suggest that Jain temples were built in the Mathura region between the second century BCE and the third century CE. Worship in these temples seems to have included images of the *jinas*. Standing images of the *jinas* found in the state of Bihar seem to come from the first century.

While some images are only a few centimetres or inches in length, the colossal statue of Bāhubali, carved from a single block of stone, measures 21 m (68 ft) tall. Bāhubali, a son of the first *tīrthaṅkara*, Ṛṣabha, fights with his brother Bharata for the title of universal emperor. Just as he is about to the win the duel, Bāhubali sees the futility of worldly life and becomes a renunciant.

Bāhubali's austerities are well known in the Jain tradition, especially among the Digambaras. He stands for years in unbroken meditation. So intense is his meditation that no part of his body moves. Vines grow on him, and some snakes, lizards, and even a scorpion live on his body, believing it to be something inanimate.

The enormous statue was erected on the summit of Indragiri hill in Sravana Belgola, 65 km (40 mi.) north of Mysore in the southern state of Karnataka. It depicts Gomatta (Bāhubali) standing naked in meditation, with creepers growing around him. The first consecration apparently took place in 981. The image was bathed continuously with several kinds of liquids, and then anointed with various substances. Every twelve years or so, the Digamabaras repeat this *mahāmastābhiṣeka* ('grand head anointing'). The image is drenched with fragrant liquids, flowers are now strewn from helicopters, and hundreds of thousands of people witness the ceremonies. Such an anointing was conducted with great fanfare in December 1993.

There is debate as to what change, if any, takes place when an image is consecrated. Unlike in many Hindu traditions, the Jains do not believe that the images themselves are 'alive' after the consecration. Indeed, for many Jains, the official position as indicated in some sacred texts is that these images serve as a reminder to all human beings that the state of liberation is available to everyone

## The Great Mantra of Adoration

I bow to the *jina*, those who have attained perfection, those who have attained liberation, to religious leaders, to religious teachers (preceptors), and all the monks. This fivefold adoration that destroys all sins is the most important and the most auspicious of all auspicious things.

and that one ought to concentrate one's efforts on getting it. The orthodox position, according to many teachers, is that images are not 'inhabited' by the souls or presence of *jinas*. Nevertheless, devotees' attitudes reflect a strong feeling that images are transformed by consecration.

Devotion to *jinas*, teachers (*ācāryas*), and ascetics (*śramaṇas*) is practised both by laypeople and monks. Since monks have no possessions, however, they have no material substances to offer physically to images. Nevertheless, they encourage the building of shrines and temples as pious acts and greatly facilitate this procedure.

The Digambara writer Vaṭṭakera holds that devotion to the *jinas* causes one's past *karma* to be destroyed. Acquisition of knowledge and repetition of sacred phrases (mantras) become successful through the grace of the teachers. The most famous of Jain mantras is called the *namsaskāra mantra*. In this formulaic phrase of devotion, the Jain pays obeisance to five holy beings: the *jinas*, the other perfected beings, the ascetic teachers, the ascetic preceptors, and all Jain mendicants. This fivefold salutation is believed to destroy all bad *karma*, and the salutation ends by stating that these auspicious acts are among the holiest deeds.

Even though devotion usually involves emotion, according to Vaṭṭakera, it is unlike worldly passion because spiritual devotion is directed towards the *jinas*. Other Śvetāmbara authors like Bhadrabāhu also say that devotion stimulated by worldly desire is wrong, but when shown to the *jinas* and when prompted only through a love of liberation, it destroys *karma*. In this sense, it is as effective as the practice of asceticism. Other Śvetāmbara texts say that by singing hymns and praising the *jinas*, one gets wisdom consisting of right knowledge, faith, and conduct. These will be conducive in ending one's worldly existence and giving one a better afterlife. Devotion to the *jinas* seems to stimulate the process of internal purification that leads one to *nirvāṇa*.

Some Digambara Jains have advocated a scheme of 'tenfold' devotion. Devotion is shown towards ten objects. These include the *jinas*, the other perfect beings who have reached *nirvāṇa*, the holy words spoken by Mahāvīra, mendicants, teachers, and leaders of the Jain community, *nirvāṇa*, the five supreme beings (the *jina*, perfected beings, spiritual teachers, mendicant teachers, and all ascetics), Nandīśvara, the mythical place with fifty-two temples, and finally, Śānti,

## The *Sakra Stava* (Hymn of Indra)

*[Indra, the god of the celestial one spoke thus]:*

16. 'My obeisance to my Lords, the Arhats, the prime ones, the Tirthankaras, the enlightened ones, the best of men, the lions among men, the exalted elephants among men, lotus among men.

Transcending the world they rule the world,
think of the well-being of the world.
Illuminating all, they dispel fear,
bestow vision, show the path,
give shelter, life, enlightenment.
Obeisance to the bestowers of *dharma*,
the teachers of *dharma*,
the leaders of *dharma*,
the charioteers of *dharma*,
the monarchs of the four regions of *dharma*,
To them, who have uncovered the veil
and have found unerring knowledge and vision,
the islands in the ocean,
the shelter, the goal, the support.
Obeisance to the Jinas—the victors—
who have reached the goal
and who help others reach it.
The enlightened ones, the free ones,
who bestow freedom,
the Jinas victorious over fear,
who have known all and can reveal all,
who have reached that supreme state
which is unimpeded, eternal, cosmic and beatific
which is beyond disease and destruction,
where the cycle of birth ceases; the goal, the fulfillment,
My obeisance to the *Sramana Bhagvan Mahavira*
The initiator, the ultimate Tirthankara,
who has come to fulfil the promise of earlier Tirthankaras.
I bow to him who is there—in Devananda's womb from here—my place in heaven.
May he take cognizance of me'.

With these words, Indra paid his homage to *Sramana Bhagvan Mahavira* and facing east, resumed his seat on the throne.
(Lath 1984:29–33)

the sixteenth *jina*. To this list is sometimes added the goal of deep meditation and a special valorous devotion to Mahāvīra. 'Tenfold' devotion has parallels in Śvetāmbara practice.

Although this list of objects and goals seems comprehensive, even allowing for some repetition, there are other exalted beings who are the focus of veneration. For several centuries, Jains have venerated celestial beings known as *yakṣas* (feminine: *yakṣīs*) and built temples for them. Hindus considered these beings as demigods with limited powers. *Yakṣas* and *yakṣīs* are woven into Jain mythology and legend, and a *yakṣī* called Padmāvatī ('she who resides on the lotus') is pop-

*One of the Dilwara Jain temples on Mount Abu in Rajasthan.* (W.G. Oxtoby)

ular among Jains all over India. The Jain Padmāvatī is distinct from but resembles the Hindu goddess Lakṣmī, the bestower of worldly fortune and divine grace.

After the ninth century almost every *tīrthaṅkara* was portrayed with his own attendant. Some of them (Kālī, Brahmā, Īśvara) show Hindu influence, and others such as Vajrāṇkuśa show Buddhist influence. Ambikā Māta, the 'Mother Goddess' who is worshipped as a form of Pārvatī/Durgā by Hindus, is regarded as a guardian deity by Jains and is associated with the twenty-second *tīrthaṅkara*, Nemināth.

A powerful protector deity worshipped in many Jain temples in America is Ghantakarna Mahavir, a *yakṣa* and also one of the fifty-two *vīrs* or heroes venerated by the Jain community. He is an entity who has great powers and protects the Jain community. The temple dedicated to him in Mahudi in Gujarat, the place of his reported origin, is said to attract a million worshippers every year.

Thousands of Jain temples have been built in India, housing many images of the *tīrthaṅkaras*. Cave temples dating back to the second century BCE have been excavated in the eastern state of Orissa. Images of Mahāvīra are the most prevalent in Jain temples. Ṛṣabha, Pārśva, and Śāntināth are also enshrined in many of them. There are twelfth-century temples in Halebid, in the southern state of Karnataka.

Undoubtedly, the most beautiful examples of Jain architecture are in Rajasthan. The temple at Ranakpur and the Dilwara temples on Mount Abu rank among the finest art in India. Praised as 'hymns in marble', the Dilwara temples consist of five Śvetāmbara shrines built between the eleventh and sixteenth centuries. White marble is intricately carved with elaborate reliefs and floral designs. Sculptures of gods and goddesses, musicians, dancers, marriage processions, and scenes from the lives of the *tīrthaṅkaras* are all carved with a delicate and rich architectural vocabulary. Mount Abu is a popular place for the Jains and a major attraction for tourists.

## The Ritual Calendar

The Jain tradition has many rituals of fasting and feasting within a calendar year. Almost all observances are based on the phases of the moon, that is, practised on a particular day in the cycle of a waxing or waning moon. As in the Hindu tradition, the Jains adjust their lunar calendar to the solar one regularly.

Fasting is observed on many days of the month, especially by women. Some fasts involve total abstention, even from water, and in other modes one may refrain from certain kinds of foods. There are varying degrees of abstention from and selectivity in the foods consumed. For instance, a Śvetāmbara fast called *ayambil* can be observed for a long time. During the period of the fast, the participant eats from a common kitchen where the foods are prepared with particular care and where flavourful and tasty ingredients (including salt and oil) are avoided. Other fasts are undertaken over particular cycles of time.

This ritual of fasting is not necessarily a private domestic affair; some elaborate and difficult fasts are undertaken in public places of worship and culminate with pomp and ceremony. This form of fasting gives a sense of prestige, measurable in terms of public piety, to the entire family. In certain fasts in which large groups of people participate, there may be accompanying activities such as narration of edifying stories. Frequently, the fasting may be followed by a *pratikramaṇa*, discussed later, a ritual of confession and repentance.

Ritual giving is also an important part of Jain life. As an exercise of non-possession, Jains give away part of their riches in elaborate ceremonies. Like the act of fasting, ritual donation is a marker of the piety and prestige of an entire family.

Caturmās ('four months') coincides with India's hot, rainy monsoon season, roughly June through September. This is a time of special observances for South Asia's Buddhist, Hindu, and Jain ascetics, and is generally considered to be the monks' rain retreat. Travel is curtailed, many believe, to prevent the accidental killing of the many insects and other small forms of life that tend to come out during the rainy season. Many Jain laypeople are also involved with their religious institutions during the four-month season and undertake frequent fasts.

The eight- to ten-day period called Paryūṣaṇ is particularly sacred for the Śvetāmbara Jains. The entire *Kalpa sūtra* is read out during these days. On the final day, there is a ritual confession and seeking of forgiveness from one's family and associates. Form letters and sometimes printed cards seeking pardon are mailed to friends and relatives at this time. The Digambara tradition has a similar festival called Daśa Lakṣaṇa Parvan ('the time of the ten characteristics'), which follows shortly after Paryūṣaṇ, but during this celebration a different text is the focus of exposition.

The Hindu festival known as Dīvālī or Dīpavālī ('necklace of lamps') is celebrated by the Jains, but for reasons different from those of the Hindu tradition. Jains believe that on this day Mahāvīra reached *nirvāṇa*. During this time of festivity, the goddess Lakṣmī, an important deity in the Hindu tradition, is worshipped by the Jains. Lakṣmī is the goddess of wealth and the bestower of good fortune. Many Jains are business people and worship her with reverence. This time also marks the Jain new year and new account books are started that day.

Mahāvīra's birthday is observed on the thirteenth day after the new moon occurring between mid-March and mid-April.

Digambaras and Śvetāmbaras remember an act of giving on Akṣaya Tṛtīya, which occurs on the third day of the waxing moon coming between mid-April and mid-May. It commemorates an incident in the life of the first *tīrthaṅkara*, Ṛṣabha. In the narrative, Ṛṣabha undertakes a fast, and a holy man gives him sugar cane juice to break the fast. Many Śvetāmbaras undertake a fast during this time at Mount Satrunjaya in Gujarat, where Ṛṣabha is enshrined. Ṛṣabha's attendant, a goddess called Cakreśvarī, protects pious Jain women, especially those who undertake fasts willingly.

### *Pratikramaṇa*

One of the central rituals of the Jain tradition is the *pratikramaṇa* ('going back'). Some interpret the name to mean taking the soul back to its original pristine state, restoring virtues like compassion, peace, and equanimity. Others take the word to mean 'turning back', away from one's transgressions.

In this act, a person ritually confesses his or her transgressions of omission and commission and then seeks forgiveness. Ideally, it should be done twice a day because the longer one goes without making peace with others and with oneself, the more difficult it becomes to remove the clinging *karma*. In practice, since the whole ritual, carefully executed, can last as long as three hours, some perform it only every fortnight, or once every four months. It is considered mandatory to do it at least once a year; the Śvetāmbaras perform it on the last day of Paryūṣaṇ.

The words uttered are in the Ardhamagadhi language, which most Jains do not understand. In recent years, to make the rich meaning of the ritual more widely accessible, the words have been translated into Gujarati and also into English. Elements in the ritual as practised by 'householders' (that is, laypersons) reflect the postures and vows of Jain ascetics.

One starts by reciting the *namaskāra mantra*, verses adoring the *tīrthaṅkaras* and one's *guru*. The devotee adopts the motionless ascetical *kātyosarga* posture and meditates on the nature of the human soul. The actual *pratikramaṇa* ritual has six essential parts, each of which has to be performed completely.

*Sāmāyika* or equanimity is the first stage. During this time, the practitioner tries to achieve outer and inner purification. By bowing down before the supreme beings who have achieved liberation, and venerating the teachers and preceptors, one is freed from passions like anger, greed, and arrogance. By curtailing physical and verbal activities through meditation, one establishes a sense of tranquillity.

Second, one recites the *Caturviṃśatistava*, a hymn of twenty-four verses venerating the twenty-four *tīrthaṅkaras*. The third part, *vandana* ('prayer,' 'adoration'), is the veneration of the monks and nuns.

Next comes the central *pratikramaṇa* act of seeking forgiveness. One reaffirms the twelve vows of householders at this point. These begin with the five ancillary or 'minor vows' (*aṇuvratas*), discussed before: non-violence, truthfulness, non-stealing, sexual purity, and non-possession. These are identical to the list discussed before, except in degree. The sixth vow declares an intent to limit spatial movement, curtailing one's travels. The seventh vow, extending non-possession enjoined in the fifth one, sets limits even on essentials; in the vocabulary of Jains overseas today, it means limits on clothes and cosmetics and on indulgence in eating. This vow also implies curtailing certain kinds of occupations that lead even indirectly to violence. The other vows extend earlier ones in degree and direction. One is to refrain from purposeless violence, adopt certain forms of self-control, restrict one's physical movements within a curtailed area for a day or so, and share one's belongings with friends and guests.

After the adoption of all these vows, one formally expresses the hope that one will have the faith and courage to have a religious fast unto death in the future. After the recitation of each vow, the worshipper utters ritual words seeking forgiveness from all.

The last of the six essential acts is the *pratyākhyāna*. One vows to renounce certain activities, such as those that cause violence or harm in any way. The humble yet powerful utterance seeking forgiveness for the many sins that the worshipper enumerates is the overpowering and moving theme that comes through this ritual. Having worshipped all worthy souls, and having sought pardon from all beings, the Jain devotee emerges cleansed and purified.

# THE JAINS TODAY

## Jains in Hindu Society

In India, Jains constitute a tiny minority, numbering only half of 1 per cent of the population. There have been periods of cordial relations between Jains and Hindus. Marriages are sometimes arranged for men and women between the two traditions in some regions of India. Sometimes, at least on the American continent, there have been temples accommodating both faiths. Historically, however, there have also been times of conflict and tension.

Times of tension and intolerance have occurred in South India. Hindu devotional poets frequently converted Jain kings to become followers of Viṣṇu or Śiva. Thus Pāṇḍyan kings from Madurai in South India were persuaded to become followers of Śiva by Śaivite saints in the eighth and ninth centuries. The Hoysala king Biṭṭideva was converted to Vaisnavism by the teacher Rāmānuja and was given the name Viṣṇu Vardhana. Hindu texts in the Tamil language show considerable animosity towards the Jains, and inscriptions in the state of Tamil Nadu bear eloquent testimony to the persecution of Jains.

Although there was considerable interaction and mutual borrowing leading to a shared corpus of myth and ritual between the Hindu and Jain traditions, throughout the centuries the Jains have held fast to their own retelling and interpretations of the myth, and to rituals and beliefs that have never compromised their unique identity.

The unique characteristics of the Jain tradition have safeguarded its identity and from a fate that would have been almost inevitable: to become absorbed as one of the many sects of the amorphous Hindu tradition. The Jain and Buddhist traditions began at about the same time, but their historical roles differ. The Jains remained in India as an identifiable minority, while Buddhism eventually lost much of its identity in India but successfully spread elsewhere in Asia.

Although by the tenth century the Hindu *Bhagavata purāṇa* included (albeit patronizingly) Siddhārtha Gautama, the Buddha, as one of the many incarnations of Viṣṇu, Mahāvīra was never identified as one. However, this Hindu text did identify Ṛṣabha, the first Jain *tīrthaṅkara*, as a partial incarnation of Viṣṇu and Hinduized many of the Jain details. Ṛṣabha and Pārśva are portrayed with certain iconographic characteristics that are associated with the Hindu deity Viṣṇu. The name Ṛṣabha means 'bull', and his emblem, like that of the Hindu god Śiva, is the bull. Pārśva, like Viṣṇu, is seen with a serpent serving as his umbrella. On the other hand, the Jains have their own versions of the *Rāmāyaṇa* and the *Mahābhārata*. In recounting one of the myths, the Jain tradition associates the Hindu god Kṛṣṇa (variously seen as the eighth or ninth incarnation of Viṣṇu) as the cousin of the twenty-second *tīrthaṅkara*, Neminatha.

The relationship between the Jain and Hindu traditions has been somewhat ambiguous in postindependence India. While the religious identity of the Jains has not been compromised, their legal and social identities are somewhat blurred. Since India does not have a uniform civil code, Jains and Sikhs are included under the Hindu family law. Thus, marriage, divorce, and inheritance are all governed by the law applying to Hindus. Legal texts observe that the courts in India have always applied the Hindu law to Jain cases in the absence of a Jain custom that directly contradicts the Hindu law.

Socially, some Jains in India and especially in the diaspora, while proud of their heritage and identity, simply identify themselves as 'Hindu' when asked about their religion. They do this, they say, because many Westerners are not familiar with the Jain tradition and the explanations seem tedious in a casual conversation. Interestingly, while these Jains seem comfortable identifying themselves as Hindu to social acquaintances, they are quite clear about their distinctive religious identity at home and among close friends.

## Jainism in the Diaspora

Jainism was introduced to the Americas in 1893 when Virchand Raghavji Gandhi spoke about the doctrines of the religion at the World's Parliament of Religions in Chicago. However, neither Canada nor the United States were destinations for Jain immigrants in the beginning of the twentieth century. Jain immigrants from India primarily settled in England and in East Africa.

Only since the 1960s have Jains have settled on the American continent in significant numbers. More than two-thirds of the Jains in the Americas are reportedly from the western Indian state of Gujarat. It is estimated that there are at present about 25,000 Jains in Britain, 25,000 in the United States, and 10,000 in Canada. Like the Jains in India, many immigrant Jains are business people and bankers. About 40 per cent are engineers, and about 20 per cent are physicians. The Jain predilection to austerity has evidently contributed to the community's economic stability, and has also made philanthropy a virtue that is zealously practised.

There are more than sixty Jain centres in North America. The umbrella organization for many of these centres and groups is called Jain Associations in North America, with the felicitous acronym JAINA. Although there are sectarian, linguistic, and geographic differences among the Jains, the centres and the metaorganization seek to bridge these differences in the diaspora. The focus of JAINA and the many local centres is on the transmission of the tradition in a meaningful way to a younger generation of adherents who have been born and raised away from India. The centres also emphasize the practice and preservation of the culture through devotional rituals and lectures by scholars and visiting religious specialists.

In India, the social presence, institutional organization, and spiritual example of ascetics has figured importantly in the maintenance of Jainism as a distinct tradition over 2,500 years. Despite its cultural similarity to Hinduism, the ascetic lifestyle that is enjoined on both the renunciant and the householder gives this tradition its unique identity and distinctive flavour. Without the Jain renunciants, the religio-cultural line between Jains and Hindus may seem blurred to some eyes.

Because of the rigour of the vows they take, ascetics do not travel great distances, and never outside India. One of the main contrasts evident when Jainism is practised in other countries is the absence of the ascetics to guide, bless, and gently encourage the devotees. The Jain community is seen as composed of four *tīrthas* or social segments: monks, nuns, laymen or male householders, and laywomen or female householders. Outside India, the absence of monks and nuns deprives the Jain tradition of two of these.

The only two major spiritual leaders in North America went there despite the Jain injunctions curtailing travel for ascetics. Gurudev Chitrabhanu (b. 1922) moved further away from the ascetic tradition and has married. Ācārya Sushil Kumar (b. 1926) was born into a Hindu brahmin family, became a disciple of a Jain teacher, and at a young age was convinced of the efficacy of the *namaskāra* mantra. Siddhachalam, his hermitage and retreat centre about 95 km (60 mi.) west of New York City, attracts both Euro-American and Indo-American Jains. Summer camps are regularly scheduled for children, and the harmony between all religious world views is preached. Working to make his centre a focus of Jain pilgrimage, Sushil Kumar celebrated the installation of many *mūrtis* ('forms', i.e., images) of *tīrthaṅkaras* in 1991.

Both Sushil Kumar and the Jain centres seek to translate traditional concepts and practices into themes that are relevant to the concerns of the younger generation. Vegetarianism is spoken of as a healthful way of living, causing the least amount of harm to other living creatures and to human beings. Non-violence is applied to many areas. Current interest in protection of the environment and conservation of resources through waste reduction is compatible with traditional Jain ideals. For example, the preface of the translation of the *pratikramaṇa* ritual published in the United States says, 'For the sake of Ahimsa to trees, we have used recycled paper. Hopefully, we have spared some trees.' That book also uses soybean-based ink for printing.

During the large JAINA conventions, activists from various other organizations distribute pamphlets about causes that Jains sympathize with. These include the magazine *In Defense of Animals* and *The Compassionate Shopper*. These magazines speak out against the use of animals for clothing and medical experimentation and also list companies that avoid using animal products for cosmetics and cleaning materials. While austerity and non-possession are enjoined for liberating the soul in the traditional Jain teaching, they are congruent with current concerns about conservation and resource husbandry.

Jain conventions and celebrations of festivals invariably include a large feast for everyone along with a cultural entertainment in which young girls do classical and folk dances. Occasionally, traditional messages are also conveyed through rap. In form and content, the Jain message is being made relevant to a new generation.

In contrast with the concentration of the Jain population in England, Jains in the United States and Canada are spread out over a wide area, but with principal concentrations in New York, New Jersey, California, and Ontario. To have houses of worship in smaller towns where their numbers are sparse, they have on occasion joined with Hindus from northern India, with whom they share a common culture. Such Hindu-Jain cultural centres and temples are seen in Pittsburgh and Allentown, Pennsylvania. A close relationship is seen between the Jain Center of Northern California and the Hindu Temple and Cultural Center of Fremont, in the San Francisco Bay area. In these temples, images of Hindu gods and goddesses share space with Mahāvīra or other *tīrthaṅkaras*. Although land, money, and cultural resources are maximized in these cases and the community rewards are pleasing, there is some concern among orthoprax Jains that the ritual specialists who attend to the Hindu deities are not knowledgeable about rendering the proper service required in a Jain context.

The last century has brought a new set of challenges for the Jain community. As we have seen, the Jain practice of non-violence has been unmatched in other world religions. In the twentieth century, the emphasis has shifted from the preoccupation with vegetarianism, dietary control, and protection of sick animals to larger issues of ecology and social justice.

Many Jains now give broader scope to the interpretation of non-violence and associate it with contemporary issues such as civil rights, national security, and nuclear warfare. It is in these areas that the Jains see the large-scale challenge of violence. They see their tradition as one that offers a vision not just for the liberation of the soul, but for the survival of human beings, and indeed, this planet.

## KEY TERMS

***āgam mandirs.*** Temples dedicated to the Śvetāmbaras' sacred *āgama* texts, found especially in the western Indian regions of Gujarat and Maharashtra.

***āgama.*** 'Tradition', the Śvetāmbaras' scriptural corpus of ancient texts in Sanskrit, comprising up to forty-five treatises.

***aghātiyā karma.*** Doctrine of the effect of one's actions, understood by Jains in material terms, on the conditions of bodily existence.

***ahiṁsā.*** Non-violence, a goal pursued to remarkable lengths and applications in Jain tradition.

***anekānta.*** Many-sidedness, the notion that the objects of our knowledge are seen under varied and changing modes.

***aṅga bāhya.*** 'Outside the angas', the texts not forming part of the twelve *aṅgas* but included in the Śvetāmbaras' canonical *āgama* literature.

***aṅgas.*** 'Limbs', twelve core divisions of the Śvetāmbaras' *āgama* or scriptural tradition.

**Caturmās.** A four-month period of retreat, fasting, and religious discipline, coinciding generally with the summer monsoon (hot, rainy) season.

**Digambaras.** The 'sky-clad' branch of Jains, stronger in southern India, to whom asceticism means avoiding wearing clothes. Digambaras accept their ascetical principles as ancient, but accept fewer texts as ancient than do the Śvetāmbaras.

***ghātiyā karma.*** The influences of action, understood as material in nature, that affect the condition of the soul. Compare *aghātiyā karma.*

***guṇas.*** In Jain theory of knowledge, the changeable qualities that attach to the substance of things that we perceive, affecting their appearance to us.

***jina.*** 'Conqueror', one who has achieved an exemplary spiritual victory over the afflictions and conditions of life.

***Kalpa sūtra.*** An anthology of scriptural material, of somewhat late composition compared with the *aṅga* texts, but more widely used in ritual and cited in popular Jain devotion.

***nigoda.*** Among living creatures, the smallest, simplest form. *Nigodas* are understood by Jains to have only one sense perception, namely touch.

***sallekhanā.*** The practice of voluntary fasting to end one's life, normally undertaken by persons who have achieved a ripe age and feel that their end is due.

***samyak cāritra.*** Right conduct, implemented through the 'five practices' of non-violence, truthfulness, non-stealing, sexual purity, and non-possession.

***samyak darśana.*** Right faith, seen as an insight into truth from the right viewpoint.

***samyak jñāna***. Right knowledge, a proper comprehension of the nature of the world and our existence in it.

**Śvetāmbaras**. 'White-clad' Jains, whose ascetics wear clothing and the continuity of whose tradition reflects practices in northern and western India.

**swastika**. The four-spoked wheel or four-armed cross, symbolizing to Jains the cycle of rebirths.

***syādvāda***. 'Assertion with qualification', tentativeness in descriptions of things in Jain theory of knowledge.

***tīrtha***. A ford or crossing of a river; in the Jain context, a crossing from this existence to the 'other side', liberation; also, the structured Jain community

***tīrthaṅkara***. 'Ford-maker', a title used of the great spiritual teachers in each age.

***upāṅgas***. 'Ancillary limbs', a division of the scriptural canon alongside the *aṅgas* or 'limbs'.

***yakṣa / yakṣī***. Celestial beings figuring in Jain mythology. *Yakṣas* are masculine, *yakṣīs* are feminine.

## NOTE

I would like to thank J.E. Cort and H. Nagda for their suggestions.

## FURTHER READING

Carrithers, M., and C. Humphrey. 1991. *The Assembly of Listeners: Jains in Society.* Cambridge: Cambridge University Press.

Cort, J.E. 1991. 'Murtipuja in Svetambar Jain Temples'. In *Religion in India,* edited by T.N. Madan, 212–23. Delhi: Oxford University Press.

______. 1992. 'Śvetāmbara Mūrtipūjak Jain Scripture in a Performative Context'. In *Texts in Context: Traditional Hermeneutics in South Asia*, edited by J. Timm, 17–94. Albany: State University of New York Press.

Dundas, P. 1992. *The Jains.* London: Routledge.

Federation of JAINA. 1992. *Pratikraman.* n.p.: Federation of JAINA.

Folkert, K.W. 1993. *Scripture and Community: Collected Essays on the Jains,* edited by J.E. Cort. Atlanta: Scholars Press.

Jain, J., and E. Fischer. 1978. 'The Tirthankara in Jaina Scriptures, Art and Rituals'. In *Jaina Iconography: Part One, the Tirthankara in Jaina Scriptures, Art and Rituals*. Leiden: E.J. Brill.

Jaini, P. 1977. 'Jina Ṛṣabha as an *avātara* of Viṣṇu'. *Bulletin of the School of Oriental and African Studies* 40:321–37.

______. 1979. *The Jaina Path of Purification*. Berkeley: University of California Press.

______. 1991. *Gender and Salvation: Jaina Debates on the Spiritual Liberation of Women*. Berkeley: University of California Press.

Seeling, H. 1991. 'Authority in Translation in the "American" Jain Tradition'. Unpublished ms. Pluralism Project, Committee on the Study of Religion, Harvard University, Cambridge, Mass. 02138.

______. 1992. 'The Jain Tradition in America: Centers, Organizations and Temples'. Unpublished ms. Pluralism Project, Committee on the Study of Religion, Harvard University, Cambridge, Mass. 02138.

Settar, S. 1988. *Inviting Death: Indian Attitude towards the Ritual Death*. Leiden E.J. Brill.

Shanta, N. 1985. *La Voie jaina: Histoire, spiritualité, vie des ascètes pèlerines de l'Inde*. Paris: OEIL.

Singh, R.B.P. 1975. *Jainism in Early Medieval Karnataka*. Delhi: Motilal Banarsidass.

Kumar, S.A.B., ed. *Jinamanjari*, a journal brought out biannually by the Brahmi Society Publications, 4665 Moccasin Trail. Mississauga, Ontario, Canada (905-890-3365).

## REFERENCES

Jacobi, H., trans. 1884. *Jaina Sutras*, Part I. Oxford: Clarendon Press.

______. 1895. *Jaina Sutras*, Part II. Oxford: Clarendon Press.

Lath, M., trans. 1984. *Kalpa Sūtra*, edited by V. Sagar. Jaipur: Prakrit Bharati.

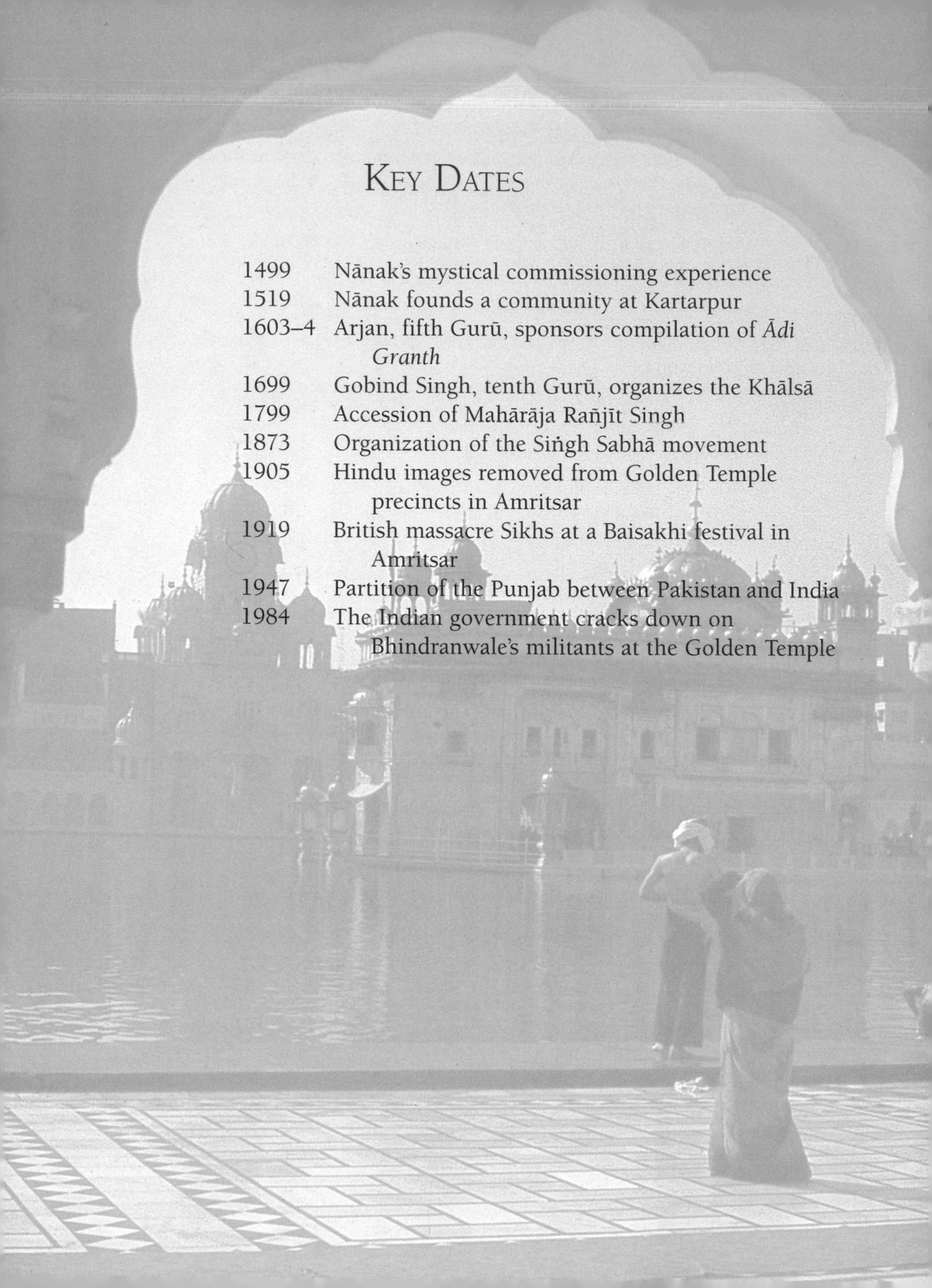

# Key Dates

1499 Nānak's mystical commissioning experience

1519 Nānak founds a community at Kartarpur

1603–4 Arjan, fifth Gurū, sponsors compilation of *Ādi Granth*

1699 Gobind Singh, tenth Gurū, organizes the Khālsā

1799 Accession of Mahārāja Rañjīt Singh

1873 Organization of the Siṅgh Sabhā movement

1905 Hindu images removed from Golden Temple precincts in Amritsar

1919 British massacre Sikhs at a Baisakhi festival in Amritsar

1947 Partition of the Punjab between Pakistan and India

1984 The Indian government cracks down on Bhindranwale's militants at the Golden Temple

Chapter Three

# The Sikh Tradition


## Willard G. Oxtoby


The Sikhs trace their religious origins to the Punjab ('five rivers') region, in north-western India, five centuries ago. Thus theirs is one of the younger of the world's religious traditions. The tradition is one-fourth as old as Christianity; its first teacher, Nānak, was a contemporary of Martin Luther. It is about one-third as old as Islam.

The attention that the Sikhs merit does not rest primarily on their numbers. They are reckoned currently at more than 15 million, or over 1.5 per cent of India's population. What makes the Sikhs significant is their situation on the political and spiritual interface between Hindus and others in India. Sikh origins lie in the shared insights of Hindu and Muslim devotional mysticism, including a denial that distinct worship forms or separate community identity are important to God. Ironically, the Sikh role more recently in India has displayed a quest for precisely such identity: for public recognition as a separate, boundaried tradition in a dominantly Hindu society.

The popular image of the Sikh is of a male wearing a turban. Many Sikhs do wear turbans to cover uncut hair, and likewise have full beards, but there are also many Sikhs who do not. And the turban is by no means a Sikh monopoly; it was part of traditional dress among Muslims in various parts of Asia and Africa.

Certain comparisons with the Jewish tradition come to mind. The Sikhs have small numbers, indeed very close to those of the Jews worldwide. Each community has struggled in the twentieth century for a political expression of its identity. In each community the hard-line militants include orthodox males with long hair and traditional headgear. But there is a marked contrast in the relation of the Jewish and the Sikh traditions to Islam: Islam in its origins drew from the already extant Jewish tradition, whereas Islam was already extant as part of the environment when the Sikh tradition was born.

# SIKH ORIGINS

## Devotional Religion in Mughal India

We situate the first Sikh teacher, Nānak, in the context of the North Indian Sant tradition. Some trace the term 'Sant' to the same linguistic origins as *sādhu*, Sanskrit for a holy ascetic, but another etymology is *sat*, 'truth'. Although the similarity of words is only coincidental, the role of these devout persons is loosely equivalent to 'saint' in English. Many Sants followed the Nirguṇa Sampradāya teaching. That implies a conception of the divine as beyond description: Brahman, as Hindus call it, does not have *guṇas* or intermediary qualities, for such would limit its transcendent character.

Three elements flowed together in the Sant tradition. One of these was *bhakti* or devotional Hinduism. This movement of devotion to the lord Viṣṇu had spread from southern India to the north. The response of the devotee to the lord is a deep, profound love. But while the love of the Vaiṣṇava for Viṣṇu was often directed to one of his *avatāras* or incarnate manifestations, such as Kṛṣṇa, the Sants disciplined themselves to offer love to the supreme lord in inward meditation without the focus of any manifest forms.

A second element was tantric yoga. Gorakhnāth, who lived sometime before the early thirteenth century, is regarded as the principal teacher of *haṭha yoga*, a system of meditation involving postures and breath control that is linked with an elaborate mapping of correspondences between the individual body and the structure of the universe. The tradition had early links with tantric Buddhism, but by the fourteenth century its North Indian practitioners called Nāths were mainly Śaivite Hindus, that is, devotees of the lord Śiva. The Nāths were among those who contributed a strong emphasis on experiencing unity to the Sant movement, bridging a duality between the practitioner and the divine. Interpreters looking at Nānak's piety see an awareness of this emphasis, to challenge if not to accept it.

A third element present in the Sant environment was Sufism, the Islamic mystical tradition. Its influence on the Sants, and through them on Nānak, is harder to pin down and is probably only marginal. On first encounter, it might seem that Ṣūfī themes indicate a direct transmission from Ṣūfīs to Sants and thence to Sikhs. Among such themes one can note the suffering felt in separation from one's beloved, the notion that selfhood is dissolved in an ultimate union, and such practices as concentrating attention on or 'remembering' God's name.

However, the Sant movement drew its specific vocabulary from Hindu far more than from Muslim sources. And when its poets mention Islam, they frequently do so more to negate its outward forms than to employ them. Yet as the Sikh tradition subsequently gained momentum, it did so in an environment in which Muslim rulers and institutions figured importantly.

Influential among the Sant poets were Nāmdev, Ravidās (Raidās), and Kabīr. Nāmdev (1270–1350) lived in Maharashtra, in western India well to the south of the Punjab, but tradition holds that he spent twenty years in the Punjab.

Ravidās (traditionally 1399–1514) was a leather worker or cobbler from Banaras; his was a low-caste occupation, since as dead animal matter, leather is considered unclean and degrading in Hindu society. Though humble about himself, Ravidās is emphatic about how caste status is irrelevant to spiritual fulfilment:

A lowly cobbler lacking skill,
Yet others bring their broken shoes …
Though others patch they yet know pain;
I lack their skill and yet know God.
Thus Ravidās repeats God's Name
And thus eludes Death's evil grasp.
(*Sorath* 7, *Ādi Granth* 659)

Kabīr (c. 1440–1518 or 1398–1494), also from Banaras and a contemporary of Ravidās, was a low-caste weaver. In the extensive body of poetry attributed to him, scholars see a background in *Nāth yoga* and a possibly superficial conversion of some of his family to Islam. Kabīr's own religious experience appears to have been deeply mystical, a sense of union with the divine, transcending differences of caste and religious community. Kabīr describes himself as 'the child of Rāma and Allāh', and says, 'The Hindu resorts to the temple and the Mussulman to the mosque, but Kabir goes to the place where both are unknown.'

He who by grace can repeat the blest Name
will enraptured receive his reward.
Led by the Guru he gathers God's riches,
true wealth which for ever endures.
Hear what Kabir says to God's faithful followers:
all other wealth must decay.
All must relinquish this worldly existence
when God sends the call to depart.
(*Āsā* 15, *Ādi Granth* 479)

To the Sants, God is formless and eternal, his love manifest both in the created world and the human heart. Devotion to God as the Sat Gurū ('true teacher') rejects social distinctions and formal ritual, and is expressed in poetry in accessible vernacular dialects. As the two passages just cited illustrate, Sants emphasized the meditative repetition of God's name. This feature of Sant Hinduism became a central feature of Sikh devotion.

## Nānak

The founder of the line of *gurūs* or inspired teachers revered by the Sikhs was Nānak (1469–1539). The content of his religious thought is clear, because more than 900 of his devotional hymns have been compiled, together with hymns by others, in the Sikh scripture known as the *Ādi Granth*. That compilation took place a century after Nānak, but his hymns may have been passed along without too much distortion. Even though reciters of poetry improvised, poetic form tends to have greater stability than does prose in oral transmission.

Representative of Nānak's thought is the following:

> Man is led astray by the reading of words; ritualists are very proud.
> What availeth it to bathe at a place of pilgrimage, if the filth of pride be in the heart?
> Who but the guru can explain that the King and Emperor dwelleth in the heart?
> All men err; it is only the great Creator who erreth not.
> He who admonisheth his heart under the guru's instruction shall love the Lord.
> Nānak, he whom the incomparable Word hath caused to meet God, shall not forget the True One.
> (Macauliffe 1909, 1:272–3)

But Nānak's hymns provide few details from which to reconstruct his life and career. For that, Sikhs rely on another body of literature, the *janam-sākhī*s, 'life testimonies'. These legendary biographies contain varied material, so that it is hard to harmonize their details completely. The traditions emerged at least a century and a half after Nānak and underwent expansion for some time until printed editions were made in the nineteenth century.

Sikhs today refer mainly to the tradition recorded in the *Purātan Janam-sākhī*. In its account, we find Nānak born in Talwandi, a village 65 km (40 mi.) from Lahore in the Punjab. He is married at twelve, his wife comes to live with him when he is nineteen, and they have two sons. While his father cannot succeed in getting Nānak to apply himself as a herdsman or tradesman, Nānak's brother-in-law arranges a job for him as a steward for a local official at Sultanpur, southeast of today's Amritsar, which Nānak discharges with reasonable diligence.

The problem with Nānak's everyday work is his preoccupation with spiritual matters. Already at the age of five he begins to ask the meaning of life. Still as a youth, he takes little interest in reading and writing (Sanskrit and Persian), even if a reading of his later work shows him clearly literate. He prefers to talk with holy men 'without confiding the secrets of his heart'. At twenty, he looks for the company of wandering ascetics.

Nānak associates with a Muslim minstrel, Mardānā, from his home town of Talwandi. Together in Sultanpur, they organize nightly singing of devotional hymns, going to bathe in the river before daybreak. In one of these morning baths, Nānak at the age of thirty has his first mystical experience. God gives him a cup of the nectar of immortality (*amrit*) and charges him with a mission to teach people the practice of devotion.

Nānak's response is the *mūl mantra* ('root statement'), the creedal affirmation that precedes his *Japjī*, repeated by Sikhs in their morning devotions:

> There is one Supreme Being, the Eternal Reality. He is the Creator, without fear and devoid of enmity. He is immortal, never incarnated, self-existent, known by grace through the Guru. The Eternal One, from the beginning, through all time, present now, the Everlasting Reality.

Nānak receives the commission to call people to an awareness of God's name, and God presents to Nānak a robe of honour.

Presumed drowned after a three-day absence, Nānak returns, gives away all his possessions but basic clothing, and repeatedly proclaims the irrelevance of religious communities in the words, 'There is no Hindu, there is no Muslim.'

In the following years, Nānak travels extensively. According to the *Purātan Janam-sākhī*, he makes a journey in each of the four compass directions. Eastward, he traverses India all the way to Assam, visiting Hindu sites in Banaras, Bengal, and Orissa. Southward, he goes to Tamil Nadu and Ceylon (Sri Lanka). To the north, he visits the highest reaches of the Himalayas. And to the west, he visits Muslim regions as far as Mecca, Baghdad, and Medina. On his journeys he seeks out Hindu and Muslim spiritual teachers, while himself wearing a mixture of Hindu and Muslim attire such that people ask him to which community he belongs.

Visiting the great mosque at Mecca, Nānak stretches out in a colonnade to sleep. When prayer time comes, a local Muslim judge reproves him for having his feet pointed in the direction of the house of God, the Ka'bah. Nānak replies, 'Then turn my feet in the direction where God does not dwell.'

Settling down at the age of fifty, Nānak founds a settlement at Kartarpur, northeast of Lahore and 90 km (55 mi.) north of today's Amritsar, where he leads a circle of followers until his death at seventy. The name Sikh is the word for 'disciple'. He conducts them in religious meditation and study, making *nām simaraṇ* ('meditation on the divine name') and *kīrtan* ('singing' hymns of praise) regular features of devotion. He also insists that his followers do practical labour and maintain regular family life.

Among the religious ideas contained in Nānak's hymns, besides his attempt to go beyond ritual and communal forms, is a notion shared with his Hindu milieu: that life entails *saṃsāra*, the cycle of rebirths, and that spiritual release or liberation from bondage to it is the goal of religious discipline.

## The Ten *gurūs*

Nānak's appointment of a successor inaugurated a spiritual lineage each of whose members was accorded the title Gurū and served for life. Counting Nānak, the succession of ten *gurūs* extended for two centuries. During that period, the leadership and core membership of the Sikh community underwent considerable development, from a rather informal circle of disciples to a strictly defined and disciplined order. Different steps in this process took place under different *gurūs* in the succession.

The second Gurū, Aṅgad (b. 1504, r. 1539–52), reportedly began collecting Nānak's hymns and making use of the *gurmukhī* ('from the *gurū*'s mouth') script, an alphabet related to the *devanāgarī* used for Sanskrit and for North Indian vernacular languages. Aṅgad may have also institutionalized the communal kitchen or *laṅgar* to feed disciples who came to the hostelry or *dharamsālā* that had developed under Nānak. Community meals have remained a feature of Sikh practice, making a primarily moral and social rather than ritual statement: that all, regardless of caste, are welcomed and expected to eat together. Under the third Gurū, Amardās (b. 1479, r. 1552–74), the community developed its religious observances and began a shrine tradition.

The fourth Gurū, Ramdās (b. 1534, r. 1574–81), founded a town and dug a large reservoir called Amritsar, 'pool of the nectar of immortality'. Amritsar became an important centre, and during the time of the Mughal emperor Akbar (r. 1556–1605), Ramdās enjoyed a leadership position among the people of the Punjab. Appointing his son Arjan, Ramdās set a hereditary precedent for the office of Gurū. Its subsequent incumbents all came from his family, the Soḍhī family.

A more distinct Sikh identity began to emerge under the fifth Gurū, Arjan (b. 1563, r. 1581–1606). Relying on earlier collections, Arjan supervised the compilation of the sacred scripture, the *Ādi Granth*, consisting of devotional hymns. He built a new temple at the site his father had founded, Amritsar. This was the Harmandir Sāhib (i.e., the honoured temple of Hari or God). The Golden Temple, as the eighteenth-century building now on the site is popularly known, is reached by a causeway and stands in the middle of the large rectangular reservoir or pond, called a 'tank' in Indian usage. Surrounding the tank are porticoes and other buildings of the temple complex, which has come to serve as the administrative centre of the Sikhs.

Arjan's contributions were not limited to the devotional practice of religion.

Tradition holds that he also organized a system of charitable contributions somewhat like the Muslim *zakāt* and established trading links across India's northwestern frontier into Afghanistan and points farther west. Under him, community leadership was developing from the meditative example of a spiritual virtuoso to the politico-military role of a princely ruler. Arjan was charged with having supported a rebellion by Khusro, a son of the Mughal emperor Jehangir (r. 1605–27), and was put into prison in Lahore. Sikhs see his death there as martyrdom and a call to arms.

The shift from devotional spirituality to political involvement persisted. Arjan's son Hargobind (b. 1595, r. 1606–44), the sixth Gurū, donned a pair of swords, one symbolizing traditional religious authority and the other the new temporal authority. An emblem of two sabres flanking a double-edged sword and a discus or quoit has become the symbol of the Sikhs.

Maintaining a bodyguard 300 strong, Hargobind took the community in a political direction. It now began to have some of the functions of a state, as Hargobind sought to assert himself over against Jehangir, the emperor in Delhi, fighting and winning three skirmishes.

Under the seventh and eighth Gurūs, confrontation receded, but the ninth Gurū, Tegh Bahādur (b. 1621, r. 1664–75), had to cope with the increasingly restrictive policies of the emperor Aurangzeb (r. 1658–1707). These included enforcement of Islamic laws and taxes and sometimes the replacement of local Hindu sanctuaries by mosques. Tegh Bahādur's agitation against such policies brought him imprisonment. His refusal to become a Muslim brought him execution and in Sikh history the status of a martyr for the freedom of worship.

Involvement with the community's political concerns alongside or as an expression of spiritual ones came to a climax with the tenth Gurū, Gobind Singh (b. 1666, r. 1675–1708). He redefined the core of the Sikh community as a military order, the Khālsā, so termed from the Persian word (from the Arabic for 'pure') meaning 'special', applied to the ruler's landholdings. It was the *gurūs*' own élite guard, with a strict discipline. We shall discuss it in more detail below. Gobind Singh's militant following disturbed neighbouring Hindu chieftains as well as the Mughal rulers, who dispatched forces against him. Two of his sons died in battle, and the remaining two were captured and executed. Gobind Singh escaped, and reportedly sent the emperor, Aurangzeb, a message, the *Zafar nāmā* (Victory Letter). Its spirit is invincible, despite Gobind Singh's reverses: 'What use is it to put out a few sparks when you raise a mighty flame instead?'

Gobind Singh may have backed Bahadur Shah (r. 1707–12) against Aurangzeb's other sons in the succession on that ruler's death; Bahadur befriended him. Later Gobind Singh was stabbed by an assassin while accompanying Bahadur on a campaign against one of the brothers. As he neared death, he reportedly declared the line of *gurūs* to be at an end, exhorting the community to look to the scriptural texts for authority.

The Golden Temple in Amritsar is built in the middle of a large pool in which devotees bathe before proceeding to the temple for worship. (W.G. Oxtoby)

## Politics under the Mughals

The Sikhs became a politico-military force following Gurū Gobind Singh's formation of the Khālsā, or 'special' corps (which will be discussed later) at the beginning of the eighteenth century. Their slogan was '*Rāj karegā Khālsā*' ('the Khālsā shall rule'). The phrase appears in the *Tankhāh-nāmā* (Book of Penances) attributed to Nand Lāl Goyā (1633–c. 1712), and may have been popularized in the eighteenth century. Basically, their fortunes turned on the extent to which they could assert themselves in dealings with the Mughal rulers to the southeast in Delhi and the Afghans to the northwest, at the same time as they jockeyed for position *vis-à-vis* local Hindu princes in the Punjab.

In the middle of the eighteenth century, Sikh forces formed into twelve militia units called *misls*. At first democratic, the *misls* became hereditary as the Sikhs dislodged the Mughals and took over landowning. They were disintegrating in rivalries when the Sikhs' most illustrious ruler, Rañjīt Singh (r. 1799–

1839), dissolved them, unified the Sikhs, took Lahore, and proclaimed himself *mahārāja* of the Punjab. After consolidating strength in other quarters, he secured India's northwestern frontier in campaigns against the Afghans and Pathans in the 1820s and 1830s. The temple in Amritsar was covered with gold leaf during his reign.

Mahārāja Rañjīt Singh enjoys a place in Sikh affection not only for his military accomplishments but for his common touch. He was short and unattractive, and blind in one eye from smallpox. There are stories of his stepping down from his throne to use his own beard to wipe the feet of Muslim *faqīrs* ('poor ones', i.e., ascetics). But he was a daring ruler, and shrewd in his handling of human relationships. His favourite courtesan reportedly asked, 'Where were you when God was handing out good looks?' His reply: 'I was busy seeking power.' But the Sikh kingdom fell into disorganization on his death, and ten years later, in 1849, Britain annexed the Punjab.

## The Sacred Scriptures

The principal sacred literature of the Sikhs is the collection of hymns called the *Ādi Granth* ('first book', hence 'original book') or alternatively the *Gurū Granth Sāhib* ('revered book that is the Gurū'). It consists of devotional poems from the first five *gurūs* as well as comparable verses from North Indian Hindu and Muslim saints such as Nāmdev, Kabīr, and Ravidās.

The collection is organized according to the different *rāgas* or musical modes in which it is to be sung, and includes musical directions. Essentially, for each *rāga* in turn, the hymns of each *gurū* are given in order, followed by the hymns of Kabīr and the other non-Sikh saints.

The fifth Gurū, Arjan, is credited with having compiled the *Ādi Granth* in 1603–4. The text was placed in the Harmandir Sāhib at Amritsar and attended by a reciter called a *granthī*. It went through various recensions during the following hundred years, during which some material not universally recognized was added or deleted. Widely accepted was the eventual inclusion of hymns by the ninth Gurū, Tegh Bahādur

Next in scriptural rank after the *Ādi Granth* is the *Dasam Granth* ('the book of the Tenth'), a collection whose compilation is attributed to the tenth Gurū, Gobind Singh, but can have taken place a generation after his death and included the writings of others as well as his own. Gobind Singh acknowledged the priority of the *Ādi Granth*, reportedly saying, 'The real *Granth* is the *Ādi Granth*; mine is only a poetic pastime.'

The *Dasam Granth* contains the long *Jāp Sāhib* ('master recitation'), which some Sikhs recite as a morning prayer along with the shorter *Japjī* ('honoured recitation'), Gurū Nānak's creed quoted above. It contains other devotional

## From the Sacred Writings of the Sikhs

*[Gurū Nānak exalts the divine Name.]*

If in this life I should live to eternity, nourished by nothing save air;
If I should dwell in the darkest of dungeons, sense never resting in sleep;
Yet must your glory transcend all my striving; no words can encompass the Name.
*[Refrain]* He who is truly the Spirit Eternal, immanent, blissful serene;
Only by grace can we learn of our Master, only by grace can we tell.
If I were slain and my body dismembered, pressed in a hand-mill and ground;
If I were burnt in a fire all-consuming, mingled with ashes and dust;
Yet must your glory transcend all my striving; no words can encompass the Name.
If as a bird I could soar to the heavens, a hundred such realms in my reach;
If I could change so that none might perceive me and live without food, without drink;
Yet must your glory transcend all my striving; no words can encompass the Name.
If I could read with the eye of intelligence paper of infinite weight;
If I could write with the winds everlasting, pens dipped in oceans of ink;
Yet must your glory transcend all my striving; no words can encompass the Name (*Siri Ragu* 2, *Ādi Granth* 14–15).

*[Though the following passage has been construed as telling Muslims that they should worship at their mosque, Nānak declares that there is no need for outward religious observance.]*

Make mercy your mosque and devotion your prayer mat, righteousness your Qur'an;

hymns as well, comparable to the *Ādi Granth*. But it also contains a large amount of narrative material not used in prayer: Gobind Singh's autobiography, plus poetic and verse accounts of feats by Sikh heroes, and by various *avatāras* of Hindu deities in the genre of the Hindu *Purāṇas*.

If today we consider such material Hindu rather than Sikh, we might think it out of place in the *Dasam Granth*. Clearly Sikhs feel the need to explain the material. One recent author apologizes for it, writing, 'The Puranic lore in the tenth *gurū*'s poetry did not necessarily emanate from his beliefs; it stands as a powerful poetic exercise in itself' (Kohli 1987:242). But poetic merit aside, its inclusion in this collection illustrates how fluid some boundaries between religious communities were three centuries ago, as compared with what has developed in the twentieth century. To be Sikh in the early eighteenth century was to have a particular affection for the spiritual lineage of Nānak while sharing aspects of Hindu religion and culture. To be a Sikh today, however, is to consider

Meekness your circumcising, goodness your fasting, for thus the true Muslim expresses his faith.
Make good works your Ka'bah, take truth as your pir, compassion your creed and your prayer.
Let service to God be the beads which you tell and God will exalt you to glory (*VārMājh* 7:1, *Ādi Granth* 140–1).

*[The third Gurū, Amar Dās, directs his words to brahmins, allegedly proud of the traditional learning that they have monopolized.]*

He who is truly a dutiful Brahman will cast off his burden of human desire,
Each day performing his God-given duty, each day repeating God's Name.
To such as submit God imparts divine learning, and those who obey him live virtuous lives.
He who is truly a dutiful Brahman wins honour when summoned to God (*Malār* 10, *Ādi Granth* 1261).

*[The tenth Gurū, Gobind Singh, praises the sword. This passage, often repeated at Sikh functions, has now come to serve as the national anthem of the Khālsā.]*

Reverently I salute the Sword with affection and devotion.
Grant, I pray, your divine assistance that this book may be brought to completion.
Thee I invoke, All-conquering Sword, Destroyer of evil, Ornament of the brave.
Powerful your arm and radiant your glory, your splendour as dazzling as the brightness of the sun.
Joy of the devout and Scourge of the wicked, Vanquisher of sin, I seek your protection.
Hail to the world's Creator and Sustainer, my invincible Protector of the Sword! (*Bachitar Nātak*, *Dasam Granth*, 39)

oneself emphatically not a Hindu. We shall have more to say later about the conditions under which this shift took place.

There is a section in the *Dasam Granth* that describes 'the wiles of women', taking them as a metaphor for the temptations we encounter in this world. The inclusion of this gossipy material alongside the religious compositions attributed to Gobind Singh was questioned. A story about its acceptance relates that in 1740 when the premises of what is now the Golden Temple were occupied by a Muslim, Massā Raṅghaṛ (and profaned by carousing and erotic dancing), Sardār Mehtāb Singh (d. 1745) vowed to kill Massā. The learned Sikhs agreed that if Mehtāb were successful, the objectionable passages could be included. He was, and they were.

Next after the *Ādi Granth* and the *Dasam Granth* come the hymns of two early Sikhs, Gurdās Bhalla (d. c. 1633) and Nand Lāl Goyā. (1633–c. 1712). So highly esteemed is their poetry that it is approved for recitation in gurdwaras

(Sikh houses of worship), and in that sense it stands as a third body of scriptural material. The title Bhāi ('brother'), regularly used with their names, is a mark of honour accorded them.

Bhāi Gurdās was an assistant to the fifth Gurū, Arjan, in the compilation of the *Ādi Granth*. More than a scribe, he ranks next after the *gurūs* as the Sikh tradition's principal theologian. His own poetic compositions include thirty-nine *vārs*, long heroic poems, as well as more than 500 shorter verses. They provide an insight into the ways in which the teachings of the *gurūs* were received and perceived.

Bhāi Nand Lāl served the militant tenth Gurū, Gobind Singh. But there is no clear evidence that he entered the Khālsā, he seems not to have taken the name Singh, and his verses were not included in Gobind Singh's *Dasam Granth*. By contrast, the tone of his works is broadly spiritual, even pacifist. The *Dīvān-i Goyā*, his collected poetry, includes sixty-one compositions. Another of his works is his *Zindagī-nāmeh* (Life Story).

The Sikh tradition has given a very high place to its scriptures, especially the *Ādi Granth*. In every gurdwara, the sacred book is chanted and its contents studied. Its text is considered inspired, reflecting and containing divine guidance. The centrality of the book in Sikh worship and the notion of scriptural authority accorded to it call to mind at once comparisons with the authority of the written text in Islam.

At the same time, the copy of the *Ādi Granth* in a gurdwara receives respect that an observer can best describe by analogies with Hindu rather than with Muslim devotion. In the gurdwara (the word means 'the Gurū's doorway'), and also in the private homes of Sikhs who can afford to set aside the space, there is a room where the sacred book is kept. In the gurdwara the book is provided with comforts one would give a guest: a bed, a light, and, because of India's hot climate, a fan. A student of religion can hardly overlook parallels to the way in which Hindus in the temple and the household offer these amenities, as well as the hospitality of flowers and food, to the deity believed present and manifest in the image.

Besides, the Ik Oṅkār monogram, described later, ornaments the canopy over the book in just the way that the *Oṃ* monogram is placed over images or pictures of Hindu deities. *Kaṛāh praśād*, a sweet food distributed at rituals after having been placed in the presence of the scripture, is like *prasāda*, the Hindu temple food first offered to the deity manifested in the image and then distributed to the worshippers, in both name and function. And on festival days, the book is carried through the town at the head of a procession on a wagon or truck decked with flowers.

One way the scripture is consulted for guidance is to open it at random and read whatever hymn one comes upon. At the name-giving ceremonies for a newborn child, for instance, the *granthī* opens the book and reads out the first word of the first hymn on the left-hand page to the parents. They then select for the child a name starting with the same letter.

# SIKH INSTITUTIONS

## The Khālsā

Not all Sikhs have been members of the Khālsā or followed its dress code, but the institution of the Khālsā has come to define the image of the Sikh to outsiders and to be regarded by many within the community as the orthodox expression of its identity.

The story of the Khālsā's origin is set in 1699. Gurū Gobind Singh calls his followers to assemble at the time of a festival in Anandpur, 280 km (175 mi.) east of Amritsar. There he accepts five followers who pass the test of absolute loyalty and as the *pañj piāre* ('the five cherished ones') become the core of his disciplined force.

Just what happened in the selection is told in various ways. Gobind Singh asks for someone's head, a volunteer comes forward, they enter Gobind Singh's tent, and the swish of a sword and the thump of a falling head are heard. This is repeated four more times. After this, according to one account, the curtain is drawn aside to reveal five very brave volunteers and five very headless goats. In another account preferred by many Sikhs, the Gurū actually decapitates the five volunteers, but then brings them back to life intact.

Five items of dress mark the initiated male Khālsā Sikh. The words for these all begin with *k* in Punjabi; hence they are called the *pañj kakke* or 'five K's':

- *kes*, uncut hair and beard
- *kaṅghā*, a comb worn in the hair
- *kirpān*, a steel dagger or sword
- *kaṛā*, a steel ring worn on the right wrist
- *kachh*, shorts

Khālsā initiation is performed in a baptismlike ritual that includes sipping a drink of consecrated sweetened water. Termed nectar or *amrit*, the beverage is thought to resemble the sacred nectar offered to Gurū Nānak at the moment of his vision and call. Hence a fully initiated or Khālsā Sikh is referred to as *amrit-dhārī*, 'nectar-bearing'.

The Khālsā way of life came to be summarized in a set of rules of faith and practice called the Rahit ('path'). Its formulation can be documented in manuals termed *rahit-nāmās*, with varying lists of these rules, produced since the eighteenth century. The content of the texts covers four areas: doctrine regarding the deity, the ten *gurūs*, and the sacred scripture; rules of personal conduct from hygiene to social behaviour; directions for the observance of community rituals; and procedures for disciplining violators of the code.

The *amrit-dhārī* Sikhs, 'baptized' into the Khālsā, are an influential minority both in the Punjab and overseas. Two other categories within the community make up its principal constituency. A *kes-dhārī* ('hair-bearing') Sikh is a male who keeps his hair uncut, but has not undergone the Khālsā initiation; such are a majority among Sikhs in parts of India and a sizeable minority overseas.

A Sikh male who has always shaved and cut his hair is termed *sahaj-dhārī*, a term explained by many Sikhs today as 'gradualist'. One sense of the word is 'instinctive' or 'innate', but scholars also interpret *sahaj* as serenity or bliss experienced in following the spiritual discipline of Gurū Nānak. Many Sikhs in India and the majority overseas are of this category. Technically, a Khālsā initiate who cuts off his hair does not become a *sahaj-dhārī* but is considered *paṭit* or 'fallen'; the percentage of these ex-*amrit-dhārī* individuals is not large. Another group, numerous overseas, are the ex-*kes-dhārī*s.

Unshorn hair, then, is common to Khālsā Sikhs and to many unshorn but non-Khālsā Sikh males. Both groups gather the hair in a knot on top of the head, sometimes with a handkerchief-sized white cloth and then wrap it with a strip of cloth several metres or yards long, usually of a solid colour, forming a turban. Some also support the beard in a hammocklike net, but that is unacceptable to some orthodox Sikhs, who insist that the beard show fully.

To Sikhs themselves as well as to others, the turban has come to be a distinguishing mark. Wherever Sikhs have migrated, in India's larger cities and overseas, especially in the English-speaking world, it has been the most visible sign of Sikh identity. Of course Sikhs have no monopoly on the turban; Muslim males in Central Asia, for instance, still wear varieties of turbans, and so do Zoroastrians in India in traditional settings. And as indicated, not all Sikh males have worn it. Moreover, it is not the turban as such but uncut hair that is the requirement for Khālsā membership.

Nonetheless, the turban itself has received a large measure of acceptance as a symbol of community identity carrying religious meaning. Under British rule in India, it became part of the uniform of Sikh units in the police and army, and subsequently an option for individual Sikhs serving in other units. Sikhs overseas who wish to wear it where uniform or safety regulations require something else make a claim for its retention as being mandated by their observance of religion. They also raise a practical consideration: it is a simple matter to doff a hat upon entering a place or at a moment when such action is called for, but one cannot quickly remove and replace a fabric intricately bound around the hair.

As for women's dress, Sikhs in the Indian subcontinent often wear the *salwar-kamīz*, a tunic-and-slacks combination with a long flowing neck scarf of light material. This, however, is a general regional costume, shared especially with Pakistani Muslim women, rather than a mark of religio-communal identity. The Indian *sāri* and Western dress are also seen.

Gobind Singh instituted that all male Sikhs should take the name Singh, meaning 'lion', as a surname, and all Sikh women the surname Kaur, 'princess'. Hence 'Singh' by itself is often a surname, but often Sikhs will also use after the name Singh another name denoting a clan, home town, or other association. So Sikh males who do not have 'Singh' as their surname can be expected to have 'S.' as a middle initial, and Sikh women likewise the middle initial K.

## Four Notions of Guruship

Spiritual authority in the Sikh tradition is vested in the Gurū. On first encounter, this may seem a way of respecting Nānak as an insightful teacher, but Sikhs mean far more than Nānak when they speak of the Gurū, in a cluster of doctrines that developed in the course of time.

Sikhs came to acknowledge four focal points of authority, referring to each as *gurū*. We should consider them complementary rather than contradictory: one eternal Gurū is manifested in different forms. Some of the specific conceptions are distinctively Sikh, but the general activity of asserting unity among diverse manifestations is familiar in other traditions such as Hinduism and Buddhism.

### *God as Gurū*

To experience the deity is to experience divine guidance. For Nānak, the Gurū is the divine voice, speaking within the consciousness of the devotee. As in the Sant tradition, God is formless and invisible. Philosophically speaking, the indescribable reality is beyond and unqualified by attributes or characteristics, but its transcendence does not stop Sikhs from being guided by a meditative or mystical sense of its personal presence, and a variety of names and attributes can be found in Sikh literature and devotion. We can best depict the Sikh conception of the Supreme Being on the basis of these names, rather than merely importing from Western religion and philosophy the theological freight that the English word 'God' has accumulated.

God is Akal Purakh, the 'timeless person', and characterized as *niraṅkār* or formless. He is Sat Kartār, 'true creator', Sat Gurū, 'true teacher', and Sat Nām, 'true name'. In devotional hymns Nānak also uses the Hindu names Hari and Rām for God, a usage we see continued in Sikh reference to the Golden Temple as Harmandir Sāhib, 'the honoured temple of Hari', but Sikhs today have often tended to drop these names. On the other hand, Nānak refers to God as Oṅkār, 'the expression of *oṃ*', that is, of the sacred syllable of the Hindus, a conception that actively continues as Ik Oṅkār, 'the one *oṃ*-expression' (a name picked up as Eckankar and used by others in the twentieth century); it is symbolized in a Sikh rendering of an *oṃ*-like monogram in the *gurmukhī* script. After Nānak's time, the devotional expression *Vāhigurū*, 'hail to the Gurū', came into use as yet another name for God, the eternal Gurū.

In these designations, we should clarify the implications of *nām*, the word 'name'. The theological concept sees God's 'name' as much more than a culturally determined series of sounds (arbitrary in the sense that a rose by any other name, such as *gol* in Persian, would smell just as sweet). God's 'name' is his essence and identity, his power and majesty. It is his acknowledged reputation, much as in the biblical Hebrew connotations of the Lord's name. *Nām* is the link between absolute transcendence and worldly manifestation.

Thus worship itself is understood as 'remembering the name' (*nām simaraṇ*), that is, making the deity the focus of one's awareness and motivation. This may be routinized by the repetition of a word or formula as a mantra, such recitation being called *nām japaṇ*. Worship also consists in congregational chanting and singing from the tradition's rich repertory of devotional hymns, a practice called *kīrtan*. It does not exclude earnest but less structured meditation and prayer.

### A Teacher as Gurū

According to Sikh doctrine, the spiritual guidance or guruship of the deity was vested in Nānak, who became a living embodiment of it. Not only, then, was his religious insight a model for the insight that others might gain through reflection, but he personally became a model of authority in conduct that others might emulate or obey.

This authority was transmitted from Nānak to the succession of nine *gurūs* who followed him. Guruship was passed like a torch from one runner to another. No matter how many disciples at any moment had an understanding of the teaching, only one as *gurū* could be the locus of authority; indeed, the hymns of the different *gurūs* in the *Ādi Granth* are cited by referring to their composers as sequential *mahālas* ('places') of manifestation of guruship. As indicated earlier, after the fourth Gurū the office became hereditary, continuing to and including the tenth.

It also came to be the accepted view that when the tenth Gurū, Gobind Singh, was stabbed by an assassin and about to die, he specified that the authority of guruship should no longer pass to a designated personal heir but reside in the scripture (the doctrine is called *Gurū Granth*) and in the collective wisdom of the community (*Gurū Panth*).

### The Scripture as Gurū

In this context, the *Ādi Granth* came to be also called the *Gurū Granth Sāhib*. Seen as a gift from God, it embodies one of the ways in which divinity manifests itself: as *śabad* or divine word. The doctrine is laden with symbolic association, offering parallels to Jewish and Christian notions where the word of God is the divine intention as well as expression. But such parallels should not divert our attention from the equally rich understandings of word as creative and revelatory speech in the *Veda*s and other Hindu texts.

Sikhs clearly treat the *Granth* as inspired, that is, of divinely guided human authorship. Its devotional hymns are explicitly attributed to individuals, not all of them even Sikhs. But doctrine confers on the *Granth* an authority not only of inspiration but of revelation, that is, of divine authorship, in the following manner.

As indicated, each of the personal *gurūs* in the succession beginning with Nānak was respected by his followers as an incarnate embodiment of the eternal Gurū. From these *gurūs* come the devotional compositions compiled especially in the *Ādi Granth*; the textual legacy of each *gurū* is referred to as his *bāṇī*. So the doctrine developed that the *bāṇī* of the *gurūs* as a group was a textual, literary embodiment representing what had been serially their incarnate personal embodiment of the Gurū.

The *Praśan uttar*, a composition in Punjabi verse traditionally attributed to Bhāi Nand Lāl of Gobind Singh's entourage at the beginning of the eighteenth century, reflects the doctrine as it emerged during that century. In it his Gurū declares:

> This [the *Granth*] you must accept as an actual part of me, treating its letters as the hairs of my body. This truly is so. Sikhs who wish to see the Guru will do so when they come to the Granth. He who is wise will bathe at dawn and humbly approach the sacred scripture. Come with reverence and sit in my presence. Humbly bow and hear the words of the Guru Granth (Piara Singh Padam in McLeod 1989:53).

The doctrine of *Gurū Granth*, holding the text to be the ongoing embodiment of the personal Gurū, has remained important to Sikhs. Today, it functions to heighten respect for the *Ādi Granth*, particularly for the profoundly spiritual hymns of the *gurūs* contained therein. For the Khālsā of the eighteenth century, however, the divine authority ascribed to the *Granth* was considered the direct bequest of the tenth Gurū. Thus they held the *Dasam Granth*, attributed to Gobind Singh as compiler, virtually on a par with the *Ādi Granth* of his predecessors. Gobind Singh, after all, was the key link in the tradition's pedigree that transferred guruship from the person to the text.

### *The Community as Gurū*

Sikhs regularly call their community the *panth*. The term, meaning 'path' or 'way', reflects a nearly universal feature of religions. Almost all speak of following their precepts or tradition as one would follow a road or path. In the Sikh case, the word for path became the word for the group: initially, followers of Nānak's way were referred to as the *Nānak-panth*, and subsequently the community became simply the *panth*.

Also widespread among religions is the idea that the consensus of the community or of its leadership core has some form of authority. More varied is the rationale or manner by which that consensus is validated or connected to a divine source. In the Sikh case, the orthodox Khālsā view is that the tenth Gurū, when he was nearing death, formally designated it as the collective embodiment of his divine mandate.

A narrative poem from the first half of the eighteenth century, titled *Gur Sobhā* (Radiance of the Gurū) and attributed to an author named Sainapati, reports this transfer. In it, Gobind Singh says:

> Upon the Khalsa which I have created I shall bestow the succession. The Khalsa is my physical form and I am one with the Khalsa. To all eternity I am manifest in the Khalsa. They whose hearts are purged of falsehood will be known as the true Khalsa; and the Khalsa, freed from error and illusion, will be my true Guru (Sainapati in McLeod 1989:52).

In the view of Khālsā Sikhs, this passage validates the élite corps of the Khālsā as possessing the authoritative guidance for the community; many of them have claimed to speak for the community as a whole. Non-Khālsā Sikhs, meanwhile, have interpreted the doctrine of *Gurū Panth* as conferring spiritual authority on a community more broadly defined.

## Customs and Rituals

### *Worship in the Gurdwara*

In the gurdwara or Sikh house of worship, the principal congregational activity is attendance at *kīrtan*, the singing of hymns from the scriptures. Any adult Sikh, male or female, may in principle conduct religious ceremonies. The specialized readers of the sacred texts, called *granthī*s, and the career singers, called *rāgī*s, who perform congregational duties when demand calls for it, are qualified for their roles by skill rather than by ritual ordination.

Architecturally, the gurdwara structure is a rectangular hall, usually with a side room adjoining the dais, to which the copy of the *Gurū Granth Sāhib* is retired at hours other than congregational worship.

### *Daily Prayer*

The dawn meditation includes the *Japjī* or prayer containing Gurū Nānak's creed, as well as the *Jāp* or hymn of Gurū Gobind Singh. A devout Sikh will also pass by the gurdwara in order to recite hymns from the scriptures. In the *Ādi Granth* the fourth Gurū, Ramdās, describes a Sikh's morning prayer routine:

> He should rise early, take a bath and make an effort to wash himself clean in the Pool of Nectar. By repeating God's name according to the Guru's instruc-

*Within the Golden Temple of Amritsar, the* granthī *reads from the* Gurū Granth Sāhib, *the sacred Sikh scripture.* (W.G. Oxtoby)

tion all his evil deeds and mistakes will be washed away … The Guru's disciple (Gursikh) who with each breath and every morsel of food contemplates my Lord God becomes pleasing to the Guru's mind (*Gauṛī* 11, *Ādi Granth* 305).

### *Special Days*

In India, Sikhs have followed their own rituals at the time of three seasonal Hindu festivals. Important since the time of the third Gurū, Amardās, are Baisakhi and Dīvālī. The tenth Gurū, Gobind Singh, is held to have added the day after Holī.

Baisakhi, celebrated as New Year's day in India, follows a solar calendar and usually falls on 13 April. While it had been a grain harvest festival for Hindus, it has acquired historical associations for Sikhs. Since Gobind Singh formed the Khālsā at a Baisakhi assembly in 1699, Sikhs have celebrated the festival as a historical birthday for their community. Further Baisakhi assemblies have added to the deposit of historical memory, particularly when a crowd in Amritsar in 1919 were fired on as political agitators by the British, with 378 fatalities.

The date of Dīvālī varies across a month's range because it follows the

Indian lunar calendar, but it generally falls during October. Dīvālī is the Hindu festival of lights, traditionally oil-lamps. Sikhs, too, light lamps on Dīvālī, including outlining the architectural features of gurdwaras with strings of electric lights.

While *Rāmāyaṇa* and *Mahābhārata* narratives are what Hindus associate with the occasion, Sikhs tell a story about the sixth Gurū, Hargobind, imprisoned under the Mughal emperor Jehangir. When the emperor orders Hargobind's release, it does not include fifty-two Hindu princes also imprisoned. Hargobind refuses to leave unless they are also freed. Jehangir agrees to release only as many of them as can hold on to Hargobind's clothing, whereupon Hargobind has a cloak made with tassels long enough to provide freedom to all.

The date of Holā Mohāllā, the day after Holī, likewise follows a lunar reckoning and varies across late February and early March. For Hindus, Holī is a time to splash coloured powder or water on everyone and everything in sight, and Sikhs do follow this custom to some extent. The emphasis Gobind Singh gave to Sikh observance of the day after Holī was to channel people's energies into military exercises and organized athletic and literary contests.

Besides celebrating at these Hindu holidays, Sikhs have introduced a number of observances of their own during the year. The three most important and most widely observed all follow lunar reckoning, with a month's range of variation in their solar dates. Observance of Gurū Nānak's birthday generally falls in November, thus according with one *janam-sākhī* tradition about him while other traditions place his birth in April. The birthday of Gurū Gobind Singh is observed usually in December, and the martyrdom of the fifth Gurū, Arjan, in May or June.

On occasions such as these, the preparation is an *akhaṇḍ pāṭh* ('unbroken reading'), an uninterrupted two-day reading of the *Gurū Granth Sāhib*. The text is read aloud in its entirety by relays of readers, each in turn reading for up to two hours. The reading is scheduled to conclude just before dawn on the anniversary day, so that the conclusion of the reading leads right into the morning *kīrtan* for which the worshippers have gathered.

An *akhaṇḍ pāṭh* can also be scheduled for ceremonies other than anniversaries, such as just prior to a wedding or just following a funeral. In a private home, where non-stop reading is often not practical, the cover-to-cover reading can take seven days and is called *saptāhak pāṭh* or *sahaj pāṭh*.

### *Life-Cycle Rituals*

In India, marriages have traditionally been arranged between families, with family loyalty bulking larger than romantic love in the considerations. In this sense, as well as in having a procession through the streets of the town, Sikh weddings follow general Indian custom. What is distinctive about the Sikh ceremony is that it is conducted in the presence of a copy of the sacred scripture, the *Gurū Granth Sāhib*. At a stage in the ceremony, the couple circle four times around it.

One of the marriage hymns in the *Granth* was used by the fourth Gurū, Ramdās, for his daughter's wedding. It is called the *lāvāṅ* ('circling'). While it is read and sung, the couple slowly walk in a clockwise direction around the sacred book four times, once for each stanza of the hymn. In its first stanza, the text affirms the Hindu conception of responsibilities in the householder stage of life, though it instructs the couple to 'sing the *bāṇī* instead of the *Vedas*'. Subsequent stanzas dwell on the devotee's awareness of divine love as present in the fellowship of the community and in the blissful experience of mystical union.

Sikh funeral practices follow Indian custom in cremating the body within a day after death, with the pyre lit by the deceased's eldest son or a close relative. Preparation of the body for cremation includes washing and often also making sure that the five symbolic articles of attire, the five K's, are present. Following cremation, ashes are generally thrown into a river, though numerous shrines are built at the presumed burial sites of the ashes of holy men. An oral reading of the *Granth* can follow in the days after a funeral. Sikhs understand death to be followed by rebirth, unless through faith and through divine favour one achieves release from the cycle.

Another major stage of life for some Sikhs is initiation into the Khālsā, performed at or after the age of fourteen. The officiants are five persons, men or women, recalling the *pañj piāre* or 'cherished five' original members of Gurū Gobind Singh's Khālsā, plus a *granthī* or reader. During a recitation of hymns and prayers lasting about two hours, the five mix the *amrit* or nectar, stirring sweetened water in an iron bowl with a short double-edged sword. The initiates then come forward, sip *amrit* five times from their cupped hands, and have it sprinkled five times on their eyes and hair.

The initiates are then instructed regarding obligations of conduct, four of which have come in the twentieth century to be listed as major offences against the Rahit or code. These include prohibitions that an observer would consider moral, such as adultery (one of the major offences) and profiting from an arranged marriage. They also include smoking (another of the four) and the use of narcotics and alcohol. Then there are prohibitions we might associate with religious group identity: cutting one's hair and eating meat slaughtered in the Muslim style where the animal bleeds to death (the other two major offences), and breaking one's vows, joining breakaway sects, performing ceremonies incompatible with Sikhism, and eating with non-Khālsā or lapsed Sikhs. Less clear is the moral or group-identity force of another prohibition: dyeing or pulling out gray hairs.

Some interpreters see the Khālsā initiation as a symbolic reversal of ascetic practices in other Indian communities. Rather than shaving their heads, Sikh initiates are unshorn. Rather than espousing pacifism, they are always armed with a dagger. Rather than having a personal, secret mantra whispered to them at initiation, they take their vows publicly. Perhaps this is to be expected, as early Sikh leadership came from a mercantile rather than a priestly class.

## From Sikh Hymns and Prayers

*[Despite his militancy, Gobind Singh shares with Nānak a sense that religious boundaries are irrelevant to God.]*

There is no difference between a temple and a mosque, nor between the prayers of a Hindu and or a Muslim. Though differences seem to mark and distinguish, all men are in reality the same.
Gods and demons, celestial beings, men called Muslims and others called Hindus—such differences are trivial, inconsequential, the outward results of locality and dress.
With eyes the same, the ears and body, all possessing a common form—all are in fact a single creation, the elements of nature in a uniform blend.
Allah is the same as the God of the Hindus, Puran and Qur'an are the same. All are the same, none is separate; a single form, a single creation (*Akal Ustat, Dasam Granth*, 19–20).

*[Bhāi Gurdās likewise declares the irrelevance of external religious observances.]*

If bathing at tiraths procures liberation, frogs, for sure, must be saved;
And likewise the banyan, with dangling tresses, if growing hair long sets one free.
If the need can be served by roaming unclad the deer of the forest must surely be pious;
So to the ass which rolls in the dust if limbs smeared with ashes can purchase salvation.
Saved are the cattle, mute in the fields, if

## The Sikhs and Caste Identity

The Sikh tradition speaks with two voices about the stratification that has been so characteristic of Indian society. Sikh thought has denied the importance of caste identity at the same time as some in Sikh society have assumed its presence.

Caste in Indian society has affected people's occupational status and eligibility for marriage, and its boundaries have been so rigidly enforced that many will not share a meal with someone from another social group. The etymology of an English word hints at the social reality: a 'companion' is literally someone with whom one shares bread. Some Hindus are so reluctant to eat food prepared by a person of a different or unknown caste that even in today's urban commuting society, they eat lunches prepared in their own homes; and in cities like Bombay many, who for status reasons consider themselves above carrying their own lunchpails, support an entire industry of porters who deliver those pails during the morning from suburban home to downtown office.

Seen in this context, the Sikh sharing of food amounts to a strong declaration that all regardless of caste have access to the spiritual benefits that accrue to a disciple of the Gurū. This sharing occurs in Sikh rituals, as *kaṛāh praśād* (a mix-

silence produces deliverance.
Only the Guru can bring us salvation; only the Guru can set a man free.

*[The Sikh prayer called the* Ardas, *standardized by the 1930s, contains a roll-call of the ten gurūs. Siri Hari Krishan, included in it, is the child who became the eighth Gurū, and should not be confused with the Hare Krishna movement arising from Hindu Vaisnavism in Bengal.]*

Having first remembered God, turn your thoughts to Guru Nanak;
Angad Guru, Amar Das, each with Ram Das grant us aid.
Arjan and Hargobind, think of them and Hari Rai.
Dwell on Sri Hari Krishan, he whose sight dispels all pain.
Think of Guru Tegh Bahadur; thus shall every treasure come.
May they grant their gracious guidance, help and strength in every place (*Chandi di Vār 1, Dasam Granth*, 119).

*[The theme of martyrdom abounds in the pages of Sikh history and motivates Sikhs to persevere in struggles today.]*

These loyal members of the Khalsa who gave their heads for their faith; who were hacked limb from limb, scalped, broken on the wheel, or sawn asunder; who sacrificed their lives for the protection of hallowed gurdwaras never forsaking their faith; and who were steadfast in their loyalty to the uncut hair of the true Sikh: reflect on their merits, O Khalsa, and call on God, saying, *Vahiguru*! (*Chandi di Vār*)

ture of whole grain meal, sugar, and ghee or clarified butter, which has been placed in the presence of the sacred scripture) is then considered blessed and is distributed to all in attendance. It also takes place in a non-ceremonial context, as the *laṅgar* or kitchen attached to a gurdwara produces meals in which all present are to share. Sikhs also tell of the tradition that their *mahārāja* ('great king') was to eat with all his subjects before becoming their ruler.

The institution of the common kitchen is credited to the second if not the first Gurū, the distribution of *kaṛāh praśād* may have been practised by the time of the fifth Gurū, and the sipping of *amrit* from a common bowl at initiation was instituted by the tenth Gurū. But already in the words of Gurū Nānak, caste is useless for spiritual fulfilment:

Kingship, possessions, beauty, and riches—all are but transient clouds
And when the Sun's chariot ascends the true landscape comes into view.
In the hereafter name and caste count for nothing.
(*Malār* 8, *Ādi Granth* 1257)

And again:

Observe the divine light in a man and ask not his caste
For there is no caste in the hereafter.
(*Āsā* 3, *Ādi Granth* 349)

A similar point is made by the fifth Gurū, Arjan, in the compilation of the *Ādi Granth*. He includes compositions by Hindu poets in the Sant tradition, several of whom were explicitly low-caste like Ravidās and Kabīr and speak of access to divine grace despite their low status. And Sikh tradition holds that the first five initiated into the Khālsā by the tenth Gurū represented a range of castes.

Yet the ten *gurūs* were Khatrīs, that is, of a high-caste Indian mercantile class claiming the ancient status of the warriors or *kṣatriyas*. The *gurūs* held that the religious framework of caste (*varṇa*), institutionalized in India in four strata of society, is of no benefit in the hereafter. But in this life they operated within the kinship framework of clan or birth groups (*jātis*). They married within their own broad class, and as their office was made hereditary after the fourth Gurū, no members of other castes became designated as *gurūs*. And a number of the other leading figures among Nānak's early followers were also Khatrīs.

The formation of the Khālsā changed the visible profile of the Sikh community. Enough of the Khālsā members in the eighteenth and nineteenth centuries were drawn from the farming population, who belonged to the middle-range Jaṭ class, that when a census was taken under British auspices in 1881, two out of every three persons enumerated as Sikhs (that is, as *kes-dhārī* or turbaned Sikhs) were Jaṭs. The remainder counted as Sikhs in that census were scattered across two dozen castes, with the Khatrīs accounting for just over 2 per cent of the Sikh population.

What had happened to the Sikh tradition among the ten *gurūs*' people, the Khatrīs? They had evidently been less inclined to accept Khālsā initiation and the outward symbolic attire of the five K's. They were among the wider circle of Nānak-panthīs, that is, followers of the teachings of Nānak. They considered themselves fully able to follow these as *sahaj-dhārī* or turbanless Sikhs. Part of what the Khālsā symbolism offered—an egalitarian sense of dignity and worth regardless of caste—may have been less urgent for a group already high on the social scale.

## Sikhs in the Modern World

### Sikh Identity under the British

British rule in the second half of the nineteenth century saw three Sikh reform movements, each seeking to restore a sense of spiritual identity to a people no longer masters of their own kingdom. They also helped to keep Sikh identity distinct among the vast array of religious communities and teachings in India. They did this at a time when most such traditions were beginning to be thought of collectively as Hinduism.

### *The Niraṅkārīs*

Born a Hindu, Dyāl Dās (1783–1853), of the northwestern frontier city of Peshawar, was engaged in Sikh issues but never underwent the Khālsā initiation ritual. His followers were called Niraṅkārīs ('worshippers of the Formless One') because he condemned the worship of images; he also condemned the practice of Hindu rituals by Sikhs. The group was especially strong around Rawalpindi, where they revered his *Hukam-nāmā* (Book of Ordinances) alongside the *Gurū Granth Sahib*. That was enough to cause them to be rejected by orthodox Sikhs. The Niraṅkārīs were located in a region from which they were uprooted a century later in 1947 with partition and the formation of Pakistan; thereafter, they transferred their headquarters to Chandigarh, in the eastern Punjab.

### *The Nāmdhārīs*

Rām Singh (1816–84) became the Nāmdhārī ('Name-bearing') leader on the northwestern frontier and moved his headquarters to a village near Ludhiana in the Punjab. The movement became a separate group in 1857 when it created its own baptismal ritual and rule of conduct. Rām Singh promoted vegetarian diet, the wearing of all-white dress, austere discipline, and extensive chanting. 'Nāmdhārī' alludes to their repetition of the divine Name; they were also nicknamed Kūkās ('shouters') because of spontaneous outbursts in the devotional trances that they cultivated.

As the number of his followers increased, Rām Singh began to hold court and regulate public practice. The British had permitted the reintroduction of cattle slaughter, which had been banned under Mahārāja Rañjīt Singh. In 1871, the Nāmdhārīs moved to suppress it, and Muslim butchers in Amritsar and Ludhiana were killed. The British put down the Nāmdhārīs, ransacked their headquarters, blew sixty-five of their men to pieces by tying them over the mouths of cannons, and deported Rām Singh to exile in Rangoon. The execution and deportation made political martyrs of the Nāmdhārīs in the Indian independence movement.

The Nāmdhārīs developed a doctrine of religious authority reminiscent of the Shī'ī Muslim teaching about the hidden Imām. They hold that Gobind Singh was not assassinated in 1708 but went into hiding, and that Rām Singh was his successor as the twelfth Gurū. Moreover, he is believed to be alive in hiding and expected to return some day. In the meantime, authority for them is vested not in the scripture but in a descendant of Rām Singh as a personal representative of the living Gurū. They refer to their houses of worship as *dharamsālās*, reserving the term 'gurdwara' for buildings actually used by the historical *gurūs*.

## Defining the Tradition

The Siṅgh Sabhā movement began in 1873 as an effort to counter losses by the Sikh community to the missionary activity of Christians and especially of Ārya Samāj Hindus. The British colonial administrators patronized their work, which included founding educational institutions, such as Khalsa College in Amritsar (1892). Vir Singh (1872–1937), a poet and philosopher, became one of the movement's leading intellectuals and launched its publication activity.

The Siṅgh Sabhā movement redefined the Sikh tradition in more ways than one. In social and institutional terms, it transformed the means by which the heritage was communicated. As late as the mid-nineteenth century, there was no centralized group that articulated the Sikh tradition for all of its adherents. In different clan and caste groups, in different villages, there were bards and minstrels, diviners and healers, and saintly ascetics. The tradition was the sum of what these and others taught, but no one central agency attempted to add up its total.

But under British rule, the Siṅgh Sabhā became a new leadership élite. By 1900 it developed a network of more than a hundred chapters extending across the major cities and towns of the Punjab and adjoining regions, from Delhi to the northwestern frontier. The British colonial administration was sympathetic to it, but equally important to its emergence were the new realities of transportation, communication, and commerce.

The sense of Sikh identity today as a community distinct from Hindus is in no small measure due to views promoted by the Tat Khālsā of Lahore, one of the elements in the Siṅgh Sabhā. 'We are not Hindus', its scholar Kahn Singh Nabhā (1861–1938) declared in 1897 in a Hindi-language pamphlet with that title, *Ham Hindū nahīn*. A century later, it is hard to imagine how novel such views were in Kahn Singh's own day.

It has never been hard to tell Sikhs and Muslims apart. This is partly because Islam itself is a religion with well-defined doctrinal requirements and community boundaries. Moreover, Islam condemns as apostasy any participation in other communities' worship. Sikh politico-military activity in Mughal times clearly underscored the conflicts between local Sikh units and the interests of the Muslim emperors.

But well into the nineteenth century, the boundary between Sikh and Hindu identity was difficult to draw. Sikhs and Hindus shared much in their outlook on human existence in the universe, in their standards of personal and social conduct, and in their ritual practices. It was not uncommon for those who esteemed Nānak's spiritual insight to revere Hindu saints as well; even the compilers of the Sikh scriptures did so. At the end of the century, one could still find Hindu images in many gurdwaras.

Under the Mughals, in Persian, the term 'Hindu' was primarily an ethnic term, meaning 'Indian', although in specific group contrasts, it could imply non-

Muslims. Under the British in the nineteenth century, it was put into service in English as an explicit religious designation for most Indians—those who did not belong to boundaried, identifiable minorities in the population. (See the opening of the chapter on the Hindu tradition, where in Indian law the Hindu Family Act continues to define a Hindu in this fashion, specifically excluding Muslims, Christians, Parsis [Zoroastrians], and Jews—but not Jains or Sikhs.) A follower of Gurū Nānak was in no way administratively excluded from Hindu identity.

By the same token, as long as a diversity of views of Sikh identity prevailed, it would be hard to exclude any follower of the teachings of Nānak from Sikh identity. There were, and are, many who bear the name Singh but do not wear the turban. The Siṅgh Sabhā movement, by presenting the Khālsā as the ideal of Sikh identity and interpreting the term for the turbanless followers of Nānak, *sahaj-dhārīs*, to mean 'slow adopters', had the effect of drawing just such a line. Khālsā Sikhs, who had been a core element among the Sikhs for two centuries, were beginning to be considered the only true Sikhs.

What reform meant in intellectual terms was a kind of neoconservatism. The Siṅgh Sabhā undertook to speak for the Sikhs as a whole and to define the entire community's identity in terms of observance of the Khālsā Rahit or rule. What is more, they presented this as the explicit intent of the tenth Gurū, Gobind Singh, as well as the implicit intent of Nānak and of Gobind Singh's other predecessors. Provisions contained in texts of the Rahit that can be seen by a historian to have accumulated during the eighteenth and nineteenth centuries are held by twentieth-century orthodoxy all to have been in place when Gobind Singh organized the first Khālsā in 1699.

## Twentieth-Century India

The Siṅgh Sabhā undertook to 'purify' the Sikh community by purging it of Hindu cultic and ritual influences. Hindu images were removed from the precincts of the Golden Temple in 1905. Agitation for recognition of the Sikh wedding service as a distinct form resulted in the Anand Marriage Act of 1909.

The Chief Khalsa Diwan was formed as a political structure in 1902 and continued to identify with the British government's position. But since its chief base was in the educated classes, it lost grass-roots support in the second decade of the twentieth century as popular sentiment shifted towards Indian independence.

In 1920, the Akal Takht in Amritsar (the most highly respected of then four, now five, chief *takhts*, 'seats', among Sikh shrines) announced the formation of a committee to manage all Sikh shrines. Called the Shiromani Gurdwara Prabandhak Committee (i.e., central gurdwara management committee) or SGPC, this body has continued to be viewed as the central religious administrative authority of the Sikhs. Not only administrative matters but questions of religious discipline are referred to it.

A kind of Sikh vigilante movement came into being, calling itself the Akali Dal ('army of the immortal'). Sworn to defend the gurdwaras to the death, it undertook to seize control of the gurdwaras from local *mahants* or proprietors, many of them *sahaj-dhārīs*, and centralize it. Its militancy was reminiscent of the Khālsā and the *misls* of earlier times, but an embarrassment to twentieth-century pro-government intellectuals. Responding to its initiative, the government passed the Sikh Gurdwaras Act of 1925, enumerating gurdwaras and giving the SGPC regulatory authority over them.

Partition upon the British withdrawal from India in 1947 carved out the Indus Valley and East Bengal, Muslim-majority regions, as a separate constitutionally Islamic state, Pakistan. Partition was particularly hard for the Sikhs, as it split the Punjab in two. Most Sikhs in the western Punjab, from Lahore west, numbering 2.5 million, fled Pakistan as refugees and were absorbed in the eastern portion, from Amritsar east. This produced increases in the demographic ratio of Sikhs in the receiving areas, heightening political consciousness. It also meant that certain sites figuring in a sense of Sikh history were no longer readily accessible.

What remained as independent India was now constitutionally 'secular'. In practice that meant not antireligious but multireligious or pluralistic. In principle the government sought to be sensitive to local custom but not to grant privilege to any one group over another. Preferential treatment that Sikhs had enjoyed under the British for military and civil-service positions was curtailed. Electoral representation by religio-communal identity was abolished in favour of representation by region; in many districts where Sikhs were a minority, they thus lost their representatives. But in business and particularly in agriculture, Sikhs prospered according to their energy, merits, and luck. Many farmed in a fertile region where the government was building irrigation canals.

In the 1980s, calls for an independent Sikh homeland or Khalistan were considered extreme by most, but many Sikhs in India harboured grievances over what they took to be the central government's failure to acknowledge adequately the Sikhs as a distinct religio-communal entity. The Punjab was wracked by strife, with a kind of Gresham's law operating as hard-line views drove conciliatory positions out of circulation. Armed Sikh militants holed up in the Golden Temple were routed and their leader, Jarnail Singh Bhindranwale (1947–84), killed when the precincts were stormed and heavily damaged by government forces in 1984.

Many Sikhs had renounced Bhindranwale and his methods, but they discovered even greater depths of grief at the assault on their holiest shrine. The mix of politics and religion was heated yet further that same year with the assassination of India's prime minister, Indira Gandhi (r. 1966–77, 1980–4), by her Sikh bodyguards. Sikhs in Delhi and elsewhere were victims of the anti-Sikh rioting that followed. Feelings of insecurity spurred Sikh emigration overseas. The demand in India for recognition of communal identity remains an explosive issue.

## The Sikhs Overseas

The advent of British rule in the nineteenth century brought communications and transportation links through the British Empire. Sikhs made their way to Singapore and Hong Kong, and from there across the Pacific. From 1903 to 1907, more than 5,000 Sikhs arrived in British Columbia. Sikhs also arrived in California in the same years.

Most of the migrants were farmers of the Jaṭ class who had done well enough to afford transpacific steamship passage. In California, they found work in the farmlands of the state's interior. In British Columbia, most found jobs in the lumber industry. In the first decade, virtually all the migrants were young males, who came without families. Some had left wives and children in India, and some after establishing themselves eventually returned to India to find mates, but others in the first wave married English-speaking (or, in the agricultural regions of California adjoining Mexico, Spanish-speaking) North American women. Canadians and Americans, both in the lay public and in the immigration bureaucracy, considered the migrants as Hindus, and some called the Sikh-Hispanic offspring in California 'Mexidus'.

Economic recession in 1913 reduced the attractiveness of Canada and the United States as migration destinations, and restrictive immigration policies also reduced opportunities for migration. It was only in the 1950s that immigration, particularly to Canada, became an opportunity for many. This time, the pattern was different. Many Sikhs who migrated to North America after mid-century did so as families, or sent for relatives once they became established. Air travel, international telephone links, and eventually video cassettes of Indian movies made it much easier to keep in touch with one's Indian roots, but as families the new migrants were even more committed to putting down new roots in the Western hemisphere.

The Sikh presence in North America has both contributed to and benefited from the emerging climate of religious pluralism in the late twentieth century. On the whole, religious acceptance of turban-wearing males has been covered by the same type of interfaith etiquette as has, for instance, the acceptance of the Jewish *yarmulke*. On the other hand, there has been strong sentiment against turban-wearing by police and the military on the ground that government officials should not only operate on strictly secular principles but should be perceived to do so. And there has been strong opposition to *kirpān*-wearing by children in schools where not only must the use of knives and weapons be eliminated from school premises but the tolerance of even their possession be perceived as absolutely zero.

At the time of India's partition in 1947, Britain was an open destination for Sikhs whom partition uprooted. From then until the 1960s, many Sikhs, like other South Asians and West Indians, settled in England and worked largely as unskilled labourers. Some wrote home to describe their work as simply pushing buttons to start and stop a machine, for which they were paid exponentially more than what they could earn by farming in India. But especially after the influx of South Asians expelled from Uganda in 1972, mass attitudes in Britain became hostile to immigration.

Whereas the earlier migration of Sikhs to North America had been to rural locations, Sikhs in Britain gathered in the large industrial cities. Among the acculturation issues was the disposal of ashes from cremating the dead, as scattering them on English rivers was prohibited. Shipping companies offered to arrange their disposal at sea outside British waters, but many families fly the ashes back to India. Turban-wearing has occasioned more conflict with safety regulations than with uniform regulations; Sikh motorcyclists have been exempted from wearing crash helmets if they wear turbans.

Doubtless because of the population size (at least half a million) and urban visibility of the Sikh community in England, British education has tended to list the Sikh tradition among the half dozen principal religious traditions studied in schools, along with Buddhism, Christianity, Hinduism, Islam, and Judaism. The Sikh tradition's presence in the accepted canon assures it the opportunity to survive and prosper in the diaspora. How well it will prosper will depend on the choices that Sikhs themselves make as they continue to articulate for themselves in decades to come what it means to be a Sikh.

## Feminine Dimensions of Sikh Faith

Sikh religious literature is almost completely the work of males, and the community's institutions have been almost completely staffed by males. In this the Sikh tradition differs little from other major religions. And where the Sikhs are most visibly distinguished from other groups, in hair and headgear, the masculine attire is prominent. Moreover, to think of the Khālsā as a military brotherhood is to confirm an impression of the Sikh tradition as male-centred.

Of course half the Sikhs through the centuries, including many members of the Khālsā, have been women, and feminine perspectives in the tradition are crucial for any picture of it to be adequate for today's needs. Encouraged by advances in scholarship on other religious traditions, some recent interpreters of the Sikh experience, especially Sikhs overseas, have begun to assemble a picture that allows scope for women's perspectives. Their insights have followed several lines.

First is the evaluation of women's historical roles. Discussing caste, we have already characterized the *gurūs* as socially egalitarian. Today, interpreters are recruiting them as forerunners of women's liberation as well, seeing in the early Panth a community of equal spiritual access for male and female. Pivotal in such a reading is the hymn by Gurū Nānak:

> Of woman are we born, of woman conceived,
> To woman engaged, to woman married.
> Woman we befriend, by woman do civilizations continue.
> When a woman dies, a woman is sought for.
> It is through woman that order is maintained.
> Then why call her inferior from whom all great ones are
> born?
> Woman is born of woman;
> None is born but of woman.
> The One, who is Eternal, alone is unborn.
> (*Āsā* 19, *Ādi Granth* 473; Singh 1993:30)

To Sikh women today, these words signify a stance that was revolutionary in Gurū Nānak's time, when Muslim women were secluded and many Hindu widows were expected to join their deceased husbands on the funeral pyre. Sikh women are seen as partners, not property. Married family life—not asceticism or celibacy—is extolled as the ideal for human social fulfilment. And because women and men shared the practical and symbolic roles associated with the community meals of the *laṅgar*, interpreters argue, women were equally valued in religious contexts.

While appreciating the positive side to these ideals, we urge caution in supposing that they were fully implemented. Women and men did gather together for worship in the early Panth, but gurdwara practice today still often segregates the sexes. And the hymn above indicates that a widower seeks to remarry, but is silent about what a woman is to do when her husband dies.

A second aspect to modern thinking about women's place in the tradition is the evaluation of women's roles as distinctive. Women, not men, give birth, as the hymn above states. Gurū Nānak's word for woman here is *bhaṇḍu*, etymologically 'vessel'. Creation pours forth from woman. But—importantly in Indian tradition—so does pollution, particularly with the discharge of blood in childbirth and menstruation. On this point, a feminist reading of Nānak makes him a revolutionary who condemns the notion of pollution as false:

> If pollution attaches to birth, then pollution is everywhere
> (for birth is universal).
> Cow-dung [used as fuel] and firewood breed maggots ...

How can we then believe in pollution, when pollution
inheres within staples?
Says Nānak, pollution is not washed away by purificatory
rituals;
Pollution is removed by true knowledge alone.
(*Āsā* 18, *Ādi Granth* 472; Singh 1993:32–3)

Still open to discussion is whether such a text denies the existence of pollution through bodily discharges or whether it assumes it in order to state that spiritual insight is of higher value.

A third line of interpretation is to value the metaphorical or symbolic role of femininity. Here again Gurū Nānak's hymns offer a resource, as they are rich in bridal imagery. The created universe is the bride, and God is the groom. Modern Sikh fiction writing likewise finds religious analogies in the adornments of South Asian bridal costume and the focus of anticipation that weddings provide. And again the question to ask of such imagery is whether the feminine role is one of true equivalency: is not the groom, or God as groom, the master in the relationship? On this point, Sikhs do see God as either male or female.

But we can set birth imagery against bridal imagery. On a descriptive level, many references in Sikh religious literature speak of humans as born of women and as first nurtured by women. Symbolically, however, they evoke a sense of deity as giving birth to, and nurturing, creation.

Who is our Mother? Who the Father?
Where have we come from?
(*Gāuṛī* 17, *Ādi Granth* 156; Singh 1993:54)

The child's first attraction is to the mother's breast milk;
Second, to the recognition of the mother and father.
(*Vār Mājh* 2, *Ādi Granth* 137; Singh 1993:57)

The divine, giving birth to the human, has a bond with its offspring that many today wish to read as uniquely feminine. It is the womb from which we come, the breast at which we suckle. The bond between divine and human is like that between mother and child. Interpreters see the primacy of the female explicit in the second of the passages above, where our initial experience is of the mother. They see it also implicit in the mention of mother before father in numerous references like both of the above.

For interpreting the divine as mother, or mother as divine, the Sikh heritage offers a treasury of material useful in today's discussions of women's role in religion. Indeed, the Sikh sacred literature, comprising mainly poetry, has poetry's advantage of multiple meanings and associations. It speaks of the tangible things of everyday life, at the same time evoking a sense of the intangible and transcendent. Finding a perspective of God as feminine to be symbolically present in Sikh poetry is an option partly because poetry is multivalent.

A question is still open. Is such a reading compatible with the rest of Sikh theology? If, as Sikh thought holds, divinity is truly formless—if it is beyond the categories and images that we humans use to describe it—then it is beyond femininity as well. It may be useful to speak of God as mother, and also as father, when operating poetically or metaphorically, but God is beyond both when we speak of ultimates. Feminist consciousness may bring out for Sikhs a new awareness of the female, but classical Sikh doctrine already provides the resources for devotion to an ultimate reality that relativizes gender.

## Punjabi Sikhs and White Sikhs

In four centuries in India, the Sikh tradition developed from a mystical teacher's spiritual following into a structured religio-ethnic community. As such, it became a movement increasingly difficult or unlikely for an outsider to join. However, the heritage is not without its modern converts.

The family of Harbhajan Singh Puri (b. 1929) lived in the western Punjab before partition and then settled in Delhi. Puri worked as a customs officer at the New Delhi international airport, but quit in 1968 to take a job in Canada as a yoga instructor. On arrival in Toronto, he discovered that the position he had been promised had fallen through, but he was able to make his way to Los Angeles and find work there teaching yoga.

The times were ripe for religious exploration in America, and Puri was in step with the times. Instantly successful as a teacher, he organized a spiritual commune for a group of his students. He took the name Yogi Bhajan and promoted tantric yoga as 'Kundalini Yoga: The Yoga of Awareness'.

For his followers he laid out a discipline that he described as 'the healthy, happy, holy way of life', which included vegetarianism. He incorporated his movement as 3HO, that is, the Healthy, Happy, Holy Organization. As new chapters or ashrams were founded in North American cities, the experiential and lifestyle benefits of a meditational practice were the principal initial message.

Puri's background in the Sikh tradition surfaced as a second stage in the development of his leadership. He took eighty-four of his followers to Amritsar in 1971, where they were welcomed at the Akal Takht and where Puri was commended for his missionary activity. Back in North America, he now took the title Siri Singh Sahib, claiming he had received it from the SGPC. He succeeded in having his organization legally registered in 1973 as the Sikh Dharma Brotherhood, a religious organization that could ordain ministers so that the marriages they performed would be valid.

Puri's followers from the 1960s had come initially for tantric yoga, but most were ready to be persuaded that it was the essence of Sikh teaching. Sikh Dharma's members (with inclusive language, 'brotherhood' was dropped), male and female alike, wore white turbans, tunics, and tight trousers, with coloured cloth used at most for a sash, belt, or trim. Members kept their first names, used Singh as a middle name, and took Khalsa as a last name (they did this to reject Sikh clan or caste names, but since they were the only group to use 'Khalsa', it has come in effect to denote them as a caste). They lived and raised families in communal houses, spending long hours in chanting and meditation. Many, with good educational backgrounds, worked at white-collar jobs; all presented a disciplined and diligent image to the wider public. In several American and Canadian challenges to safety and uniform requirements, the white Sikhs of 3HO were recognized by government or regulatory agencies as legitimate Sikhs and granted the appropriate exemptions under the freedom of religion.

Acceptance by the mainstream population has not, however, meant entrée to the ethnic Sikh community of Punjabis who are in North America. In the Punjab it is unusual for Sikh women to wear turbans, and a sign of mourning for anybody but a Nāmdhārī to dress entirely in white. (In recent struggles white turbans have also been seen as a sign of sympathy with the policies of the Indian government.) Yoga seems more Hindu than Sikh and thus alarms Punjabis still attempting to assert the distinction between Sikhs and Hindus. And though the converts memorize some hymns in attempting to sing *kīrtan*, most lack any real ability to read the sacred texts. Harbhajan S. Puri (Yogi Bhajan, Siri Singh Sahib) is viewed as an entrepreneur more than as a spiritual teacher.

Initially, some Punjabi Sikhs were impressed by the strict Khālsā-style discipline of the converts and took imitation to be a sincere form of flattery, but before long, many kept an arm's-length distance from the '*gorā*' ('white') Sikhs, considering them pseudo-Sikhs. One is unlikely to see a single white turban when the Sikh community turns out by the thousands for a Baisakhi assembly in Toronto, though the local 3HO ashram is not far from where the 1992 assembly was held.

The presence of a small number of converts on the North American scene to a form of faith evoking the Sikh heritage illustrates for us that religious traditions continually diversify. Often a community's normative legislation for itself does not anticipate new cultural environments or challenges. Often a descriptive self-definition needs to be revised practically before its ink is dry. No one can predict with full certainty the specific form that the Sikh tradition will have in India or overseas a century from now, but it will surely still be bearing a witness of faith: in the eternal creator who is beyond all forms.

## KEY TERMS

**Akal Purakh**. 'Timeless Person', a principal description or name for God.

***amrit-dhārīs***. 'Nectar-bearers', fully initiated Sikhs, members of the Khālsā. Their induction rite includes sipping the beverage *amrit*, 'nectar of immortality'.

**Baisakhi**. An Indian New Year's day, observed by Sikhs around 13 May annually on a solar calendar. (Vesak for Buddhists follows a lunar date.)

***bāṇī***. The corpus of a particular *gurū*'s hymns contained within the *Ādi Granth*.

**gurdwara**. A Sikh house of worship, containing a prayer hall and housing a copy of the sacred scripture.

***gurmukhī***. The script devised for writing the hymns of the *Ādi Granth*. Its forms are similar to the *devanāgarī* used for Sanskrit and North Indian vernacular languages.

**Gurū**. The authoritative guide. Sikhs recognize guidance from God, from the succession of ten teachers beginning with Nānak, from the sacred scriptures, and from the community.

***Gurū Granth Sāhib***. Title for the *Ādi Granth*, a collection of devotional hymns, as authoritative sacred scripture.

**Harmandir Sāhib**. The temple at Amritsar, which was built under the fifth Gurū, Arjan. The name calls it the honoured temple of 'Hari', a Hindu manifestation of deity. It was gilded during the reign of Rañjīt Singh, the building is also called the Golden Temple.

**Ik Oṅkār**. 'The one *Oṃ*-expression', a designation of God. The words, written in the *gurmukhī* script, serve as a symbolic monogram.

***janam-sākhīs***. Traditional accounts of the life of Gurū Nānak.

***Jāp Sāhib***. A hymn of the tenth Gurū, Gobind Singh, a regular part of morning prayer.

***Japjī***. A prayer associated with the *mūl mantra* or creedal statement of the first Gurū, Nānak, also a regular part of morning prayer.

***kaṛāh prasād***. A food made of whole grain meal, sugar, and ghee or clarified butter, placed in the presence of the sacred book during prayer and then shared by the worshipping congregation.

**Khālsā**. The 'special' core of the Sikh community, organized along the lines of a military brotherhood by the tenth Gurū, Gobind Singh. Male initiates wear five marks of membership, including unshorn hair covered by a turban.

***kīrtan***. The singing of hymns from the scriptures in worship.

***laṅgar***. A kitchen attached to a gurdwara, producing meals in which all present are to share.

***mūl mantra***. A declaration of the eternity and transcendence of God, the creator, the wording of which is ascribed to Nānak's commissioning experience.

**_nām simaraṇ_**. 'Remembering the Name', a meditation on the character of God that together with *kīrtan* or hymn-singing is part of worship.

**Panth**. The Sikh community as the locus of religious commitment and consensus.

**_Rahit-nāmas_**. Manuals of the rules of faith and practice of the special community corps or Khālsā.

**_sahaj-dhāris_**. Sikh males who have always shaved and cut their hair, in contrast to *amrit-dhārī* or Khālsā Sikhs.

**Sants**. Ascetic holy men at the time of Gurū Nānak, many of whom spoke of divinity as beyond all forms or descriptions.

**Siṅgh Sabhā**. A revival movement among the Sikhs in the latter part of the nineteenth century that succeeded in defining the tradition more explicitly and strictly.

**_Vāhigurū_**. 'Hail to the Gurū', an expression that came to be used as a name for God.

## FURTHER READING


Cole. W.O., and P.S. Sambhi. 1978. *The Sikhs*. London: Routledge and Kegan Paul.

McLeod, W.H. 1968. *Guru Nanak and the Sikh Religion*. Oxford: Clarendon Press.

______. 1975. *The Evolution of the Sikh Community*. Delhi: Oxford University Press.

______. 1989. *Who Is a Sikh? The Problem of Sikh Identity*. Oxford: Clarendon Press.

______. 1991. *Popular Sikh Art*. Delhi: Oxford University Press.

Oberoi, H.S. 1993. *The Construction of Religious Bounderies: Culture, Identity, and Diversity in the Sikh Tradition*. Delhi: Oxford University Press.

O'Connell, J.T., M. Israel, and W.G. Oxtoby, eds. 1988. *Sikh History and Religion in the Twentieth Century*. Toronto: University of Toronto Centre for South Asian Studies.

Singh, K. 1963–6. *History of the Sikhs*, 2 vols. Princeton: Princeton University Press.

Singh, N.-G.K. 1993. *The Feminine Principle in the Sikh Vision of the Transcendent*. Cambridge: Cambridge University Press.

# REFERENCES

Kohli, S.S. 1987. 'Dasam Granth'. In *The Encyclopedia of Religion,* edited by M. Eliade, vol. 4:241–2. New York: Macmillan.

Macauliffe, M.A. 1909. *The Sikh Religion,* 6 vols. Oxford: Clarendon Press.

McLeod, W.H. 1984. *Textual Sources for the History of Sikhism.* Manchester: University of Manchester Press.

Singh, H., ed. 1992–. *The Encyclopaedia of Sikhism.* Patiala: Punjabi University.

Singh, N.-G.K. 1993. *The Feminine Principle in the Sikh Vision of the Transcendent.* Cambridge: Cambridge University Press.

# Key Dates

| | |
|---|---|
| c. 531 (or 589 or 413) BCE | Śākyamuni's enlightenment, followed forty-five years later by his *parinirvāṇa* or passing |
| c. 395 BCE | Council at Vaiśālī |
| c. 273 BCE | Accession of King Aśoka |
| c. 225 BCE | Mahendra takes Theravāda Buddhism to Sri Lanka |
| c. 100 CE | Emergence of Indian Mahāyāna, including Pure Land |
| c. 200 | Nāgārjuna, Mādhyamika philosopher |
| c. 350 | Asaṅga and Vasubandhu, Yogācāra philosophers |
| 372 | Introduction of Buddhism from China into Korea |
| d. 413 | Kumārajīva, translator of Mahāyāna texts into Chinese |
| c. 500 | Emergence of *tantra* in India |
| d. 597 | Chih-k'ai, founder of T'ien-t'ai in China |
| d. 622 | Prince Shōtoku, Japanese regent and patron of Buddhism |
| d. 712 | Fa-tsang, founder of Hua-yen in China |
| c. 750 | Padmasambhava takes Vajrayāna Buddhism to Tibet |
| d. 835 | Kūkai, bringer of Shingon (tantric) Buddhism to Japan |
| 845 | Persecution of Buddhism in China |
| d. 1262 | Shinran, Japanese Pure Land thinker |
| d. 1281 | Nichiren, Japanese sectarian Buddhist leader |
| 1603 | Start of Tokugawa regime, Japanese state control of Buddhism |
| c. 1617 | Dalai Lamas become rulers of Tibet |
| 1824 | Accession of Rama IV, reorganizer of Thai lineage |
| c. 1900 | Beginning of Buddhist missionary activity in the West |
| d. 1956 | B.R. Ambedkar, promoted Buddhism among low castes in India |
| 1959 | Chinese takeover of Tibet, destroying temples and monasteries; Dalai Lama and other Tibetans flee to India |
| 1963 | Thich Quang Doc's political protest suicide in Vietnam |

CHAPTER FOUR

# THE BUDDHIST TRADITION

ROY C. AMORE (southern Asia)
JULIA CHING (East Asia)

## OVERVIEW OF CONTEMPORARY BUDDHISM

'Everything that arises also passes away, so strive for what has not arisen.' With these last words to his disciples, Śākyamuni (the sage of the Śākya clan) passes into everlasting *nirvāṇa* almost two and a half millennia ago. He has become enlightened at thirty-five, and is thus known as the Buddha (i.e., 'the Enlightened One'). He has spent the next forty-five years teaching that all worldly things, including humans and human consciousness, are passing phenomena caught up in a process of arising and passing away. His teachings have 'set the wheel of *dharma* [teaching, truth] in motion', and he has instituted a religious order (*saṃgha*) with both ordained and lay divisions.

The Buddha charges his disciples to carry the *dharma* to all regions. Consequently, today there are millions of people who identify themselves as Buddhists. There are Buddhists in nearly every country in Europe, Asia, and North America. Buddhists form a high percentage of the population in many countries in South and Southeast Asia, and also in East Asia. Outside Asia, Buddhists are an important minority in Hawaii, mainly because of the Japanese-American population there. And in the land of its origin, India, Buddhism has all but disappeared. In this last respect, Buddhism's experience is like that of another major missionary religion, Christianity.

Buddhism as a worldwide religion reflects a vast diversity. In its patterns of teaching and practice, it is split into three major traditions or 'vehicles'. These include first the Theravāda (or, pejoratively, Hīnayāna), which spread from India to Southeast Asia and is dominant today in Sri Lanka, Myanmar, Thailand, Cambodia, and Laos. Second, there is the Mahāyāna, which spread from India to central and eastern Asia, and has a significant presence today in China, North and South Korea, Mongolia, Japan, Taiwan, Vietnam, and Singapore. A third tradition, which developed out of the Mahāyāna, is the Vajrayāna, found in Tibet, Bhutan, Nepal, and also Mongolia.

Buddhists today, as in the past, are divided by cultural, linguistic, and political boundaries. Nonetheless there is a common core to be found among all Buddhists regardless of language or vehicle. Buddhists are those who 'take refuge' in what they call the 'Triple Gem' or 'Three Jewels' or alternatively call the 'Three Refuges'. Buddhists pay respect to (1) the Buddha, (2) the *dharma* or Teaching, and (3) the *saṃgha* or Order of Disciples. In so doing, they dedicate themselves to following the path of the Buddha towards enlightenment. As they progress on the path, they seek to become more compassionate, more generous, more detached from worldly desires, more focused mentally, and especially more full of spiritual wisdom and purity.

**Table 4.1**
**Buddhist Vehicles and Schools**
**Discussed in This Survey**

1. Hīnayāna (the 'Little Vehicle',
   now dominant in Sri Lanka and Southeast Asia)
   - Eighteen third-century-BCE sects;
     of these, only Theravāda survives today
2. Mahāyāna (the 'Great Vehicle',
   now dominant in East Asia and Vietnam)
   - Mādhyamika in India, San-lun in China
   - Yogācāra in India, Fa-hsiang in China
   - T'ien-t'ai in China, Tendai in Japan
   - Hua-yen in China, Kegon in Japan
   - Shingon in Japan
   - Pure Land, Jōdo in Japan
   - Ch'an in China, Son in Korea, Zen in Japan
     - Lin-chi in China, Rinzai in Japan
     - Ts'ao-tung in China, Sōtō in Japan
   - Nichiren
3. Vajrayāna (the 'Diamond Vehicle',
   now dominant in Tibet and the Himalayas)
   - Gelugpa ('Yellow Hats')
   - Kargyu ('Red Hats')
   - Karma-pa ('Black Hats')

The regional distribution of Buddhism in Asia today can be said to reflect the development and diversification of the tradition over time. There is a substantial though by no means total correlation between the type of Buddhism that is found in different lands and the type that was dominant in India at the time of the spread of the tradition to those lands.

Theravāda Buddhism prevails in Sri Lanka and Southeast Asia. Missionaries reportedly began to go to these regions beginning in the third century BCE, in the time of Aśoka, before the emergence of Mahāyāna.

Following the emergence of Mahāyāna as a favoured teaching in northwestern India in about the first century, the principal form of Buddhist teaching that spread through Central Asia to China was Mahāyāna. After further development in China, this branch was carried to Korea and Japan and eventually also Vietnam.

The Tibetan tradition, often referred to as Vajrayāna, reflects the situation of Buddhism in northeastern India from the eighth century onward. By that time, Hindu thought and institutions largely prevailed over Buddhist ones in India. Vajrayāna Buddhism itself reflects the development of tantric Hinduism, with ritual techniques promoting the achievement of a privileged union by the practitioner.

Buddhism began and remains a monastic religion. Large monasteries still function as institutions of higher learning, where monks study the words of the *sūtras* and debate their meaning. With the increase in the number of monks as well as of lay adherents, Buddhism underwent some division. The major difference between the Theravāda or 'school of the elders' (sometimes pejoratively called Hīnayāna or 'Smaller Vehicle') and the Mahāyāna or 'Greater Vehicle' has to do with whether enlightenment or salvation is universally accessible. The Theravāda school teaches that salvation is difficult to attain, and quite impossible unless one embraces the monastic life; the Mahāyāna school teaches that all can become enlightened.

# THE BUDDHA AND HIS TEACHINGS

## Religious Life in Ancient India

One of the active centres of civilization 2,500 years ago was the plain of the river Ganga (Ganges) in northern India. In the Indian literature of the time, the area was known as the Middle Region because it lies halfway between the Bay of Bengal to the east and the Arabian Sea to the west. The name of the modern Indian state is Madhya Pradesh, meaning 'middle country'. Buddhist texts refer to the whole Indian subcontinent as Jambudvīpa, the 'Rose-apple Continent'; the rose-apple, a tropical fruit with a roselike fragrance, is still found in the markets of India.

During the seventh and sixth centuries BCE, this Middle Region underwent political transformation. A region with numerous small kingdoms and republics began consolidating into a region consisting of four large kingdoms. The economy of the region flourished; it enjoyed a rich agricultural base, with large estates owned by ruling-class landlords and worked by commoners and slaves, and it developed trade along a caravan route that crossed the Middle Region from east to west, and produced one of the world's first banking industries.

The emergence of the large kingdoms created great wealth as well as power among the ruling *kṣatriya* (warrior) class, as did the thriving trade for the merchant class. Furthermore, some members of the hereditary priestly class, the brahmins, owned land and also cattle, the traditional forms of wealth. While upper-class males held most power and influence, some upper-class women were well educated and also enjoyed wealth and prestige.

Hidden beneath the peace and prosperity were social and ideological divisions, however. There were tensions between the upper and lower classes, as we would expect, but the new money economy had created a large urban merchant class whose wealth and financial power outstripped its social status. The brahmin class, being more conservative, was critical of money-lending, and the ruling class looked down upon the merchants for being landless. The brahmins and *kṣatriya*s saw their high status as legitimated by the Hymn to the Supreme Person in the *Ṛg Veda*, which understood them to be the mouth and arms of the cosmic Person (see the chapter on the Hindu tradition).

In addition to the tension between the new urban rich and the traditional landed rich, the region had been assimilating an infusion of Aryan culture for some centuries. The *kṣatriya* and brahmin classes were the élite of an Aryan culture that had entered the region from farther west. Its language, pottery, marriage customs, and social conventions were new to the Middle Region.

Perhaps the most important cultural tension was between the brahmin priests and the traditional spirituality of the region. It is very difficult to prove that a distinct regional religious tradition did exist, because the written sources we now have are the products of the brahmin élite. However, linguistic and archaeological data lend support to the claim that the religion of the brahmins had been superimposed on the traditional spirituality of the region. An attempt to reconstruct the traditional religion of the area is important, for it forms the basis of two of the world's living religions, Buddhism and Jainism.

Along the Ganges were camps that served as the centres for various religious teachers. Many of the teachers were brahmins, but these open-air seminaries admitted non-brahmins as well. Only males were admitted, it seems, but later as Buddhism developed it instituted monastic orders for women as well as men. Each camp had its spiritual master, who laid down a discipline (*vinaya*) and a set of teachings (*dharma*). There were fierce rivalries among the masters as they competed for students and respect. The students of ancient India, perhaps like university students today, shopped around for teachers, looking for one who seemed to be superior in spiritual attainment, more astute in philosophical discourse on *dharma*, or perhaps less demanding in discipline.

There were areas of general agreement among the masters. All the students were required to take a vow of celibacy. There were dietary restrictions, the most common being the avoidance of meat eating on the grounds that killing animals caused them suffering. Most masters required their disciples to rise quite early and to spend many hours at manual labour (to sustain the camp) as well as at meditation and study. In short, these religious training camps were the forerunners of later monasteries, which play a large role in Buddhism and many other religions.

Students were expected to engage in ascetic practices. That is, they were expected to deny themselves bodily pleasures for the sake of spiritual development. Some of the ascetic practices were relatively mild, by their standards, such as standing or sitting in a fixed posture for several hours at a time, or fasting during full-moon days, or sleeping on the ground. Other practices were quite severe, such as exposing oneself to rain for long periods of time in the cool season, or standing naked in the sun for hours during the hot season, or piercing one's skin with metal objects, or going without food or water for very long periods of time.

The ethical values of the masters were rooted in the concept of *ahiṁsā*, non-harming or non-violence. The brahmin masters continued to make animal sacrifices as called for by their tradition, but some other masters took the ethic of *ahimsa* so seriously that they denounced even the sacrificial killing of animals. Some masters went so far as to require their disciples to wear cloth over their mouths and noses, and to strain their drinking water, in order to avoid even accidental killing of insects. The Jain leader Mahāvīra advocated these extreme forms of *ahiṁsā*.

Leaving the world of day-to-day concerns in favour of a path of spiritual pursuits, the disciples thought of themselves as having 'departed the world'. They were *śramaṇas* (disciples) and no longer 'householders' (laypersons). Their vows of celibacy and poverty could, however, be nullified if they chose to return to householder life.

Gods and goddesses played a surprisingly small role among these ascetic students along the ancient Ganges. People who held to the brahmin religious worldview worshipped the gods and goddesses of Hinduism. Among the non-brahmins there was a belief in various gods, especially the creator god Brahmā and the storm god Indra. We shall see that minor gods function somewhat like archangels in the Buddha's life story.

For the most part, though, the students followed a path that was based upon one's own efforts and not upon saving grace from a god or goddess. As an East Asian Zen Buddhist master put it much later, 'If there is anything to take hold of, you must take hold of it for yourself.' Basically, a spiritual master is the path maker, the one who goes on ahead, but the disciples have to walk the path themselves. One of the verses of the *Dhammapada*, a collection of verses that is a favourite of Buddhists everywhere, puts it this way: 'You must strive for yourselves. The Tathāgatas [*buddhas*] are only your guides. Meditative persons who follow their path will overcome the bonds of Māra [death]' (*Dhammapada*, no. 276).

So Buddhism did not originate in a vacuum but in the religious milieu of sixth-century-BCE India. Some features of Buddhism, as we shall see, represent innovations: a teaching of the impermanence of the human self or soul, for instance, and a notion of social egalitarianism. Other features of Buddhism were shared with Buddhism's Indian milieu. These include, for example, the idea that one is reborn in successive lives, the spiritual ideal of the ascetic who has withdrawn from household life, and the references to numerous gods, demons, and spirits in the narratives of folk tradition.

Among the students along the ancient Ganges was Siddhārtha Gautama, a prince from a small kingdom, in what is now southern Nepal, of a people called Śākya. Putting one's trust in the Buddha, as the first of the three 'gems' or 'refuges' of the Buddhist tradition, entails appreciating Siddhārtha's achievement as Śākyamuni, 'Śakyan sage', and as Samyaksambuddha, a 'fully enlightened person'.

## First of the Three Gems, the Buddha

### *The Bodhisattva Vow and Previous Lives*

The Buddhist view of the cosmos is that universes arise and pass away in endless succession. Our current universe, having evolved long ago, moves through major periods of time, just as have all the others. These great eras can last for centuries, but things slowly tend to expand and stabilize, then decline and disappear as an era unfolds. For example, the human life span and human morality are declining in our age.

The law of *karma* (actions) causes living creatures to be reborn again and again, for better or worse according to their good or bad moral conduct. Whenever morality and truth, that is, *dharma*, have declined badly, a new highly developed being is born and becomes the *buddha* for that era. (Compare the *Bhagavad Gītā*, in which the lord Kṛṣṇa explains that he comes down to save the earth when *dharma* has declined.)

Although many Buddhists believe in gods and spirits, no almighty God is needed to mastermind the appearance of a new *buddha*. The highly developed being who becomes the new *buddha* is aware of the needs of the world and knows when to be reborn. Buddhists tell the story of Gautama Buddha, or Śākyamuni, as the Buddha for our era, with the understanding that there have been *buddhas* in previous eras and there will be *buddhas* in subsequent ones. We shall see later that some Mahāyāna Buddhists venerate a *buddha* of a previous age, named Amida, and that Buddhists look to Maitreya as the *buddha* to come in the next era.

Although each era is considered to have only one fully enlightened, teaching *buddha*, there are numerous beings in each era thought to have achieved some degree of enlightenment. They are known by such titles as *arhats* ('worthy ones', frequently translated as 'saints'), *bodhisattvas*, or *pratyeka buddhas* (enlightened hermits who do not teach others).

The Buddhist traditions all agree that Śākyamuni lived to the age of eighty, but scholars are not certain when he lived. In Sri Lanka and Southeast Asia he is dated at 624–544 BCE, while Indian and Western Buddhologists correlating the Buddhist chronicles with Greek evidence date him at 566–486 BCE or, according to some scholars, 563–483 BCE. Meanwhile, Japanese scholars, relying on Chinese and Tibetan texts, have adopted the dates of 448–368 BCE.

Significantly, Śākyamuni achieves enlightenment through his own reflective and meditative efforts. He has, however, nearly perfected his 'mind of enlightenment' through hundreds of previous lives. Unlike Hindu or Christian notions of incarnation as the manifestation of deity in a human life, the Buddha, Śākyamuni, is not a god on earth but simply a human being who has perfected the spiritual potential of all living creatures. What is special and transhuman about the Buddha's enlightenment does not reside in the quality of his body or of his personality so much as it does in the spiritual and intellectual power of his insight. That manifestation of power, power to free people from entrapment in suffering, is what Buddhists have in mind when they say that they take refuge in the Buddha.

Before we relate the narrative of Śākyamuni, we must clarify an item of terminology. Usage distinguishes between a *buddha* as an already enlightened being and a *bodhisattva* as one who is still on the path to enlightenment, who has vowed to become enlightened. Thus for the period of his younger years in quest of enlightenment, Siddhārtha is termed a *bodhisattva*, but in his mature teaching following his enlightenment, he is referred to as the Buddha. In this chapter we shall refer to Śākyamuni as 'the Buddha' (capitalized), but to any other enlightened being as 'a *buddha*' (italicized).

The story of the Buddha, as Buddhists tell it, has its beginning in earlier ages. During the lifetime of one previous *buddha*, a young man comes upon a crowd of people filling mud holes in the road in anticipation of the arrival of the *buddha* of that era. But the *buddha* comes before one mud hole is filled, and so the young man puts himself into the hole for the *buddha* to use him as a stepping-stone. Rather than stepping on him, the *buddha* pronounces that the young man will become a *buddha* in the distant future.

The young man takes the startling prophecy to heart and vows to work towards full enlightenment. The act of solemnly promising to work towards buddhahood is called taking a *bodhisattva* vow. The term *bodhi* in the first part of the compound means 'enlightenment', and *sattva* means 'being', as in the phrase 'human being'. A *bodhisattva* is a person who has vowed to become a *buddha*. (One of the characteristics of Mahāyāna Buddhism, as we shall learn, is to encourage all Buddhists to take a *bodhisattva* vow.) After the young man in our story dies, his *karma* complex, that is, the matrix of his past actions, gives rise to a new being. Simply put, he is reborn, as are all living beings. Over many lives he makes progress towards purifying his inner nature. Stories of over 500 of his lives are preserved in the Buddhist text called *Jātaka*, meaning 'birth stories'.

The last *Jātaka* story is the best known and most loved among Buddhists. Here the *bodhisattva* is reborn as a prince named Vessantara. The young *bodhisattva* decides to use this particular life to work towards the perfection of generosity, so he takes a vow to give away anything he has if asked to do so. This is relatively harmless to others while he is a child, but when his father retires and turns the throne over to him, following an old royal custom of India, the trouble starts. No one complains much that he gives food and clothes from the public treasury to the poor, for righteous kings are expected to provide for the poor in the kingdom, but when Vessantara gives away the crown jewels to brahmins, who are already rich, people complain. Finally a taxpayer revolt breaks out when he gives away large amounts of jewellery and even the kingdom's lucky white elephant to citizens of a rival kingdom. The people demand that his father resume the throne and that Vessantara be exiled. In exile he continues to give away anything requested, even his wife and children. In the end, he is reunited with his family and again becomes king, and we learn that the gods have been guiding the events to provide him with the opportunity to test his resolve. Vessantara's strict adherence to his vow provides a model for Buddhist self-discipline.

### *Siddhārtha's Birth and Childhood*

When Vessantara dies, his *karma* complex gives rise to a being in one of the layers of heaven, where he waits until the earth needs a new *buddha*. The idea is that a new *buddha* comes only well after the *dharma* or teaching of the previous *buddha* has been lost. At such a time, a new 'wheel-turner' is needed to set the wheel of *dharma* (termed the *dharmacakra*) rolling once again. So, because the world needs him, he chooses his prospective class, parents, birth date, and so on. The story of the birth and subsequent childhood events varies to some extent among the Buddhist traditions. Here we tell the story very briefly, following the account preserved in the Pali writings of the Theravāda tradition. In general, the versions of the story written in later centuries tend to be longer and recount many more miracles associated with the events.

According to the story, Queen Mahamaya, his prospective mother, is napping one afternoon during a festival when she dreams that the four world-protectors carry her and her bed to a pleasant grove of trees. (The world-protectors are gods who look after the earth, one in each direction. Although Buddhists do not attribute a significant role to any god in the process of enlightenment, they do think of minor gods such as the world-protectors as active in the unfolding of events.)

In the grove, her dream continues, a spiritual being in the form of a white elephant—albino elephants being considered sacred and a source of good fortune—descends from the heavens and miraculously enters through her side, becoming the embryo of the *bodhisattva*, of the Buddha-to-be. This is not a normal conception because she has kept a strict vow of sexual abstinence in observance of the festival.

Certain miraculous events surround the pregnancy. For example, Mahamaya does not get tired, and she can see the child within her womb. When it is nearly time to give birth, Mahamaya travels towards her home city, but actually gives birth *en route*, while holding onto a branch of a tree in a park. Later Buddhist stories hold that the tree miraculously lowers its branch to assist her, that flowers appear out of season, and that hot and cold streams of water rain down from the sky to wash the baby.

The birth occurs on the full-moon day of the month Vaiśākha ('rains'), which usually falls in May of the Western calendar. A bright light is said to illuminate the world that night, to mark the holy event. We note that in the ancient world, the birth of special persons was often seen as marked by astral events, such as a bright light or an auspicious alignment of a constellation with the planets.

It is interesting to compare the birth stories of Buddha and Jesus. Both are conceived asexually, without normal human intercourse. Buddha's mother is married, but is under a vow of celibacy, whereas Mary is said to be an unwed virgin. Both infants are born outside the house, Jesus in a stable and Buddha in a grove. A bright light announces both births, and sages forecast their future greatness. Also, angels appear in the sky to announce the births, to shepherds in the case of Jesus and to a meditating sage in the Buddhist case.

The *bodhisattva* is presented to the father, King Śuddhodana, who soon holds a naming festival. He names the child Siddhārtha, which refers to achieving success or prosperity. But Buddhists do not make much use of this childhood name. They prefer the names that derive from his later accomplishments, such as Śākyamuni or (Lord) Buddha.

During the naming ceremony, various brahmins offer predictions about the child based upon their reading of his bodily signs. Later Buddhist texts say that he has thirty-two major bodily signs and over eighty minor ones. Some of the more important major ones can be seen in the Buddha statues that became popular about 500 years later. His unusually long ear lobes are a sign of great spiritual wisdom, his golden complexion shows his inner calmness, and the wheel patterns on the soles of his feet suggest his role as a wheel-turner. On the basis of such signs, the brahmins predict that he will be outstanding. If he stays 'in the world', he will be destined to become a great emperor, ruling far more than the little Śākya kingdom. But, if he 'departs the world', he will reach the highest achievement of a monk, becoming a fully enlightened *buddha*.

His father, the king, wants Siddhārtha to become a great emperor, so he orders that no evidence of sickness, old age, or death be allowed near the boy. Being sheltered from life's inevitable suffering might prevent the boy from becoming a monk. Evidently the early Buddhists, in relating this story, presumed what some modern interpreters have also argued: that religious involvement arises as a response to the adversities of human life, and that if life posed no problems, there would be little impetus to become serious about religious matters. The Buddhist narrative stresses the youth's pampered life.

> I was delicate, most delicate, supremely delicate. Lily pools were made for me at my father's house solely for my benefit. Blue lilies flowered in one, white lilies in another, red lilies in a third.
>
> I had three palaces; one for the Winter, one for the Summer and one for the Rains (*Aṅguttara Nikāya* iii.38; Ñāṇamoli 1972:8).

Only a few childhood events are recorded. One claim is that the young *bodhisattva* amazes his first teacher because he already knows the various alphabets. Another is that he wins a martial arts tournament held at court for warrior boys his age, even though he has shown little interest in war. The event of most significance is described quite simply by the Buddha in one text. He relates that one time when he was young, he entered a meditational trance state while sitting in the shade of a rose-apple tree as his father ploughed. Buddhists understand the ploughing to be part of the spring ground-breaking ceremony, and while he is in the meditational trance the shadow of the tree miraculously stands still even though the sun moves. We shall see that his memory of this wakeful meditation state plays a role in his achievement of enlightenment.

### *The Four Sights and Great Departure*

King Śuddhodana's plan backfires. Though he protects the prince from life's great sorrows for years, the bitter truth must come out. It happens when Siddhārtha is about twenty-nine. By then he has been happily married and is father to a son named Rāhula.

Going for a chariot ride through the royal park, the prince happens to see the four great sights that will alter the course of his life. The first three sights are negative. He sees a sick man, an old (suffering) man, and a dead man. His chariot driver gives him straight answers when he asks about these three. He credits these three sights with overcoming his vanity of youth, health, and life. His statements on all three run along these lines:

> When an untaught ordinary man, who is subject to sickness, not safe from sickness, sees another who is sick, he is shocked, humiliated and disgusted; for he forgets that he himself is no exception. But I too am subject to sickness, not safe from sickness, and so it cannot befit me to be shocked, humiliated and disgusted on seeing another who is sick. When I considered this, the vanity of health entirely left me (*Anguttara Nikāya* iii. 38; Ñāṇamoli 1972:8).

Then he sees a monk, whose calmness and detachment from the world suggest to him a path for overcoming suffering. To this day, Buddhist monks often say that what first attracted them to join the *saṃgha* (the monastic order) was seeing, as children, the calmness and serenity of the older monks and nuns going through the streets for alms.

The *bodhisattva* returns to the palace, where he ponders the four sights. That night he flees the palace, along with his horse and servant and with the help of the four world-protectors. Buddhist temples often have a mural depicting this event, called the Great Departure.

Having departed the worldly life, the *bodhisattva* dismisses his servant and horse, exchanges his princely clothes with a poor hunter, obtains an alms bowl, and begins living the life of a wandering student seeking spiritual truth. He travels south towards the Ganges, bent on achieving all eight of classical yoga's levels of concentration. He chooses a yoga teacher and soon accomplishes the six levels of yogic trance known to the teacher. He then switches to a teacher who has mastery of the seventh level as well, but even achieving the deep tranquillity of the seventh level is not satisfactory to the thirty-year-old *bodhisattva*.

So he undertakes an independent program of very strict ascetic practices. He reportedly stands in the cold rain and hot sun and follows the other extreme practices of the Ganges area. Most of all, he excels in the discipline of fasting. He claims to have lived for a long period of time on only one palmful of water and one of food per day. Doing this, he becomes extremely thin and loses consciousness at least once due to his weak condition. However, the four world-protectors look after him. Statues of the *bodhisattva* during this period of emaciation may be seen in some temples, even though such severe fasting was later denounced by the Buddha.

### *Enlightenment*

The *bodhisattva* is now at a loss for a way to achieve the spiritual breakthrough for which he has been striving for several years—or, Buddhists might say, for the previous 500 or more lives. He has tried yoga and found it good but not appropriate to his needs. He has done ascetic practices with great zeal for six years, without a breakthrough.

Ceasing to torture himself with ascetic practices, he resumes eating and drinking. Then he remembers the wakeful meditational trance he had experienced spontaneously as a child under the rose-apple tree.

> I thought of a time when my Sakyan father was working and I was sitting in the cool shade of a rose-apple tree: quite secluded from sensual desires, secluded from unprofitable things I had entered upon and abode in the first meditation, which is accompanied by thinking and exploring with happiness and pleasure born of seclusion. I thought: Might that be the way to enlightenment? Then, following up that memory there came the recognition that this was the way to enlightenment (*Majjhima Nikāya*; Ñāṇamoli 1972:21).

Trying this method, he chooses a pleasant spot beside a cooling river and meditates under a *pīpal* tree, a variety of large fig tree considered sacred in India at least as far back as the Harappa civilization. As he sits, he vows that he will not get up until he has achieved *nirvāṇa*.

According to some versions of the story, it is at this point, just before dusk on the evening of the full-moon day in the month of Vaiśākha (Vesak), that Māra, the lord of death, comes to tempt him. Māra plays a role in Buddhism somewhat like Satan's in Christianity. Māra's main function is to come for people at death and oversee their rebirth in an appropriate place. But Māra thinks of himself as somehow lord of the earth, and by his superhuman powers he knows that the *bodhisattva* is sitting at a special place on a decisive occasion.

Māra tries to get the *bodhisattva* to move. To tempt him to give up his mission, Māra first sends his daughters, whose names suggest psychological forces such as greed and boredom and desire. When that fails, Māra offers him any worldly wish if only he will go back home and live a life of good *karma* (merit) as a householder. The *bodhisattva* refuses.

Now Māra becomes violent. He sends in his sons to attack him. Their names suggest negative psychological powers, such as fear and anger. The *bodhisattva*'s spiritual power is so great, however, that it protects him from the attack.

Having failed in his efforts to tempt and threaten the *bodhisattva*, Māra challenges him to a debate. Māra himself claims to be the one worthy to sit on the Bodhi Seat on this auspicious night and accuses the *bodhisattva* of being unworthy. In ancient debates, it would seem, the audience's cheering determined the winner of the debate, and so Māra gains the upper hand when his daughters and sons yell support for him. Māra then presses his advantage, thinking that the *bodhisattva* has no one present to lend him support.

At this point, the *bodhisattva* works a miracle by the power of his great merit and by having truth on his side. Miracles worked by such 'acts of truth' are a feature of Hindu stories as well. In this case, the *bodhisattva* claims to be the one with generosity, courage, wisdom, and so forth, perfected through countless previous lives. He calls upon the Earth herself (conceived of as feminine in Indian tradition) as a witness on his behalf. The resulting earthquake is powerful enough to drive Māra away.

Buddhists of an earlier time may have taken this temptation story literally, but many Buddhists today understand it symbolically as the surfacing of the last remnants of the mind's deep impurities, which the *bodhisattva* must overcome.

With Māra defeated, the *bodhisattva* begins to meditate in his own way, the reverse of the yoga trances he has been taught. A yogi goes deeper and deeper into levels of unconsciousness, drawing in the consciousness as a turtle draws in its head and limbs and in a sense shutting out the world. But the *bodhisattva* meditates to become more conscious, more aware, more mindful. Some today would call his method an 'upper' in contrast to a 'downer'.

In ancient India, the soldiers divided the night into three watches, and this term shows up in Buddhism. During the first watch, the *bodhisattva* remembers his own past lives. The ability to do this is considered one of the psychic powers of a spiritually advanced person in Buddhism, but one should not make it a goal in itself. During the second watch, he has an insight into the working of the law of *karma*. He has known about *karma* before, but now he *sees* the past lives of various other people, noting that evil deeds in one life lead to a bad rebirth, and so forth.

During the third watch of the night, he turns his awareness to understanding how to put an end to suffering. In due course he comes to see the Four Noble Truths, which we will discuss later.

Just before dawn, the *bodhisattva* enters a state of complete awareness, of total insight into the nature of reality, called *bodhi*. After hundreds of lives, he has fulfilled his *bodhisattva* vow. He is no longer a being (*sattva*) striving for *bodhi*; he is now a *buddha*, a 'fully enlightened one': 'I had direct knowledge. Birth is exhausted, the Holy Life has been lived out, what was to be done is done, there is no more of this to come' (*Majjhima Nikāya*; Ñāṇamoli 1972:25).

He now also has earned the title Tathāgata ('the thus-gone one'), meaning that he has completed the pattern that a fully enlightened holy one must follow. In the Buddhist texts the Buddha usually uses the title Tathāgata when referring to himself. For example: 'Whatever a Tathāgata utters, speaks, and proclaims between the day of his enlightenment and the day he dies, all that is factual, not otherwise, and that is why he is called "Tathāgata"' (*Anguttara Nikaya* ii.22; Dhammika 1989:50).

In the effort to understand Buddhist teaching, one has to get accustomed to many terms, including those in the Sanskrit language. Sometimes several terms denote virtually the same thing, such as enlightenment (*bodhi*) and *nirvāṇa*, with the nuance being that *nirvāṇa* refers to a final and definitive enlightenment. Other words, like 'liberation' and 'buddhahood', have basically the same meaning as well.

There are several ways to describe the new Buddha's momentous achievement. The most common way is to say that he achieved or experienced *nirvāṇa*. The etymology of the word *nirvāṇa* is controversial, as there are both positive and negative connotations to the term. Put in negative terms, on the one hand, *nirvāṇa* has the sense of 'putting out the fire', where the fire is the three evil roots of the deep consciousness—greed, hatred, and delusion.

On the other hand, the positive meaning of the term *nirvāṇa* is the experience of transcendental happiness. A poem, by one of the early Buddhist ordained women named Patacāra, expresses how the positive and negative meanings of *nirvāṇa* (*nibbāna* in Pali) go together, in that perfect happiness comes when one's evil desires have been extinguished.

> With ploughshares ploughing up the fields, with seed
> Sown in the breast of earth, men win their crops,
> Enjoy their gains and nourish wife and child.
> Why cannot I, whose life is pure, who seek
> To do the Master's will, no sluggard am,
> Nor puffed up, win Nibbana's bliss?
>
> One day, bathing my feet, I sit and watch
> The water as it trickles down the slope.
> Thereby I set my heart in steadfastness,
> As one doth train a horse of noble breed.
> Then going to my cell, I take my lamp,
> And seated on my couch I watch the flame.
> Grasping the pin, I pull the wick right down
> Into the oil ...
> Lo! the Nibbana of the little lamp!
> Emancipation dawns! My heart is free!
> (Rhys Davids 1964:73)

The Buddha considers the experience and reflects on whether or not enlightenment is teachable. Is it possible to help others achieve a breakthrough? The answer is yes, and so at thirty-five years of age, the new Buddha begins a teaching career motivated by his great compassion for all living beings. Some versions of the account describe the creator god Brahmā coming to encourage the Buddha to teach.

### *Setting the Wheel in Motion*

The newly enlightened Buddha's first concern is to seek out and teach his two former yoga teachers, but through his psychic powers he perceives that both have died. So Śākyamuni decides to begin by teaching five students who have been his friends during his period of ascetic practices. Again using clairvoyance, he determines that they are staying at the deer park outside of Banaras. On his journey towards Banaras, two merchants, sometimes said to be Burmese, pay respect to the newly enlightened Buddha and offer him food.

One can say that institutional Buddhism begins with this act, for the tradition is marked by a reciprocity of giving. The laypeople give gifts of material support (food, medicine, robes, and the like), while the ordained Buddhists give spiritual gifts (the *dharma*, advice, chanting, and so on). This pattern is central to all forms of Buddhism to the present day.

Upon arriving at the deer park, the Buddha is at first shunned by his five friends because he has abandoned the hard ascetic practices they so value, but when they see his aura, to use a Western word, they realize that he has attained *nirvāṇa*, and ask to know how he did it. The reply is known, in its short form, as his 'first sermon', but Buddhists usually refer to it in its longer form, the 'Wheel-turning Sermon' (or discourse). The Wheel of true *dharma*, as taught by the previous *buddha*, needed to be set in motion once more for the benefit of all living creatures.

The discourse is also called the 'Instruction on the Middle Path' because the Buddha begins by telling the five ascetics that the proper way to treat one's body is to follow a path of moderation between indulgence and asceticism. Buddha says that while he lived the life of a pampered prince, there was no spiritual development. Likewise, all of his ascetic self-torturing gained him little, but after he began to eat, drink, and sleep in moderation, he made progress.

In the later development of Buddhist thought, this principle of moderation was broadened into a general ethic of the Middle Way. It holds that in all material things 'enough is better than too much'. As we shall see, the principle was also applied to Buddhist philosophy. Some Buddhist interpreters have considered it so central that they have referred to Buddhism itself simply as 'the Middle Way'.

Having told the five first disciples to abandon their ascetic practices, the Buddha instructs them. He articulates the Four Noble Truths, which state in a nutshell how suffering is caused and can be overcome. He details the Eightfold Path, spelling out the means for overcoming suffering. After a few days of instruction, the disciples are formally accepted and sent forth to teach *dharma* to others. The number of ordained disciples grows quite rapidly.

### *Entering parinirvāṇa*

The Buddha travels throughout the four countries of the Middle Region during the next forty-five years. He ordains hundreds of disciples and accepts thousands of lay followers, including members of his own family and the kings of the region, but not everything is perfect. His cousin Devadatta leads a group of dissident disciples in revolt, and there is an attempt on his life.

His body is getting weak as he reaches eighty, but he continues to travel. As he travels through one region, a leader of a local tribal group invites him and the disciples travelling with him to a meal. The Buddha notices that one of the dishes, made from a particularly pungent local mushroom, is going bad. So he tells the host to serve it only to him, not to his disciples, and then bury the rest. This dish gives him severe dysentery and later leads to his death. Before dying, the Compassionate One tells his disciples not to blame the host, who meant well, for the illness. They ask whom they should follow if he dies, and he tells them to follow the *dharma*. This means that in Buddhist doctrine overall, no individual has the status of absolute authority. There are, however, supreme leaders in particular countries or traditions, the most famous being the Tibetan Dalai Lama.

After giving his final instructions to his disciples, the Buddha meditates up through the eight yoga stages, back down through them, and then back up through the first four. From this point, he is said to experience *parinirvāṇa*: the complete ending of rebirth, the total cessation of suffering, the perfection of happiness. Between the time of his enlightenment and his death, he has been in the state known as '*nirvāṇa* with remainder', that is, the level of *nirvāṇa* possible for one still living as a human.

But upon dying, he enters the *parinirvāṇa* state of '*nirvāṇa* without remainder'. Buddhism refuses to elaborate on this state. It dismisses as unanswerable questions such as 'Where did Buddha go?' or 'What exactly was it that entered *nirvāṇa*?' But it would be a distortion of Buddhism to say the Buddha became extinct or ceased to exist. The reality of *nirvāṇa* and the possibility of its achievement by all living beings are fundamental to Buddhism, although descriptions of *nirvāṇa* escape human understanding.

## Second of the Three Gems, the *dharma*

> Avoid doing all evil deeds,
> cultivate doing good deeds,
> and purify the mind—
> this is the teaching of all buddhas.
> (*Dhammapada* 183)

Taking refuge in the *dharma* implies for Buddhists a reliance on the order of things as articulated in the Buddha's teaching. *Dharma* is a central organizing concept in Buddhist thought, and the range of its meanings and associations has extended considerably beyond the meaning of *dharma* in the Hindu milieu in which Buddhism arose.

As background to a Buddhist understanding of *dharma*, one should recall that in classical Indian culture generally, *dharma* has the sense of social and moral obligation. The *Bhagavad Gītā*, for instance, presumes that one's *dharma* is the

## The *Dhammapada*

*[The* Dhammapada *is a collection of poems drawn from various talks given by the Buddha. Chapter One contains couplets about developing a pure mind.]*

1. The mind is the source of all mental actions [*dharmas*],
mind is the chief of the mental actions, and they are made by the mind.
If, by an impure mind, one speaks or acts,
then suffering follows the mind as a cartwheel follows the footprint of the ox.
2. The mind is the source of all mental states,
mind is their leader, and they are made by the mind.
If, by a pure mind, one speaks or acts,
then happiness follows the mind like a shadow.
3. 'I was abused.' 'I was beaten.' 'I was hurt.' 'I was robbed.'
Those who dwell excessively on such thoughts never get out of their hating state of mind.
4. 'I was abused.' 'I was beaten.' 'I was hurt.' 'I was robbed.'
Those who leave such thoughts behind get out of their hating state of mind.
5. In this world hatreds are never ended by more hating.
Hatreds are only ended by loving kindness.
This is an eternal truth [*dharma*].
6. Some people do not know that we must restrain ourselves.
But others know this and settle their quarrels.
7. One who dwells on personal gratifications, overindulges the senses, overeats, is indolent and lazy,
that person is overthrown by Mara [Death] like an old, weak tree in a windstorm.
8. One who dwells in meditation on the bodily impurities, keeps the senses under control, eats moderately, has faith and disciplined energy,
that person stands against Mara like a rocky mountain.
9. Whoever puts on the ochre robe but lacks purity, self-control, and truthfulness,
that person is not worthy of the robe.
10. Whoever puts on the ochre robe and is pure, self-controlled, and truthful,
that person is truly worthy of the robe.
11. Mistaking the unessential for the important,
and mistaking the essential for the unimportant,
some persons, dwelling in wrong-mindedness,
never realize that which is really essential.
12. Knowing the essential to be important,
and knowing the unessential to be unimportant,
other persons, dwelling in right-mindedness,
reach that which is really essential.

> **ITIVUTTAKA**
>
> Even if one should seize the hem of my robe and walk step by step behind me, if he is covetous in his desires, fierce in his longings, malevolent of heart, with corrupt mind, careless and unrestrained, noisy and distracted and with sense uncontrolled, he is far from me. And why? He does not see the Dhamma, and not seeing the Dhamma, he does not see me. Even if one lives a hundred miles away, if he is not covetous in his desires, not fierce in his longings, with a kind heart and pure mind, mindful, composed, calmed, one-pointed and with senses restrained, then indeed, he is near to me and I am near to him. And why? He sees the Dhamma, and seeing the Dhamma, sees me (Dhammika 1989:49–50).

duty appropriate to the caste and the life situation into which one is born. The *dharmaśāstras* are law codes governing the conduct of Hindu society.

It should be no surprise, then, that translators of Buddhist texts sometimes choose 'law' as the equivalent for *dharma*, but Buddhist usage reflects the root meaning of the word *dharma*: 'that which holds'. The Sanskrit term *dharma* is related to Latin *firma*, and so in English we could understand *dharma* to mean 'the teachings that are firm', that is, eternal truths. For Buddhists, these eternal truths apply to many realms, including the laws of nature, the reality of spiritual forces such as *karma*, and the rules of moral conduct or duty.

Buddhists attribute to Śākyamuni the definitive understanding of these matters, something then studied, cited, and systematized by generations of thinkers. The Buddha delivers a penetrating insight into how things are, and he spells out a program of how people can bring their attitudes and actions into line with them. Some Buddhist teachers use medical imagery, suggesting that the Four Noble Truths diagnose the human predicament, with the Eightfold Path being the prescribed therapy.

### *The Four Noble Truths*

- The first truth is that suffering (*duḥkha*) is inevitable for living beings. This means not that everything is suffering, but that no one can escape suffering sooner or later. Birth, sickness, senility, and death are all occasions of suffering and pain. And there is the psychological grief that comes from the loss of loved ones, the experience of failing, and so forth. All these and other aspects of the human predicament are summed up in this 'truth of suffering'.

- The second is the truth of the origin of suffering, which sees that suffering arises from *tṛṣṇā* ('desire', 'craving'). For this reason, the second truth may also be called the truth of craving.
- The third is the truth of cessation, which sees that it would be possible to end suffering totally if desires ceased.
- The fourth is the truth of the Eightfold Path, which lays down eight areas of self-improvement to be undertaken. The eight are not to be taken in order, like climbing a ladder, but must be developed in concord, like the petals of a flower opening together and blossoming.

### *The Eightfold Path*

The eight areas for self-improvement are: right view, right thought, right speech, right conduct, right livelihood, right effort, right mindfulness, and right meditation. In this list, 'right view' (or right understanding) refers mainly to properly grasping the Four Noble Truths. 'Right thought', by contrast, means freeing the mind from sensuous desire, ill-will, and cruelty.

### *The Characteristics of Existence*

Existence has three marks or characteristics, according to the Buddhist *dharma*: suffering, impermanence, and no-soul.

Suffering as a characteristic of existence is what is referred to by the Four Noble Truths. We experience all sorts of pain and deprivation, physical and psychological. Some Buddhist interpreters classify and catalogue the varieties of human suffering in detailed ways.

The characteristic of impermanence refers to the passing nature of all things. Remember the last words of the Buddha with which we began: 'Everything that arises also passes away, so strive for what has not arisen.' All things, other than empty space and *nirvāṇa*, are best seen as in process rather than as static entities. In contrast with some philosophies, both in India and the West, where permanence is attributed to what is valued most highly, Buddhist thought treats change as a fact rather than as a problem.

The no-soul characteristic applies the notion of impermanence to humans as well. The Sanskrit term *anātman* means 'without *ātman*', but what is *ātman*? In the Hindu *Upaniṣads*, some of which were composed around 500 BCE, about the time of Śākyamuni, *ātman* means the eternal self or soul in humans. Through religious awareness, *ātman* is apprehended as related to Brahman, the underlying energy of the universe. For many Hindus, the innermost self is the most stable and abidingly real feature of a person because it participates in the reality of the universe.

To this teaching, which was current at the time he lived, the Buddha proposed a striking and sharply contrasting alternative. Buddhists deny that any such eternal, unchanging self exists. The importance of this for Buddhists is not

## QUESTIONS OF KING MILINDA

*[A legacy of the military campaigns of Alexander the Great in the late fourth century* BCE *was a number of Greek-derived regimes in eastern Iran and northwestern India over several succeeding centuries. These may have been the 'Yavanas' (presumably 'Ionians') to whom King Aśoka, a convert to Buddhism, reports having sent missions. The following text depicts a situation, real or imagined, in which a king inquires into Buddhist teaching. Scholars take his name to be an Indian rendering of the Greek name Menander.]*

Now Milinda the king went up to where the venerable Nāgasena was, and addressed him with the greetings and compliments of friendship and courtesy, and took his seat respectfully apart.

And Milinda began by asking, 'How is your Reverence known, and what, Sir, is your name?'

'I am known as Nāgasena, O king. But although parents, O king, give such a name as Nāgasena … [it] is only a generally understood term, a designation in common use. For there is no permanent individuality (no soul) involved in the matter.'

'If, most reverend Nāgasena, there is no permanent individuality (no soul) involved in the matter, who is it, pray, who gives to you members of the Order your robes and food and lodging and necessaries for the sick? Who is it who enjoys such things when given? Who is it who lives a life of righteousness?'

'You tell me that your brethren in the Order are in the habit of addressing you as Nāgasena. Now what is that Nāgasena? Do you mean to say that the hair is Nāgasena?'

'I don't say that, great king.'

'Or is it the nails, the teeth, the skin, the flesh, the nerves, the bones … or any of these that is Nāgasena?'

And to each of these he answered no.

so much to deny Hindu teachings as it is to reject selfishness. The no-soul characteristic of existence means that one should not think of things as 'mine', for there is no 'my'.

The Buddhist teaching of *anātman* does not mean that there is 'no person' or 'no personality' in the ordinary English sense of those terms. Buddhist teachings about the self, in fact, go into extensive detail about the *skandhas* or components of personality. They stress that personality can be the product of shifting, arbitrary, and fluid circumstance; personality is more modular than integral. In that respect, Buddhist notions of personality resemble modern Western psychological theory far more than they do either Hindu or Western religious notions of an eternal soul. What Buddhist personality theory implies is that wise people, realizing the impermanence of all things including themselves, should not become emotionally attached to things. Wise people are detached from both material goods and images of themselves.

'Is it the outward form then (*rūpa*) that is Nāgasena, or the sensations, or the ideas, or the confections, or the consciousness, that is Nāgasena?'

And to each of these he answered no.

'Then is it all these *skandhas* [physical and mental 'heaps' or processes] combined that are Nāgasena?

'No! great king.'

'But is there anything outside the five *skandhas* that is Nāgasena?'

And he still answered no.

'Who then is the Nāgasena we see before us?'

'... if you came in a chariot, explain to me what that is. Is it the pole that is the chariot?'

'I did not say that.'

'Is it the wheels, or the framework .. ?'

'Certainly not.'

'Then is it all these parts that are the chariot?'

'No, Sir.'

'Then ... I can discover no chariot. Chariot is a mere empty sound.'

'It is on account of its having all these things—the pole, and the axle ...—that it comes under the generally understood term, the designation in common use, of "chariot".'

'Very good! Your Majesty has rightly grasped the meaning of "chariot". And just even so it is on account of all those things you questioned me about ... that I come under the generally understood term ... 'Nāgasena'. For it was said, Sire, by our Sister Vajira in the presence of the Blessed One:

'"just as it is by the condition precedent of the coexistence of its various parts that the word 'chariot' is used, just so is it true that when the *skandhas* are there we talk of a 'being'."'

'Most wonderful, Nāgasena, and most strange. Well done, well done, Nagasena' (abridged from Rhys Davids 1890:40–55).

### *The Three Instructions*

There is a story about a young Buddhist named Buddhaghosa, who comes to the main monastery in ancient Sri Lanka, requesting permission to use its library for his research and writing on the *dharma*. To test him, the abbot assigns him the task of commenting on a verse to the effect that once one has become established in morality (*śīla*) one should go on to perfect one's concentration (*samadhi*) and wisdom (*prajñā*). In response, Buddhaghosa writes *The Path of Purity*, which became a very famous commentary, in which he explains that following the moral precepts and basic moral principles is an essential foundation. This forms the first level of training or instruction.

Concentration, the second instruction, refers to the development of a mental state in which one is focused, tranquil, and alert. This *samādhi* state of mind is very helpful in every aspect of life, but it is especially helpful if one is to go on to the state of higher wisdom, the third instruction, without which one cannot attain *nirvāṇa*. One important insight that is gained through higher wisdom is the notion of causality.

The principle of causality is an important thread that runs through Buddha's *dharma*. To appreciate its function, think of a pool table. Being born into this world of changing circumstances is like glimpsing a pool table where the balls are colliding with one another and the cushions, repeatedly causing one another to change directions. Each time you blink, you see a new configuration of pool balls, caused by the previous configuration. With this image in mind, we can now turn to one of the more difficult expressions of Buddhist higher wisdom, which should be understood as a way in which the principle of causality manifests itself.

## Dependent Origination

A distinctive way of expressing insight about reality, according to Buddhist *dharma*, is to say that everything that arises does so in dependence upon other factors. This doctrine of *pratītya-samutpāda* ('dependent origination' or, as it is sometimes put in English, 'conditioned coproduction') grows out of the Buddhist understanding that all things are constantly changing and that their changes effect subsequent changes in other things. Buddhism depicts this state of flux as a wheel with twelve spokes—not to be confused with the wheel with eight spokes that symbolizes the Eightfold Path. The twelve spokes stand for twelve interconnected stages or dimensions of dependent origination.

The twelve links of the chain of dependent origination are given here in a way that divides them into three groups according to whether they refer to a past life, the present, or the future:

| | |
|---|---|
| Past | 1. Ignorance, leading to |
| | 2. *karma* formations, leading to |
| Present | 3. a new individual 'consciousness', leading to |
| | 4. a new body-mind complex, leading to |
| | 5. the bases of sensing, leading to |
| | 6. sense impressions, leading to |
| | 7. conscious feelings, leading to |
| | 8. craving, leading to |
| | 9. clinging to (grasping for) things, leading to |
| | 10. 'becoming' (the drive to be reborn), leading to |
| Future | 11. rebirth, leading to |
| | 12. old age and death |

The process does not stop with the twelfth link, for old age and death just lead to yet another birth, and so the twelve-spoke wheel turns on and on. Buddhists have analysed this wheel of rebirth from many viewpoints and with many similes, but the heart of the matter is always the same: all living beings are in process and will be reborn repeatedly until they realize *nirvāṇa*.

For the purpose of *dharma* instruction, Buddhists may employ various lists, including the three instructions, the twelve stages of dependent origination, the Four Truths, and Eightfold Path. These are alternative ways of expressing the Buddhist understanding of reality. After all, to Buddhists *dharma* is reality, and so *dharma* teaching is supposed to bring one into true awareness of reality.

## Third of the Three Gems, the *saṃgha*

### *The Order of Bhikṣus and Bhikṣuṇīs*

The third gem or refuge is the *saṃgha*, the community of ordained men (*bhikṣus*) and women (*bhikṣuṇīs*). As already mentioned, Śākyamuni began accepting disciples from the time of his first sermon in the deer park at Banaras. Within a short time, an ordination ritual took shape in which the new disciples took the Triple Refuge—in the Buddha, *dharma*, and *saṃgha*—and took vows of chastity, poverty, obedience, and so on. (Similar vows later played an important role in Christian monasticism.) A new disciple was first accepted into the category of *śrāmaṇera*, or novice, and called by a term that means 'one who has gone forth from living in a home'. Each novice is assigned a teacher, who is usually demanding, and also a spiritual guide, who is supportive. The novice receives a lower-level ordination, with fewer vows, but is permitted to wear the special robes that mark one as having 'gone forth'.

In early Indian Buddhism, these robes were dyed with vegetable dyes, especially saffron, which resulted in the bright orange-yellow colour known by that name. Most *bhikṣus* and *bhikṣuṇīs* in Southeast Asian countries still wear saffron robes, but as Buddhism spread into East Asia, other colours came into use, such as red and brown. There is no special meaning to the colour choice, but the members, whether *bhikṣu* or *bhikṣuṇī*, of a particular branch of Buddhism or ordination lineage would normally all use cloth of the same colour.

Śākyamuni himself seems to have accepted disciples right into the higher level of ordination, but later, institutionalized Buddhism found it advantageous to wait until the novices had mastered the basics of *dharma* and the textual language before ordaining them to the higher level of *bhikṣu* or *bhikṣuṇī*. This ordination ritual can be performed only in certain designated areas, which some ordination traditions still mark off with 'boundary stones', as in ancient India. There are special rituals for these stones. The ceremony of higher ordination takes several hours to complete. Friends and relatives of those being ordained attend and pay their respects to the new *saṃgha* members, who give presents to their teachers and counsellors in gratitude for their assistance. Seniority plays a large role in monastic life, so careful attention is paid to the exact time and date of the ordination.

### *The saṃgha of Laypeople*

Lay Buddhists are considered members of the *saṃgha* in its wider sense, which includes all those following the path laid down by the Buddha. The *saṃgha* of all disciples includes eight categories of 'noble persons', according to which of four levels they have achieved. The four levels are 'those who have entered the stream (to *nirvāṇa*)', those who have advanced enough to return (be reborn) just once more, those who are so advanced that they will never return, and those who have advanced to the state of realizing the *arhat* (worthy) path. At each of the four levels, Buddhists distinguish the person who has just realized the new level from one who has matured at that level, making a total of eight classifications of noble persons.

In all Buddhist traditions, laypeople are thought to be able to make good progress towards *nirvāṇa*, although some forms of Buddhism expect that one eventually needs to take ordination in order to devote oneself full time to the spiritual quest. In Mahāyāna Buddhism, as discussed later, the role of the layperson was upgraded and stressed.

## Controversies, Councils, and Sects

Sectarian divisions developed within the *saṃgha*. The defection of some *bhikṣus* under the leadership of Devadatta shows that sectarian problems could arise even while the Buddha was alive. We do not know the precise history of the *saṃgha*'s divisions, but it is possible to reconstruct some details.

Trouble surfaced when a *bhikṣu* noticed, while visiting the city of Vaiśālī, that the *bhikṣus* there accepted gold and silver donations from the laity. He criticized them publicly for this, and they demanded that he apologize in front of their lay supporters. In so doing, he managed to turn this molehill into a mountain, and a meeting of all the *bhikṣus* in the area had to be convened, early in the fourth century BCE.

Because there was no central person, court, or committee that held authority in Buddhism, the monks collectively had to settle disputes on the basis of their interpretations of the discourses given by the Buddha. This was more problematic than one might now imagine, however, for the scriptures had not yet been written down. Writing in ancient India, as in many other ancient civilizations, was thought to be a tool more appropriate to commercial records than to sacred teachings. In the Hindu tradition, the most sacred ritual texts, the *Vedas*, were memorized and recited orally rather than written down.

The meeting, called the Vaiśālī Council, decided that the *vinaya*, the discipline tradition, did indeed forbid the acceptance of gold and silver by *bhikṣus* (and *bhikṣuṇīs*). Most of the Vaiśālī *bhikṣus* agreed to abide by the ruling, and so there was no schism over the matter of accepting donations in the form of money. Before adjourning the council, the *bhikṣus* recited the *Vinaya* ('discipline') and *Sūtra* ('discourse') divisions of what would become the scriptures.

Some *bhikṣus* evidently dissented from the council's decision, and more troubling issues soon arose. The first schism occurred shortly after the Vaiśālī Council. A certain monk listed five points of controversy, mostly having to do with whether or not an *arhat*, a 'worthy one' or saint, was subject to certain limitations. For example, was an *arhat* susceptible to sexual misconduct? Was it possible for an *arhat* to be ignorant of some doctrine, or to have doubts about doctrine? Could one become an *arhat* merely by instruction, rather than by spiritual practice?

Many of the *sthavira* ('elders' or senior monks) dissented from the majority opinion on the five points, and so a division arose between the majority group (forming the Mahāsāṃghika or 'Great *Saṃgha*' sect) and the Sthavira group (forming the Sthaviravāda sect). The disputed five points may seem somewhat trivial, but behind them lay an important issue that fuelled even more serious divisions in later Buddhism. That issue concerns the understanding of what level of attainment is possible for Buddhists in this life. The more conservative position held that enlightenment (attaining the *arhat* level) was very difficult and beyond the reach of almost everyone, whereas the more liberal position held out the prospect of arhatship in this life. This debate gave the *saṃgha* a foretaste of the split that later led to the distinction between Mahāyāna and Theravāda Buddhism.

By the time of Aśoka, in the third century BCE, there were eighteen sects. Each had its oral version of the Buddhist teachings, although from the few later written texts that have survived, we can imagine that the versions did not differ very much. They all shared a similar ordination tradition and all followed more or less the same *vinaya* rules. Also, it is unlikely that the laity paid very much attention to the divisions. For this reason these sects were not so much like the denominations in Protestant Christianity as they were like the various religious orders in Roman Catholicism. The *bhikṣus* of the various sects sometimes lived together in one monastery, especially at the major training centres, which evolved into Buddhist universities.

## The Three Baskets of Sacred Texts

Śākyamuni did not write down any of his teachings or rules of discipline, nor did he assign anyone the task of recording his words. As we have indicated, this situation followed the pattern of India's Hindu milieu. The sacred teachings of the Hindus were committed to memory by the brahmin priests. There was a sense that the Hindu ritual formulas had an acoustic effectiveness, that they were the exclusive preserve of the priests, and that they should therefore explicitly be oral rather than written. In the case of Buddhism, for the first 400 years or so, the *saṃgha* was content to recite the teachings from memory.

To manage the task of passing along the large numbers of teachings without losing them, various *bhikṣus* were assigned the task of memorizing selected portions. When the early conferences of all *saṃgha* members were held, one of the most important tasks was to recite the teachings in their entirety. *Bhikṣus* with especially good memories were essential, of course.

At the first council, *Bhikṣu* Ānanda, who had been Śākyamuni's travelling companion, is credited with reciting the section on monastic rules (*vinaya*). *Bhikṣu* Upāli is credited with reciting the discourses (*sūtras*) on *dharma* ascribed to Śākyamuni. At a later meeting, another disciple is credited with reciting the systematic treatises (*abhidharma*) that were composed after Śākyamuni's *parinirvāṇa*. The Theravāda monks in Sri Lanka put the teachings into writing in the first century CE after a famine reduced the *bhikṣu* population so drastically that there was a danger that the oral tradition might not survive to the next generation.

Eventually the material that had been orally transmitted was written down. The activity may have been spread over more than a century, but was apparently completed by the first century BCE. The manuscript copies of the texts in the three divisions, written on palm leaves strung together and bundled like Venetian blinds, may have been stored in three baskets. At least, that would explain why the Theravāda Buddhists refer to their scriptures as the *Tripiṭaka* ('three baskets'). The collection survives in the Pali language, a vernacular related to and partly derived from Sanskrit, and is therefore referred to as the Pali canon.

The *Sūtra Piṭaka*, or 'discourse basket', contains the talks on *dharma* attributed to Śākyamuni or his early disciples. The discourse is often given in response to a question from a disciple or outsider. The beginning of the *sūtra* gives the setting in a stylized manner. The following opening of the 'Discourse on the Lesser Analysis of Deeds' is typical:

> Thus have I heard: At one time the Lord was staying near Savatthi in the Jeta Grove in Anathapindika's monastery. Then the brahmin youth Subha, Todeyya's son, approached the Lord; having approached, he exchanged greetings with the Lord; having conversed in a friendly and courteous way, he sat down at a respectful distance. As he was sitting down at a respectful distance the brahmin youth Subha, Todeyya's son, spoke thus to the Lord:
>
> 'Now, good Gotama, what is the cause, what the reason that lowness and excellence are to be seen among human beings while they are in human form' (Horner 1967, iii:248–9)?

Subha has asked the timeless question of why bad things happen to apparently good people. Śākyamuni, called by the title *bhagavan* ('Lord') here, then instructs Subha about how *karma*, the influence of actions from past lives, accounts for the fact that some people suffer short, unhappy lives, while others enjoy long, blessed lives.

There are five sections (*nikāyas*) of the *Sūtra Piṭaka*, the first 'basket'. Chronological or alphabetical ways of organizing texts were seldom used in the ancient world. Instead, the *sūtras* are organized according to a system commonly used: from the longest to the shortest. (Notice that in Islam the same principle applies in the sequence of the *sūrahs* or chapters of the *Qur'ān*.) Other organizational schemes are used as well. One section, 'Kindred Sayings', contains *sūtras* collected around topics, while the 'Gradual Sayings' section contains *sūtras* organized according to numerical lists (four truths, four kinds of humans, and so on).

The *Vinaya Piṭaka*, or 'discipline basket', contains both the rules of monastic discipline and stories about how Śākyamuni came to institute each rule.

The *Abhidharma* (Further Discourses) *Piṭaka* contains seven books by unnamed early Buddhists who systematically analysed every conceivable aspect of reality from the standpoint of various Buddhist principles. For example, the first book of *abhidharma* classifies all mental phenomena according to whether each is good, bad, or neutral karmically. Other books deal with the various physical elements of nature by classifying them under numerous rubrics.

The development of *abhidharma* is associated with Śāriputra, one of the brightest of the Buddha's disciples. He lived in a city named Nālandā, where a large university flourished by the first century. It may have been the world's first university.

The *abhidharma* books formed the basis of the physical and psychological sciences taught at Nālandā and other Buddhist universities of India. The goal, however, was not so much the advancement of the physical sciences as it was the spiritual advancement of the student. Throughout the *abhidharma* works runs the basic Buddhist teaching that all physical and mental realities are devoid of eternal nature and are subject to constant change. However, the *abhidharma* scholars were later criticized by some Mahāyāna Buddhists on the grounds that they seemed too preoccupied with classifying reality and not concerned enough with enlightenment.

## Moral Discipline: The Precepts

Moral discipline is basic to progress on the path, as mentioned in the section on the three instructions. The rules of moral discipline (*śīla*) are usually called 'precepts' in English. Buddhists think of the precepts not as commandments from a god or the *buddhas* but as basic moral principles that one should discipline oneself to follow. As part of most Buddhist rituals, Buddhists recite in unison the five precepts (*pañca śīla*), as follows:

I undertake to observe the precept of abstaining

1. from destroying the life of living creatures
2. from taking things not given
3. from sexual misconduct
4. from false speech
5. from liquors that cause intoxication and heedlessness

On the holy days of the Buddhist calendar, some pious Buddhists may undertake to observe the eight precepts. The list of eight includes the basic five, except that the precept of abstaining from sexual misconduct is changed to abstaining from unchastity. This means that during the holy day(s) the lay observant practices celibacy, even though married. The additional three precepts involve the following abstentions:

6. from eating after noon
7. from dancing, singing, music, and unseemly shows, and from the use of garlands, perfumes, and ointments, and from things that tend to beautify and adorn the person
8. from using high and luxurious seats

On full-moon days, the holiest days of the Buddhist lunar calendar, many Buddhists go to their local temple, where they take the eight precepts together in a ritual, and then spend the day meditating, listening to *dharma* talks and reading about *dharma*, while being careful to avoid eating after noon, sitting on chairs, and so forth. For that one day each month, the layperson lives a holy life similar to that of a *bhikṣu* or *bhikṣuṇī*.

The Buddhist prohibitions against stealing, adultery, lying, and drunkenness are similar to those of other religions. The precept against killing any living creature, however, is not found in most religions, except Jainism and Hinduism, which also have roots in the *ahiṁsā* (non-violence) ethic of the ancient Ganges region.

The ideal of *ahiṁsā* must, of course, be compromised in real life. Buddhists never went so far as to wear masks to avoid breathing in, and therefore harming, microscopic insects, but meditating *bhikṣu*s and *bhikṣuṇī*s will blow mosquitoes off their arms rather than swat them. And Buddhists tell stories about *bhikṣu*s and *bhikṣuṇī*s who go to great trouble to save the life of animals, no matter how small or commonplace. Buddhists do not normally say—as some non-Buddhists imagine they might—that they do this because the animal might be a deceased human now reborn as an animal. Rather, Buddhists usually give the straightforward explanation that they wish to avoid bringing harm to all living beings.

Buddhists who choose to practice *ahiṁsā* rigorously have been known to give up their occupations as hunters or fishermen, or even as farmers because of the worms and insects killed when ploughing and tilling the soil. Most Buddhist laity do eat meat and do kill insects and small animals as necessary to make life bearable, but there remains in Buddhism to this day the ideal of minimizing the harm one brings to other creatures, no matter how small.

***The Divine Virtues***

While the five precepts summarize what Buddhists want to avoid doing, the four divine virtues (*brahmavihāras*, 'abodes of the god Brahmā') express Buddhist values in positive terms. Buddhists are to strive towards a consciousness having 'lovingkindness', compassion, altruistic joy, and equanimity.

The first two of these are often linked in the phrase *maitra-muditā*, meaning 'love and compassion'. The first means being friendly towards other 'sentient beings', that is, both animals and humans. Compassion means not merely caring when they suffer, but taking action to help them. The third virtue, altruistic joy, means pleasure rather than envy or jealousy when good things happen to others. Equanimity means being neither upset by criticism nor egotistical when praised.

The four virtues are deemed possible only when some control over the three evil roots of greed, hatred, and delusion has been accomplished. The complete eradication of these three evils from the unconscious is expected to result in the attainment of the level of *nirvāṇa* that is possible for a person in the present life.

## Meditation

It is important for the novice to learn to meditate. One sits in the 'lotus' position: legs and hands crossed, hands resting on the lap, soles of the feet resting on top of the thighs. The spinal column is kept erect, the tip of the tongue touches the back of the upper front teeth, and the eyes are downcast and eyelids partially closed.

Once able to maintain this position, one concentrates on the process of breathing. This can be done by sensing air passing through the nose or, as in Burmese teaching, by becoming aware of the rising and falling of the diaphragm with each breath—the yoga practice that is mocked in the West as 'contemplating one's navel'. The student is told not to slow down or control the breathing consciously, but rather to be aware or mindful of the breathing as it happens.

After progress in 'mindfulness of breath', the novice proceeds to develop mindfulness of body and mind. The mindfulness of body involves an enhanced awareness of oneself from head to toe. Mindfulness of mind means, for example, becoming aware of what or whom one hates and for what reasons, with the goal of eradicating the hatred from one's deep mind.

The novice may also meditate on objects or concepts. Buddhist meditation manuals list the objects of meditation, including various colours and shapes. In early Buddhism, novices were sometimes told to meditate on corpses in various states of decomposition, in order to develop an awareness of death, including their own. Some meditation centres today display a skeleton or other death object for this purpose. The practice of meditating on statues or paintings of various *buddhas* and *bodhisattvas* became popular in some forms of Mahāyāna and Vajrayāna Buddhism, which will be discussed later. Among the concepts, the most popular were the basic *dharma* teachings, such as *karma* or *samsāra*.

The goals of meditation are to enhance the power of concentration and develop insight (*vipāsyana*) into truth, including truths about oneself and all reality. The goal of developing this insight is so important that many Buddhists today refer to meditation in general using the Pali form of the term, *vipāssana*.

The novice is expected to continue doing *vipāssana* meditation after full ordination as a *bhikṣu* or *bhikṣuṇī*, but historically meditation was not stressed for laypeople. This is changing today, with the creation of meditation centres that open their doors to laypeople who come for instruction in meditation during intensive weekends or longer periods of time. Such lay retreat sessions may be found across Asia, from Sri Lanka to Japan, and the pattern has proven especially popular in Western countries.

## Aśoka's Establishment of Buddhism

The spread of Buddhism within India was quite remarkable. Unlike many reformers, Śākyamuni had succeeded in gaining converts across a broad social spectrum ranging from the lowest classes of labourers and tribal members through the rich merchant class to the powerful kings of the newly emerged major kingdoms of the rose-apple continent. The conversion of the kings in Śākyamuni's lifetime did not mean that all subsequent kings were Buddhists, however. There was a long-standing Indian tradition that the king had a duty to defend and support all the legitimate religious traditions of his kingdom. After Śākyamuni's *parinirvāṇa*, it seems that Buddhism became one, among several others, of these legitimate *dharma* systems.

Approximately 150 years after the passing or *parinirvāṇa* of Śākyamuni, Greek-speaking rulers came to power in northwestern India as a result of Alexander's conquest in 326 BCE. A king of the Mauryan dynasty later drove the Greek rulers out of central India, and his son expanded the newly formed kingdom. The grandson, Aśoka (r. c. 273–232 BCE), inherited the throne and began a series of wars to expand his territory to the south and west. Eventually, he ruled an empire that included most of modern India.

The Buddhist histories claim that as a result of Aśoka's reflection on the horrible carnage of his bloody war with the kingdom of Kalinga on the eastern coast, he underwent a conversion to Buddhism and began promoting the ethic of non-violence. Probably his family had previously been supporters of other non-brahminical traditions such as Jainism, and so his conversion to Buddhism was likely not a major shift.

Under the patronage of Emperor Aśoka, Buddhism enjoyed its golden age in India. Aśoka devoted himself, according to the Buddhist histories, to a *dharma* conquest, as opposed to the military conquests previously pursued by his grandfather, his father, and himself. To spread the *dharma* of non-violence, he ordered builders to erect large stones or tall pillars at major crossroads throughout his empire and carve messages on them for the moral instruction of his subjects. Some of these stones and pillars have been recovered by archaeologists, and the messages are still readable.

In the message carved on the rock erected in the coastal Kalinga area of eastern India, he expresses remorse at having been responsible for the death and suffering of so many people.

> When the king, Beloved of the Gods and of Gracious Mien, had been consecrated eight years Kalinga was conquered, 150,000 people were deported, 100,000 were killed, and many times that number died. But after the conquest of Kalinga, the Beloved of the Gods began to follow Righteousness (*dharma*), to love Righteousness, and to give instruction in Righteousness. Now the Beloved of the Gods regrets the conquest of Kalinga, for when an independent country is conquered people are killed, they die, or are deported, and that the Beloved of the Gods finds painful and grievous. ... The Beloved of the Gods will forgive as far as he can, and he even conciliates the forest tribes of his dominions; but he warns them that there is power even in the remorse of the Beloved of the Gods, and he tells them to reform, lest they be killed (*Thirteenth Rock Edict*; de Bary 1958:146).

He then lays out his ideals for governing his new subjects, saying that he desires security, self-control, impartiality, and cheerfulness for all living creatures in his empire. Aśoka spells out his 'conquest by *dharma*' and claims that it is spreading not only within the Indian continent but westward among the various Alexandrian kingdoms, whose kings he names. Aśoka states that real satisfaction in ruling over people comes only from inducing them to follow *dharma*.

> Thus he achieves a universal conquest, and conquest always gives a feeling of pleasure; yet it is but a slight pleasure, for the Beloved of the Gods only looks on that which concerns the next life as of great importance. I have had this inscription of Righteousness engraved that all my sons and grandsons may not seek to gain new victories, ... that they may consider the only [valid] victory the victory of Righteousness, which is of value both in this world and the next (*Thirteenth Rock Edict*; de Bary 1958:147).

He pledges his intent to be just and moderate in punishment when necessary. As we have seen, he does remind his Kalinga subjects and the tribal people of the surrounding forest areas that despite his commitment to non-violence, he will not hesitate to deal firmly with rebels and criminals. His punishments will be just and moderate, however.

Aśoka's promotion of *dharma* became a model for later Buddhist rulers. Like 'Dharma-Aśoka', as Buddhists later called him, they were willing to sentence criminals (and rebels) to punishment or even death, but they remained committed to non-violent practices in other matters. Aśoka himself went so far as to encourage his subjects to become vegetarian and give up occupations such as hunting.

## Buddhism and the State

### *The King as Wheel-Turner*

Indian tradition prior to 500 BCE and perhaps even in the Vedic age prior to 1000 BCE employed the term *cakravartin* or 'wheel-turner' to refer to kings as world rulers. On one level, the imagery implicit in the term is that of a ruler whose chariot wheels encounter no opposition. On another level, the wise ruler is seen as one who in meditation perceives a wheel turning in the heavens, and gains an understanding of the orderly process of the universe. Thus a world-ruler has both the spiritual wisdom to perceive order as a norm and the political power to implement it in practice.

Śākyamuni is described as of noble birth, even though he turns his back on affairs of state in favour of the insights of meditation. When the early Buddhists began to refer to him as a *cakravartin*, they were in one sense according to him the honour one would bestow on a king, an honour that Śākyamuni may not have sought. His followers did think that they were following his wishes when they adopted an architectural form (which will be discussed later), the stupa or burial mound of the sort used for royalty, to entomb his remains. But in another sense, the Buddhist tradition was directing the focus of the concept of political power away from unchallenged military strength and towards the notion of wisdom in the guidance of society.

From the time of Śākyamuni, Buddhism understood the king to have a special role with regard to the *dharma*. The king was supposed to provide for the basic welfare of his citizens by setting up food distribution centres and clinics. And the king was to promote *dharma* by setting a good example and by sponsoring lectures, translations, and the distribution of literature. By thus promoting *dharma*, the ideal king would be in a real sense a successor to Buddha, the definitive wheel-turner.

As Buddhism spread throughout Asia, it advocated an ideal role for kings to play in society. An East Asian Zen Buddhist story shows how one particular king adopts the Buddhist model of royal support for Buddhism. The story is set around the third century at the court of a Chinese ruler named Wu. The king has converted to Buddhism and dedicated himself to doing all the things a good Buddhist king does, probably with the goal of winning a long and pleasant rebirth in heaven. When Emperor Wu learns that Bodhidharma, a monk newly arrived from India, has taken up residence in his kingdom, Wu summons him to court and proudly shows the monk his good Buddhist works. Wu has established rice kitchens for feeding the poor, a new wing of the palace with rooms filled with scribes busy translating and copying the sacred Buddhist texts, a Buddhist altar for daily worship, and the practice of having the texts read aloud and explained to the citizens on holidays. After the tour of the palace, Emperor Wu asks Bodhidharma, 'How much merit do you think I have made from all this?' 'None whatsoever!' is the famous response. Bodhidharma proceeds to explain that true merit comes only from activities that increase one's wisdom and purify the mind. Emperor Wu, it seems, was doing all these good things for the wrong reason.

With regard to Buddhism and the state, we learn from this story of Emperor Wu that the rulers were encouraged to support the *saṃgha* and actively promote *dharma* in their realms, but that they were sometimes challenged to go beyond that to higher levels of achievement. This explains why Buddhist kings sometimes abdicated the rule at a fairly early age in order to take ordination as a *bhikṣu*.

### *Non-violence as a Public Ethic*

One characteristic of Buddhist political rule, at least ideally, was the special attention given to non-violence. Unnecessarily harsh punishments were forbidden, and kings released prisoners during Buddhist festivals. Also, justice was to be administered fairly, regardless of social status, and quickly, even if that inconvenienced the king. A particularly pious king of ancient Sri Lanka is remembered for instructing his staff to wake him even in the middle of the night if a citizen came seeking justice. A rope was installed outside the palace walls so that a common person could pull it to ring the bell and awaken the king to hear the complaint. Non-violence rituals continue in some Buddhist festivals to this day. For example, caged birds or other animals may be released into the wild, on the basis that keeping wild animals caged is hurtful to them.

The Buddhist king was expected to maintain an army and a police force, however, on the grounds that the public needs to be defended against criminals and foreign enemies. There is no such thing in Buddhist scripture as a 'just war' of aggression, but many Buddhists have believed that a defensive war is not against *dharma*. They argue that the state may use force as necessary to maintain law and order. However, a modern Thai Buddhist writer points out that the scriptures do not support the use of violence, even in self-defence.

With very few exceptions, Buddhism spread by missionary conversion rather than by force. However, there were territorial wars among various Buddhist kingdoms of Southeast Asia, and in Sri Lanka the conflict between the Buddhist Sinhalese and Hindu Tamils has a long history.

# THERAVĀDA

## Theravāda in Sri Lanka

One of the eighteen divisions of early Indian Buddhism called itself the 'Way of the Elders', which is Sthaviravāda in Sanskrit and Theravāda in Pali. We know very little about this school's early history, but suspect that it was widespread in India by the time of Aśoka in the third century BCE. On the one hand, archaeological evidence suggests it was known in regions of southern India. On the other hand, it preserved the scriptures in a North Indian dialect now known as Pali. Since the name Pali etymologically alludes merely to the language of the 'lines' of the text, it gives no clue as to the origin of the dialect itself. It is claimed that the dialect came from the ancient Indian kingdom of Magadha, one of the four where Śākyamuni himself taught, but archaeology has not yet confirmed this.

We do know that the Theravāda tradition was conservative, as its name suggested, and considers itself as preserving Buddhism in its original form. It refuses to deify the Buddha, for example, as did some later forms of Buddhism, and it rejects scriptures written after the formation of the *Tripiṭaka*. A monk named Mahinda (in Sanskrit, Mahendra), who was Aśoka's son, took this version of Buddhism to Sri Lanka in the third century BCE. The story of his converting the Sri Lankan people to Theravāda is told in the island's *Great Chronicle* (*Mahāvaṃsa*).

In the *Great Chronicle*, Mahinda and his assistant *bhikṣus* travel through the air, using one of the psychic powers, and arrive on a large hill near the Sri Lankan capital, Anuradhapura. The king of Sri Lanka and his hunting party discover the *bhikṣus* on 'Mahinda's Hill' and are soon converted to the Buddha's *dharma* as taught by Mahinda. This hill, Mihintale, is an active centre for monks and lay pilgrims in Sri Lanka today. The day after his conversion, Mahinda enters the capital and teaches *dharma* to the members of the king's court, who are converted. On the following day the biggest hall available (the royal elephant stable) is put into service, after suitable cleaning, as a hall of *dharma* instruction, whereupon everyone is converted.

These legends presumably reflect history from the mid-third century BCE. King Aśoka probably sent his son to the island kingdom to the south. In one of his inscriptions, Aśoka claims to have sent missionaries in groups of five so that they could ordain converts far and wide, even to the Hellenistic kingdoms to the west.

**Figure 4.1**
**SPREAD OF BUDDHISM**

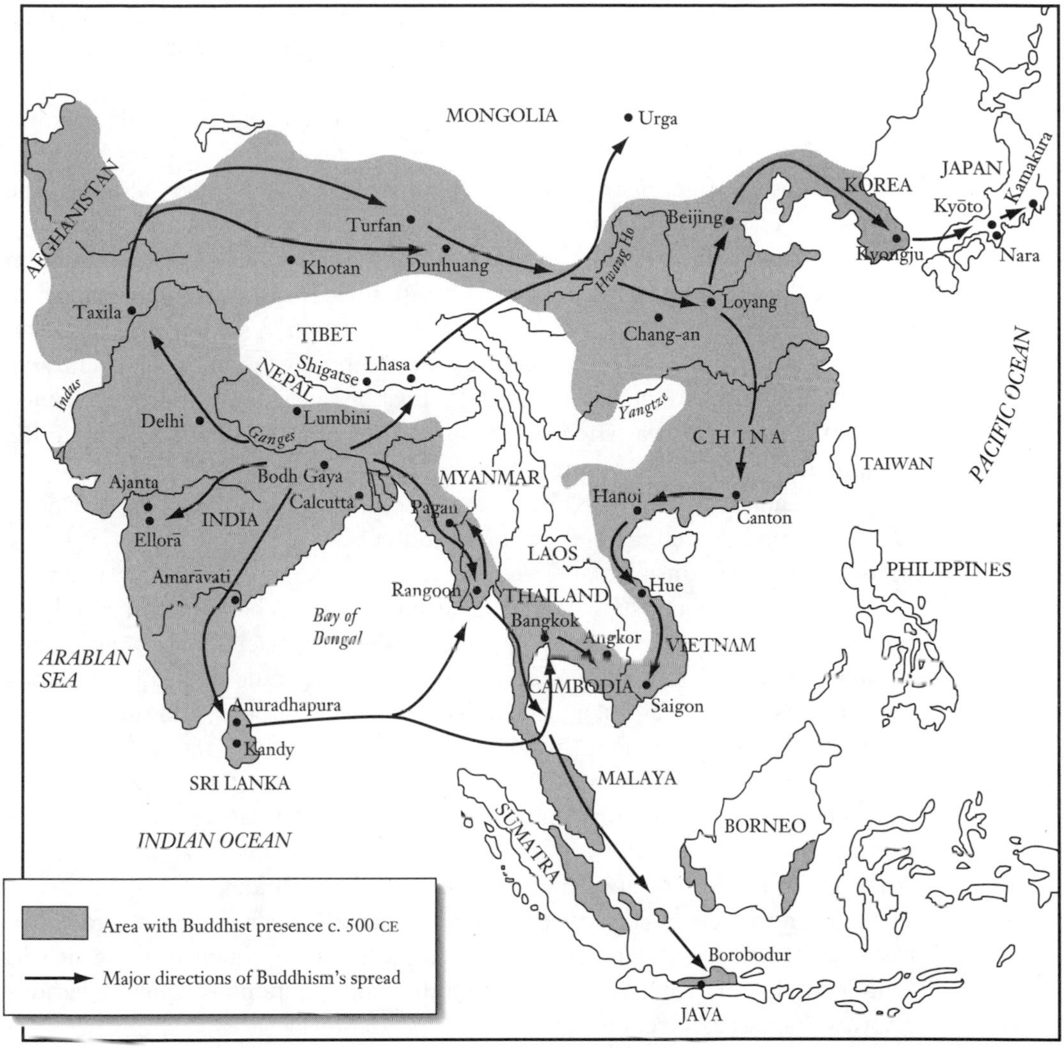


*Source:* Adapted from N.C. Nielsen et al., eds, *Religions of the World*, 3rd ed. (New York: St Martin's Press, 1993):196.

The king of Sri Lanka may have been quite receptive to forming an alliance with the powerful emperor on the mainland, and what better way than to adopt the empire's religion and court rituals? To effect the adoption of the religion, the king ordered the building of a proper stupa, temple, and *dharma* hall, and the temple grounds were made complete with the arrival of a Bodhi tree sapling brought from India by a *bhikṣuṇī* who was Mahinda's sister.

The adoption of Indian-style court rituals was accomplished when, after receiving the proper equipment from India, the Sri Lankan king submitted himself to a new enthronement ritual carried out according to Aśoka's instructions. In this way the island of Sri Lanka became a cultural extension of Aśoka's empire while maintaining its sovereignty. This uniting of Buddhist leadership and Indian forms of kingship set the pattern for subsequent Buddhist rulers in mainland Southeast Asia. The king is considered the lay leader and chief financial supporter of Buddhism in his kingdom.

Theravāda Buddhism is still the main religion of Sri Lanka, although the *saṃgha* fell on such hard times in the eleventh century due to famine that there were not enough ordained *bhikṣus* to continue. Buddhist rules require a minimum of five senior *bhikṣus* to officiate at an ordination. So, *bhikṣus* from Burma had to be imported to Sri Lanka to conduct a proper ordination. A similar appeal to *bhikṣus* from Siam in the eighteenth century led to the revitalization of Theravāda, with the establishment of a new *nikāya* ('ordination lineage') appropriately named the Siyam (Siam) Nikāya. The majority of Sri Lankan *bhikṣus* today belong to the Siyam Nikāya, which has control of many of the major temples.

Sri Lanka was populated by various peoples from India, and many aspects of Sri Lankan art, architecture, customs, and cuisine reflect the close ties to the predominantly Hindu mainland. A version of the Indian caste system is one of these Hindu transplants to Sri Lanka. Śākyamuni taught that a person should be judged by his or her character rather than birth (birth refers to the social status of one's hereditary occupational or clan group). In keeping with this principle, Śākyamuni's *saṃgha* was open to members of all social groups, and the names of his early disciples reflect that this policy was indeed put into practice.

Surprisingly, the Siyam Nikāya of Sri Lanka, the most prestigious ordination lineage, today accepts only members from the Goyigama caste. The Goyigama, considered the highest caste among the Sinhalese, is a caste of landowners and would rank among the *vaiśya* castes of India.

There are other *nikāyas* in Sri Lanka that accept members regardless of caste background. The Ramañña Nikāya is the most important of these. It was founded in the nineteenth century as an ordination tradition dedicated to various reforms, including the elimination of caste restrictions.

## Theravāda in Southeast Asia

The spread of Buddhism into Southeast Asia took place in stages spread out over many centuries. The names and boundaries of the region's kingdoms have changed frequently during two millennia. 'Southeast Asia' is a modern name for the region, used for an area of Allied military command during the Second World War. Earlier European usage termed the region 'the Indies', reflecting the perception of explorers and traders from the sixteenth century onward that the culture they encountered there was in some sense Indian. Today, Buddhist culture remains dominant in Southeast Asia in such mainland countries as Cambodia, Thailand, and Myanmar, while Islam now overlies earlier Buddhist influence in the Indonesian islands and the Malay peninsula.

The traditional Buddhist claim is that Buddhism's introduction in Southeast Asia dates back to the third century BCE, when King Aśoka reportedly sent missionaries to the kingdom of the Mon people, who ruled a large region spanning present-day Cambodia and Thailand, yet there is little historical evidence of Buddhism in Southeast Asia until the sixth century or so, long after Aśoka's era. The kingdoms of Southeast Asia during the early centuries CE are termed 'Indianized'. The religious adherence of the Indianized kingdoms was sometimes Buddhist, sometimes Hindu. For example, the rulers of the impressive temple complex in Cambodia known to us as Angkor Wat were Hindu in the ninth to twelfth centuries, but the rulers after the late twelfth century were Buddhist. Similarly, the island of Bali in Indonesia is still Hindu.

From the account of a seventh-century Chinese Buddhist pilgrim and from a few archaeological remains, we may conclude that several of the early Buddhist sects were established in Southeast Asia. This diversity reflects the pattern in India, where various Buddhist sects coexisted for centuries. Eventually, Theravāda sects prevailed. Some accounts of early Buddhism in Southeast Asia stress the working of miracles, a feature of Buddhist missionary expansion found later in Tibet and elsewhere. The use of powerful chants and other protective powers also was a feature of Southeast Asian Buddhism, partly because some who came to the region followed the Vajrayāna school, which will be discussed later.

From the eleventh through the fifteenth centuries, Buddhism consolidated its position in the region, with the Theravāda tradition of Sri Lanka emerging as the normative form. By the end of this period, Theravāda Buddhism was the majority religion of the Thai, Khmer (Cambodian), Burmese, and Lao (Laotian) people, and has remained so.

### *Burma*

Burma was the region most easily reached by Buddhist missionaries from India. By the eleventh century, the kingdom of Pagan, in what is today Myanmar, developed ties with the Theravāda rulers of Sri Lanka. A temple enshrining a sacred relic, a tooth alleged to be from the Buddha, became the guardian and legitimizer of the kingdom.

With the dominance of Theravāda, the Pali-language version of the *Tripiṭaka* was established as the official one in Burma, but in keeping with Buddhist practice elsewhere, the text was written in the local script, in this instance Burmese. The Thai and Khmer *saṃghas* likewise copied the Pali texts using their own scripts. These alphabets bear little resemblance to one another at first glance, but they are all derived from Indian scripts and are distantly related to the alphabets of Semitic origin used in the Mediterranean world.

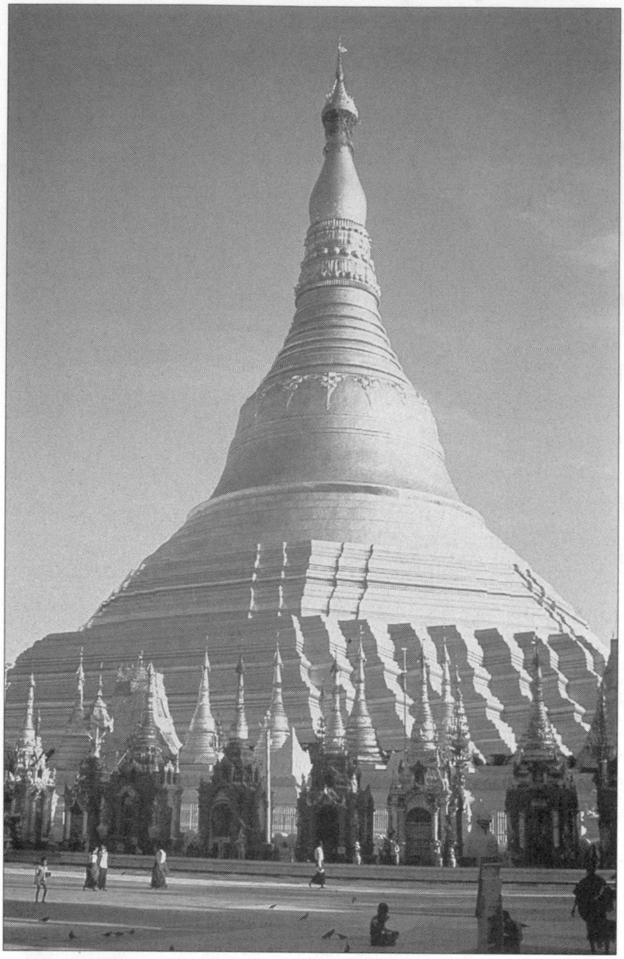

*The massive Shwe Dagon pagoda stands amid satellite pagodas in Yangon, Myanmar.*
(W.G. Oxtoby)

### *Cambodia*

The area of Southeast Asia that corresponds to modern Cambodia was also influenced by some various forms of Indian Buddhism as well as Hinduism prior to the fifteenth century. Since then, the Theravāda school has been well established in Cambodia. Recently the legitimacy of Buddhism has been sought by all sides of the political spectrum in war-torn Cambodia. By 'paying respect' to the *bhikṣus*, the political leaders can express their continuity with Cambodia's rich Buddhist tradition.

### *Thailand*

The Thai people are thought to have migrated into Southeast Asia from southern China, where tribal groups speaking dialects of Thai still live. The history of the Thai spread into Thailand, formerly Siam, traces the gradual southward movement of the Thai people and their capital cities. During the fifteenth century, Thai monks returning from Sri Lanka, where they were ordained in the Theravāda tradition, gained favour with King Tiloraja, who ruled central Thailand from Chiangmai, a city well north of the modern capital, Bangkok.

Two of the most important kings of nineteenth-century Siam were Mongkut and his son Chulalongkorn. Both were active in reforming the *saṃgha*. King Mongkut (r. 1824–51) is revered by Thais under the name Rama IV and is known in the West as the king portrayed in 'The King and I'—which has never been screened in Thailand because it portrays Mongkut in a disrespectful way.

Having been a *bhikṣu* for over twenty years, Mongkut set out to restore discipline and direction to the *saṃgha* after he became king. This endeavour led to the founding of a new ordination lineage called the Thammayut Nikāya. The name is a Thai spelling for a Pali word meaning 'those who adhere to the *dharma*'.

This reform movement set the tone for modern Theravāda not only in Thailand but elsewhere in Southeast Asia. For example, the king of Cambodia arranged for the establishment of the Thammayut Nikāya in his country in the nineteenth century.

Following in his father's footsteps, King Chulalongkorn, Rama V (r. 1851–68), undertook to unite the various ordination lineages (*nikāyas*) under a central administrative authority and standardize the training given to novices in meditation, *dharma* instruction, and the Pali language. The training standards and central administration are still important features in the Thai *saṃgha*.

Thai kings in the modern period, even in the late twentieth century, have always spent time in a monastery. Their prior monastic training is taken by the Thais to be an important preparation for their rule, both in the king's capacity as lay head of the *saṃgha* and in his capacity as leader of Thai cultural life.

Buddhist discipline and orthodoxy are maintained through control of the right to ordain. Historically the kings of Burma, Cambodia, Siam, and Laos sought to regularize and consolidate religion in their kingdoms by establishing the Theravāda ordination lineage as normative. Theravāda may have appealed to the rulers because of its purity, in keeping strict discipline and traditions, and because by adopting it the rulers could bring their kingdoms into political alliance with other powerful kingdoms in Sri Lanka and mainland Southeast Asia.

### *Laos*

Laos is a small country with close linguistic, racial, and cultural ties with Thailand. There is inscriptional evidence of Sri Lankan *bhikṣus* bringing Theravāda orthodoxy to Laos over 500 years ago. This is similar to the pattern of Sri Lankan influence we have encountered in Burma, Cambodia, and Thailand. However, due to its proximity and common language, Thai Buddhism was the most influential upon Laos. For example, Laotian *bhikṣus* in modern times have travelled to Bangkok to attend one of the two large universities there that train *bhikṣus*.

The history of Buddhism in mainland Southeast Asia may be summarized along the following lines. Prior to 1000, various sects of early Indian Buddhism as well as Mahāyāna and Vajrayāna schools competed for support among the royalty and the peasantry. By the fifteenth century the rulers of the major kingdoms of the area embraced the Theravāda form of Buddhism and imported senior *bhikṣus* from Sri Lanka to reordain the indigenous monks in the Theravāda lineage. Other forms of Buddhism gradually died out in most of Southeast Asia, and Theravāda Buddhist training centres and temples of national importance flourished under royal patronage.

Island Southeast Asia, in contrast to the mainland countries, has become predominantly Muslim over the course of the past five centuries, but both Buddhist monuments and Buddhist minorities survive. For example, Buddhism is no longer practised in Indonesia, although tourists still flock to the ruins of the majestic temple of Borobudur, which covers a hilltop with a geometrical arrangement of stupas. It models in stone the mountains that anchor the world, according to traditional Buddhist cosmology. In Malaysia, there is a sizeable Buddhist minority.

## Theravāda Rituals

Buddhism has rituals, but at the same time is critical of ritualism. The critique of rituals takes two forms. First, the Buddha was quite critical of the rituals conducted by the brahmins of his day. He condemned animal sacrifices because they violated the ethic of non-violence. With regard to the brahminical rituals that do not involve animal sacrifice, such as kindling a sacred fire or praying towards the various directions, Śākyamuni merely encouraged the substitution of rituals that he felt were better suited to the promotion of *dharma*. For example, to brahmins accustomed to offering prayers in the six directions (the four cardinal compass directions, plus the nadir and zenith), Śākyamuni suggested substituting a ritual in which one affirmed proper behaviour towards six different classes of people—parents, rulers, servants, and so on. However, with regard to rituals that called for the sacrifice of animals, Śākyamuni condemned them as compromising the ethic of non-violence.

The second form of Śākyamuni's critique of rituals applies to any rituals—even ones used by Buddhism. The *dharma* principle underlying the critique is that one should not be overly dependent upon anything, including doctrine or rituals. It is not the ritual itself that is bad, but rather a person's clinging to it.

The Buddha used an image drawn from a common experience of travelling to make his point. Travel during the rainy season in ancient India could be very difficult because of the high water in rivers and streams. At the major crossing points there were ferrymen who would take travellers across for a fee, but in other places one would have to build a raft and then pole oneself across. Śākyamuni's parable of the raft tells of a man who builds a raft, uses it for crossing, and then foolishly decides to carry it with him over dry land because it has been so useful. Doctrine and rituals are like rafts. They are to be used, but should not become a burden for one's journey towards mental purification and *nirvāṇa*.

### *Merit-Making Rituals*

All Buddhist rituals are opportunities for making merit. The term 'merit' (Sanskrit *puṇya*) means good *karma*. Any action in thought, word, or deed may be good, bad, or neutral with regard to *karma*. Good actions produce good *karma*, that is, merit. Most of our everyday actions are neutral, which means that they make our minds neither better nor worse. Therefore such neutral actions do not give rise to any *karma*, good or bad. Bad actions, arising from some combination of our deep-seated mental conditions of greed, hatred, and delusion, make our minds less pure and therefore produce bad *karma* (demerit or evil). Actions that arise from a good state of consciousness (Sanskrit *kuśala citta*) are good and produce good *karma*, or as English-speaking Buddhists usually say, 'make merit'.

Buddhism's criticism of craving or desiring does not mean that there are no good desires. It is acceptable, even necessary, to desire to make progress on the path to mental purification, and each step towards purification is at the same time an instance of making merit. So, Buddhists are motivated to go to the temple, listen to the scriptures being chanted, make offerings to the *saṃgha*, and so forth because they wish to make merit. Each merit-making opportunity brings one slightly closer to *nirvāṇa*.

Three of the most important merit-making rituals are those of Almsgiving, *Dāna*, and the Buddha Day (Viśākhā) Festival.

### Almsgiving

Traditionally, Buddhist *bhikṣus* and *bhikṣuṇīs* leave the monastery early each morning and walk in a single-file procession through the streets for their daily food. They move slowly, with their eyes focused on the ground in front of them. They do not speak to anyone, nor look around or otherwise do anything to disturb their tranquil, composed state of mind. The laypeople come out of their houses and put cooked food into the alms bowls carried by the *saṃgha* members. After putting the food into the bowl, the laypeople bow low or prostrate themselves as a way of paying respect to the *saṃgha*. The *saṃgha* members silently move on to the next house, where they receive more food. As mentioned earlier, the tranquil appearance of the *saṃgha* members while going for alms has played a role in the recruitment of new members to the *saṃgha*.

Unfortunately for Buddhism, this ritual, which has been an important point of contact between ordained and lay Buddhists, is disappearing from contemporary practice. In many Buddhist countries today, few *saṃgha* members go for alms on a regular basis. However, in some countries such as Sri Lanka, there has recently been an effort to revive this ritual, with the assistance of some *bhikṣus* from Thailand, where the almsgiving ritual is still in use. In other countries, such as Malaysia, the ritual is performed in the vicinity of the temple on important Buddhist occasions. People bring rice from home and then put it in the alms bowls of *bhikṣus* as they process along the road near the temple. Everyone then returns to the temple, where the *saṃgha* members are served first and then the laypeople eat a festive meal, including the rice that was blessed by the ritual.

### Dāna

The practice of giving food and other necessities to the *saṃgha* has developed into a ritual called *dāna*, from the Sanskrit word for 'giving'. A *dāna* might be held at a temple, usually as part of a major festival, or at a pilgrimage site, but it is very

*A procession of* bhikṣus *in Bangkok at an almsgiving ritual.*
(R.C. Amore)

common to hold a *dāna* in a private house. The following description of a *dāna* as held in Sri Lanka provides us with a glimpse of several other Buddhist rituals as well, such as foot-washing, chanting *paritta*, and merit transfer.

Prior to the *dāna*, a family will invite a certain number of *saṃgha* members to conduct the ritual in their home on some special occasion, such as a birthday, wedding anniversary, or the anniversary of the death of a family member. The family also invites a large number of relatives and friends.

On the chosen day, *saṃgha* members process from the temple to the home around ten in the morning. Upon arriving at the door to the home, the men in the family wash the monks' feet. This foot-washing ritual is a vestige of ancient hospitality practices, similar to those mentioned in the New Testament of the Christian Bible. The reason that only men can do the foot-washing is that one of the *vinaya* rules prohibits the *bhikṣus* from being touched by members of the opposite sex, and in Sri Lanka there are only *bhikṣus* today, although there were *bhikṣuṇīs* in the past. If *bhikṣuṇīs* were attending a *dāna*, their feet would be washed by women only.

Upon entering the Sri Lankan home, the *bhikṣus* pay respect to the home's

*A member of the* saṃgha *is given rice as he and the other* bhikṣus *make their way to the temple.* (R.C. Amore)

Buddha altar, then seat themselves on the floor around the room. They then conduct a Buddha-*pūjā* (a service honouring the Buddha), along the lines described below, after which they chant from the *paritta* collection.

The practice of *paritta* chanting is very important to Buddhism and is incorporated into most lengthy Buddhist rituals and festivals. The Pali term *paritta* refers to a collection of Buddha's teachings, which are thought to be especially good for bringing a blessing upon those who hear them. The *sutras* in the *paritta* collection seem to have been chosen originally because they either deal with basic moral instruction or mention blessings.

One might ask how 'blessing chants' fit into the *karma* doctrine that one has to do good on one's own behalf. People raised in a Buddhist culture seldom see any conflict here. They hold that listening to chanted Buddha teachings helps purify the mind, which means that it 'makes merit'. By developing blessing chants and blessing rituals of their own, Buddhists were presumably better suited to compete with rival religious communities.

After the chanting, which may take an hour or so, the *bhikṣus* conduct a merit-transfer ritual, in which the merit made by all present through their partic-

*Men of the household wash the feet of monks as they arrive to begin their chanting at a* dāna *ritual.* (R.C. Amore)

ipation in the rituals and listening to the *dharma* talk is transferred 'to all living beings': 'May the puñña [merit] made by me now or at some other time be shared among all beings here infinite, immeasurable; those dear to me and virtuous as mothers or as fathers are, ... to others neutral, hostile too ...'

The merit-transfer ritual has roots in early Buddhist history. The words of transfer are carved in stone in a Sri Lankan temple dating from the fifth century.

Somewhat like the traditional Roman Catholic practice of transferring the merit of penances or indulgences for the benefit of deceased relatives, the Buddhist merit transfer is said to help one's ancestors in their afterlife state. The concept of merit transfer to the deceased may seem to violate the early Buddhist principle that each person must purify his or her own mind, but according to scriptures, Śākyamuni himself advocated this ritual.

The next ritual involves a string that, before the chanting began, had been run from the Buddha image on the home altar to a pot containing holy water, to the *bhikṣus* and finally to all the laypeople. The *bhikṣus* and laypeople hold the string in their right hand during the chanting and *dharma* talk. After the merit-transfer ritual, the *bhikṣus* cut the string into short pieces, which they tie around the right wrist of each male. A layperson ties a string around the wrist of the women—again, this is because the *bhikṣus* are not supposed to come into contact with members of the opposite sex. (Buddhists do not think of this as implying inferiority for women.) The string is not taken off, but is left on one's wrist until it wears thin and falls off.

### *Buddha Day Festival*

Taking shape in traditional, largely rural societies, Buddhism developed plenty of festivals. Many are adapted from pre-Buddhist seasonal festivals, and there is variation from country to country. However, Buddhists in every country celebrate the day of the full moon around early May, known in Sanskrit as Vaiśākhā and in Theravāda countries as Vesak (or Wesak). (Buddhists in English-speaking countries often call the day 'Buddha Day'.) According to Buddhist tradition, three major events in the life of Śākyamuni occurred on that day—his birth, enlightenment, and passing or *parinirvāṇa*.

One of King Aśoka's rock edicts, from 259 BCE, states that he organized a procession to be held annually on Viśākhā day, and so the modern celebration in all Buddhist countries may be traceable back to Aśoka. The procession Aśoka began was like other religious processions in India's Hindu milieu and throughout the world. Special carts are constructed to carry temple images, and people line the streets to watch as they pass by.

In contemporary Sri Lanka, the custom is for Buddhists to travel from place to place to see special paintings depicting scenes from the life of the Buddha. Talks are given in which the main events in Śākyamuni's life are discussed. And of course there are special Buddha-*pūjās*, which draw large crowds. People make merit by participating in these events and feeding the crowds that come to the festivals. As with festivals the world over, in addition to the religious content, there is a street-fair atmosphere, with food stalls, entertainers, and, of course, people watching.

### *Death Rituals*

Every society expends a great deal of its energy and resources in staging rituals that form 'rites of passage', marking stages in an individual's life. These rituals' purposes include warding off evil powers (exorcism), creating a community of support for the individual (in, for instance, the child-naming ceremony), and reminding everyone involved that the individual has now achieved a new social status (puberty rituals).

Early Buddhism did not have any special rituals to meet the needs of the life cycle. The traditional customs of India met those needs, which means that early Indian Buddhists merely continued the use of the life-cycle rituals of what we now call Hinduism. As Buddhism spread to other countries, the new converts in each country simply kept using their respective traditional life-cycle rituals. Therefore, there is no 'Buddhist wedding' or 'Buddhist childhood ritual' *per se*. This partly explains why Buddhism has typically existed alongside the traditional ritual system of each country. For example, Sri Lankan Buddhists continue Hindu rituals; Thai Buddhists still worship the traditional spirits; and Japanese frequent Shinto rituals and shrines.

Although Buddhism did not develop its own childhood or marriage rituals, there is a Buddhist funeral ritual. It is based upon the cremation procedure of ancient India, but the active role of the *bhikṣus* has ensured that the funeral has taken on strong Buddhist characteristics. The Buddhist funeral includes a procession, ritual prayers, a water-pouring ritual, the cremation, final prayers, and a communal meal. The pattern varies from country to country. For example, it is not mandatory to cremate, and so burial in the ground is practised where the cost of wood is prohibitive.

The conduct of a typical Buddhist funeral in Sri Lanka illustrates the ceremony's principal features. On the day of burial, the corpse is taken in a procession to the cemetery. The route of the procession is specially prepared by filling in potholes, cutting the grass and weeds alongside the road, and placing flowers along the way. These preparations continue ancient ritual traditions that have parallels in India as well as beyond South Asia. They recall to mind the account of the procession in ancient India in which the person who is to become reincarnated as Śākyamuni throws himself into a pothole to prepare the road for the procession of the *buddha* of that era, and they parallel the preparations made for Jesus's procession into Jerusalem on Palm Sunday.

While some assistants have prepared the procession route, others have built a cremation structure on a special site at the cemetery. Wooden poles and paper are used to build the frame and walls of a cubicle-shaped structure over a large pile of firewood. When the procession arrives, the body is placed in this structure through an opening, which is then covered with more paper. By doing this the body is no longer visible as it rests, in a wooden coffin, above the funeral pyre.

A brief funeral service is then held in a small open-air building located close to the pyre. The service includes chants from the *paritta* and Buddhist prayers. As usual in Buddhist services, everyone present recites in Pali the Triple Refuge and the five precepts. The distinctive feature of the funeral observance, however, is a water-pouring ritual, in which various family members and friends take turns pouring holy water out of a container while a long prayer is chanted. As in the case of the *dāna* ritual discussed earlier, the water becomes blessed through this chanting of the words of Buddha.

After the service, the pyre is lit. According to Indian tradition, the honour and responsibility of lighting the fire belongs to the eldest son of the deceased. The paper walls and wooden frame catch fire quickly, of course, but they serve their purpose of providing some visual distance between the burning corpse and the mourners.

The use of a traditional funeral pyre as just described is giving way to the use of crematoria in contemporary Sri Lanka. One or more *bhikṣus* still come to recite prayers over the body, but some of the other funeral rituals, such as the water-pouring ritual, are postponed until the *dāna* held on the seventh day.

The loss of a loved one is always a difficult experience, but Buddhists prepare for it by years of prayer and by meditating on the inevitability of death. One of Buddhism's strengths is the way it helps its followers to accept the death of others and of themselves.

On the sixth night after the death, a *dharma*-preaching service is held at the home, followed by a *dāna*, as previously described, on the morning of the seventh day. Other memorial *dāna* rituals are held at the home of the deceased after three months, on the eve of which *bhikṣus* may be invited to chant all night long, and after one year. Family members and friends who live too far away to attend the funeral itself are able to participate in these memorials. After the passage of time has lessened the pain (*duḥkha*) of losing a loved one, the memorial services provide an occasion for the family and friends to remember the happy times with the deceased and to enjoy a family reunion.

## Buddhist Architecture in South Asia

### *The Stupa*

After the *parinirvāṇa* of the Buddha, several kings requested the honour of enshrining his cremated remains in their kingdoms. This created a dilemma that was brilliantly solved by the Buddhist in charge of funeral arrangements. He divided the remains into seven portions. The urn that had held the cremated remains and the cloth that had covered it were given the status of primary relics as well, and so nine memorials were originally built over the nine relics. But as Buddhism spread to other parts of India, additional memorials were needed to provide a place for Buddhist rituals. These memorials were built over other sacred objects, such as the cremated remains of Buddha's major disciples, or even portions of the Buddhist scriptures.

The architecture of the memorials has a rich history. The Buddha had been asked before his death about the proper way to bury him, and his response was that a Tathāgata's remains should be enshrined in a memorial stupa, like that of a great ruler. There is evidence, from as far as Ireland to India, that the preferred form for burying Indo-Aryan rulers was to place their remains in an above-ground crypt, which was then covered with earth to form a large burial mound. Tables or platforms for offerings were then constructed in each of the four cardinal directions near the mound.

The funeral itself lasted seven days—the twenty-eight-day lunar month was divided into four such weeks—during which time people walked ceremonially around the mound and placed food, water, and flower offerings on the altars. Circumambulation is always clockwise, the devotee keeping the shrine to one's right, a much more auspicious side than the left in Indian tradition. Monks' robes, moreover, keep the right shoulder bare while covering the left.

The Buddha's royal disciples made eight such memorials. A group of brahmins also made memorials, bringing the total of original monuments to ten. They buried his cremated remains in small caskets, about the size of shoe boxes, richly decorated with jewels, which they placed in a crypt made of stone slabs. The crypt was then covered over with a large mound of earth and a layer or two of bricks, which were plastered and finally whitewashed.

The builders erected a pole, which was fixed in a square frame atop the mound and positioned over the crypt. The pole represents Mount Meru, Indian mythology's cosmic mountain that reaches from earth up towards the pole star, and around whose axis the world is thought to turn. The part of the pole that extends above its support base symbolizes the upper reaches of the heavens. The pole runs through disks of wood that symbolize the layers of heaven. (In European thought, the comparable feature is the 'heavenly spheres'.) There are usually nine such layers, in keeping with Indian astrology and cosmology, which envision nine layers among the heavenly spheres and nine orbiting planetary bodies. The frame, the pole, and its planes later came to be built of stone because wooden parts were difficult to maintain.

There are several ways of referring to these white memorial mounds. The Sanskrit term *stūpa* and its Pali-language equivalent *thūpa* are cognate with the English word 'tomb'. Another name is *caitya*, which means 'shrine', or in this case 'burial shrine'. The name used throughout East Asian Buddhism is 'pagoda', which derives from another Sanskrit word for a monument, *dagoba*. It connotes 'womb' in the sense that burial is the forerunner of a rebirth. Whether the memorial structure is called stupa, *thūpa*, *caitya*, or pagoda, nearly every Buddhist temple precinct in the world has one.

Legends arose claiming in each case that the relic of a particular stupa was traceable back to the Buddha himself. For example, important temples in Sri Lanka and Burma claimed to have an eye-tooth of the Buddha enshrined in their stupas. Major Buddhist temples developed long chronicles giving the legendary history of the relics enshrined in their stupas.

In addition to the large main stupa, a temple complex may often have smaller ones built as memorial crypts of important Buddhists of that particular temple. These small votive stupas add to the beauty and spiritual atmosphere of the temple grounds. In popular piety, Buddhists sometimes strew flower petals at such locations and vow that they, too, will some day overcome death and achieve *nirvāṇa*.

Building small stupas as an act of devotion was especially popular as a merit-making practice in Myanmar, where thousands of devotional stupas have been built through the centuries. Some are built to last, such as the ones located near the ancient Burmese city of Pagan, but most are temporary structures, such as the ones devout Buddhists make from sand at the shore. The merit comes from purifying the mind while one builds the stupa in a devotional state of mind, and so it is not necessary that it endure for long.

The shape of the stupa or pagoda underwent changes through the centuries, especially when Buddhism spread to East Asia. There, pagodas eventually developed into elegant five- or seven-storied stone or wooden towers that devo-

*A landmark in Buddhist architectural history is the stupa complex at Sanchi, northeast of Bhopal.* (W.G. Oxtoby)

tees could climb up or circumambulate. The stories of the East Asian pagoda derive from the various levels of the heavens symbolized by the wooden disks of the original Indian stupas. Such pagoda architecture exaggerated the 'heavenly' levels at the expense of the lower parts of the original stupa, including the mound itself.

### *Temples*

Buddhists did not have their own temples during the time of Śākyamuni, but in subsequent centuries, stupas or *caitya*s were one focus of construction, and monks' quarters or *vihāra*s were another. As it developed into an established religious tradition in and after Aśoka's time, Buddhism elaborated its shrine buildings, and the characteristic *caitya* hall, or temple, gradually evolved. Early surviving *caitya*s include those at Bhaja and Bharut. Cave sanctuaries at Ajanta in western India supply evidence that a stage in the temple's development was as a shrine room at the back of a *vihāra*. In more populated areas, the number of Buddhists coming to such shrines may have made it necessary to build buildings whose sole feature was the shrine area. That is, monks' quarters and shrines became distinct buildings.

Early cave temples carved in stone were clearly modelled after the shapes of wooden structures. Simple huts that earlier *saṃgha* members had dwelt in during the rainy season, when they settled down for a period of intense study and meditation, may have been a prototype. By the Gupta period in India (ca.

320–540), temples took on the rectangular shape and other architectural features of Hindu temples of the time.

There are some similarities among temples in different areas of the ancient world. The typical ancient temple—whether in Israel, India, or elsewhere in southern and western Asia—is a rectangular building that one enters from one of the shorter sides. (In East Asian temples, access is from one of the longer sides.) Upon entering through a tall portico, one comes into an outer open chamber that in some cases is open to the air and can hold large numbers of people. At the far end of the building is an image of the revered figure—or, in the Hebrew temple, some sort of throne but no image—flanked by attendant deities, angels, or supernatural animals. Often, but not always, an altar in front of the image is where worshippers, or priests representing them, place flowers and other offerings. Songs of praise were usually sung, and lights and incense were lit.

### *Temple Grounds*

The stupa and temple are usually located close together in a sacred area that in English may be called the temple grounds, the temple complex, or simply the temple. The boundary around the temple grounds, normally a square or rectangular area, is marked by an ornamental wall or fence. The people enter through high gates on the sides, and usually go first to a side shrine dedicated to the guardian spirit of the temple grounds.

Besides the stupa and temple, the grounds usually contain a Bodhi tree and a hall used for *dharma* talks and other large gatherings of Buddhists on full-moon and festival days. There is also usually a monastery with small rooms where the *bhikṣus* live. Large temple grounds also have a library, a refectory, and various service buildings.

Buddhists place flowers on altars or platforms at the base of the stupa and near the Bodhi tree, and proceed into the temple to place flowers on the altar(s) there. They may put coins into an offering box in the temple, and they say prayers expressing their dedication to living according to the *dharma*.

## Theravāda Art

### *Buddha Images*

It was almost 500 years after the *parinirvāṇa* of the Buddha before his first image appeared. Up to that point it was evidently assumed, particularly in Theravāda Buddhism, that no physical form could or should depict him. In the intervening years, the Buddha and his teaching were symbolized by the stupa and other non-iconic forms such as his footprint, the Wheel of the Law, the Bodhi Tree, or an empty seat. These representations played an important role in the decoration of the stupa as well as its surrounding fence and gates.

Scholars suggest that the representations in stone and terracotta that came later may have been developed from wooden models of this period. The masonry of the important stupa complex at Sanchi in central India reflects this copying of wooden patterns in stone. The detail of its carvings, with scenes from Śākyamuni's life, hints at another transition as well, for some of the teaching scenes might be interpreted as showing the *bodhisattva* in human form prior to his enlightenment, while the enlightened Buddha is still not depicted.

The first Buddha icons in stone emerged during the first century CE, at a time when the devotional aspects of Mahāyāna Buddhism were becoming increasingly popular. Images in statues and reliefs are depicted standing, seated in the lotus position of yogic meditation, seated with dangling legs, or reclining at the *parinirvāṇa*.

Hand gestures or *mudrās*, like those found in Hindu portrayals of deities, became an important feature of Buddhist art. In one, the Buddha touches the earth with the fingers of his right hand, 'calling the earth to witness', as he is reputed to have done in his encounter with Māra on the eve of his enlightenment. Another popular image depicts the Buddha in a posture of teaching. One *mudrā* shows the Buddha with his right hand raised, with his palm outward and fingers upward, in a gesture indicating the 'granting of protection'. This is usually combined with a *mudrā* where the left hand is extended downward, with the palm outward and fingers pointed down, interpreted as 'fulfilling a wish'.

In some cases, the Buddha reclining on his side is simply thought to be Śākyamuni asleep; Hindu temples also often include a statue of the sleeping deity. More commonly, a reclining figure represents the *parinirvāṇa* of the Buddha. The iconography of the Buddha figure is said to include some thirty-two major signs of Śākyamuni's status, the most obvious of them being the *uṣṇīṣa* (the protuberance atop his head as the locus of his supernatural wisdom) and elongated ear lobes. He is often robed like a monk, with his left shoulder covered and his right shoulder bare.

### *Story Illustrations*

Buddhist art, especially painting and relief carving, often illustrates scenes from the life of the Buddha or from the *Jātaka* ('birth story') collections recounting the previous lives of Śākyamuni Buddha. The walls of temples are often lined with such art. The story of the Buddha's life may, for example, be viewed chronologically as one circumambulates the stupa or moves around in the temple.

In ancient India when stupas were located away from temple grounds, they were surrounded by an ornamental fence with beautiful relief carvings of scenes from the *Jātaka*s and the Buddha's life. The great stupa in the complex at Sanchi, in central India, offers the most important example of such art. The fences that can be seen after 2,000 years are those that were made of stone, whereas their wooden prototypes have not survived. Stupas today do not normally have ornamental fences, but narrative illustration panels in temples continue the ancient pattern.

# Mahāyāna in India

## The Rise of Mahāyāna

Beyond the diverse interpretations of the Buddha's teaching that resulted in different Buddhist monastic schools 2,000 years ago, a vast cultural movement arose that affected monastic and lay Buddhists alike. Called Mahāyāna, it spread northwestward into Central Asia and then east to China. It now dominates the Buddhist world from Japan and Korea to Vietnam. Theravāda, as we have seen, spread to the south and southeast from India and now dominates the Buddhist world from Sri Lanka to Cambodia.

Ultimately, Theravāda and Mahāyāna went their separate ways not only geographically but in many matters of doctrine and practice. While Theravāda maintained a strong focus on the Śākyamuni of the present historical age and his spiritual insight and discipline, the Mahāyāna emphasis saw the principle of his insight as attained by enlightened beings of past and future worlds. While Theravāda doctrine was reticent to speculate about transhuman powers and realities, Mahāyāna populated the heavens with them. While Theravāda stressed the role of disciplined *bhikṣus* as a necessary condition for liberation, Mahāyāna offered spiritual benefits to the laity as a reward for simple trust or declaration. There are hardly greater contrasts than those between Theravāda and Mahāyāna, and yet these two traditions were developing side by side in India 2,000 years ago. Moreover, they continued to be practised together in monastic and lay communities for centuries.

The precise history of Mahāyāna Buddhism's emergence is difficult to reconstruct. We know that by the third or fourth century CE, there were Buddhist ordination lineages that distinguished themselves from earlier forms of Buddhism. The new form of Buddhism called itself the 'Great Vehicle' (Mahāyāna), in contrast to the older forms to which it now referred collectively (and pejoratively) as the 'Little Vehicle' (Hīnayāna). We also know that the Mahāyāna Buddhists had new scriptures, new forms of the *dharma*, new rituals, and new meditational practices, but why and how did all this arise?

A possible explanation is that one of the eighteen or more early Indian sects developed into Mahāyāna Buddhism. There is some evidence for a close connection between early Mahāyāna and two or three of the early Indian sects, especially the Mahāsāṃghika (Great *Saṃgha*). However, it seems more likely that Mahāyāna Buddhism arose in southern India as a movement that spread across several of the early Indian sects. In the following paragraphs, we shall sketch several characteristics that figure in its development.

### *Stupa Veneration*

Mahāyāna placed emphasis on pilgrimage to stupas. The veneration of Śākyamuni at stupas enshrining relics had been a part of Buddhism from the earliest days after the *parinirvāṇa*, his passing from worldly existence. By the time of Mahāyāna's origin, however, some lay Buddhists had come to place great emphasis upon making pilgrimages to stupas. This development may have been influenced by the significant role played by pilgrimages to shrines in Hinduism. In any case, lay Buddhists were fond of making pilgrimages and came to believe that the merit made by participating in the pilgrimage could greatly influence one's future karmic state.

### *The Role of Lay Disciples*

Closely related was an emphasis upon the role of lay Buddhists. In early Indian Buddhism, the role of laypeople was primarily one of giving support to the *saṃgha*. Any layperson who wished to pursue the purification of the mind more seriously was expected to 'depart the world' and enter the *bhikṣu* or *bhikṣuṇī saṃgha*. Mahāyāna Buddhism, in contrast, held out the promise of making serious spiritual progress, possibly even attaining enlightenment, while remaining a layperson. This meant an improvement, especially in the status of lay-women.

### *Doctrine of the Three Bodies*

Mahāyāna developed a doctrine of the 'three bodies' (*trikāya*) of the Buddha to account for the various ways in which one could experience or refer to buddhahood. The earthly manifestation body of a *buddha* is called the Appearance Body or Transformation Body (*nirmāṇakāya*). The heavenly body of a *buddha* that presides over a Buddha-realm, that can communicate in the heavens with other *buddhas*, and is an object of devotion for Mahāyāna Buddhists is called the Body of Bliss (*sambhogakāya*).

These are supported by the Buddha as the absolute essence of the universe, called the Dharma Body (*dharmakāya*). This doctrine called attention not only to the oneness of all the *buddhas* that have appeared on earth, but also to the unity of the Buddha-nature or Buddha-potential in all its forms. That is, the *trikāya* or three-bodies doctrine envisions one cosmic reality (Dharma Body) that manifests itself as grace-filled heavenly beings (Body of Bliss) and as humans such as Śākyamuni (Appearance Body).

By making a connection between the earthly Buddha and the Dharma Body or Absolute, the doctrine of the three bodies also moved Mahāyāna Buddhism in the direction of a theistic religion, in contrast to the Theravāda Buddhist understanding of things.

### *Expedient Means*

The Sanskrit term *upāya* ('stratagem') forms part of an expression frequently translated as 'skill in means' or 'skilful means'. Sporadic occurrences of '*upāya*' in Theravāda's Pali texts seem to have a non-technical meaning, but the building blocks of the later idea are already present. Śākyamuni's teachings are practical, even pragmatic. Their variation appears to be somewhat tailored to people's capacity to grasp them. Śākyamuni's followers are urged to use skill in guiding people to spiritual attainment, like the skilful boatman ferrying people to the other side of the river. Already in the analogy of the raft or boat, we see the implication that when one has reached the other side, there is no further need of the raft for the onward journey.

As Mahāyāna teachings developed, the temporary, provisional, and expedient nature of doctrine came to be asserted explicitly. A Mahāyāna text that places major emphasis on *upāya* is the polemical *Lotus sūtra*, which treats many Buddhist teachings as provisional, relativizing them as steps towards its own perspective. As an illustration, the *Lotus sūtra* tells a story about a father whose children are inside a burning house. He gets them to come out by offering them chariots—a deceptive lure, but an expedient rescue. Similarly, ultimate spiritual truth is obscured from persons just starting the path with temporary formulations, but spiritual advancement enables one to put earlier stages in their place. Moreover, even Śākyamuni's teaching is merely provisional, and his earthly life almost a mirage, a mere device to get human beings started. In other texts besides the *Lotus sūtra*, handling earlier teachings as expedient means made it possible for Mahāyāna thinkers to redirect Buddhism's emphasis from Śākyamuni to celestial *buddha* figures and a notion of cosmic wisdom.

### *Merit Transfer*

Other important characteristics of Mahāyāna Buddhism centre around a new interpretation of merit transfer. Early Buddhism taught that good or bad *karma* (merit or demerit) is made by oneself, and not by an outside agent such as a god. However, early Buddhists did allow one instance of the transfer of merit from one person to another, namely, the transfer of merit for the benefit of one's dead relatives and the welfare of all beings. For example, recall how a ritual merit transfer is incorporated into a *dāna* ritual in Theravāda Buddhism.

## The *bodhisattva* in Mahāyāna

Many of the most important features of Mahāyāna centre around the important roles *bodhisattvas* play in thought and practice.

There was in early Buddhism a sense in which a *bodhisattva* could be helpful through instruction and example in assisting others on the right path because of the *bodhisattva*'s store of past merit. Mahāyāna greatly developed this notion, to the point where one of the key characteristics of Mahāyāna is the idea that *bodhisattvas* share their merit with all beings. Having advanced very close to total enlightenment, they are reborn in one of the heavens, and from there they stand ready to share their great merit with all who turn to them for help. Mahāyāna cosmology envisions many spiritually advanced *bodhisattvas*, each presiding over a heavenly region, from which the *bodhisattva* is prepared to bestow merit (grace) upon those humans who pray for help.

### *Bodhisattva* Vows

Another Mahāyāna characteristic follows directly: the practice of taking *bodhisattva* vows. As we have seen, early Indian Buddhism taught that in a previous era, Śākyamuni had vowed to become a *buddha* one day. Śākyamuni's '*bodhisattva* vow' was taken as a rather special case in early Buddhism. Few Buddhists dared to think of themselves as destined to be the *buddha* of some future era. Rather, they were content to hope that they could in some future life enter the *saṃgha* and achieve the status of *arhat* ('worthy one') or saint.

Mahāyāna Buddhism sharply criticized the *arhat* ideal on the grounds that it seemed too self-centred. The *arhat*, they argued, was out only for his own liberation and was not striving to save all beings. In contrast, they claimed, those who take *bodhisattva* vows are dedicating themselves first and foremost to the salvation of all living beings. All Mahāyāna Buddhists, whether male or female, lay or monastic, were encouraged to take the *bodhisattva* vows. During the ritual, one vowed to become a *buddha* some day, but one also vowed to remain active in helping to liberate all beings.

### Veneration of *Bodhisattvas*

In practical terms, the vows meant that one hoped to be reborn in a heaven, from which one could transfer merit to others. Although the possibility of helping others by being reborn on earth as a human was not ruled out, the advanced *bodhisattvas* were thought of as residing in a heavenly realm. This provides the background for another Mahāyāna characteristic, the veneration of *bodhisattvas*.

Early Indian Buddhism paid respect to the Buddha, but thought of Śākyamuni, after the *parinirvāṇa*, as being beyond the realm of direct involvement with human lives, so Theravāda Buddhists do not think of themselves as praying to the Buddha. Theravāda does not have prayers of petition in the way that theistic religions such as Christianity, Islam, devotional Hinduism, or Shinto do. Mahāyāna Buddhism, in contrast, holds that numerous *bodhisattvas* are available to respond to the needs of worshippers. Mahāyāna Buddhists can petition the *bodhisattvas* for blessings, and comparisons have sometimes been made with the Roman Catholic veneration of the saints.

Mahāyāna holds that there are countless heavenly *bodhisattvas* ready to help all sentient beings, but only a few are venerated by name, and these important *bodhisattvas* have their special functions. Bodhisattva Maitreya, the 'Friendly One', is destined to be the next *buddha*. He will come after the *dharma* wheel set in motion by Śākyamuni has stopped. That is, when the world needs a new Fully Enlightened Buddha to teach *dharma*, the *bodhisattva* Maitreya will be reborn. Some Mahāyāna Buddhists pray to Maitreya, requesting that they be reborn when he comes to earth as the next *buddha*, for it is easier to become enlightened when there is a living *buddha* to follow.

With the coming of Mahāyāna Buddhism, the difference in meaning almost disappears between the Buddha figure as an enlightened being ready for *nirvāṇa* and the *bodhisattva* who is ready but forgoes it and returns to *saṃsāra* to save more beings. In some of the philosophical schools, words like 'Buddha-nature', 'mind', or 'Buddha-mind', also became substitutes for 'enlightenment'. A Westerner could appreciate the importance of such issues when it is understood that Buddhism is essentially a religion of salvation, with doctrinal disputes focused on the accessibility of such salvation, which is also explained as *nirvāṇa*, buddhahood, or enlightenment.

The *bodhisattvas* have exercised enormous appeal as saviour figures in Mahāyāna Buddhism. In their compassionate activity of self-sacrifice, they have been compared to the Christ figure. The difference between the two is the essentially historical character of Jesus as a saviour. While certain *bodhisattva* figures are believed to have become historically incarnate, their role for devotees is more like that of medieval saints or angels. Bodhisattva Mañjuśrī is the guardian of Buddhist wisdom. In their quest for it, Buddhists entering monastic training can call upon him to guide and inspire them.

The *bodhisattva* known especially for compassion is Avalokiteśvara, whose name according to one etymology means 'the Lord who looks down'. This *bodhisattva* has a long and widespread history of veneration. His image is prominently featured at Borobudur, Indonesia, for example, as well as in Indian and early Southeast Asian places. Yet Avalokiteśvara's story is the most interesting in China, where the *bodhisattva* eventually came to be venerated in feminine form under the name Kuan-yin. This gender shift is one example of the power to take any shape that is needed to benefit believers, and a famous *Lotus sūtra* chapter lists thirty-three examples of such 'shape-shifting'.

Whether manifest as masculine or feminine, Avalokiteśvara has been the most venerated *bodhisattva* in Buddhist history. She has been called the 'virgin Mary of East Asia' by Westerners since graceful statues of her are found everywhere. The special closeness many Mahāyāna women feel towards Kuan-yin is based on her promise to bring children to those who lack them and on her care for infants who die and for aborted foetuses.

### *Buddha-Realms*

The heavens in which a *buddha* or *bodhisattva* resides are known as 'fields', which we might better translate as 'realms'. The belief in such 'Buddha-realms' is another characteristic of Mahāyāna. The Buddha-realm gained special significance with the development of the belief that a *buddha* or *bodhisattva* has the power, through merit, to cause the devotee to be reborn in his realm. Simply put, if one venerates a certain *buddha*, one may be reborn into that *buddha*'s heaven. As we shall see, this is a key belief underlying the popular Pure Land movement in Buddhism.

#### *Meditation and Visualization*

Another characteristic of Mahāyāna is the emphasis upon meditational practice. For example, the practice of 'vision meditations' became very popular. This practice grew out of the belief in various *buddhas* and *bodhisattvas*, each with his or her own heaven. In vision practice, the meditator concentrates upon a particular *bodhisattva* or *buddha*, trying to focus the mind so that one would be granted a vision of that *buddha* or *bodhisattva*. In this way the practitioner could achieve a heightened state of consciousness and develop special rapport with the *bodhisattva* or *buddha*. The Vajrayāna school also made great use of vision practices.

## Mādhyamika

The Mahāyāna movement gave rise to several specific schools of Buddhism. One of the most important was Mādhyamika.

Early Buddhism taught that there were six perfections (*pāramitās*), with the sixth and most important being the perfection of wisdom. The word for wisdom here is *prajñā*, which should not be confused with worldly wisdom or scientific knowledge. It connotes a state of highly developed consciousness or awareness. One tendency in Mahāyāna Buddhism was to put great emphasis upon the development of *prajñā*, and a number of perfection-of-wisdom texts were written from as early as the first century BCE. The *Perfection of Wisdom in Eight Thousand Verses* is the oldest such text. The most important in later Mahāyāna were the *Heart sūtra* and the *Diamond Cutter sūtra*. Throughout these texts, the emphasis is upon developing the highest form of spiritual wisdom through an awareness of the emptiness (*śūnyatā*) of all things.

Sometime during the later part of the second century, a brahmin from southern India converted to Buddhism, taking the ordination name Nāgārjuna. He wrote Buddhist devotional hymns and ethical guides, but his fame is based upon his philosophical works, such as the *Mūlamādhyamaka-kārikā* (Fundamentals of the Middle Way).

Nāgārjuna's philosophical position is called the 'Middle Way' (Mādhyamika) because it refuses to take a position either affirming or negating statements about reality. All statements fall short of being expressions of ultimate truth. All realities (*dharmas*) are equally 'empty' of absolute truth or 'self-essence'. Nāgārjuna taught the doctrine of Emptiness, chiefly that everything in the phenomenal world is ultimately unreal. By a process of paradoxical logic, he claims that Emptiness as ultimate reality is itself unreal, although it may be experienced in meditation with directness and certainty.

Nāgārjuna summed up in a famous eightfold negation:

> Nothing comes into being,
> Nor does anything disappear.
> Nothing is eternal,
> Nor has anything an end.
> Nothing is identical,
> Or differentiated,
> Nothing moves hither,
> Nor moves anything thither.
> (Ch'en 1964:84)

For Mādhyamika and the later Mahāyāna schools it influenced, such as Zen Buddhism, enlightenment involves the realization of the *śūnyatā* or Emptiness of all *dharmas*. The subject as discussed by these schools is also often translated as 'the Void' or 'Nothingness' or, especially in Zen, 'Buddha-nature'.

Being a very consistent thinker, Nāgārjuna realized that such all-embracing criticism would apply to his own thinking as well. Nāgārjuna's philosophical 'position' is to refuse to take a position. A modern Japanese Buddhist professor reports that as a graduate student, he was very uncertain of himself in relation to the various Buddhist philosophical schools. When he told his teacher this, the teacher said, 'Your position is to have no position.' This illustrates the continuing influence of Nāgārjuna and the admiration shown in early Buddhist texts for those who avoid dogmatism.

Through his paradoxical logic, Nāgārjuna asserts that Emptiness or *nirvāṇa* is actually dialectically identical to *saṃsāra*, or the phenomenal world. In other words, each is present in the other. This is the most characteristic and most puzzling Mādhyamika teaching. Early Indian Buddhism had taken these to be opposites, *saṃsāra* being the temporal, worldly process of 'coming to be and passing away', and *nirvāṇa* being the eternal, unchanging goal of one's spiritual quest, and yet Mādhyamika holds that '*saṃsāra* is *nirvāṇa*, and *nirvāṇa* is *saṃsāra*'. From the point of view of conventional wisdom, they may be distinguished, perhaps, but from the point of view of higher wisdom, no such distinction is tenable, nor, claims Mādhyamika, are any other distinctions tenable in higher wisdom.

By the sixth century, a split in the Mādhyamika school developed around the teachings of two teachers, each of whom considered himself to be the true follower of the master, Nāgārjuna. The school of Bhāvaviveka (or Bhavya, c. 490–570) was willing to talk about levels of reality and degrees of insight, as long as it was understood that the distinctions applied only to the realm of conventional truth. That is, they accepted the mind's ability to make distinctions about reality within the realm of conventional truth. Nāgārjuna's insistence upon the identity of *nirvāṇa* and *saṃsāra* kept them from making distinctions in the realm of absolute knowledge. This school founded by Bhavya was known by the name Svātantrika because it accepted the validity of independent (*svātantra*) inference.

The rival Mādhyamika school founded by Buddhapālita (c. 470–550) rejected independent inference and the other positions taken by Bhavya. It was called the Prāsaṅgika school because it stressed the position that all statements of knowledge, or theories, were ultimately self-contradictory (*prāsaṅga*).

## Yogācāra

A *bhikṣu* named Maitreyanātha (c. 270–350) and two *bhikṣus* who were brothers, Asaṅga (c. 315–90) and Vasubandhu, wrote important Mahāyāna texts in the late fourth century. The new school of Mahāyāna they founded has two names. It is called Yogācāra, meaning 'Practice of Yoga', after one of its many texts, the *Yogācārabhūmi*. As the name suggests, this school was particularly devoted to meditational practice.

The other name is Vijñānavāda, which means 'Way of Consciousness' or 'Consciousness Only'. The latter name derived from the school's unusual theory of consciousness (*vijñāna*), in which it is argued that apparent realities are really only objects of consciousness derived from a 'storehouse consciousness' (*ālaya-vijñāna*). The net effect of this is that one can never know the external world itself, nor know oneself, if they even exist. All one can ever know is images in one's consciousness. These ideas come from a repository, a 'storehouse of consciousness', that has been shaped by past karmic actions and attachments.

On first glance, the Yogācāra school seems to resemble the pure idealism of the philosophers George Berkeley (1685–1753) and David Hume (1711–76) in eighteenth-century Europe. For them, the universe exists only in the mind of the perceiver; it is but a fabrication of consciousness. But for Yogācāra, the universe and the perceiver exist only in the perceptual process. Even one's 'self' and one's *karma* are but a reification of momentary awareness. Impressions are 'seeds' that lead to acts or thoughts.

> A seed produces a manifestation,
> A manifestation perfumes a seed.
> The three elements (seed, manifestation, and perfume) turn
> on and on,
> The cause and effect occur at the same time.
> (Ch'en 1964:323)

According to Yogācāra, mountains and rivers, other people and ourselves—all are such manifestations. Through yoga and spiritual cultivation, one can purify the process of awareness from false substantialization. Such discipline would exhaust consciousness until it became identical to the ultimate reality called 'Thusness' or 'Suchness' (*tathatā*) that also corresponds to the Emptiness of the Mādhyamika or the indefinable character of awareness in what Westerners term the I-Thou experience.

Critics from rival schools of Buddhism claimed that the concept of a storehouse consciousness seemed to run counter to the traditional Buddhist doctrine of no-self (*anātman*) and came too close to affirming the Hindu notion of *ātman* that the Buddha had negated. The Yogācāra writers, however, were careful to point out that although the storehouse consciousness transmigrates from birth to birth (like the *ātman* in Hinduism), it has no eternal or unchanged substance (in that respect, unlike the *ātman*). Buddhist ideas of the link between one birth and the next as a '*karma* complex' or 'migrating consciousness' were developed by Yogācāra into the notion of a storehouse consciousness.

The Yogācāra emphasis upon the 'consciousness only' teaching and the psychological origin of all one's perceptions may have arisen out of their experience of emptying one's mind during meditation. This contrasts with other meditation traditions, in which one concentrates on visualizing an image. Yogācāra's most important contribution to later Mahāyāna Buddhism in China and Japan may have been as much its emphasis on meditation practice as its doctrine of Consciousness-only.

## Indian Pure Land

A sectarian movement within Buddhism developed in the first century around the veneration of a celestial *buddha* known in Sanskrit as Amitāyus or Amitābha, and subsequently as O-mi-t'o-fo in Chinese and Amida in Japanese. It may have emerged around the first century, about 500 years after the *parinirvāṇa* or passing of Śākyamuni. Although Amitābha, the *buddha* of 'infinite life' and 'infinite light', is a popular figure in many Mahāyāna texts, the *Larger Sūtra on the Pure Land* contains an account by Śākyamuni of Amitābha before his enlightenment when, as a young prince named Dharmākara, he takes a series of forty-eight *bodhisattva* vows.

The vows detail the *bodhisattva*'s avowed intention to achieve higher enlightenment and help others in specific ways. In form some resemble a medical oath not to deny service to people who have no money to pay the doctor. In one of the most important, the eighteenth vow, Amitābha promises to establish a country (i.e., heaven) for those who desire to be reborn there by thinking of him (i.e., through faith in his compassionate power):

> If, after my obtaining Buddhahood, all beings in the ten quarters should not desire in sincerity and trustfulness to be born in my country, and if they

> should not be born by only thinking of me for ten times, except those who have committed the five grave offences and those who are abusive of the true Dharma, may I not attain the Highest Enlightenment (Bloom 1965:2–3).

Taken collectively, the essence of Dharmākara's vows is that he will strive to become a completely enlightened *buddha*, but on the condition that he can remain active in the work of bringing all living beings towards liberation. To do this, he vows to establish a Buddha-realm in the western region of the heavens, a paradise to which all his followers can be reborn. Once in the Western Paradise, they will be spiritually uplifted by Amitābha's great store of merit and will be able to make easy progress towards *nirvāṇa*.

Beings reborn in the Western Paradise will experience only bliss because suffering, old age, and death are unknown there. Amitābha's paradise is a Pure Land or Happy Land (*sukhāvatī* in Sanskrit) where the streets and buildings are made of semiprecious jewels, trimmed with gold, diamonds, and other precious stones. One can hear whatever music one wishes, have water any temperature one likes, and so forth. And while enjoying sensual pleasure, one can learn true *dharma* from all these adornments as well as from the *buddha* Amitābha himself.

In Pure Land, the idea of heaven has undergone a remarkable transformation. In early Buddhism, a meritorious person hoped to enjoy being reborn in a heaven. However, while in heaven one could not 'make' new merit or develop one's higher wisdom, and so there was no path leading from heaven to *nirvaṇa*. One always had to come back to earth in a human rebirth when one's merit was exhausted. Only as an earthly human could one achieve the final goal, *nirvāṇa*. However, in Amitābha's heaven, the Pure Land, one can listen to *dharma* talks by Amitābha and otherwise go on to the perfection of one's mind that leads directly to *nirvāṇa*. Amitābha's great store of merit supports ideal conditions for enlightenment, and *nirvāṇa* is reachable, so it is not necessary to be reborn on earth again.

The *Shorter Sūtra on the Pure Land* spells out the nature of what is to be done to benefit from Amitābha's great store of merit. One who has recollected and repeated Amitābha's name before death will, upon dying, be reborn in his Pure Land. This rebirth is not won by one's own meritorious works, as was the case with the path laid down by Śākyamuni. Rather, one wins rebirth in the Pure Land by means of the infinite merits of the *buddha* Amitābha.

The third text of early Pure Land Buddhism, the *Meditation on Amitāyus sūtra*, is a manual of sixteen different ways of meditating in order to be granted a vision on Amitāyus (Amitābha). This text is an example of a Mahāyāna vision text, which teaches ways to meditate on a certain *bodhisattva* or *buddha* until one sees him or her in a vision. The promise of the *Meditation sūtra* is that one who has achieved such a vision will be reborn in the Pure Land. To encourage religious development, nine levels of practice are outlined.

Yet not everyone had the time to undergo the training in vision meditations, so the *Meditation sūtra* offers an easier path intended for the laity. This was the formula characteristic of Pure Land Buddhism: 'Homage to Amitābha Buddha'. The *Meditation sūtra* prescribes that the phrase be repeated at least ten times, but later Japanese Pure Land writers taught that three, or even one sincere, faithful repetition of the sacred formula would suffice for rebirth in the Pure Land. People, even meritless or wicked ones, may gain rebirth in the Pure Land by sincerely taking refuge in Buddha Amitāyus.

The Pure Land school introduces into Buddhism a path of devotion in which one trusts and praises the deity. It employs a sacred mantra (chant) to bring that faith to expression. The mantra is 'Homage [*namo*] to Amitābha Buddha'. The most important time to repeat the 'Homage to Amitābha Buddha' prayer is shortly before dying, but followers of this path have never thought it wise to wait until one's deathbed. Rather, the consciousness should always be directed towards Amitābha, and the best way to do this is to repeat the sacred prayer throughout one's life.

The Pure Land school spread to East Asia, where it remains the most popular of all forms of Buddhism. Much as Christians do, Pure Land Buddhists strive to be good, but are assured that the divine being will bestow divine compassion upon them. Important East Asian writers in the Pure Land tradition have looked upon the major thinkers of early Indian Mahāyāna Buddhism as forerunners of Pure Land practice. There is no parallel to this approach in Theravāda Buddhism, nor is there any mantra practice that compares closely with uttering the 'Homage to Amitābha Buddha'. However, as we have seen, Theravāda Buddhists always include a refuge-taking homage to the Triple Gem as part of their rituals.

## Vajrayāna

Half a century ago, most of the West's discussions of Buddhism divided it into two traditions, Theravāda and Mahāyāna. Since then, Tibetan Buddhists have fled or migrated to India and the West. Tibet itself has become more accessible. Tibetan texts have been studied and translated. Hence one now regularly encounters reference to Tibet as preserving a third branch of Buddhism. The name Vajrayāna has come into widespread use for this branch, but other descriptions of it have also been used to designate it.

### *The Third Turning*

Its advocates and converts refer to it as the 'third turning of the wheel of *dharma*', after Theravāda as the first and Mahāyāna as the second. They see Vajrayāna as the culmination of the other two. This self-understanding gave rise to a system of Vajrayāna training with three stages named after the three Vehicles. First, in the

'Hīnayāna' phase of practice, the beginner concentrates upon basic moral discipline. In the second or 'Mahāyāna' stage, the practitioner gets instruction in basic Buddhist doctrines. In the third and highest stage, the Vajrayāna, one is taught what from a Vajrayāna point of view are advanced doctrines and practices.

Vajrayāna's role as the third turning of the wheel also makes some sense in historical terms, for it emerged and was diffused from India at a later period than Theravāda and Mahāyāna, Buddhism's two main branches. Arising in India around the third century, the techniques and emphases of Vajrayāna subsequently were taken to virtually all the Buddhist world: to Southeast Asia, Central Asia, and in the course of time to Japan. In many of these regions, however, Vajrayāna remained a minor influence or died out. It disappeared from Southeast Asian (Theravāda) countries centuries ago, and in East Asia it had to settle for a minor role, alongside more popular forms of Mahāyāna.

### *'Northern' Buddhism*

In the region of the Himalayan mountains, however, Vajrayāna ultimately became the majority religion. In the course of time, it achieved dominance in Nepal and Bhutan, and across the Himalayas in Tibet and Mongolia. Hence some refer to Theravāda as 'southern', Mahāyāna as 'eastern', and Vajrayāna as 'northern' Buddhism—north, that is, at least from the Buddha's birthplace on the frontier between India and Nepal.

### *Diamond Vehicle, Thunderbolt Vehicle*

The name Vajrayāna means 'Diamond' or 'Thunderbolt' Vehicle. A connotation of the diamond is that it is hard, unbreakable, or unsplittable. A connotation of the thunderbolt in India before Buddhism was that it was the sceptre of the Hindu deity Indra. Indra's power as ruler of the heavens was perceived particularly in thunderstorms. The thunderbolt (*vajra*) was Indra's sceptre, the symbol of his power. It came to be represented stylistically as an hourglasslike wand, regularly used by Vajrayāna Buddhists in ritual. It is shaped somewhat like a planetarium projector or like a three-dimensional version of our conventional symbol for infinity. Its associations are, however, not physical, astronomical, or mathematical. The curved prongs, for instance, represent various *buddhas*, and the power it symbolizes is the power of the enlightened awareness: itself unbreakable, but capable of shattering spiritual obstacles.

### *Mantrayāna*

Vajrayāna incorporates numerous elements that have a background in India, in both Hindu and Buddhist usage, but often gives its own emphasis to them. An example is the use of mantras, on account of which this Vehicle is sometimes known as Mantrayāna. Mantras are magical chants, or sacred syllables. They are thought to be evocative of great spiritual blessing when properly spoken or intoned. In many respects, they continue the notion of efficacy that attached to the performance of Vedic rituals by brahmin priests in ancient India and that is paralleled in the claims made for chanting of the Zoroastrian ritual texts.

### *Esoteric Buddhism*

But the mantras of Vajrayāna Buddhism take on a more esoteric or secret connotation. The meaning of the Vajrayāna mantras was presented as a closely guarded, secret teaching, passed along in a lineage from master to initiated pupil. For this reason the Vajrayāna tradition is also frequently described as 'esoteric' Buddhism.

### *Tantric Buddhism*

Another designation used in English for Vajrayāna is 'tantric' Buddhism. This points to another link that the tradition has with Indian antecedents. Like Buddhist tantrism, Hindu tantrism comes to light at around the third century, but, like many innovations in religion, it was presented as the intended meaning of the much older *Veda*s from the outset. Like Hindu tantrism, Buddhist tantrism possesses a set of practical techniques relating to a religious manifestation of universal power, often conceived of in masculine and feminine form. The techniques aim at spiritual union with that figure and the manipulation of the spiritual force tapped in the union. And these techniques are matters of initiation and training at the hands of a master in a spiritual lineage.

Some of the symbolic and meanings of Vajrayāna reflect the emphases of tantric Hinduism, including practices of sexual yoga. Some texts suggest that since the world is bound by lust, it is to be released by lust. 'Right-hand' tantrism tended to take masculinity and femininity as symbolic, while 'left-hand' tantrism tended to act things out explicitly. Rites included ritual unions where the partner was visualized as a deity; a couple, not celibate, would visualize themselves as a divine being and consort. Such practices properly undertaken, were to confront lust, defeat it, and transcend it. Not surprisingly, practices associated with 'left-hand' tantrism gave tantra a bad reputation in some quarters, contributing to the need for secret transmission of the tradition. Whereas earlier Buddhism in India had been 'establishment', tantric Buddhism was 'underground'.

The texts in which such techniques are laid out for Vajrayāna Buddhists are termed *tantra*s, contrasting with the previous Mahāyāna terminology referring to the Buddha's discourses and similar texts as *sūtra*s. Etymologically, the term *sūtra* connoted the thread or string by which texts were bound together, and *tantra*, 'loom', also connotes a fabric of continuity in teaching and practice.

The Vajrayāna canon adds numerous *tantra*s to the previous Mahāyāna *sūtra*s. The best-known version of the Vajrayāna canon is the Tibetan one, edited by Bu-ston in the early fourteenth century. It includes a vast library of *tantra*s under the heading *Kanjur* and various commentaries under the heading *Tanjur*. It was printed on slips of paper from wooden blocks, one carved for each page. The pages themselves were long and horizontal, reflecting the form and layout of manuscripts in the Indian tradition, written on palm leaves.

The Buddhist *tantras* classify the many *buddhas* and *bodhisattvas* into various families, and Vajrayāna Buddhists use these groupings in their spiritual practices. For example, the 'head' of the family is given the honoured place in the centre of a geometrical arrangement called the *maṇḍala*, a sacred design used in meditation. The other members of the Buddha family are placed diagrammatically in specific directions around the central figure. *Maṇḍalas* map divine beings in their cosmic connections. One goal of meditating on a particular *buddha* or *bodhisattva*, as we have seen, is to achieve a vision of that spiritual entity. The vision in turn helps one come closer to achieving enlightenment.

The *guru*, spiritual master, initiates the disciple into the symbolic meanings of members of the family of *buddhas* and their relationships. The texts themselves do not necessarily reveal the whole of the teaching, and in fact the texts are sometimes deliberately incomplete. Special guidance by the meditation master plays a role in the other two Vehicles, but the secret, supplemental teachings passed along from master to initiated disciple give Vajrayāna its secretive or esoteric characteristic. In this it contrasts with Theravāda, which has no secret teachings and is therefore termed exoteric. Vajrayāna is very ritualistic, but the rituals are meant to enhance the practitioners' inner wisdom. That is, Vajrayāna stresses both ritual and its version of yoga.

Vajrayāna spread throughout India and to most of the countries where other forms of Buddhism had gone before. There were Vajrayāna monasteries in Burma and elsewhere in Southeast Asia until the Sri Lankan form of Theravāda came to dominance. Vajrayāna even had some followers in ancient Sri Lanka, the stronghold of Theravāda. A major centre of Vajrayāna learning was located in island Southeast Asia, in an area that is now part of Indonesia, and the influence of the *maṇḍala* practice can be seen in the temple at Borobudur, on the island of Java, whose ground plan resembles an elaborate *maṇḍala*.

Vajrayāna includes the practice of magic, invoking the spirits either to increase prosperity or attack one's enemies. This is often done with the help of mantras or mystic syllables, chanted and repeated, and with *mudrās* or gestures. Mantras do not need to be spoken orally to be activated; they can be written on banners or slips of paper and hung on trees or lines or rotated in cylindrical containers referred to as prayer-wheels.

The best-known mantra is the expression *Oṃ mani padme hūṃ*, 'O the Jewel in the Lotus'. Vajrayāna Buddhists bring many interpretations to this phrase. Some understand it to refer to the *bodhisattva* Avalokiteśvara in feminine form as the 'jewelled-lotus lady'. Some count its six syllables as referring to six realms of rebirth or six spiritual perfections.

Meditation plays an important role in tantric Buddhism. One of its principal techniques is visualization. The devotee trains or allows the consciousness to focus on a view of a chosen celestial *buddha* or spiritual being. For instance, one may visualize rays of light emanating from the celestial beings in their realms. Frequent as a focus of visualization meditation are geometrical arrangements of *buddha* figures in chartlike *maṇḍalas*. Tibetan wall hangings or *thangkas* may portray an individual deity or often an arrangement of many in a *maṇḍala*.

Having built up a visualization of the deity in the first stage, the meditator then moves to a stage in which he or she may identify with the visualized being, losing the sense of duality or distinction with respect to that being and tapping its spiritual energies. Visualizing oneself as identical with the being, one senses several *cakras* or centres of power within one's own body and may perceive oneself to be at the centre of a pure land defined by a *maṇḍala*. On conclusion of this process of awareness, one exits by dissolving it slowly into nothingness, so that one is free from ego-attachment.

Tantric Buddhism gives particular emphasis to the *Mahāvairocana sūtra* (The Great Sun *sūtra*), the basis of the 'womb *maṇḍala*', with its thirteen divisions and 405 deities. In a tantric *maṇḍala*, the central figure is Mahāvairocana, or the Great Sun *buddha*. He is flanked by the *buddhas* of the four directions, Akṣobhya in the east, Amitābha in the west, Amoghasiddhi in the north and Ratnasambhava in the south, all of them together demonstrating the various emanations of buddhahood itself. Besides, it is characteristic of tantric Buddhism to give to the *buddhas* and even the *bodhisattvas* (for each *buddha* is accompanied by a *bodhisattva*) female counterparts, thus increasing the number in the pantheon.

Also, these deities have dual aspects, pacific and angry, according to the functions they have to perform, such as to repel evil forces or to assist in beneficial functions. Indeed, the union of wisdom and compassion, considered as key to Mahāyāna enlightenment, is represented by the father-mother image, i.e., the deity locked in embrace with its consort. Initiation is very important to this school, and is done, among other things, by a series of baptisms.

### *Tantric Buddhism in East Asia*

Esoteric Buddhism was introduced into China in the eighth century, at about the same time it was introduced into Tibet. An important difference is that at that time, the T'ang dynasty in China (618–907) was already dominantly Buddhist, while Tibet was more nearly virgin territory for Buddhist missionary activity. What had been established in China was Mahāyāna, which as we shall see had already adapted itself to the Chinese environment through several centuries of assimilation and systematization. Tantrism as a novelty enjoyed only a very brief period of prosperity in China, in the form of the Chen-yen/Zhenyan ('true word' or 'mantra') tradition, but soon died out.

But while it lasted, Chen-yen was transmitted to Korea, which was receiving massive Buddhist influences from T'ang China. In Korea the Chen-yen teaching, known as Milgyo, maintained a distinctive identity until amalgamation with Mahāyāna schools in the fourteenth century.

Much more important was tantric Buddhism's transmission from T'ang China to Japan. Japan had come relatively recently into China's cultural orbit when at the turn of the ninth century, Kūkai brought tantric Chen-yen to Japan. Hence Shingon, as Chen-yen came to be called in Japan, was on a much more even footing *vis-à-vis* Mahāyāna than it had been in China. Shingon prospered in Japan, and has survived to the present. Its tantrism is of the 'right-handed' type.

## Vajrayāna in Tibet

Śākyamuni had been born in the foothills of the Himalayas, and he had converted his home region (now part of Nepal) a few years after his enlightenment, but travel to the high Himalayan plateau was so difficult that Buddhism made little impact there for the first 1,200 years of its history. From the late eighth century a few Buddhist texts and missionaries found their way to Tibet at the invitation of Tibetan kings.

A *bhikṣu* named Padmasambhava, among others, was successful in bringing Vajrayāna to Tibet. He is revered as a *guru Rinpoche* ('precious teacher'). He combined instruction in *dharma* with magical practices concerning the world of the spirits. The figure of Padmasambhava and the practices attributed to him are claimed in retrospect particularly by a school of Tibetan Buddhism known as the Nyingma (in technical transliteration, Rñiṅ-ma-pa). His activity tipped the balance from the priests of the indigenous religion to the Vajrayāna form of Buddhism.

The indigenous religion that existed in Tibet in the eighth century when Buddhism arrived is known as Bon (a name meaning 'truth' or 'reality'). We have only fragmentary information concerning it, but scholars are in general agreement that its ritual objectives included the safe conduct of the soul of a dead person to an existence in a land beyond death. To get the soul to that realm, the Bon priests sacrificed an animal such as a yak, a horse, or a sheep during the funeral ritual. These rituals were performed on behalf of commoners, but especially of kings, for whom large funeral mounds were built that are similar to Chinese tomb mounds.

The Bon religion appears to have combined and interacted with Buddhism in Tibet, and elements of it have continued to the present day. One way teachers who have preserved the Bon tradition have differentiated it from Buddhism is by claiming that it originated not in India but in a mythical region west of Tibet named Ta-źig (the same name as in Tajikistan) or Shambhala.

One of the interesting practices of Tibetan Buddhism is its development of written instructions about the afterlife state. In Tibetan, these instructions are known as the *Bardo Thodol*, the 'Liberation by Hearing on the After-Death Plane', and have been translated under the title *The Tibetan Book of the Dead*. The instructions are meant to be read aloud to dying persons as a means to help them achieve liberation during the three stages of the *bardo* state between death and subsequent rebirth.

During the first stage (*chikhai bardo*), the dying person loses consciousness, experiences a transitional time of darkness, and then emerges into a very different world filled with strange objects unknown on the earthly plane. A colourless light appears that is so bright that, due to bad *karma*, one usually turns away in fear. But if the bright light is recognized as the *Dharma* Body of Buddha, liberation will occur and one will experience *nirvāṇa* rather than rebirth. Tibetan Buddhists often represent *saṃsāra* by a twelve-spoked wheel (recall the earlier discussion of causality and Dependent Origination) held in the teeth of a fierce animal symbolizing the ravages of time.

Due to their *karma*, most persons cannot recognize the *Dharma* Body, however, and so they pass on to the *chonyid bardo* stage, in which some consciousness of objects is regained. One may be aware of one's own funeral, for example. During this stage, peaceful deities appear for seven days, and then wrathful deities appear for seven more days. These are all the Buddha as well, in the Body of Bliss form, and liberation comes to those who meditate on them as such. The *sidpa bardo* is the third stage, during which one experiences judgement according to *karma*. This is followed by a gradual assumption of a new bodily form within a few weeks of death. Liberation is possible right up to the moment of rebirth, but *karma* keeps most people in the grip of *saṃsāra*, the wheel of death and rebirth.

Vajrayāna, accustomed to 'underground' status in India, maintained its esoteric mode of transmission when taken to Tibet. For a long time after Padmasambhava in the late eighth century, the tradition was in the minority, but even when it became established and dominant some centuries later, it retained the notion of transmission through esoteric lineages.

Tibetan Buddhism is divided among several ordination lineages, or orders. The best-known order is the Gelugpa (the frustratingly technical transliteration of its name, Dge-lugs-pa, reflects sounds that are written in the Tibetan script but no longer pronounced). The order was founded by the reformer Tsongkhapa (1357–1419). Members of this order are also known as the Yellow Hats, due to their large, cloth hats, whereas members of their main rival orders, such as the Kargyu (technically, Bka'-brgyud) and Karma-pa, wear red or black hats. The Gelugpas are rather scholastic, in that they lay heavy emphasis on the study and interpretation of texts.

### *Lamas and Mongols*

The Mongols ruled in China from 1222 to 1368, but did not invade Tibet.

Instead, they began to appoint the head of the Śākya monastery as their *tisri* or viceroy for the region. Tibetan missionary activity among the Mongols did not begin in earnest until Sonam Gyatso (1543–88) went to Mongolia and converted Altan Khan. The ruler gave him some temporal power and named him the Third Dalai Lama (Ocean of Wisdom), his two predecessors being designated Dalai Lamas retroactively. With the sponsorship of the Mongol princes, the Gelugpas dominated in Mongolia and Tibet.

The Dalai Lamas became the rulers of Tibet from the time of the fifth Dalai Lama, Ngawang Logsang Gyatso (1617–82). With Mongol aid he subdued the challenge of the rival Karma-pa lineage and constructed the Potala palace in Lhasa. But he recognized his teacher, Lobsang Chögye Gyaltsen (1569–1662) as an incarnation of the *bodhisattva* Amitābha and titled him the Panchen Lama, thus providing a rallying point within the Gelugpa lineage for opposition to the religio-political authority of the succession of Dalai Lamas.

The Fifth Dalai Lama also established diplomatic relations with the Manchu (Ch'ing) dynasty, which came to power in China in 1644. This relationship subsequently involved Tibet in the eighteenth-century rivalry between the Manchus in Beijing and the Oirots of Mongolia, such that Tibet became a Manchu protectorate. Inner Mongolia came into the Chinese orbit too, while Outer Mongolia was torn between Chinese economic influence and Russian political protection.

The Dalai Lama is considered to be a reincarnation of a *bodhisattva*, and each Dalai Lama is said to be the reincarnation of the previous Dalai Lama. The other orders make similar claims, and use a procedure similar to the following to pick a new head lama. When a Dalai Lama dies, a long and complicated search is undertaken to find a young boy who appears to show signs of being the reincarnation of a former Dalai Lama. After initial canvassing identifies a number of suitable candidates, various techniques are employed to narrow the list to one boy. That boy must show appropriate intellectual qualities and certain personality characteristics similar to the departed Dalai Lama. Various objects are presented to the boy to see if he chooses ones that were favourites of the former Dalai Lama. Finally, a man who holds the office of State Oracle goes into a trance in order to contact the spirits to confirm the selection.

Tenzin Gyatso (b. 1935), the fourteenth Dalai Lama, was chosen in this manner from a family of Tibetan descent who lived in China. Once chosen, he was raised in Tibet, where he received extensive training in Buddhist doctrine and practice as well as in the duties of a ruler. When he came of age, he assumed his full role as both head of the Gelugpa order and ruler of Tibet. When the Chinese took over Tibet in 1959, he escaped to northern India, where he and many of his followers settled near Dharamsala, northwest of Delhi. Other Tibetans have established communities elsewhere in northern India.

# Mahāyāna in East Asia

## Buddhism's Introduction in China

Throughout its history, China can be described as a cultural and, much of the time as well, a political unity. Early on, China was quite insulated and isolated from outside influences, even though trade along the 'Silk Road' was developing in Central Asia, and there was some contact with India. Buddhism acted as a harbinger of civilization in many areas, introducing knowledge of Sanskrit and other Indian languages and scripts and eventually a technical vocabulary in Chinese for translation purposes, as well as inspiring art, literature, and philosophy.

The possibility that the Chinese sage Confucius and the Indian historical Buddha, Śākyamuni, lived in the same century gives some substance to the hypothesis of the German philosopher Karl Jaspers (1883–1969) regarding the 'Axial Age' in human civilization. Jaspers thought it more than coincidental that a number of great teachers lived at approximately the same moment in world history, but with the distance that separated the two countries, the Indian religion only reached China roughly 500 years after the deaths of the two men.

There are parallels and contrasts between the Buddhist encounter with Chinese culture and the meeting of Jewish Christianity with Hellenistic culture. For its part, Greek culture contributed to the speculative legacy of the interpretation of Judaeo-Christian doctrines. Chinese culture, by contrast, rendered simpler and more pragmatic the highly speculative and analytical doctrines of early Buddhism. It also attempted to harmonize the inconsistencies in teaching that had crept in through factionalism in India.

When Buddhism was introduced, China was already home to a vigorous civilization with an ancient canon—the Confucian classics—and time-hallowed traditions. The meeting of the Buddhist religion and Chinese culture became the occasion for conflicts and controversies. These were resolved only as Buddhism adjusted itself to the Chinese context, taking account of Confucian moral and social values, while making use of Taoist ideas and terminology for its own survival and advancement.

The Buddhist presupposition of rebirth or transmigration and the practice of monastic life were introduced to a society that venerated ancestors and valued descendants. The consequent change in Buddhism was that monastic service was adopted as a way to benefit ancestors in the other world. The Chinese affirmed this life and this world, including the values of family and posterity. They considered Buddhist meditation helpful in the quest for longevity.

A legend associates Buddhism's advent in China with the interpretation of dreams. In it a Chinese emperor, Ming-ti / Mingdi (r. 57–75), of the Han dynasty, sees in a dream a golden giant entering his palace. On asking courtiers for an interpretation of this dream, he is told that the giant represents none other than

Śākyamuni, the wise man from the west. Immediately the emperor sends a delegation to India to inquire after this wise man. Buddhist monks from India are also invited to China to preach their religion to the Chinese.

In spite of imperial welcome, Buddhism met resistance. Adherents of the Confucian tradition found it hard to believe that any wisdom might come from outside of the country, nor had the teachings been mentioned in the Chinese classical texts. The Chinese were revolted that Buddhist monks went against the demands of the ancestor cult and filial piety, injuring their bodies (received from parents) by shaving their heads and abandoning family and society by embracing celibacy and asceticism. And the Indian belief in transmigration, many feared, was also incompatible with the Chinese veneration for ancestors as well as with the Chinese custom of eating meat.

There were also misgivings among China's followers of the Taoist tradition. In the rivalry and competition, a Taoist claim was that the Buddha was none other than the Taoist master Lao-tzu/Laozi, who had reportedly gone west into Central Asia and preached to the barbarians. Taoists were also disappointed that Buddhism, so ready to give up attachment to this life, had no great contribution to make to the Taoist quest for elixirs of immortality. Indeed, the earliest Buddhists most welcome in China turned out to be those with magical and healing powers, that is, wonder-workers.

With their own preference for solitude, the Taoists were better able than the Confucians to appreciate Buddhist asceticism and monasticism; the Taoist Ch'üan-chen/Quanzhen tradition adopted celibacy, monasticism, Buddhist precepts, and Buddhist rituals. Taoist philosophy, which we discuss in the section on East Asian religions, displayed metaphysical interests and used a language of negation. With these features it was much more compatible with Buddhist teachings than was Confucianism. Eventually, Taoist ideas and expressions were used in the translation of Buddhist scriptures into Chinese, resulting in a blending of Indian and Chinese thought.

## The Translation of Scriptures

Buddhist literature was translated from the Indian vernacular language of Pali and also from the literary Sanskrit into the Chinese language. The activity hastened the process of acculturation of Buddhism in China. This may sound simple, but it was not. Buddhism had already undergone several centuries of development both in theory and practice, and its corpus of books was vast. The translation effort took over a thousand years. Indeed, such an effort defies comparison with the translation of any other body of religious texts in the world.

A difference between the Chinese and the Indian civilizations is that India had a slower transition from an oral tradition to a written one. It therefore took longer for Buddhist scriptures to be written than it took the Confucian classics or the Christian New Testament. There were also major differences between the Indian languages and Chinese.

At the time that Buddhism, especially Indian Mahāyāna, was first introduced, the Chinese knew nothing of its previous history. They were ignorant of the fact that Buddhism had already splintered into sects in India and Central Asia, and that the scriptures were to a large extent sectarian writings long after the Buddha's death that attributed various teachings to him. Instead, they imagined that all the scriptures were the Buddha's very own words, recorded by disciples around the time of his death and stored in caves and libraries before they were discovered and taken to China.

The facts, however, were quite different, especially where Mahāyāna is concerned. It had no fixed corpus, no early *Tripiṭaka* like the texts of Theravāda, which were gradually being translated. The ensuing difficulties experienced by Chinese converts led to the creation of a distinctively Chinese Buddhism, a response in part to the problems of textual interpretation. These problems far exceeded Christianity's, which claims a much smaller corpus of texts as definitive.

Important in the translation process were the texts chosen for translation and the quality of the work, as well as who did the translating. Actually, many of the translations are all that remain of texts that have been lost in their original Indian languages. Indeed, with its 3,053 entries, but including many commentaries as well as so-called original scriptures, the Japanese *Taishō* edition of the Chinese *Tripiṭaka* (1922–33) has become essential for the study of the Buddhist religion.

At the start, the Chinese had little choice to exercise about what to translate and what not, as they knew too little. The matter was left to the discretion of foreign monks, but as the translations were read, there was little doubt as to which books were preferred. We see the repeated translation of more popular texts, a fact marking the character of Chinese Buddhism. The *Great Perfection of Wisdom* was translated four times, the *Suraṅgama sūtra* nine times, the *Lotus sūtra* three times. The *Small Perfection of Wisdom*, introduced earlier, had been translated nine times. The number of times depends also on how early the scripture was first introduced, and the versions varied in length.

By the end of the T'ang dynasty (906), the formation of the Chinese Buddhist canon was virtually completed. We use the word 'canon' because the collective work did have some normative value. It was believed to contain the religious founder's teachings, and includes monastic rules and discipline as well. But we should remember that the word 'canon' does not have the same restricted sense it has with the Hebrew or Christian scriptures, or even with the Theravāda (Pali) scriptures. The specific normative value of many entries, including commentaries, is open to question, and we have not discovered a serious effort to define scriptural authority.

The Chinese Mahāyāna canon still keeps something of the tripartite structure of Theravāda's Pali canon. True, this has become artificial on account of the great influx of new discourses or *sūtras* composed much later that were purported to be the words of the historical Buddha and translated as such into Chinese. The Chinese added new works to the corpus, including one work given the status of a *sūtra* without being ascribed to the historical Buddha: the *Platform Sūtra of the Sixth Patriarch*, a Ch'an work. Subsequently, Japanese Buddhists added many texts, taking the writings of such figures as Nichiren to be authoritative.

An East-West comparison that some have made, though overstated, is suggestive: for Western religions such as Christianity, if something is in the canon, it is taken as true; while for Chinese traditions such as Buddhism, if something is taken to be true, it becomes part of the canon. Frequently inclusion was decided on the basis of similarity to the content of scriptures already known through earlier and shorter versions.

What attracted the Chinese to these scriptures? The Chinese found certain Mahāyāna doctrines appealing, especially that of the *bodhisattva* as a compassionate saviour who refrains from entering *nirvāṇa* in order to help more people. A related doctrine is the universal accessibility of buddhahood, a prominent theme in the *Lotus sūtra*. There is also the ideal of the lay Buddhist in the *Vimalakīrti sūtra*. Chinese Buddhists developed such ideas further, to include in the pale of salvation all sentient beings, even stubborn unbelievers, and expressed this metaphorically to embrace the entire universe also.

Why did the state support translations and promote their spread? There were, of course, pious sovereigns who did this for merit and devotion, or to please the believing multitudes, but patronage was also a way of controlling the religion. The state exercised its prerogatives by making the final decision about which translations were fit for inclusion in the canon. Such decisions were made on the advice of the experts, but it was the state's *imprimatur* that made a collection of books the 'Buddhist canon'. The canon was useful to the state, serving as a 'constitution' for the *saṃgha*. The state used it as a sanction, punishing members of the *saṃgha* for moral or ritual transgressions against the prescriptions and proscriptions of the scriptures.

## Early Translators

Little information is available regarding the authorship of the Mahāyāna texts in India. By comparison, there is ample information about the process of translation that built up the Chinese Buddhist canon, and about the men who translated the Buddhist scriptures into Chinese. We know the names of over 200 translators, not to mention their assistants, who were important since in most cases the translators cannot be said to have personally done the work word for word, but worked with teams.

In the beginning, texts were copied by hand, sometimes from dictation, but printing was used from very early on to help with wide dissemination. A page would be carved in a single wood block. Movable blocks, a technical advance, were developed in the eleventh century. New books, always attributed to the Buddha himself, were taken to China for translation as soon as they were written, almost before the ink was dry. There was what amounted to a '*sūtra* industry' in India, meeting the demand in China for Buddhist scriptures for translation. To the Chinese, it must have seemed a miracle that so many texts should claim to give the Buddha's own words.

After the foreign monks who knew little Chinese, there came successors like Dharmarakṣa (232–309), born in Dunhuang, on China's western desert frontier. He translated over a hundred Mahāyāna texts, often dictating from memory to his Chinese copyists. In 286, he translated the *Lotus sūtra*, called in Sanskrit the *Saddharmapuṇḍarīka*, a text of paramount importance for the development of Mahāyāna. The task of translation was spurred on by a succession of monks who were Chinese. They travelled on pilgrimage westward through Central Asia and then south to India.

The first of these actually to reach India was Fa-hsien, who went in search of an original monastic code in 399. Till then, it appears that the *Vinaya Piṭaka* had been passed down only by oral transmission. By the time of Fa-hsien's return to China, and unknown to him, the entire *Vinaya Piṭaka* had already been translated by someone else. The fact that more than one person was dedicated to finding and translating it shows the strength Chinese Buddhism had achieved.

### *Kumārajīva*

The monumental enterprise of translating scriptures required the support of the state and its enormous resources. It also called for a certain kind of genius, and one such was the famous Kumārajīva (344–c. 413), a native of Kucha in Central Asia. This region is historically important for religious encounters, including those of Buddhism with Christianity, with Manichaeism, and with Islam. Kumārajīva's fame as a Buddhist scholar reached the northern Chinese court (the country was then politically divided), and the ruler literally plotted wars to 'kidnap' him. Eventually, he was brought to Ch'ang-an (today's Xi'an) by another ruler in 402, honoured with the title of National Preceptor, and surrounded by a thousand monks and laypeople, including some of the best scholars in the country.

Kumārajīva retranslated the most influential Mahāyāna scriptures and produced definitive editions with authoritative interpretation. Until his death in 413, he and his collaborators poured forth a steady stream of translations, including not merely scriptures but also commentaries that helped to explain the primary texts. Their output included the *Amitābha sūtra*, basic text of the Pure Land school in China, the *Perfection of Wisdom in 25,000 Lines*, as well as the massive *Treatise on the Great Perfection of Wisdom* and the two important Mahāyāna scriptures, the *Lotus sūtra* and the *Vimalakīrti sūtra*.

Until then, translators of Buddhist scriptures had sought mainly to make use of words and concepts coming from Taoist texts to make the Buddhist scriptures more comprehensible as well as more acceptable. This was the method called *ko-yi/geyi* ('matching of meanings'), but it did not always permit the accurate communication of the content of the original texts, and sometimes even distorted them. Kumārajīva's translations were different.

Yet it appears that Kumārajīva could not read or write Chinese. After all, he was already forty-six years old when he arrived in Ch'ang-an. His greatness lay in his immense learning and understanding, and the leadership he exercised in the translation project, a task he accomplished with the assistance of his teams of assistants. His reputation as a genius was such that the Chinese ruler in the north thought it a waste for him not to have progeny, and offered him concubines. Kumārajīva acquiesced to the royal wishes, for which he has been severely criticized by other Buddhist monks. However, we know of no child prodigies from him.

### *Hsüan-tsang*

The T'ang dynasty (618–907) witnessed a flowering of translation activity. The most famous contributor then was a Chinese. Hsüan-tsang/Xuanzang (602–64), pilgrim and translator, personally brought back from India hundreds of *sūtras*. He remained after that for twenty years in the capital, Ch'ang-an. A man of peerless energy and determination, Hsüan-tsang took care to translate entire works, rather than only parts of them. Through his work, the corpus of Mahāyāna scriptures was made available, as well as its most important treatises and commentaries. In the twenty years before he died, he finished the translation of seventy-five works.

Having left China for India without official permission, Hsüan-tsang returned to a royal welcome and had to decline offers of high office. He was a traveller and pilgrim, and was nearly killed on his way from China to India by some cannibals, who only spared him at the last minute for fear of reprisals from a higher power. His adventures eventually inspired the famous novel, *Travels to the West*. In this piece of fiction he is given as companions a monkey, representing quick wit and loyalty, and a pig, representing sensuality. As things unfold, the monkey becomes the hero in the novel, whereas the monk seems quite helpless in difficulty, resorting only to prayer and meditation.

## Chinese Buddhist Schools

Diverse schools of opinion developed in China, seeking mainly to reconcile a difficult range of often contradictory teachings attributed to the Buddha. In Chinese, the term translated either as 'school' or as 'sect' is *tsung/zong*, which refers to lineage—doctrinal lineage. Interestingly, the modern Chinese term for 'religion' is *tsung-chiao/zongjiao* (literally, 'the teachings of the lineages'), which some scholars think has a Buddhist resonance.

The doctrinal situation can be contrasted with that of Christianity. In the early history of Christianity, the emergence of doctrine was marked by sharp controversies. The Christian ecumenical councils of the first several centuries sought to draw lines between orthodox and heretical doctrines. A synthesis or combination of teachings, such as those that Chinese Buddhists frequently attempted, would be anathema to many a jealous defender of the Christian faith in the West.

In modern times, with the growth of the ecumenical spirit, Christians of different persuasions have shown a genuine desire to find common ground, and even to enter into active dialogue with people of other traditions, such as Buddhists. Still, an important difference exists. For Buddhism, truth means religious insight, which is potentially plural. It includes myths as well as divergent doctrinal formulations. These are secondary to salvation, as the means are secondary to the end. For Christianity, on the other hand, centralized institutional authority and an emphasis on revelation combine to force an uncompromising attitude on certain points of doctrine as factual assertions.

The concern with lineage offers a parallel to the concern for apostolic succession in the case of Christianity, whether it be the Greek Orthodox Church, the Roman Catholic Church, or the Church of England. Each wishes to demonstrate its descent from the apostles of Jesus, through proper sacramental lineage. In the case of Buddhist groups (or sects), such lineage also has a sacramental dimension. Often, the attempt was made arbitrarily to link the sect to the historical Buddha himself.

Both Theravāda and Mahāyāna schools developed in China, but the Theravāda had little influence and soon disappeared, whereas the Mahāyāna prospered and grew. Of the Chinese Mahāyāna schools, two (San-lun and Fa-hsiang) were basically Indian imports, reducing everything either to Emptiness or Consciousness.

## San-lun, Chinese Mādhyamika

The San-lun ('Three Treatises') school is the Chinese extension of Nāgārjuna's Indian Mahāyāna philosophy known as Mādhyamika ('Middle Doctrine'). Kumārajīva introduced this teaching into China with the translation of two treatises by Nāgārjuna, and a third by his disciple Āryadeva (or Deva, c. 300). These became the foundation of the San-lun or Three Treatises school.

Basically a restatement of Nāgārjuna's ideas, the chief teaching of the San-lun school was that everything is empty (*śūnya*), as nothing has any independent reality or self-nature. An entity can be identified only through its relation to something else. Hence relations and dependence constitute this unreal phenomenal world. On such a relative level of truth and understanding, one is as in a dream, making distinctions between subject and object, *saṃsāra* and *nirvāṇa*. However, the Buddha can lead to an understanding of this emptiness, which is intuitive wisdom (*prajñā*), a higher level of absolute truth called *śūnyatā* or Emptiness.

Kumārajīva was fortunate to have a disciple who became an outstanding exponent of this system in China: Seng Chao/Seng Zhao (374–414). Seng Chao produced three treatises on (1) the immutability of things; (2) the emptiness of the unreal; (3) *prajñā* is not knowledge. For him, the Middle Doctrine represents an effort to reconcile extremes, for things both exist and do not exist, which can be known through sagely wisdom, not knowledge.

## Fa-hsiang, Chinese Yogācāra

In Chinese, the Fa-hsiang/Faxiang ('Dharma Character') school is also known as Wei-shih/Weishi ('Consciousness Only'). It corresponds to the Yogācāra school in India, discussed earlier. First introduced into China by Paramārtha (499–569) in the sixth century, the school grew up around Asaṅga's *Compendium of Mahāyāna*. It was perplexity over the meaning of this work that spurred Hsüan-tsang to set out for India to find more scriptures.

Like the San-lun, the Fa-hsiang school survived until the ninth century, and then quickly declined. This happened in part because of the persecutions against Buddhism, the worst one taking place in 845. However, Fa-hsiang was also too abstract to maintain long-term appeal, although some of its ideas, especially regarding *ālaya* consciousness and *tathatā*, influenced other schools of thought. In our modern period, especially in the 1920s–30s, there has been a revival of interest in this school, initiated by a group of monks and laypeople, including the monk-reformer T'ai-hsü/Taixu (1890–1947) and the philosopher Hsiung Shih-li/Xiung Shili (1895–1968), who became even more interested in Wang Yang-ming's (1452–1529) Neo-Confucian philosophy.

San-lun and Fa-hsiang exercised some importance, but did not survive as vital sects, even if their doctrines influenced the subsequent development of other schools of thought, including Neo-Confucianism in the case of Fa-hsiang. By contrast, T'ien-t'ai and Hua-yen, two other great Mahāyāna schools that developed in China, may be regarded as the responses of the new converts to the great diversity of doctrine they discovered in the scriptural corpus.

## T'ien-t'ai

As translations of Buddhist texts were proceeding at an uninterrupted rate, there was at first little time for reflection, but once people realized the complexity of the doctrines, serious problems presented themselves. What should one do when contradictory teachings were all ascribed to the Buddha himself? The translation of the two huge scriptures, the *Mahāparinirvāṇa* and the *Avataṃsaka*, especially presented problems of understanding. How to sort out, coordinate, and systematize these new strands of Buddhist doctrine became the burning question.

The T'ien-t'ai/Tiantai school is named after its place of origin on a mountain in Chekiang, in southeastern China. It is also called the Lotus school. It had a great systematic thinker in Chih-k'ai/Zhikai or Chih-yi/Zhiyi (538–97), who enjoyed imperial patronage as well. He proclaimed himself a practitioner of meditation rather than a philosopher, but he left behind a truly architectonic synthesis in his attempt to reconcile and harmonize all Buddhist teachings.

According to Chih-yi, doctrinal divergence within Buddhism and its many scriptures comes from the Buddha's having taught different things at different times. Besides, each of the *sūtra*s speaks on several different levels because each is addressing a different audience. So he distinguishes among five approaches in the Buddha's life of preaching (which we shall presently explain), four methods of teaching the *sūtra*s or scriptures (sudden, gradual, secret indeterminate, and explicit indeterminate), and four modes of doctrine (Hīnayāna, Śūnyavāda or the teaching of Emptiness, Yogācāra or Special Teaching, and the perfect teaching that is given in the *Lotus* and *Nirvāṇa sūtras*).

According to later interpretation, Chih-yi's five approaches became five periods in the Buddha's teaching. After enlightenment, the Buddha remains in an ecstatic state and preaches first the *Avataṃsaka sūtra*, which teaches that the universe is the revelation of the Absolute, but few can understand him during those three weeks. So the Buddha decides to accommodate his teachings to the listeners, and spends the next twelve years teaching the *Āgama*s, his discourses in the Pali canon, with the Theravāda doctrines of the Four Noble Truths, the Eightfold Path, and Dependent Origination. Thus he gathers together huge crowds, who are converted. After that, he moves to another period of eight years, teaching the simple Mahāyāna truths, especially of the *bodhisattva*, who forgoes his own *nirvāṇa* to save others. Then come twenty-two years of the fourth period, when he discusses metaphysical problems like those taught in the *Prajñāpāramitā sūtra*s. The fifth or last period of eight years is spent on the reconciliation of apparent contradictions, in accordance with the *Lotus* and *Nirvāṇa sūtra*s.

T'ien-t'ai Buddhism thus represents an attempt to establish a great eclectic school recognizing all forms of Buddhism, giving a place to all the scriptures by regarding them as the product of a gradual process of the Buddha's revelations. It harmonized the many differences found in the diverse scriptures. It formulated a classification of the *sūtra*s and their doctrines. Its synthesis is an instance of the Chinese propensity for asserting the harmony of opposites.

But, like so many religious attempts at a universal synthesis, T'ien-t'ai gave a place of privilege to a particular outlook. In asserting the universal accessibility of enlightenment and buddhahood, it claimed that the *Lotus sūtra* represents the culmination of the Buddha's teaching. The perspective is reminiscent of Islam's view that God speaks through many prophets, but definitively and climactically through Muḥammad. T'ien-t'ai was introduced into Japan in 804, where it came to be known as Tendai. We shall discuss its history in Japan later.

## Hua-yen

The Hua-yen or Flower Garland school is most saliently represented by Fa-tsang/Fazang (643–712), who worked as a translator with Hsüan-tsang and served as preceptor to four emperors. It relies particularly on the *Avataṃsaka* or Flower Garland *sūtra*, focusing attention on the conception of the *dharma* realm. It finds in that realm the two aspects of *li*, the fundamental patterns or principles, and *shih/shi*, the expressions in phenomena. This conception later exercised a profound influence on the later Neo-Confucian metaphysics of *li* and *ch'i/qi*.

Fa-tsang enjoyed the patronage of Empress Wu (r. 684–705), who frequently listened to his sermons. Once he pointed to the figure of a golden lion to explain Hua-yen philosophy, namely that *li* and *shih* interpenetrate each other, just as gold, which has no nature of its own, is present everywhere in the lion.

> If we look at the lion [as lion], there is only the lion and no gold. This means that the lion is manifest while the gold is hidden. if we look at the gold, there is only the gold and no lion. This means that the gold is manifest and the lion is hidden. If we look at them both, then both are manifest and both hidden … In each of the lion's eyes, ears, limbs, joints, and in each and every hair, there is the golden lion … Thus in each and every hair there are an infinite number of lions, and in addition all the single hairs, together with their infinite number of lions, in turn enter into a single hair (Chan 1963:412).

Another time he had a statue of a golden Buddha placed in the middle of a palace room, with mirrors surrounding it on all sides, as well as above and below. A burning torch was placed next to the statue. He then explained that the Buddha is present in all of its images and reflections just as *li* is present in the *shih*: 'In each and every reflection of any mirror you will find all the reflections of all the other mirrors, together with the specific Buddha image in each …' (Chang 1971:24). One is in all and all is in one. Hua-yen established a totally integrated philosophical system, in which everything leads to the Buddha in the centre, as Fa-tsang demonstrated in his hall of mirrors. Whereas T'ien-t'ai had accounted for diversity in the received texts by saying that the Buddha said essentially different things at different times, Hua-yen asserted that in the scriptures, the Buddha said the same essential thing in different ways.

## Ch'an in China

The last two Mahāyāna schools we have described, T'ien-t'ai and Hua-yen, had no equivalents in India. They were philosophical schools, developing the Buddhist philosophical genius in a Chinese context. They were also practical religious movements, preaching methods of meditation and devotion. Indeed, Indian doctrinal differences were often harmonized or subordinated to devotional practice through the Mahāyāna emphasis on *upāya* ('skill in means'), which relativizes the importance of dogma as such in favour of practical results.

We turn now to the Ch'an and thereafter to Pure Land teachings. Together with T'ien-t'ai and Hua-yen, these two teachings exemplify the Chinese assimilation of and response to Indian religiosity. We shall treat them more as denominations than as philosophical schools. The terminology 'sect' or 'movement' is appropriate here because in these cases the doctrinal content is less prominent, compared with T'ien-t'ai or Hua-yen. With their popular followings, Pure Land and Ch'an have remained living forms of Chinese Buddhism, surviving many persecutions. And they spread in turn outside China, to develop further in Korea and Japan.

We shall see the harmony of opposites reflected once more in the success of Ch'an and Pure Land. A kind of 'merging' eventually took place between these two sects in China, but a similar merger did not happen in Japan, to which Chinese Buddhism was exported. To the present day, Japan has retained a multiplicity of sects and lineages, with their claims of unbroken succession.

We shall also argue that the success of Ch'an and Pure Land has to do with their emphasis on meditative and devotional practices rather than on scriptural knowledge. On the one hand, the growth of Chinese Buddhism required the translation and interpretation of the Buddhist canon. On the other hand, the intellectual emphasis of scriptures and hermeneutics (the study of the principles of interpretation) became an obstacle to spiritual experience and devotional fulfilment. At issue, indeed, was the central Mahāyāna question of whether salvation is really accessible to all. Must one first know all the scriptures? Is there not a more direct approach—dare we say, a shortcut?

The name Ch'an is the Chinese transliteration of the Sanskrit *dhyāna*, meaning 'meditation'. It refers to the religious discipline that is aimed at calming the mind, permitting the person to penetrate into his or her own inner consciousness. Continual practice can allegedly induce an ecstatic experience or a blissful state of equanimity and enlightenment. As the exercise of meditation, *dhyāna* was developed in India over the ages, and the Ch'an tradition as it developed in China certainly did include meditation. However, the emphasis of the tradition shifted from meditation, which some Ch'an teachers criticized as inadequate, to taking some bold new steps to achieve enlightenment in life.

In common with other Mahāyāna systems, Ch'an teaches that ultimate real-

## CH'AN BUDDHISM: MEDITATION AND WISDOM

Good friends, how then are meditation and wisdom alike? They are like the lamp and the light it gives forth. If there is a lamp there is light; if there is no lamp there is no light. The lamp is the substance of light; the light is the function of the lamp. Thus, although they have two names, in substance they are not two. Meditation and wisdom are like this (*The Platform Sutra of the Sixth Patriarch*, sec. 15; Yampolsky 1976:137).

ity—*śūnyatā* (Emptiness), sometimes called Buddha-nature—is inexpressible in words or concepts. It is apprehended only by direct intuition, outside of conscious thought. Such direct intuition requires discipline and training, but is also characterized by freedom and spontaneity. This has led Ch'an to become a somewhat iconoclastic movement, relativizing practices that others take seriously. These include studying or reciting the Buddhist *sūtras*, worshipping the Buddha images, and performing rituals. Ch'an conducts these activities, but insists that there should be no dependence on them as a means to spiritual enlightenment (in Chinese, *wu*; in Japanese, *satori*).

Ch'an's claim to a direct legacy from the historical Buddha is based upon its story of a discourse given on Vulture Peak. On this occasion, surrounded by a huge crowd of gods and humans, the Buddha keeps silent while holding up a lotus flower, the symbol of purity. Most disciples are puzzled by the gesture, a wordless sermon, but the wise Kāśyapa 'understands'. Then the Buddha smiles at him, to acknowledge a special transmission of the school to be known as Dhyāna ('meditation').

By the early sixth century, a semilegendary master, Bodhidharma, reached China, where he was known especially for meditating while facing the wall of a cave monastery for nine years. The tradition that this caused his legs to atrophy is popularly recalled in the legless, egglike Japanese dolls termed *darumas* after him. His teaching is summed up in these four lines:

> A special transmission outside of doctrines.
> Not setting up the written word as an authority.
> Pointing directly at the human heart.
> Seeing one's nature and becoming a *buddha*.
> (Robinson 1959:332)

These lines reflect Kāśyapa's 'flower sermon' experience of the transmission of enlightened consciousness by direct contact between master and disciple, without the need for textual or doctrinal study.

## CH'AN BUDDHISM: SUDDEN AND GRADUAL ENLIGHTENMENT

Good friends, in the Dharma there is no sudden or gradual [enlightenment], but among people some are keen and others dull. The deluded commend the gradual method; the enlightened practice the sudden teaching. To understand the original mind of yourself is to see into your own original nature. Once enlightened, there is from the outset no distinction between these two methods; those who are not enlightened will for long kalpas be caught in the cycle of transmigration (*The Platform Sutra of the Sixth Patriarch*, sec. 16; Yampolsky 1976:137).

On account of its distaste for book learning, Ch'an became known as a special tradition 'outside the scriptures', not dependent on 'words or letters'. It is only transmitted 'from mind to mind', that is, from master to disciple without the intervention of rational argumentation. It advocates the 'absence of thoughts' to free the mind from external influences.

Often cited is a competition in verse between a young kitchen boy or apprentice monk Hui-neng (638–713) and the older and more learned Shen-hsiu/Shenxiu (606–706), a senior disciple. The fifth patriarch (counting from Bodhidharma) has announced the poetry contest to choose his successor. The senior monk emphasizes the need for disciplined meditation as preparation for the enlightenment-experience in the poem he writes on the wall:

> The body is the *Bodhi* tree,
> The mind is like a clear mirror.
> At all times we must strive to polish it,
> And must not let the dust collect.
> (Yampolsky 1976:130)

After the others have gone to sleep, Hui-neng counters with a poem that asserts the non-duality of mind and body, and the immediate character of enlightenment:

> *Bodhi* originally has no tree,
> The mirror has no stand.
> Buddha nature is always clear and pure;
> Where is there any dust?
> (Yampolsky 1976:132)

After winning the contest to become the sixth patriarch, Hui-neng returns

*Central among the features of this Japanese Zen Buddhist home altar is a scroll portraying Bodhidharma.* (R.C. Amore)

to his home in southern China. Travelling from village to village, he gives instruction, resulting in a wide popular following for Ch'an.

Ch'an Buddhism continued to divide into many subsects or branches, depending on the varying emphasis on methods and techniques. The difference between Shen-hsiu and Hui-neng embodies an issue that divided Ch'an: whether enlightenment is the fruit of gradual cultivation or comes all at once. Shen-hsiu, the gradualist, was recognized in northern China as the sixth patriarch, but his school later died out. Meanwhile, Hui-neng's 'southern' school focused on the abrupt character of enlightenment. This, plus southern Ch'an's iconoclastic attitude towards *buddhas* and *bodhisattvas*, Buddhist literature and rituals, contributed to the spirit of Zen in Japan.

The account of Hui-neng in the *Platform sūtra* stresses the importance of ordinary life, and even the possibility of finding enlightenment outside of meditation. A logical development for the Mahāyāna movement, which acknowledges the presence of the Absolute in the relative, of *nirvāṇa* in *saṃsāra*, Ch'an Buddhism had the result of affirming the value of this life and this world. Chinese Ch'an, especially as represented by Hui-neng's school, became known for freedom of expression and respect for the natural. Similar characteristics are associated with Taoism. These attitudes can be traced, not only in spirituality and mysticism but in art and culture.

However, the problem is whether Ch'an should be considered authentically Buddhist when it does not give a prominent place to scriptures, images, and even the Buddha himself. Ch'an masters, of course, reply in the affirmative. According to them, the religion is defined not by its scriptures but by the realization of the experience of enlightenment, which can be done best by looking inside one's own nature. After all, Ch'an represents an effort to return to the sources of Buddhist inspiration—and hence to certain features of early Buddhism, especially that of 'saving oneself by one's own efforts'.

## Ts'ao-tung and Lin-chi

Two subsects of southern Ch'an prospered, each concentrating on practical matters of spirituality. Their rival teachings on enlightenment and how this might be acquired attracted much attention.

Tsao-tung/Caodong proposed a gradual transformation of life and character. It emphasized silent enlightenment (in Chinese, *mo-chao/mozhao*; in Japanese, *mokusho*), a reference to the 'silently shining' inner light. As a discipline leading to mystical enlightenment, it stressed the importance of sitting in meditation (in Chinese, *tso-ch'an/zuochan*; in Japanese, *zazen*).

*Mo-chao* or 'silent illumination' underlines the importance of meditation as a spiritual exercise, and the Ts'ao-tung Buddhists were eager to point out that it did not refer to inactivity or passivity. Rather, silence is considered to be the primal stillness of the ultimate ground of the enlightened mind, which is naturally radiant and 'shining'. According to them, silent meditation and the quiet deeds of ordinary life are preferable to a riddlelike expression of the limits of rational thought. The effort of quiet meditation has been compared to that of 'the bird hatching the egg' and the inner light as 'a ray penetrating past and present'.

The Lin-chi sect, which had a much wider following, aims for sudden enlightenment through the use of shouting, beating, and paradox. These are considered aids in provoking mystical experience, for which no slow preparation is necessary or possible.

A story traces the Lin-chi sect's use of hitting, shouting, and paradox to its founder and namesake, Lin-chi (d. 867). When he is a young novice, the monastery trainer sends him to get instruction from the master, Huang-po. In response to his question about Ch'an, Huang-po strikes him. When this has happened three times, Lin-chi decides to leave training. He is allowed to do so on the condition that he visit a hermit master at his mountain hut.

Lin-chi complains to the old hermit of being hit three times. The hermit laughs and says, 'Poor old Huang-po, exhausting himself by hitting you.' The element of the unexpected in this response triggers Lin-chi's enlightenment. He now also laughs and shouts, 'There isn't so much to old Huang-po's Ch'an after all!' Returning to Huang-po's monastery, Lin-chi takes Huang-po's master's staff and hits him with it, whereupon Huang-po invites him to continue his training.

Lin-chi went on to succeed Huang-po as master, and masters in his sect continued to find that they could stimulate a breakthrough to Ch'an consciousness by delivering unexpected blows and shouts, or otherwise confounding their trainees.

A paradoxical thought exercise, called *kung-an/gongan* (in Japanese, *koan*), poses an insoluble problem to reason and the intellect. By doing so, it is supposed to dissolve the boundary between the conscious and the unconscious in the human psyche. This brings about a sudden experience, described metaphorically like the blossoming of a lotus, or like the sun emerging from behind the clouds.

However, excessive reliance on the *kung-an* itself also has its defects. Lin-chi followers accused Ts'ao-tung of a passivity in meditation. Ts'ao-tung adherents, for their part, accused the Lin-chi of playing dangerous mental games. Lin-chi, they said, allowed possibly illusory experiences to be mistaken for enlightenment. Of course, the Ts'ao-tung Buddhists did not ignore *kung-an* altogether, and Lin-chi Buddhists did meditate. The difference between them was more nuances of emphasis than practice, yet the nuances were important enough, having to do with maintaining a balance between the 'gradualist' preference for spiritual cultivation and the 'subtilist' focus on mystical enlightenment. A steady exchange of Chinese and Japanese monks, from the middle of the twelfth century on, took these two Zen Buddhist subsects to Japan. Rinzai (from Lin-chi) and Sōtō (from Ts'ao-tung) are still active there today, with Rinzai commanding a larger following.

During the Sung dynasty (960–1269), the vigorous growth of Ch'an Buddhism was reflected in the written word. Ch'an produced numerous recorded dialogues that gave the words of wisdom of its various masters. While Ch'an Buddhists placed less importance on the study of the *sūtras* as a means to enlightenment, they sought to shed any impression of being heretical. They wanted to prove themselves the legitimate heirs of the historical Buddha, and they did study the *sūtras*. They produced numerous works outlining the transmission of Ch'an insights through allegedly correct lineages. Nevertheless, the proliferation of Ch'an writings was in direct contradiction to original Ch'an principles of not establishing written directives, and some have seen in this the beginning of the decline of the true Ch'an spirit.

## Chinese Pure Land

The name 'Pure Land' (in Chinese, Ching-t'u/Jingtu) comes from *sukhāvatī*, a Sanskrit word naming an ideal Buddhist paradise this side of *nirvāṇa*. The Indian origin of this teaching has been discussed already. We shall elaborate here on its development in the Chinese context. Its development in Japan as Jōdo will be discussed later.

The celestial *buddha* who is believed to preside over the Pure Land is known in India as Amitābha. He is held to have lived much earlier than the historical Buddha. He is assisted by a *bodhisattva* (in Chinese, *p'usa*). This *bodhisattva* is Avalokiteśvara in India, Kuan-yin in China, and Kannon in Japan.

Recall that the *Shorter Sūtra on the Pure Land* says specifically that all that is necessary for one to be reborn in Amitābha's Western Paradise is faith in the infinite compassion of the *buddha*, shown in prayerful and meditative repetition of his name. Pure Land Buddhism's reliance is not on the self but on outside or 'other' power, referred to in India as 'cat grace'.

The recitation of praise to Amitābha is called *nien-fo/nianfo* in Chinese and *nembutsu* in Japanese. In it the devotee invokes with faith the name of Amitābha. The practice is usually done while fingering beads. Thus Pure Land Buddhism shows strong resemblances to devotional Christianity, with a God-figure (O-mi-t'o-fo), a mediator (Kuan-yin), a doctrine of faith and grace, and a prayerful devotion that resembles the rosary.

In its development in China, Pure Land Buddhism has especially appealed to the masses who seek not only ultimate salvation but also a power that responds to their ordinary needs. In this respect, the *bodhisattva* Kuan-yin attracts the most devotion. Originally a male figure in China, it eventually became transformed into a female in religious iconography, probably through Tibetan influences around the tenth century. Clad in white, this 'goddess of mercy', to whom women pray, soon became a symbol of the 'giver of children'. This offers a curious contrast to the otherworldly thrust of Indian Buddhism, and shows how Chinese the religion has become in a totally different cultural environment.

It is associated with the medieval legend of the Chinese princess Miao-shan, who is killed by her parents for wanting to become a nun. The female figure, sometimes seen holding a child, bears a resemblance to the Christian figure of the Madonna (Mary) with child. And indeed, it is claimed that in this pose, the Kuan-yin figure was influenced by missionary Christianity in the late seventeenth or early eighteenth century.

### *Fusion of Ch'an and Pure Land*

Emphasizing, as it does, faith in O-mi-t'o-fo as a God-figure and a dispenser of grace and salvation, Pure Land differs immensely from Ch'an and its more pantheistic tendencies. However, in spite of obvious differences between Ch'an and Pure Land, the Chinese tendency towards harmonization led to a gradual combination of Ch'an with Pure Land. Devout Buddhists combined the Ch'an practice of meditation with the Pure Land practice of reciting the beads while invoking with faith the name of Amitābha. This joint practice considered invocation as another form of meditation, involving visualization of the *buddha* Amitābha and combining self-reliance with reliance on other power. The argument was that since *nien-fo* could terminate discursive thought, it could lead as well to enlightenment, a Ch'an goal. In this way, the Western Paradise was interiorized and became an absolute, just as the Ultimate and the Buddha-nature had become interiorized absolutes in Ch'an, in T'ien-t'ai, and in Hua-yen Buddhism.

## Folk Buddhism and the Mi-lo Cult

To speak of folk Buddhism is to speak about a process of syncretism, that is, of the combination of religious elements from various sources. We find it within Buddhism, as well as between Buddhism and other Chinese religions. What emerges is a folk religion that embraces various strands from all three Chinese traditions: Buddhist, Taoist, and Confucian. A well-known example of this is the metamorphosis of the Maitreya cult.

The figure Maitreya, the *buddha* of the future, is well known in the Indian Buddhist *sūtras*. Maitreya may have originated under the influence of movements beyond India, perhaps in Persia, anticipating a coming saviour. A god named Mitra or Mithra appears in Indo-Iranian religion, where, however, future saviour roles are ascribed to figures with other names. Because of messianic connotations, Maitreya has been the focus of certain political rebellions in China, including one that eventually led to the founding of the Ming dynasty (1368).

The image of Maitreya underwent a transformation somewhat akin to that of the Indian Avalokiteśvara into the Chinese Kuan-yin. Before the seventh century, Maitreya was a large and heroic figure, but he reappeared in the fifteenth century and afterwards in the shape and appearance of an alleged historical figure in China, the 'hemp bag monk'. The image is that of a wrinkled, laughing, reclining monk, with an exposed pot-belly, carrying a hemp bag, with small children climbing on top of him and surrounding him.

According to the legend, Mi-lo used to travel from village to village, putting interesting objects into his sack along the way. Upon arriving at the next village, he would give them out as presents for the children. At night he would sleep in his sack. This explains his happy-go-lucky nature (in Sanskrit, *maitri* means happy or friendly). It also explains his association with children. His image is extremely popular, not only in a devotional cult in the whole of East Asia, but also as an artistic decoration. It often presides over monastic dining halls as well as ordinary Chinese restaurants.

We see here once more the embodiment of Chinese values within a Buddhist image, used so differently from the original Indian depiction of a princely figure. This Maitreya figure, called Mi-lo, affirms the importance of worldly happiness and prosperity. It performs the same function as the goddess figure Kuan-yin, since it is alleged to have the power of giving children to those who pray to it. This desire for posterity, so much a part of the Chinese ancestral religion, stands in diametrical opposition to the Buddhist call for renunciation of worldly desire.

In fact, with his happy expression and carrying a bag on his shoulder, Mi-lo bears a resemblance to the Western Santa Claus, a figure with Christian religious links, who has come also to represent worldly prosperity. Indeed, the metamorphosis of both Kuan-yin from Avalokiteśvara and Mi-lo from Maitreya indicates a Chinese appropriation of the Buddhist religion. If Buddhism survived in China, it did so by serving Chinese goals, including the great importance Chinese gave to continuing the family line. It confirmed a basically Chinese affirmation of the importance of this life and this world.

## Buddhism's Adaptation in China

Did Buddhism conquer China? Buddhism introduced China to ideas and vocabulary that were entirely new to the Chinese. Through Buddhism, China was introduced to Indian languages, especially Sanskrit, whose script is phonetically based and quite different from the Chinese. Eventually, the translation of Buddhist scriptures required many transliterations and produced a new literary genre as a side effect.

New converts developed their own philosophies concerning various scriptures in order to appreciate and absorb the new ideas. The result was a new harmonization of alien teachings with the indigenous, especially with Taoism. Buddhist philosophy brought such synthesis to a higher level of intellectual sophistication. Buddhism became sufficiently Chinese to survive and prosper. Buddhist monks who have studied under T'ien-tai and Hua-yen lineages are still found today, even if Chinese Buddhism as a religion no longer boasts a multiplicity of schools or sects. Yet in the end, it was not just philosophical sophistication that would condition the religion's survival. If Buddhism conquered China, China also transformed Buddhism.

An example is what happened to the Theravāda doctrine regarding the non-existence of the soul (in Sanskrit, *anātman*). In Chinese Buddhism, this received a radical reinterpretation that borrowed from Taoist concepts. East Asian Mahāyāna Buddhists, while continuing to use the Theravāda vocabulary of the denial of the existence of the soul, equated Emptiness with Nothingness (in Chinese, *wu*; in Japanese, *mu*), which, in turn, was interpreted in terms of fullness or the Absolute.

There were other factors. There were continuing problems with ideas like rebirth and practices like monasticism, which were alien to the Chinese ancestral and family system. Buddhism extended the Chinese sense of moral retribution beyond the present life and into future rebirths. In doing so, it offered the Chinese a new way to interpret and accept present sufferings.

Moreover, Buddhism extended the Chinese worldview beyond a vague

*The laughing Mi-lo and his retinue are carved out of solid rock in a hillside in Hangzhou, China.* (W.G. Oxtoby)

notion of the underworld and a home with their ancestors into a system of many-layered heavens and hells. To provide a prospect of hope rather than despair, Mahāyāna added a series of saviour figures. Although Kuan-yin assists in the other world equally as well as in this world, the *bodhisattva* Ti-tsang/Dizang ('earth-store'; in Japanese, Jizo) adopted as his special mission the role of relieving the suffering of anyone unlucky enough to be born in hell. Accordingly, his scripture, the *Ti tsang ching/Dizangjing*, describes not only the many hells but also his many vows to rescue others from suffering. It promises that anyone who recites his vows will gain protection from sundry disasters. Hence it became adopted as part of the devotional core of Chinese Buddhism, and is regularly recited by clergy and laity alike.

Several scriptures that have been accepted in East Asia as coming from the Buddha in India were actually composed in China. A few of these expressed East Asian values so well that they became very popular and came to define the distinctiveness of East Asian Buddhism. For example, the *Yu-lan-p'en ching* is a short text that tells the story of the monk Mulien, who after his enlightenment seeks to help his mother, who is in hell. This Buddhist expression of filial piety forms the basis for the 'all souls' day', the fifteenth day of the seventh month of the year, not only in China and Korea but in Japan, where it is known as Obon.

Another text that became part of the core curriculum for East Asian Buddhism was the *Fan-wan ching*, which lists ten major and forty-eight minor vows. Like the *Yu-lan-p'en ching*, it was presented as taught by the Buddha, but was actually composed in China. Although it includes the standard rules against killing, stealing, sexual misconduct, and lying, it also expresses various ideals for vegetarianism and saving others. The text became so popular that everyone who became a monk or nun in East Asia repeated its vows as a way of expressing Mahāyāna ideals, supplementing the traditional monastic prohibitions of the Indian *vinaya*. This text was used as the basis for Japanese liberalization of the monastic discipline beginning in the eighth century, and is also used by laypeople on occasions of high devotion.

Buddhism also influenced Chinese Taoism and folk religion. For example, rebirth on a higher or lower level of life is often aligned with ideas of retribution for good and evil in folk religious teachings. The Chinese, in their turn, transformed the monastic life. Whereas Indian society respected the monks who begged for their living, Chinese society looked down on those who did no work. South Asian monks ate what they received, including meat. The Chinese monks eventually incorporated manual labour into their discipline, growing their own food where possible, and became committed vegetarians.

There were also problems arising from the religion's prosperity. The big monasteries acquired much land from endowments and donations, and used serf labour to work the fields. The poet Po Chü-i's/Bo Juyi's (772–846) visit to a monastery in 814 evoked this poem, reflecting the wealth of Buddhism:

> Straight before me were many Treasure Towers,
> Whose wind-bells at the four corners sang.
> At door and window, cornice and architrave
> A thick cluster of gold and green-jade …
> To the east there opens the Jade Image Hall,
> Where white Buddhas sit like serried trees.
> We shook from our garments the journey's grime and dust,
> And bowing worshipped those faces of frozen snow
> Whose white cassocks like folded hoar-frost hung,
> Whose beaded crowns glittered like a shower of hail.
> We looked closer; surely Spirits willed
> This handicraft, never chisel carved!
> (Waley 1946:143)

It is no surprise that imperial officials might resent a foreign religion's prosperity. Early in the seventh century the administrator Fu Yi addressed the following memorial to T'ang Kao-tzu (r. 618–26), the first T'ang emperor:

> In Han times these barbarian writings were translated, [the government] being led astray by their specious hypotheses. Thus people were made disloyal and unfilial, shaving their heads and discarding their sovereign and parents, becoming men without occupation and without means of subsistence,

> by which means they avoided the payment of rents and taxes ... I maintain that poverty and wealth, high station and low, are the products of a man's own efforts, but these ignorant Buddhist monks deceive people, saying with one voice that these things come from the Buddha. Thus they defraud the sovereign of his authority and usurp his power of reforming the people (Hughes and Hughes 1950:77).

Such discomfort eventually turned to opposition and persecution. From its zenith of prosperity, the religion entered a decline in the ninth century. A decree in 845 led to the destruction of over 40,000 temples and the laicization of 260,500 monks and nuns.

There are a number of reasons why Buddhism prospered in China. It received the patronage of various rulers. Its rich and elaborate imagery and concepts fascinated many Chinese, who strongly preferred the Mahāyāna teachings of universal salvation. Perhaps this had to do with the character of Chinese society, which was less stratified and more open than that of India. Perhaps it also had to do with another preference that developed within Confucianism, for human perfectibility and the universal accessibility of the goal of sagehood. Moreover, Buddhism tackled the big questions of life and the universe (as did Taoism, to an extent), and offered interesting speculative answers (which Taoism did not).

The practical nature of the Chinese also influenced the development of this religion in their country. Certain practices were favoured, especially that of mindfulness and meditation, as pursued in Ch'an, and that of devotional piety and prayer, as recommended in Pure Land. So these two practices survived and continued to prosper, even after the great persecution of 845, which virtually wiped out the institutional dominance of the Buddhist religion in China, together with the influence of other foreign religions like Zoroastrianism.

## Korean Buddhism

Korea's relations with China were especially close. Ancient trade routes linked it with China's feudal states. In the late second century BCE, the Han dynasty conquered northern Korea and established command posts there from which Chinese culture was diffused during the following four centuries. Confucian texts were adopted and preserved there in Chinese, and the ideographic Chinese writing system was also used for Korean, which actually belongs to a different language family, closer to Japanese than Chinese. Eventually, in the fifteenth century, Korea introduced Hangul, a phonetic alphabet of their own. However, though they use them today less than the Japanese do, Koreans have not given up Chinese ideograms completely.

A Chinese monk brought Buddhism to Korea in the fourth century, and to this day Chinese versions of the Buddhist scriptures continue to be used there as well as in Japan. While there is a wealth of diverse Buddhist sects and lineages in Japan, in Korea there is much more evidence of syncretism with local shamanistic religion. A feature of Korean Buddhism is the integration of folk religious elements, such as popular shamanic cults, which have become inseparable from Buddhist practice.

At a time when the country was split into three kingdoms, Buddhism was first introduced to Koguryo in the north, then to Paekche in the southwest, and later to Silla in the southeast. It was most influential after Silla conquered the other two kingdoms and united the country (668–935).

An interesting story regarding Korea and Buddhism is that of a Silla prince, who became a monk and settled in China. The monk, named Kim Chijang (696–794), was an exemplary ascetic and hermit. His cult is connected with the sacred Chin-hua mountain in Anhwei, China, where he allegedly died at the age of ninety-nine. He eventually was (and is still) worshipped as the *avatāra* of the *bodhisattva* Kṣitigarbha (Chinese Ti-tsang/Dizang, Korean Chijang), who saves beings from the Buddhist hells. The figure of Kṣitigarbha ('womb of the earth') is second only to that of Avalokiteśvara (Chinese Kuan-yin) in its appeal to popular devotion. The association of this figure with the historical Korean monk occurred only in China, but was not commonly made in Korea. Images of him are still venerated in Chinese Buddhist temples around the world.

During the Silla period, the new religion expanded on an unprecedented scale. Major schools of scholastic Buddhism were introduced from China, including the Yogācāra, the Flower Garland (Hua-yen; in Korean, Hwaom), the Theravāda tradition of the *vinaya* (monastic discipline), and others. The Fa-hsiang (Yogācāra) school eventually developed into a syncretic tradition. And from Korea, it and other forms of Buddhism made their way to Japan.

Korean monks like Wonhyo (617–86) and Uisang (625–702) also contributed to Buddhist exegesis, especially on the *Avataṃsaka* or Flower Garland *sūtra*. Wonhyo wrote a famous scriptural commentary. He propounded a teaching that sought to harmonize the various doctrinal trends of the period. According to Wonhyo, the different teachings all complement one another, and together make up one whole truth, just as the Buddha-nature is present in all human beings and in the whole world.

> The world itself is, essentially speaking, in everlasting Enlightenment. In other words, the essential base upon which the whole complex of relationships among the different living beings is standing, is the ultimate eternal reality which is ... the source of life and light,... which make it possible for our life ... to be truly human, to be enlightened (Rhi 1977:202).

There is a distinctive Korean representation of Maitreya, the *buddha* of the future. This is the image of Maitreya as a pensive prince, very trim, with one leg crossed over the other knee. Possibly this is the identification of the *bodhisattva* with a 'flower boy' (*hwarang*) or member of a semimilitary organization in a sixth-century story.

This kind of image also spread to Japan, at the time of Shōtoku Taishi (574–622). An example is the famous statue, regarded as National Treasure Number One, in Kōryuji temple (also called Uzumasadera), Kyoto, which was founded in 622 for the repose of Prince Shōtoku's soul.

The introduction of Ch'an (in Korean, Son) in the early seventh century was especially memorable, as it was to become the strongest force, and eventually to represent the whole of Korean Buddhism. Nine Son monasteries were established, known as the Nine Mountains, derived from various lineages and periods of Chinese Ch'an.

The city of Kyongju in southeastern Korea, the former Silla capital, is still rich with Buddhist sites and remains. These include the nearby Pulguksa, founded in 561 and, near the summit of a mountain not far away, the cave temple of Sokkuram, founded in 751, which houses one of the finest Buddha images in East Asia.

During the period 937–1392, the Koryo court continued to favour Mahāyāna Buddhism and ordered the printing of the Chinese Buddhist canon, known as the Koryo edition. During this period, efforts were made to unify the religion. A renowned Korean monk, Ch'egwan (d. 971), who was invited to T'ang China to reintroduce T'ien-t'ai (in Korean, Ch'ont'ae) manuals that were lost after China's persecution of 845, systematized Ch'ont'ae philosophies through his own exegetical work.

Following him, the monk Uich'on (1054–1101) further revived Ch'ont'ae Buddhism in Korea and was subsequently regarded as its founder in the country. He considered meditation as the ideal vehicle for accommodating the various concerns of Son Buddhism and the other scholastic schools, including Ch'ont'ae.

Still later, the charismatic monk Chinul (1158–1210), fired by a syncretic vision of the unity of Buddhism, meaning the unity of Son and the scholastic schools, founded the Chogye sect. To this, he introduced the practice, which was made famous by Lin-chi Buddhism in China, of the *kung-an* (in Japanese, *koan*) paradoxical exercise, also called in Chinese *hua-tou/huadou*, from which comes the Korean name *hwadu*. This marked the ascendancy of Son Buddhism in Korea, and Chogye Buddhism remains today the orthodox form of Korean Buddhism.

However, the Yi dynasty, ruling from 1392 to 1910, adopted Confucianism as its state ideology, and Buddhist influence withered for several centuries. Neo-Confucian metaphysics flourished, and the emergence of thinkers like Yi T'oegye (1501–70) and Yi Yulgok (1536–84), like their Chinese mentor Chu Hsi (1130–1200), criticized Buddhism for its lack of worldly interest.

Confucian scholars also petitioned the court to restrict the number of Buddhist temples, supervise more closely the selection of monks, and reorganize the ecclesiastical system while reducing the number of sects to facilitate state control. This policy was especially adopted in the fifteenth century, so that the Chogye, Ch'ont'ae, and Vinaya (monastic discipline) sects were amalgamated into a single Son school, while remaining scholastic schools were merged into the Kyo (doctrinal) school. Temple properties were confiscated and the legion of serfs retained by monasteries drafted into the army. Buddhist monks were banned especially, in Seoul, the capital. What has survived is mainly Chogye Buddhism, which had incorporated much of Hua-yen teachings as well.

As in other countries, there was the emergence of new cults that owed their inspiration to Buddhist teachings. The best-known is Won Buddhism, which was founded in the early part of the twentieth century. Its focus of interest is an image of a black circle in a white background, representing the cosmic body of the Buddha, the *dharmakāya*. This new religion seeks to modernize the old religion by translating *sūtras* into modern Korean, by concentrating its work in the cities, by permitting monks to marry, and by emphasizing social service. It has attracted hundreds of thousands of followers.

In contrast to Japan, Buddhism in Korea lacks the wealth of the historical schools or sects, which merged under government auspices. The ensuing institutional Buddhism, the Chogye sect, comprises all the common forms of Buddhist religious practice in the country. In South Korea today, the monks worship the *buddha* Amitābha of the Pure Land, make Son meditation, or recite *sūtras*, in the same monastery, each according to his own inclinations. The situation somewhat resembles that in Chinese Buddhism, where sectarianism has also generally disappeared.

## Buddhism's Introduction in Japan

Buddhism was first introduced to Japan from Korea during the mid-sixth century. Korea, for its part, received Buddhism from China two centuries earlier. This originally Indian religion had taken about 600 years to travel to the extremities of East Asia, becoming transformed along the way. Japanese Buddhism, like Korean and Chinese Buddhism, is Mahāyāna Buddhism, the 'larger vehicle', the kind that permits more cultural adaptation than Theravāda. Today, Japan offers a rich spectrum of Buddhist schools and practices. Indeed, among the lands to which Mahāyāna Buddhism has spread, Japan offers the broadest surviving range of its varieties.

An important landmark for Buddhism in Japan was the welcome proffered to the religion by the then regent, Prince Shōtoku (574–622), in the sixth century. He allegedly formulated the Seventeen-Article Constitution, which extolled the value of harmony and urged reverence for the Three Gems or Refuges of Buddhism: the Buddha, the *dharma* ('teachings'), and the *saṃgha* ('community').

He also allegedly wrote commentaries on Buddhist *sūtras*. Japan welcomed Buddhism for its civilizing benefits.

Shōtoku's personal preference for the *Lotus sūtra* has left its mark. Praised for its mystical as well as magical character, this *sūtra* has maintained an enduring place in Japanese Buddhism. Another important *sūtra* was the *Kegon sūtra* (from Chinese Hua-yen; in Sanskrit, the *Avataṃsaka sūtra*). The Kegon ideal of the unity and interpenetration of all things greatly impressed the Japanese. As for the prince himself, he became the centre of a Buddhist cult that still endures.

The Taika reforms (645–50), inspired by Prince Shōtoku, institutionalized Chinese influence on the Japanese state and society. After them, Buddhism from Korea and directly from mainland China continued to spread throughout Japan. Japanese monks travelled to China to pursue further study. Meanwhile, the state continued to protect the religion and build its temples.

During the Nara period (710–94), Japan experienced its first golden age of culture under Buddhist influence. However, Buddhists were very involved in politics and eventually corrupted by their involvement. The state limited the number of monks and forbade them from proselytizing among the general populace. Buddhism therefore became a religion mainly for the aristocracy. The situation changed with time.

## Heian Buddhist Sects

### *Tendai*

In the Heian period (794–1185) the capital was moved from Nara to Kyoto. Buddhism reached its climax in Japan during those relatively peaceful years. The most influential Buddhist sect was Tendai, which made Mount Hiei, northeast of the capital, its base of operations. This school or sect traces its origins to the monk Saichō (766–822), who had studied in China and returned eager to reform a Buddhism that was manipulated and corrupted by secular power. Saichō attacked the older sects that were established in the Nara period. The temples on Mount Hiei eventually became a kind of fortress with their own monk-soldiers overlooking the capital.

As in Chinese T'ien-t'ai, followers of Japanese Tendai believed in the universal attainment of buddhahood or salvation, as taught in the *Lotus sūtra*, and the harmonization of Buddhist teachings. This means that there was no effective difference between *buddhas* and *bodhisattvas*. But unlike Chinese T'ien-t'ai, Tendai incorporated esoteric beliefs and rituals associated with certain forms of tantric Buddhism related to those found in Tibet and Mongolia. In this sense, Tendai uses both public or 'exoteric' elements (*kenkyo*) and secret or 'esoteric' elements (*mikkyo*) in its teachings and practices. Mount Hiei also became a centre of Buddhist studies, and eventually served as a cradle to the new sects that were to emerge much later.

### *Shingon*

A more important influence of tantric Buddhism in Japan is in another sect, the Shingon ('True Word', i.e., mantra) sect. This, too, came from China, where it was known as Chen-yen, but where it died out. Brought to Japan by the monk Kūkai (774–835), also known as Kōbō Daishi, Shingon Buddhism made Mount Koya, not far from Osaka, its base. Unlike Saichō, Kūkai did not attack the older Nara sects, and was especially on good terms with Kegon.

The Shingon school emphasized the Buddha's teachings in his *Dharma* Body (*dharmakāya*), whom it recognized as Mahāvairocana, called the Great Sun *buddha* in Japan. The realization that one's own Buddha-nature is identical with Mahāvairocana is enlightenment, and can be achieved in this life and this world through the esoteric doctrine of Shingon.

This teaching is founded on the three ritual mysteries of body, speech, and mind. These invoke the cosmic forces embodied by *buddhas* and *bodhisattvas*, with which the devotee identifies. The mystery of the body involves *mudrās* (hand gestures). The mystery of speech involves the recitation of mantras and *dhāraṇīs* (mystical sounds and verses). The mystery of mind involves yogic contemplation of the *buddhas* and *bodhisattvas*. A large number of Japan's warriors, the *samurai*, turned to Shingon to prepare themselves for military success.

Shingon, with its worship of masculine deities, has been described as right-handed tantrism. As such it is distinguished from the left-handed type (like Mongol-Tibetan Buddhism), which emphasizes the feminine side of divinity. Presumably Shingon drew its beliefs and practices not just from China and India, but also from Japanese popular religion. Its healing rituals make it popular among laypersons. And on Mount Koya, Kōbō Daishi, who is believed to be still alive and meditating, is a source for blessing and aid.

Both Shingon and Tendai taught the universal attainment of buddhahood and affirmed life in this world. Like Nara Buddhism before them, both sought the favour of the court and the support of the nobility, and both had magical rites that were believed to be effective in assuring material prosperity and earthly happiness. These two sects became the prototypes of all later Japanese Buddhist sects.

## Syncretism with Shinto

Besides its civilizing benefits, Buddhism appealed to the Japanese because of its access to sacred powers. It included a dimension of magic aimed at achieving practical advantages in day-to-day life. Also, it became associated with Shinto, the indigenous shrine tradition of Japan.

Japan witnessed the confluence of Buddhism, Shinto, and Confucianism. The introduction of Buddhism did not oblige the Japanese to pick and choose between competing systems of beliefs and rituals. Instead, over time, a syncretic

### SHINGON BUDDHISM: KŪKAI ON THE DIFFERENCE BETWEEN INNER AND OUTER

There are three bodies of the Buddha and two forms of Buddhist doctrine. The doctrine revealed by the Nirmanakaya Buddha [Śakyamuni Buddha] is called Exoteric; it is apparent, simplified, and adapted to the needs of the time and to the capacity of the listeners. The doctrine expounded by the Dharmakāya Buddha [Mahāvairocana] is called Esoteric; it is secret and profound and contains the final truth …

The teachings expounded by the Nirmāṇakāya Buddha in order to help others, responding to the needs of the time, are called Exoteric. What was expounded by the Dharmakāya Buddha for his own enjoyment, on his innermost spiritual experience, is called Esoteric (Hakeda 1972:151–4)

system developed, sometimes called Dual Shinto, by which Buddhist and Shinto elements were combined.

With the patronage of the imperial court, Shinto shrines honouring local *kami* were built within Buddhist temples. Buddhist *sūtras* were also chanted at Shinto shrines. Eventually *jingu-ji*, the 'shrine-temple' system, spread throughout Japan, typified by a small Buddhist temple within a larger Shinto shrine. The red lintel-type gateways called *torii*, which are characteristically Japanese, were put up at the entrances to Buddhist as well as Shinto shrines.

Both Tendai and Shingon Buddhism in Japan were harmonized with the indigenous Shinto beliefs and practices. Shinto gods were worshipped alongside *buddhas* and *bodhisattvas* as their Japanese 'incarnations'. A rationale for this fusion was the concept called *honji suijaku*, or 'original site and local manifestations', referring to the Buddhist deities as original and the Shinto deities as their local forms. We discuss this development in more detail under Shinto in the chapter on East Asian religions. In addition, Confucian morality, especially its teachings of filial piety and political loyalty—in Japan, feudal loyalty between lords and vassals—also continued to prosper and was accepted by the resulting Shinto-Buddhist syncretism.

## Zen in Japan

Heian Buddhism, like Nara Buddhism earlier, was a religion of the élite. Buddhism became a popular force only during the Kamakura period (1185–1333). During this time, several sects emerged and became influential. One was

Zen, from Chinese Ch'an. As it happens, the important figures of Kamakura Buddhism all started their religious training on Mount Hiei, but many of them taught doctrines that were quite different from Tendai Buddhism, which had nourished them.

Northern Zen teachings from China had also been introduced earlier by Saichō, but southern Zen, with its emphasis on sudden enlightenment, was brought from China to Japan by Eisai (1141–1215), who was originally a Tendai monk. He founded Rinzai, from Chinese Lin-chi. Eventually, other Zen lineages were also introduced, but the most important forms in Kamakura Japan and later periods were the Rinzai (Chinese Lin-chi) and Sōtō (Chinese Ts'ao-tung) schools.

Rinzai advocated practices like the use of *koans* to facilitate a breakthrough experience in one's consciousness. The moment is a sudden discovery of one's intrinsic nature and the attainment of enlightenment. Rinzai's followers were urged to renounce external formalism and challenged to discover their inner selves.

Rinzai won the confidence of the Kamakura *samurai* through its emphasis on succinct doctrines and personal discipline. While the monk sought spontaneous enlightenment, the warrior looked for a transcendence of the fear of death in combat.

The Sōtō school of Zen preferred gradual spiritual cultivation. Its founder in Japan was Dōgen (1200–53), who had entered Buddhist training at the age of thirteen in search of an answer to death, as both his parents had already died. As a young novice, he worried about why one had to train so hard to develop buddhahood if presumably one innately possessed Buddha-nature. In time, he received an answer from Master Eisai: 'All the *buddhas* in the three stages of time are unaware that they are endowed with the Buddha-nature, but cats and oxen are well aware of it indeed!' (Yokoi 1976:28).

Dōgen learned the value of the Zen practice of everyday life from a monastic cook in China. Upon returning to Japan, he founded the Sōtō sect, which is based upon strict discipline and meditation. His thought features several 'identities', such as the identity of self and others, life and death, and most importantly of practice and enlightenment. Therefore, Sōtō Zen monks are told to get on with daily practice and not to think of enlightenment as a separate goal towards which one should work.

Dōgen advocated *shikantaza*, sitting up straight without vain thoughts, and believed that meditation alone is sufficient, rather than the quest for a sudden experience, since practice and realization are regarded as one. Dōgen was a purist who rejected ritualism. Later, however, esoteric rituals were also introduced into the sect.

Japanese Zen, like its counterpart in China, has always promoted hard work. It is often said, in the spirit of the sixth patriarch Hui-neng, that 'in carrying water and firewood, there is the Tao ('the Way')'. Thus, all work, including work considered secular, is really Buddhist practice. Zen is for 'self-power', that is, the acquiring of enlightenment through one's own efforts.

In later developments, Rinzai and Sōtō diverged even further. Rinzai flourished on the patronage of high-ranking *samurai*. Its chief temples in Kyoto and Kamakura served as centres for Zen education and even for the spread of a new Chinese learning, Neo-Confucianism. Sōtō had adherents mainly among provincial *samurai* and peasants, adapting to their needs by departing from Dōgen's more élitist stance. It devised funeral and memorial services for the dead, and in doing so established a trend that became important for all Buddhist sects in Japan.

## Japanese Pure Land

Pure Land is called Jōdo in Japanese (from Chinese Ching-t'u), and is also called Amida Buddhism from the Japanese name for the *buddha* called Amitābha in Sanskrit. Although Zen, with its emphasis on meditation and the use of *koans*, is better known to foreigners, Pure Land Buddhism in Japan commands greater numbers of adherents.

Japan's Pure Land Buddhism owes its emergence to the Buddhist monk Hōnen (1133–1212), a man of saintly reputation, who wanted to provide everyone with a simpler way to salvation. He taught a devotional form of Buddhism. It relied on the figure of the *buddha* Amida, on faith in Amida's power of salvation, and the use of a rosary for devotion while reciting the name of Amida with full faith in his power to save. This recitation was called the *nembutsu*. Pure Land Buddhism in both China and Japan has much in common with Christianity, for the religion looks to the grace of a saviour for deliverance.

Honen's disciple Shinran (1173–1262) further transformed Pure Land Buddhism in Japan. In contrast to Zen's 'self-power' (*jiriki*), he emphasized 'other-power' (*tariki*), in this case Amida's. Believing Amida's salvation necessary in this degenerate age called *mappō*, Shinran condemned the magical and syncretistic Buddhism of Mount Hiei. Like Honen, he taught the use of the *nembutsu*, the invocation of Amida's name and power. He emphasized its function as an act of faith and thanksgiving. In a moving passage about the salvation of the wicked, Shinran says:

> People generally think ... that if even a wicked man can be reborn in the Pure Land, how much more so a good man! This latter view may at first sight seem reasonable, but it is not in accord with the purpose of the Original Vow, with faith in the Power of Another. The reason for this is that he who, relying on his own power, undertakes to perform meritorious deeds, has no intention of relying on the Power of Another and is not the object of the Original Vow of Amida. Should he, however, abandon his reliance on his

## Pure Land Buddhism: Hōnen's One-page Testament on the Nembutsu

The method of final salvation that I have propounded is neither a sort of meditation, such as has been practiced by many scholars in China or Japan, nor is it a repetition of the Buddha's name by those who have studied and understood the deep meaning of it. It is nothing but the mere repetition of the "Namu Amida Butsu," without a doubt of his mercy, whereby one may be born into the Land of Perfect Bliss. The mere repetition with firm faith includes all the practical details, such as the three-fold preparation of mind and the four primordial truths. If I as an individual had any doctrine more profound than this, I should ... be left out of the Vow of the Amida Buddha (Tsunoda 1958:208).

> own power and put his trust in the Power of Another, he can be born in the True Land of Recompense ... Amida made his Vow with the intention of bringing wicked men to Buddhahood. Therefore the wicked man who depends on the Power of Another is the prime object of salvation (*Tannishō*; Tsunoda 1958:217).

Both Honen and Shinran met with opposition from the monks of Mount Hiei and were exiled by the authorities, only to find support from the masses. Shinran founded a new sect called the Jōdo Shinshū or True Pure Land sect, also referred to as Shin Buddhism. He also did something revolutionary: like Martin Luther in Europe, he took a wife, claiming that husband and wife are to each other as the *bodhisattva* Avalokiteśvara (in Japanese, Kannon) is to the believer. In doing so, he laicized Buddhism. At the time, he met with strong opposition for breaking with the tradition of monastic celibacy. Since then, however, Japanese Buddhism—not just Pure Land—has had a mainly married Buddhist clergy. Even today, Japanese temples are usually controlled by married priests through the principle of hereditary succession.

Shin Buddhism grew especially under the fifteenth-century patriarch Rennyo (1415–49), who wrote pastoral letters to the faithful and rebuilt the Honganji temple in Kyoto. Today it is the largest Buddhist sect in Japan, although it is split into different lineages, with head temples in Kyoto, especially the Honganji with its East and West branches.

## Nichiren

Nichiren Buddhism was founded by the controversial monk with the religious name Nichiren ('Sun and Lotus'; 1222–82). He, too, had studied on Mount Hiei, but left Tendai because he felt it had abandoned the teachings of the *Lotus sūtra*. His own message was very simple. Where Pure Land Buddhism places its trust in the figure of the *buddha* Amida, Nichiren preferred to place his in the power of the *Lotus sūtra*, the main scripture of Tendai Buddhism.

Nichiren sought to invoke that power by calling on the name of the *Lotus sūtra* itself. He inscribed his formula, *Namu myōhō renge kyō* (Homage to the *Lotus sūtra*) as a *maṇḍala* on a calligraphic scroll, the *Gohonzon*, kept at the temple of the Nichiren Shōshū sect at Taisekiji, near Mount Fuji. This formula, called the Daimoku, is repeated as a chant or mantra by his followers.

Starting out as a reformer, Nichiren established a new, characteristically Japanese form of Buddhism that associated religion with nationalist fervour at a time when the Japanese feared a Mongol invasion. Nichiren Buddhism was popular among the merchants of Kyoto and other cities. In the fifteenth century, with the collapse of political order, Nichiren Buddhists rose up in arms. This marked the sect's involvement in politics and society.

Nichiren was aggressive in attacking other Buddhist sects, especially Pure Land and Zen. For this, he was sent into exile. For him, Japan was a sacred land, the land of the *Lotus sūtra*. Many forms of Buddhism that are still vital in Japan today, including the new religions of Reiyūkai, Risshō Kōseikai, and Sōka Gakkai, are derived from Nichiren Buddhism.

### *Ji*

Ji Buddhism is associated with the monk Ippen (1239–89), a practitioner of the *nembutsu* and a preacher of simple sermons. 'Ji' refers to 'occasions', like those that gave rise to groups or assemblies that he gathered together for ritual purposes. These groups had no fixed abode and no consolidated organization. Ji Buddhism also advocated the integration of Shinto divinities with Buddhist worship.

During the Kamakura period, Buddhist development reached its zenith in Japan. Certain features were common to all forms of Buddhism that developed during that time. These include the simplicity of teachings and the emphasis on personal adherence rather than state support. In this sense, it was only during the Kamakura period that Buddhism really became a religion for the common people in Japan.

To recapitulate, we should note that three important sects of Japanese Buddhism were not well known in China. Of these, the esoteric, tantric Shingon sect, though it was an import from China in the early ninth century, has since disappeared there. The other two are native products in thirteenth-century Japan: Shinran's Jōdo Shinshū or True Pure Land sect, and the Nichiren sect.

When Christianity reached Japan in the mid-sixteenth century, it was at first regarded by the Japanese as a form of Buddhism. This perception no doubt contributed to Christianity's initial success in Japan. The confusion was due to the use of Buddhist and Shinto terms to refer to Christian concepts. Moreover, in their learning and discipline, the Jesuits conducted themselves in a manner resembling Zen monks, but Japanese rulers eventually turned against the foreign religion, fearing foreign political encroachment.

## Tokugawa 'Temple Buddhism'

The political involvements that affected the destiny of Buddhism in Japan were more domestic than foreign. By the late sixteenth century, Buddhism, with its great monasteries and armed warrior-monks, had become an important political and military force in Japan, but it encountered opposing forces.

Buddhist power was hardly tolerated by Japan's seventeenth-century warlords. Oda Nobunaga (administrator 1573–82) and Toyotomi Hideyoshi (administrator 1782–98) struggled to break the temporal power of Buddhism, especially Tendai and Shingon, on the battlefield. A new Tokugawa shogunate established its capital at Edo, the location of today's Tokyo.

The Tokugawa family assumed power with Tokugawa Ieyasu's accession as *shōgun* in 1603. In the Tokugawa period (1603–1867), the government turned more to Confucianism for ideological guidance. However, many of the well-known Confucian (or Neo-Confucian) thinkers and scholars of that time were former Buddhist monks, and continued to show the influence of Buddhism in their teachings, even though they criticized Buddhism for its perceived lack of social virtues like loyalty and filial piety.

The government required that each household be registered with a Buddhist temple, an act that paved the way to what has been called 'temple Buddhism'. This was initiated to prevent any revival of missionary Christianity, which had enjoyed a period of prosperity, but which the Tokugawa regime persecuted. The government also made efforts to monitor and control the many sects or schools of Buddhism while favouring the Jōdo sect for political reasons.

Registration and control tended to separate further the different Buddhist schools in Japan. They became distinct legal and property-owning entities, much like the status of Protestant denominations in the West. By comparison, individual Buddhist temples in China remained much freer to change their identity and affiliation from one teaching to another or vary their ritual practice, depending on the views of the abbot or active lay supporters.

Although Jōdo dominated, Zen Buddhism also prospered, with the monk Hakuin (1685–1768), known for his revival of Rinzai. Also, there was the introduction of a new form of Zen from China: the Obaku (in Chinese, Huang-po) sect. The Chinese monk Yin-yüan (in Japanese, Ingen; 1592–1673) arrived with some twenty followers in 1654 and built a temple at Uji, southwest of Kyoto, in the Ming architectural style. This sect honours Amida, but as the Buddha-spirit in daily life, and teaches that Pure Land exists in the heart only. In practice, it has much in common with Rinzai.

Among other things, Japanese Buddhism tolerated Shinto influences and had its soldier-monks. Although the Tokugawa *shōguns* at first competed with the Buddhists for military power, eventually they sponsored an institutional role for Buddhism in Japanese society. When the Meiji restoration of 1867–8 reduced the *shōguns*' power and increased that of the emperor in efforts to strengthen Japan against possible Western encroachments, institutional Buddhism's identification with shogunate rule did not help the religion. It was disestablished and largely disendowed. Buddhist emblems were removed from the imperial palace, and Buddhism was confronted with a nationalism that opposed a religion of foreign origin. Instead, the Meiji government greatly favoured Shinto, and removed Buddhist images from Shinto shrines.

Under these circumstances, Buddhism gave birth to new forms of religious identity. A number of new popular movements, independent of the established institutions, appear as Buddhist responses to the changed climate. Some of these Japanese movements are discussed as new religions in the chapter on East Asian religions.

## East Asian Buddhist Art and Architecture

The introduction of Buddhism from India to China brought two large civilizations into contact. Some of the more enduring contributions of Buddhism can be found in art and architecture. The religion's expansion created the need for temples, especially during the third and fourth centuries. Two basic types of structures developed in China.

The rectangular wooden *buddha* hall was essentially modelled on Chinese prototypes. The earliest Chinese Buddhist architecture still surviving in wood was built at the mountain of Wu-t'ai (Shanxi) in the eighth and ninth centuries. *Buddha* halls were built like tile-roofed imperial halls of state, with the *buddha* statue enshrined in the posture of an emperor. The best-known example in Japan is the Todaiji, the Great East Monastery, built in the 740s, which reflects Chinese T'ang influence. Its *buddha* hall houses a bronze image of Vairocana, the cosmic *buddha*, which is over 16 m (52 ft) high. The Byodoin in Uji, built c. 1000, has a small central hall and a false second story flanked by two-story corridors with corner towers. This is dedicated to Pure Land Buddhism. This sect prefers smaller structures, which dot the country.

The pagoda developed from the Indian stupa, which was originally a repository for relics. The closest structure to it in earlier China was the watch-tower, which goes back to the Han dynasty (206 BCE–220 CE). By the sixth century, square-, octagonal-, and dodecagonal-plan pagodas with up to thirteen eaved tiers could be found in China.

A solid pagoda of the Korean style in Pulguksa, near Kyongju in southeastern Korea.
(W.G. Oxtoby)

Pagodas abound at the Korean site of Pulguksa. The Korean style of pagoda construction is distinctive; their pagodas are generally scarcely taller than a single-storey house and are solid stone monuments—pagoda models, one could say. Their exterior form depicts in miniature the architectural details of their prototype, the multistoreyed pagoda tower with tiled roofs at each level, which in China are constructed of masonry or wood and, in Japan, usually of wood. One can climb up stairs inside a Chinese or Japanese pagoda. While Korean pagodas look East Asian in style, their solid-monument function has much more in common with the smaller solid pagodas of Theravāda Buddhism in Myanmar and Thailand.

Still another Buddhist introduction was the rock-hewn cave temple. Following the model of famous Indian and Central Asian sites, Buddhist rock-cut cave temples were created at Tun-huang/Dunhuang in the northwest in the fourth century, at Yün-kang/Yungang, near today's city of Ta-t'ung/Datong, in the fifth century, and others later.

Besides the main worship hall, Buddhist temple complexes in China came to include repositories for the scriptures, storage for temple treasures, as well as pavilions dedicated to individual *bodhisattvas*, residences for the monks, refectories, towers for the bell and drum, Chinese ceremonial gates, and a stable. As comprehensive institutions, the Buddhist monasteries served a role comparable to the medieval monasteries of Europe.

Buddhist iconography in China is interesting in its evolution from an Indian to a Chinese style. In rock temples and on frescoes, the Chinese depicted the Buddha encircled by his company much as they would an emperor at court. As the central figure, the Buddha, with a crop of curly hair, is usually seated in a

*A colossal sculpture of the Buddha is a central feature of the monks' grottoes known as the Yün-kang/Yungang caves in Datong.*
(W.G. Oxtoby)

serene posture, flanked by two shaved and ascetic-looking monks, the older Kāśyapa and the younger Ānanda. Next to these stand the *bodhisattvas*, who eventually assumed feminine characteristics, looking like court ladies in delicate apparel. Next to these are the *arhats* (in Chinese, *lohans*), looking older, darker, and starker.

The popular figure of Avalokiteśvara or Kuan-yin was transformed in China from a male to a female, but Indian influence remains, as Kuan-yin often has multiple heads and arms, called 'a thousand hands and a thousand eyes', often with eyes marked on the many hands.

A contribution of Buddhist ritual to the Japanese cultural aesthetic is the ceremonial drinking of tea. Introduced by Zen monks, the tea ceremony has become an occasion in which religion and patriotism are inextricably intertwined. Zen influence also reinforces the use of empty space and minimal statement in Japanese painting. Some Zen paintings are a simple brush-stroke circle. Famous among Zen influences in Japanese gardening and architecture are the raked-gravel gardens (the space accented only by the occasional boulder) in the courtyards of Zen temples such as Ryoanji in Kyoto.

### The Buddhist Calendar in East Asia

In Japan and other Mahāyāna countries, the three anniversaries of the Buddha—his birth, his enlightenment, and his entrance into *nirvāṇa*—are remembered on separate days (8 April, 8 December, and 15 February). Festivals honouring other *buddhas* and *bodhisattvas* are also observed, especially Kuan-yin's birthday in China, the date of which varies with the lunar calendar. Also celebrated are anniversaries of a sect's patriarch, for example, Nichiren in Japan.

Under the influence of the ancestor cult in China and Japan, the dead are honoured by an 'all souls' day'. In China on this day, which is called P'u-tu/Pudu, paper boats are burned to free the *preta* or 'hungry ghosts' who perished in violence. In Japan, during the feast called the Bon, two altars are built, one for offerings to the dead ancestors and the other for the *preta*.

Buddhism also adopted local customs such as New Year, when visits to the temple are more frequent, especially among the Chinese. In China, pilgrimages are made to the four sacred mountains of O-mei, Wu-tai, P'u-t'o, and Chin-hua, each dedicated to a different *bodhisattva*.

## Buddhism in the Modern World

### Women in Buddhism

In most countries, historical Buddhism has been a monastic religion with celibate monks. The exception is Japan, where monastic celibacy has long been abolished. As a monastic tradition, Buddhism has emphasized otherworldly values while also encouraging almsgiving and the protection of life. In our own time, the Buddhist religion worldwide has been active in promoting global peace. While it is not possible to deal with the entire range of Buddhist attitudes towards a variety of social problems, we shall single out for discussion a special issue: the position of women.

There is a profound ambiguity about the status of women in Buddhism, as is the case in most traditional religions. This ambiguity may be found in the early texts themselves. Śākyamuni cautions the *bhikṣus* against women as a distraction:

'How are we to conduct ourselves, Lord, with regard to womankind?'
'Don't see them, Ānanda.'
'But if we should see them, what are we to do?'
'Abstain from speech, Ānanda.'
'But if they should speak to us, Lord, what are we to do?'
'Keep wide awake, Ānanda'.
(Rhys Davids 1881:91)

On the one hand, Śākyamuni is said to have resisted the formation of the *bhikṣuṇī saṃgha*, and when he reluctantly agreed to institute it, he predicted that its existence would prove detrimental to the length of time that his teachings would endure. On the other hand, he did institute such a *saṃgha* and encouraged his stepmother and other close relatives to join it. The main reason for starting a *bhikṣuṇī saṃgha* was that women were as capable as men in attaining levels of higher spiritual achievement, including the spiritual goal of becoming an *arhat*.

Early Buddhist history has other evidence of women's ambiguous status. On the positive side, the texts describe approvingly the important role played by some rich women who were early benefactors of Buddhism. One book of the Pali canon, the *Therigathā*, is devoted solely to the poems of early *bhikṣuṇīs*. The ethic of non-violence discouraged the physical abuse of women and children. Buddhism did not define women as the 'property' of men in the way that many traditional religions did:

And be it woman, be it man for whom
Such chariot doth wait, by that same car
Into Nirvana's presence shall they come.
(Horner 1930:104)

On the negative side, female monks had a lower status. The *bhikṣu saṃgha* officially outranked the *bhikṣuṇī saṃgha*, an individual *bhikṣu* outranked an individual *bhikṣuṇī*, and *bhikṣuṇīs* were not allowed to teach *bhikṣus*. The *bhikṣuṇī saṃgha* has died out in many Buddhist countries for various reasons. In general, the *bhikṣuṇī saṃgha* was more vulnerable because it was smaller and less connected to political power, so when times were hard, its survival was precarious.

The case of Sri Lanka illustrates the difficulties of maintaining a *saṃgha* for women. Saṃghamittā, the daughter of King Aśoka, is credited with establishing the *bhikṣuṇī saṃgha* in Sri Lanka. By the eleventh century, after a long period of economic downturn and rule by Hindu Tamils, there were not enough senior *bhikṣus* left to conduct an ordination for the males, and there were no *bhikṣuṇīs* left at all.

A Buddhist king came to the throne in 1065 and invited a party of *bhikṣus* from Burma to reinstate the *bhikṣu saṃgha* in Sri Lanka. He was not able, or perhaps did not try hard enough, to import Theravāda *bhikṣuṇīs*, so the female *saṃgha* in Sri Lanka was lost. Similar stories account for the loss of the *bhikṣuṇī saṃgha* in many other Theravāda countries.

Currently the biggest obstacle to re-establishing a *bhikṣuṇī saṃgha* is that Buddhist rules require ordinations to be performed by at least five senior *saṃgha* members of the same sex as those being ordained. This rule has worked well as a way of discouraging schismatic ordination lineages, but whenever the main female ordination line has been lost, the only way to restore it has been to import senior *bhikṣuṇīs* from another country. Now, there are no available Theravāda *bhikṣuṇīs*.

Despite this drawback, Theravāda Buddhist lay-women are very active in their religion, both at home and in the temples. There are organizations of women Buddhists, in Thailand, for example, who live a pious life and devote themselves to the service of others. They are not ordained *bhikṣuṇīs*, but they typically may have taken vows of poverty and service, somewhat along the lines of Roman Catholic nuns. Some of these women are not interested in becoming *bhikṣuṇīs* because they feel they have more freedom to serve others if they are not bound by the *vinaya* rules. This option is especially appealing to women whose children are grown or who are otherwise free of family responsibilities.

The status of women in some of the Mahāyāna texts is somewhat higher than it is in the earlier texts. The Mahāyāna movement was more sympathetic than earlier forms of Buddhism towards the laity and the rituals the laity practised, such as stupa worship. It elevated the status of all lay Buddhists, but the increased status of the laity is especially noticeable in the case of female Buddhists, as the texts mention outstanding lay-women. Women were seen as capable of making spiritual progress towards enlightenment.

One reason for this change may be that Mahāyāna tended to be less dominated by monasticism, which is typically a stronghold of patriarchal attitudes. But the elevation of lay-women's status must have positively influenced women's status in the *saṃgha* too, as Mahāyāna scriptures include references to wise *bhikṣuṇīs*. The reverse must have been true as well. We should not overstate the case, however. The status of women in the Mahāyāna tradition was not equal to that of the men, and the ancient role of laymen and lay-women in Hīnayāna was probably not all that lowly. Certainly contemporary Theravāda lay Buddhists revere the *saṃgha*, but they do not feel that their own status in comparison is a lowly one.

Another reason for the improved status of women in Mahāyāna is that both men and women were encouraged to take the *bodhisattva* vow. Also, many Mahāyāna Buddhists believed that they could benefit by receiving help from a *buddha* or advanced *bodhisattva*'s store of merit.

In one text, a princess named Jewel Brocade cleverly uses the Mahāyāna doctrine of the Emptiness of all things to refute a male disciple, who represents

## A Woman's Compassionate Wisdom

Once, while the Lord was staying among the Bhaggis on the Crocodile Hill ..., the good man Nakulapitā lay sick, ailing and grievously ill. And his wife Nakulamātā said to him: 'I beg you, good man, do not die worried, for the Lord has said that the fate of the worried is not good. Maybe you think: "Alas, when I am gone, my wife will be unable to support the children or keep the household together." But do not think like that, for I am skilled in spinning cotton and carding wool, and I will manage to support the children and keep the household together after you are gone.

'Or maybe you think: "My wife will take another husband after I am gone." But do not think that, for you and I know that for sixteen years we have lived as householders in the holy life [that is, as celibates].

'Or maybe you think: "My wife, after I am gone, will have no desire to see the Lord or to see the monks." But do not think like that, for my desire to see them shall be even greater.

'Or maybe you think: "After I am gone, my wife will not have a calm mind." But do not think like that, for as long as the Lord has female disciples dressed in white, living at home, who gain that state, I shall be one. And if any doubt it, let them ask the Lord.

'Or maybe you think: "My wife will not win a firm foundation, a firm foothold in this Dhamma and discipline. She will not win comfort, dissolve doubt, be free from uncertainty, become confident, self-reliant, and live by the Teacher's words." But do not think like that, either. For as long as the Lord has female disciples dressed in white ... I shall be one.'

Now, while Nakulapitā was being counselled thus by his wife, even as he lay there his sickness subsided and he recovered. And not long after, he got up, and leaning on a stick, Nakulapitā went to visit the Lord and told him what had happened. And the Lord said: 'It has been a gain; you have greatly gained from having Nakulamātā as your counsellor and teacher, full of compassion for you, and desiring your welfare' (Adapted from Dhammika 1989:111–13.)

the stereotypical patriarchal position. No distinction between male and female spiritual abilities is valid, she rightly argues, because all distinctions are ultimately invalid.

> You have said: 'One cannot attain Buddhahood within a woman's body.' Then, one cannot attain it within a man's body either. What is the reason? Because only the virtuous have eyes of Emptiness. The one who perceives through Emptiness is neither male nor female. The ears, nose, mouth, body, and mind are also Empty (Paul 1979:236).

For reasons such as these, women were encouraged to strive towards enlightenment, despite the earlier Buddhist prejudice that one could not make serious spiritual progress as long as one was in a female body. Later Mahāyāna texts not only reflected a greater acceptance of female spiritual potential, but they also took the position that ideally the *bodhisattva* would advance to the point where the mental state was beyond sexual characteristics, to a state of being spiritually neither male nor female. Theravāda Buddhism also progressed towards the full acceptance of the possibility of high religious achievement by women. In Thailand, for example, one particular woman is highly revered for her mastery of meditation, and young *bhikṣus* go to her meditation centre for instruction.

## Buddhism in Modern India

### *Remnants of Buddhism in India*

Buddhism's intellectual and institutional influence within India lasted over a number of centuries. The reign of Aśoka, 273–232 BCE, marks the emergence of Buddhism as an established religion, approximately three centuries after the time of Śākyamuni. Aśoka was of the Mauryan dynasty, which continued for half a century after him. Buddhism continued to flourish under their successors in northern India, the Śuṅga dynasty, in the second and first centuries BCE and the first century CE, and then under the Kushans, who entered northern India from the Iranian region. Northern India was unified by the Gupta dynasty from the fourth to the sixth centuries, and Mahāyāna thought and institutions continued to be strong during this period.

Buddhism subsequently declined throughout most of India. It had enjoyed royal patronage, but that patronage was lost in many regions of India due to the invasion of Islamic rulers in much of northern India and the preference for Hinduism among the rulers of other regions. Muslim armies overran and destroyed many Buddhist universities. The scholar-monks and their students were under pressure to convert to Islam or face death. Some scholars fled to Tibet or elsewhere. With its centres of learning gone and the population converting to Islam, Buddhism dwindled.

A related factor may have been the loss of lay support for the monasteries. As many of the Buddhist teachings were absorbed into Hinduism and Indian tantric practices reshaped Buddhism, laypeople may have lost their motivation to support Buddhism rather than Hinduism. We know that some of the most famous Buddhist scholar-monks emigrated to Tibet from the eleventh century onward. Their departure to Buddhist universities abroad suggests that the great Buddhist universities of India were in decline.

Those remaining *bhikṣus* who did not wish to disrobe and return to lay life fled from the persecution of the Muslim rulers or the apathy of the people by going either to the Himalayan countries or to the far eastern regions of India. As a result of this migration by *bhikṣus* and the loss of lay adherents, Buddhism no longer survives in most of India. It does survive, however, in Tibet, Nepal, Bhutan, Sikkim, Assam, and in a few regions of eastern India.

### Hindu Appreciation of the Buddha

More recently an Indian intellectual of low-caste background, Bhimrao R. Ambedkar (1893–1956), led a Buddhist revival among Indians who had been denied access to Hindu temples and rituals due to their low-caste or outcaste status. Beginning in the 1950s, many ex-untouchables converted to Buddhism. Buddhism appeals to the 'Ambedkar Buddhists' because it is an indigenous Indian religion that does not advocate discrimination according to social or birth status.

The Buddha is respected as a social reformer who advocated equal opportunity for all, regardless of caste and class. Śākyamuni taught that in making judgements about someone's ability, one should 'Ask not about one's caste, ask about one's character.' This rejection of the caste system, combined with the denunciation of the hereditary brahmin priesthood, provides a viable alternative to low-status Indians to this day, although the number of Ambedkar Buddhists is not great. Some low-status Indians have turned to Islam instead, while others remain Hindu.

For similar reasons, there has been a growing appreciation among Indian scholars of the place of Śākyamuni in Indian history. During the period of Buddhist-Hindu competition, Hindus had claimed that Buddha was actually an *avatāra* ('descent', 'incarnation') of Viṣṇu. However, unlike the other *avatāras* of Viṣṇu such as Rāma or Kṛṣṇa, the Buddha was said to have played a negative role, namely, that of attracting undesirable people away from Hinduism, the true religion. In contrast, modern Hindu scholars see the Buddha's critique of social inequity as a much-needed reform movement. That is, the Buddha is now accepted among Hindu scholars as an important and admirable figure in the religious history of India.

### Restoration of Monuments

Under the leadership of Buddhists from Sri Lanka, the Mahabodhi Society of India was formed in 1891 with the purpose of restoring the Buddhist pilgrimage sites of India and revitalizing Indian Buddhism. With the permission of the Indian government, the Mahabodhi Society in 1953 took charge of Bodh Gaya, the once-grand pilgrimage spot that commemorates Śākyamuni's enlightenment. It has restored several of the ancient stupas at Bodh Gaya, with financial contributions from Buddhists around the world, and has made the site an active pilgrimage and learning centre. The ancient pilgrimage site that commemorates Śākyamuni's birth at Lumbini has been identified in southern Nepal (on the border with India, northeast of Lucknow and southwest of Kathmandu) and has likewise been returned to active use. Buddhists can now also visit the other two major pilgrimage places: Sarnath (near Varanasi), the site of the first sermon, and Kusinara (near modern Gorakhpur), the site of the *parinirvāṇa*.

## Theravāda in Modern Sri Lanka

In the period of European expansion after the fifteenth century, Sri Lanka was colonized by the Portuguese, Dutch, and British, in that order. During the last 500 years of rule by powers promoting various kinds of Christianity, Buddhism declined in prestige.

While Buddhism lost the competition with Hinduism in India, it maintained its hold on Sri Lanka. The Sinhalese population remains loyal to Theravāda Buddhism despite the presence of largely Hindu India to their north and 500 years of Christian missionary efforts under the European colonial rulers. The Sinhalese take pride in viewing their island as a stronghold of Buddhism.

Despite the political problems on the island, Sri Lankan Buddhism continues its rich intellectual and ritual life. Henry S. Olcott (1832–1907) and other members of the Theosophical Society helped revitalize Buddhism in Sri Lanka during the late nineteenth century, and Sinhalese Buddhists have been very active ever since in publishing English-language materials on Buddhism.

The symbolic centre of Buddhism in Sri Lanka is the Temple of the Tooth in Kandy. The Sinhalese hold that the relic enshrined in this temple is an actual eye-tooth of Śākyamuni. The tooth is kept in the temple's shrine room under a number of stacking, miniature gold stupas.

Celebrations at Kandy illustrate the cross-fertilization of Hindu and Buddhist custom in Sri Lanka. At the full moon in August, the tooth, represented by one of the miniature gold stupas that houses it, is paraded on an elephant through the streets of Kandy for several nights. Each night the parade gets larger and grander, and on the final night the sacred relic is given a ritual bath in a nearby river. This reflects a worship pattern that is widespread in India in which a temple's image is paraded annually to a river for bathing. Three other Buddhist temples and one Hindu temple participate in the Kandy Perahera, as the event is called. These processions by torchlight, complete with over a hundred richly costumed elephants parading in groups of three interspersed by musical and dancing groups, constitute one of the world's most famous religious processions.

Since independence in 1948, there has been a revival of Buddhist influence on Sri Lankan politics and the policies of the ruling parties, which draw support from the Sinhalese Buddhist majority. This has led to feelings of oppression on the part of some of the Hindu minority. These are for the most part Tamils, whose ancestry is traceable to various periods of migration over the past two millennia across the narrow stretch of water that separates the Tamil area of India from the northern tip of Sri Lanka. A Tamil separatist movement aimed at creating an independent country for Tamils in the northern and northeastern parts of the island has led to recurring flare-ups of violence and bloodshed throughout the island since 1978. This civil conflict has severely strained the relationship between Buddhists and Hindus on the island and provoked many individuals of both religious communities to take up arms, despite the teaching of non-violence held by both Hindus and Buddhists.

## Theravāda in Modern Southeast Asia

Theravāda Buddhism also remains strong in most of mainland Southeast Asia, but there are challenges to be met. European colonial rule in the nineteenth and twentieth centuries brought heavy Christian influence to Southeast Asia. Britain, exerting Protestant influence, was the dominant power in Burma. The French brought Roman Catholic influence to Cambodia and Laos. Thailand, though, was never a colony of Europe. Most Theravada Buddhists resisted conversion, and the Christian presence in postcolonial Southeast Asia is not especially significant. The largest number of Christian conversions were among the tribal peoples of Burma, who had previously followed their traditional tribal religions and not Buddhism.

The Chinese populations settling in Vietnam and Malaysia brought an East Asian form of Buddhism with them from China, and over the past century Theravāda missionaries from Sri Lanka, Burma, Cambodia, and Thailand have converted some of the Malaysian Chinese Buddhists to the Theravāda tradition. Some of the Chinese Mahāyāna Buddhists of Singapore have also turned to Theravāda Buddhism because it is regarded as pure in contrast to Chinese forms of Mahāyāna that have incorporated large amounts of Chinese folk religion into their practice.

The end of Burmese kingship in the late nineteenth century, the years of British rule, and long periods of military rule since independence have weakened the Burmese *saṃgha*'s traditional political influence. Lately, the economy of Myanmar has remained out of the mainstream of modernization and industrialization, and over the past few decades its *saṃgha* members have been cut off from significant contact with other Buddhist countries. Its people are poor and the temples have fallen into disrepair, but its *bhikṣus* are still important in the traditional village-centred society.

In modern Cambodia, the overthrow of Prince Norodom Sihanouk (r. 1941–55) meant the end of Buddhist kingship with its ideal of a government that provides the basic human needs for all citizens. The subsequent periods of civil war and dominance by Vietnam have disrupted the Cambodian *saṃgha*'s influence. The period of Khmer Rouge power under Pol Pot (r. 1975–9) was a low point for the Cambodian *saṃgha*.

By the late 1980s, the monthly newsletter of the coalition of resistance movements, which included the communist Khmer Rouge faction that was responsible for slaughtering many *bhikṣus* and innocent laypeople in the 'killing fields', proudly pictured Khmer Rouge soldiers and *bhikṣus* working together on village projects. The Cambodian *saṃgha* has been split by the country's civil war, but most laypeople of all political factions remain Buddhists. All appeal to Buddhist values to help legitimate their claim to power. At the village level, Buddhism maintains its tradition role.

Buddhism in Thailand maintains some political influence. The tradition of monastic training for the king still holds, and members of the royal family take part in Buddhist ceremonial occasions. The most important are the rituals in which the king, at the beginning of each season, changes the clothing on the Buddha image in the famous Temple of the Emerald Buddha and gives the Buddha image a ceremonial bath. These rituals symbolize the interlocking relationship among Thai Buddhism, the Thai royalty, and Thai nationalism.

Since the 1960s in Laos, communist rule, under the control of Vietnam's communist government, has cut Laos's previous close ties with Thailand. Buddhism in Laos has lost its political influence, but the traditional relationship of *bhikṣus* and laity holds in the villages. The *saṃgha* continues in Laos, but without the governmental support that Buddhist *saṃghas* throughout Southeast Asia have traditionally enjoyed.

Theravāda Buddhism never gained control in Vietnam, where various kinds of Chinese Buddhism are still found. The Chinese population of Malaysia and Singapore also follow Chinese forms of Mahāyāna Buddhism, but Theravāda missionaries have successfully spread Theravāda Buddhism, especially among English-speaking Chinese. Recently the Young Buddhist Association of Malaysia has been very active in encouraging *dharma* study among young Buddhists.

Several Buddhist reform movements are having an impact on Theravāda Buddhism today. For example, retreat centres have been established in Thailand in an effort to reintroduce the practice of meditation among laypeople. The Thai reformer *bhikṣu* Buddhadasa (1906–93), by severely criticizing the compla- cency of popular Buddhist practices, has influenced many Thai laypeople and ordained Buddhists to be more diligent in meditation and the study of *dharma*. Other Theravāda Buddhists have concentrated on social reforms. The Thai intellectual Sulak Sivaraksa (b. 1932) has argued effectively for a Buddhist vision of society in which the means of development are harnessed for the good of everyone rather than the profit of a few capitalists. He has started several Buddhist organizations dedicated to that goal, such as the Asian Cultural Forum on Development.

## Mahāyāna in Vietnam

Because of China's influence, Vietnamese Buddhism bears more resemblance to so-called northern Buddhism (Mahāyāna) than it does to the Theravāda variety we find in the rest of Southeast Asia, as well as in Sri Lanka.

It is difficult to say exactly when Buddhism was introduced to Vietnam. Presumably, Buddhist missionaries representing both the southern and northern branches of that religion went to Champa in southern Annam (Vietnam) from both India and China. However, by the ninth century, Mahāyāna Buddhism became dominant, although older Theravāda images and monastery foundations have since been discovered. Theravāda Buddhism remains today only as the religion of the Khmer minority in Vietnam, although it is the majority religion in the Khmer state of Cambodia. Theravāda also dominates in the other Southeast Asian countries of Laos, Thailand, and Myanmar.

The insight that *nirvāṇa* is to be found in *saṃsāra*, that the ultimate is to be found in the relative, means that salvation is to be found here and now. This feature, which we can observe also in Korean and Japanese Buddhism, is likewise found in Buddhism in Vietnam.

The leading Buddhist sects or schools in Vietnam are the same as those in China since the ninth century—that is, Thien (from Chinese Ch'an) and Tinh-do (from Chinese Ching-t'u, 'Pure Land'). In contrast with Thien, Tinh-do has been predominantly a lay movement that spread especially during those periods when there was a dearth of educated Thien monks. However, Vietnamese Buddhism is syncretistic, and the two sects have influenced each other, to the extent that all Thien monasteries also teach Pure Land practices.

In the early part of the twentieth century, Vietnamese Buddhism attempted to reform itself in the face of modern challenges, including those coming from the West—secularism and the rival Christian religion—but this was interrupted by the Second World War, followed by the country's division (1954) and the Vietnam War (1965–73). Under the anticommunist Catholic president Ngo Dinh Diem (r. 1954–63), the Buddhist reform movement in the south was forced to make a political response to official restrictions.

It was then that the fiery suicide of Buddhist monks took place as expressions of protest against the government. Apparently, the Buddhists found themselves in conflict with the regime, and several were shot and killed for carrying the Buddhist flag in public during a procession. Then the world witnessed the self-immolation of several monks and nuns, events that made headline news everywhere and eventually contributed to the fall of the Diem government.

In May 1963 the first suicide involved an elderly monk, Thich Quang Duc, who, accompanied by other monks and nuns, assumed the cross-legged lotus position on a busy street in Saigon and had gasoline poured over him. Then he calmly struck a match and became a human torch. Throughout it all, until he expired, he maintained a calm and meditative composure, in contrast to the wailing of the spectators.

What about Buddhist attitudes towards suicide? This question has become urgent in the twentieth century with the self-immolation of monks in southern Vietnam. The answer is ambiguous. When we search the scriptures, we find the Buddha forbidding suicide in these words: '[Monks], let no one destroy himself, and whosoever would destroy himself, let him be dealt with according to law' (Warren 1896:437).

However, when we turn to the Mahāyāna tradition in East Asia, we find the *Lotus sūtra* apparently accepting suicide when it is undertaken for a good cause. This is the case with the *bodhisattva* Medicine King, a popular figure in China, who vows to offer his own body to heal the sicknesses of human beings. For this, we turn once more to the *Lotus sūtra*:

> ... he wrapped his body in a garment adorned with divine jewels, anointed himself with fragrant oils, with the force of supernatural penetration took a vow, and then burnt his body. The glow gave light all around to the world-spheres equal in number to the sands of eighty millions of Ganges rivers. Within them the Buddhas all at once praised him (Hurvitz 1976:294–5).

Historically, a few Buddhist monks in China committed suicide as a demonstration of their piety or to protest persecutions. Sometimes, they offered a part of themselves, such as cutting off their arms or fingers. It was in fact such instances, together with the veneration of relics, that the Chinese Confucian scholar Han Yü (786–824) cited in his criticism of the Buddhist religion, in a text called the *Memorial on the Bone of Buddha*. The tradition of self-immolation in Vietnamese Buddhism seems stronger, although it is hoped that such acts will not be necessary in the future.

A well-known contemporary Vietnamese monk is Thich Nhat Hanh (b. 1926), who entered a monastery at the age of sixteen. Living in troubled times, he became a Thien master, a poet, and a peace activist. In 1961, he visited Columbia and Princeton universities in the United States, and returned to Vietnam two years later. In response to the war and its atrocities, he developed what he called an 'engaged Buddhism' to bring the resources of Buddhist wisdom and meditation to bear on contemporary conflicts.

In 1966, he visited the United States again to speak to important government leaders and propose peace without siding with any of the warring parties. Subsequently, he was unable to return home and had to live in exile in France. There, he continued to promote peace and help refugees, while also meditating, commenting on the scriptures, and writing short stories, poetry, and one-act plays to communicate his teachings.

For Thich Nhat Hanh, the self-immolation of Vietnamese Buddhists in 1963 was not intended as suicide but rather as a strong statement of self-sacrifice to call attention to the suffering of the people in Vietnam. This is to be understood in the context of the belief in the continuity of life beyond one human life span. Such an explanation, however, may be difficult for non-Buddhists to accept.

For Thich Nhat Hanh, changing the world means first changing our awareness of ourselves and the world, especially through meditation and the 'art of mindful living'. Commenting on the *Heart sūtra*, he says:

> If you are a poet, you will see clearly that there is a cloud floating in this sheet of paper. Without a cloud, there will be no rain; without rain, the trees cannot grow, and without trees, we cannot make paper. If we look even more deeply, we can see the sunshine, the logger who cut the tree, the wheat that became his bread, and the logger's father and mother. Without all of these things, this sheet of paper cannot exist ... Everything co-exists with this sheet of paper. So we can say that the cloud and the paper 'inter-are'. We cannot just be by ourselves alone; we have to inter-be with every other thing (Nhat Hanh 1988:3).

In 1992, Buddhist dissidents protested against the communist effort to support a Vietnamese Buddhist church subordinate to the government. It had been promoted as a replacement for the Unified Buddhist church, which was active in the south during the Vietnam war, calling for peace and human rights.

## Buddhism in Modern China and Korea

From the seventeenth century onward, the Manchu rulers of China took a strong interest in Vajrayāna, and served as patrons. During the Ch'ing or Manchu dynasty, each successor as Dalai Lama was confirmed by the Chinese government. The Manchus used Tibetan motifs in their architecture, including stupas in the Tibetan style. In the environs of their summer capital, Chengde, some distance east of Beijing, a monastery temple is enclosed in a multistoreyed wall reminiscent of the Potala, the Dalai Lama's residence in Lhasa.

In the early twentieth century, Tibet was caught up in Anglo-Chinese conflicts. After the invasion of Tibet by the Chinese Communist army, the fourteenth Dalai Lama fled to India in 1959. An approachable and warm personality, he has emerged as a world figure, becoming a spokesman not only for Tibetan Buddhism in particular, but also for Buddhism in general.

In the 1920s, while Chinese intellectuals were calling for intellectual pluralism and a greater openness to Western ideas, the monk T'ai-hsü also started a reform movement within Buddhism. Prominent lay devotees dedicated to furthering the knowledge of Buddhism extended their activities to social work and popular education. Such activity has become part of the Buddhist mission in those areas and countries where the monks and believers still have the freedom to pursue these goals.

Buddhism's historical transformation in China leaves behind many questions for students of the history of religions. On the one hand, as we have seen, Buddhism adapted itself to Chinese culture to the extent of becoming a Chinese religion while maintaining its distinct identity in the company of Confucianism and religious Taoism. On the other hand, it was never completely accepted by the country's political and intellectual élite, suffered severe persecutions, and has been threatened with near-extinction. Has the Buddhist openness to acculturation served the religion well? What would have happened if the religion had been less adaptable?

Buddhism probably would not have survived in China the way it did if it had not adapted itself culturally to the environment. Acculturation also accounts for its transformation and its ability to contribute positively to Chinese civilization. Buddhism has been on a steady road of decline since the ninth century, and, despite all its efforts at renewal and revival, it has generally been regarded in the twentieth century as peripheral to the concerns of Chinese society and even irrelevant to modern life. However, without acculturation, such decline could have set in much earlier, perhaps even a thousand years ago. Despite its decline, its strength may be discerned in its continual ability to resurrect itself after persecutions. We should be cautious in estimating the importance of Buddhism in today's China, but we ought not to overlook its resilience.

### *Korea*

In speaking of the contemporary religious situation in Korea, we are limiting ourselves to South Korea, since the north has been governed by a communist regime. Under Japanese occupation (1910–45), Korean Buddhism was freed from its subjugation to Confucianism. Monks, who had been banned from Seoul during the Yi dynasty, were allowed entrance to the city. However, the religion was controlled and manipulated by the occupying power. Japanese influence led to the breakdown of monastic discipline, as monks began to eat meat and marry. The renewal of Korean Buddhism followed the country's liberation from Japan, although this was a slow process because of the devastating civil war (1950–3).

The more conservative Chogye Buddhists struggled against the married monks of T'aego, who were based in the cities, and sought to restore the meditative, disciplinary, and scholastic orientations of traditional Korean Buddhism. It finally won official support for its efforts in 1954, regaining control over virtually all the major monasteries. Indeed, Korean Son is supposedly the most disciplined. Later, partly as a response to the growing influence of Christianity in Korea, Buddhists made good efforts to influence students and intellectuals, especially through the spread of Son meditation.

## Buddhism and Modernity in Japan

In some ways, modern Japan resembles a museum of the history of religions. It exhibits many cultural traditions, including those of ancient Japan, Indian and Chinese Buddhism, Christianity, and the secularized ideologies of the West. However, there is relatively little interaction among the religions. This is why Japan is not a 'Buddhist country' in the same sense as Sri Lanka and Thailand. Although Buddhism has left an indelible mark on Japan for fourteen centuries, inspiring art and literature as well as an entire way of life, it was never the state religion, or even the religion of the people as such. However, in many ways, it has become identified with the history of Japan and the life and customs of the people.

So closely is Buddhism associated with the memory of the dead and the ancestor cult that the family shrine dedicated to ancestors is called the *butsudan*, literally, the Buddhist altar. Buddhism is frequently called the religion of the dead, whereas Shinto is called the religion of the living because of its association with the joys of life. It has been the custom in modern Japan to have Shinto weddings and Buddhist funerals.

### *The Role of Buddhist Temples*

The rich history of Buddhism in Japan is reflected in the country's many temples and other art treasures, but the temple system has led to much religious formalism. The Japanese tend to regard Buddhism as a funerary religion. Buddhist sects are associated with rituals of death and mourning. Temple shrines honour the ashes of the departed.

In certain Buddhist temples, the memory of aborted foetuses is honoured at special shrines. Parents offer children's toys to placate the foetuses' spirits for fear that they might become vengeful and damage the prospects of living siblings.

### *The West and the Kyoto School*

An interesting development in modern Japan is the Kyoto school of Buddhist philosophy. Its founder was Nishida Kitarō (1875–1945), who sought to fuse Japanese Buddhist ideas with continental European philosophy, with an emphasis on 'pure experience'.

> ... 'pure' is used here truly to signify the condition of experience just as it is without the addition of the slightest thought or reflection. For example, it refers to the moment of seeing a color or hearing a sound that takes place not only before one has added the judgment that this seeing or hearing is related to something external ... When one has experienced one's conscious state directly, there is not as yet any subject or object; knowing and its object are completely at one. This is the purest form of experience (Nishida, *Zen no kenkyū;* Takeuchi 1987:456).

The Kyoto school developed further under his successors, Nishitani Keiji (1900–90) and others, who were professors of philosophy or religion at Kyoto

University. Nishitani was also interested in Christian theology and addressed it often in his writings, but the Kyoto school still remains Buddhist in its main inspiration.

During the Pacific War of 1941–5, the philosophers of the Kyoto school sided with the militarist government. They were not alone; so did most Buddhists, and many Confucian scholars, as well as many Japanese Christians. This demonstrates that religion in modern Japan has been politically correct or conservative, despite any interest in the Western world. On the other hand, many socialists protested the war and went to prison for their beliefs.

### *Buddhism's Contemporary Relevance*

Some have asked whether Buddhism has any contemporary relevance in Japan, aside from ministering to the memory of the departed. Its influence in speculative thought is evident in the Kyoto school's blend of Buddhism with continental European philosophy. Buddhism has been termed a conservative force that is associated with nationalism and is little interested in the problems brought about by social change. However, Japanese Buddhism has made efforts to adapt to modern needs. In modern times, as a spirit of critical inquiry flourished in the country, Japanese intellectuals pursued a process of demythologizing beliefs such as rebirth and mythological descriptions of the Pure Land. Yet traditionalists still cling to the idea of rebirth because it is rooted in the teaching of *karma*, which is so central in Buddhism.

On the other hand, many others have reinterpreted both ideas. They understand *karma* more simply as a theory of causality that asserts every effect to be the result of earlier actions. Rebirth appears to have become only metaphorical for the rationalists. Even Amida and the Pure Land are regarded as metaphorical, or an ideal to be achieved. All this can be done in the spirit of the Buddhist understanding of *upāya* (in Japanese, *hoben*) or expediency, since salvation is much more important than truth.

Buddhism has become uniquely Japanese in Japan, as it became Chinese in China. Japaneseness is an important dimension of all Japanese religions, in spite of discernible Chinese influences. Theoretically, one finds similarities between China and Japan, in the case of both Confucianism and Buddhism. However, the blending of traditions, such as Shinto and Buddhism, has given Japanese Buddhist sects a new visage, different from their Chinese antecedents.

The fundamental Mahāyāna insight that *nirvāṇa* is present in *saṃsāra*, the cycle of birth, life, death, and rebirth, has always been central to Japanese Buddhism. Indeed, this is reflected in the abolition of monastic celibacy. The sacred is so all-pervading for the Japanese that the line between the sacred and the secular is often hard to draw. Nevertheless, with Japan as with China, the student of Buddhism is not helped by any attempt to assert that religion, culture, and society are so intertwined that it is not possible to study them separately. The religious phenomenon in culture and society still merits distinct attention.

## Buddhism in the West

Alfred North Whitehead (1861–1947), the Anglo-American philosopher, has said that Christianity is 'a religion seeking a metaphysic', in contrast to Buddhism, which is 'a metaphysic generating a religion'. Indeed, for Westerners, Buddhism was initially very difficult to comprehend. For a long time, scholars were not certain whether it fit their definition of 'religion', since the place of God, so central to Western beliefs, has been ambiguous, especially in Theravāda, and yet Buddhism produced many scriptures and rituals, as well as important monastic orders—all of which Westerners would call religious.

Only with increasing openness, especially in the twentieth century, has the West learned to accept Buddhism with more appreciation. In this respect, the German theologian Paul Tillich (1886–1965) has contributed his own understanding of religion as 'the state of being grasped by an ultimate concern, a concern ... which itself contains the answer to the question of the meaning of our life' (Tillich 1963.4). As such, a religion need not always profess personal theism. The essential thing is to be concerned with the ultimate meaning of life.

Knowledge of Buddhism in Europe and North America was almost non-existent before the middle of the nineteenth century. The first scholarship on the Buddhist texts and the textual languages began in the 1840s in Europe. The 1879 publication of Edwin Arnold's (1832–1904) *The Light of Asia*, a very moving poetic account of the life of Buddha, brought widespread attention to Buddhism. The book became so popular that one Christian writer countered with a book about Jesus entitled *The Light of Asia and the Light of the World*.

First-hand accounts of Buddhist meditational practice were not available in Western languages until the beginning of the twentieth century when a few Western seekers independently found their way to various Asian countries and were ordained as Buddhists. Among the most important of these early converts were two members of the Theosophical Society, Helena P. Blavatsky and Henry S. Olcott. By the 1930s, Buddhist societies had been established in Great Britain, France, and Germany.

Buddhist influence in North America has come more from the East Asian Mahāyāna than from the South and Southeast Asian Theravāda. It dates from the World's Parliament of Religions meeting in Chicago in 1893, and the influence was evident a hundred years later as large-scale centennial observances were held in Chicago and India in 1993.

A Zen delegate to the Parliament was a Japanese monk named Shaku Sōyen (1856–1919), who later returned to America to spread Buddhism. His bright young translator, Daisetsu T. Suzuki (1870–1966), became the most influential Buddhist writer in North America.

Suzuki made two extended visits to the United States and wrote many books and articles. These caught the attention of English readers looking for an alternative to the personal theism or institutional structures of Christianity. Suzuki sprinkled his books with stories of Zen masters who challenged their disciples to transcend words and distinctions. The Zen strategy of relativizing words and viewpoints may be traced back to the Mādhyamika emphasis upon the Middle Way as a critique of all 'viewpoints'.

Zen attracted Western interest for its teachings, which some consider a form of mysticism. Others are less comfortable with this term as a description of the Zen experience of spiritual enlightenment. Christians and Mahāyāna Buddhists alike have long been accustomed to describing a mystical experience as union with a personal God, but such is not present in Zen, as Suzuki himself acknowledges. However, a broader understanding of the term 'mysticism' describes the spiritual experience as a transformation of human consciousness. Here there is common experiential ground between Zen practitioners and Christian mystics like Johannes 'Meister' Eckhart (c. 1260–1327), Henry Suso (c. 1295–1366), and others.

Westerners have been interested in Zen meditational practice both for its own sake and to emulate it. Catholic missionaries and theologians, coming from a long contemplative tradition, have sought to learn from Zen insights and techniques. Many have looked for a religious awareness or wisdom common to the two traditions. At the same time, the Zen experience has attracted the attention of experts in depth psychology, as Taoist meditation has also done.

Suzuki's writings were popularized through the lectures, books, and media appearances of author Alan W. Watts (1915–73). By the 1970s, Western-born, Japan-trained Zen masters, such as Philip Kapleau (b. 1912) in Rochester, New York, and Robert Aitken (b. 1917) in Honolulu, established Zen training centres.

Zen was the first form of Buddhism to make significant numbers of converts in North America, but was by no means the only form. Another import from Japan has been Nichiren Shōshū, whose tradition of meditation contrasts with Zen's rejection of particular forms. In Nichiren practice, one chants a specific mantra praising the *Lotus sūtra*, a Mahāyāna text that envisions the heavens filled with celestial *buddhas*, and meditates on a *maṇḍala* or diagrammatic design representing it.

Since the 1960s, different lineages of Tibetan (Vajrayāna) Buddhism have also gained converts in North America. Although a congregation of such converts is often made up largely of Americans or Canadians of European descent, frequently its spiritual guidance will be given by a visiting or resident *rinpoche*, a senior priest, from among the Tibetans who settled in India after the flight of the Dalai Lama from Lhasa in 1959. The Naropa Institute in Boulder, Colorado, of the Kargyu lineage, is well known. This lineage group of Tibetans and converts established its North American headquarters in Halifax, Nova Scotia. The Gelugpa lineage (of the Dalai Lama) is also represented, with centres in New York and elsewhere.

Existing alongside and independent of the converts to Buddhism were Chinese and Japanese Buddhist populations that immigrated to North America in the late 1880s. Hawaii, California, and British Columbia were the main centres of these ethnic Buddhist populations, and they gradually found the financial resources to build Buddhist temples similar to those of their homelands. The ethnic congregations were quite diverse. First generation immigrants from different lands spoke different Asian languages, and their overseas-born descendants tended to speak English. In ritual and teaching, these congregations represented many branches of Buddhism. The most popular form of East Asian Buddhism is the Pure Land or Amida branch, and that popularity is reflected among the ethnic Buddhist congregations of North America. There are networks of particular ethnic groups like the Buddhist Association of America and the Buddhist Association of Canada, which serve mainly immigrants of Chinese origin, and the Buddhist Churches of America (and of Canada), which serve True Pure Land followers, who are mainly ethnic Japanese. Smaller groups among immigrants from Vietnam and Laos also have their networks.

With acculturation over time, ethnic Buddhists have tended to adapt their tradition along lines of North American Christianity. Some have adopted Christian styles of worship, with pews, hymnals, and a leader who takes on the roles expected of North American clergy. Frequently they have named their congregations 'churches', and have purchased older Christian church buildings or built their own new sanctuaries using contemporary styles of church architecture. Buddhist Sunday schools were founded, Buddhist cemeteries have been consecrated, and Buddhist wedding rituals have been brought under the supervision of a *bhikṣu*, now called a 'priest'.

In North America, ethnic Buddhists use their temples as centres of their ethnic identity as well as places of worship. Outsiders are welcome, but the ethnic language service and the exotic look of the altars and other furnishings generally limit the appeal for outsiders. Buddhist meditation centres, on the other hand, have been successful in attracting occidental converts to Buddhism. Umbrella organizations, such as the Buddhist Council of Canada, are helping to bring the occidental 'meditation Buddhists' into closer contact with the ethnic Buddhists.

The influence of Buddhist meditation and doctrine has been more widespread than expected, given the relatively small number of Western Buddhists. Without necessarily becoming Buddhists, many people in the West have adopted modified versions of Buddhist meditational practices in order to become more calm-minded or to focus the mind before athletic or artistic performances. Also,

Buddhist (and Hindu) values such as non-violence and notions of rebirth and *karma* have been influential in the West in circles outside what have traditionally been considered religious communities, such as various popular self-help movements that stress diet and meditation.

## Prospects for the Future

### *A Renewed Sense of Mission*

According to the Buddhist understanding of long-term historical cycles, we are in a period of decline. The coming of a new *buddha*, such as Śākyamuni, begins a new era by setting the wheel of *dharma* in motion again. Having been re-established under a living *buddha*, the *dharma* then goes into a holding operation, but it will eventually decline so much that another *buddha* will be needed. This somewhat pessimistic picture of Buddhism's future is in sharp contrast with many religions, including Christianity, but the notion that organized Buddhism will eventually decline does not in any way diminish Buddhists' zeal in strengthening the religion. There seems to be a renewed sense of mission among Buddhists, as volunteer associations are organized to promote Buddhist solutions to modern problems.

The volunteer associations fill the gap left by the loss in most Buddhist countries of a Buddhist kingship that provided both financial support and leadership in education, economic development, or social values. For example, the modern problems of stress and an overdependence on material possessions are being addressed by providing meditation retreat centres for laypeople. The centres offer instruction in basic meditational posture and breathing techniques in order to help achieve calmness, mental focus, and insight into *dharma* truths. Most of them emphasize the teaching of *anātman*, in the sense that the meditator should break through the normal bonds of ego, self-centredness, and the general sense of permanence. *bhikṣu* Buddhadasa summarizes the problem as the attitude of 'me and mine'. According to Buddhist analysis, this problem, although characteristic of the human condition, is made worse by the materialistic and individualistic emphasis of contemporary values.

Another problem being addressed by some Buddhist organizations is the need for an alternative to modern schemes of economic development. The Buddhist alternative calls for a middle path (of course!) between the environmental and social disasters of overdevelopment on the one hand and the poverty of not making any economic improvements on the other. This middle path prefers local-level, low-tech, people-oriented projects that will help everyone. It criticizes megaprojects that uproot humans or animals, and all projects that make the rich richer and the poor poorer.

### *Cooperation among Buddhists*

The Buddhist world is currently undergoing the Buddhist equivalent of the Christian ecumenical movement. There is a growing spirit of cooperation among the branches of Buddhism within most countries, and networks of Buddhists from various countries are being formed. One example of this is the International Network of Engaged Buddhists, with headquarters in Bangkok.

Many Buddhists now identify themselves first as Buddhists and only secondarily as Zen Buddhists or Theravāda Buddhists. This tendency is strengthened by the way many Buddhist periodicals now include articles by writers from various Buddhist traditions.

The sense of common purpose among Buddhists has been greatly helped by the Dalai Lama's international exposure. He has travelled to most Buddhist countries, and in every case has been very well received. Strictly speaking, the Dalai Lama is the spiritual head of just one order of Tibetan Buddhists, but by virtue of the stature of his office and his outstanding personal qualities, he is recognized by Buddhists everywhere as their spokesperson in some sense. His forced exile from Tibet due to the Chinese takeover is seen as a loss for Tibet, but in the long run it may provide the impetus that Buddhism needs to regain its traditional role as one of the world's most vigorous and successful religions.

We have traced South Asian Buddhism through 2,500 years of history from the time of Śākyamuni. The tradition has enlisted the dedication and challenged the intellect and imagination of millions of people. It has enjoyed imperial patronage and rich artistic expression. It has spread far beyond the land of its origin. Buddhism, one might say, has done some things right.

However, there have been setbacks. Most notably, it lost out to Hinduism and Islam in the competition for support in India. Furthermore, in Sri Lanka and Southeast Asia under European colonial dominance it was weakened and challenged by Christian missions and Western values. Also, the loss of kingship in most of the Buddhist countries of southern Asia has undermined the political support system to which Buddhism had been accustomed since the days of the Buddha.

Buddhism, like other religions today, has also been challenged and called into question by modern, secular ways of life. *Bhikṣus* are no longer the main educators, social workers, dispute settlers, or advisers to the people in Buddhist countries, especially in the major cities. Their role has been reduced to that of ritual leaders, directors of religious education, and representatives of the Buddha.

Buddhism has met and is meeting these modern challenges rather well. Buddhists are not converting in any significant numbers to the other two main missionary religions, Christianity and Islam. Even Buddhists who do not go to the temple very often still think of themselves as Buddhists and make some effort to live according to Buddhist values.

What gives Buddhism its energy? What makes Buddhism work for so many people in so many countries? The answer may lie in the continuing power of the Triple Gem to shape people's spiritual life. Buddhists feel confident in their act of 'taking refuge' in the Buddha, not as a god but as a great human being who perfected his mind and broke through to a level of superconsciousness held to be attainable eventually by us all. Buddhists still feel confident in taking refuge in the *dharma*, not merely as a set of scriptures to be studied, but as a living set of teachings that go to the heart of reality itself. And Buddhists still feel confident in taking refuge in the *saṃgha* as a community of people who have set aside family and economic life in order to follow the Buddha's path as closely as possible.

The mythology of old India, with its gods and sacred mountains, is not so important to contemporary Buddhists as is their effort to make merit by participating in rituals, keeping the precepts, and gaining wisdom. These modern Buddhists do not find the scientific worldview to be a serious challenge, for the Buddha himself taught that everything is in process and subject to causation. Buddhists do hold to the idea of *karma* and rebirth, although those that do are not a part of the West's scientific worldview, and many Buddhists venerate local spirits or gods and goddesses without feeling that these conflict with the teaching of *karma*.

In the Buddhist countries of modern Asia, Buddhism will most likely continue for many centuries to be respected as the highest expression of spiritual wisdom. However, in the distant future, when the wheel of *dharma* set in motion by Śākyamuni ceases to turn, Buddhists expect that the next *buddha*, Maitreya, will appear on earth and turn the *dharma* wheel yet again for the benefit of the next era.

## Key Terms

***abhidharma***. 'Advanced doctrine', one of the three divisions of the early Buddhist scriptural canon. See *Tripiṭaka*.

***anātman***. No-soul, the doctrine implying that the human person is impermanent, a changing combination of components.

***arhat***. A worthy one or saint, someone who has realized the ideal of spiritual perfection in Theravāda Buddhism.

***bhikṣu*** and ***bhikṣuṇī***. An ordained Buddhist monk and nun respectively. Compare with *saṃgha*.

***bodhisattva***. In Theravāda, a being who is on the way to enlightenment or buddhahood but has not yet fully entered it. In Mahāyāna, a celestial being who forgoes *nirvāṇa* to save others.

**Ch'an / Zen**. A tradition involving meditative practice and the teaching that ultimate reality is not expressible in words or logic, but is to be grasped through direct intuition, either gradual or sudden.

*dāna*. A 'giving' ritual, characteristic in Theravāda family homes, involving gifts of food to the *bhikṣus* who conduct chanting, and involving a ceremony for the transfer of merit.

*dharma*. In Buddhist usage, the teaching or truth of the religion concerning the ultimate order of things.

*duḥkha*. The suffering that characterizes human life, from both physical and psychological causes.

*Gohonzon*. The Nichiren sect's calligraphic scroll containing the words, 'Homage to the *Lotus sūtra*', which this Japanese sect repeats as a mantra.

**Hīnayāna**. 'Lesser Vehicle', the description of a group of early Indian Buddhist sects of which the Theravāda became the most important.

*jiriki*. Japanese for 'self-power', a description of the Zen emphasis on achievement of insight through meditation. Compare with *tariki*.

*Kanjur*. The Tibetan scriptural collection of texts called *tantras*. The corresponding Tibetan collection of traditional commentaries is termed the *Tanjur*.

*karma*. The energy of one's past good or bad thoughts and actions; it operates in the 'wheel' or continuing cycle of *saṃsāra* or rebirth, ended only by *nirvāṇa*.

*kung-an/koan*. A paradoxical thought exercise in the Ch'an/Zen tradition that is aimed at impressing on the disciple that religious insight goes beyond the limitations of verbal formulations and logic.

*lama*. Title meaning 'wise teacher', given to heads of different Tibetan ordination lineages.

**Mādhyamika**. Teaching of the early Mahāyāna thinker Nāgārjuna, termed the 'Middle Way' because of refusal either to affirm or to negate statements about reality.

**Mahāyāna**. 'Greater Vehicle', designation of the form of Buddhism that emerged around the first century in northwestern India, which spread to China and later to Korea and Japan.

*maṇḍala*. A chartlike representation of cosmic Buddha figures often serving as a focus of Mahāyāna or Vajrayāna meditation and devotion.

*mudrā*. A pose or gesture in artistic representations of Buddha figures. Different *mudrās* have conventionalized symbolic meanings.

*nembutsu*. Japanese term for the recitation of praise to the celestial *buddha* Amida in Pure Land.

*nikāya*. A division, such as of the *saṃgha* or of a textual collection like the discourses attributed to the Buddha.

*nirvāṇa*. The state of absolute bliss associated with final enlightenment.

**pagoda**. A multistoreyed tower that is characteristic of Southeast and East Asian Buddhism, historically developing out of the South Asian mound or stupa.

*pāramitā*. A perfection of effort or the like. Of early Buddhism's list of six perfections, Mahāyāna emphasized the perfection of wisdom.

*parinirvāṇa*. The ultimate perfection of bliss. It is achievable only on departing this life, as distinct from the *nirvāṇa* qualified by 'remainder' achievable while one is still in the present existence.

*paritta*. A collection of chants used for blessing.

*prajñā*. Spiritual wisdom or insight necessary for enlightenment.

**Pure Land**. The comfortable realm in the western region of the heavens for those who trust in the merit and grace of its lord, the celestial *buddha* Amitābha (Amida).

*rinpoche*. Title of respect for Tibetan teachers or leading monks.

**Śākyamuni**. 'Sage of the Śākya clan', a title used by Buddhists to refer to the historical figure of Siddhārtha Gautama, the Buddha.

*saṃgha*. The community of Buddhist monks and nuns.

*satori*. Japanese for spiritual enlightenment in the Zen tradition.

*skandhas*. The shifting, fluid components that make up personality.

**stupa**. Hemispherical mound built to mark or contain a Buddhist relic. In time, towerlike forms, including Southeast and East Asian pagodas, were added to or developed out of stupas.

*śūnyatā*. The Emptiness that is held to be ultimately characteristic of all things, according to Mādhyamika doctrine.

*sūtra*. A discourse attributed to Śākyamuni or to an important disciple.

*tariki*. Japanese for 'other-power', a description of Pure Land's reliance on the grace and compassion of the celestial *buddha* Amida. Compare with *jiriki*.

*tathāgata*. One who has 'gone thus', that is, fulfilled the pattern of a *buddha*.

*tathatā*. 'Suchness' or ultimate reality. Yogācāra thought holds it to be the only proper focus of consciousness, as distinct from the false objects derived from the 'storehouse consciousness' or *ālaya-vijñāna*.

*thangka*. A Tibetan wall hanging, portraying either an individual deity or a *maṇḍala* arrangement of many, used for meditation.

**Theravāda**. 'Teaching of the elders', the dominant form of Buddhism surviving in Sri Lanka and Southeast Asia.

*Tripiṭaka*. 'Three baskets', the collection of early Buddhist sacred writings in Pali. Its three sections contain discourses attributed to the Buddha, rules of monastic discipline, and treatises on doctrine.

*upāya*. 'Skilful means', a strategy used especially by Mahāyāna regarding doctrinal positions as provisional only, in favour of practical results.

**Vaiśākha (Vesak)**. Theravāda Buddhist festival at the full moon around early

May, observed as the triple anniversary of Śākyamuni's birth, enlightenment, and *parinirvāṇa* or passing from this life.

**Vajrayāna.** The tantric branch of Buddhism that became established in Tibet, spreading later also to Mongolia and now India.

***vihāra.*** A dwelling or abode, the term used for monasteries and temples in parts of the Theravāda world. In Thai usage, the term for a temple complex is *wat*.

***vinaya.*** The rules of practice and conduct for monks, forming a section of the Pali canon.

***vipāsyana.*** Meditation practised by Theravāda Buddhists in order to gain insight.

**Yogācāra.** A Mahāyāna school that interprets the world as the product of consciousness and that practises a meditation technique emptying the mind of objects of consciousness.

## FURTHER READING

Amore, R.C. 1978. *Two Masters, One Message.* Nashville: Abingdon.

Bechert, H., and R. Gombrich, eds. 1984. *The World of Buddhism: Buddhist Monks and Nuns in Society and Culture.* London: Thames & Hudson; New York: Facts on File.

Ch'en, K.K.S. 1964. *Buddhism in China: A Historical Survey.* Princeton: Princeton University Press.

Conze, E. 1951. *Buddhism: Its Essence and Development.* Oxford: Bruno Cassirer.

de Silva, L.A. 1974. *Buddhism: Beliefs and Practices in Sri Lanka.* Colombo: L.A. de Silva.

Dumoulin, H., ed. 1976. *Buddhism in the Modern World.* New York: Collier Books; London: Collier Macmillan.

Fields, R. 1981. *How the Swans Came to the Lake: A Narrative History of Buddhism in America.* Boulder: Shambhala.

Fisher, R.E. 1993. *Buddhist Art and Architecture.* London: Thames & Hudson.

Gross, R.M. 1993. *Buddhism after Patriarchy: A Feminist History, Analysis, and Reconstruction of Buddhism.* Albany: State University of New York Press.

Harvey, P. 1990: *An Introduction to Buddhism: Teaching, History and Practices.* Cambridge: Cambridge University Press.

Paul, D.Y. 1979. *Women in Buddhism: Images of the Feminine in Mahayana Tradition.* Berkeley: Asian Humanities Press.

Saunders, E.D. 1971. *Buddhism in Japan; With an Outline of Its Origins in India.* Philadelphia: University of Pennsylvania Press.

Takasaki, J. 1987. *An Introduction to Buddhism.* Tokyo: Toho Gakkai.

Thomas, E.J. 1951. *The History of Buddhist Thought.* 2nd ed. London: Routledge and Kegan Paul.

Zürcher, E. 1962. *Buddhism: Its Origin and Spread in Words, Maps and Pictures:* London: Routledge and Kegan Paul.

## References

Bloom, A. 1965. *Shinran's Gospel of Pure Grace.* Tucson: University of Arizona Press.

Chan, W. 1963. *A Source Book in Chinese Philosophy.* Princeton: Princeton University Press.

Chang, G.C.C. 1971. *The Buddhist Teaching of Totality: The Philosophy of Hwa Yen Buddhism.* University Park: Pennsylvania State University Press.

Conze, E. 1959. *Buddhist Scriptures.* Harmondsworth: Penguin.

de Bary, W.T., ed. 1958. *Sources of Indian Tradition.* New York: Columbia University Press.

______. 1960. *Sources of Chinese Tradition.* New York: Columbia University Press.

Dhammika, S., ed. 1989. *Buddha Vacana.* Singapore: Buddha Dhamma Mandala Society.

Embree, A.T., ed. 1988. *Sources of Indian Tradition,* 2nd ed. New York: Columbia University Press.

Fung, Y. 1958. *A Short History of Chinese Philosophy.* New York: Macmillan.

Hakeda, Y.S. 1972. *Kukai: Major Works.* New York: Columbia University Press.

Horner, I.B. 1930. *Women under Primitive Buddhism.* New York: Dutton.

______. 1967. *The Collection of the Middle Length Sayings,* vol. 3. London: Luzac & Co.

Hughes, E.R., and K. Hughes. 1950. *Religion in China*. London: Hutchinson.

Hurvitz, L. 1976. *Scripture of the Lotus Blossom of the Fine Dharma*. New York: Columbia University Press.

Ñāṇamoli, trans. 1972. *The Life of the Buddha as It Appears in the Pali Canon, the Oldest Authentic Record*. Kandy: Buddhist Publication Society.

Nhat Hanh, T. 1988. *The Heart of Understanding: Commentaries on the Prajnaparamita Heart Sutra*. Berkeley: Parallax Press.

Malalasekara, G.P., et al., ed. 1961–. *Encyclopaedia of Buddhism*. Colombo: Government of Ceylon.

Reynolds, F.E., ed. 1981. *Guide to Buddhist Religion*. Boston: Hall.

Rhi, K. 1977. 'Wonhyo and His Thought'. In *Korean and Asian Religious Tradition*, edited by C. Yu, 197–207. Toronto: Korean and Related Studies Press.

Rhys Davids, C.R. 1964. *Psalms of the Early Buddhists: The Sisters*. London: Luzac for Pali Text Society.

Rhys Davids, T.W. trans. 1881. *Buddhist Sutras*. Oxford: Clarendon Press.

____, trans. 1890. *The Questions of King Milinda*, Part I. Oxford: Clarendon Press.

Robinson, R.H. 1959. 'Buddhism: In China and Japan'. In *The Concise Encyclopedia of Living Faiths*, edited by R.C. Zaehner, 321–47. London: Hutchinson.

Shaw, R.D.M., trans. 1961. *The Blue Cliff Records: The Hekigan Roku [Pi yen lu] Containing One Hundred Stories of Zen Masters of Ancient China*. London: Joseph.

Takeuchi, Y. 1987. 'Nishida Kitarō'. In *The Encyclopedia of Religion*, edited by M. Eliade, vol. 10, 456–7. New York: Macmillan.

Tillich, P. 1963. *Christianity and the Encounter of the World Religions*. New York: Scribner.

Tsunoda, R., ed. 1958. *Sources of Japanese Tradition*. New York: Columbia University Press.

Waley, A. 1946. *Chinese Poems*. London: Allen and Unwin.

Warren, H.C. 1896. *Buddhism in Translations*. Cambridge: Harvard University Press.

Yampolsky. P., trans. 1976. *The Platform Sutra of the Sixth Patriarch*. New York: Columbia University Press.

Yokoi, Y. 1976. Zen Master Dogen: An Introduction with Selected Writings. New York: Weatherhill.

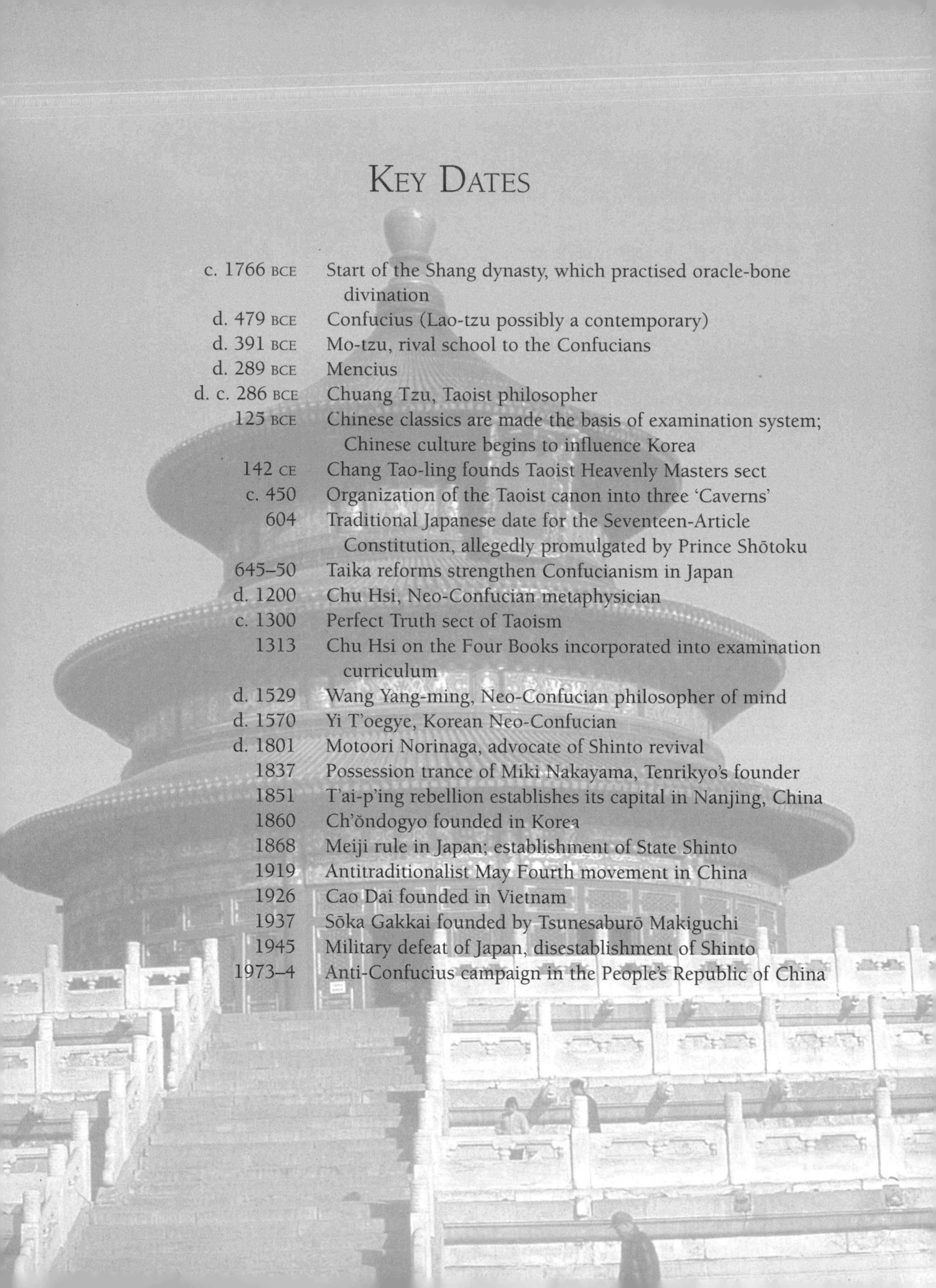

# KEY DATES

| | |
|---|---|
| c. 1766 BCE | Start of the Shang dynasty, which practised oracle-bone divination |
| d. 479 BCE | Confucius (Lao-tzu possibly a contemporary) |
| d. 391 BCE | Mo-tzu, rival school to the Confucians |
| d. 289 BCE | Mencius |
| d. c. 286 BCE | Chuang Tzu, Taoist philosopher |
| 125 BCE | Chinese classics are made the basis of examination system; Chinese culture begins to influence Korea |
| 142 CE | Chang Tao-ling founds Taoist Heavenly Masters sect |
| c. 450 | Organization of the Taoist canon into three 'Caverns' |
| 604 | Traditional Japanese date for the Seventeen-Article Constitution, allegedly promulgated by Prince Shōtoku |
| 645–50 | Taika reforms strengthen Confucianism in Japan |
| d. 1200 | Chu Hsi, Neo-Confucian metaphysician |
| c. 1300 | Perfect Truth sect of Taoism |
| 1313 | Chu Hsi on the Four Books incorporated into examination curriculum |
| d. 1529 | Wang Yang-ming, Neo-Confucian philosopher of mind |
| d. 1570 | Yi T'oegye, Korean Neo-Confucian |
| d. 1801 | Motoori Norinaga, advocate of Shinto revival |
| 1837 | Possession trance of Miki Nakayama, Tenrikyo's founder |
| 1851 | T'ai-p'ing rebellion establishes its capital in Nanjing, China |
| 1860 | Ch'ŏndogyo founded in Korea |
| 1868 | Meiji rule in Japan; establishment of State Shinto |
| 1919 | Antitraditionalist May Fourth movement in China |
| 1926 | Cao Dai founded in Vietnam |
| 1937 | Sōka Gakkai founded by Tsunesaburō Makiguchi |
| 1945 | Military defeat of Japan, disestablishment of Shinto |
| 1973–4 | Anti-Confucius campaign in the People's Republic of China |

Chapter Five

# East Asian Religions

Julia Ching

East Asia is a cultural region in much the same way as Europe. Its various parts have a shared heritage and a long history of mutual interaction. One could compare China with Rome, for each was a major empire 2,000 years ago, contributing a writing system, literary traditions, and a religio-philosophical heritage to the surrounding region. One could compare Japan with Britain, an offshore archipelago that has been a spark-plug of industrialization and modernization in more recent centuries.

Analogies such as these are initially useful to stimulate investigation, but if maintained for too long, they risk forcing a preconceived interpretation of the data. For East Asia, as for all cultural and historical study, a more accurate picture takes into account not just shared features but distinctive ones. The Japanese in particular take pains to point out the ways in which they think their situation is unique. Still, we find a number of features shared widely in the preclassical background of East Asian religions. These include nature myths, divination or fortune-telling, cultivation of trance states, worship of ancestor spirits, and ritual roles for kings, queens, and princes.

A unifying feature in the classical era, and even today, has been the ideographic Chinese writing system, which was already in ancient times the product of a long development in China. As it is not tied to the sounds of particular words, the Chinese writing system represents ideas in Korean, Japanese, and Vietnamese as well. In the nineteenth century Vietnam switched to the Latin alphabet, introduced by a French Jesuit missionary in the seventeenth century. In the fifteenth century Korea developed its own phonetic alphabet, Hangul. The Japanese continue to use Chinese ideograms while mixing in two other phonetic scripts within a single sentence. However, one is not considered truly literate in East Asia without a command of the ideographic characters. For the past thousand years, the Confucian tradition, recorded in the classic texts that were the syllabus of education, has likewise been a common thread in the fabric of East Asian culture.

The entire region has also been affected by imported traditions. Buddhism came from India, was domesticated and transformed in China, and was further differentiated in Japan, but synthesized in Korea. More recently, the political and intellectual impact of the Euro-American West has been a major force in modern developments. Christianity, which the Europeans brought, has become numerically influential chiefly in Korea, while communism dominated the East Asian mainland in the second half of the twentieth century.

## The Overlap of Religions

A major difference between East Asian religious life and that of India and the West is that its communities are not completely separate. If you ask a Japanese, for instance, whether he or she is a believer in a particular religion, you may get the answer 'no' (even the Japanese word for 'no' is not as tightly defined a denial as is 'no' in English). However, if you ask whether he or she adheres to Shinto, Buddhism, and Confucianism, you may get the answer 'yes' (albeit again a bit noncommittal compared with the English 'yes'). Many Japanese follow more than one religion, even though they do not consider themselves very religious.

Much the same can be said of the Chinese, the Koreans, or the Vietnamese. At issue is the inseparability between religion and culture in East Asia, as well as the syncretism or combination that characterizes all the major religions there. East Asians all assert the importance of cosmic and social harmony. Since harmony is highly valued, each of the religious traditions tends to meet some of the needs of the people. In spite of occasional religious conflicts, all tend to work together in a larger cultural and social context.

Some scholars go so far as to say that the Chinese and Japanese have no religion, since their 'religions' do not make the exclusive claims to truth and dogma so characteristic of Western religions. Others claim that China and Japan have no religion because their civilization is basically areligious and this-worldly. Still others, while granting that religion is present in East Asian civilization, find it so entwined in the culture itself that the two have become inseparable; they hold therefore that speaking about religion in such places as China is a useless exercise. Others are not always sure whether they should speak of 'religion' in the singular or the plural.

We should make our own position clear. There is ground for confusion, we grant, because of the close ties between religion and culture. It is not easy to separate religion and culture in our discussions. This does not mean, however, that East Asian civilizations are areligious. Some people dismiss customs and rituals as superstitious, but others in the same culture see them as practical means of securing benefit in life. We should be aware that definitions of these traditions in the region are fluid, as distinct from the roles of religions of West Asian origin, like Christianity or Islam. Moreover, we think that the word 'religion' need not be defined in exclusivist terms, in theist terms, or even in doctrinal terms.

We consider as religion all forces and institutions that function in East Asian society as does 'religion' in Western society. That is why we include Confucianism and rival teachings in our discussions, while acknowledging that some regard them more as philosophy than as religion. We also call this section 'East Asian Religions' in the plural because traditions exercising certain roles of 'religion' can be identified as distinct and cohesive, despite intertwined origins and historical interactions. This is the case especially with Confucianism and Taoism.

Is there anything called East Asian religion in the singular? The answer is, strangely, yes. And what is this religion? Chinese, Korean, Japanese, and Vietnamese religions include variations on the well-known ancestor cult as well as a dimension of nature worship. There is as well some collaboration between Confucianism and Taoism in China, and between Buddhism and Shinto in Japan. Age-old traditions were incorporated into each system in a different way. To see these, we must go back to the remote past to examine the status of ancient religion before the other traditions developed.

# ANCIENT RELIGION AND ITS ECHOES

## Archaeology and Antiquity

Chinese civilization is best understood when we see the whole picture against 4,000 years of historical background. Chinese religion does not consist only of the 'great traditions' of Confucianism, Taoism, and Buddhism. We must also include an earlier 'great tradition', using the singular term in a composite sense. The religion of antiquity's mythology, divination, and sacrifices, and 'ecstatic' or shamanistic character has been rediscovered through archaeological artefacts. Of course not all of it is yet known because much remains to be discovered. What has come to light so far is important not only for its own sake but also because it enables us to understand later developments.

China has extensive archaeological remains from its preliterary past, and thus offers a very fruitful field for scholars interested in antiquity. Indeed, China is an archaeologist's paradise. Archaeological finds have yielded the records of an early civilization that is possibly 5,000 years old. The so-called Shang oracle-bone inscriptions offer evidence of unmistakable early religiosity, including an ancestor cult, divination, sacrifice, priesthood, and shamanism. We shall recount a few of these findings and the world of antiquity they have opened up to scholars in the twentieth century.

Prehistoric China spans a period that was contemporary with the Ancient

Near East. Archaeological discoveries have thrown light on the religious character of its civilization. From the late fourth and early third millennium BCE, we have evidence of potters' marks resembling writing, and of scapulimancy (shoulder-bone divination) that used a variety of animal bones. There are also clay phallus objects that were apparently used in ancestor worship.

Archaeological discoveries in recent years have revolutionized our knowledge of ancient China as a whole. The Yellow River basin is no longer considered the source of China's ancient civilization, since many very early finds have been unearthed some distance from that area. In 1986, archaeologists discovered altars and other remains in Chekiang (Zhejiang) that date back 5,000 years ago, that is, long before the Shang dynasty. They also unearthed remains in San-hsing-tui/Sanxingdui, Szechwan, that date back 3,000 or more years, back to the early Chou/Zhou dynasty, but at a time before this region was incorporated into China.

Because of the various finds in different areas of China, far from the Yellow River basin, archaeologists think that Chinese civilization may have had multiple origins. Perhaps it is more accurate to call this civilization the composite of many regional cultures, each with its special features. Although no writing system earlier than the oracle bones has been discovered or deciphered to date, such may yet be uncovered.

## Gods and Spirits

The Chinese, it has sometimes been said, knew no gods, and Chinese civilization has been termed inherently secular. This assertion, often made in the past, is no longer tenable. The study of archaeology and textual philology has yielded a hierarchy of gods and spirits that were worshipped in Chinese antiquity, which nearly rivals that of the Greeks and Romans. We now know that the ancient Chinese believed in many gods and spirits belonging to the cosmic as well as the ancestral or human order.

### *The Supreme Deity*

Part of the confusion about a supreme deity in ancient Chinese religion stems from the fact that different populations used different names. A name we translate as 'Lord' or 'Lord-on-high' dominated during the Shang era (c. 1766–1122 BCE). However, when a different people prevailed in the subsequent Chou era (1122–249 BCE), a name we translate as 'Heaven' came into use. Many of the earlier Shang conceptions of the Lord became fused with the Chou conceptions of Heaven. In its broad outlines the process resembles cultural assimilation and association that one can observe elsewhere, such as in the ancient Middle Eastern and Mediterranean world.

Let us review the Chinese situation in more detail. In Shang times, the supreme deity of ancient Chinese religion was called Lord (Ti/Di) or Lord-on-high (Shang-ti/Shangdi). Shang-ti reigns over a host of nature deities, just as an earthly king rules over his court. The exact etymological meaning of the term Ti is not clear, and various explanations have been offered, especially those pertaining to a sacrificial cult. He is usually understood anthropomorphically, and considered the supreme deity. He is also frequently referred to as God in Western literature. In divination, questions regarding eclipses of the sun and the moon were posed to him because such natural events were regarded as manifestations of heavenly displeasure with earthly conduct.

The Lord-on-high was represented in Shang times as a remote and impersonal being, perhaps a creator god. I am not suggesting that the ancient Chinese believed in any clear doctrine of creation. There is scant evidence for this. The speculation is based on a comparison between this figure and the later Chou figure called T'ien (Heaven), which was much closer to the people who worshipped it, and was more characteristic of an ancestral deity.

T'ien, 'Heaven', became the preferred term for a divine power or god during the Chou period, by the time of Confucius in the sixth century BCE. According to the pictorial etymology of Chinese characters, the term probably referred to a human with a big head. The word was often found on bronze inscriptions, designating a personal god who was interested in human affairs, and possibly the supreme ancestor figure worshipped by the Chou royal family.

The Chou conquest of the Shang was actually a western people's conquest of an eastern people in northern China. It probably led to the confusion and combination of two originally distinct cults, and to the subsequent usage of both Ti and T'ien to designate the supreme being, regarded as a personal god.

We can compare these two names for God with what we see in the religion of ancient Israel. There, two different names for God have been interpreted by modern scholarship as characteristic of the Yahwist and Elohist sources in the *Pentateuch*, the Five Books ascribed to Moses. In the account of the burning bush in the sixth chapter of *Exodus*, the name Yahweh (written with the Hebrew letters YHWH) is explained to Moses as 'I am who am', according to the early translators, or 'I shall be what I shall be', according to some modern interpreters. The other name was Elohim, a plural but used with the singular verb, meaning God or Godhead. These two were later used interchangeably in the Hebrew scriptures: 'that you might know the LORD (Yahweh) is God [Elohim]; there is no other besides him' (*Deuteronomy* 4:35). In the Jewish case, both terms had personal connotations, whereas, in the Chinese case, the term T'ien later took on pantheistic tones.

### *Nature Deities*

In addition to this supreme deity, there were other classes of gods or spirits in ancient China. Inscriptions on the Shang oracle bones refer to nature deities. These include heavenly deities such as the sun, moon, wind, clouds, rain, and snow. There were earthly deities such as the earth (*she*) and its product, grain (*chi/ji*), rivers, and mountains. The so-called 'Queen Mothers of the East and West' were perhaps goddesses identified with the sun and moon; perhaps they were also the spouses of the Lord-on-high. These nature deities were all under the direct control of Ti. Their ancient cult and the veneration they continued to receive in later ages typify the mixed character of Chinese religion, which was never exclusively an ancestor religion but a combination of the cult of ancestors with that of other spirits.

### *Mother Goddesses*

There is archaeological evidence in Europe, India, and Africa that worship of a mother goddess was widespread in palaeolithic, neolithic, and early historical times. Such a figure had its place in the ancient civilizations of Sumer, Babylon, and Egypt.

Recently there has been a similar discovery in China. In 1986, such a figure was allegedly found in Liaoning province, northeast of Beijing, at excavation sites of the Hongshan culture, which existed about 4500 to 2500 BCE. The area adjoins today's Inner Mongolia. The artefacts were small statues of a pregnant goddess figure, significantly often surrounded with jade dragons, tortoises, birds, and cicadas. Somewhat northwest of this main site, in Niu-he Liang, a life-sized head of a female figure from 3000 BCE was also unearthed. It is considered the oldest deity figure discovered in China and possibly the first tangible evidence of an archaic female goddess cult.

The meaning of this find is still under discussion. The sites of the discoveries are some distance from the Yellow River basin, which was long believed to be the cradle of Chinese civilization. Predating these finds, there is textual evidence of female deity figures, a 'Western Mother' and an 'Eastern Mother', which were mentioned in oracle inscriptions. There are also different descriptions of the 'Queen Mother of the West' in such texts as *Chuang Tzu/Zhuangzi* and *Huai-nan Tzu/Huainanzi*, as well as in *Lieh Tzu/Liezi* and in *Shan-hai ching/Shanhaijing* (Classic of Mountains and Oceans)—a text that contains some parts going back to 400 BCE, and other parts of about 300 CE.

However, there is a problem in linking records to these remains. Unlike the statues, the texts do not refer clearly to this goddess figure in fertility terms. Nevertheless, the textual figure has a clear connection to life and motherhood, and would later represent the power and wisdom connected with longevity. Certainly, these finds must give pause to any scholars who still assert the absence of a mother-goddess figure in ancient China.

There is also another female deity figure in the myths: Nü-wa (etymologically suggesting 'woman'), sometimes alleged to be the consort of Fu-hsi/Fuxi, the culture hero. A second-century text describes her making human beings with the yellow earth; when she gets tired, she just strings many figures together with mud. Hence it is said that the nobles are the ones made with some care, while the commoners are strung together with mud. The second-century-BCE text *Huai-nan Tzu* also describes an early cosmic catastrophe involving a male god who breaks the pillar attaching earth to heaven. Nü-wa's task is to repair the universe, which she does, using multicoloured pebbles to mend the blue skies, cutting turtle legs to establish the four compass points, and killing the black dragon that has been causing a flood.

To have humankind created by a goddess is a story feminists can endorse, even if it enshrines social distinctions between nobility and lesser folk. Moreover, if it takes a male figure to bring catastrophe to the universe, it takes a female deity to restore order and completion. If Chinese religion lacks a formal doctrine of creation, mythology provides food for thought in this story and in others.

### *Female Deities Today*

The role of the female appears more prominent in popular religious manifestations than in the so-called 'great' traditions. In the chapter on Buddhism, we referred to the universal importance of Kuan-yin, the Buddhist goddess of mercy.

There is also the mother-goddess Wu-sheng Lao-mu (literally, 'the Uncreated Old Mother'), a creator as well as saviour figure who is sometimes called the 'Eternal Venerable Mother'. Her role reflects a high status for women in society, since so much power is ascribed to a goddess. According to popular belief, celebrated in some 'spirit-writing' divination texts, she first creates the world and then engenders human beings, who are her children. Their misbehaviour and contention, however, brings her grief. With great compassion, she continues to send messages to them through inspired leaders and revealed books, calling on them to recover their true nature and return home. In the I-kuan-tao/Yiguandao, discussed later, this cult has been traced back to the Ming dynasty (1368–1644). To quote from one text:

> [Mother], thinking of her children with great pain and limitless sorrow, from the cool native land of utmost bliss has sent all the immortals and Buddhas to save the imperial [children] … She sighs that they are lost … and in pity has descended in person to save the world, sending down from on high books written in [her] blood in many thousands of words (Jordan and Overmyer 1986:222–3).

Ma-tsu, whose name is the Hokkien dialect's expression for 'grandma', has special importance in Taiwan and Fukien. Allegedly, the historical figure was born on an island off the Fukien coast and died at a young age. She is said to have saved her father and brother when their fishing boat collapsed, and commands much loyalty among the fisherfolk. In the early summer of 1989, an image of Ma-tsu was carried back for a visit to the Fukien temple by the fishing community of I-lan, on Taiwan's east coast. This was done in flagrant violation of the law that forbade direct contact with communist China. However, the whole event was televised, and those involved suffered only nominal penalties. Television coverage of the impressive fishing fleet that carried her image featured it as the goddess's 'visit to her parental home'.

## Mythological Figures

The myths of some cultures, such as the Greek, Roman, and Japanese, have survived largely intact. Chinese myths of antiquity, in contrast, remain scattered and fragmentary, frequently interspersed in later texts bearing the mark of a demythologizer's editing.

### *Ancestral spirits*

The high ancestors were frequently semidivine figures to whom the royal lineage was traced. The later ancestral spirits, both male and female, as well as the spirits of deceased ministers, looked up to them. The Three Dynasties were each allegedly founded by members of a different clan—people who traced their descent from the same mythological ancestor. The Hsia/Xia dynasty (third millennium BCE?) goes back to the sage-hero Yü, reportedly born out of a rock. The Shang dynasty had for its principal high ancestor a mythical hero whose mother becomes pregnant after devouring a dark bird's egg. The Chou dynasty goes back to Chi/Ji, the 'Lord Millet', whose mother treads on Ti's divine footprint.

Less easy to pinpoint at an early stage are the ancestral spirits of the common people. Their cult was little known until a much later age, as the practice was not meticulously recorded. One might associate with these departed spirits the term for 'ghost' (*kuei/guei*), the pictograph for which shows a human being wearing a huge mask, possibly to signify a feeling of strangeness.

### *The Sage Kings*

Archaeological discoveries indicate a past of war and violence, when warriors were buried with horses and chariots. Mythological records support an age of legendary gods and heroes, especially those sage figures traditionally known as the Three Sovereigns (San-huang) and the Five Emperors (Wu-ti), who are also venerated as ancestral leaders of the Chinese people.

Classical texts refer to the role of wise and virtuous men, usually rulers. The term *sheng*, translated as 'sage', was represented by a character derived from the oracle-bone pictograph of a big ear and a small mouth. It is closely associated with acute hearing, perhaps hearing the voices of the spirits and communicating what has been heard.

The so-called Three Sovereigns are legendary figures whose names connote

## CHINESE THEORIES OF THE UNIVERSE

Heaven is like an egg, and earth is like the yolk of the egg. Alone it dwells inside. Heaven is great and earth is small. Inside and outside of heaven there is water. Heaven wraps around the earth as the shell encloses the yolk. Heaven and earth are borne up and stand upon their vital force, floating upon the water (From Chang Heng, *Hung-t'ien-i*; de Bary 1960:210).

Heaven is like an umbrella, earth like an overturned dish. Both heaven and earth are high in the middle and slope down at the edges. The point beneath the north pole is the center of both heaven and earth. This is the highest point of earth, and from here it slopes down on all sides like water flowing downward. The sun, moon, and stars alternately shine and are hidden and this makes the day and night (From *Chin Shu* 11A:1b; de Bary 1960:210).

Heaven is flat just as the earth is flat, and the rising and setting of the sun is due to the fact that it revolves along with heaven ... To the gaze of men it appears that heaven and earth unite at a distance of no more than ten *li*. This is only the effect of distance, however, for they do not actually come together (From Wang Ch'ung, *Lun heng*, Sec. 3; de Bary 1960:211.)

this status and imply their contributions to culture. They are sometimes called the Heavenly Sovereign (T'ien-huang/Tianhuang), the Earthly Sovereign (Ti-huang/Dihuang), and the Human Sovereign (Jen-huang/Renhuang). They have also been identified with such figures as Fu-hsi, 'Animal Tamer'; Sui-jen/Suiren, 'Fire-maker'; and Shen-nung/Shennong, 'Divine Farmer', who bear names that bespeak their merits. As a group, these figures might represent the personifications of certain stages in the development of early culture, and are hailed as culture heroes in later texts.

The next group of figures who appear in the classical texts are the Five Emperors. They usually include the Yellow Emperor, Chuan-hsü/Zhuanxu (his obscure grandson) and the famous Yao, Shun, and Yü. We introduce each of these briefly.

- The Yellow Emperor is often portrayed as the conqueror of evil forces and the bearer of civilizing benefits, including the invention of the compass needle. His wife teaches the people to rear silkworms, while his chief minister invents writing.
- Chuan-hsü is little known, and is sometimes said to be another name for Emperor Yao, the third of the group of five.
- Yao is remembered as a benevolent ruler who decides to pass the throne on to Shun, the worthiest man in the realm.

### A Female Creator of Humankind

It is popularly said that when Heaven and Earth had opened forth, but before there were human beings, Nü-kua created humans by patting yellow earth together. But the work tasked her strength and left her no free time, so that she then dragged a string through mud, thus heaping it up so as to make it into humans. Therefore the rich and the noble are those humans of yellow earth, whereas the poor and the lowly—all ordinary people—are those cord-made people (Adapted from Yang Shao, *Feng-su t'ung-yi*; Bodde 1961:388–9).

- Shun is the legendary filial son who has a blind father and an evil stepmother. In his turn, he makes Yü his heir.
- Yü is the great flood-controller. The Yellow River overflowed its banks and flooded large areas. Yü is the model hard worker who labours for thirteen years and finally succeeds in channelling the waters of the Yellow River into the ocean. He is also the founder of the first dynasty, the Hsia, after he is urged by a grateful populace to depart from tradition and make his son the heir to the throne.

In the middle of the twentieth century, a group of critical Chinese historians proposed the theory that these legendary sages were gods. According to them, the Three Sovereigns and Five Emperors belong to the realm of mythology, but became regarded as human beings during the later Chou period. This would be the reverse of the process known as euhemerism, in which early human figures are divinized.

Should we consider the ancient sages as human or divine? The answer depends on whether we define 'divine' as a supreme deity or as an ancestral spirit or deity of a tribal group. Scholars who consider the ancient sages as deity symbols do not always agree on what it means to be a deity. Scholars like Ku Chieh-kang (1893–1980) and Yang Shang-k'uei (b. 1910) think that the Three Sovereigns (and perhaps also the Five Emperors) all represented a supreme deity, a personal god.

There are others who prefer to regard the same sages as ancestral spirits or god-ancestors, occupying a position lower than that of the supreme deity. This is closer to a totemic theory, in which an animal or plant species is associated with a particular tribal group's identity. In any case, the primordial sages were obviously ancestral figures in a country where the people considered themselves as children of a divine or semidivine origin. The sages are from an age when communications between the human order and the divine were central to all life, with sages either representing the divine order or serving as mediators—and also as ancestral spirits.

### *Domestic Deities Today*

In popular religion the gods often overlap with those of traditional religion, including Taoism and even Buddhism. Lord Heaven or the Jade Emperor, for example, are the popular names for the supreme deity, names that are obviously from ancient religion or Confucianism and Taoism. He is regarded as too remote for most people, who only dare approach him through other intercessory powers, but the pantheon also embraces many other deities, some of whom have special influence in certain regions. In rural Taiwan, traditional families burn three sticks of incense every morning and evening.

> One of these is placed in a niche outside the back door for the benefit of wandering ghosts; one is dedicated to the Stove God, whose image resides above the large brick structure on which all meals are prepared; and the third is placed in a burner before the tablets of the family's immediate ancestors (Wolf 1974:131).

The stove god, also called the kitchen god, goes back to time immemorial; his cult used to be found all over China. Its survival to the present is testimony to the continuity of Chinese religion. His presence is actually more like that of a policeman sent from above to watch over the behaviour of the family and its members, each of whom he reports on at the end of the year. Glutinous rice cakes are offered to him on New Year's Eve—literally, to shut him up and forestall any unfavourable reports he might make to Lord Heaven (T'ien-kung/Tiangong) or the Jade Emperor, i.e., the supreme deity. This practice is also an example of the bureaucratization of religion, the organization of heaven as the equivalent of organization on earth. That is, the world beyond is a mirror image of traditional Chinese society, with an emperor above, who rules over officials, who in turn rule over the commoners.

The earth god is another deity with a widespread cult. Tablets marked with his name are found in many places, urban and rural, even in overseas communities. A tutelary deity, he is also alleged to be the escort of the dead to the nether world. His role is to protect the living from dangerous, wandering ghosts, while keeping a watch over the behaviour of those he protects. He, too, reports on them to a higher authority, usually the city god. There are those who ask his permission to build a new house or demolish an old one. Often the family's ancestor altar has the stove god in the lower left-hand corner and the earth god on the lower right-hand corner. The city god, on the other hand, governs all the spirits in a major administrative district.

### *The Higher Bureaucracy*

In popular religion, the city god is represented as a higher bureaucrat in the robes of a scholar-official. Presumably, he ranks above the local earth gods. He is traditionally named by the imperial government from among deceased notables. The city god of Shanghai, for example, was a high scholar-official called Ch'in Yü-po/Qin Yubo (1295–1374), who was so honoured by the founder of the Ming dynasty.[1]

The various deities usually have their own temples or shrines, which serve as their palaces or mansions. Incense is offered to them and dramatic performances are sometimes staged nearby for their entertainment. They are believed to inspect the regions they govern; there are processions in which the statue of the city god is carried around the city's borders, and there is a similar procession for the local earth god in his neighbourhood. They are usually preceded by noisy bands and firecrackers. It can be seen in these representations of jurisdictional territory that the gods' powers are not infinite but rather explicitly and carefully defined.

## Shamans' Access to the Divine

Ancestral spirits enjoyed a dominant place in life in ancient East Asian society. The bond between the human and the divine was assured by communication between the ancestral spirits and their living descendants, or communication between the human and the divine through the mediumship of diviners or shamans, which was at the heart of all rituals. The formal celebration of the ritual reveals its ecstatically shamanic character.

The bond between the human and the divine, the natural and the spiritual, was experienced in trances or spirit possession. This primordial state of intimacy with spirits is similar to what philosophers later termed the continuum between Heaven and human beings—*T'ien-jen ho-yi/Tianren heyi*. Indeed, the latter may well represent a philosophical transformation of a primordial ecstatic experience.

In ancient China all religion, whether divination, sacrifice, rain-dance, or so-called magical healing, was predicated upon this special relationship between certain gifted persons and the deities. All ritual referred symbolically, and sometimes also actually, to a primeval union between humans and the gods, a union that was shamanic and ecstatic, a union that would be celebrated in a different way in later philosophical humanism.

1. Interestingly, this god is among the ancestors of the author of this chapter. See Ching (1988), ch. 4.

### *Priests*

The English word 'priest' denotes a religious specialist with a special ability to mediate with the divine, someone who is devoted especially to cultic worship and belongs to both a profession and a class. As such, the priest may occasionally appropriate the function of other specialists, whether medicine men, diviners, or magicians, but operates usually as someone with specialist knowledge of the deity and expert skills in performing cultic duties. The priest's mediating powers depend upon his ability to influence the supernatural powers or the deity, whereas the magician's powers to manipulate nature rest upon techniques properly applied, such as spells and incantations.

In the case of China, scholars have often remarked on the absence of a powerful priestly caste, unlike other ancient societies, especially in the Near East and India. While we know of Taoist priests, few of them had much power, whether in the past or present, but the ancient sacrificial cult had powerful ministers, whether they were specialists or not. Who were the persons called *chu/zhu* dedicated to that cult? There is no Chinese term that is the equivalent of the English word 'priest'. Instead, practitioners in ancient Chinese religion tend to be characterized as 'shamans'.

### *Shamans*

By 'shamanism' scholars mean trance states that some societies interpret as possession by or intimate rapport with gods and spirits. The word 'shaman' comes from a North Asian, specifically Siberian, context (Tungusic *saman*). A person, male or female, is said to have a special ability to commune with the gods, or with one of the gods, through knowledge and mastery of a 'technique of ecstasy'. Indeed, people become shamans through initial ecstatic experiences like pathological sicknesses, dreams, and trances, followed by theoretical and practical instruction at the hands of the old masters.

Shamans are believed to be able to receive visions, see the spirits of deceased humans or animals, and communicate with them. They are also described as able to levitate and make magical flights into the sky and descents into the underworld. They have control over rain, fire, and the cure of sicknesses. All of these abilities are usually exercised in a trance state. Arthur Waley (1889–1966) has described the shamans (*wu*) of ancient China as intermediaries in spirit cults, experts in exorcism, prophecy, fortune-telling, rain-making, and the interpretation of dreams, as well as magic healers. A shaman is a person who apparently reaches a state of trance through ritual dance, and is able afterwards to transmit the wishes of the spirits to human beings.

The *wu*'s special gift is described in the collection of poems called the 'Nine Songs', derived from the *Songs of the South*. The poems came from the mid-fourth-century-BCE kingdom that comprised parts of today's provinces of Hunan, Hupei, Anhwei, Honan, and Szechwan, amounting to about a third of the then-known

China. In the poems, the relationship between the shaman and the deity is described as a fleeting love affair, either between a female deity and a male shaman, or between a male deity and a female shaman.

Another important function the shamans performed was summoning back the soul of a sick or deceased person. At one time, the soul was summoned whenever death occurred. A relative would climb onto the roof, holding the deceased's garments, and cry out for the person to return.

The term *wu* is often used in association with another word *chu/zhu*, signifying oral communication with the divine. Indeed, the oracle-bone script for *chu* shows a picture of a human being kneeling in front of an altar. One explanation is that the word *wu* refers to a mediator between the human world and the divine, while the word *chu* refers to the mouthpiece of the Lord who transmits his messages to human beings through an expert in ritual incantations.

The *chu* were presumably members of the official clergy, who were entrusted with the worship of ancestors. They may be described as the priests and deacons of the state cult, with special responsibility for sacrifices. Their status appears to have risen, at the expense of the *wu*, by the end of the Chou dynasty. Their duties included praying for the gods' blessings, especially for a good harvest. These persons may also be called magicians, to the extent that their incantations were considered effective in themselves. Unlike the *wu*, however, they did not have the gift of ecstasy.

In the traditional religion of East Asia in general and in ancient Chinese religion in particular, there is much that may be described as 'ecstatic' (from the Greek for 'standing outside'). I use the term in the technical sense when referring to states of religious consciousness, that is, a feeling of displacement from one's ordinary awareness and conduct. In my opinion, ancient Chinese religion may be defined as ecstatic religion, to the extent that it had an essentially shamanic character. Even the later religious Taoism and certain forms of Buddhism, together with the product of their union, which is called popular or folk religion, continued to manifest features that can be identified as shamanic and ecstatic. We could say that shamanism persists in today's folk religious tradition wherever the Chinese live and thrive.

### *Kings as Shamans*

Basically the function of the shamans and priests of antiquity was to hear and transmit the messages of the gods. Perhaps not all the historic kings in China or Japan had the special gift of communicating with the divine, but they appeared to have been descended from ancestors with such shamanic and ecstatic powers. It was a case of institutionalized shamanic (and ecstatic) charisma. In this charismatic role, the king served as the chief diviner, the chief priest, and the chief shaman—at least in name. If certain later kings lost their powers, they continued to use religious professionals who possessed and exercised the gift of ecstasy to call down the deity at will.

Ultimately, the king was in charge of divination and diviners. Given that the king was a religious and political leader, was his office charismatic as well as shamanic? Was the first king of each dynasty a powerful shaman in his own right? Were his descendants considered shamans as well? Here we examine kingship itself.

Early connotations of kingship are illustrated by the pictographic writing on the oracle bones. The pictograph for the Chinese word *wang* ('king') sometimes represents a fire in the earth, at other times an axe, but in any case designates without doubt the political ruler and his royal ancestors. The French scholar Léon Vandermeersch (b. 1928) sees a relation between this word and another term, originally denoting 'male', and explains it as the 'virile king', father of the ethnic group, heir of the founder-ancestor's power. Thus he places kingship in a familial and patriarchal context.

As already explained, the ancient kings also claimed some kind of divine descent. The symbolism of divine descent entails direct access to the supernatural. The kings of antiquity were called *t'ien-tzu/tianzi*, literally 'the sons of Heaven', although the kings and other rulers of historical China, unlike the emperors of Japan, never claimed any personal divinity for themselves. This is like the contrast between the Mesopotamian and Egyptian concepts of kingship. Whereas in Egypt the king was a god descended among humans, the Babylonian king was not a god but a human deputy of the gods, charged with upholding the cosmic harmony in a mundane realm.

The information about King T'ang, the founder of the Shang dynasty, in classical texts is much more rational. According to several accounts, T'ang's conquest of Hsia is followed by many years of drought, during which he is told by the diviners that T'ien (Heaven) can be placated only by a human sacrifice. Thereupon he purifies himself, places himself on the firewood, and prepares to offer himself to the Lord-on-high, but rain starts to fall and quenches the fire.

T'ang's gesture of self-sacrifice is a supreme example of a king acting as both priest (*chu*) and victim while serving a shamanic (*wu*) role to elicit rain. He does so after divination, as would have been expected. The sense of expiation for sins, committed either by himself or the people, should especially be noted.

Although little is known of King T'ang, he might almost be regarded as a historical figure. In the cases of the other wise kings of the Chou dynasty, we have clearly historical personages, even if the stories about them—such as those about T'ang—may not be historically accurate. Examples of such kings are Wen and Wu, the eleventh-century-BCE father-and-son pair who began the Chou dynasty, and Wu's younger brother and chief minister, the Duke of Chou, Confucius's favourite historical figure.

A story about the Duke of Chou, who was also alleged by some to be a shamanic figure, demonstrates his diligent practice of prayer and divination while his royal brother the king is seriously sick. The duke prays to the ancestral spirits, begging them to spare the king and take himself instead as their servant in death. The text of his prayer is then locked into a golden casket. The response to his divination is a favourable one, and King Wu recovers temporarily.

Today's critical historians are not inclined to accept the virtuous tales regarding the ancient kings and nobles, whether legendary or historical. We mentioned earlier that Yao, Shun, and Yü have been called deity symbols or god-ancestors. The kings T'ang and Wu, each a dynastic founder, have also been described as ambitious men eager to supplant their overlords and install their own family in place. Even the Duke of Chou has been debunked as an eager usurper of royal power. The evidence for these assertions (as well as for the divinization of the more remote sage kings) will probably remain circumstantial.

### *Female Shamans*

It is interesting that in examining the shamanic character of rulership, we have been able to speak only of male rulers in ancient China. Female shamanic figures are abundant, especially in mythology, but the shaman-queen in ancient Japan, discussed later, appears as an exception to the historical rule of male kingship in China.

As time passed, the role of the professional shaman declined. My hypothesis is that this decline was linked to a general decline of the role of women in society. Female shamans were increasingly assigned to one area of responsibility: rain-making. It remained an important responsibility, indeed the official responsibility of the ruler. However, as the ruler's secular duties became increasingly important, kingship or rulership itself became more and more secularized.

In the patriarchal clan-family system, the practice of the ancestor cult rested very much on the shoulders of the male heirs. As the cult developed, female ancestors were also venerated together with their spouses, and women could participate in certain auxiliary aspects of the cult, but sons (or in their absence, sons-in-law) were the chief priests in the family.

The differing ritual receptions of sons and daughters in the early Chou times are described in the following song, which is in the *Book of Songs*:

> So he bears a son,
> And puts him to sleep upon a bed,
> Clothes him in robes,
> Gives him a jade sceptre to play with …
> Then he bears a daughter,
> And puts her on the ground,
> Clothes her in swaddling clothes,
> Gives her a loom-whorl to play with
> (Waley 1937:283–4)

The gender roles were clearly determined from birth, with the male as a future ruler, to be honoured and pampered, and the female educated to be subservient and destined for the work force.

## Divination: Advice from the Spirits

Divination is the search for information about the causes of present conditions or about what to expect in the future. It relies on the wisdom of a spirit, through the mediumship of a specialist known as a diviner. The intent is usually practical: the seeker desires to know the wise way of acting, be that in war, marriage, or treatment of an illness. Presumably the diviner has a special skill, including extrasensory perception, to look into symbols and events and make utterances, disclosing certain patterns of action that those who consult him or her should follow.

Does divination really work? Though modern life may treat reliance on divination as somehow gullible or ineffective, we do not seem altogether ready to give it up. In today's society, the practice is quite widespread, even in high places, for example, Nancy Reagan's (b. 1923) efforts to consult an astrologer on behalf of her husband, the former United States President Ronald Reagan (r. 1981–9), in finding proper dates and times for certain actions. Many people believe in the influence of the stars under which they were born.

### *The Oracle Bones*

The people of northern China in the neolithic period (starting from the late fourth millennium BCE) appear to have been the first anywhere to use animal shoulder-blades for divination by heating them and interpreting the cracks that ensued. The practice reached its height by Shang times, towards the middle of the second millennium BCE. There was widespread use of turtle shells in addition to the shoulder-blades of oxen. The bone remains received sophisticated preparation, chiselled to produce hollows and grooves to facilitate the application of fire and also structure the omen cracks. Inscriptions were added after the event, noting not only the occasion and result of the particular divinatory act, but also sometimes the occurrence of events confirming the efficacy of the oracle. After the fall of the Shang, the Chou continued to use divination by shells and bones for a while before the practice died out.

The divination ritual was usually supervised by the king at his court, perhaps in the ancestral temple. The questions were usually addressed to ancestral spirits, the fire was applied to the bones and shells, and the cracks appeared. So far, the notations in the inscriptions do not offer enough correlation with the shapes and angles of cracks. Although there is evidence that divination manuals were followed, these are no longer extant. Besides, we do not know whether the manuals explain the logic of prognostication, or whether such was left to a so-called higher form of reasoning.

Were the diviners of Shang China mere ritual specialists, or were there also shamans, alleged to have superior powers and given to trancelike sessions? According to the shells and bones and the ritual texts of later ages, such as the *Institutes of Chou* (*Chou-li/Zhouli*) and especially the *Ceremonials* (*Yi-li*), divinatory functions were divided between the person(s) who posed the question (*chen-jen/zhenren*), the person(s) in charge of the specific ritual itself, including the burning, and the person(s) who interpreted the results. In the case of royal divination, there were also official recorders or archivists. Since royal divination was relied upon for decisions concerning state matters or the ruler's private life, the idea was to involve the supernatural order in the human and natural order so as to receive blessings from above and avoid punishments and calamities. In this sense, it differed little from divination elsewhere, such as in ancient Sumero-Babylonian religion.

### *Yarrow Stalks and Hexagrams*

The materials used for divination in Shang times were mainly shells and bones, and occasionally yarrow or milfoil stalks. With the fall of the Shang, the tortoises gradually fell into disuse, while the stalks were increasingly used in the Chou and later times, especially in association with the *Book of Changes*. However, yarrow plants are perishable materials and have not survived in the company of oracle bones. Our knowledge about them comes from the texts and from their usage in the present.

It appears that the diviner had the dual responsibility of performing the ritual and interpreting its outcome. Today's diviners still employ yarrow stalks, using them like a deck of cards. This time-consuming process is being replaced in many parts of Taiwan and Southeast Asia by the use of coins, placed in turtle-like containers.

Many even in the West consult the Chinese *Book of Changes* (*I-ching/Yijing*), a divination manual that also ranks as a Confucian classic. It has as its kernel the sixty-four hexagrams, representing all the combinations of six broken and unbroken lines, derived in turn from the eight possible trigrams.

### *Astrology*

Today we distinguish between astronomy or the study of the heavens, and astrology or the attempt to discern the influence of heavenly bodies on human life and society. In ancient China, there was little separation between these two enterprises. Indeed, observation of the heavens was motivated by the belief that heavenly laws and astral bodies have influence on earth. Besides, a calendar based on astronomical knowledge was important, as it was the basis of the seasonal arrangement of religious rituals and agricultural work.

According to tradition, the culture hero Fu-hsi was the maker of the first calendar, and the Yellow Emperor its reformer and the rectifier of intercalation. The Chinese knew about the five principal planets and carefully determined solstices and equinoxes some 4,000 or more years ago. Two thousand years ago, they had the twelve zodiacal signs. Comets and eclipses were considered divine warnings to human beings, especially rulers, to reform their personal conduct as well as their conduct of government.

### *Dream Interpretation*

Dreams were another source of warnings from the spiritual world. Oracle-bone inscriptions often refer to dreams. Sometimes it was believed the spirits demanded sacrificial offerings. Thus the interpretation of dreams often involved divination itself. In ancient Egypt, this was done with help from astrology. In China, there was a multitude of techniques, including consulting oracle bones, or the *Book of Changes*, or meteorological phenomena. Even more interestingly, there was the practice of divination by dreams that was then verified by oracle divination. In Chinese antiquity, there were also officials (*chan-jen/zhanren*) who were in charge of dream interpretation and performed their duties using their knowledge of the stars.

## The Decline of Divination

Following the time of the Shang, the practice of divination lost some favour at court, but spread widely among the common people. Nevertheless, the more intellectual voiced disbelief. From the third century BCE, we have the story of Ch'ü Yüan/Qu Yuan (c. 343–c. 289 BCE), the minister exiled from the court of the state of Ch'u, who called upon the Great Diviner Chan Yin to settle the turmoil in his mind. His questions were phrased to allow for simple affirmative and negative answers:

> Is it better to be painstakingly honest, simple-hearted and loyal,
> Or to keep out of trouble by welcoming each change as it comes? …
> Is it better to risk one's life by speaking truthfully and without concealment,
> Or to save one's skin by following the whims of the wealthy and high-placed? …
> Is it better to be honest and incorruptible and to keep oneself pure,
> Or to be accommodating and slippery, to be compliant as lard or leather?
> (Hawkes 1959:89)

The Great Diviner reportedly threw aside the divining stalks, excused himself, and said:

> There are cases in which the instruments [of divination] are of
> no avail,
> and knowledge can give no enlightenment.
> There are things to which my calculations cannot attain,
> over which the divinity has no power.
> My lord, for one with your mind and with resolution such as
> yours,
> the tortoise and the divining stalks are unable to help.
> (Hawkes 1959:90)

Though simple enough, the answers Ch'ü Yüan sought were obviously not what the tortoise and the stalks could provide. He was ruminating over ethical decisions, and these were not meant for oracles. The diviner readily admitted impotence, indicating the limits of divination as well as, perhaps, the rise of a new age when human beings were to rely more on their own moral intuitions than upon the instruments of divination.

## Spirit Mediums Today

> He who shakes the Heavens comes from the west riding on a tiger and a dragon, bearing a holy seal ... Your voice like thunder makes the *shen* (spirits) and devils tremble ... You can save a myriad of people. Now we invite you ... to come before this altar. With your sword you can kill evil spirits ... Wake, wake, and save us (Elliott 1955:170).

This quotation comes from one of the invocations used to call for a spirit in a Chinese spirit-medium cult in Singapore, where the majority population is ethnic Chinese. There, the male spirit-mediums, called *tang-ki* (or *dang-ki*) are subject to involuntary possession by one or more spirits. The *tang-ki* flout Confucian customs by deliberately causing self-injury in public performances. This behaviour is accepted as they are considered instruments of higher powers, cut off from the world of ordinary mortals.

There are also more private or semiprivate seances, often involving communications with the recently deceased, usually through female mediums, who exhibit ecstatic or trance behaviour while they pray for assistance in seeking out a specific soul.

In popular religion, divination is a widespread practice. There are also more mechanical ways of divining. For example, in Taiwan diviners use crescent-shaped 'divination blocks'. The combinations of their positions when dropped on the floor indicate responses from the deity. Sometimes these are used in conjunction with joss sticks, that is, sticks covered with incense. People may also use divination verses in temples. They take out a numbered slip from a vase, to which corresponds a verse of four lines, usually composed of rather cryptic words with added explanations.

For even more serious consultation of the spirits, there is the 'divination chair'. A miniature wooden chair is held upright before an altar while incense is burned and the spirit is asked to descend into the chair, which then crashes onto a prepared table and traces messages from the possessing deity. However, they are not easily understood.

Spirit-writing (*fu-chi/fuji*) is a ritual that has been traced back to the Sung dynasty. Today, such writing ranges from housekeeping procedures and liturgical instructions through moralistic verses and commentary on the classics, to rare but elaborate mythological explorations of heaven and hell.

Geomancy (*feng-shui*, literally 'wind and water') is a popular divinatory practice that is widespread. A legacy from ancient times, it was applied earlier especially when choosing burial sites. Today, *feng-shui* is also consulted to locate sites for the activities of the living. The specialist uses a magnetic compass in a disc with concentric circles, the symbols of *yin* and *yang*, and the eight trigrams. Incongruous though it may seem to the outsider, the ancient practice is today considered a crucial step in the design and construction of modern office towers, hotels, restaurants, and shopping centres in Hong Kong, Taiwan, and among overseas Chinese.

## Sacrifice

The ancient Chinese had a three-tiered world-view: of heaven above, the abode of the dead below, and earth, the abode of the living, in between. They believed that at death, the upper or ethereal soul (*hun*) rises to heaven while the lower or material soul (*p'o/po*) descends into the earth. While this belief was formulated only in Chou times, it was already implicit in the religious beliefs of Shang times and in Shang practices of divination and sacrifice. This is not to say that the dead were supposed to be 'imprisoned' down under. The royal ancestors were often represented as in the presence of the Lord, and continued to have power over the living, whether to protect and bless them or punish and curse them. They were also represented as expecting their descendants to provide sacrificial 'blood' offerings to them.

Different forms of sacrifice developed very early. What was already present in the archaic cultures evolved in the later cultures as very complicated rituals, complete with detailed instruction manuals. In China and Israel, offerings of animal victims were brought to the altars, sanctified, and often destroyed, in order to achieve contact with an invisible power and thereby avert evil or invite beneficial influence.

In the Chinese writing system, the character for *chi/ji* ('sacrifice') is said to derive from a pictograph representing the offering of meat and possibly also wine to some spirit. Originally the practice began as a simple act of providing food for the dead. Later ritual texts describe an elaborate system of state sacrifices, each with its own name, offered to heavenly and earthly deities as well as to ancestral spirits.

There is ample evidence from both oracle and bronze inscriptions as well as from later classical texts regarding what victims were used and how rituals were carried out. The usual victims were cattle, goats, and pigs, with young bulls preferred for the most important sacrifices. Other objects, like jade and silk, were also offered. The selected animal had to be the best available, perfect in itself. It was led to the site, killed, and opened up by the chief priest celebrating the event, with some assistance from the other participants. The fat was burned to make smoke, inviting the spirits to descend, and the internal organs were prepared and cooked. In the royal ancestral temples, special halls and yards were available for various kinds of sacrificial rituals, with bronze vessels of different sizes and shapes to hold the raw and cooked offerings.

A sense of sin is often implicit in sacrificial action. Everywhere—not just in China or Japan—an animal or a human victim could serve as a scapegoat and take upon itself and expiate the sins of the community or individuals. This becomes evident when we examine the case of King T'ang, the Shang dynastic founder, who offered himself to the supreme deity to save the people from a long drought. We should emphasize at this stage that sin did not necessarily imply moral evil, but simply some offence against God or the ancestors. Indeed, ancient religion showed little interest in questions of moral good or evil. Its ritual practices were aimed at pleasing the spirits, rather than inculcating moral values.

### *Human Sacrifice*

There is evidence of human sacrifices in Aztec Mexico, the Ancient Near East, China, and Japan. Seen in a comparative perspective, the story of King T'ang bears some resemblance to the biblical account of Abraham's offering of his son Isaac in a sacrificial ritual commanded by God but also interrupted by God, who calls for an animal to be substituted for the human victim. Abraham's story in *Genesis* 22 is all the more relevant as it hints at an early practice of human sacrifice in ancient Israel. It is often interpreted as a test of the patriarch's faith, but it can also be said that the final outcome shows divine disapproval of human sacrifice.

Human sacrifice is now regarded among scholars to have been a universal religious phenomenon in antiquity. In China's case, the *Historical Annals* of the Ch'in mention the capture of the duke Hui of Chin, who was nearly offered in a ritual sacrifice to the Lord-on-high, but was saved after the intervention of the Chou king as well as the Ch'in duchess, his own sister (645 BCE). Even though the proposed victim in this instance, an aristocrat, escaped the fate proposed for him, such textual evidence confirms the practice at the time. Presumably, royal or noble captives were not the usual sacrificial victims. Since the number of victims was often high, even in the hundreds, the unfortunate were often war captives, perhaps sometimes even criminals, and sacrificial rituals thereby resemble civil punishments.

Some other textual evidence indicates that human victims were not always offered on altars of sacrifice. There were also those who accompanied their lords and ladies to the other world, in the burial chambers of ancient Egypt and China. Such a practice might not formally rank as ritual sacrifice, but served a purpose that is also based on religious belief in the afterlife, as well as the human desire for companionship in the afterlife. The chosen victims were from different classes. Some belonged to the nobility, either as spouses or were part of the retinue of the deceased, while others were slaves or captives.

Burial companions were frequently women. They might be concubines of the deceased or just ladies of the court. In 210 BCE, the first Ch'in emperor and dynastic founder took with him all those who constructed his underground mausoleum—and with them went the secret of access to the mausoleum. He also took all the childless ladies of his harem, presumably because they were not needed by the next generation and might better serve him underground. In spite of the difficulties in finding his vast subterranean hideaway, a veritable underground city, archaeologists have successfully unearthed many things from it. Near Xi'an today is the impressive life-size terracotta army of men and horses, exhibited in their burial place. These statues served as secondary burial companions to the dead emperor.

That human sacrifice was practised in antiquity is confirmed by the classical texts, but they do not approve of it. One story in the *Book of Rites* gives the example of a disciple of Confucius who tells his brother's widow that burying the living with the dead is contrary to the rites and should not be followed. Another gives the instance of a son who refuses to follow his father's dying wish to be buried in the same coffin with two living concubines. These reflect the result of ethical consciousness, which accompanied the evolution of Confucian humanism.

## The Ancestor Cult and Filial Piety

In many regions around the world, respect for ancestors is expressed in a religious duty. Ancestor veneration is part and parcel of ancient Roman religion and African tribal religion, as well as the religions of East Asia. It is therefore not uniquely a Chinese phenomenon. In the later nineteenth century, scholars thought that it was possible to find historical evidence for the existence of one primitive religion for all humankind. Many agreed with the Englishman Herbert Spencer (1820–1903) that an ancestor cult could be at the root of every religion. Such a view implicitly sees religion as a conservative force, with an emphasis on venerating the authority of the ancients, stressing traditional attitudes and affirming the importance of social control.

An ancestor cult still underlies much religious practice in China, Korea, and Japan, even if the term 'ancestor' does not always refer to a lineal progenitor. Today it may instead represent a close deceased relative. The practice has not often been observed in mainland China since the Communists took power in 1949, but memories of it linger. Formerly, wooden tablets with the names of the deceased male and female ancestors inscribed on them were placed on a home altar. Anniversary feasts, complete with prostrations and libations, were held before these family altars. Today, photographs or paper tablets might grace a special spot in a home. In this way consciousness of ancestors remains strong in a society where age still commands respect.

In a study of religions, belief in immortality or an afterlife is often a core question. It appears that the ancients in China, both in the Shang and the Chou dynasties, believed in a heavenly abode for the good. Both the oracle inscriptions and the *Book of Poetry*, a classical text, mention the deceased kings ascending to heaven to be near the Lord-on-high.

### *Ancient Ancestral Rituals*

Ancestor religion was central to Chinese society 4,000 years ago. The royal ancestral temple was also the centre of political administration. There the great feasts were held, the weapons of war were stored, and the vassals were enfeoffed. The gods and spirits were also invited to participate in each of the great occasions. Departed ancestors were not the only ones worshipped. Many other spirits were venerated, including a supreme deity, astral spirits, and spirits of the mountains and rivers.

Oracle-bone divination involved consultations with ancestral spirits. Its practice permeated daily life in Shang times. There are inscriptions on ritual vessels cast in bronze, from the early part of the Chou dynasty when the court diviners had diminished in influence but the ancestor religion was still widely practised.

Later literature, such as the classic texts of the Confucian tradition, offers evidence of the performance of ancestral rituals. Often the son served as the family priest, while a grandson or nephew was appointed, after divination, to serve as *shih/shi* (literally, 'corpse') or ancestor impersonator, that is, to act as a living reminder of the ancestor to whom sacrifice was being offered. In fact, this impersonator was much more than an actor in a drama. He was regarded as the carrier of the ancestor's soul. He was called *shen-pao/shenbao*, 'possessed by the soul of the ancestor', just as shamans were sometimes called *ling-pao/lingbao*, 'persons possessed by spirits'. It was believed that the ancestral spirit in this person received the offerings made to him, and also spoke through this person, who acted as a mouthpiece, expressing gratitude for the offerings and promising protection and happiness to the family.

### *Ancestors and Other Ghosts*

Ancestral spirits today are remembered at a domestic altar. It is usually a large table holding ancestral tablets, whether in wood or on paper, venerating the deceased ancestors, male and female. Photographs are sometimes placed there when tablets are absent. Every morning incense is offered, usually by the woman of the house. The same table holds a statue of Kuan-yin (a feminine representation of the *bodhisattva* Avalokiteśvara), and one of the deified Kuan-kung, 'god of war'. Food offerings are made on special occasions such as the anniversary of a death, with communal meals afterward either at home or in a restaurant. One asks the ancestors for blessings, and fears punishment or retribution from them. Offerings are occasionally made of imitation paper money, even paper houses with appropriate furnishings and servants, as well as clothing, which are usually burned in outdoor rituals.

One class of spirits resembles the Hindu and Buddhist *preta* or 'hungry ghosts', from which they are actually derived. In Hindu or Buddhist religion, they suffer deprivation as punishment for avariciousness in life. In Chinese popular beliefs, these frustrated and sometimes angry ghosts often require solace and appeasement. They are spirits who have no living relative to care for them, and may turn vicious to get attention and offerings. Spirits of unmarried women and children who died as victims of violence before they completed a natural life span are not included in the normal domestic cult. People's fear of these ghosts is similar to the Western fear of ghosts and spirits, as manifest in customs such as on Hallowe'en.

### *Filial Piety*

The virtue of filial piety is usually perceived as central to Confucian teachings, but it was already implied in the pre-Confucian ancestor cult. Filial piety, a child's respect for a parent, was important not only in the patriarchal religion of China but also in that of ancient Israel, with its deeply rooted sense of duty towards father and mother, as reflected in the fourth of the Ten Commandments. How did this virtue take up centre stage in China? Was it related to the ancestor cult? Again, the study of antiquity is helpful, and gives surprising findings.

The term for filial piety is *hsiao/xiao*. The pictograph for it is found not in oracle inscriptions but on later bronze artefacts, presumably from the Chou times, that depict a hand resting upon the head of a child. This image may represent an older person supported by a younger one, and may also portray affection. Interestingly, too, some of the older bronzes were cast by Chou rulers as acts of filial piety to ancestors, and other more recent ones were presented to parents and grandparents, even to other living members of the family. Thus it appears that the scope of filial piety was widening to include others in addition to direct ancestors.

A historian may well be surprised by ancient attitudes towards aging and the elderly, as well as attitudes towards death and dying. On the one hand, death and burial rituals have always been more elaborate than those surrounding birth. On the other hand, while sorrow has always been associated with death, as shown in oracle inscriptions from the Shang, there is also evidence in prehistoric China, carbon-dated at one site to 5630 BCE, of the custom of clubbing the elderly to death. Similar customs have been found elsewhere in the world as well. Scholars have linked this practice to a ritual to release the soul of the victim, which would make such an act euthanasia.

Scholars have also concluded that unwanted children, especially female infants, were often disposed of at birth. Filial piety went through transformations over the centuries, affecting not only the attitude towards one's parents but also the attitude towards one's children. Unfortunately, female infants have long been the victims of a patriarchal society in which filial piety makes the male heir, who serves as family priest, the foundation of the ancestor cult.

No

## Korean Shamanism

Korea's traditional name, Cho-sen, means 'morning dew' and also refers to the country's geographical position just east of China, which called itself the 'Middle Country'. Centuries ago, particularly after the Chinese Han dynasty (206 BCE–226 CE), Korea was influenced by China's Confucianism, Taoism, and Buddhism. In Korea, which was divided in the fourth century into three independent kingdoms—Koguryo in the north, Paekche in the southwest, and Silla in the southeast—the traditions introduced from China were transformed in their development, so that they became distinctively Korean.

Korea has preserved the age-old veneration for the god of heaven, a personal deity, the most important of the three main gods—the other two being the god of earth and the god of ancestors. Indigenous Korean religion has a pantheon or roster of deities. In contrast to China, these deities have not been organized into a supernatural hierarchy reflecting a bureaucracy on earth.

Korea has its own mythology, which includes a shaman-king called Tangun, the 'Sandalwood Prince', who is born of a bear-woman and is descended from the god of heaven; he is also the founder of the country in 2333 BCE. He rules over the tribes of Dragon, Horse, Deer, Crane, Eagle, and Egret and is a mediator between them and heaven. Other myths include the 'cosmic egg', from which an ancestral figure of the Silla royal house emerges.

What may be shamans are mentioned in the earliest Korean records, the

## Korean Mythology: The Birth of Tangun, First Ruler of Korea

In those days there lived a she-bear and a tigress in the same cave. They prayed to [the heavenly king] to be blessed with incarnation as human beings. The king took pity on them and gave them each a bunch of mugwort and twenty pieces of garlic, saying, 'If you eat this holy food and do not see the sunlight for one hundred days, you will become human beings.'

The she-bear and the tigress took the food and ate it, and retired into the cave. In twenty-one days the bear, who had faithfully observed the king's instructions, became a woman. But the tigress, who had disobeyed, remained in her original form.

But the bear-woman could find no husband, so she prayed under the sandalwood tree to be blessed with a child. [The son of the heavenly king] heard her prayers and married her. She conceived and bore a son who was called Tangun Wanggom, the King of Sandalwood.

... [Sometime before 2000 BC] Tangun came to P'yongyang (now Sogyong), set up his royal residence there and bestowed the name Chosun upon his kingdom.

(From the late thirteenth-century account *Samguk yusa: Legends and Histories of the Three Kingdoms of Ancient Korea*; Ha and Mintz 1972:32–3).

*Samguk sagi* (Records of the Three Kingdoms) and the *Samguk yusa* (Stories of the Three Kingdoms), which were compiled in the twelfth and thirteenth centuries.

## Korean Popular Religion Today

The word 'shaman' comes from the language of the Tungus of Siberia. In religion as well as in language, Koreans share many characteristics with the southern Tungus, a branch of the Altaic-speaking peoples of northern Asia. In early Korean records, the shamans are called *mu* (in Chinese, *wu*), usually in the term *mudang*. The *mudang* were often female shamans. Today the term *mudang* designates a ritual specialist of folk religion.

There are two types of professional *mudang*. In early times, some of the *mudang* were allegedly called to the profession by spirits that took control of them, while other *mudang* came from shamanic families. The distinction between possessed and hereditary *mudang* continues today.

The possessed *mudang* or shaman, usually a woman, implores the deities for good fortune or for the removal of misfortune. The hereditary *mudang*, who are less numerous than the other type, perform rituals without becoming possessed by spirits.

The faithful make offerings of food and beg for the welfare of the household, the recovery of sick family members, or the safe conduct of the deceased to a happier existence. The *mudang* play an important role in divination by serving as mouthpieces for supernatural beings.

Korean folk deities may have names similar to their Chinese counterparts (stove god, Dragon King god, and so on), but are not organized into a vast supernatural bureaucracy. As in China, ancestor worship has always been an important part of Korean religion, with clearly established rites of the dead, based on Confucian texts.

## Vietnam Past and Present

As a country, Vietnam depends on the land for its agriculture and the sea for its fishing. Not surprisingly, legends say the Vietnamese people go back to King De Minh, a descendant of the mythical Chinese Shen-nung ('Divine Farmer'). The union between De Minh's son and the daughter of the Dragon Lord of the Sea produces Lac Long Quang, regarded as the first Vietnamese king. He in turn marries a Chinese immortal, who produces a hundred eggs, from which issue a hundred sons. When the parents separate, the wife takes fifty sons with her and moves into the mountains, whereas the husband and his other fifty sons remain in the lowlands, over which they rule. The eldest of these sons allegedly begins the first Vietnamese dynasty, the Hong Bang.

Scholars have speculated that these stories could very well represent in mythological form the early experience of population movements in the geographical area that we now call Vietnam. 'Viet' is the name of the people, and 'Nam' refers to the south, that is, with reference especially to China. The region ruled over by the Hong Bang was later incorporated into the Chinese kingdom of Nam Viet in 208 BCE. Its territory then extended into much of southern China. Its capital was near today's Chinese city of Guangzhou (Canton).

Today's Vietnam, centred around the Red River delta along the Southeast Asian coastline, has a history that was shaped by Chinese rule for about 1,000 years (111 BCE–939 CE). Then there was independence for about 900 years, followed by French colonial rule till the mid-twentieth century. The land, which the French called Indochina, was known earlier by the Chinese as Annam (the 'Peaceful South'—a euphemism). It received cultural influences from India and especially from China. In this regard, Vietnamese culture is essentially influenced by the same outside forces as Japanese and Korean cultures, notably by the language and religion of China.

Vietnam adopted the Chinese writing system and much of Chinese culture as well. The Vietnamese language, which belongs to the Austro-Asiatic family, is different from Chinese, although it has had to rely on the Chinese script. Situated at a point of contact among different populations, Vietnam has experienced its own distinctive syncretism or combination. Its population includes the Brahmanist and Muslim Chams of the coastal Champa, and the Theravāda Buddhist Khmers of the Mekong delta, who have contributed elements of Brahmanism, Islam, and southern Buddhism to religion in Vietnam.

Among the rural population, animism and a spirit-cult with their own beliefs and rituals have survived. Generally, the Vietnamese, like the Chinese, venerate their ancestors and pay much attention to funerary rites. Ancestor worship occupied a central place in the family cult. Confucian influences have always been strong in Vietnam, especially when it became the state ideology under the Ly dynasty (1009–1225) and the later Le dynasty (c. 1428–1787). Worship of the Jade Emperor was also introduced by Taoism. As mentioned earlier, the Vietnamese were and continued to be involved in spirit medium cults.

## SHINTO

The word *Shinto* means 'the way of the gods'. The 'gods' are Japan's countless spirits, the *kami*. Shinto originated in nature worship, and with spirits related to nature: the spirits of heaven and earth, of the mountains, rivers, seas, islands, or forests—just as in Greek or Hindu religion. The *kami* also include deified clan ancestors, especially the sun goddess Amaterasu, and the spirits of deceased emperors, saints, and heroes.

Shinto is a name coined in the sixth century and subsequently used to refer to the indigenous religious heritage of the Japanese, in contrast to the traditions imported from mainland Asia, especially Confucianism and Buddhism, whose influence was increasingly felt.

In a sense Shinto underlies all the religious traditions in Japan. Nevertheless, Shinto, Buddhism, and Confucianism each take care of a certain sphere of life. The Japanese rely on Shinto birth rituals. They develop their moral principles from Confucian teachings. They usually marry in Shinto shrines (although today many do so in Christian churches, without becoming Christians), and turn to Buddhist temples for funerals.

Japan borrowed many religious beliefs and practices from China, integrating them with the indigenous Shinto heritage in a distinctive synthesis, blending Buddhism and Shinto. Later, Japanese intellectual patriots and political nationalists challenged foreign influences, creating new self-consciously Shinto institutions from the seventeenth century onward.

Through all this, Japanese religion has remained in many senses uniquely Japanese. It gives a high priority to ritual purity, which does not have such an important place in Chinese religion. Japanese culture also differentiates itself from

**Figure 5.1**
**JAPAN AND KOREA: Major Cities and Religious Sites**

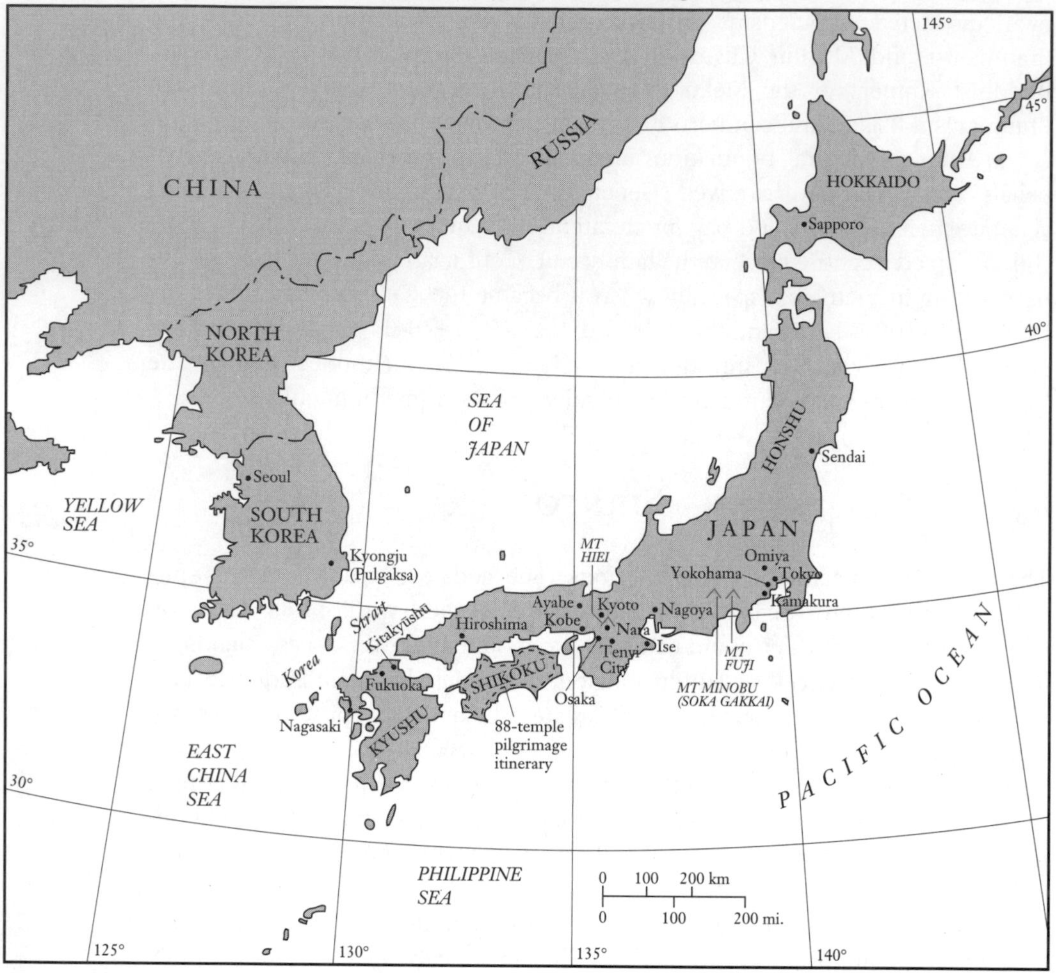


*Source*: Adapted from W.A. Young, *The World's Religions* (Englewood Cliffs: Prentice-Hall, 1995):211.

Chinese culture, with its more martial spirit, its aesthetic leanings, and its predisposition for ritualized behaviour. Indeed, the uniqueness one may ascribe to Japan cannot be assigned to only one factor or practice.

## Shinto's Narratives of Origins

We begin with Japanese mythology. Myths play an important role in Japanese culture, much more so than they do in Chinese culture. The recorded history of Japan, the 'Land of the Rising Sun', started around the seventh century, much later than the recorded history of China and Korea. The sources of Japanese

## Japanese Mythology: The Marriage of Izanagi and Izanami

Now the male deity turning by the left, and the female deity by the right, they went around the pillar of the land separately. When they met together on one side, the female deity spoke first and said: 'How delightful! I have met with a lovely youth.' The male deity was displeased, and said: 'I am a man, and by right should have spoken first. How is it that on the contrary thou, a woman, shouldst have been the first to speak? This was unlucky. Let us go round again.' Upon this the two deities went back, and having met anew, the male deity spoke first and said, 'How delightful! I have met a lovely maiden.' ... Hereupon the male and female first became united as husband and wife (Aston 1896:12–13).

mythology are correspondingly late. The *Kojiki* (Record of Ancient Matters) and the *Nihongi* or *Nihonshoki* (Chronicles of Japan) both date from the early eighth century. These record myths that tell us about the origin of Japan, the people, and the state.

In the beginning, heaven and earth are not separate but together form an inchoate mass containing the life principle. The purer and clearer part then rises to become heaven, while the grosser and heavier part settles down as earth. Scholars who find this part of the narrative abstract, a discussion of principles rather than personifications, see it as influenced by ancient Chinese cosmological theory.

The birth of the gods, however, is much more concrete. Something resembling a sprout of vegetation, also referred to as the 'pillar of the land', springs up between heaven and earth, and becomes a god referred to as the one who established the eternal land. Propagated for six generations, it gives rise to the primal couple, who introduce male-female reproduction.

These first parents are Izanagi, the male principle, and Izanami, the female principle. As they descend from heaven, their union produces the islands of Japan, as well as many gods or *kami*. These include deified powers and features of nature, ancestral spirits, and the spirits of well-known historical figures.

Correct ritual behaviour is closely intertwined with the notion of purity. In the creation narrative, on their initial tour of the 'pillar of the land', Izanami speaks first. As this is a ritual offence, it bodes ill for their first offspring, which turns out to be a leech. They set it adrift and start over. The second time, Izanagi, the male, speaks first, whereupon the Japanese archipelago and the rest of creation are born.

After Izanami dies from burns while giving birth to the fire spirit, Izanagi goes to the underworld to look for her. Finding putrid decay and maggots, he turns back and goes to cleanse his body by diving deep into the sea. In doing so,

## JAPANESE MYTHOLOGY: THE BIRTH OF THE SUN GODDESS

After this Izanagi no Mikoto and Izanami no Mikoto consulted together, saying, 'We have now produced the Great-eight-island country, with the mountains, rivers, herbs and trees. Why should we not produce someone who shall be lord of the universe?' They then together produced the Sun Goddess, who was called [Amaterasu no Oho kami] ...

The resplendent lustre of this child shone throughout all the six quarters. Therefore the two Deities rejoiced, saying: 'We have had many children, but none of them have been equal to this wondrous infant. She ought not to be kept long in this land, but we ought of our own accord to send her at once to Heaven, and entrust to her the affairs of Heaven.'

At this time Heaven and Earth were still not far separated, and therefore they sent her up to Heaven by the ladder of Heaven (Aston 1896:18).

he produces another generation of deities. Washing his left eye, he produces the sun goddess, Amaterasu. Washing his right eye yields the moon god, Tsukiyomi. And rinsing out his nostrils, he generates the god of the hot summer wind, Susano-o.

Central to the narrative, and to Shinto, is the notion of purity and pollution. In general, the sun is associated with life, fertility, and benefit. Not associated with the sun are death, sterility, and misfortune. The narratives refer to heaven as a higher region reached by a bridge from Japan. By purification one is brought closer to the divine realm.

The Japanese as an island people subsisted through fishing and farming. Agriculture figures among the ritual taboos built into the origin narratives. Susano-o is the withering hot summer wind and, as such, is a threat to crops. He has a fiery nature and perpetrates various offences against his sister, the sun goddess Amaterasu. He blocks the irrigation channels and breaks down the dividing ridges in her rice paddy. He removes the hide from a colt and tosses it at Amaterasu. He deposits excrement under her throne, nauseating Amaterasu.

Angered by her younger brother's offences, Amaterasu withdraws to the Rock Cave of Heaven and bars its door. The 800 spirits confer on how to coax her out and decide to have the ancestors of two Japanese clans set up a *sakaki* tree outside her cave. A mirror is hung high on the tree and jewels on the middle branches, while white and blue ribbons decorate the lower branches. The 'Terrible Woman of Heaven', from whom ritual dancers are descended, then performs a dance with lewd routines and gestures. When the noise of the spectators lures Amaterasu from her cave, the clan ancestors string up a rope to prevent her from going back.

Interpreters see the sun's hiding in a cave as a solar eclipse, a threatening and unexpected sign to an ancient population. They also find ritual details of Shinto built into this account. A tree festooned with white—though not blue—paper ribbons is a characteristic feature of Shinto shrines. And the mirror and jewels form part of the regalia of the emperor, who is regarded as a descendant of the sun goddess. The reflections in a mirror, it is also argued, were thought to be the work of *kami*; moreover, the mirror might enable one to keep on the lookout for malevolent spirits, or to frighten away those that came close enough to find themselves reflected in it.

The sun goddess is acknowledged as the ancestor of Japan's first emperor, Jimmu, the Yamato ruler traditionally dated to 660 BCE. By extension, she is the ancestor of the Japanese people. In effect, she also becomes the supreme Shinto deity. The three insignia of the imperial throne—the mirror, the jewel, and the sword—are her gifts to the Yamato rulers.

## Shamanic Queenship in Ancient Japan

In early Japan, certain women were greatly respected for their shamanic powers, and several founders of new religions in modern Japan were women alleged to have shamanic powers. Unlike early rulers in China, those in Japan were considered divine beings by virtue of the shamanic powers associated with their position. Interestingly, the position was not reserved only for men, and there are early records of women rulers. Presumably these rulers served the gods (*kami*) and were their mouthpieces. The best-known is the charismatic Queen Himiko of the Yamato state, who reigned during the late second and early third centuries. Her story is described in the Chinese chronicle, *Wei-chi/Weiji*:

> [The people of Wo] elected a young girl as their queen who was then named Himiko [literally, 'child of the Sun']. She attended and rendered service to the gods or spirits [literally, the way of the ghosts] and had a special power that bewitched the people. She never married even in her youth and her brother helped her administer the affairs of the Kingdom. After she was enthroned only a few persons were able to see her. Only one man always attended her, served her meals, transmitted her words, and had access to her dwelling (*Chronicle of Wei*, ch. 30; Hori 1968:188).

This charismatic queen was probably enthroned when only fourteen or fifteen, and her reign continued for sixty-eight years. Her personality and character appear typical of a shamanic queen. Some historians have even identified her with Amaterasu, the great sun goddess and reputed ancestor of the imperial family. Today, rituals involving the imperial family, especially the heir to the throne, still remind us of the shamanic character of the royal institution.

## Shinto Ritual

Shinto has no historical founder, no official scriptures, and no organized teachings, but it has a hereditary priesthood, which is important for the performance of ritual action and facilitates communication with the *kami*. Shinto also includes ascetic disciplines, social service, and other activities. Basically, Shinto implies a way of life inextricably woven into Japanese thought and culture. The Japanese usually go to Shinto shrines at the birth of a child, marry according to Shinto rituals, and visit the shrines on New Year's day.

Shinto displays a strong aesthetic sense. We associate with Japan the art of flower arrangement, the tea ceremony, and the martial art of swordsmanship. Some of these different arts have a Chinese origin. For example, the tea ceremony allegedly began in Ch'an monasteries in China, where monks took tea rather than liquor as a stimulant. However, the Japanese were responsible for ritualizing these arts.

According to Shinto, spirits are present in all nature and life, but some natural manifestations are more noticeable than others. Changes in the weather, such as storms and winds, demonstrate the power of the *kami*. Outstanding parts of the terrain, such as mountains, promontories, and offshore rocks, are likewise places where one senses the *kami*. These are prime places for establishing shrines; some are elaborate, but a very simple sign of awareness of the *kami*'s presence is to tie a straw rope to a rock or tree.

Ancient Shinto included a positive attitude towards nature and life. What must be cleansed is pollution, especially the pollution associated with decay and with substances separated or discharged from the human body. Spilled blood is a defilement, but the ritually guilty party is the victim who spills it by bleeding, not the person who inflicts the wound. Physical, ritual impurity, which is a Shinto concern, is different from moral guilt; there is no concept of sin in classical Shinto. There is hardly any element of real morality in the mythological and ritual lists of offences, but in time, Shinto taught the need to purify the heart and keep it true.

If pollution is physical and dealt with through ritual, it follows that the outward action is more important than the internal attitude of the petitioner. For a purification ritual to be effective, it needs to be correctly recited by a qualified practitioner, like a charm or mantra. The correctness, precision, and beauty of the recitation are what are thought to impress the *kami*. Indeed, the followers of the Shingon ('true word' or *mantra*) sect of Buddhism, which shares roots with Tibetan and Mongolian tantrism, found this aspect of Shinto congenial.

Usually Shinto priests preside at rituals after having purified themselves by bathing and abstinence from sex and certain foods. Some of the principal objects associated with Shinto ritual are mentioned in the sun-goddess myths. These include the mirror (representing a sun disk), the jewels (talismans), and the use of branches from the sacred *sakaki* tree. The goal of the festivities is to assure harmony between human beings and nature.

Shinto holds a basic assumption about human beings. Since people receive life from *kami*, they are the children of *kami*. The Shinto concept of community links ancestors to descendants and individuals to other members of society. Indeed, in early times, the role of the clan was central, and the *kami* worshipped were ancestral spirits and local agricultural deities.

Communication with the spirits or *kami* takes place during seasonal ritual celebrations called *matsuri*, with various offerings made to the *kami*. Some of these celebrations have fertility overtones, for example, those that involve young girls carrying phallic objects in ritual processions.

In Shinto rituals, food and drink are offered, and music and dancing are performed for the spirits in return for their blessings and protection. Presumably, the spirits descend on the shrine to receive the gifts. Afterwards, the priest dips a branch from a sacred evergreen (*sakaki*) tree in holy water, waves it over the people, and sprinkles them with the *kami*'s blessings. Together, everyone then partakes of the meal prepared for the *kami*.

Communication with the *kami* also occurs through the female mediums called *miko*, who are often blind and have shamanic powers to act as the spirits' mouthpieces. The fact that *miko* have always been women is interesting and can be traced back to the religious role of early women rulers. The *miko* are called upon for their services in times of crisis such as sickness, war, or natural disaster, or to make decisions regarding marriage or other important events. The *miko* are still consulted in contemporary Japan, especially in the rural areas of the northeast, where shamanic rituals are more important.

Today, ascetics in Japan are more numerous than the mediums. These men and women, living alone or in groups, use ancient techniques of trance and exorcism. They often spend their days making pilgrimages on foot to various holy places, healing the sick, and resolving spiritual problems for those who consult them. While they are heirs to a very ancient tradition, many are now ordained Buddhist priests of the Tendai, Shingon, or Nichiren sects.

Although Shinto is an indigenous religion in Japan, it has been subject to Taoist, Buddhist, Confucian, and other influences. Taoism spread from China to Korea, and eventually to seventh-century Japan when Japan opened itself to Chinese influences. Taoism was never an organized religion in Japan; its influences appear to be more diffused there than in Korea.

Shinto's animistic beliefs and magical practices were reinforced with the introduction of Taoism. Taoism's *yin-yang* and Five Agents theory (metal, wood, water, fire, and earth) are already reflected in such early Japanese works as the *Kojiki* and the *Nihongi*, with their myths and legends. These theories made a lasting impact on divination and other practices. Taoist influences can be discerned in the Shinto veneration of such sacred temple objects as the sword and the bronze mirror, which are used in Taoist rituals. Taoist influences are less readily distinguishable from indigenous shamanism, for Shinto has strong affinities with Taoism in shamanism and nature worship.

## Dual Shinto

The introduction of Buddhism did not oblige the Japanese to pick and choose between competing systems of beliefs and rituals. Instead, a syncretism or fusion eventually developed between the two. Ryōbu Shintō or Dual Shinto, as it is called, incorporated Buddhist elements.

Under imperial patronage, shrines were built within Buddhist temples honouring local *kami*, and Buddhist *sūtras* were chanted at Shinto shrines. Eventually the custom of building a small temple within large Shinto shrines became widespread. This was the *jingu-ji* ('shrine and temple') system, which retained the old and the new side by side. The red *torii* gateways were erected at many Buddhist temples as well as at Shinto shrines.

As Shinto gods were worshipped alongside *buddhas* and *bodhisattvas*, Buddhists began to assert that the *kami* were manifestations of universal Buddhist powers. This development was under way in Japan by 937 when two *kami* were declared to be incarnations of *bodhisattvas*. Eventually all the important *kami* were identified with a *buddha* or *bodhisattva*.

The principle of this identification was described in Japan by the phrase *honji suijaku* (the 'original site' and the 'local manifestations'). In a sense, Shinto was represented as a Japanese manifestation of Buddhist truths. As the many Shinto deities or *kami* became regarded as manifestations of *buddhas* and *bodhisattvas*, the bond between the two religions became so close that it became quite difficult to tell them apart. Shinto, we may say, was absorbed into Buddhism, as Buddhism adapted itself to Shinto. The *kami* were *avatāras* of the *bodhisattvas*, and *buddha* figures were treated as guests of the *kami*.

Different Buddhist sects offered different conceptions of assimilating the Shinto *kami*. For Tendai Shinto, the Buddha-nature, the reality behind all phenomena, includes the Shinto *kami*. For Shingon Shinto, the cosmic Buddha or Mahāvairocana, symbolized by the sun, unites the two aspects, the masculine and the feminine. Shingon Shinto holds that the original form of Amaterasu (the sun goddess) worshipped at Ise was the feminine aspect, while the original form of the deity of the Outer Shrine was none other than the Buddhist figure Mahāvairocana. Shingon developed particularly intimate ties with Shinto, and many of the associations of *kami* with their 'original sites' were with the thirteen *buddhas* of Shingon.

Shinto priests not only adopted certain Buddhist practices but were also prompted into developing their own doctrines. In 1274 and 1281, the Mongols attempted to invade Japan, but were frustrated in their attempt by storms at sea.

The Japanese interpreted the 'winds of the gods' (*kamikaze*) as protection given by Japan's local deities, and some began to assert the superiority of Japan over mainland Asian influences. The consequence of this was a strengthened claim for the place of Shinto.

Yoshida Kanetomo (1435–1511), an advocate of Shinto, sought to assert the priority and primacy of Shinto over Buddhism. For him, the *kami*, not the *bodhisattvas*, were the 'original site.' In the process, Yoshida also considered another import, Confucianism, which by his time was influential in Japan. Yoshida writes,

> Prince Shōtoku stated in a memorial that Japan was the roots and trunk [of civilization], China its branches and leaves, and India its flowers and fruit. Similarly, Buddhism is the flowers and fruit of all laws, Confucianism their branches and leaves, and Shinto their roots and trunk. Thus all foreign doctrines are offshoots of Shinto (Tsunoda 1958:271).

For Yoshida, the *bodhisattvas* were indeed the guests of the *kami*.

## Shinto and National Identity

From the seventeenth century onward, antiquarian and patriotic interests combined in a shift of cultural emphasis. Indebtedness to China was replaced by pride in what was originally and distinctively Japanese. Certain scholars switched from the study of ancient Chinese learning to the study of Japanese antiquity. They emphasized ancient poetry and mythology in their desire to believe in a Japan with an uncontaminated native Shinto tradition. This movement was known as Kokugaku, the National Learning school, which preferred Shinto to Confucianism. The school, which sparked a Shinto revival, blossomed particularly in the eighteenth century.

A precursor of the Kokugaku movement was Yamazaki Ansai (1618–82), considered a scholar of Shushigaku (the Neo-Confucian Chu Hsi school). Although he offered a synthesis of Confucian ethics and Shinto prayers, the movement took a distinctive turn with Kamo Mabuchi (1697–1769), whose strategy was more one of rejection. He wrote in Japanese, criticizing the Chinese language and repudiating Chinese literary influence.

Motoori Norinaga (1730–1801) pursued the issue further. He, too, criticized earlier efforts to link Shinto with Buddhism and Confucianism. He emphasized the study of Japanese origins in the mythological classics, the *Kojiki* and the *Nihongi*. His urge for a thorough study of Japanese classical literature became central to the agenda of the National Learning school. He also gave special veneration to the sun goddess Amaterasu. His efforts and those of his successors led to a revival of Shinto in the National Learning school.

*Priests bow at a Shinto shrine, Tokyo.*
(W.G. Oxtoby)

Interestingly and ironically, it was the Confucian-inspired virtue of loyalty to the emperor that encouraged the restoration of imperial rule under Emperor Meiji (1868), and also paved the way to the establishment of Shinto as the state cult.

## State Shinto

State Shinto existed from the late nineteenth to the mid-twentieth century. It was an official cult, sponsored by the government after the Meiji restoration for political and ideological purposes. As such, it was declared to be not a religion but above religions. It revered the emperor as the alleged descendant of the sun goddess, and consisted of rituals performed by the emperor and also those performed as devotion to him.

In spite of its ancient origins, the emperor cult was rarely practised for centuries prior to the Meiji restoration in 1868. When the country was dominated by the warlords called *shōguns*, the imperial family lived in obscurity, but following the Meiji restoration, the ruler of Japan was described in some contexts as the ruler of the universe by divine mandate.

The defeat of Japan in the Second World War (1945) resulted in the abolition of State Shinto. As part of the terms of surrender to the Americans, the emperor was forced to renounce his divinity. What may have seemed to the

Americans a logical and natural distinction between religion and the state was perceived by many Japanese as a humiliation.

Although the cult of the emperor was eliminated, the imperial family rituals continued. So-called 'Imperial Family Shinto' can be considered distinct from the political ideology of the emperor's divinity. As such, it was not abolished after the Second World War. It involves rituals and ceremonies, including funerals and accessions. It is centred on four palace shrines associated with the sun goddess and other deities as well as imperial ancestors. The Japanese are divided on the value of these ceremonies, but those who consider them worthwhile find in them the satisfaction of the continuity of tradition.

## Main Types of Contemporary Shinto

The Shinto tradition is a grab-bag of varied elements, meaning different things to different people and in different social contexts. Beyond the rituals of the imperial household, Shinto today is classified into three main interrelated types: Sect Shinto, Shrine Shinto, and Folk Shinto.

### *Sect Shinto*

Sect Shinto is comprised of thirteen groups formed during the nineteenth century, some of which have few Shinto features. Founded among the common people by shamanic individuals who had special religious experience, these groups do not have shrines but use congregational meeting halls as their centres of religious activity. They came under the supervision of a Meiji government office. Later, most of the principal groups became independent religious bodies, and for this reason were officially classified as 'Sect Shinto'. Nevertheless, it is not always easy to distinguish a Shinto sect. Tenrikyō, described as a 'new religion', for example, has often been treated as a Shinto sect, although since the end of the Second World War, its followers have asserted that it is not.

Shinto sects include mountain-worship sects, such as those that grew out of the cult of Mount Fuji; faith-healing sects, usually centred around a founder and his or her religious experience and activity (like that of Tenrikyō); purification sects that perpetuate the tradition of water purification to cultivate the body and mind; Confucian sects that arise from the merging of Confucianism and Revival Shinto; and Revival Shinto sects, based on Motoori Norinaga's National Learning school.

### *Shrine Shinto*

Shrine Shinto is the oldest and most prevalent. Shrines throughout Japan venerate numerous spirits associated with nature worship. Shrine Shinto has always been part of Japanese history, and constitutes the main current of Shinto tradition. Of these shrines, the best known is that dedicated to the sun goddess at Ise,

*Containers of sake donated by Japanese companies, at a Shinto shrine in Omiya.* (R.C. Amore)

south of Nagoya. Under the laws governing State Shinto, control over the shrines was taken away from the families that had served them for centuries and transferred to the government. This action 'secularized' the shrines, although after the Second World War, this change was reversed. Shinto shrines, with their red *torii* or free-standing lintel gateways, are seen all over the countryside today.

Worship at Shinto shrines is divided into four main parts: purification, offering, prayer, and a symbolic feast. As a devout worshipper, one usually pauses at the ablution basin to wash one's hands and rinse one's mouth. One removes one's hat, coat, and scarf. Entering the gate to the inner precincts, and facing the main sanctuary from outside, one bows, throws a coin in the offering box, claps one's hands twice to attract the attention of the *kami*, and pauses in brief prayer. Before leaving, the worshipper usually makes an offering to a priest, who gives him or her a branch of the sacred *sakaki* tree or a paper imitation of it. Besides money, one might also offer food or drink, flowers or some symbolic offering like a tree sprig.

At specific rituals or ceremonies, the prayers recited by the Shinto priests are usually in classical Japanese, an older form of the language than the current vernacular. They praise the spirits and make reference to the ritual involved. At the end of a ritual, there is a sacred feast, consisting at least of formally drinking a sip of rice wine served by a priest or an attendant. Shinto shrines receive many faithful visitors during feast days, especially on New Year's day.

Shrine Shinto also includes the family worship of ordinary Japanese, who often maintain a small shrine, the *kamidana*, in their home. It serves as a family altar, on which are placed sacred tablets from Shinto shrines, candles, and other offerings.

### *Folk Shinto*

Folk Shinto includes the numerous (if fragmented) folk beliefs in deities and spirits, and the practices connected with these. Practices include divination, spirit possession, and shamanic healing. Sometimes they are usages borrowed from religious Taoism, Buddhism, or Confucianism. Other times, they represent the survival of ancient local traditions.

Some customs are more closely associated with the foundation of Shinto itself. They include the worship of household and village deities, and customs of abstinence and purification. Abstinence and purification specifically pertain to Folk Shinto. The worship of household and village deities is a general characteristic of folk religion.

Folk religion in Japan is the product of the interaction between so-called indigenous elements (Shinto) and foreign ones. For example, folk religion embraces Buddhist practices like the *nembutsu* or invocation, as well as Shinto practices such as the worship of sacred mountains. Folk religion has shamanic characteristics like spirit possession and healing practices. We shall examine these in more detail later, in the context of the modern world.

# CONFUCIANISM

yes

## Confucian Origins

What do we mean when we speak of 'Confucianism'? A Western designation of a Chinese tradition, the term itself is ambiguous, representing an ideology developed by a man called Confucius (552?–479 BCE). It is actually a misnomer. The Chinese themselves have usually preferred *Ju-chia/Rujia* or *Ju-chiao/Rujiao*, the school or teachings of the scholars. Etymologically, it has been claimed that the word *ju/ru*, 'scholars', is related to the word for 'weaklings' or 'cowards'. It is supposed to have referred originally to those dispossessed aristocrats of antiquity who were no longer warriors but lived off their knowledge of rituals or history, music, numbers, or archery. Eventually, 'the school of *ju*' came to refer to the ethical wisdom of the past that Confucius transmitted to later ages, as well as to the entire development of the tradition after his time.

The questioning of religious belief is reflected in the philosophical thinking of the times. Some of the great thinkers of the sixth century BCE and afterwards further contributed to the rationalist atmosphere of philosophical reflection by focusing on humanity's place in the universe and the need for social order and harmony. Confucius and the school named after him offered a moral or ethical answer to the question regarding life's meaning and order in society, an answer that dominated Chinese philosophical thinking for more than 2,000 years.

Obviously, this answer was not produced in a vacuum, yet the search for its genesis in the society of its times is beset with problems. Many of the sources for the period in which Confucius and his followers lived are coloured by Confucian ideas, and either come from a later age or were edited at a later period. What can we say about Confucius's life, given the paucity of solid historical evidence and the abundance of legendary materials?

## The Historical Confucius

'Confucius' is the Latin rendering of K'ung fu-tzu/Kongfuzi, or 'Master K'ung', whose name was K'ung Ch'iu, also styled K'ung Chung-ni. He was a native of the small state of Lu, and was born near modern Ch'ü-fu (Qufu, Shandong). Details of his biography are at least as elusive as the life of Jesus. Little can be confirmed about the exact year of birth or about his forebears and immediate family. However, legends (including very early ones) are abundant. He is sometimes said to be a direct descendant of the Shang royal house. By the time of his parents, however, the family's circumstances were far from comfortable, and the country was divided among feudal lords under a nominal Chou suzerainty.

He describes his own situation as humble. The highest public office he occupied was that of a police commissioner in his home state, and that was only for about a year. In over ten years of travel, K'ung visited many feudal states, seeking but never finding a ruler who would follow his advice. In his later years, he devoted more time to teaching disciples, while also occupying himself with music and poetry, and occasionally conversing with rulers or ministers.

Like Jesus, K'ung became historically influential only after his death, but it was from natural causes when he was about seventy. Also like Jesus, K'ung did not develop any systematic doctrinal structure in which manners, morals, law, philosophy, and theology were clearly separated. In K'ung's case, the teachings were systematized only with Mencius (c. 371–289 BCE) and with Hsün-tzu (c. 312–238 BCE).

For an insight into K'ung's consciousness, we can examine a passage from the *Analects*, the collection of his discourses with his disciples. The text reveals his high regard for rituals, and for the virtue of propriety that is associated with them. His profound reverence for the will of Heaven (T'ien) should help us appreciate the basically religious orientation of his life and character.

At fifteen I set my heart on learning [to be a sage].
At thirty I became firm.
At forty I had no more doubts.
At fifty I understood Heaven's Will.
At sixty my ears were attuned [to this Will].
At seventy I could follow my heart's desires, without
overstepping the line.
(*Analects* 2:4; adapted from Waley 1938)

The mention of K'ung's ears as attuned, presumably to Heaven's will, is of particular interest. Was not the pictograph for 'sage' originally a large ear and a small mouth? While K'ung consistently exalted the sages of the past, such as the Duke of Chou, one might also infer that he recognized himself as a wise man.

In this account of his spiritual development, we can see K'ung as a believer in Heaven. We might infer that he regarded Heaven as a personal god, as a higher power, order, and law that displaced the many forms or patterns of the old gods. In fact, the word 'Heaven', which occurs eighteen times in the *Analects*, is mentioned only once in association with Shang-ti/Shangdi ('Lord-on-high'), its earlier equivalent. It is the will of Heaven that people (especially rulers) are to understand and obey. 'He who offends against Heaven has none to whom he can pray' (*Analects* 3:13; Legge 1893, 1:159).

K'ung sought to understand and follow Heaven's will. He lived in an age of turmoil, during which the ancient religious beliefs, with their emphasis on divination and sacrifice, were questioned. Understandably, K'ung reacted to the ambiguous heritage of the past by distancing himself from it. The manner in which he referred to the legacy of the ancients heralded a new age of ethical wisdom. Was he, then, a conservative or a reformer, or perhaps a revolutionary?

'I am a transmitter', he said, 'not an innovator; I believe in antiquity and love the ancients' (*Analects* 7:1; Waley 1938). His rhetoric was conservative. However, in spite of his love for the rites, he also asserted that human beings should respect the gods and spirits, but keep a distance from them. If we focus on his attention to the rituals, we might decide that he was basically a traditionalist, but given his own ideological preferences, we might also regard him as a selective heir to the legacy of the past, which he transmitted to the future.

When it came to actual beliefs and actions, Confucius often had reformist or even revolutionary preferences. His teachings on the virtue of *jen* ('humaneness') contributed to a social revolution by putting the nobility of virtue ahead of the nobility of birth. His general preference for education and philosophy over a military career eventually influenced the entire society. It is interesting that Confucius should use the term for a nobleman or gentleman (*chün-tzu/junzi*, literally 'the ruler's son') to denote a person of high moral character. Today, the term still retains this meaning. The word for scholar (*shih*) originally meant a warrior—as with the Japanese *samurai*.

In historical China, however, the scholars became the top class, ahead of farmers, artisans, and merchants, while soldiers were nearly social outcasts. (To be sure, the military usually decided the fate of successive dynasties. Nevertheless, a disdain for military service persisted in Chinese families until modern times, when the communist government made efforts to raise the public prestige of soldiers.) Confucius, it would seem, was a traditionalist by avocation, a reformer by choice, and a revolutionary in some of the consequences that his teachings produced.

In a book by the German philosopher Karl Jaspers (1883–1969), Confucius is mentioned among the great philosophers, the 'paradigmatic individuals', along with Socrates, Jesus of Nazareth, and Gautama Buddha. In each case, we have a man who lived in a time of social crisis and sought to respond to such through special teachings aimed at all people. In each case as well, disciples were gathered, regardless of their social backgrounds. In all cases, Jaspers argues, the teachings were not of abstract metaphysics but concerned with the higher order of things (the Rites or *li*, the Law or Torah, or the Dharma). These individuals offered their own critical interpretation of this higher order in opposition to external conformism and hypocrisy and in favour of a moral disposition. All lived what they preached, and represented a very high personal ethic, which expressed itself in clear moral demands.

## The Confucian Classics

While Confucius's teachings are best found in the *Analects* (the record of his conversations with his disciples), early Confucianism regarded a prior group of works called the Five Classics as its primary special texts. These books, of widely divergent genres, reflect a range of concerns in Confucius's day and a clear sense of the authority of past tradition. They include the *Book of Changes* or *I-ching*, the *Book of History* or *Shu-ching*, the *Book of Poetry* or *Shih-ching*, as well as the *Classic of Rites* or *Li-ching*, and the *Spring-Autumn Annals* or *Ch'un-ch'iu*. (A sixth classic, the *Book of Music*, is no longer extant.)

- The *Book of Changes* is also called *I-ching/Yijing*. It is a divination manual attributed to the sages of old. The manual centres upon short oracles arranged under sixty-four hexagrams, symbols made up of combinations of broken and unbroken lines in groups of six. Commentaries were later added to the oracles, offering early cosmological and metaphysical speculation in a cryptic language that makes reference to *yin-yang* and other ideas.

- The *Book of History* is also called the *Book of Documents* or *Historical Documents* (*Shang-shu*, literally 'ancient documents'). It is mainly an assortment of speeches from royalty and chief ministers, as well as certain narrative accounts of royal achievements and principles of government, arranged chronologically. Some of the allegedly older chapters have been discredited.
- The *Book of Poetry* is also called the *Book of Songs*, or the *Odes* (*Shih-ching/Shijing*). It is basically a collection of 305 songs. It includes four sections, with various genres, such as folk songs of love, courtship, and desertion, as well as hunts and dances. There are also banquet songs or state hymns. For many centuries, its love songs were interpreted as political allegory, and it took the twelfth-century philosopher Chu Hsi to restore their correct interpretation.
- The *Classic of Rites* is an entire corpus. It includes the *Ceremonials* (*I-li/Yi-li*), an early manual of etiquette for the nobility, detailing such occasions as marriages and funerals, sacrifices and archery contests. There is also the *Book of Rites* (*Li-chi/Liji*), with its forty-nine sections of ritual and government regulations, as well as treatises on education, the rites, music, and philosophy. Then there is the *Institutes of Chou* (*Chou-li/Zhouli*), apparently an idealized description of government offices in early Chou times.
- The *Spring-Autumn Annals* (*Ch'un-ch'iu/Chunqiu*) are basically a chronicle of the state of Lu, the Master's native state. Didactically and laconically written, they purport to explain the decline of the ancient political and moral order. The annals cover the period dating from 722 to 481 BCE, a period accordingly named the 'Spring-Autumn Period'. It is usually associated with three commentaries, or rather appendages: the vividly narrative *Tso-chuan/Zuozhuan* or Tso Commentary, and the catechetical (question-and-answer) Kung-yang Commentary and Ku-liang Commentary.

Indeed, all the Five Classics have in the past been attributed to Confucius, either as their editor or, in the case of the *Spring-Autumn Annals*, as the author. He is also alleged to have added the 'Appendices' to the *Book of Changes*, and to have expurgated the *Book of Poetry* of its more licentious contents. Contemporary scholarship no longer takes this seriously. True, the core of many of these classical texts goes back to the time of Confucius and even prior to him. The antiquity of the texts shows the ancient lineage of the school of *ju*, 'scholars'. But each of them underwent a long period of evolution, receiving additions after Confucius's time.

The textual situation was complicated in 213 BCE by the ruthless unifier of China, the Ch'in emperor Ch'in Shih Huang-ti (r. 221–210 BCE), who burned many books. He also unified the writing system, which made it difficult for later scholars to read more ancient scripts even when certain texts that had survived in hiding were unearthed. In the Han dynasty, which followed, restoration of the texts was a long process, complicated by forgeries and the diversity of schools of transmission. During the Han dynasty's reign, the Five Classics were made the basis of examinations in the imperial college in 125 BCE. The requirement that aspiring scholar-officials master their contents established the supremacy of the Confucian school. To assure proper transmission, the classical texts were inscribed in master copies, literally on stone, more than once. In time, a corpus of commentaries and subcommentaries developed, establishing various traditions of textual exegesis.

Other texts, not formally included in these five, have also been very influential. They include the *Analects* of Confucius and the *Book of Mencius*, which we shall describe later, and the *Classic of Filial Piety* (*Hsiao-ching/Xiaojing*), which resembles the *Book of Rites* in style and content. It is basically a brief purported dialogue between Confucius and a disciple, Tseng Tzu, which presents the virtue of filial piety (the duty of children towards parents) as the foundation of all knowledge and action. We shall give more attention to these four other texts as a second canon later on when we examine the development of Neo-Confucianism.

## The Virtue of Humaneness

The great merit of Confucianism, it has sometimes been said, is its discovery of the ultimate in the relative—that is, in the moral character of human relationships. Confucius himself taught a doctrine of reciprocity and neighbourliness: to regard every one as a very important guest, to manage the people as one would assist at a sacrifice, *'never do to others what you would not like them to do to you'* (*Analects* 15:23; Waley 1938:198). The last part of this quotation, which I have italicized, offers what has come to be called the 'negative Golden Rule'.

Confucianism characteristically speaks of the 'Five Relationships', each with its norms and duties. The relationships are those of ruler and minister, father and son, husband and wife, elder and younger brother, and friend and friend. Three of these are family relationships, while the other two are usually conceived in terms of the family models. For example, the ruler-minister relationship resembles the father-son, while friendship resembles brotherliness. For this reason, Confucian society regards itself as a large family: 'Amidst the four seas all men are brothers' (*Analects* 12:5; adapted from Waley 1938:163–4).

The responsibilities implied by these relationships are mutual and reciprocal. A minister owes loyalty to his ruler, and a child filial respect to the parent, that is, 'filial piety'. But the ruler must also care for his subjects, and the parent for the child. All the same, the Five Relationships emphasize a vertical sense, a hierarchy. Even in the horizontal relationship between friends, seniority of age demands a certain respect.

And though the husband-wife relationship would seem more naturally to resemble that between siblings, it is more usually compared to the ruler-minister relationship. The duty derived from filial piety to have progeny in order to perpetuate the ancestor cult has served for centuries as the ethical justification for polygamy. The obligations of filial piety have also promoted mutual help among family and more distant clan members, and even among persons from the same ancestral town, or descendants of the same ancestor who bear the same surname.

Confucius's central teaching, which became his main legacy, is the virtue of *jen/ren*. Etymologically, '*jen*' is written with the component 'human' and the component for 'two', or, if one prefers to read the sign thus, 'above'. It is pronounced the same as the word for human being. Understandably, *jen* is always concerned with human relationships, with relating to others. It may also be explained as the virtue of the 'superior man', the gentleman. It is associated with loyalty (*chung/zhong*)—loyalty basically to one's own heart and conscience, rather than a narrower political loyalty. It is also associated with reciprocity (*shu*)—respect and consideration for others (*Analects* 4:15).

*Jen* is also related to *li*, a term that has been translated both as 'propriety' and as 'ritual'. The latter of these two connotations has more to do with social behaviour, and the former more with the inner orientation of the person. *Jen* is translated variously as 'goodness', 'benevolence', 'humanity', and 'human-heartedness'. It was formerly a virtue expected of particular individuals, the *noblesse oblige* kindness that was the mark of a gentleman in his behaviour towards his inferiors. Confucius transformed it into a universal virtue, the quality that can make a human being a sage. The later application of his teachings would draw from this a social implication: that moral merit, not noble birth, should be the criterion for status as a gentleman. Like many a moral philosopher, Confucius offers both a description of human nature and a standard for it. *Jen* means affection and love. Descriptively, it is rooted in human sentiment, Prescriptively, it is a fundamental orientation for life.

While the natural feelings underlying kinship call for special consideration, the natural feelings aroused by a neighbour's need for help are also recognized. To help a neighbour is to act with empathy. This is similar to the Christian parable of the Good Samaritan, which illustrates the meaning of universal love.

Familial relations provide a model for behaviour in the wider society. Respect others' elders as you would respect your own; be kind to the children and juniors of others as you would be to your own. This philosophy has been a basis not only for the strong sense of solidarity in the Chinese family but for the familylike solidarity of Confucian social organizations, even among overseas Chinese communities today.

## A Religion of Ritual

Ritual was important in Confucius's teachings, and was recognized as such by his

*The hall of prayer in the Temple of Heaven complex in Beijing is built in a style similar to pagodas.* (W.G. Oxtoby)

disciples, who were also teachers of rituals. Thus, Confucianism also became known as the 'ritual religion' (*li-chiao/lijiao*), as it emphasized both doctrinal and ritual prescriptions for proper behaviour within family and society. Confucian teachings helped to maintain the older ancestor cult. Confucianism also perpetuated the worship of Heaven, a formal cult practised by China's imperial rulers.

Confucius also stressed the need to have the right inner disposition, without which ritual propriety becomes hypocrisy (*Analects* 15:17). He insisted that sacrifice was to be performed with an awareness of the presence of the spirits (*Analects* 3:12), and he emphasized that the importance of the rites does not reside in their external observance, such as in the offering of gifts and the accompaniment of musical performances: 'What can rites do for a person lacking in the virtue of humanity (*jen*)? What can music do for a person lacking in humanity?' (*Analects* 3:3).

In the matter of ritual, we should note Confucius's stated distaste for making human effigies or wooden burial figures (*yung*). These were made with movable limbs, to represent human beings capable of serving their lords and ladies in the world of the dead. Confucius is reported to have said that whoever made such figures did not deserve to have posterity (*Mencius* 1A:4). I interpret this as an unequivocal condemnation not only of human sacrifice but the symbolic representation of it.

### *The Cult of Heaven*

We have already mentioned the worship of Heaven in Chou times prior to Confucius. The worship included the emperor's annual sacrifices. Today, one may still visit the site in Beijing (Peking) where these rituals took place. The building complex of the Temple of Heaven, dating back to the Ming dynasty (1368–1661),

*The circular open-air terraces at the Temple of Heaven in Beijing, site of the emperor's annual ritual sacrifice to Heaven.* (W.G. Oxtoby)

is situated in a spacious park to the southeast of the former 'forbidden city'. There are several old structures there, including the well-known circular hall of prayer for good harvests, with its blue tiles (blue being the colour of the sky). Nearby, even more impressive, are three concentric circular open-air marble terraces, under the sky itself. They are the altar for the cult of Heaven. The middle of the topmost terrace is the place where the emperor used to make sacrifices to Heaven (the Lord-on-high) at the time of the winter solstice.

The cult of Heaven involved the sacrifice of animals as burnt offerings. In that respect, and also because it was a once-a-year performance, it is more similar to ancient Jewish temple sacrifice than to later Jewish or Christian ritual practice. Attendance was strictly limited. The population in general was not permitted, and individual citizens would be guilty of high treason should they attempt to perform such a rite. Rather, the performance was the privilege as well as sacred duty of the Son of Heaven, the emperor. This itself was proof that there was no separation between political and religious powers—between the *imperium* and the *sacerdotium*, as ancient and medieval Europeans would put it. It also shows that the office of emperor was basically a continuation of the ancient office of the priest-shaman-king.

In speaking of the ritual offerings to Heaven, one should not neglect the other cult, which offered sacrifices to earth. The dual cults give an impression that Heaven and earth are equals, each accepting a sacrifice, but the reality is not quite like that. While the sacrifices of Heaven and earth both belonged in the category of 'great' sacrifices, performed by the emperor himself as Son of Heaven, Heaven takes on greater importance than the earth and is addressed as Lord-on-high. It would appear that these cults represented a mixture of beliefs, a legacy from Shang and Chou times. So sacrifices were offered to both Heaven and earth as cosmic forces, and to Heaven in particular as a supreme deity.

### *Other State Cults*

An elaborate state cult began during the Han dynasty. Rightly or wrongly, it has been attributed to Confucian teachings. There are expressions of very ancient beliefs, not only in a supreme deity but in natural powers as deity symbols, as well as in the intercessory powers of deceased worthies or heroes. The great rituals performed by the emperor himself honoured Heaven, earth, and the imperial ancestors. There were also intermediate rituals for the worship of the sun, moon, and numerous spirits of earth and sky. There were the lesser sacrifices to minor gods, such as deities of mountains, lakes, and rivers.

Well-known historical figures, particularly wise and honest magistrates, were honoured as 'city gods'. Confucius himself, surrounded by his disciples and later worthies, became the centre of an elaborate cult, which very likely would have been repugnant to him. While not deified, he received official sacrifices as the teacher *par excellence*, and was especially venerated by the scholarly class. In sum, the Confucian emphasis on rituals assured a continuity with the past, and also offered a ritual as well as moral education for the would-be gentleman.

With the end of imperial rule and the establishment of a republic in China in 1912, the cult of Heaven and the other state cults came to an end, but their memory remains as witness to a theistic belief (either monotheism or polytheism, depending on one's interpretations) at the heart of traditional Chinese religion. This basic religiosity persisted throughout the ages, in spite of the changes in philosophical formulation and interpretation.

### *The Ancestor Cult*

The ancestor cult envisions a realm where ancestors reside. The traditional Confucian understanding regarding the hereafter posits that a human being has two 'souls'. The upper, or intellectual, soul, called the *hun*, becomes the spirit (*shen*), and ascends to the world above. A lower, or animal soul, called the *p'o/po*, becomes the ghost (*kuei*) and descends with the body into the grave.

Such ideas are found in the Tso Commentary (*Tso-chuan*), in a record of a conversation dated 534 BCE, suggesting that 'souls' were also presumed to be possessed by everyone, not just the nobility. Such ideas are confirmed by archaeological findings of tomb paintings of a heavenly realm, like those found at Mawangdui, a Han site. They were also accepted by the Taoist religion, which elaborated on them. The Taoist cult of immortality, involving the dead's physical immortality or the ascent to heaven as immortals, developed from these beliefs, especially regarding the *hun*.

The ancestor cult functioned as a memorial service. It was held first at ancestral temples, and subsequently at grave sites or at home. Wine and food libations were usually offered, with silent prostrations in front of the tablets that represented the ancestors. The ancestors were alleged to have tasted the food before the whole family partook of the meal. Conversion to Christianity frequently represented a break with this tradition, since the converts were either forbidden or no longer expected to continue the cult.

The cult of ancestors, much better known than the cult of Heaven, goes back to the dawn of Chinese history and thus likely antedates the cult of Heaven. Originally it was the exclusive privilege of the nobility to practise the rituals. It became associated with the state orthodoxy, while remaining very much a family practice—an expression of a community that included both the living and the beloved deceased. While the ancestor cult may be regarded as a religion in itself, its persistence has also been considered another indication of the religious character of Confucianism. Until recently, the ancestral shrine was maintained in many Chinese homes in Hong Kong, Taiwan, and Southeast Asia, as well as in Korea and Japan.

### *Family Rituals*

There are other rituals recorded in the *Book of Rites* that have also been practised throughout many centuries. They include the male adolescent's 'capping' ritual, which takes place sometime between the ages of fifteen and twenty, when he receives his formal hat and ceremonial gown, as well as his formal name. A wine libation is made and the young man is formally presented to his ancestors, an act that gives the ceremony its religious aspect. It is similar to the Jewish Bar Mitzvah. After that comes marriage, which is a union of families. It begins with the announcement of the event to the ancestors in the temple, accompanied by a wine libation. The *Book of Rites* has a very clear emphasis on marriage and the family:

> The respect, the caution, the importance, the attention to secure correctness in all the details, and then [the pledge of] mutual affection—these were the great points in the ceremony, and served to establish the distinction to be observed between … husband and wife. From that righteousness came the affection between father and son; and from that affection, the rectitude between ruler and minister. Whence it is said, 'The ceremony of marriage is the root of the other ceremonial observances' (Legge 1885, 2:430).

Family rituals are inseparable from the veneration of departed ancestors. The ancestors receive reports from the family regarding births and weddings, as well as the occasions that mark the adolescent's entry into adult society. There are also other rituals dedicated specifically to the deceased, such as mourning and funerary rites, and anniversaries marking the memories of departed family members. The *Book of Rites* concentrates on these occasions and how such associated rituals should be enacted.

## Later Followers: Mencius and Hsün-tzu

The Confucian school was further developed by its followers, notably including Mencius and Hsün-tzu, in the centuries after Confucius. These two men differed not only with Confucius regarding certain issues but even more so between themselves, yet they had enough in common with him that they are credited with building the Confucian tradition. On the other hand, Mo-tzu, who started as a follower of the Confucian school, departed sufficiently from it that his ideas are regarded as distinctive.

The name Mencius, like the name Confucius, is a form with a Latin ending; it gained currency in Europe after Roman Catholic missionaries made contact with China. The Chinese element is the title Meng-tzu/Mengzi, 'Master Meng', and Meng's own name was Meng K'o. Meng, who lived from 372 to 289 BCE, was a native of a small state adjacent to Confucius's Lu. Like Confucius, he travelled from one feudal state to another, looking for a ruler who would accept his advice. Unlike Confucius's way of giving advice, his advice was often given bluntly, and, of course, there was much greater turmoil in his lifetime than in earlier times. It appears that feuding lords regarded Mencius as hopelessly impractical. He preached benevolence and righteousness at a time when might was making right in the struggle for political survival. The *Book of Mencius*, with its passages of lofty idealism and even mysticism, has more eloquence than the *Analects* of Confucius.

In the *Book of Mencius*, we find an evolutionary shift in the meaning of the term 'Heaven'. Whereas Confucius seldom mentions the personal deity, Mencius speaks much more of Heaven—but not always as a personal deity. According to Mencius, Heaven is present within the human's heart, so that one who knows one's own heart and nature, knows Heaven (*Mencius* 7A:1). Heaven therefore has a greater immanence. The term also increasingly refers to the source and principle of ethical laws and values, but this shift in emphasis towards the ethical is not really at the expense of ritual. Mencius continues to hold in esteem the practice of offering sacrifices to the Lord-on-high and to ancestors. 'Though a man may be wicked, if he adjusts his thoughts, fasts and bathes, he may sacrifice to the Lord-on-high' (*Mencius* 4B:25).

Hsün-tzu/Xunzi, 'Master Hsün', named Hsün K'uang or Hsün Ch'ing/Xun

Qing, lived from about 312 to 238 BCE, which means that he belonged to a later generation than Mencius. However, he was from the same region in northern China, the state of Chao, from which virtually all early Confucians and even Mohists originated. Hsün-tzu was appointed magistrate of Lan-ling, in the powerful state of Ch'i, and served in that capacity for a short period. He left behind a work known by his name, *Hsün-tzu*, which contains thirty-two sections. The extant version appears to include sections written by him as well as by his disciples. The work is organized around specific topics such as the nature of Heaven and the wickedness of human nature.

Some of Hsün-tzu's teachings were controversial, as they were diametrically opposed to those of Mencius. Hsün-tzu observes a difference between the educated gentleman, who uses his rationality, and the common people, who believe in fortune and misfortune. Hsün-tzu was the beginning of the upper class's movement away from religious practices such as divination in the royal ancestral temples of the Shang dynasty and rain dances sponsored by the state, which became identified with the practices of 'superstitious' commoners. It is the beginning of the separation between Confucianism as an élite tradition and the so-called popular religion at a grass-roots level.

> You pray for rain and it rains. Why? For no particular reason, I say. It is just as though you had not prayed for rain and it rained anyway … You consult the arts of divination before making a decision on some important matter. But it is not as though you could hope to accomplish anything by such ceremonies. They are done merely for ornament. Hence the gentleman regards them as ornaments, but the common people regard them as supernatural (Watson 1963a:85).

In 'A Discussion of Heaven', Hsün-tzu has this to say about the ways of Heaven: 'Heaven does not suspend the winter because men dislike cold; earth does not cease being wide because men dislike great distances; the gentleman does not stop acting because petty men carp and clamor' (Watson 1963a:82).

Although apparently reducing Heaven's ways to the laws of nature, he maintains the importance of rituals and attacks Mo-tzu's criticisms of such:

> … if a man concentrates upon fulfilling ritual principles, then he may satisfy both his human desires and the demands of ritual; but if he concentrates only upon fulfilling his desires, then he will end by satisfying neither. The Confucians make it possible for a man to satisfy both; the Mo-ists cause him to satisfy neither (Watson 1963a:91).

In the process of education, the rites are supported by music. The *Book of Rites* shows evidence of Hsün-tzu's influence. Its chapter on music extols music as a way of gaining inner equilibrium and tranquillity; the equilibrium reflects the harmony of music. Together, music and rituals maintain or restore an inner harmony that is, or ought to be, a reflection of the harmony between Heaven and earth. This reflects the teachings of the *Doctrine of the Mean*, also a chapter from the same ritual text.

The philosophical assumption here is the correlation between the microcosm and the macrocosm, between the inner workings of a person's mind and heart and the creative processes of the universe. The mystical dimension is obvious. Here, we touch upon the heart of the Chinese meaning of harmony, on which Mencius and Hsün-tzu would agree. Here, too, we may recall the place of music in religion. Liturgical worship in most places offers a union of ritual and music that is expressive of the heart and human culture.

## Human Nature: Good or Evil?

The Chinese word for human nature is *hsing/xing*. The character representing this is written as a compound that includes the terms for mind or heart and life or offspring. Philological scholarship demonstrates the association between this etymology and early religious worship. A human being receives from Heaven the gift of life and all the innate endowments of human nature, especially the shared faculty of moral discernment. Mencius says that the sense of right and wrong is common to all (2A:6), which is what distinguishes humans from animals. A related belief is that all are equal, despite any social hierarchy or distinction between the 'civilized' and the 'barbarian'.

The Confucian tradition has sometimes been criticized for not explaining the role of evil in human existence. Traditional thought affirms the presence of evil: Mencius explains it as the product of contact between an originally good nature and its wicked environment, while Hsün-tzu believes that it is inherent in human nature.

However, the two thinkers agree that human perfectibility is possible. Mencius declares that everyone has the potential to become a sage. Hsün-tzu explains that the evil in human nature desires its opposite, and that education can train human nature to seek goodness. He says:

> Man's nature is evil; goodness is the result of conscious activity. The nature of man is such that he is born with a fondness for profit … Therefore, man must first be transformed by the instructions of a teacher and guided by ritual principles … It is obvious … that man's nature is evil, and that his goodness is the result of conscious activity (Watson 1963a:157).

In the Han dynasty (206 BCE–220 CE) and generally in early Confucianism, Hsün-tzu was more influential than Mencius. The situation changed after the

### Mencius on Human Nature and Virtue

Mencius said: 'No man is devoid of a heart sensitive to the suffering of others ... Suppose a man were ... to see a young child on the verge of falling into a well. He would certainly be moved to compassion, not because ... he wished to win the praise of his fellow villagers or friends, nor yet because he disliked the cry of the child ...

'The heart of compassion is the germ of benevolence; the heart of shame, of dutifulness; the heart of courtesy and modesty, of observance of the rites; the heart of right and wrong, of wisdom. Man has these four germs just as he has four limbs' (2A:6; Lau 1970:82–3).

tenth century with the development of Neo-Confucianism. When Christian missionaries arrived in China, they discovered that Confucian scholars usually followed Mencius in upholding the basic goodness of human nature. Evil was explained as a deflection from the good, a perversion of the natural. The Europeans were confused by the lack of a Chinese word equivalent to 'sin'. A word used in this connection, *tsui/zui*, has a double significance: crime, as well as sin.

This ambiguity has led some people to the mistaken belief that the Chinese and the Japanese had no guilt-oriented morality (in which a consciousness of moral evil is internalized), but only a shame-oriented one, based externally and superficially on the desire to be respected by others. Certainly, Confucian education sought to instil a strong sense of moral responsibility, inseparable from consciousness of guilt. Contemporary mainland Marxist scholars have tended to emphasize Hsün-tzu's concept of the original wickedness of human nature, in order to justify political and social control.

The belief in human perfectibility is the combined legacy of Mencius and Hsün-tzu. Mencius has centred this teaching on the mind and heart. The Chinese word for this unity is *hsin*, originally represented by a pictograph for fire. The heart comes to us from Heaven (*Mencius* 6A:15) and leads us back to Heaven. It represents both the symbol and reality of humanity's oneness with Heaven. More so than Christianity, Mencius has expressed a continuity between the mind's knowledge and the heart's willingness in levels of conscience that unite in the heightened moral faculty of the sage.

## Mohism: A Rival School

Inevitably Confucius's successors developed his thought in various directions. There was a considerable amount of diversity, such as that between Mencius and

## SELF AND SOCIETY IN THE WAY OF THE GREAT LEARNING

The Way of the Great Learning consists in clearly exemplifying illustrious virtue, in loving the people, and in resting in the highest good …

The ancients who wished clearly to exemplify illustrious virtue throughout the world would first set up good government in their states. Wishing to govern well their states, they would first regulate their families. Wishing to regulate their families, they would first cultivate their persons. Wishing to cultivate their persons, they would first rectify their minds. Wishing to rectify their minds, they would first seek sincerity in their thoughts. Wishing for sincerity in their thoughts, they would first extend their knowledge. The extension of knowledge lay in the investigation of things. For only when things are investigated is knowledge extended; only when knowledge is extended are thoughts sincere; only when thoughts are sincere are minds rectified; only when minds are rectified are our persons cultivated; only when our persons are cultivated are our families regulated; only when our families are regulated are states well governed; and only when states are well governed is there peace in the world (de Bary 1960:129).

Hsün-tzu. In some instances, though, the differences of opinion put their proponents outside Confucianism, as history defines that tradition.

What is called Mohism, the school of Mo-tzu/Mozi ('Master Mo'), is such a case. Like Confucianism, Mohism is an ancient school of philosophy with strong moral and religious overtones. Mo's dates of birth and death are not certain, but he lived some time after Confucius and died in the early fourth century BCE (c. 470–391 BCE). Mo-tzu initially was a student of the Confucian school. Unlike Confucius, who came from minor aristocracy, Mo was a commoner. Much more importantly, Mo-tzu tended to extremes, while Confucius was a moderate. Indeed, Mo-tzu became a severe critic of the Confucian school as he knew it, and developed his own independent thinking. This is evident in the work called *Mo-tzu*, which was presumably composed by disciples of his school.

*Mo-tzu* is organized around specific topics, sometimes with three-part elucidations from the diverse schools of transmission. Its later chapters have more to do with logic and military strategy. The teachings are exceptional and the style is clear, though somewhat dull and repetitious. Some of the teachings are derived from ancient religion, like the belief in ghosts and spirits. Others sound modern, like non-aggression and even militant pacifism.

Where Confucius had been discreet about Heaven and the afterlife, Mo-tzu is religiously outspoken. He believes in Heaven as the Supreme Being, and in the will of Heaven as the guide to human existence. He also believes in a hierarchy

## IN EVERY SITUATION, A GENTLEMAN

The gentleman acts according to the situation he is in and does not desire what is out of it. If he is wealthy and honorable, he acts like one wealthy and honorable, if poor and lowly, he acts like one poor and lowly. If he is among barbarians, he does what one does among barbarians ... There is no situation into which the gentleman enters in which he is not himself. In a superior position he does not abuse his subordinates; in an inferior position he does not hang on his superiors. He makes his own conduct correct and seeks nothing from others, and so he has no resentment. He neither complains against Heaven nor blames men (*The Mean* 14; de Bary 1960:133).

of spirits and ghosts, like those popular in ancient China. For this reason, he is sometimes said to be the direct heir to early Chinese religion.

A believer in Heaven and spirits, Mo-tzu places importance on rituals, including sacrificial rituals, for which he would spare no expense. However, when it comes to the ancestor cult and funerary rituals, he criticizes the extravagance lavished on Confucian funerals. These were a re-enactment of ancient practices, such as searching for the spirits of the deceased before preparing the body for burial, presumably to call the spirits to return to life:

> When a parent dies, the Confucians lay out the corpse for a long time before dressing it for burial while they climb up onto the roof, peer down the well, poke in the ratholes, and search in the washbasins, looking for the dead man. If they suppose that they will really find the dead man there, then they must be stupid indeed, while if they know that he is not there but still search for him, then they are guilty of the greatest hypocrisy (Watson 1963b:125).

Confucius taught the virtue of humanity (*jen*), which has sometimes been called 'graded' love, since it begins with the family and extends outward. Mo-tzu taught universal love, equal love (*chien-ai/jianai*) for all, on the basis that Heaven loves all equally. Mencius found Mo-tzu's idea of universal love to be subversive of family values.

> How do we know that Heaven loves the people of the world? Because it enlightens them universally. How do we know that it enlightens them universally? Because it possesses them universally. How do we know that it possesses them universally? Because it accepts sacrifices from them universally (Watson 1963b:81–2).

Mo-tzu believed in authority even more fervently than Confucius, and certainly much more so than Mencius. Like Confucius and Mencius, Mo-tzu considered it a duty to offer advice to rulers. However, Mo-tzu actively devoted himself to the cause of maintaining peace and opposing war. He was a militant pacifist who did his homework: he became a specialist in weaponry and military strategy, in order to use these skills to bring about peace. For example, when Mo-tzu heard that the state Ch'u was planning an attack on a smaller state Sung/Song, he walked for ten days and ten nights to the capital of Ch'u. There he convinced the ruler to call off the expedition, after having organized his disciples with better weapons to help protect the smaller state. This demonstrates Mo-tzu's tireless devotion to his causes. It also highlights the good organization of his band of disciples, who are sometimes described as knights religiously devoted to their leader.

Over time, the Chinese people preferred Confucius to Mo-tzu as a teacher. Confucius was a man of moderation, while Mo-tzu was an extreme pacifist, carrying things to excess and expecting others to do the same. Mo-tzu was a great man and a great teacher. If anything, his problem was his excesses in virtue:

> Mo-tzu wrote a piece 'Against Music', and another entitled 'Moderation in Expenditure', declaring that there was to be no singing in life, no mourning after death. With a boundless love and a desire to insure universal benefit, he condemned warfare … His views, however, were not always in accordance with those of the former kings, for he denounced the rites and music of antiquity … A life that is all toil, a death shoddily disposed of—it is a way that goes too much against us (Watson 1968:365–6).

Although he was important in his own times, Mo-tzu and his teachings were overshadowed by Confucianism and eventually by Taoism and Buddhism. Mohism enjoyed some revival of interest with the introduction of Christianity and its similarity to Mo-tzu's teaching on Heaven and universal love. Certain scholars in modern mainland China have also tried to exalt Mohism, although they have been unable to approve of his religious teachings

## The Mandate of Heaven

Traditional China adhered to certain political principles with implicit religious sanctions. That is, the Chinese believed that Heaven bestows a mandate on rulers to govern. They forfeit it if they become tyrants. Each ruler, as custodian of the 'Mandate of Heaven' to govern, functions as a kind of high priest, mediating between the human order and the divine.

Originally aimed at advising the rulers themselves, Confucian teachings in time were increasingly applied to training the rulers' advisers. The problem for the minister or would-be minister is what one should do if the ruler is not only unwise (as most rulers turned out to be) but even despotic and tyrannical, as some of them definitely were.

Confucius himself offers a doctrine of rectification of names, which has sometimes been misunderstood. In eight cryptic words, he says: 'Ruler, ruler; minister, minister; father, father; son, son' (*Analects* 13:3; Waley 1938). These have been misinterpreted as representing a caste system in which the ruler is always ruler, the minister always minister. However, this is obviously a mistake, since every son is expected to become a father.

The correct interpretation is that the ruler should be a *good* ruler, the minister a *good* minister, and so on. This double sense is evident in English when the first occurrence of the noun is the example, and the second one the norm or standard: 'That car is a [real] car', for instance. But sometimes our norms or standards are un-Confucian, as in 'Boys will be boys.' The Confucian teaching is that names should represent realities, and that human relationships are only real when the persons involved strive to live up to the ideal.

Mencius offers an explicit teaching about the legitimation of political power. It is authorized by a mandate bestowed by Heaven. Mencius is articulating a theory that is already implicit in the accounts of dynastic changes given in the classical *Book of History* and reflected also in the *Book of Poetry*. Mencius also offers a clear doctrine of justified rebellion or revolution, known popularly as the 'removal of the mandate' (*ko-ming/geming*). It is Mencius who says that killing a tyrant is not regicide, since the tyrant no longer deserves to rule (*Mencius* 1B:8). It is Mencius who declares, 'The people come first; the altars of the earth and grain come afterwards; the ruler comes last' (*Mencius* 7B:14). The idea of a justified rebellion is implicit in the notion of authority delegated by Heaven. Not too surprisingly, the fourteenth-century founder of the Ming dynasty sought to delete from the *Book of Mencius* the passages that approve of tyrannicide.

In the Confucian classics, we sometimes find 'the one man' as the expression used by the emperor to refer to himself as the individual who alone holds the exalted office. In Confucian China, the emperor is Son of Heaven, governing by a mandate from above and mediating between the powers above and the people below. His high position and awesome responsibilities make him a solitary individual. In another sense, he is the collective man, alone guilty of fault whenever his people offend Heaven (as in the case of King T'ang.)

The Confucian tradition bridged the two ends of China's political spectrum; it included political conservatives as well as moderate and radical reformers. There were those whose priority was to serve the state. There were also those who remained independent of the state, while seeking to change or transform it. Confucian scholars were usually activists, either serving the government, advising and admonishing the ruler or engaging in reforms, or even protesting against tyranny through passive or active resistance.

## Confucianism in the Han Era

The Han dynasty, like its contemporary the Roman Empire, marked an important period for the emerging relationships between religion and the state. During this time, Confucianism became a state orthodoxy—some would say, the state religion. (Taoism at that time became an institutional religion, and Buddhism was introduced into the country.) Han China represents an epoch when 'all under Heaven' was unified under one emperor, who ruled by Heaven's mandate with the help of Confucian orthodoxy. It was a development parallel to Christendom under Constantine and his successors, who had a 'political theology' of one God, one *logos*, one emperor, and one world. That monotheistic ideology undergirded the monarchical order and remained a European ideal for centuries. In the Roman case, the prestige and authority of Rome long outlasted the fall of the empire. Perhaps we should not be surprised that the name Han has continued to be identified with the majority population of China.

Among Han scholars, the one reputed to be most influential in consolidating Confucian gains was Tung Chung-shu/Dong Zhongshu (179–104 BCE). With philosophical arguments he sought to persuade the ruler to govern benevolently. Systematizing traditional thought, he established Heaven, earth, and humans as a horizontal triad or trinity, with kingship as the vertical link among them.

> Those who in ancient times invented writing drew three lines and connected them through the middle, calling the character 'king'. The three lines are Heaven, earth and man, and that which passes through the middle joins the principles of all three ... Thus the king is but the executor of Heaven. He regulates its seasons and brings them to completion (*Ch'un-ch'iu fan-lu*; de Bary 1960:179).

The Han Confucians also incorporated ideas from the Yin-Yang and Five Agents schools. These were independent and ancient schools of philosophical speculation, but their ideas gradually fused with one another and were absorbed into both Taoism and Confucianism.

### *The Yin-Yang School*

The Yin-Yang school elaborated ideas of two pervasive forces in the universe, opposing yet complementary. There is a duality between *yin* and *yang*; *yin* is feminine, shadowy, soft, moist, passive, and so on, while *yang* is masculine, bright, hard, dry, aggressive, and so on. However, this is not 'dualism', which often connotes a struggle between good and evil where one side must prevail. In the case of this cosmology, what is desirable or beneficial consists in proper harmony and balance, not in the replacement or eviction of one side by the other (although in action, not in cosmology, Taoists prefer a *yin* style as opposed to a *yang* style).

### *The Five Agents School*

The Five Agents school viewed five primal elements as active cosmic agents engaged in interaction and change. These five agents are water, fire, wood, metal, and earth. Each has power over another, that is, water is over fire, fire over earth, earth over metal, metal over wood, and wood over water.

These five agents thus differ from the Greek or Hindu 'four elements' of earth, fire, air and water. Not only does the Chinese group include an organic substance, wood, but it appears to exclude the very important and all-pervasive air. Actually, air or *ch'i* had always been regarded as fundamental and indeed all-pervasive.

Together with *yin* and *yang*, the Five Agents integrated life and the universe. For example, each of the agents was associated with a dynasty: metal with the Hsia, water with the Shang, wood with the Chou, and so on. The agents were also associated with cyclical signs for designating years, days, and hours. They were associated, moreover, with the Chinese zodiacal cycle of twelve animals, listed later in this chapter.

The religious discourse of Han Confucianism was tolerant of exaggerations and superstitions. Many apocryphal texts were also accepted, together with the reconstructed Five Classics. Indeed, each classic had at least one apocryphal text associated with it. We hear of Confucius's alleged miraculous birth and many other legends. There were also widespread beliefs in omens and portents, supported by a wide array of prognostication and divination texts. Even Tung Chung-shu demonstrated credence in portents and omens.

> The creatures of Heaven and earth at times display unusual changes and these are called wonders. Lesser ones are called ominous portents ... Portents are Heaven's warnings, wonders are Heaven's threats ... If we examine these wonders and portents carefully, we may discern the will of Heaven (*Ch'un-ch'iu fan-lu*; de Bary 1960:187).

## Neo-Confucian Response to Buddhism

During and after the Han dynasty, many commentaries and subcommentaries were written on the classical Confucian texts, which became the core of the civil-service examination curriculum. Much of this activity was the work of scholars striving for detailed literary and linguistic analysis of the ancient material. This activity continued into the T'ang dynasty during the seventh through ninth centuries when Buddhism became prominent in Chinese intellectual life.

After that, a succession of influential philosophers took up the commentary activity during the Sung/Song dynasty, which ruled from the middle of the tenth through to the late thirteenth centuries. These philosophers were more than literary and linguistic philologists; they were innovators and synthesizers. Their goal was to find answers in the classical heritage to a number of questions that had been raised during the centuries of Taoist and then Buddhist dominance. The philosophers attributed to Confucius their own new thinking, which they developed in response to Taoist and Buddhist influences.

These thinkers are known as the Neo-Confucians. The principal figures in this school are Chou Tun-yi/Zhou Dunyi (1017–73), Chang Tsai/Zhang Zai (1021–77), the brothers Ch'eng Hao (1032–85) and Ch'eng Yi (1033–1107), and the synthesizer Chu Hsi/Zhu Xi (1130–1200). A further contributor to this school was Wang Yang-ming (1472–1529).

### *The Four Books as a New Canon*

The combined challenge of Buddhism and Taoism led the Confucian scholars to look for the spiritual legacy within Confucianism itself. The Five Classics were a body of works of different literary genres, which stimulated philological exegesis but did not promote sufficient philosophical and religious commentaries. The Sung dynasty Neo-Confucian philosophers reformulated Confucian philosophy on the basis of a smaller corpus of texts, the Four Books: the *Analects of Confucius*, the *Book of Mencius*, the *Great Learning,* and the *Doctrine of the Mean*. For them, these contained a 'legacy of the mind and heart'.

- The *Analects of Confucius* (*Lun-yü*) includes twenty chapters, divided into nearly fifty sections, some of which are very brief. As the earliest text with any historical information about Confucius, it goes back to about one century after the Master's death and records conversations between Confucius and his disciples. The chapters are not organized systematically, and the dialogues they offer are fragmentary.
- The *Book of Mencius*, a work in seven chapters, presents conversations between Mencius and his disciples. Probably compiled after Mencius's death, although perhaps not that much later, it, too, is not systematically organized, but the passages are longer and the contents livelier, including many anecdotes.
- The *Great Learning* and
- The *Doctrine of the Mean* were both originally chapters with philosophical content in the *Book of Rites*, which, in its present form, probably came from the early first century BCE, although the materials included could be much older. The *Great Learning* makes moral and spiritual cultivation the beginning of good rulership; the *Doctrine of the Mean* concentrates on the inner life of psychic equilibrium and harmony.

Chu Hsi and the other Neo-Confucian philosophers gave these texts preeminence at a time when Buddhism had made great inroads. In doing so, they increasingly oriented Confucian scholarship to the kind of metaphysical and spiritual questions that Buddhism dealt with. By metaphysics we mean one's philosophical speculation about the nature of ultimate reality. In fact, these Confucians' speculation shows signs of Buddhist and Taoist philosophical influence. The result is a new synthesis, a *Weltanschauung* or worldview that builds on the old moralist answer to questions about life and the world, but achieves a clearer metaphysical framework and spiritual profundity.

## The Contribution of Chu Hsi

Chu Hsi was probably the greatest mind and the most prolific author among the Neo-Confucians. Though he was not accepted as an orthodox thinker during his own life, his commentaries (on the Four Books) were eventually integrated into the curriculum of the civil-service examinations (1313), making his philosophy the new state orthodoxy for the subsequent six centuries.

Chu Hsi's philosophy is all the more representative of the Chinese humanist tradition as it is a conscious synthesis of previous philosophies. It combines the 'naturalist' legacy of the Taoists and Buddhists, and what may be called the 'psychist' and 'culturalist' legacy of the Confucians themselves, modified also by an undercurrent of Buddhist influences. His theory of human nature draws from both sides. For Chu Hsi, as for the mainstream of Chinese philosophy, the human being and the cosmos are paradigms of each other, so that evil loses its significance in the affirmation of human perfectibility, as expressed through the doctrine of sagehood.

### *The Absolute*

A compact expression of the world regarded as an ontological paradigm is given in the philosophy of the Great Ultimate (*T'ai-chi/Taiji*), which Chu Hsi took over from Chou Tun-yi. This is a symbolic expression of cosmology that emphasizes the interrelatedness of the world and people in macrocosm-microcosm terms.

In interpreting the *T'ai-chi*, Chu Hsi uses the concept of *li*, those 'principles' that constitute all things and that were given prominence by the Ch'eng brothers, especially Ch'eng Yi. *Li* may be defined as forms or essences, as organizing and normative principles, belonging to the metaphysical realm, 'above shapes'. It is logically, not chronologically, prior to its coordinate, *ch'i/qi*, translated sometimes as 'ether', or 'matter-energy', which belongs to the physical realm, 'within shapes'. All things are constituted of both *li* and *ch'i*, somewhat like Aristotelian form and matter, except that *li* is passive and *ch'i* is dynamic. They are not in conflict, but rather are metaphysical coordinates.

The Great Ultimate is described as the most perfect *li*, a kind of primal archetype. It is also the sum total of the principles (*li*) of everything. In Chinese philosophy, it serves the function that the Form of the Good does in the thought of Plato, and that God does in the writings of Aristotle. In place of a personal deity, Chu Hsi discussed an Absolute that he clearly identified with both Heaven and the Lord-on-high. He asserted that it is not correct to speak about a man in heaven who is lord of the world, but that it is equally wrong to say that there is no such ruler. He was removing the anthropomorphic overtones of these terms while affirming the presence of a higher power, a metaphysical more than a personal absolute.

### *Human Nature*

In Chu Hsi's metaphysics, the human being, who represents the summit of the universe and is part of the excellence of the Great Ultimate, has a nature that is the result of the interaction of *yin* and *yang* and the Five Agents. Human nature is originally good, or 'sincere' (*ch'eng*). In this respect, Chu Hsi, following Mencius, has a more optimistic view of human nature that what we learn from Christian, and especially early Gnostic, teachings. Where, then, does evil come from?

The explanation is that *li*, though wholly good in itself, loses its perfection in its relationship to *ch'i*. When actualized through *ch'i*, it becomes constrained by the limitations of *ch'i*. This is true of physical things as well as of human nature. People with pure or translucent *ch'i* are endowed with a natural ease for sageliness; those who have impure *ch'i* will be more attracted to evil.

The remedy for the imperfection of existence is the spiritual task of self-cultivation. Chu Hsi proposes the double effort of maintaining an attitude of reverence (*ching/jing*) towards one's own inner nature and its capacity for goodness, as well as developing knowledge about oneself and the world. This is disputed especially by his contemporary and rival thinker, Lu Chiu-yüan/Lu Jiuyuan (1139–93), as well as by Lu's spiritual heir three centuries later, Wang Yang-ming. They point out that this doctrine of cultivation makes intellectual pursuit the cornerstone of moral striving: that is, sages must be intellectuals. This implies that sagehood is inaccessible to all those who are deprived of the possibilities of intellectual development. Chu's critics prefer to emphasize the potential for greatness in each and every human being, and the power of the human mind and heart to choose good (*liang-chih/liangzhi*) and to perfect itself by practising virtues; they regard intellectual pursuits a useful but unnecessary component of cultivation. They prefer the dynamism of moral action as the expression of the whole personality, oriented to the highest good.

### *Meditation*

Clearly showing Buddhist influence, Chu Hsi gives some importance to the practice of meditation, returning to one's original nature, recapturing the source of one's being, and enabling this original equilibrium of nature and the emotions to permeate one's daily life. Such a form of meditation differs from the scripture reading that precedes much of Christian meditation and the tradition of point-by-point reflection on the gospel episodes. It also differs from the Buddhist tradition of meditation by visualization, in which the person imagines the presence of *buddhas* or *bodhisattvas*, but it is similar to the Ch'an (Zen) ideal of emptying the mind or heart of its concepts and feelings. Unlike Buddhist meditation, however, Confucian meditation concentrates more on enhancing one's moral nature and less on attaining mystical experience. Here we are referring to spirituality as well as moral doctrine. This dual concern is also in Christian (especially Catholic) theology, but is not often understood in the West by Protestants or secular philosophers.

## The Contribution of Wang Yang-ming

Wang Yang-ming (1452–1529) lived three centuries after Chu Hsi. His philosophy may be called a protest philosophy because of his criticisms of Chu Hsi and the state orthodoxy that was making use of Chu Hsi. Wang's orientation was not manipulated by the state because it was more subjective. According to Wang Yang-ming, the mind cannot be easily controlled, whereas Chu Hsi's emphasis on *li* in human nature and everything else—including classical texts—lent itself more to such control through the state examination system.

### *Wang Yang-ming on the Absolute and Human Nature*

Chu Hsi speaks of the Great Ultimate as present in both the world and the self. By contrast, Wang Yang-ming, following in the footsteps of Lu Chiu-yüan, prefers to begin with the self and speaks of ultimate reality in terms of a subjectivity that infuses all objectivity. Such an approach has been described as the school of mind (*hsin/xin*), in contrast to Chu Hsi's school of *li*, which is sometimes translated as principle.

The Chinese character for *hsin* is derived etymologically from a flame symbol. As a philosophical concept, it occurs frequently in the *Book of Mencius* and Buddhist scriptural texts, where it refers to ultimate reality. Neo-Confucian thinkers restored *hsin* to its meaning as a psychic principle, while retaining the overtones of Buddhist metaphysics. Metaphysically, Chu associated *hsin* with *ch'i*. Lu Chiu-yuan, however, identifies it with *li*, while also speaking about the mind of the sages as the moral mind or the mind of Tao.

> Sages appeared tens of thousands of generations ago. They shared this mind; they shared this *li*. Sages will appear tens of thousands of generations to come. They will share this mind; they will share this *li* (*Hsiang-shan ch'üan-shu*, ch. 22, adapted from Chan 1963:580).

## THE NEO-CONFUCIAN WANG YANG-MING

Master Wang said: The great man regards Heaven and earth and the myriad things as one body. He regards the world as one family and the country as one person. As to those who make a cleavage between objects and distinguish between the self and others, they are small men. That the great man can regard Heaven, earth and the myriad things as one body is not because he deliberately wants to do so, but because it is natural with the humane nature of his mind that he should form a unity with Heaven, earth, and the myriad things. This is true not only of the great man. Even the mind of the small man is no different ... Therefore when he sees a child about to fall into a well, he cannot help a feeling of alarm and commiseration. This shows that his humanity (*jen*) forms one body with the child (de Bary 1960:571).

As Lu's spiritual heir, Wang Yang-ming continued the process of interiorizing this metaphysical principle. For him, the mind explains the meaning of both the world and people and contains levels of profundity in meaning and presence.

> The original substance (*pen-t'i/benti*) of the mind is nothing other than the heavenly principle (*T'ien-li/Tianli*) ... It is your True Self. This True Self is the master of [your] physical body. With it, one lives; without it, one dies (*Ch'uan-hsi lu*, part 1, adapted from Chan 1967:80).

We do not find such philosophical terms as 'original substance', 'heavenly principle', or 'True Self' in Confucius or Mencius because they come from Buddhist and Taoist vocabulary. In using them, Wang Yang-ming, like Chu Hsi before him, was integrating Buddhist and Taoist insights into the Confucian tradition. For him, one must take good care of the True Self, always keeping its original substance intact. As one takes down the barricades erected by the 'false self'—the ego—that one hides behind, one clears away the selfishness that hinders the inner vision and discovers the innermost core of one's own being. This in turn will lead to the realization of perfect goodness, which is the ultimate revelation of the Absolute in the self.

There is also a very pragmatic dimension to this philosophy: making sagehood accessible to all. For Lu and Wang, Chu Hsi's emphasis on the priority of *li* and *ch'i* masks an overintellectualism and élitism, since the cultivation of *li* requires intellectual pursuit and the pursuit of knowledge. Instead, they wanted to offer a philosophy that assures the possibility of perfection to everyone, whether educated or illiterate.

## Confucianism in Korea

The Confucian influence is more evident in Korea than in Japan. Historically, Confucianism in Korea, like its counterpart in China, has been associated with education and a civil-service examination.

Confucian texts and ideas from China were introduced in Korea before the Common Era. Confucian ideas were taught in schools and practised in government even during the periods when Buddhism was more influential. Under the Silla dynasty (668–935), official examinations were instituted at the Royal Academy and became a vehicle of Confucian learning. Such influence continued during the Koryo dynasty (918–1392).

Confucianism became the ideology of Korean state and society during the Yi dynasty (1392–1910). The Four Books and Five Classics became the basis of the civil-service examination and the curriculum of the Royal Academy.

The Neo-Confucian philosophy propounded in China by Chu Hsi became dominant in the Yi era. It was called *Songni hak* ('the learning of human nature and principle'). Discussions centred on the relationship between human nature and the emotions. Indeed, this subject very much absorbed the attention of Korean thinkers, dividing them into different schools. Their divisions were reflected as well in political factions, which affected the course of politics over several centuries.

The problem that most interested—and divided—Korean philosophers concerned emotions. It is usually referred to as 'the Four and the Seven': the Four Beginnings of Virtue (*Mencius* 2A:6), namely, commiseration, shame, modesty, and moral discernment as the beginnings of the virtues of humanity, righteousness, prosperity, and wisdom; and the Seven Emotions (*Book of Rites*), namely, joy, anger, sadness, fear, love, repulsion, and desire.

Chu Hsi had discussed this matter rather generally. Chu acknowledges that the Four Beginnings of Virtue are also emotions but manifest *li*, whereas the Seven manifest *ch'i*. Korean philosophers focused their attention on this subject, devoting several centuries to debates over the distinctions—if any—between the Four and the Seven, and over whether these distinctions are actually real or arbitrary.

The best-known of these Korean philosophers was Yi Hwang, also called Yi T'oegye (1501–70). He was conservative in his strict adherence to Chu Hsi and especially devoted to Chu's dual teaching of *li* ('principle') and *ch'i* ('matter/energy'). But Yi Yi, also called Yi Yulgok (1536–84), was more independent and preferred to speak in more monistic terms concentrating on human nature. In general, Korean intellectuals were so faithful to the Chu Hsi school that the writings of his important Chinese successor Wang Yang-ming were seldom read or discussed, and a small Yang-ming school in Korea survived only as an underground current. The writings of Chong Hagok (1640–1736), a seventeenth-century Yang-ming scholar and important court official, were first published only late in the twentieth century.

In the late Yi dynasty, Korean Confucian scholars, like their counterparts in China and Japan, were confronted with the challenges of the West. While some were unable to adapt to the changing times, others issued a call for understanding Western learning. This entailed putting Neo-Confucian principles like Chu Hsi's 'investigation of things' into practice in the context of the modern world. Today, Confucianism is stronger than Taoism and even Buddhism in Korea.

## Confucianism in Japan

Confucianism provides an ethic for Japanese society, just as Shinto provides a mythology and aesthetic, while Buddhism offers a view of the afterlife. According to Japanese chronicles, Confucianism was first introduced in Japan near the end of the third century when a Korean from the southwestern realm of Paekche brought the *Analects* of Confucius to the Japanese court. Whether or not that particular date is correct, the Confucianism the Japanese learned about was clearly an already evolved form. It had been influenced by *yin-yang* and Taoist teachings.

Confucian teachings became important at the time of Prince Shōtoku (573–621), who was also a patron of Buddhism. His Seventeen-Article Constitution emphasized harmony and administrative efficiency, which reflected the Confucian cosmology of Heaven, earth, and humankind. Confucianism was further strengthened by the Taika reforms (645–6) and the introduction of a legal and administrative system modelled on that of T'ang China. Over time, Confucianism encouraged ancestor worship, spreading the practice from the aristocracy to the common people, and provided society with a system of ethics that became the basis of Japanese feudalism.

Still, Confucian teachings were not always in harmony with the Japanese way of doing things. Japanese Confucianism is more hierarchical than its Chinese counterpart, rigidly distinguishing vassal from lord, and woman from man. The result was a Japanese Confucianism suited to the society of the feudal warriors. For example, the Confucian doctrine of the Mandate of Heaven, with its implicit approval of rebellion against tyranny, seemed incongruous in Japan. It conflicted with the Japanese concept of an imperial house that commanded people's loyalty. Besides, the feudal character of traditional Japanese society, where the *samurai* were in charge, differed from the traditional Chinese society, which was dominated by the scholar gentry. Understandably, Confucian ethic in Japan especially supported *bushidō*, the ethical code of the warriors or *samurai*.

### *Neo-Confucianism in Japan*

Neo-Confucian ideas were introduced to Japan by Buddhist monks who went to China for training. Zen monks played an important role in spreading Neo-

Confucianism in Japan. The ideas of reverence (in Japanese, *kei*) and meditation (in Japanese, *seiza*) were easily assimilated by Zen adherents and well understood in a Zen context. Neo-Confucianism achieved a wider cultural influence, a kind of dominance, only when it emerged from the shadow of the Zen Buddhist umbrella. This happened mostly during the Tokugawa period.

The Tokugawa shogunate, eager to preserve order and stability, encouraged the development of Confucianism and Neo-Confucianism at the expense of Buddhism as well as Christianity. Whereas the Chinese and the Koreans were scholar-officials, the Japanese Confucians were scholar-*samurai*s. They were fighting men who always wore swords and lived in readiness for an honourable death, according to *bushidō*, which was influenced by Confucian principles.

This illustrates a principal difference between Confucianism in Japan and the same tradition in China and Korea. Of the 'five relationships', the Chinese have emphasized the parent-child relationship, thereby celebrating filial piety. On the other hand, the Japanese *samurai* have focused more on the ruler-minister relationship, with the commitment of absolute loyalty from generation to generation. In this light, we can better understand the Japanese tradition of deep respect for the emperor, and its tendency to divinize the emperor—a cult that was never found in China.

Important figures in Japanese Neo-Confucianism include Hayashi Razan (1583–1657), who turned from Zen to the study of Chu Hsi (in Japanese, Shu Shi). He found much in Chu's thought to his liking: rationalism and humanism, an ethics focused on human relationships, and an emphasis on patriotism and good government. His son shared these preferences and became a noted historian. His grandson was named head of the state university, a title that became hereditary under the Tokugawa *shōguns*. In this way, Neo-Confucianism became the official ideology for education.

Another figure was Yamazaki Ansai (1618–82), whose so-called 'southern school' popularized Chu Hsi's ethics and gave it a religious significance. He stressed reverence, purity of mind, prayer, and loyalty to the emperor.

Chu Hsi had been a philosopher and a scholar. Wang Yang-ming, the soldier-philosopher, attracted many intellectuals in Japan, all educated *samurai*. Unlike the followers of the Shushikagu (Chu Hsi school), those of the Yōmeigaku (Yang-ming school) were from lower strata among the *samurai* and tended to be less attached to the shogunate establishment and more likely to follow their individual consciences.

Among these was Nakae Tōju (1608–48), known as a religious teacher and a son who preferred devotion to his mother over service to the feudal lord. Nakae's doctrine of innate or intuitive knowledge comes directly from Wang Yang-ming, but he combined it with a strong personal theism, drawn from Shinto. He was praised as a sage (*seijin*): 'He was the Sage of Ōmi province; but is he not also the Sage of Japan, the Sage of the East, and indeed, the Sage of the entire world? For a sage is a sage in the same way in the present as in the past, in the east as in the west' (Tsunoda 1958:369).

Kumazawa Banzan (1619–91), his disciple, was a *samurai* who served in the government of Lord Ikeda of Okayama. His views on politics and economics are known especially through his dialogue on the *Great Learning*.

In the eighteenth century Ōshio Heihachiro (1793–1837), also known as Ōshio Chūsai, a Yōmeigaku scholar serving the government in Osaka as a lower-level bureaucrat, started a rebellion during a famine. The rebellion failed, but the act received symbolic attention for its defiance of the shogunate in the name of higher authority, including that of one's conscience. As Ōshio puts it:

> In face of a crisis, a hero certainly transcends considerations of fortune or disaster, life or death. But even when [the crisis is over and] the work is accomplished, he should still question [the importance of] fortune or disaster, life or death. This is the same with the gentleman whose learning has beome refined and genuine (Ching 1976:252).

The Neo-Confucian teachings of Wang Yang-ming (in Japanese, Ō Yōmei) emphasized action. Interestingly, scholars leaning towards the Yang-ming school were also influential in shaping a modern Japan. This happened after Matthew C. Perry (1794–1858), the American commodore, demanded in 1853 that Japan open up to foreign trade and commerce. Sakuma Shōzan (1811–64) and his disciple Yoshida Shōin (1830–59) called for the study of Western science and its union with Eastern ethics. Presumably, it was the protest value of Yang-ming philosophy that inspired them to stand up to the shogunate.

### *Neo-Confucianism and Shinto*

The Neo-Confucian schools in Japan, whether following Chu Hsi or Wang Yang-ming, were all influenced by Shinto. Scholars made an effort to interpret Shinto in the Neo-Confucian language of Chinese philosophers like Chu Hsi and Wang Yang-ming. This Confucian Shinto made the greatest advances in the seventeenth century during the early Tokugawa period.

Yamazaki Ansai started Suiga Shinto, a new Confucian-influenced Shinto, which offered an interesting blend of the two traditions. Yamazaki combined Confucian ethics with prayers to Shinto gods for blessings. Moreover, he equated Shinto creation legends with Chinese cosmology, and the Shinto pantheon with Neo-Confucian metaphysics. Yamazaki's fondness for Chinese sages did not dampen his love of Japan. He once said that should Confucius and Mencius lead a Chinese invasion into Japan, he himself would put on arms and fight to capture them alive, as this 'is what Confucius and Mencius teach us to do'.

The Neo-Confucians had their rivals in the school of Ancient Learning (in Japanese, Kogaku), which preferred Confucianism. Its representatives include

Yamaga Sokō (1622–85), who went back to Confucius and Mencius and is known as a founder of *bushidō*.

Another was Itō Jinsai (1627–1705), who also returned to the study of Confucius and Mencius; he took issue with Neo-Confucian metaphysics for its deviation from early Confucian teachings. He focused on *jen* (in Japanese, *jin*), which he interpreted as 'love', including in its meaning the virtues of loyalty, good faith, reverence, and forgiveness. He also emphasized the importance of philology (the study of language and texts) over philosophy in his approach to the early classics. There was also Ogyū Sorai (1666–1728), an eminent scholar of ancient Chinese texts, who turned to early Confucianism for inspiration on social ethics and political institutions. Interestingly, Kogaku or Ancient Learning scholars eventually shifted their focus from ancient China to ancient Japan. This gave rise to the National Learning school (Kokugaku), discussed under Shinto as having a strong impact on its development.

## The Status of Women

When one reassesses the relevance of Confucianism and of Neo-Confucianism to the concerns of today, certain obvious problems are not to be overlooked. In the Confucian social order, human relationships tended to become hierarchically fixed and rigid—with the superior partners—the fathers, husbands, and rulers—exercising more right and privilege than the inferior partners, who performed their duty with submission. Historically speaking, this was the combined product of Confucian philosophy, the Legalist theory of power (discussed later in the context of the modern world), and *yin-yang* philosophy with its schematic correlation of cosmic forces and human relationships.

Confucian ideology was used to consolidate the patriarchal family system and assign an increasingly subordinate role to women. The obligation of providing a male heir became women's sacred duty in order to assure the continuation of the ancestor cult. It also offered an excuse for the husband to marry secondary wives in case the principal wife was childless, or had only a daughter.

It appears that women, especially noble women, had much more freedom in Shang than in Chou times, and in Chou than in later times. In other words, the more Confucian the society became, the less freedom women enjoyed. The *Appendices to the Book of Changes*, with their *yin-yang* ideas, represent the male-female relationship in terms of the superiority of Heaven over inferior earth. The ritual texts sum up woman's place in society—which means family—in the 'Three Obediences': she is to obey her father while at home, obey her husband when married, and obey her son if widowed. Female chastity, or loyalty to one husband, was equivalent to political loyalty, or the man's commitment to one dynastic government.

Society's double standards for men and women increased in importance.

**Figure 5.2**
**INDIGENOUS CHINESE RELIGIONS**

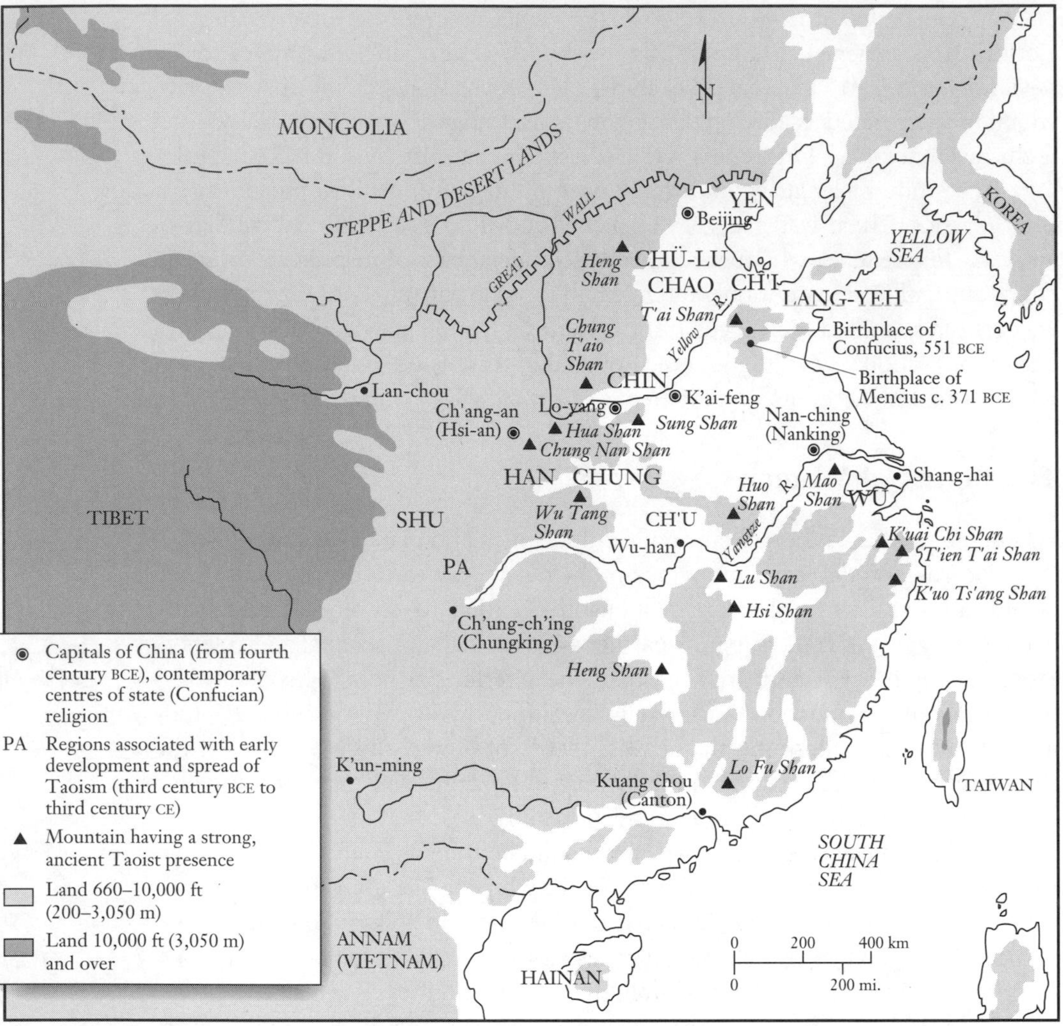


*Source:* I. al Fārūqī and D.E. Sopher, eds, *Historical Atlas of the Religions of the World* (New York: Macmillan, 1974):111.

Only in modern times, and especially with the May Fourth movement of 1919, which espoused Western ideas of science and democracy and attacked the old Confucian order for stifling individual freedom, did women begin to be liberated from some of society's harshest rules.

## TAOISM

A definition of Taoism is elusive. In his 1970 book called *What Is Taoism?* Herrlee G. Creel explains that it is foolish to try to propound a single definition of Taoism since the term denotes not one school but a series of doctrines. In fact, the word *Tao/Dao* ('the Way') is used by every school of Chinese thought.

Nor can Taoism properly be limited to doctrine. There is a doctrinal side to the tradition, philosophical Taoism, but there is also a practical side involving physical and spiritual techniques, religious Taoism. Any adequate account of the tradition must include both and sketch their interrelationships.

The English word 'Taoism' is used to refer to both Taoist philosophy (in Chinese, *Tao-chia/Daojia*) and Taoist religion (in Chinese, *Tao-chiao/Daojiao*). Taoism has also contributed much to traditional science and medicine, as well as to *ch'i-kung/qigong* or breathing techniques and martial arts. Indeed, Taoism may designate anything and everything.

Still another problem concerning definition is the secrecy surrounding Taoism. It is a philosophy of and for recluses. Its followers preferred anonymity and chose to articulate Taoist teachings in riddles. As an esoteric religion, Taoism's secrets and techniques are disclosed only to the initiated. Only recently has this shroud of secrecy been penetrated as some of the initiates have begun to publish their knowledge and expertise to share with a wider audience.

We shall discuss the philosophical aspect of Taoism first. Classical Taoist philosophy is found in two texts, *Lao-tzu* (also called *Tao-te ching*) and *Chuang-tzu*. These bear the names of their alleged authors, about whom we possess only fragmentary and uncertain information. Scholars today cannot be sure whether Lao-tzu ever lived and what his dates were if he did. However, he is still venerated as a wise man and the patriarch of the Taoist school. Similarly, in the case of Chuang-tzu, there is little that is historically verifiable about the man and the text bearing his name, which some would attribute to composite authorship.

## The Philosophy of Lao-tzu

Lao-tzu/Laozi has been cited by the philosopher Karl Jaspers as an original thinker in the company of several pre-Socratic Greek philosophers, Plotinus (c. 205–70), Nicholas of Cusa (c. 1400–64), and the second-century Indian Buddhist Nāgārjuna. Traditionally, it has been held that Lao-tzu (literally, 'old master') was an older contemporary of Confucius, to whom Confucius went for advice (sixth century BCE), but scholars tend to place him, if he was a historical person, in a later period. Among other problems, the best biography we have of him, written by in a first-century-BCE historian, is a composite life of three persons.

Here we are not even certain of the actual name of this figure, and whether his surname was Lao (Lao Tan/Lao Dan) or Li (Li Erh, Li Tan). He was allegedly a native of Ch'u, in southern China, and a court archivist for the Chou house before he retired from the civilized world that China was and went west. He supposedly left behind a small book at the border, at the request of the keeper of the

*The goal of local youths to jump up and touch Lao-tzu's nose on this sculpture is no challenge for this tall Westerner.* (W.G. Oxtoby)

pass. It contains unmistakably political statements.

This text is *Lao-tzu*/*Laozi*, also called *Tao-te ching*/*Daodejing* (Classic of the Way and Its Power). Brief but cryptic, it contains about 5,000 words, presented in parallel verses and poetic stanzas. In spite of the difficulties of dating, authorship, and interpretation, it is one of the most translated texts in the world. Some scholars prefer to treat it as a secular text, with no religious content or dimension.

However, this position is not accepted by all. After all, religion means many things, and *Lao-tzu* offers a vision that we may call religious. It asks for humans to return to nature and reconcile themselves with it. This vision has also been described as salvific, and the word 'sage' in the text, usually referring to the sage ruler, has even been translated as 'saint' with all the religious connotations of the term because, as J.J.L. Duyvendak (1889–1955) says, 'it gives more emphasis to the magical power, which is proper to a saint' (Duyvendak 1954:24).

The concept of the Tao gives the school its name, Taoism. The text *Lao-tzu* begins with the famous line: The Way (Tao) that can be spoken of is not the constant Way (Tao).' Here is a double play of words, since the term *tao* is also a verb, 'to speak'. It is really saying: 'The Tao that can be articulated (*tao*-ed), is not the constant Tao.' And also:

> There is a thing confusedly formed,
> Born before heaven and earth.
> Silent and void
> It stands alone and does not change,
> Goes round and does not weary.
> (Lau 1963:82)

Here, the Tao is described as existing before the universe came to be, an unchanging first principle, even the ancestor of all things, by which all things come to be. This appears to be a philosophical attempt to conceptualize an earlier religious belief. In the Confucian classics, the Lord-on-high has been a supreme deity, while Heaven has sometimes been given a creator's or at least a great ancestor's role, as that which gives birth to all things. The term 'Heaven' did not completely disappear from Taoist philosophical writings, appearing especially in *Chuang-tzu* alongside the term 'Tao', but 'Tao' has obviously replaced 'Heaven' in *Lao-tzu*, as the natural Way as well as the human way, even the political way. Even though the Tao is no longer a personal deity, it still remains a model for human behaviour.

The classic also refers to the Tao as the mother of all things, and shows preference for images of the weak (water, valley, emptiness, etc.) over their opposites. Even more explicitly, it says,

> Know the male,
> But keep to the role of the female
> And be a ravine to the empire.
> (Lau 1963:85)

Such contemplation of the universe leads to the discovery of the nameless first principle and the disposition that should accompany such contemplation and also the whole of life. This is expressed by the term *wu-wei*, literally, non-action. It does not signify the absence of action but rather acting without artificiality, without overaction, without attachment to action. This is the practical part of *Lao-tzu*, the *way* of living according to the Way. This is the power of the natural, the simple, even the weak. It teaches the lesson of survival, of keeping one's own integrity in a time of disorder. This is the most important practical lesson of Taoist philosophy, which has had immense importance in the development of Taoist religion.

The text suggests a measure of asceticism, of withdrawal from the world and its pleasures, even its cherished values. For the person seeking the knowledge of the Tao, the senses and passions are in need of purification or moderation. After all,

> The five colours blind man's eyes.
> The five notes deafen his ears.
> The five tastes deaden his palate.
> Riding and hunting make his mind go wild.
> (adapted from Lau 1963:68)

Civilization marks a departure from the Tao. The virtues preached by the

Confucians, such as benevolence (humanity) and righteousness, are also relativized. Instead, we are to follow nature. If we are to employ *yin-yang* classifications, we may associate Confucianism and its emphasis on action with the *yang* force, and Taoism and its preference for peace and quiet with the *yin* force. Many interpreters have drawn this contrast. Taoism as a philosophy and religion gives women a higher status than does Confucianism. The claim is supported by an examination of passages in *Lao-tzu* that admire or give privilege to *yin*.

*Lao-tzu* also offers controversial political teachings, ostensibly to the ruler. The work appears to advocate a small pacifist, village state. There the sage-ruler seeks to undo the cause of troubles that result from too many prohibitions, prescriptions, and philosophical contentions, especially the ethical teachings of Confucianism. By practising non-action, he keeps the people healthy yet ignorant, protecting them from the excesses of knowledge. If this sounds like a 'back to nature' romanticism, it has also given rise to political authoritarianism.

In 1973, archaeological discoveries confirmed the greater political importance of the text *Lao-tzu* in early history. At the site Mawangdui, near today's Changsha (Hunan), archaeologists unearthed two manuscript recensions of the oldest extant text of the *Tao-te ching*, handwritten on silk and dating back to the second century BCE. Unlike the text to which we have become accustomed, it places Part Two (more concerned with *te*, the power by which the universal Tao becomes particular) before Part One (more theoretically concerned with the Tao). In other words, it gives greater priority to the specific applications of the Tao in politics. This version from the Han dynasty, while very useful to the scholarly world, is not regarded as the original text, which is presumed to have the same order of Tao before *te* that we have been accustomed to. Scholars now associate the use of the Han text with an early esoteric school, the Huang-Lao school. They trace the text back to the fourth- and third-century-BCE Warring States period, which preceded the Han.

## The Philosophy of Chuang-tzu

Chuang-tzu/Zhuangzi was a contemporary of Mencius and a native of Meng. Scholars are not certain where Meng was; some would place it in Honan, south of the Yellow River, possibly in the former feudal state of Sung given by Chou to the descendants of the Shang kings. But then, scholars are not sure of any of the other information, such as the dates, allegedly concerning Chuang-tzu. It is often speculated that Chuang-tzu, like Lao-tzu, came from a different part of China than Confucius and Mencius, and that this explains why their perspectives were different from those of the classical Confucian thinkers. Usually the Confucian thinkers are regarded as northerners, more rationalistic and systematic, whereas the classical Taoist thinkers are regarded as southerners, who are quite nonconformist and prefer imagination and fantasy to strict reason and moderation.

As in the *Lao-tzu*, the central concept here is of the Tao as the principle underlying and governing the universe. On the other hand, the work shows a hermit's distaste for politics. The *Chuang-tzu* is ascribed to a thinker presumably of the fourth or third century BCE and resembles a collection of essays. It makes abundant use of parable and allegory, as well as paradox and fanciful imagery. It makes an ardent plea for spiritual freedom: not merely the freedom of the individual from social conventions and restraints but rather a self-transcending liberation from the limitations of one's own mind—from one's self-interested inclinations and prejudices. According to *Chuang-tzu*, such freedom can only be achieved in embracing nature itself, in the Tao.

### *Chuang-tzu's Mysticism*

Both Lao-tzu and Chuang-tzu have been termed mystics. Whereas the text *Lao-tzu* was addressed to rulers and contains political teachings, the text *Chuang-tzu* is quite different. It defines true happiness as a mystical union with nature that presupposes withdrawal from politics and society. It speaks of a blissful trance state like mysticism described in Christianity. In the Taoist case, more meditative techniques have been developed, and the trances are usually described as self-induced.

*Chuang-tzu* teaches that absolute happiness comes with transcending the distinctions between one's self and the universe by uniting perfectly with the Tao. This involves a higher level of knowledge, the knowledge of wisdom, which goes beyond the distinctions among things, including that between life and death. This may be called mystical knowledge, since it is unitive and not acquired by ordinary rational means. Indeed, it comes only with 'forgetting' the knowledge of all things—especially that of the self. There is mention in the text of 'sitting and forgetting' (*tso-wang/zuowang*), as well as of a 'fasting of the mind', which is different from the fasting of the body. This requires emptying the senses and the mind itself: 'Let your ears and your eyes communicate with what is inside ... Then even gods and spirits will come to dwell' (Watson 1968:58).

*Chuang-tzu* even attributes words to Confucius to give expression to Taoist teachings and ideals. The practice of 'sitting and forgetting' as well as the 'fasting of the mind' are thus explained in an imaginary conversation between Confucius and his favourite disciple, Yen Hui:

> [Yen Hui said:] 'May I ask what the fasting of the mind is?'
>
> Confucius said: 'Make your will one! Don't listen with your ears, listen with your mind. No, don't listen with your mind, but listen with your spirit. Listening stops with the ears, the mind stops with recognition, but spirit is empty and waits on all things. The Way gathers in emptiness alone. Emptiness is the fasting of the mind' (Watson 1968:57–8).

### Taoism: Reality and Illusion

Once Chuang [Tzu] dreamt he was a butterfly flitting and fluttering around, happy with himself and doing as he pleased. He didn't know he was Chuang [Tzu]. Suddenly he woke up and there he was Chuang ... But he didn't know if he was Chuang ... who had dreamt that he was a butterfly, or a butterfly dreaming he was Chuang ... Between Chuang ... and a butterfly there must be *some* distinction! This is called the transformation of things (Watson 1968:49).

Like mysticism everywhere, the experience takes one beyond discursive knowledge and even beyond distinctions of good and evil. On another occasion, Yen Hui and Confucius have the following conversation:

> Yen Hui said, 'I'm improving!'
> Confucius said, 'What do you mean by that?'
> 'I've forgotten benevolence and righteousness.'
> 'That's good. But you still haven't got it.'
> Another day, the two met again and Yen Hui said, 'I'm improving!'
> 'What do you mean by that?'
> 'I've forgotten rites and music!'
> 'That's good. But you still haven't got it!'
> Another day, the two met again and Yen Hui said, 'I'm improving!'
> 'What do you mean by that?'
> 'I can sit down and forget everything!'
> Confucius looked very startled and said, 'What do you mean, sit down and forget everything?'
> Yen Hui said, 'I smash up my limbs and body, drive out perception and intellect, cast off form, do away with understanding, and make myself identical with the Great Thoroughfare. This is what I mean by sitting down and forgetting everything.'
> Confucius said, '...So you really are a worthy man after all! With your permission, I'd like to become your follower' (Watson 1968:90–1).

When one lives according to nature, one must respect its laws, including the inevitability of death. But a superior wisdom frees the sage from the emotional vicissitudes of life and the world. He has not lost his feelings, but he has risen above them. His acceptance of the natural enables him to regard life and death with equanimity and frees him from the desire to prolong life. On the other hand, some passages in *Chuang-tzu*—in particular the lyrical descriptions of the Perfect

### TAOISM: THE PRICE OF FREEDOM

Once when Chuang Tzu was fishing in the P'u River, the king of Ch'u sent two ministers to go and announce to him: 'I would like to trouble you with the administration of my realm.'

Chuang Tzu held on to his fishing pole and, without turning his head, said: 'I have heard that there is a sacred tortoise in Ch'u that has been dead for three thousand years. The king keeps it wrapped in cloth and boxed, and stores it in the ancestral temple. Now would this tortoise rather be dead and have its bones left behind and honored? Or would it rather be alive and dragging its tail in the mud?'

'It would rather be alive and dragging its tail in the mud,' said the two officials.

Chuang Tzu said, 'Go away! I'll drag my tail in the mud' (Watson 1968: 187–8)!

Man who has become 'immortal'—may be interpreted to suggest that conquering death and helping others to overcome sickness are not undesirable goals.

Yet another dimension in *Chuang tzu* goes beyond the self-effacing and quietist connotations of 'nature' mysticism. There are passages that evoke the memory of more ancient customs, involving ecstasy and shamanism. These 'shamanic' passages include the lyrical description of the holy or Perfect Man, who has also been called an immortal.

> There is a Holy Man living on the distant Ku-she Mountain, with skin like ice or snow … He does not eat the five grains, but sucks the wind, drinks the dew, mounts the clouds and mist, rides a flying dragon, and wanders beyond the four seas. By concentrating his spirit, he can protect creatures from sickness and plague and make the harvest plentiful (Watson 1968:33).

This could very well refer to a shaman of traditional antiquity, his dietary habits, his shamanic 'flights', and his healing and other magical powers. From these lines, it would seem that the shamanic tradition has become peripheral to the society in which it had once flourished, while acquiring in the meantime the kind of prestige that comes from being a rarity.

## The Faces of Neo-Taoism

The legacy of Taoist philosophy is interesting if ambiguous. This may be discerned if we look at the commentaries on *Lao-tzu* and *Chuang-tzu*. Indeed, few books have received as much attention as these two. Like the Confucian classics, each has attracted a tradition of commentaries, some of which are very important,

## SEEKING LONGEVITY AND IMMORTALITY

In the fourth-century *Shenxian zhuan* (Biographies of Immortals), recounted the legend of Wei Boyang. Allegedly, he had made an elixir in the mountains, and decided to try it first on his dog, which died instantly. He turned then to his disciples, and said, 'I have abandoned worldly ways and forsaken family and friends ... I should be ashamed to return without having found the Dao of the Immortals. To die of the elixir is no worse than living without having found it.' And so he, too, took the elixir and fell dead. On seeing this, one disciple commented, 'Our teacher is no ordinary person. He must have done this with some reason.' So he followed the master's example, and also died. The other two disciples said to each other, 'People prepare elixirs for the sake of gaining longevity. But this elixir has brought on death. It would be better not to take it, but live a few more decades in the world.' So they left the mountains to procure coffins for the burial of their master and fellow disciple. After they were gone, however, both Wei Boyang and the loyal disciple, together with their dog, revived, became real immortals, and went away! They left behind a message for the other two, who were then filled with remorse (*Shenxian zhuan* [Biographies of Immortals], fourteenth century).

not only for understanding the original text but also for what the commentators themselves have to say. After all, recalling the example of Confucius, we can assert that a great deal can be said by creative thinkers who attribute their ideas to the ancients. There are also important questions asked about the original texts. For example, is *Chuang-tzu*'s Tao the same as *Lao-tzu*'s? The answers can be diametrically opposite, depending on which chapters one focuses on and whether one agrees or disagrees with some of the chief commentators.

When we speak of 'Neo-Taoism', we are dealing with a period in which Taoism was transformed during the third to sixth centuries. That was when the country was politically divided and in turmoil after the order imposed by the Han dynasty had collapsed, especially at the hands of invading barbarians. Ideas associated with the Taoist tradition were a force in and an expression of the general unrest. Taoism, after all, had protest value, just as *Lao-tzu* and *Chuang-tzu* both criticized Confucius. If rulers in that period made use of Taoist tenets in their government, ordinary people also appealed to Taoist ideas in revolts and rebellions. This has remained the case, so much so that even in our own time the Taoist religion in Taiwan has been associated with the movement for an independent Taiwan.

Neo-Taoism was a multifaceted movement. It has a 'rationalist' side, with exegesis and philosophical discussions, and an 'aesthetic' side, with poetry and art. It was also an iconoclastic movement, resembling in some ways the antinomian spirit of modern off-campus hippies or on-campus student protesters in the 1960s. Respect for authority, including the centrality of the Five Relationships, was collapsing. Children were calling their parents by their personal names, while poets and philosophers found solace in drink and unstructured conversation. We can discern rationalist, sentimentalist, and iconoclastic aspects in the philosophical positions that Taoist writers attempted to draw out of the earlier texts.

## A Protest Movement

Neo-Taoism was a protest movement in a world of disunity and chaos. The commentator Wang Pi/Wang Bi (226–49) had iconoclastic attitudes towards the social authority of the past, even if he based his arguments on an ancient text. Others included Hsiang Hsiu and Hsi K'ang/Xi Kang (223–62), who belonged to a group called the Seven Worthies of the Bamboo Grove. Many of these were opposed to what is called *ming-chiao/mingjiao* (literally, 'names and doctrines', referring to the intellectual establishment, while also reviving interest in an ancient school of logic, *ming-chia/mingjia*. Theirs was a kind of Taoist-influenced Confucianism that permitted its followers to enter public service. Their view reinterpreted Confucius as a sage united with the Tao—even giving him a place higher than Lao-tzu.

There is a chapter entitled 'Yang Chu' in the text *Lieh-tzu/Liezi*, which is attributed to a fifth-century-BCE Taoist. It uses Yang Chu/Yang Zhu, who was denounced by Mencius as an egoist, to give voice to a pessimistic view of life and an approval of hedonism: 'Whether one lives for ten years or for a hundred, and whether one is a benevolent sage or a stupid criminal, everyone dies ... Let us enjoy this life. Why be concerned about the hereafter' (de Bary 1960:291)? *Lieh-tzu* voices fatalism and scepticism, especially regarding the existence of a higher power. In it, the Taoist idea of *wu-wei,* non-action, degenerates into 'doing nothing' and living according to one's impulse, certainly the direct opposite of Lao-tzu's teachings.

The Seven Worthies of the Bamboo Grove were known for their non-conformist behaviour. One of them, Liu Ling, preferred to remain naked in his house. When visitors found this strange, his response was: 'I take heaven and earth for my pillars and roof, and the rooms of my house for my pants and coat. What are you gentlemen doing in my pants?' (Mather 1976:374). Juan Chi/Ruan Ji (210–63) and his nephew Juan Hsien/Ruan Xian were great drinkers and used to sit around a large container and drink from it. Sometimes the pigs also shared their drinks.

These are examples of what one might term a romantic spontaneity, expressed by the term *feng-liu* ('wind and stream'). In traditional China, this term means an aesthetic attitude towards life and the universe. Taoist philosophy has had a profound influence on many aspects of culture, inspiring creativity in art and poetry and a fascination with the grotesque. Taoists in particular had a penchant for gnarled trees and odd-shaped rocks. This focus greatly influenced East Asian Buddhist gardens, notably those of Zen. Taoist emphasis on insightful awareness no doubt contributed to the domestication in China of ideas drawn from Indian Buddhism.

## Taoist Religious Practices

The Taoist religion originated in early times—indeed, in the era of oracle bones and divination. However, this does not mean that Taoism is identical to ancient religion, but it does highlight the difference between Taoist activity and the philosophical Taoism of *Lao-tzu* and *Chuang-tzu*. In those writings, the ancient religion was partially eclipsed by a process of philosophical rationalization and speculation.

Although the Taoist religion that developed after these philosophical texts revered Lao-tzu (both the man and the text), it radically reinterpreted his teachings as well as those of *Chuang-tzu*. Philosophical Taoism is only one of several intellectual strands that converged in religious Taoism. There are also ideas from the Yin-Yang school, which regards the natural order as under two complementary yet antithetical aspects of the Tao. There is also a discernible influence of the Five Agents school, which pursued proto-scientific theories and experiments.

In early Han times, Taoism was known as the cult of the Yellow Emperor and Lao-tzu, i.e., Huang-Lao. In ascribing its teachings to these earlier figures, its proponents did what so many others in religion, including Confucius, have done: they attributed authority to the distant past. As religious Taoism developed, it exhibited characteristics we associate with religions of salvation. It instructs its faithful in healthy living, and also seeks to guide its believers beyond this transitory life to a happy eternity. It professes a belief in an original state of bliss, followed by the present human condition, that is, the fallen state. It relies on supernatural powers for help and protection. Some of these features might, of course, represent Buddhist influence in Han times and later.

## The Heavenly Masters Sect

Often the formal beginning of the Taoist religion as an institution is identified with the founding of the Heavenly Masters sect. In later Han times (second century), a significant religious movement developed in Szechwan under Chang Ling (also called Chang Tao-ling/Zhang Daoling, 34?–156?). He claimed that Lao-tzu appeared to him in a mountain cave in 142, complaining of the world's lack of respect for the true and the correct, and of people's worshipping pernicious demons. In this alleged revelation, Chang was made the Heavenly Master and told to abolish the influence of the demons and install true orthodoxy.

The new sect opposed the bloody sacrifices that were offered to the spirits of the deceased at that time, and substituted offerings of cooked vegetables. To heal sicknesses, it instituted the confession of sins in secluded rooms, where the priests prayed for the sick, who wrote down their sins. These documents were then offered to heaven (on mountain tops), to earth (by burial) and to the rivers (by 'drowning'). The sect levied and collected a tax of five pecks (about 35 kg) of rice from the members of its congregation. For this reason, it was called the Five Pecks of Rice sect.

Later, the Heavenly Masters became a hereditary institution. The sect eventually moved its traditional base from Szechwan to the Dragon-Tiger Mountain of Kiangsi. It has been especially popular in southern China, and has continued to the present. After the communist takeover in 1949, its headquarters were moved to Taiwan. Interestingly, the Heavenly Masters sect includes women in its clergy, but excludes them from certain rituals such as the rite of cosmic renewal and from higher office. It has always been known for its good organization: there are hereditary instructors, assisted by parish councils of Taoist notables, including men and women who take part in various ceremonies, and there are secular patrons of the organization as well. The Heavenly Masters sect was only one of many Taoist sects that eventually developed. We shall discuss another, the Perfect Truth sect, later in this chapter.

## The Taoist Pantheon

Taoism can be called a 'salvation' religion. Salvation implies a 'fallen' state, from which one is to become 'whole' again, or healed. This comes about with the help of a saviour or healer, or, in the case of some non-Western religions, through one's own effort. True, the quest for physical immortality may seem rather earthly, yet the wish for immortality contains within itself a quest for transcendence. To become godlike—powerful like the gods, or immortal like the gods—has always been the deepest of human longings. In this perspective, the Taoist religion echoes the Latin phrase *eritis sicut Deus,* 'you shall be like God'. In its quest for wholeness, religious Taoism tends to associate human weakness and sickness with sin. Taoists consider such ills an offence against both the conscience and the deity, and associate their healing with the confession of sin and the forgiveness and help of higher powers.

Taoism evolved a pantheon of innumerable spiritual beings, gods, or celestials and immortals, as well as deified heroes and forces of nature. They make up a divine hierarchy, resembling in its functions a state bureaucracy. The hierarchy includes mythical figures, as well as many who were divinized human beings, under the supremacy of the highest deity. During the second century BCE, this was the T'ai-yi/Taiyi ('Great One').

A triad of gods came to be worshipped, and assumed different names in different periods. In early Han times, these three gods were known as the T'ien-yi/Tianyi ('Heavenly One'), the Ti-yi/Diyi ('Earthly One'), and the T'ai-yi ('Great One'). They are sometimes interpreted as the supreme deity (a direct emanation of the Tao itself), his disciple, the Lord Tao (the Tao personified), and *his* disciple, the Lord Lao (Lao-tzu deified). Lao-tzu appears as the third in a hierarchy of gods, and the cult honouring him is very old. Many believe that he revealed all the principal texts in the Taoist canon.

Later, the Taoist trinity received other names, such as the 'Three Pure Ones' (San-ch'ing/Sanqing), who were the lords of the Three Life Principles or 'Breaths' (*ch'i*). Their names were the Primal Celestial One (Yüan-shih t'ien-tsun/Yuanshi tianzun), the Precious Celestial One (Ling-pao t'ien-tsun/Lingbao tianzun), and the Way-and-Its-Power Celestial One (Tao-te t'ien-tsun/Daode tianzun). They each represented some aspect of the ineffable Tao, transcendent and yet capable of becoming 'incarnate', especially through Lao-tzu's revelation. More recently, the supreme deity has been called the Jade Emperor, or, in today's Taiwan, T'ien-kung/Tiangong (colloquial for Lord Heaven).

Has there been any Western influence on the Taoist trinity? A Gnostic connection has been suggested, but the ancient origin (second century BCE) of the Taoist trinity makes this hypothesis questionable. The Taoist trinity was well established by T'ang times. Nestorian Christianity was also active and well known in China at that time. There was contact and interaction between the two religions, and it is no surprise that the Taoist trinity is compared by some scholars to the Christian trinity: the Primal Celestial One, controlling the past, to God the Father; the Precious Celestial One, controlling the present, to God the Son, and the Way-and-Its-Power Celestial One, controlling the future, to God the Holy Spirit.

Taoism places importance on a messiah figure, especially in the *T'ai-p'ing ching/Taiping jing* (Classic of the Great Peace), which looks forward to a future epoch of Great Peace. In an incomplete and partially restored version from the seventh century, it is sometimes regarded as the most important text in religious Taoism after the *Lao-tzu*. It offers a doctrine of salvation, with a saviour or divine man who possesses a celestial book.

The book's teaching calls for a return to ideal government while awaiting the arrival of the Great Peace. The divine man has the mandate of passing the revealed words on to the 'true man' (*chen-jen*), a prophet figure who is to transmit the texts to a ruler of high virtue. This prince is to rule by the Tao and its power. Specifically, he is to govern with the help of his ministers and the people at large, careful to maintain harmony within the realm but slow to exercise coercion or punishment.

Perhaps this text originated with those individuals who attempted to influence the ruler in the direction of reform during the Han dynasty. Their lack of success then led to the widespread Yellow Turbans revolt (184–215), which involved hundreds of thousands of Taoists wearing yellow kerchiefs. The revolt failed, but Taoist messianism became the inspiration for successive movements of political protest, organized by secret societies throughout history. This is one reason why the religion has been regarded with suspicion by the various governments even until today. It has been severely persecuted in communist China and carefully supervised in Taiwan.

## Rituals and Priests

Rituals and liturgical expressions have always been the soul of the Taoist religion. It involves a complex system that includes a quasi-sacramental regard for ritual initiation, for purification and renewal in the life cycle, and for development of the human being. Already under development in Han times, Taoist liturgy was further transformed with the emergence in the later fourth century of the cult in Mao-shan (Kiangsu).

In this setting the early collection of ecstatic scriptural texts, which contain visions and inspired writings, was influenced by Buddhist literature. New hymns were introduced, together with Buddhist customs like circumambulation and the chanting of sacred texts called *ling-pao/lingbao* ('sacred treasures'). This literature gives assurances of salvation to the initiated at the time of expected cataclysms. There is also the expression of eschatological hopes: Lao-tzu's new advent is to establish a reign of peace and equality for the elect, the very 'pure'.

Taoist priests are licensed to perform particular rituals. Since the Sung dynasty, the authorization to perform these rituals has usually come from the Heavenly Master and is made after an examination of the individual's ritual knowledge. Exorcism rituals are often carried out in cases of sickness, with the exorcist struggling for a victory over the evil spirits. Many other rituals are regularly performed throughout the lunar year and its festivals. The best-known ones take place around the lunar New Year, with dragon dances and firecrackers to chase away the demons, and prayers to the stove god—a very important Taoist deity who was known in ancient religion. There is also the rite of cosmic renewal, celebrated at the winter solstice, symbolizing the cosmic rebirth in the sun's return. Some of the priests who lead the rituals and say the prayers are also shamans, soothsayers, or spirit-mediums. They assist the faithful with their counsels and fortune-telling, explain the influence of the stars, and communicate with the spirits of the beloved dead.

Incense and the sacrificial offering of sacred writings, such as the burning of paper talismans, are central to Taoist ritual. Sometimes the papers sacrificed bear the prayers of the faithful, giving their names and the intentions for which the service is being performed. While the religious leaders' ritual expertise is important, the faithful who participate in such rituals are usually urged to prepare for them by fasting and developing a spirit of forgiveness and reconciliation.

## The Taoist Canon

Taoism claims a vast number of texts as having scriptural value. Drawing teachings from various sources, the Taoist tradition accumulated a huge body of scriptures called the *Tao-tsang/Daozang* ('Taoist canon'). This collection eventually included over 1,000 volumes compiled over fifteen centuries. Because of its size, it is consulted rather than read in its entirety. Western scholars often refer to it as a 'canon' because it is a collection in which the tradition finds normative authority.

Interestingly, if we search Taoist writings for 'scripture', our scope could widen to what may be the world's largest body of such texts, the *Tao-tsang*, or, on the other hand, narrow to one of the shortest texts tucked away in it, the *Tao-te ching*. Taoists allege that the principal books in the canon are divine revelations made to Taoist adepts when they were in a trance. None bears the name of the author or the date of composition. Many are written in a coded, esoteric language that can only be understood by the initiated. Philosophical treatises like *Lao-tzu* and *Chuang-tzu* have been incorporated into the Taoist canon and given distinctive interpretations. The *Book of Changes*, which is both a Confucian classic and a divination manual, is also part of this canon.

The structure of the Taoist canon, which comes from the fifth century, sheds light on its sectarian character. There are seven sections, placed under the tripartite division of the so-called Three Caverns, each of which originally developed around a particular scripture or group of scriptures:

The Three Caverns:

(Each is divided into twelve subsections):

- The First Cavern (Tung-chen/Dongzhen) has as its nucleus the Shang-ch'ing scriptures, surrounding a liturgical poem with secret names of gods and spirits. It is associated with the Mao-shan movement, which originated near Nanking in southern China.
- The second (Tung-hsüan/Dongxuan) has as its nucleus the Ling-pao/Lingbao scriptures, which also originated in the south. With talismans and added texts, these show a strong Buddhist influence and have been associated with the Ling-pao sect.
- The third (Tung-shen/Dongshen) has as its nucleus the San-huang ('Three Sovereigns') scriptures. Their origins are less clear; they might have come from the Taoist masters who served at court. At their core they contain tal-

ismans and ancillary exorcism texts. These have been connected with the Heavenly Masters sect.

The Four Supplements:

- The T'ai-hsüan/Taixuan is a supplement to the First Cavern. Its central text is actually *Lao-tzu* itself (which shows the curiously subordinate place of this treatise).
- The T'ai-p'ing/Taiping is a supplement to the Second Cavern. Its central text is the well-known *T'ai-p'ing ching* (Classic of the Great Peace), a utopian and messianic text.
- The T'ai-ch'ing/Taiqing is a supplement to the Third Cavern. Its central texts deal more directly with alchemy.
- The Cheng-i/Zhengyi is a supplement to all three. Its texts are made up of the canonical texts of the Heavenly Masters sect.

We think the term 'cavern' (*tung/dong*) is used because of the claim that the principal texts were allegedly revealed to or discovered by hermits in caves. Each of the Three Caverns is placed under the protection of one of the three members of the Taoist trinity. Indeed, all the central texts in the Supplements are older than the Three Caverns texts. The Four Supplements were perhaps added to the Three Caverns in a reform movement that resisted Buddhist influences on Taoism.

## The Search for Immortality

Religions are usually concerned with life after death, and this is true of Taoism, but Taoists do not conceive of eternal life only in terms of spiritual immortality. Because they look forward to the survival of the whole person, including the body, we can say that there is no strict separation of spirit and matter in their thought. This is the authentically Chinese core of the Taoist religion.

Taoists have also developed the doctrine of the three life principles: breath (*ch'i*), vital essence or semen (*ching/jing*), and spirit (*shen*). Each of these principles has two dimensions: they are present in the human being as a microcosm and at the same time in the cosmos as a macrocosm. The Taoist trinity is not only a pantheon of deities but is also represented as a manifestation of these cosmic principles.

Taoist techniques have been developed for healing and breath circulation, meditation, and sexual hygiene (a blending of sex and yoga). Much of this teaching is transmitted in secret from master to disciple, like Tibetan and Mongolian tantric Buddhism. These teachings gave rise to Chinese healing techniques and the martial arts, as well as herbal medicine. This is a truly holistic healing system, based on an age-old text, the *Inner Classic of the Yellow Emperor* (*Huang-ti Nei-ching*), which goes back to the sixth century BCE. It gives a clear list of priorities for maintaining health: first treatment of the spirit, then proper nutrition, and finally healing.

China's belief in immortals is an ancient one, going back at least to the third century BCE. It was elaborated after Taoism became an institutional religion. 'Heavenly immortals' are said to roam the sacred forests and mountains. There are also some human beings who appear to die, but actually only leave behind their physical frames (*shih-chieh*). The search for immortality continues. It is interesting to note that the beginning of modern China's Cultural Revolution in 1966 was marked by Mao Zedong's displeasure with a play that he believed contained a criticism of his desire to live forever. I refer to Wu Han's (1909–69) historical drama, *Hai-jui pa-kuan/Hairui baguan*, in which a Ming official tries to deter the emperor from favouring alchemists and elixirs, and loses his official position for doing so.

The Taoist belief that men and women could become immortal led to the practice of alchemical experiments like transmuting cinnabar (mercuric sulphide). This is mentioned in early treatises, such as the *Ts'an-t'ung-ch'i* of Wei Po-yang (second century) and the *Pao-p'u-tzu*, written by Ko Hung (c. 250–330). Taoists have described this effort as the attempt to 'steal the secret of heaven and earth', that is, to wrest from nature the mystery of life. They might not have found the elixir of immortality, but, like the medieval European alchemists, they became pioneers of scientific experimentation. Their attention to physiology as well as to chemistry and pharmacology has led to many contributions in several fields, including Chinese medicine.

In fact, alchemical information and experimentation contributed to the preservation of the physical body. Metallic components like mercury and lead can be fatal when swallowed, but they also have preservative powers. Well-preserved bodies from Ming times and earlier have been discovered with perfumed mercury in their abdomens. Perhaps Chinese aristocrats swallowed mercury to ensure that their physical bodies would be preserved, so that their 'souls' and bodies would eventually attain immortality together.

In 1972 in Mawangdui, near Changsha, Hunan, archaeologists discovered the well-preserved body of an approximately fifty-year-old noblewoman from the second century BCE. The body, whose condition was like that of someone dead only a week or two, had been immersed in a liquid containing mercuric sulphide. Might it be that she had died of elixir poisoning in an effort to gain immortality? Together with the body, archaeologists also found various talismans designed to conduct the deceased to her eternal destination after burial, into the presence of the Lord-on-high. Such finds are important for reconstructing the beliefs of the time.

## Taoist Meditation and Inner Alchemy

Taoist meditation also involved experiments with one's self, including the body.

One could regard the body as a kind of 'furnace' in which to make the elixir of immortality. This was possibly the natural development when Taoists realized the physiological dangers associated with ingesting a chemical or 'outer' elixir and failed to find the ultimate pill or potion for immortality. The techniques of 'inner' alchemy are the methods associated with Taoist yoga and meditation, which were developed during T'ang and Sung times. The theory behind inner alchemy is nourishing the *yin* and the *yang* of the human body, uniting the two in an effort to recover the primordial energy (*ch'i*) that permeates and sustains all life.

In theory, the human body is divided into three 'cinnabar fields': head, chest, and abdomen. (The terminology associates inner alchemy with the function of mercuric sulphide in outer alchemy.) Each field is inhabited by a large number of gods, but under the supervision of a member of the Taoist trinity. Methods of meditation include visualizing light, which represents energy or *ch'i*, and conducting it through the three cinnabar fields in a 'microcosmic orbit' or extending this circulation to the extremities of the limbs in a 'macrocosmic orbit'.

By doing *ch'i-kung* exercises and meditating, the Taoist practitioner seeks a vision of the gods—there are thousands of them—and a visit with them within the body. Through such contact, the Taoist may obtain their help in curing sicknesses by ridding the body of toxins or 'evil spirits'. One might even acquire an inner elixir through spiritual illumination and produce an ethereal and immortal body within oneself. These are traditional practices that are similar to exercises taught today.

'Embryonic respiration' was an advanced stage of Taoist practice involving complex techniques that consciously imitate the life of the foetus in the mother's womb. It also involved the quest for inner peace and the integration of the personality. Taoists speak of finding the 'True Self' within and achieving greater harmony with the rhythm of the external cosmos. This 'True Self' is often envisaged in terms of a new birth within.

Taoists incorporate ethical behaviour into their practices. They speak of the need for a moral life of good works and ritual penance for wrongdoing. Such an ethical dimension shows the historical interaction between Taoism and Confucianism. Buddhist influence resulted in more advanced doctrines of spirituality as well as meditative exercises.

## Monasticism: The Perfect Truth Sect

The Taoist religion produced many sects and subsects. However, sectarian differences were not doctrinal but practical. The sects and subsects placed varying emphases on outer and inner alchemy, sexual hygiene, and meditative exercises. For example, the Ling-pao tradition gave special attention to rituals at court, while the Mao-shan tradition is better known for its meditative preferences. While the Taoist canon represents the union of these groups in one large eclectic tradition, sectarian distinctions on the basis of style and performance of rituals have persisted until today.

Taoism has steadily declined since the seventeenth century. The two sects that have survived are the southern school, represented by the Heavenly Masters sect (sometimes called the Cheng-i), and the northern school, known as the Perfect Truth (Ch'üan-chen/Quanzhen) sect, which developed during the Yüan (Mongol) dynasty of 1269–1378.

The Perfect Truth sect shows the greatest Buddhist influence. Its monks are required to practise frequent fasts, abstain from alcohol, and pursue the techniques of inner alchemy and meditation. The Heavenly Masters sect has maintained a married and often hereditary priesthood and few food taboos. It is active in the use of charms and talismans, while other sects are more concerned with personal cultivation (including the cultivation of longevity) and the more difficult exercises of healing and exorcism.

## Korean Taoism

Taoism has been practised in Korea since the seventh century. It has been influenced by the popular practice of ancient Chinese religion. It also resembles in many ways, and has interacted with, the indigenous folk religions of Korea and Japan, which are dominated by shamanistic beliefs and practices.

Together with Confucianism and Buddhism, Taoism constituted one leg of the 'tripod' of religions in Korea. Even during the fourteenth-century unification of Korea under the Yi dynasty, which preferred Confucianism, Taoism suffered less than Buddhism did. Its followers, particularly the common people, continued to worship Taoist deities. Korean Taoism is basically of the Heavenly Masters sect, with a married clergy. Because of its amalgamation with popular shamanism, described earlier, Taoism has continued in Korea till today, exercising an influence on the newer cults that have emerged during the last two centuries.

# The Modern World

## Chinese Popular Religion

'Popular religion' is the faith and practice of the common people, as contrasted with the sophisticated doctrines and institutional structures of the three so-called 'great' traditions. While popular religion may be easy to characterize, it is often impossible to isolate. This is partly because it not a formally boundaried tradition with a centralized authority. Its interaction or combination with anything that people find useful from other traditions is a characteristic of popular religion.

More than any of China's other traditions, popular religion represents the survival of the native traditions as well as their fruitful union with the foreign.

*A pagoda overlooks the Taroko Gorge on the east side of Taiwan.*
(W.G. Oxtoby)

The combination, called 'syncretism', is possible because popular religion has little need to defend its own orthodoxy. It is less self-conscious. China's religious practices and rituals on an unsophisticated level, together with their implied beliefs and theories, have never been entirely assimilated into the doctrinal systems of institutional Confucianism, Taoism, or Buddhism. The people's expressions of religiosity have proved to be remarkably long-lasting. Thus popular or folk religion incorporates an apparently amorphous mass of accumulated tradition from the past and the surviving—sometimes thriving—beliefs and practices of the present.

Popular religion crosses the boundary lines between Confucianism, Taoism, and Buddhism, and has no single sacred text or set of documents. Its basic ideas and values consist of those that pervade the culture as a whole, with particular focus on human concerns for personal and communal survival in a sometimes harsh world. These concerns relate to health, children, education, finance, violence, even war and peace. Popular religion and mainstream Confucianism and Taoism share the belief that somehow the spirits have power over this life and yet require sustenance from those who are alive, so offerings and promises are made to them in return for their help, and offerings may be with-

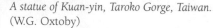

A statue of *Kuan-yin, Taroko Gorge, Taiwan.* (W.G. Oxtoby)

held if help is not forthcoming. The 'ghosts', in their turn, may harass the living and demand propitiation.

Religious ritual and practice on the folk level often remind us of ancient religion and its practice of divination and shamanism. The understanding of priesthood changed with the historical development of Confucianism, Taoism, and Buddhism. The state religion of divination, shamanism, and sacrifice lapsed centuries ago with the Shang dynasty, but the practice of divination, having trances, and making sacrificial offerings of cooked food, especially to the ancestors, persists.

In Taiwan today, the country's prosperity is reflected in the abundance and wealth of its temples and popular shrines. After all, temples and shrines are the supposed earthly palaces of the deities and spirits. Often, the temple is the modern town's or village's only architectural structure that still follows the traditional style of roofs with curved eaves. It is a rectangular tile-roofed structure, usually with its longer sides aligned across a north-south axis. The image of the deity faces south, enthroned like a ruler or emperor in a Chinese palace centuries ago. The entrance is usually a three-arched gate.

Large temples are situated in walled compounds with many courtyards. The main central structure with the images of the deities is flanked or surrounded by courtyards or long halls. These temples are very visible structures when they are well maintained, with strong colours like green roof tiles and red pillars. Statues of deities, especially of *buddha* figures, are often gilded. In fact, there are so many temples, even in communist China today, that one wonders how the Chinese could ever have been described as an irreligious people. Shrines are even more common, in the form of miniature temples, the dwellings of more humble deities like the local earth god.

## Interactions with the Great Traditions

### *The Influence of Confucianism*

Confucian influence on the popular level has been exercised by osmosis over the centuries. This has occurred especially through the institution of the family. Families have generally urged their children to work and study hard, and to behave according to the rules of propriety in order to uphold the family's good name. This kind of moulding has been supported as well by the state, with its own emphasis on political loyalty and civil obedience. Popular sects are also known to call themselves Confucian. In Taiwan, there is the 'Confucian lineage spirit religion' (Ju-tsung Shen-chiao/Ruzong Shenjiao), which was introduced from the mainland. This is a salvation religion with shamanic features that honours, among other figures, the Taoist Jade Emperor and the divinized Kuan-kung/Guan Gong. Its scriptures are regarded as revealed from above, sometimes through a form of spirit writing with a heavenly bird as medium.

#### *Buddhist Figures*

Certain *buddha* and *bodhisattva* (in Chinese, *p'u-sa/pusa*) figures are prominent in the popular cult. These include the historical Buddha himself, and also O-mi-t'o-fo (Amitābha), the *buddha* of the Pure Land, the future *buddha* Mi-lo (Maitreya), sometimes called the Laughing Buddha, as well as the famous female figure, the *p'u-sa* Kuan-yin. Kuan-yin, the female *bodhisattva*, ranks ahead of Mi-lo, ahead of O-mi-t'o-fo, and ahead of the historical Buddha in popular devotion. Among the healing figures, there is the Healing Buddha, called Yao-shih.

#### *The Eight Taoist Immortals*

An interesting group of 'deities' are the Eight Immortals, of Taoist fame, all allegedly historical individuals, who collectively signify happiness. They include men and women of different ages and stations in life and therefore appeal to a variety of people. Among them are the crippled Li, holding an iron crutch, the patron of pharmacists; the imperial relative Tsao, a military commander, patron of actors; the androgynous-looking Lan, formerly a street singer and now patron of florists; the fairy maid Ho, daughter of a storekeeper; Chung-li Ch'üan/Zhongli Quan, a stout man holding a peach in one hand and a feather fan in the other, a patron of silversmiths; Old Man Chang, carrying a fish drum; the famous Lü Tung-pin/Lü Dongbin, carrying a sword and a fly-whisk; and his disciple, the young Han, carrying a basket of flowers and a jade flute, a patron of musicians.

As patrons of special groups of people, especially in the various trades, the Eight Immortals are similar to the Christian saints in the Catholic tradition. They are not so much deities as they are individuals of merit; they are role models as well as protectors. As with the ancestor cult, their existence represents the close ties between the living and the deceased, since the spirits of the deceased are always within reach when help is needed.

#### *Buddho-Taoist Hells*

Taoism is more concerned with life on earth, while Buddhism is more concerned with life after death. Thus popular beliefs in afterlife rewards and punishments bear Buddhist influences. The well-known Chinese hells, derived from Buddhist beliefs, have become part and parcel of Taoism, with Taoist priests hanging scrolls depicting the hell scenes during funeral services.

The figure may vary, but Chinese hells are usually said to be ten in number. They are sometimes said to be situated under a high mountain in Szechwan, in southwest China. Each is ruled by a king serving as judge, surrounded by ministers and attendants who implement his decisions. In these hells, justice is meted out impartially. Punishments are usually described as corporal, exercised with the use of torture instruments. Supposedly, the soul of the deceased goes through the series of hells until it is ready for rebirth, so Chinese hells are not final and bear resemblance to the Catholic purgatory. As in Catholic belief, offerings and prayers for the dead can mitigate punishments.

### *Syncretism: The 'Unity' Sect*

I-kuan-tao/Yiguandao illustrates that popular religion represents the ultimate expression of syncretism. The term means 'Unifying Tao' and is sometimes translated simply as 'Unity Sect'. I-kuan-tao is an ethical society devoted to the salvation of its members and of all humankind. It claims to embrace Taoist, Buddhist, and Confucian teachings, as well as the cult of the Eternal Venerable Mother. Adherents engage in chanting and meditation, participate in scriptural studies, including those of morality books, and do *T'ai-chi* or *ch'i-kung* exercises and abstain from meat.

The syncretistic character of the Unity sect is reflected in its texts. These include spirit-writing tracts and scriptural texts borrowed from Confucianism, Taoism, and Buddhism as well as from other small sects. They deal with doctrine, ritual, and the important issue of lineage or apostolic succession. Part of its claim is similar to that of the Neo-Confucian thinkers: that the proper transmission of ancient doctrine, through both Confucius and Lao-tzu, ceased with the death of Mencius. But it maintains that this Tao blended with Buddhism in the West (i.e., India), and proceeded through Ch'an in China, to the Sixth Patriarch Hui-neng, after which it was once again lost, to be recovered by the 'common people' who received his teachings and managed to continue the transmission.

### *The Compassion Society*

The Eternal Venerable Mother, also called 'Golden Mother' or 'Queen Mother', is the special protector of certain sects, including besides I-kuan-tao the 'Compassion Society' founded on the east coast of Taiwan in the mid-1950s. The Canadian scholar Daniel Overmyer (b. 1935) describes a chapel of this sect. There are six images on an altar, arranged in two transverse rows of three. In the front, the Jade Emperor is flanked by Kuan-yin on his right and the Earth Mother on his left. The back row has the Queen Mother in the centre, with two female figures flanking her: on the right, the Mysterious Woman of the Nine Heavens from Taoist mythology, and on the left, the ancient creator goddess Nü-wa. This appears to be a faith-healing sect that also relies on spirit-mediums. Members are both male and female, and considered adopted children of the goddess Mother.

Popular religion has a history, although its past has until now been less studied than that of the more institutionalized and 'established' traditions. It also has a present, which is an important proof of its continued survival and vitality, and this vitality is also an indication that it has a future. Chinese popular religion includes beliefs and practices that are still part of Chinese life among ethnic Chinese communities in Taiwan, Hong Kong, Singapore, Southeast Asia, and beyond. This also includes mainland China when religion is recognized and permitted there. Official guarantees of religious freedom have permitted religious faith in theory, but the implementation of those guarantees in fact has varied from time to time and from place to place. Here and there, one can find evidence of the re-emergence of religious expressions formerly dismissed as 'superstitions'.

## The Chinese Religious Calendar

The Chinese religious calendar reflects the syncretic character of popular religion. In Chinese culture, years are designated by animals, in a twelve-year cycle: mouse (or rat), ox, tiger, hare, dragon, snake, horse, sheep, monkey, cock, dog, boar (or pig). These animals are the constellations of the ancient Chinese zodiac.

Within each year, the calendar follows a lunar cycle, with the first of the moon or month coinciding with the new moon and the fifteenth coinciding with the full moon. It also parallels the agricultural cycle. Even with the official adoption of the solar calendar, the traditional Chinese almanac remains an important book. The lunar calendar, which would otherwise run eleven days short of the solar year, is kept in phase with the solar by adding an intercalary or second lunar month in seven of every nineteen years when the sun finishes a lunar month in the same sign in which it began it.

The cycle begins with preparations for the lunar New Year, which usually takes place in late January or early February. About a week before the New Year, i.e., the first day of the first moon, the stove god, whose portrait decorates the kitchen, has to be sent off to heaven with his report on the family members. After bribing him by smearing his lips with honey or sticky candy, the family then removes his picture and burns it. He returns on New Year's eve when a new picture is pasted over the stove. New Year rituals originally include worship of various deities as well as the ancestors. Today, they include dragon dances (to encourage rain and fertility) and firecrackers (originally to chase away demons). The New Year's celebrations usually extend to the fifteenth day of that month, which is called the Feast of the Lanterns.

'Double Two'—the second day of the second moon—is celebrated as the birthday of the local earth god, to whom incense, candles, and paper offerings are

*The* yin-yang *symbol is encircled by the animals of the Chinese zodiac in this sculptured panel at a Taoist temple in Chengdu, China.* (W.G. Oxtoby)

made. He is considered the local registrar for births, marriages, and deaths. The birthday of Kuan-yin is celebrated on the nineteenth of the same moon. This female figure is sometimes represented as having a thousand eyes and a thousand hands, to better hear and respond to prayer.

Ch'ing-ming, the 'clear and bright' festival, is the next big occasion on the calendar. It falls fifteen days after the spring equinox. This is the time for visiting and repairing the tombs, and sometimes offering sacrifices of cooked food at the burial sites.

Śākyamuni's birthday is celebrated on the eighth day of the fourth moon, which usually falls in May. The principal rite is the 'bathing of the Buddha', in which a small Buddha image is cleansed with scented water in a temple ritual of Indian origin. In late spring, a popular custom honours the ancient poet and minister Ch'ü Yüan/Qu Yuan (c. 343–289 BCE), who drowned himself in a river. This is the dragon boat festival on 'Double Five', the fifth day of the fifth moon. It is alleged to be a re-enactment of the search for the dead poet's body, sometimes as an effort to placate dragons living in the waters. Cooked rice, wrapped in leaves, is eaten today, commemorating the custom of offering food to the spirit of the drowned man. This has become quite a secular celebration.

A feast special to women is 'Double Seven'—the seventh day of the seventh moon—commemorating the love story of the cowherd and the weaving maid, who is allegedly the youngest daughter of the stove god. Granted only one reunion a year with her husband, she meets him on a bridge of magpies over the Milky Way. Also in the seventh moon is the Buddhist P'u-tu/Pudu ritual, a kind of 'All Souls' Day'. Its name (literally, 'ferrying across to the other shore') reflects concern for the spirits of all the departed in their next abode.

In the eighth moon, there is a harvest festival similar to the American Thanksgiving. It coincides with the harvest moon, so round moon cakes are eaten. Traditionally, women made offerings to the moon, but the day has now become mainly a secular family feast. The ninth day of the ninth moon is reserved for climbing heights with opportunities for picnics and kite-flying, as well as for remembering the deceased.

In the tenth moon, the ancestors are remembered once more during ritual visits to the tombs. Mock paper money and paper clothing are burned, representing what is needed for the cold season. After that comes the winter solstice during the eleventh moon. Traditionally, thanksgiving offerings were made at the family altar to Heaven and earth, the household gods, and the ancestors, followed by a sumptuous dinner for the family.

Soon after that, the preparations for the lunar New Year begin the whole cycle once again. While many may not observe all the events in this liturgical calendar, every family usually observes some of the festivals, especially New Year's. The calendar evokes the rhythm of nature's seasons and of human life, giving meaning and fulfilment to life itself. A comparison can be made with the post-Christian West and its own yearly cycle. Even though Christmas is secularized, the observance of seasonal festivals indicates a need for traditions that still inspire peace and sharing.

## The T'ai-p'ing Rebellion

The ideal of *t'ai-p'ing/taiping* ('Great Peace'), which comes from a Confucian text and refers to a golden age of the past, has served as a rallying point for Taoist and Buddhist popular movements with a messianic thrust. However, the T'ai-p'ing rebellion of 1850–65 near the end of the Manchu dynasty combined native and Protestant Christian impulses, including monotheism, the Ten Commandments, and Sunday worship.

Under the leader Hung Hsiu-ch'üan/Hong Xiuquan (1813–64), who called himself the younger brother of Jesus Christ, the T'ai-p'ing rebels from southern China took over a large part of the country and established their capital in Nanking in 1851, calling their theocratic domain the Heavenly Kingdom of Great Peace.

Like twentieth-century Protestant fundamentalism, T'ai-p'ing Christianity has prohibitions against smoking, drinking, and illicit sex, advocates compulsory education for both boys and girls, and enforces monogamy—although some of their leaders exempted themselves from the general rule. They had a revolutionary vision for the country, even if it was naïve in its implementation.

The movement's iconoclasm towards Chinese traditions provoked the enmity of the Confucian gentry, who, with some Western help, came to the aid of the Manchu rulers and defeated the rebels. However, the syncretism of the T'ai-p'ing religion remains a precursor to other cults found even in today's China, where nature and Christian beliefs sometimes blend with faith healing and other practices.

## Rethinking Confucius

Neo-Confucianism has been the official philosophy in China for much of the last thousand years. The textual commentaries written or compiled by its representatives have also served as the basis of the civil-service examination system. However, Matteo Ricci (1522–1610) and other Jesuit missionaries in the sixteenth century preferred classical Confucianism to the later development. They also opposed the metaphysical dimensions of Neo-Confucian philosophy, which bore the pantheistic imprint of Buddhist influence. More recently, however, leading Chinese scholars of the twentieth century have complained that this missionary attitude overlooked the rich spiritual dimension of the Neo-Confucian tradition. Indeed, Neo-Confucianism is a defining feature of the Confucian tradition today.

When China was shaken politically and psychologically by Western intrusion in the late nineteenth century, Chinese intellectuals began a soul-searching questioning of their cultural heritage, particularly Confucianism, which many regarded as a weight and a burden—an intellectual shackle on the mind, preventing the country from modernization. Its strongest critic was probably the writer Lu Hsün/Lu Xun (1881–1936), whose short stories attacked the 'cannibalistic' ritual religion that stifled human freedom and individual initiative in the name of passive, conformist virtues.

These antitraditionalist, anti-Confucian voices of the 1919 May Fourth movement gave birth to the Chinese Communist party in 1921. What began as a search for intellectual freedom also involved a repudiation of the monopoly of tradition, especially that of the Confucian social structure. With the communist takeover of the mainland in 1949, vigorous discussions and debates took place over the advantages and disadvantages of the Confucian tradition.

While mainland Marxist scholars were criticizing the entire traditional legacy, a group of philosophers and scholars in Taiwan and Hong Kong expressed their concern for the survival of Chinese culture, which they identified with Neo-Confucianism.

A plea for a return to Neo-Confucian sources was made public in 'A Manifesto for the Reappraisal of Sinology and Reconstruction of Chinese Culture' by a group of Chinese philosophers in Hong Kong and Taipei in 1958. The manifesto refers to the harmony of the 'way of Heaven' (*t'ien-tao/tiendao*) and the 'way of man' (*jen-tao/rendao*) as the central legacy of Confucianism. It also challenges Western sinologists to give greater attention to Confucian spirituality as the core of Chinese culture, which it claims was not properly understood by the missionaries of the sixteenth and seventeenth centuries. In this manifesto, these scholars interestingly concurred with mainland scholars that Neo-Confucianism in particular possesses an undeniably spiritual and religious character.

The group of philosophers associated with this movement for Confucian revival included Carsun Chang (Chang Chün-mai, 1886–1969), T'ang Chün-i (1907–78), Mou Tsung-san (1909–95), and others. These men analysed traditional Chinese ideas using European philosophical concepts from Immanuel Kant (1724–1804) and others. Their legacy remains important for Chinese intellectuals outside the mainland, and their achievement parallels that of the early twentieth-century Kyoto school of Japanese philosophers who merged Buddhist ideas with European (especially German) philosophy. However, the Chinese philosophers defend the religious and spiritual dimensions of the Confucian legacy without engaging in real dialogue with other traditions like Christianity in the manner of the Kyoto school. On the other hand, scholars in the West studying the Confucian tradition, including Neo-Confucianism, whether they are Chinese or not, are more open to such dialogue.

## Legalism and the Criticism of Confucius

'Legalism' (Fa-chia/Fajia) should not be confused with the rule of law. It refers to an ancient school of thought, almost as old as Confucianism, that advocated using harsh penal law to deter political opposition and enhance and maintain power, so it is no surprise that Legalism was the favourite of despots. Its key thinker is a prince known as Han Fei Tzu (d. 233 BCE). This is the title also of a work attributed to him and his school.

Legalism does not address questions about the meaning of life. Rather, it offers a political answer (despotism and power politics) to the problem of order in society. Devoid of any religio-moral belief, it deals exclusively with *Realpolitik*, political power. A ruler's goal justifies all means. Legalist writings tend to be handbooks for rulers, teaching them how to manipulate people and circumstances to keep themselves in power. In this respect, the text *Han Fei Tzu* has frequently been compared to a European Renaissance work, *The Prince*, by Niccolò Machiavelli (1469–1527).

According to biographies, several Legalist thinkers were betrayed by others. Han Fei Tzu, for example, was prevented by a jealous high minister from meeting with a ruler who had invited him. Han was thrown into prison, where he was unable to defend himself against trumped-up charges. Reportedly, that was where the book bearing his name was written.

The followers of Legalism are great cynics who put no faith in any power higher than that of the state or ruler. They subordinate all human relations to the one between ruler and minister and divest it of any moral significance. They also recommend that the ruler ascertain the loyalty of his subjects by using rewards and punishments. The ruler is to take no one into his confidence, not even his immediate family, in case that person becomes his foe.

Liu Shaoqi (1898–1969), who served as head of state in communist China, lauded both Confucian and Neo-Confucian ideas in his address, *How to Be a Good Communist*.

> The Chinese scholars of the Confucian school had a number of methods for the cultivation of their body and mind. '…the cultivation of the person, the regulation of the family, the ordering well of the state and the making tranquil of the whole kingdom' as set forth in the Great Learning also means the same. All this shows that in achieving one's progress one must make serious and energetic efforts to carry on self-cultivation and study (Liu 1951:24).

But for much of communist rule in China, Legalism has been regarded by scholars in the People's Republic as a 'progressive' school of thought, while Confucianism has been described as 'reactionary'. Mao Zedong was frequently and approvingly compared to Ch'in Shih Huang-ti, the ruler who unified China in 221 BCE and who is known, among other things, for having burned books and buried scholars. Chinese communists described Legalism as engaged in a life-and-death struggle with Confucianism and praised it for its materialist preferences and modernizing potential.

A particularly vituperative phase of the Cultural Revolution of 1966–76 was the Anti-Confucius campaign of 1973–4. Diatribes linked the fallen defence chief Lin Piao/Lin Biao (1907–71) with Confucius. Liu Shaoqi became enemy number one for Mao, and the Confucian and Neo-Confucian writings that Liu praised came under heavy attack. In the Anti-Confucius campaign, Legalism was exalted as the heroic ideology. In the 1990s, Legalism continued to be reflected in China's policy of using the judicial system to impose severe punishments for crimes large or small, real or imagined.

In the late 1970s the excesses of the Anti-Confucius campaign were discredited, and Confucianism has since been restored to a degree of respectability. However, because Confucianism is concerned with the state and society, it has continued to be viewed more as political and philosophical ideology than as religion. What are considered religions in contemporary mainland China are the more ritualized and institutionalized traditions of Taoism and Buddhism, and the religions of identifiable minorities such as Islam or of definable membership like Christianity.

## Korea's New Religions

An interesting phenomenon in modern times is the number of Christian conversions in Korea, the result of missionary activity during the last century. The figure has been proportionally much higher than in China or Japan, giving Korea a significant Christian minority in comparison with all the other countries of eastern Asia—with the sole exception of the Philippines, where Christians are the majority.

Christian evangelistic activity in Korea has been mainly Protestant, especially Presbyterian, although Catholics have also made inroads. Today there are about 7 million Christians in Korea, with Protestants outnumbering Catholics by about four to one.

### *The Unification Church*

Sun Myung Moon's (b. 1920) Holy Spirit Association for the Unification of World Christianity has Christian (especially Presbyterian) roots and an overseas following. The word 'Unification' is ambiguous. It can refer to political reunification of North and South Korea, divided since the end of the Second World War. The name can also refer to the twentieth-century ecumenical movement in which branches of Christianity that had been separated for centuries found grounds for conversation if not for full merger. Though the name suggests ecumenical reunion, the Unification Church is centrifugal rather than centripetal. Moon's book *Divine Principle* proposes to unite all religions through an interpretation of the Bible currently held by the 'Moonies' alone.

The Church, which grew after the mid-twentieth century, has been dogged by controversy because of its aggressive—some also say deceptive—recruitment methods and financial scandals. Somewhat notorious in the West, the Unification Church is not so strong in Korea itself.

### *Ch'ŏndogyo*

Another movement, much stronger within Korea, is Ch'ŏndogyo ('religion of the heavenly way'). Founded by Ch'oe Suun (1824–64) in 1860 under the name Tonghak ('eastern learning'), it demonstrates both Confucian and Taoist influence. In 1905 the movement's name was changed to Ch'ŏndogyo. Although the founder was killed by a government suspicious of his political intentions, his two successors made the religion a major force in the country, and the writings of all three form the scriptural canon for Ch'ondogyo.

Ch'ŏndogyo proclaims faith in a heavenly lord called Hanullim or Ch'onju ('lord of heaven'). It sees human nature as a reflection of divinity, and thus deserv-

*The gateway to the Ch'ŏndogyo complex in the vicinity of Kyongju in southeastern Korea.* (W.G. Oxtoby)

ing of all respect and concern. On its altar is placed a bowl of clear water, to reflect heaven to the bowing worshipper. An injunction is to treat human beings as God. It also envisions a cooperative human community world-wide.

Ch'ŏndogyo involves certain prayer formulas, purification rituals, and rice offerings. Sunday worship includes hymns, prayers, scriptural readings, and a sermon. It also emphasizes moral discipline and sincerity. It teaches how to regard others, especially family members:

> There is nothing that is not the Way in daily activities. The divine spirit of the universe moves together with all things. Therefore, practice the principle of respecting people and things ...
>
> If a guest comes to your house, think that God has arrived.
>
> The peaceful harmony of husband and wife is the heart of our way, and therefore, if a wife is disobedient, bow before her with all earnestness. If one bows once, twice and repeatedly, even the wife who has the hardest heart will be reconciled ...
>
> Do not strike a child, for striking a child is striking God ...
>
> Especially respect your daughter-in-law like God (Kim 1977:243).

Considering the low position traditionally accorded to women in Korea, especially wives in relation to husbands, and daughters-in-law living together with parents-in-law under the same roof, these instructions are unusual.

Ch'ŏndogyo was behind the Tonghak revolution of 1894, a popular uprising that contributed to the modernization of Korean society. The religion also played an important role in the 1919 independence movement against Japanese rule. Currently, it has about a million followers, with its headquarters in Seoul.

## Cao Dai and Modern Vietnam

Around 1620, the Nguyen family, who ruled southern Vietnam from Hué, declared independence from Hanoi in the north. Eventually, in 1802, a Nguyen gained control of the whole country, with some help from the French. He was Emperor Gia Long.

In the seventeenth century, the French Jesuit missionary Alexandre de Rhodes (1591–1660) introduced to Vietnam a system of writing using the Latin alphabet. It gained slow acceptance, but became universal in the twentieth century. With it came Christian teachings and conversions, followed by French colonization (1883–1939). Next to the Philippines, Vietnam is an Asian country with a large Catholic population, though a minority.

Cao Dai, a religion in southern Vietnam, was supposedly revealed by the god Cao Dai ('Great Palace'). It is a syncretic teaching that merges Confucianism, Taoism, Buddhism, and Catholicism—all the religions known to the people of Vietnam. It also has a strong shamanic aspect.

Ngo-van-Chieu (1878–1932), the founder of Cao Dai, was a Vietnamese working for the French colonial bureaucracy. With the assistance of women spirit-mediums, he held sessions during which spirits were summoned. In 1919 in Phucoq, on the Gulf of Siam, he claimed that the spirit of Cao appeared, whom he recognized as a god to be worshipped. On Christmas night in 1925 in Saigon, Cao Dai allegedly revealed himself once more during a 'table-moving' spiritualist session, and instructed the group to go to Ngo-van-Chieu for instruction.

After that, the god also reportedly announced that a wealthy scholar, Le-van-Trung (c. 1875–1934), was to be regarded as the head of the new religion. A profligate opium smoker, the fifty-year-old Le converted to a very moral life and attracted many followers. The new religion was officially proclaimed in November 1926, with Le as a pope figure. The sect built a great temple at Tay-ninh and organized a hierarchy on the Catholic model, except that all positions, save that of the pope, were open to both men and women. A council elected a successor to the pope on Le's death in 1934.

Cao Dai continues to have some 2.5 million followers. It teaches the brotherhood of humankind, and the doctrine of transmigration of souls, as well as kindness to animals and even to plants. It involves incense sacrifices and spirit-mediums for 'table-moving' and 'spirit-writing' sessions. Revelations are written down during trances. Spirits that have reportedly been contacted have included Chinese poets (Li Po, 701–62), French writers (Victor Hugo, 1802–85), and Christian heroes (Joan of Arc, c. 1412–31). In a few decades, it has already developed into many sects. Despite years of communist suppression, it appears to be alive and well today.

The prosperity of Cao Dai attests to the importance of the spirit cult, which is so widespread throughout East Asia. With the recent religious revival in Vietnam, there has been an increase in folk religious activities, including those of spirit-mediums outside of Cao Dai. According to reports, even in the northern capital of Hanoi there is a revival of making offerings at ancestral altars in family homes, as well as consulting spirit-mediums during crises.

In the twentieth century, communism isolated Vietnam from the Western world for a long time. To forestall challenges to its leadership, the Communist party took over Vietnamese schools, hospitals, and orphanages that were previously run by religious groups, first in the north, and then also in the south after the fall of Saigon in 1975. Religious personnel were sent to prison or to re-education camps, while Buddhist as well as Christian communities sought to survive through compromises and collaboration with the government. All these developments were parallel to developments in communist China.

Since 1986, Vietnam's communists have gradually adopted free-market economics, and eased the tensions with Catholic and Buddhist groups, who have taken in new recruits, repaired their places of worship, and published religious books and periodicals. Unlike the case in China, Vietnam's Catholic bishops have not broken off relations with the Vatican.

## Popular Religion in Japan

Simultaneous or alternating adherence to various religious traditions is manifest in Japan. Three-quarters of all Japanese households have either a *kamidana* (Shinto household shrine) or a *butsudan* (Buddhist household altar), but nearly half the households have both. As we have indicated, people characteristically follow Shinto birth rituals and turn to Buddhist institutions for funerals. Weddings are most often associated with Shinto, though Christian or Christian-style weddings have become fashionable. People regularly observe ritual customs, such as clapping their hands twice when entering a Shinto shrine (and may transfer this practice also to Buddhist temples), even though they profess no attachment to religion.

As in Korea, Japanese popular religion has a shamanic aspect, as it is associated with trances, healing, and asceticism. Like Korea, Japan also has had female shamanism of a northern, Siberian type, as with Queen Himiko of antiquity and with some women founders of Japanese new religions more recently. It is also home to the cult of mediums, which is more familiar in southern China and regions farther south. Japanese popular religion is also conditioned by influences from Polynesia or Melanesia.

As with folk religion elsewhere, Japanese practice presumes that the spirits need to be placated, lest they become angry and inflict misfortune on the living. Ancestors' spirits are served with offerings and memorials at the household *butsudan*.

Other living creatures are believed to have spirits too, that may be offended if they are not thanked for the service that they have given to people. For example, there is a restaurant serving eels, whose management engages the local Buddhist temple from time to time to perform memorial rites for the souls of the eels sacrificed to be eaten by humans. Keeping the eel spirits happy is an investment in the restaurant's continued prosperity.

Utilitarian objects are similarly treated. A time-honoured custom is cremating worn needles and other tools in a ritual resembling a funeral. The spirits associated with these implements are thanked for the wear and tear they have suffered while giving benefit to humans. We now think of such objects as inanimate, but in pre-modern Japan such items were most often made of wood, bone, or straw, that is, of formerly living material.

In recent years, obsolete or worn-out computer parts and other electronic gear have received similar funerary ceremonies in urban Tokyo. A modern wrinkle, however, is that plastic and other substances in such equipment have been deemed unsuitable for burning because of current air-pollution concerns. Therefore, photographs of the equipment have been substituted for the items in the cremation ceremonies.

## Shugendō

It is difficult to place Shugendō in any category other than popular or folk religion. Literally 'the way of mastering religious power [through asceticism]', Shugendō is an age-old Japanese tradition that combines native Shinto and imported elements, especially Buddhism. The religion's main focus is in the sacred mountains, and its practice includes magical and ritual techniques. Its semilegendary seventh-century founder, En no Gyōja, is the subject of miracle stories.

Its principal practitioners are the so-called *yamabushi* or mountain monks. They are wandering ascetics who practise austerities like fasting, going without sleep, and standing under cold waterfalls. Strengthened by their discipline, they emerge from the mountains to serve as itinerant healers and exorcists among the nearby villagers. They demonstrate their powers by such actions as walking barefoot through the hot embers of a ritual bonfire, claiming special protection or control.

*A shaman in Omiya, a northern suburb of Tokyo, counsels a newly married couple.*
(R.C. Amore)

By the thirteenth century, Shugendō was already a highly organized tradition with many local variations. There were pilgrimages to the sacred mountains, where purification and other rituals were enacted. The Shugendō fire ritual may originate from Japanese folk religion, but is also related to esoteric Buddhism—Shingon or Tendai. Shugendō dispenses charms and blessings, especially for healing sicknesses.

An example is a woman ascetic who is a professional healer and exorcist. She lives in her own house, which is also a temple to her tutelary deity. She makes occasional visits to the Buddhist temple to which she is formally affiliated. She is visited by sick persons who attribute their problems to malignant spirit possession and ask for exorcisms and cures.

Sometimes she performs fire rituals—even indoors—before a Buddhist altar where Fudo, a guardian figure, is honoured. Wooden sticks, with the prayers of individuals written on them, are burned and thus dispatched to the deities. The flames rise dangerously close to the ceiling, where paper decorations are hung (the Japanese word for paper, *kami*, sounds just like the word for spirits). While she petitions for cures, the sick person's clothing, such as pajamas, is passed quickly through the fire. The ritual may be attended by close to a hundred people in a crowded apartment and can last for more than an hour.

Shugendō was banned by the Meiji government in 1872, which was intent on restoring Shinto to a 'pure' state, free from Buddhist influence. The government was also interested in uprooting what it took to be superstition. Since 1945, however, some Shugendō traditions surviving in Shinto and Buddhism have been revived, and new forms of Shugendō have appeared. Today, however, many of those who seek spiritual healing turn to the new religions rather than to Shugendō practitioners.

## Japan's New Religions

Over a hundred new religions have emerged in Japan. Though they have often sprung from Shinto or Buddhist roots, they are distinct organizations and recognized as such. Some started in the nineteenth century, but they have flourished since the middle of the twentieth century as Japan experienced urbanization and social change.

A factor in their growth was the restructuring of Japanese life after the Second World War. In 1942 Japan controlled an empire that stretched from Manchuria to Burma and practically to Australia. By 1945 its industrial cities were in ruins from bombing raids, including the atomic explosions at Hiroshima and Nagasaki. Rule by foreigners brought a break with the past. The new constitution of 1946, actually drafted by the American occupation, mandated the separation of religion and the state, but also guaranteed freedom of religion. This environment, which uprooted institutions and individuals, was also one that offered officially recognized status to extant marginal movements as well as to the array of new groups that sprang up. Any would-be religion could register with the Ministry of Education.

Practically none of the new religions claims an exclusive possession of truth. Each accepts the others on the basis of equality. Generally, they represent an effort at doctrinal simplicity and appeal mainly to those not interested in excessive intellectual sophistication. They also tend to be lay organizations without a complex hierarchy, making them accessible to the masses. Also, one can follow these new religions without abandoning any traditional faith.

The new religions characteristically promise personal benefit. Much of their appeal is to the person facing a stressful situation: illness or death in the family, trouble in a marriage, problems with a job or business, and the pressures of school admission and examinations. A co-worker or neighbour active in the group proposes that the person facing hardship would have little to lose by trying what the group has to offer, whether it is meditation, a regime of self-denial, shared activities, or the group's counselling services. Many of these resources existed in the extended families and communities of premodern Japan, but they are not easily available in big cities.

Some of the new religions are of mainly Shinto inspiration. Like Shinto itself, they tend to be preoccupied with purification rituals, and have a strong sense of Japanese culture and nationhood. Whether at home or abroad, the new religions appeal mainly to people of Japanese descent. Besides, an important characteristic of the new religions is their shamanic aspect, which is usually a part of their founders' reported experiences. It is also evident in their emphasis on faith healing, a significant factor in their popular appeal. Women played an important role in founding several of the new religions, even though men usually took over in their subsequent organization.

### *Tenrikyō*

Some religions categorized as 'new' have been in existence for more than a century and have developed established institutions. In institutional maturity, for instance, Tenrikyō in Japan can be compared with the Mormon Church in the United States.

Tenrikyō ('religion of the heavenly principle') was founded by the woman Miki Nakayama (1798–1887), who had a Pure Land Buddhist background. There are accounts of her being in a possession trance in 1837, when she declared her body was the temple of God, saying, 'I am the True and Original God. I have been predestined to reside here. I have descended from Heaven to save all human beings, and I want to take Miki as the Shrine of God and the mediatrix between God and men' (Thomsen 1963:34). Her husband reportedly asked the deity to leave her, but without success. When she subsequently began giving away the family's possessions, the family was equally unsuccessful in dissuading her. People thought her mad, but eventually she developed a following for her activity in spiritual healing and in reducing the pain of childbirth.

Miki and her nineteenth-century followers experienced government harassment, partly because their exuberant dances attracted attention at a time of peasant unrest. Dances, now more ritualized, have continued to be a feature of Tenrikyō worship. They dramatize ideas present in Miki's writings, especially the notion that we have allowed strife and greed to settle on our minds like dust. Dance rituals rid the mind of them with a sweeping action.

While the religion Miki founded urged its faithful to give up personal possessions, it acquired much wealth as a group. Today, its headquarters is in Tenri city, not far from Kyoto and Nara, where the religion has built libraries, hospitals, and even a university. It has over 1.5 million followers.

### *Konkōkyō*

Konkōkyō was founded by Akazawa Bunji (1814–83), who assisted Shinto priests coming to his village from the Ise shrine and made the pilgrimage itinerary of eighty-eight temples on the island of Shikoku. He became very ill when he was about forty.

Akazawa's illness was understood as the result of having in some way offended a malevolent mountain deity, Konjin, and his subsequent recovery the result of prayer to the deity. He believed that Konjin did not desire suffering and indeed was the one true God of the universe, Tenchi-Kane-no-kami. He began to claim revelational instruction and guidance from the deity, and to communicate also on behalf of others who asked for his assistance. He gave up farming in 1859 and spent the next two decades at an altar in his house, offering prayer for the people who came for help and healing. His followers called him Konkō Daijin, the mediator between the divine and the human, sent by God.

Konkō Daijin's spiritual healing earned him the resentment of the *yamabushi*, Shugendō ascetics, who had been the principal healers in the region and saw him as a threat to their income. For protection, he registered under Shinto auspices, even though the one god he recognized was not a traditional Shinto deity.

Konkō Daijin denied that his religion was a form of Shinto, but his successors and disciples succeeded in getting the movement recognized as one of the Meiji government's thirteen official Shinto sects. Some became active supporters of State Shinto and its militarism, a fact that since the Second World War has been an embarrassment to its recent leaders, who have repudiated it, eliminating Shinto ritual and costume.

Konkōkyō ('religion of golden light') developed an extensive organization, produces publications, and conducts missionary activity. One is said to know the love of God if one knows how parents love their children. A distinctive teaching of Konkōkyō is the interdependence of God and humans; our suffering is God's suffering too, and our salvation is God's joy.

### *Ōmoto*

Like Tenrikyō, Ōmoto (the great 'root' or 'foundation') was founded by a rural person. Deguchi Nao (1837–1918) led a life of misfortune and poverty, worked as a maid at the age of eleven, and had eight children before becoming a widow and a rag seller at thirty. Of her children, three died in infancy, two sons ran away from home, and two daughters went mad.

Driven to despair by her favourite daughter's mental illness in 1892, Deguchi Nao reportedly received from Tenchi-Kane-no-kami (the god of Konkōkyō) a trance vision of the end of the world, the coming of a messiah figure, and the ushering in of a new day. The *Scripture of Ōmoto* speaks of this renewal:

> The Greater World shall be reconstructed and transformed into an entirely new world. After going through a complete cleaning-up, the Greater World shall be changed into the Kingdom of Heaven, where peace reigns through all eternity. Be prepared for it! The Word of God given through Deguchi Nao shall never fail (Thomsen 1963:129).

Ueda Kisaburō was an able student of literature and a dedicated follower of ascetic practices and spiritualism. He claimed that in a mountain cave experience, his soul took leave of his body in a heavenly ascent to learn all the mysteries of the universe and to become aware of his mission as the saviour of humanity. When he met Nao in 1898, she declared him to be the expected messiah and adopted him. He took the name Deguchi Onisaburō (1871–1948), soon married her youngest daughter, and collaborated with Nao to systematize their movement.

The chaos in the present world, according to Ōmoto teaching, is the result of strife among the primordial *kami*. The summer wind Susano-o and the *kami* Kunikotachi-no-Mikoto, the original rulers of Japan, have been driven out by evil *kami*, and one awaits their future restoration. This teaching was a clear challenge to the national ideology of a line of descent from Amaterasu and to the legitimacy of the emperor.

Onisaburō feuded with others in the movement and left for a time to become a Shinto priest, but returned in 1908 to lead it in opposition to the government, capitalism, and the Russo-Japanese war. He wrote, 'Armament and war are the means by which landlords and capitalists make their profit, while the poor must suffer. There is nothing in the world more harmful than war and more foolish than armament' (Thomsen 1963:130).

Onisaburō increasingly acted as though he intended to take over the country and reform it. He used a form of writing for his name that only kings and princes used, and called himself 'Kimhito', as though he were royalty. This could be regarded as harmless megalomania as long as he lacked a large following, but after he bought an influential Osaka newspaper, the authorities moved in. In 1921, the police raided Ōmoto's headquarters in Ayabe, near Kyoto, destroyed its main sanctuary, and imprisoned its leaders on a charge of *lèse-majesté* (contempt for the ruler's dignity). The authorities also modified Nao's tomb because it looked too much like an emperor's.

Onisaburō emerged from jail after four months, thanks to a general amnesty on the emperor's death, but he jumped bail and went to Mongolia. There, he tried to form a state, calling himself a living *buddha* and the saviour of the world, but he ran afoul of the local warlord, and escaped being shot only thanks to the intervention of the Japanese consul. Onisaburō also began to ride a white horse, an imperial symbol, and, on his return to Japan, travelled with an imperial-style motorcycle escort and renamed the rooms of his headquarters with palace room names. By 1935 the government had again had enough: the Ōmoto buildings were dynamited, Onisaburō, his wife, and fifty followers were rounded up, and Onisaburō was sentenced to life imprisonment for *lèse-majesté*. Released in 1942, Onisaburō again spoke in the name of the divine will, criticizing Japan's participation in the Second World War and foreseeing defeat.

During the 1920s and 1930s, however, Ōmoto enjoyed worldwide visibility. It preached an internationalist message, urged the adoption of Esperanto as a world language, and asserted the common origin and essential unity of religions. Onisaburō established international contacts with like-minded movements, such as the Bahā'īs, and organized the Universal Love and Brotherhood Association. Following the Second World War, Onisaburō claimed the *kami* had preserved Ōmoto as the basis for world renewal.

### *Seichō no Ie*

Spiritual healing was important to Taniguchi Masaharu (1893–1985), who contracted venereal disease after 1914 and consulted a practitioner who claimed to cure by hypnosis. While he obtained a cure for his own condition through standard medicine, he relied on spiritual healing to prevent its spread; he denied contagion, calling it only a manner of thinking. Taniguchi obtained a job as an editor with Ōmoto, but left it after the 1921 crackdown.

In an essay, Taniguchi argues that the material world is only the shadow of the mind, and that one can eliminate suffering by concentrating on positive thoughts. This view attracted attention as Japan experienced economic distress and the severe Tokyo earthquake of 1923. For the next several years, he explored the power of mind over matter, listened to spiritualists, practised self-help cures, and read the newly translated psychological writings of Sigmund Freud (1856–1939). Launching a magazine, whose issues were reprinted as volumes of *Seimei no jissō* (Truth of Life), he argued that the material world does not exist; the only reality is the divine life of the mind.

> This manifest world, visible to the naked eye and felt with the five senses, is not God's creation. I was greatly mistaken in accusing and judging God. This world, as perceived with the five senses, is merely a production of our minds. God is love and mercy. The Real World, created by God's infinite wisdom, love, and life, is filled with eternal harmony (Thomsen 1963:154).

Taniguchi's publishing enterprise in 1930 became the basis of Seichō no Ie as an organized religion. At first he claimed it was above the other religions, and that its mandate was to help each religion to be true to its essence. In time, though, it became an eclectic religion itself, claiming to be the fundamental essence of the others. Seichō no Ie ('house of growth') amalgamates teachings from Shinto, Buddhism, and Christianity, including Christian Science. It accepts the Shinto *kami*, the Buddha, and Jesus Christ all as incarnations of the supreme deity. During the Second World War, it was strongly nationalistic, identifying the emperor with the ultimate being. Consequently its publishing activity was suspended during the American occupation of 1945–52, but it resumed thereafter, reaching a more middle-class audience than most of Japan's other new religions.

### *PL Kyōdan*

PL ('perfect liberty') provides another example of Western influence. It is named in English; the letter *l* is not part of the Japanese language. The religion was founded under the American occupation in 1946 by Miki Tokuchika (b. 1900). It worships the supreme deity, while venerating ancestral spirits. Misfortunes are taken to be divine admonitions, interpreted to the believer through counselling. PL holds that life is art, and urges its followers to cultivate appropriate self-expression in art and sports. A number of its centres have golf facilities.

### *Mahikari*

Mahikari ('true light') was founded in 1959 by Okada Kōtama (1901–74), a scion of a *samurai* family. It claims a revelation from the 'Su' god, creator of the human race, entrusting the founder with the task of purifying the world and repairing its ills. His principal successor is his daughter, Okada Sachiko. The religion grew to 50,000 adherents in 1980.

As with Japan's other new religions, miracles are very important for Mahikari. The deity cares and intervenes to provide for individuals' welfare, through the help of the true believers. Healing is practised by raising one's hand, which allegedly emits rays of light, not only to cure human sicknesses in those who have faith but even to repair damaged cars. Spirit possession, especially by deceased *samurai* of the past, is also a Mahikari phenomenon, and there are regular exorcism sessions for the possessed, who first therapeutically 'act out' their spiritual dramas.

An interesting belief of this religion is that Jesus Christ was never crucified—he just went to Japan, got married, had a family, and was buried in the country. Indeed, Mahikari followers can point out the alleged gravesite.

### *Reiyūkai*

Several new religions began as movements spawned by Nichiren Buddhism, and venerate the *Lotus sūtra*. These include the Reiyūkai (society of spiritual friendship) movement, founded in 1925 by Kubo Kakutarō (1892–1944) and Kotani Kimi (1901–71), his sister-in-law. Besides honouring the *Lotus sūtra*, Reiyūkai practises daily ancestor worship.

### *Risshō Kōsei Kai*

Reiyūkai in turn gave rise to Risshō Kōsei Kai (society for the establishment of righteous and friendly relations), founded in 1938, which emphasizes repentance as a means of breaking the chain of *karma* and practises shamanism. Today it has over 2 million members. Risshō Kōsei Kai has shed some of the chauvinism of its Nichiren heritage; its co-founder Niwano Nikkyō (b. 1906) became active in the 1950s and 1960s in initiatives to promote interreligious understanding and international peace.

### *Sōka Gakkai*

Then there is the controversial Sōka Gakkai (value-creating study group). Founded in 1937 as a lay organization by a schoolteacher, Tsunesaburō Makiguchi (1871–1944), it follows the religious teaching of Nichiren Shōshū in venerating the *Gohonzon*, the scroll that records an invocation of the name of the *Lotus sūtra*. Like many other 'new religions' in Japan, its main teaching is achieving happiness in this world, and it values profit, goodness, and beauty. Unlike other new religions, it has used aggressive recruitment tactics called *shakufuku* ('break and subdue') that have drawn criticism.

After the Second World War, Sōka Gakkai gained political influence through association with a Japanese political party, the Komeito, which attracted attention because its rapid growth in the 1950s and 1960s made it appear for a time seemingly invincible. During those years, Sōka Gakkai, under the name Nichiren Shōshū, or True Nichiren Buddhism, spread all over the world.

However, financial scandals and other problems led to Sōka Gakkai's 'excommunication' from the Nichiren parent body in Japan in 1991. It was the most dramatic event in recent Japanese religious history, the climax of a long confrontation between Nichiren Shōshū, an independent but minor branch of Nichiren Buddhism, and the Sōka Gakkai, its largest lay organization (claiming 16 million members). The ensuing fight on the part of the Sōka Gakkai, in the name of Buddhist reform, has highlighted the conflict between the laity and the clergy. As of 1993, it was unclear which side might emerge with a clear victory.

### *Agonshū*

Tsutsumi Masao (b. 1921) experienced illness, poverty, and various business failures, and was jailed in 1953 for tax charges related to illegal liquor production. He relates that he was then about to commit suicide when the rope he tossed over a beam dislodged a copy of a Buddhist text on the mercies of the deity Kannon (Kuan-yin), which he paused to read. This led to a conversion experience of being chosen for salvation through Kannon's mercy and grace.

He began to practise meditation and ascetic austerities, took the name Kiriyama Seiyū on lay ordination in the tantric Shingon Buddhist sect, and in 1970 had a vision of Kannon informing him that he had 'cut his *karma*', that is, had removed the hindrance of unhappy spirits of his deceased ancestors that had caused his failures. Now he was to help others.

Kiriyama began to write extensively; his 1971 book *Henshin no genri* (Principles of Transformation) sold widely. In it he credits esoteric Buddhist practices for his power, and offers to guide others to comparable self-realization. In 1978, he renamed his following Agonshū ('the *Āgama* sect') after claiming to discover in the early Buddhist texts called *Āgama*s a route to buddhahood that is effective not only for the living but for the spirits of the dead as well. He claimed that people can now eliminate the karmic hindrances of their ancestors' unhappy ghosts.

It has mattered little that this is not what ancient India understood the *Āgamas* (*Nikāyas*, discourses of the Buddha) to be about, nor that turning the spirits of the dead into *buddhas* is not what classical Buddhism was all about. Kiriyama's movement studies not the content of the texts but their presumed inner meaning, as discovered by Kiriyama and as implemented in esoteric discipline. However, the citation of ancient texts is regarded as a return to original Buddhism, and Agonshū's followers believe that turning the spirits of the dead into *buddhas*, making them happy, and therefore producing comfort and happiness for the living, is the central aim of Buddhism in general.

The site at Yamashima, near Kyoto, that Agonshū acquired in 1976 is believed to be spiritually validated by appearances of Buddhist deities in visions in subsequent years. In 1986, the president of Sri Lanka, Junius Jayawardene (r. 1977-88), presented Agonshū with a casket reportedly containing a bone relic of the Buddha. To Agonshū adherents, this confirms their religion's authentication and acceptance in the wider Buddhist world. Veneration of the reliquary has become their central ritual act, and they use models of it for personal devotion.

Agonshū, like other new religions, is media-conscious and uses the latest technology to broadcast its putatively ancient doctrines. The biggest spectacle occurs annually on 11 February at Yamashima, when two gigantic pyres are lit, one containing hundreds of thousands of sticks and chips of wood inscribed with prayers for the ancestral spirits contributed by adherents from all over Japan, and the other containing wishes and petitions to benefit the living. The traditional and the modern are combined in Japan as the volunteers who place these intentions on the fire, dressed in the clothing of *yamabushi*, coordinate their movements by radio telephone.

### *Religion and the Japanese Business World*

An interesting fact about Japanese religion is the interest the corporate business world takes in the religious life of its employees. This can be understood as attempting to create harmony and cohesion. Companies often send their new employees to Zen Buddhist temples for brief training periods, during which they learn discipline and loyalty. They also sponsor memorial rites for deceased employees. With company-sponsored housing and recreational activities, as well as company graves and memorials, the Japanese business world takes care of its own not only in this life but beyond.

But Buddhism has no monopoly in the corporate world. The Shinto rice god, Inari, has become the god of business, and businessmen often attach their calling cards to the doors and railings of the Inari shrines to appeal for assistance. Some companies have their own Inari shrines, at which rituals are performed regularly. Other companies have built their own shrines, at which the spirit (*kami*) of the deceased company founder is venerated.

## Religion and Modernity in East Asia

In Japan, the economy is capitalist and the government is a liberal democracy. Traditional symbols (including the emperor system and religious beliefs associated with Buddhism and folk religion), the ancestor cult, and Confucian ethical values (especially the 'work ethic') continue to dominate the life of the people, including many of their intellectual leaders. During the immediate postwar period, Japanese scholarship reflected a popular mood of uneasiness over the military defeat. An eminent Japanese scholar, Maruyama Masao (b. 1914), criticized traditional Japanese culture and thought, including Neo-Confucianism, as obstacles to modernization.

Since that time, Japanese scholars have argued about the causal factors leading to the modernization of their country and society. Their argument has favoured a 'traditionalist' interpretation focusing upon the forces that were already present in premodern Japan. Of these forces, the most prominent is Neo-Confucian rationalism, the dominant school of thought in the cultural circle that also includes China and Korea. After all, the earliest Japanese 'modernizers' were usually from the *samurai* class, which had a Confucian classical and literary education, could afford Western scientific and technological training, and were motivated by a desire to 'enrich the country and strengthen the armed forces', a slogan directly attributable to the utilitarian branch of Confucianism. This desire fostered nationalism, and in its Japanese form, nationalism was the moving force behind the country's economic success.

The same slogan and desire inspired the Chinese and Koreans as well—whether Marxist or anti-Marxist—in their modernizing efforts. They highlight the importance of finding the traditional in the modern. They are part and parcel of a continual process of cultural (including religious) integration and transformation in contemporary East Asia.

## KEY TERMS

**Amaterasu**. The sun goddess in Japanese tradition.

**Cao Dai**. 'Great Palace', name of the god in a Vietnamese religion founded by Ngo-van-Chieu in 1926.

***ch'i/qi***. Air or ether, regarded as the material component that together with *li* constitutes all things in the metaphysics of the Neo-Confucian Chu Hsi.

***ch'i-kung/qigong***. Breath control exercises, used especially by Taoists.

***chien-ai/jianai***. Universal love, according to the teaching of Mo-tzu. Heaven loves all equally without the distinction of family ties or rank.

**Ch'ŏndogyo**. A Korean religion founded in 1860 that regards human nature as a reflection of divinity and names God Hanullim or Ch'onju, 'lord of Heaven'.

***chün-tzu/junzi***. Nobleman or gentleman, Confucius's term for a person of high moral character.

**cinnabar fields**. Three regions of the body (head, chest, abdomen) in Taoist 'inner' or spiritual alchemy. The designation 'cinnabar' (mercuric sulphide) provides an association with Taoist 'outer' or physical alchemy.

**Eight Immortals**. Taoist deity figures, allegedly historical individuals, who function as patrons of various professions and crafts.

**filial piety**. Children's respect for their parents in Chinese tradition, especially Confucianism.

**Five Agents**. Metal, wood, water, fire, and earth, seen as the basic substances of nature in traditional Chinese and Japanese cosmology.

**Five Classics**. A corpus of texts considered as authoritative by the early Confucians. Their content includes poetry, historical speeches, chronicles, ritual, and divination.

**Five Emperors**. Legendary early sage-kings in Chinese tradition, including the Yellow Emperor (intro- ducer of various civilized techniques) and Yü, the flood-controller.

**Five Relationships**. Confucian roles with accompanying norms and duties of moral conduct: ruler to minister, father to son, husband to wife, elder to younger brother, and friend to friend.

**Four Books**. Earlier texts promoted as a canon by the Sung dynasty Neo-Confucians: *Analects, Mencius, Great Learning*, and *Doctrine of the Mean.*

**Heavenly Masters sect**. A lineage of Taoist teachers traced back to Chang Tao-ling as the Heavenly Master, who claimed Lao-tzu appeared to him in a vision in 142.

**hexagrams**. Sets of six straight or broken lines in their sixty-four different combinations that are consulted especially by Taoists as an aid to divination.

***honji suijaku***. 'The original site and the local manifestations', a Japanese formula interpreting Shinto as a derivative manifestation of Buddhist prototypes in Japan.

***hsin/xin***. In Chinese conceptions, the aspect of personality comprising both what Westerners refer to as 'heart' and as 'mind'. This was important for Mencius and for the Neo-Confucians.

***I-ching/Yijing***. A Chinese divination manual, one of the Five Classics, interpreting different combinations of long and broken strokes in the sixty-four hexagrams.

***jen/ren***. The Confucian virtue of humaneness.

***kami***. The gods and spirits of Japanese religion, seen as present in many forces, objects, and places encountered in nature.

***Kojiki***. 'The Record of Ancient Matters', a collection of Japanese narratives, including myths of the origin of the world and Japan.

***li***. In early Chinese thought, the concept of ritual, including propriety in behaviour towards others.

***li*** (represented by a different Chinese character). In Neo-Confucian thought, the metaphysical or formal principle or pattern in everything, a coordinate of *ch'i* (matter or energy).

**Mandate of Heaven**. The ancient Chinese idea of a divine right to rule granted by Heaven to the king, but subject to forfeiture (and hence justified rebellion) if he conducts himself as a tyrant.

**National Learning**. An eighteenth-century Japanese movement asserting pride in Shinto, the indigenous heritage, over Confucianism and Buddhism, which were considered foreign imports.

***Nihongi***. The Chronicles of Japan, along with the *Kojiki* a compilation of ancient Japanese origin myths.

**oracle bones**. Inscribed tortoise shells and ox shoulder-blades from the second millennium BCE, whose texts reflect the use of the shells and bones in divination rituals.

**Perfect Truth sect**. A Taoist sect featuring celibate monks and dating from the thirteenth-century era of Mongol rule in China.

**Ryōbu Shintō**. A syncretism or fusion between Buddhism and Shinto in Japan, in which elements of Shinto worship were incorporated into Buddhist temples and vice versa, with the principal *kami* equated with *bodhisattvas*.

***sakaki***. A type of sacred tree found at Shinto shrines.

***samurai***. The warrior élite in the feudal society of premodern Japan.

**scapulimancy**. Divination employing the shoulder-bones (*scapula*) of oxen, practised in China in the second millennium BCE.

**Sect Shinto**. Thirteen groups, characteristically founded by individuals who had shamanic experiences, that were recognized as new sects by the Meiji regime in late nineteenth-century Japan.

**Seichō no Ie**. 'House of Growth', one of the Japan's twentieth-century 'new religions', founded as a publishing enterprise in 1930.

**Shang-ti/Shangdi**. 'Lord-on-high', a supreme deity regarded in ancient Chinese religion as the ruler of a domain of nature deities and spirits.

**Shrine Shinto**. The worship of *kami* or nature deities and spirits in Japan, carried on since ancient times at shrines throughout the countryside.

**Shugendō**. A Japanese popular tradition that includes magical and ritual techniques and is associated with sacred mountain regions. Its principal practitioners are the *yamabushi* or 'mountain monks'.

***T'ai-chi/Taiji***. The Great Ultimate, viewed in Sung Neo-Confucianism as a macrocosm equivalent to the structure of the human body. The concept also underlies breathing and exercise routines practised by Taoists.

***T'ai-p'ing***. A future age of Great Peace, envisioned in a classic text that spurred Taoist and Buddhist messianic movements, as well as a modern Christian-inspired rebellion in 1851.

***Tao/Dao***. The Chinese for 'way'. For Taoists, the idea is both descriptive of the dynamic flow of nature and prescriptive for a naturalness to be implemented in human affairs.

***Tao-tsang/Daozang***. The library of texts and commentaries consulted by Taoists and referred to as the Taoist canon. It consists of over a thousand volumes, organized into three 'Caverns' and four supplementary collections.

**Tenrikyō**. A Japanese new religion whose founder, Miki Nakayama, experienced spirit possession in a trance in 1837. It seeks to purify the mind of the spiritual 'dusts' that pollute it.

**Three Sovereigns**. A heavenly, an earthly, and a human ruler in Chinese mythology and legend who precede the Five Emperors. Their roles in the origin of human culture include 'animal-tamer', 'divine woman', and 'fire-maker'.

***T'ien/Tian***. A Chinese term for Heaven or God in the first millennium BCE, when Confucius lived.

***wu***. In Chinese, the term for shamans, specialists in communicating with the spirits. Note that the Chinese Buddhist term for Emptiness or Nothingness is a *different* word, also pronounced *wu*.

***wu-wei***. Non-action, the preferred Taoist path of least resistance, allowing things to run their natural course.

***yang***. In Chinese thought, one of a pair of complementary principles manifested as masculine, aggressive, hard, dry, and bright.

***yin***. The other complementary principle: feminine, accommodating, soft, moist, and dark.

## Further Reading

Blacker, C. 1975. *The Catalpa Bow: A study of Shamanistic Practices in Japan.* London: Allen & Unwin.

Burkhardt. V.R. 1982. *Chinese Creeds and Customs.* Hong Kong: South China Morning Post.

Kaltenmark, M. 1969. *Lao Tzu and Taoism.* Stanford: Stanford University Press.

Kitagawa, J.M. 1966. *Religion in Japanese History.* New York: Columbia University Press.

Levenson, J.R. 1968. *Confucian China and Its Modern Fate: A Trilogy.* Berkeley: University of California Press

Reader, I.T. 1991. *Religion in Contemporary Japan.* Basingstroke: Macmillan; Honolulu: University of Hawaii Press.

Weber, M. 1951. *The Religion of China: Confucianism and Taoism.* New York: Free Press.

## References

Aston, W.G., trans. 1896. *Nihongi: Chronicles of Japan from the Earliest Times to* A.D.697. London: Kegan Paul.

Bodde, D. 1961. 'Myths of Ancient China'. In *Mythologies of the Ancient World,* edited by S.N. Kramer, 367–408. Garden City, NY: Doubleday.

Bowring, R., and P. Kornicki, eds. 1993. *The Cambridge Encyclopedia of Japan.* Cambridge: Cambridge University Press.

Chan, W. 1963. *A Source Book of Chinese Philosophy.* Princeton. Princeton University Press.

———, trans. 1967: *Instructions for Practical Living.* New York: Columbia University Press.

Ching, F. 1988. *Ancestors: Nine Hundred Years in the Life of a Chinese Family*. New York: Morrow.

Ching, J. 1993. *Chinese Religions.* London: Macmillan; Maryknoll, NY: Orbis.

____. 1976. *To Acquire Wisdom: The Way of Wang Yang-ming.* New York: Columbia University Press.

de Bary, W.T., ed. 1960. *Sources of Chinese Tradition.* New York: Columbia University Press.

Duyvendak, J.J.L. 1954. *Tao Te Ching.* London: John Murray.

Elliott, A.J.A. 1955. *Chinese Spirit Medium Cults in Singapore.* London: Royal Anthropological Society.

Ha, T., and G.K. Mintz, trans. 1972. *Samguk yusa: Legends and Histories of the Three Kingdoms of Ancient Korea.* Seoul: Yonsei University Press.

Hawkes, D. 1959. *Ch'u Tz'u: The Songs of the South.* Oxford: Oxford University Press.

Hori, I. 1968. *Folk Religion in Japan: Continuity and Change,* edited by J.M. Kitigawa and A.L. Miller. Chicago: University of Chicago Press.

Jordan, D.K., and D.L. Overmyer. 1986. *The Flying Phoenix: Aspects of Chinese Sectarianism in Taiwan.* Princeton: Princeton University Press.

Hook, B., ed. 1991. *The Cambridge Encyclopedia of China,* 2nd ed. Cambridge: Cambridge University Press.

Kim, Y.C. 1977. 'Ch'ondogyo Thought and Its Significance in [Modern] Korean Tradition'. In *Korean and Asian Religious Tradition,* edited by C.S. Yu, 237–47. Toronto: Korean and Related Studies Press.

*Korea: Its People and Culture.* 1974. Seoul: Hakwon-sa Ltd.

Lau, D.C. 1963. *The Tao Te Ching.* Harmondsworth: Penguin.

____. 1970. *Mencius.* Harmondsworth: Penguin.

Le Blanc, C., trans. 1985. *Huai Nan Tzu.* Hong Kong: Hong Kong University Press.

Legge, J., trans. 1885. *Li Ki. Sacred Books of the East* series, vol. 28. Oxford: Clarendon Press.

____. 1893. *The Chinese Classics*, 2nd ed., 5 vols. Oxford: Clarendon Press.

Liu, S. 1951. *How to Be a Good Communist.* Beijing: Foreign Languages Press.

Mather, R.B., trans. 1976. Liu I-ch'ing, *Shih-shuo Hsin-yu: A New Account of Tales of the World.* Minneapolis: University of Minnesota Press.

Thomsen, H. 1963. The New Religions of Japan. Rutland, VT: Tuttle.

Tsunoda, R., ed. 1958. *Sources of Japanese Tradition.* New York: Columbia University Press.

Watson, B., trans. 1963a. *Hsün Tzu: Basic Writings.* New York: Columbia University Press.

____, 1963b. *Mo Tzu: Basic Writings.* New York: Columbia University Press.

____, trans. 1968. *The Complete Works of Chuang Tzu.* New York: Columbia University Press.

Waley, A. 1937. *The Book of Songs.* London: Allen & Unwin.

____. 1938. *The Analects of Confucius.* London: Allen & Unwin.

____. 1939. *Three Ways of Thought in Ancient China.* London: Allen & Unwin.

Wolf, A.P. 1974. 'Gods, Ghosts and Ancestors'. In *Religion and Ritual in Chinese Society,* edited by A.P. Wolf, 131–82. Stanford: Stanford University Press.

Chapter Six

# Asian and Pacific Horizons

Willard G. Oxtoby

## 'Primal' Religions

A hundred years ago, people described 'primitive' religions as having survived unchanged since time immemorial, a relic even of human prehistory. Early in the twentieth century, the monumental twelve-volume *Encyclopædia of Religion and Ethics* (Hastings 1908–26) could still describe the religion of diverse tribal populations using the present tense.

Such an unchanging world—if it ever existed—is gone forever. After the middle of the twentieth century, modern transportation and communication, spearheaded by the jet airplane and the transistor radio, has left virtually no part of the world inaccessible to cross-cultural influences. The technology and the values of modernity, associated largely with the West, have produced massive change.

In these paragraphs we shall be examining the religious life of several major culture areas in Asia and the Pacific. Areas in central and northern Asia, Southeast Asia, and the Pacific inherit premodern traditions, some of whose forms survive. But these regions all eventually came into the orbit of one or more of the world's three great missionary religions, Buddhism, Christianity, and Islam.

These three all made their way along the inner Asian trade routes, so that evidence of them can be seen in Mongolian religion and to some extent in Siberian. They also spread to southeastern Asia, where in some places such as Cambodia and Indonesia they interacted with already present Hindu influences. In the Philippines, first Islam and then Christianity encountered local tribal populations. In Australia and the Pacific islands, the principal import influences have been Christian.

Hence what we shall be discussing here is the indigenous component in the experience of cultures that have been in a process of interaction with outside influence. This process has resulted in combinations sometimes labelled syncretism by observers. 'Syncretism' is a tricky term, because in the minds of some theologically inclined individuals, it connotes an illegitimate mixture, whereas to other observers, cultural borrowing and cross-fertilization are simply something to be treated as fact, whatever one's evaluation.

But what do we term this indigenous component? 'Primitive' religion? 'Primal' religion? 'Traditional' religion?

There is really no consensus concerning what terms to use. 'Primitive religion' is a term established a century ago that some still find convenient. However, nineteenth-century cultural prejudices and evolutionary assumptions cling to it like burrs to one's trouser leg, so that it is best avoided. 'Primal religion' shares the same drawbacks. 'Traditional religion' does not differentiate the topic from the literary and philosophical traditions of India and East Asia. 'Preliterate' and 'non-literate' characterize the material in terms of what it is not, as though it were unsophisticated or deficient. 'Tribal' and 'small-society religions', in taking the social group as characteristic of the culture, risk implying that it is the explanation or root cause of the patterns of religion. The question is still open; no matter what term one uses for convenient reference, one must be prepared to criticize that term as inadequate to the subtlety and variety of the material.

The Sanskrit ritual, legal, and philosophical texts of India were the work of an educated élite, not of villagers. Indeed, Sanskrit was hardly a vernacular language. To focus on the culture of the common folk, the anthropologist Robert Redfield (1897–1958) and his colleague Milton Singer (b. 1912) popularized the distinction between the élites' 'great tradition' and the village-level 'little tradition'. Thus Sanskrit text scholars and social science fieldworkers could pursue their separate investigations, each claiming to have described India. Their descriptions could be as different as in the story of the blind men and the elephant, where one grasping the tail likens the elephant to a rope, one holding the leg thinks of a tree, and so on.

The great tradition/little tradition contrast is open to criticism even apropos of India. The 'great' or Sanskrit side is identifiable enough, but the 'little tradition' may be a coherent entity only in the minds of theorists. The so-called 'little tradition' is the aggregate of a vast range of local usages, varying not only from one region of the subcontinent to another but often from one village to the next.

Since the 'great tradition' is characterized by literature and literacy, we encounter borderline and pigeonhole problems when we employ the term. Are the vernacular devotional traditions of Indian *bhakti* 'great' because they have literature, or not 'great' because they are vernacular and have mass appeal?

If we turn our attention to regions outside of India, the contrast is even harder to apply crisply. What of Chinese popular religion, which has its written texts? In China, the 'great tradition' became conceptualized as threefold: the tripod of Confucianism, Taoism, and Buddhism. But popular religion operated in a kind of syncretism especially with the latter two of these.

One strains to see a real demarcation between 'great' and 'little' traditions in Japan. There the folk tradition of the villages, if not identical with Shinto, is inextricably intertwined with it. In effect, the mythology and the aesthetic of Japan's 'little tradition' became recorded and systematized as Japan's 'great tradition'.

The aboriginal traditions to which we now turn may therefore be a 'little tradition' in their folkways and their oral character. But as with Shinto in Japan, some of them are now coming to be thought of as 'great' at least in the sense of being national traditions, and they merit attention in their own right and for their intrinsic interest.

## Mongolia and Siberia

### *Siberia*

It is tempting to propose an underlying cultural substratum among various indigenous populations in Siberia. These survived in some isolation until Russian contact in the nineteenth and twentieth centuries, when Russian researchers pioneered in the ethnographic description of them. One indicator of cultural unity across northern inner Asia was language, as many of the peoples spoke languages belonging to the Ural-Altaic group. That group is identified on the basis of linguistic similarities among Finnish and Estonian, Hungarian, Turkish, Mongolian, and Korean. Besides language, another unifying factor is environmental. Most of the tribal populations were nomadic and gained their subsistence primarily from hunting or fishing.

The universal creator God of the Siberian peoples is the lord of the heavens, indeed named 'Sky' in some of their languages. Following his role as creator, however, he tends to withdraw, except where his continuing action is seen in storms. Supervision of life on earth passes to a next generation of deities referred to sometimes as sons or daughters, sometimes as messengers, of the sky god. These deities, who watch over humans and help them, generally number fewer than ten.

We do not find much evidence of a chief mother goddess in Siberian religion, perhaps because of the nomadic and hunting focus of life. In the class of daughters or messengers of the sky god, feminine deities do appear, with spheres of influence mainly in the area of childbirth and the protection of children from disease.

Shamanism is the feature of Siberian religion that has most fascinated anthropologists and religion scholars. Among the Tungus peoples of Siberia, the word *saman* denotes a practitioner capable of going into a trance state and understood by the people to have intimate contact with the world of the spirits when doing so. Scholars use the term 'ecstasy' in a technical sense to describe this state, meaning by it that the person enters an experiential awareness outside of his or her usual stance.

Shamanism is like priesthood in that it is practised on behalf of and for the benefit of the social group by a person who is a specialist. Also, as in the case of priesthood, we find both hereditary and vocational types of eligibility for it. In either case, though, the shaman becomes qualified for his or her practice through apprenticeship to, and through obtaining the recognition of, an already practising master. Shamanism contrasts with much priestly activity in that its essential characteristic is the cultivation of a trance experience in which insight is considered received from the spirits, rather than the priest's activity of performing a ritual act involving a sacrifice or offering to the spirits.

Once identified and named in the Siberian context, 'shamanism' became a convenient term to describe comparable cultivation of trance states in other cultures around the world. Some of these, in regions adjoining Siberia, may have had prehistoric or historic links transmitting it: Korea and ancient China, for instance, and possibly across the Bering Strait to the Native peoples of North America. In more geographically distant settings, comparable phenomena have to be taken as parallels rather than as instances of common origin: Africa, the Caribbean, or the ecstatic activity of the earliest Hebrew prophets. In any event, we should be clear, 'possession' is not itself an observable phenomenon of behaviour, but is rather the interpretation given to such behaviour by societies in which it is cultivated.

The figures in other cultures with which the Siberian shaman is compared are referred to variously as sorcerers, magicians, and medicine men. These other roles are in a sense broader in their expectations than the term 'shaman'. They are result-oriented, connoting some benefit to be derived from the ecstatic activity. It is evident that shamans could be healers or could invoke curses, but the term as scholars use it suggests essentially attaining an inner experience more than causing a change in circumstances external to the practitioner.

Costume is an important feature of Siberian shamanism. The shaman wears a robe, sometimes an animal skin, draped over the shoulders. Tassels and disks or badges, sometimes of metal, are hung on it or worn over it, and are taken to represent animal spirits. Bones that form part of the paraphernalia are associated with the spirits of the human dead. Also essential for the ritual to be effective is a cap, considered a source of power. It can be decorated with antlers, an animal head, or feathers. Given that the whole costume is a sort of animal mask, it is not surprising that face masks are uncommon among Siberian shamans. And a final essential part of the shaman's paraphernalia is a drum.

The symbolism of the shaman's attire is integral with expectations of the shaman's specialist role. The shaman experiences ascent to heaven, hence the feathers suggesting flight. The shaman achieves rapport with animal and human spirits, symbolized by the tokens and bones. And the shaman summons the presence of the spirits with the drum.

### *Mongolia*

In contrast with the more northerly regions of Siberia, Mongolia lay along the inner Asian trade routes and has known many centuries of cultural and religious influence. Buddhists, Nestorian Christians, Manichaeans, Zoroastrians, and Muslims all came into contact with the Mongols. In the thirteenth century, even Latin Christians came; in southern Mongolia there are remains of a Gothic church that the archbishop of Peking, John of Monte Corvino (d. c. 1330), built for the Onggut tribe's Prince George, who converted from Nestorian to Roman Catholic Christianity.

Sometimes the Mongols found it hard, or were disinclined, to tell these different traditions apart. There was a tendency towards a syncretic identification or fusion of comparable elements from different traditions. In a Mongol source from about the thirteenth century, Muslims and Christians are said to refer to Śākyamuni, the Buddha, as Adam.

As the various traditions made their way to Mongolia, they encountered the indigenous shamanism. When they described it, they did not on the whole equate it with their own religious systems and practices, but treated it as alien. Since the bulk of the written records come from the Tibetan-Mongol Vajrayāna Buddhist era of the seventeenth century onward, it is mainly from their descriptions that we can construct a picture of traditional Mongolian religion. Today's Mongols are mostly tantric Buddhists.

Some traditions link Mongolian shamanism to the veneration of the ancestors. In one legend, an old man tells his son that after his own death he will continue to protect the son if the son conducts a proper funeral and makes appropriate subsequent offerings at his grave. The father's spirit associates with the local spirits under Atagha Tngri, the sky god. When the mother dies, the son makes similar offerings, her spirit joins other ancestral spirits and gains the power to control weather and to bring fortune or misfortune to humans. She becomes worshipped as Emegelji Elji, 'old grandmother'. As people begin to feel the power of the two ancestral spirits, they enter into a man and a girl, both of whom shake and tremble. These two experience shamanic ecstasy and fly to the ancestors' burial place, where they receive drums and feathered headgear. They announce to the people, 'We have descended from Atagha Tngri to protect all living beings on this earth.' The people subsequently make images of the shaman and shamaness as well.

Through the good offices of a Mongolian shaman, misfortunes such as illness are mitigated. The shaman invokes his Ongghot or protective spirit to fight the demon causing the trouble. The demon is banished into an image that is then burned or an animal that is then slaughtered. Similarly, demons can be expelled from animals or property. There are also formulas of blessing to promote good fortune, and the use of shoulder-bones of sheep for predictive divination.

In Mongolian popular religion, there is worship of ninety-nine *tngri* or deities, forty-four grouped to the east of the shamans and fifty-five to the west. They are also mentioned in a variety of numerically smaller groups, such as the five gods of the winds or the nine gods of anger. People turn to certain deities for quite specific benefits: for instance, to Anarba Tngri for beauty and to Kölcin Tngri for prevention or cure of boils, scabs, vermin, and worms.

Some of the names of the *tngri* appear indigenous, but others reflect influence from the great religions, such as Bisnu Tngri (the Hindu Viṣṇu) and Qormusta Tngri (the Zoroastrian Ahura Mazda). The *darqan* (blacksmith) Güjir Tngri acquires the Buddhist title Mahākāla in the following hymn:

> Great Maqa Galan Darqan Güǰir Tngri,
> Eldest brother of the ninety-nine *tngri,*
> Who arose through the blessing of Qormusta Tngri
> At the command of the holy teacher Buddha,
> You who have a glorious cast-iron shield,
> You who have a beautiful coloured throne,
> You who have a great golden hammer,
> You who have a great silver anvil,
> You, Maqa Galan Darqan Güǰir Tngri, I worship,
> Deign to come here on your blue-grey horse.
> (Heissig 1980:56)

In their shamanic folk religion, the Mongolians were not unaware of outside influences. One of the shamanic hymns contrasts the apprenticeship-based oral tradition of shamanism and the text-based character of Buddhism.

> My Master, you who have given [to me]
> the doctrine without writing
> My Master, you who have taught [me]
> the doctrine without books.
> (Heissig 1980:2)

## Australian Aboriginal Religion

Regions of the Australian continent are diverse. They range from coastal tropical rain forest in the north to hot desert in the central interior, to the Mediterranean climate of the 'gum' (eucalyptus) trees of the southeast. This last was the principal region of European settlement, so that Aboriginal traditions survived longer in the other two before undergoing the changes brought by European contact.

The overall picture of Australian Aboriginal religion is composite in two ways. First, it bridges space, bringing together the ways of inland hunters and coastal fishers, and people for whom rain is abundant with others to whom rain is scarce. Second, it spans time, from the reports of mid-nineteenth-century ethnographers to those of the present. If more than a century of contact with Europeans has made 'pristine' religion harder to find, this reduction of research data has been compensated for by a considerable refinement in theoretical approaches and assumptions.

Theorists a hundred years ago took totemism to be the most significant feature of Australian religion. By 'totem' is meant usually a species of plant or animal, or occasionally a particular place or location, to which the clan considers itself related. The totem is a symbol of the clan's identity. Under routine circumstances, members of the clan may be forbidden from killing or eating the totem, but at special times or for special personnel, such restriction can be lifted.

The general view of the universe in Australian religion conceives of earth and sky as always having existed. In the sky there is a high god, known under different names by different peoples, and given credit for supreme power, but not actively worshipped. Some tribes speak of a subordinate Great Father figure with animal feet, who has many wives and offspring who live as immortals in a paradiselike realm with abundant flowers and fruit. Though original contact with earth is posited, such contact has been broken, and heaven now functions independently without concern for earth.

Life on earth is shaped not by the heavenly spirits but by the earth spirits. In primordial time, these are asleep beneath the surface of the earth, but they then emerge in human and animal forms and fashion the world that we know. They are the 'totemic ancestors', whose task is to create humankind and instruct it in the techniques of earthly survival. This task accomplished, the spirits return to the realm below, go back to sleep, and leave humans to carry on.

This primordial time when the totem ancestors are active is called the Dream Time, or simply the Dreaming. While Australian religion devotes little attention to the supreme but remote heavenly being, it is actively concerned with recovering or reactualizing the Dream Time of the earthly totem ancestors. As these are the powers that have given form to earthly objects, the rituals are linked to specific objects and locations. Each sacred centre has its particular ceremonies, which are to be performed there and nowhere else. And to be effective, the ceremonies must be performed in the precise manner in which they have been instituted by the divine totemic ancestors. Thus initiation into one's clan consisted importantly of learning the precise location and manner of performance of rituals.

In one sense, the notion of the Dream Time as the central feature of Australian Aboriginal religion is a construct imposed on that heritage by outsiders, namely by White European and Australian ethnographers. The terms translated as 'dreaming' vary in the different Aboriginal languages, and so do the ranges of connotation of those terms. The terminology appears to have been first used as a general characterization by Baldwin Spencer (1869–1929) and Francis J. Gillen (1856–1912) in 1899, when they used it to translate the term *alcheringa* in the language of the Aranda people of arid central Australia. In the Aranda conception of things, that is time immemorial, the 'uncreated time' or primal eternity when the ancestors fashion the world and also institute practices to be followed in society.

In the twentieth century, this construct has been appropriated by Australian Aboriginal peoples themselves in speaking about their own religion. For people seeking a unified or systematic character in Aboriginal religion, it has served as a central feature about which regionally varied traditions can be assembled. Hence, while the idea of the Dream Time was not a universally recognized concept in Australia a hundred years ago, it has become such, and it gathers together several distinct meanings.

The Dream Time can be seen, first, as a narrative account of origins. It is the mythological story of the eternal (and uncreated) beings, the ancestor heroes, who form and shape the created world. Second, it is viewed as the sense of the present and continuing power of those beings in the land, localized in particular physical features of the earth's surface or in particular plants and animals that inhabit it. One of the most striking physical features of central Australia is Uluru, known to Westerners as Ayers Rock, a massive sedimentary rock outcropping. The world's largest monolith, it is 6 km (4 mi.) long and rises 350 m (1,150 ft) from the surrounding flat plain. There is evidence of its function as a sacred site in the Aboriginal drawings that decorate various recesses along its base.

A third connotation of the Dream Time is law or custom. Society's practices, both moral and ritual, go back to the timeless past of the Dreaming. The traditional activity of society today is thus given a sacred character, and actions today are to be conducted in harmony with the primal order of things. A fourth aspect of the Dreaming is the individual's personal interiorization of this sacred way. One's own clan membership or sense of relationship to the ancestral spirits can provide a personal 'way' to follow, a kind of religious calling or vocation.

Whatever individuality personal 'ways' may have, the practice of Aboriginal population groups tends to exhibit repeated patterns—patterns that we describe as ritual. Ritual serves as a re-enactment and reinforcement of the patterns of the primal Dream Time. The participant, it has been said, does not merely recall the ancestral heroes. The participant in some sense *becomes* the hero, taking on and identifying with the ancestral identity.

Much of the earlier nineteenth-century ethnography concentrated on rituals performed by the males of the society, principally because the investigators were males. Now, with a growing body of research by women anthropologists and some emerging women's voices among the spokespeople for the Aboriginal community, it has become clear that women in Aboriginal society have possessed their ritual traditions as well. It is not that there have been two systems of ritual, one male and one female. Instead, it is better to think of Aboriginal society as having a comprehensive understanding of ritual, with its male and its female roles.

The ritual life of Aboriginal Australia demarcates particular spaces and times as sacred. There is a degree of specialization by persons expert in the rituals, but generally not the sharp division that we define elsewhere as priesthood versus laity. Rather, the tribal group is involved corporately. Individuals may be the focus of rituals, especially coming-of-age rituals at puberty. In some cases, the individual may be given access to space, knowledge, or the ritual and medical uses of various articles that had previously been reserved or secret. And for the group as a whole, the function of ritual can be instructional, teaching the tradition through practice. In the long run, the essence of Aboriginal religion is more its practice than its doctrine.

## Religion in the Pacific Islands

The vast expanse of the Pacific Ocean is largely open water in its eastern half, from Hawaii and Tahiti eastward to North and South America. By contrast, the western Pacific, stretching towards Australia and the Philippines, is home to a multitude of islands.

They range in size from tiny coral reefs to substantial volcanic mountains, some such as in Hawaii rising over 4,000 m (over 13,000 ft) above sea level. Their climate, except for New Zealand, is tropical.

Geographers and anthropologists group the Pacific islands into three principal belts or zones. One is Melanesia, stretching from Papua New Guinea southeastward to Fiji. A second, parallel but more to the north, is Micronesia, a belt extending eastward from the Philippines and Guam and then turning south towards Fiji. Third, covering the largest expanse, is Polynesia, a huge triangle from New Zealand northeast to Hawaii and southeast to the islands around Tahiti.

It is possible that the Polynesians' distant ancestors migrated into the Pacific from southeast Asia or Indonesia. The resemblance of languages indicates this: throughout the region, languages are of the group identified as Malayo-Polynesian. Culturally speaking, too, Micronesia, Melanesia, and Polynesia have a considerable amount in common.

### *Micronesia*

Many of the islands of Micronesia are tiny tropical atolls. That is, they are ring-like formations composed of coral reefs around a central lagoon, whose land surface area is often at most only a square kilometre or two. Formed from marine shells, the coral has weathered into soil, which supports coconut trees and is farmed with taro or sweet potatoes. The inhabitants lead a simple life but one precariously dependent on what they can extract from the coconut, their gardens, and from the surrounding sea.

In the traditional culture of the people who live on these islands, the powers that can affect human existence are of two kinds: the spirits of the ancestors, and the gods of the forces of nature.

Like many other tribal societies, the Micronesians consider that the spirit of a human being is able to leave the body. During dreams in particular, it is experienced as travelling freely. The logic of such belief in spirits is that if they can range widely in space, they can also endure in time. The spirit survives the death of the body. The ghosts of the dead, particularly the recently deceased, are believed to be actively interested in the affairs of the living and to have the power to affect or intervene in them.

Many ghosts fade into oblivion, but some are better remembered. What keeps the memory of some ghosts alive is their connection with clan lineages. Those who are most actively remembered are those who become considered the ancestral ghosts of particular kin groups. A shrine in the house of the clan's head is dedicated to such a ghost. It is a framework of bamboo, at which offerings are left: coconut oil, left permanently; floral leis, until they wither; and turmeric and loincloths, left for twenty days and then distributed for use by family members.

Individuals may play the role of mediums, that is, persons in particularly close communication with the spirit or ghost. When a person enters such a state, he or she usually shakes and trembles, an action interpreted by the social community as spirit possession. The medium generally utters information in intelligible language, on matters of practical concern: impending weather, the conditions of travel, the safety of kin, or the cause of illness. When the medium resumes normal consciousness, he or she is unlikely to recall what has been said, but others have been paying careful attention.

Among the Caroline islanders on the Ulithi atoll studied after the Second World War by William A. Lessa (b. 1908), two ancestral spirits had achieved the rank of 'great ghosts'. One is Iongolap, born on Ulithi of a woman who creates atolls by scattering sand in the sea. His father is on the island of Yap, and visits to his father are taken to account for the custom of tribute payment to Yap. Such was told to a Russian explorer early in the nineteenth century. But by the early twentieth century, a German anthropologist reported Iongolap as the heavenly dispatcher of a mythological bird and as the teacher of fishing and cooking techniques to humans.

Another ancestral spirit elevated to deity is Marespa, whose mundane life is sufficiently documented that we know his genealogy and that he was born in 1868. Marespa dies in infancy, but his spirit takes possession of a relative and issues reliable warnings of typhoons, locates lost sailors, and successfully predicts the arrival of schools of fish. A godlike veneration for Marespa spread eastward and westward throughout the Caroline Islands, and was noted by twentieth-century anthropologists in various locales. But other beliefs have now supplanted the veneration of the ghost Marespa almost everywhere.

Besides the beneficial spirits, there are numerous demons or malevolent spirits. These are often nameless, or if named, less clearly tied to clan ancestors. Some are identified with particular locations such as dangerous shoreline rocks; others are known by the afflictions they are thought to bring, such as illness, blindness, shipwreck, or simple bad luck. They are perceived as inhabiting local haunts, they are given graphic but conflicting physical descriptions, and some are thought to pursue and accost people.

In the Gilbert Islands ('Gilbert' has become part of the local language so that the nation is now officially Kiribati) the British colonial administrator Arthur Grimble (1888–1956) lived and worked for many years, achieving a real rapport with the Native population and its ways. So well trusted was Kurimbo (as the Gilbertese pronounced his name) that he was initiated into their lineage. But so empathetic was he in his approach to Native traditions that he treated demons virtually as real; his writings relate experiences of their power. In any event, anthropologists argue, the fear of demons is a strong inducement towards ritually correct behaviour—behaviour that may also function to promote safety, hygiene, or social cohesion.

The gods are more remote than the spirits, in less direct contact with people and therefore less directly propitiated in rituals. Moreover, they are generalized in their function, belonging to the entire people rather than linked to particular lineages or locales. Some islands' narratives tell of the gods as creators, but in creation stories that assume the prior existence of a world. Creation sometimes is of species such as plants and animals in general, but creation legends also deal with how particular islands came to be located where they are.

Some of the gods spend all their time in the heavens. In the Carolines the Great Spirit, Ialulep, is envisioned as a giant white-haired man, so old that he has to be helped. When he surveys the world, two men have to prop his eyelids open. But he is still powerful; thunder is the sound of his door slamming, and death occurs when he cuts the thread of life leading to the brain of a human on earth.

Other gods are somewhat more vigorous; Iolofath, for instance, is a trickster who makes his way up the four levels of the sky world, causing fish to bite unsuspecting boys enroute. At the fourth level he is apprehended as a stranger by workers who are digging a post hole. Seeking to eliminate him, they place him in the hole and shove the post down. Red and green liquids looking like blood and bile squirt up, convincing them that they have done their job. But Iolofath has hidden in a recess in the side of the hole and has spat up mouthfuls of red earth and green apple leaves. He then gets termites to chew a passage out through the pole, surprises the workers, and is thereafter suitably respected by them.

The picture we have been sketching of religion in Micronesia is of a traditional society. It was never isolated; its language and its myths suggest diffusion or contact among Pacific cultures even before the coming of Europeans. Our knowledge of Micronesia comes mainly from outsiders who made early contact with it. Inevitably, that contact has increased, and since the middle of the twentieth century even the smallest and remotest Micronesian islands have become linked with the world outside.

### *Polynesia*

Compared with Micronesia, Polynesia includes several much larger islands, notably New Zealand and Hawaii. European contact with these was earlier and much more substantial than with Micronesia, and included extensive settlement. But through the years as the old Polynesian culture was threatened with near-extinction by British modernity in New Zealand, American modernity in Hawaii, and French modernity in Tahiti, it remained an object of anthropological investigation, tourist curiosity, and local pride. More recently, the recovery and rediscovery of the traditional heritage has been a political rallying cry both for Maoris in New Zealand and for Native Hawaiians, now minorities in their historic homelands.

Polynesian religion generally divides the universe into the earthly and the supernatural realms, further separating the supernatural into the heavens and the underworld. What goes on in the earthly realm is thought to be directed or influenced by spirits above and below. One's life as a human being, indeed, is the movement of a spirit from the other realm to take up residence in a body in this one. On death, the spirit returns to the other realm.

People's role as incarnate spirits is by no means the only contact of the spirit realm with life on earth. The gods frequently visit this world as well, making their presence manifest in places and in events. The Maoris of New Zealand refer to the gods as *atua*s, and consider them responsible for virtually every unexplained phenomenon: weather, illness, even bodily and emotional states. When Europeans came and built windmills, the Maoris even thought the *atua*s were what caused them to turn.

As far away as Hawaii, the role of the gods was the same, shaping the universe, controlling nature and humans. The British sea captain James Cook (1728–79), making the first European contact with Hawaii in 1778, remarked on the resemblance of its religion to what he had observed elsewhere in Polynesia. The principal addition to the Polynesian pantheon was Pele, the volcano goddess, since Hawaii had active volcanoes.

Four roles for the gods are often considered the principal portfolios in the Polynesian pantheon; some writers refer to them as 'departmental' gods. Tangaroa (in Hawaii called Kanaloa) is the chief god, creator of the world. In particular, he rules the ocean, dominant in the Polynesian natural environment. Tane (in Hawaii, Kane) is a male figure whose digging stick thrust into the ground releases the water of life; this action is widely seen to have sexual symbolism, and one of the representations of him is an upright cone-shaped stone, considered phallic.

Tu (in Hawaii, Ku) is not a single deity but a class of manifestations of deity. Generally male, they can be paired with female deities termed Hina. The pairs are treated as consorts or married couples in some rituals. Some of the Ku looked after routine activities, such as the supervision of fishing by the 'Ku of the sea'. The Hawaiian volcano goddess Pele was also named 'Hina of the fire'. But a main occasion for consulting the Ku deities was when there was a crisis. In times of famine or disease but particularly in war, the Ku gods were propitiated with animal and human sacrifices. The humans offered up were generally captives, slaves, or breakers of taboos.

Lono (in Tahiti called Rongo) is the deity from whom to seek two principal blessings: agricultural fertility and social peace. He is also consulted for healing. In Hawaii, his priests and tax collectors make a procession around the island, collecting offerings at local altars to Lono. The humanlike Lono figures used in the procession are mounted on poles, and when Captain Cook's ships arrived in Hawaii during the period of a Lono festival, the ships' masts were taken to be part of the annual celebration of the return of Lono to the islands for the rainy season.

Besides the nature deities, there are tutelary or guardian spirits. These look after individuals, clans, or craft groups. Humans try to discern the will of the gods by reflecting on unusual natural events such as weather or the behaviour of fish or other creatures, and through ordinary dreams and specialists' possession states.

There were also priests as specialists in ritual. In a society with kings and chieftains, such as in Hawaii and among the Maori, divine favour was sought for their general prosperity and for success in their particular undertakings. The priests served as important advisers to the chiefs, in addition to performing their ritual functions.

Rituals were conducted in open-air spaces. It was important that the space should be demarcated by a boundary wall. In Hawaii, the enclosures generally contained terraces and altars, and sometimes shelters to house the drums and ritual objects as well as to accommodate chiefs and priests. In New Zealand among the Maori, the village square was the focus of much ritual activity, with the principal building in it being an elaborately decorated or carved wooden meeting house.

One of the principal contributions of Polynesian religion to the study of religion generally is the concept of taboo. The term is Polynesian, *tapu* or *tabu*, and its range of semantic associations include both sacredness and pollution. Today the term has secular, non-ritual uses as well. In Tahiti today, private-property signs read, bilingually in French and Polynesian, 'Proprieté privé/tabu'.

One way to understand the diverse range of what can be taboo is to think of the item (or the space or the time) simply as having come under the influence of the spirits. In cases when the spirit influence is expected to be beneficial, people seek through rituals to invoke the deities, inviting them to extend their presence and influence. Their sponsorship would be sought to render auspicious a new undertaking, such as the launching of a large canoe, and sacrifices or other gifts might be offered to attract them.

In cases when the spirit influence is taken to be threatening, ritual action is devoted to recognizing and containing *tapu*. It is contagious, and can be spread through contact with a tabooed item. Death is a particularly potent source of contagion. Anything that had come into contact with a corpse, even food grown in the soil touched by one, is thought to be contaminating. Means of containment include leaving the contaminated area, washing, and the use of a latrine facing away from inhabited areas.

There are divergent views about the role of women in relation to *tapu* in Maori religion. Construction projects and warriors could be cleared of *tapu* by the ritual action of a woman, considered particularly intense during menstruation. One theory holds that the woman repels the spirits, but some of women's ritual actions, such as in various initiations, appear to attract them. The alternative interpretation would be that women attract spirits, indeed that their bodies are a kind of mysterious gateway to the spirit world.

### *Melanesia*

Contact with Europeans has been important in the history and development of Melanesia, the Pacific region closest to Australia. Westerners have sought to harvest the natural resources of its larger islands. They early brought a curiosity about Melanesian rituals, including fire-walking, the Fijian ordeal of walking barefoot across a bed of hot coals while in a spirit-possessed state.

Influential in the study of Aboriginal religion generally has been the concept of *mana*. The Melanesian word *mana* gained currency in the West after 1878, thanks to the correspondence and publications of the British missionary anthropologist Richard H. Codrington (1830–1922). Codrington described *mana* as a generalized power that is perceived in objects appearing in any sense out of the ordinary, or that is acquired by persons who possess them.

A person walking along a beach might pick up a brightly coloured or odd-shaped shell. If, while carrying that shell, the person experienced good fortune, he or she might attribute the luck to power present in the shell itself. Others observing that person's good luck might attribute it to the power of the person. So *mana* is in a sense transferable, and *mana* can generate more *mana*. Viewed analogously to electricity, *mana* is a power that can be generated, transmitted, and stored.

Codrington's theory was an effort to view all Melanesian religion as an attempt to generate *mana*, that is, to acquire and direct power magically towards the purpose of personal benefit. Other writers at the end of the nineteenth and beginning of the twentieth centuries took *mana* as paradigmatic of the sense of supernatural power present in all religion generally, and some even employed the concept as evidence to support speculation that magic lies at the origin and essence of all religion. More recent anthropological work has questioned the centrality of *mana*, suggesting that Codrington did not correctly understand the term, and has concentrated instead on the structures of kinship and social organization among the Melanesians. Religious outlooks are of interest in such research primarily when they can be taken as symbolic reinforcements of social patterns.

Another important development in Melanesian religion can hardly be generalized to serve as a characteristic of all religion, but it has been traced in various occurrences across the Melanesian culture area. This is the appearance of what are termed 'cargo cults'. In these, people look forward to a day of fulfilment, when supplies of manufactured goods are to arrive—these goods produced not by earthly humans but by the spirits of their deceased ancestors.

Cargo cults reflect explicitly the European impact on the indigenous Melanesian people: on their civilization, their economy, and their values. They have appeared since the middle of the nineteenth century, when the colonial activity of Europeans reduced many Melanesians to poverty, cheapened their labour, and sometimes denigrated their traditional arts and crafts.

Valued instead were the trade goods and military supplies unloaded from European ships: metal tools, machine-woven cloth, canned or packaged food, motor vehicles, guns, and ammunition. All of these were associated with the power that the foreigners seemed to have. Cargoes of such material were now expected to arrive and to be distributed for the benefit of the Native population. With eager anticipation, people made ritual and practical preparations to receive the awaited consignments.

The nineteenth-century cargo movements were largely among coastal populations because the Europeans came by sea and their colonial domination was most thorough in the coastal regions of New Guinea (both Irian Jaya in the west and Papua in the east), and on islands like Vanuatu (formerly New Hebrides) and the Solomons. The local populations built docks and warehouses in anticipation.

Transportation changed towards the middle of the twentieth century. While ships remained important in the Second World War, the airplane assumed an increasingly prominent role. It was even more impressive than metal ships as a carrier of exotic cargo, and soon cargo-cult preparations meant clearing airstrips in the jungle or along the beach. Moreover, the interior highlands of Papua New Guinea began to witness some cargo-cult phenomena along with the spread of pentecostal Christianity.

Cargo-cult leaders seek word of the expected arrival. Coming from the ancestors, it may arrive at cemeteries, so they devote attention to cemetery maintenance. They sometimes also erect poles for radiolike listening for messages of the cargo. Shamanic possession behaviour is considered a sign of contact with the spirit world from which the word is to come.

Cargo cults reflect not only the material contact of Western civilization with Melanesia, but also the religious contact of Christianity with indigenous religion. When a movement is based entirely on the local traditional religion, the leader needs to show how the traditional stories lend themselves to a millenarian interpretation. The traditional rituals are performed, but with a heightened fervour.

But when there is an admixture of Christian material, that can serve as the source of the novelty. The leader can claim to have had contact with, or be a manifestation of, Jesus. Alternatively, the cargo can involve the identification of the Christian deity with a local one. In the cargo cults with a Christian component, the build-up of expectation includes forecasts of the last judgement and the flames of hell, accompanied by the return or 'second coming' of Jesus. Mass assemblies are marked by conversions and baptisms.

The social roles of cargo cults have been analysed in various ways by anthropological and political interpreters. One clear yearning that they seem to fulfil is for a feeling of Native dignity: the indigenous population, formerly used to an egalitarian economy of the exchange of gifts, has been disadvantaged in an economy of plantation labour and commercial purchase, where the foreigners have greatly outweighed them.

Cargo cults can reflect an attempt to follow out the logic of traditional Melanesian religion, including the assumption that rituals are a practical technique aimed at practical results. In line with this is what a Native informant told the investigator Peter Lawrence (1921–88):

> Everything that we have was invented by a deity: taro, yams, livestock, artifacts. If we want taro to grow, we invoke the taro goddess, and so forth. Well, then, you people come to us with all your goods, and we ask, 'Where is the god of the cargo and how do we contact him' (Lawrence 1987:78)?

But by what kinds of logic can cargo beliefs be maintained, especially in the light of the continued non-delivery of the expected cargo? One looks for support in the events of the day. During the Second World War, the Japanese forces invading Melanesia were thought to have been sent by the spirits to punish the Europeans. More recently, some politicians have taken the manifest need for economic reform as evidence of its imminence. But cargo cults, by fostering an expectation of the miraculous, can tend to distract many from pursuing more practical goals in education and economic development.

The cargo cults are a clear illustration that the contact of Europeans with the islands of the Pacific has irrevocably changed the lives of its peoples. Traditional social structures have been dislocated by the foreigner, and traditional religious patterns altered by the activity of foreign missionaries. Much of what we now say about traditional religion in the Pacific must be a description in the past tense, a record of practices now extinct or threatened with extinction.

Yet the questions religion asks and attempts to answer—the questions of origin and purpose and meaning in life and in the world—remain very much alive. New combinations of indigenous and imported symbolic patterns have emerged, and the religious vocabulary of traditional Pacific religion is still being explored for resources to answer these ultimate questions that people continue to ask.

## FURTHER READING

Charlesworth, M.J., et al., eds. 1984. *Religion in Aboriginal Australia: An Anthology.* St Lucia, Australia: University of Queensland Press.

Grimble, A. 1952. *A Pattern of Islands.* (Also published as *We Chose the Islands: A Six-Year Adventure in the Gilberts.)* London: John Murray.

Handy, E.S.C. 1927. *Polynesian Religion,* Bulletin no. 34. Honololu: Bernice P. Bishop Museum.

Lessa, W.A. 1966. *Ulithi: A Micronesian Design for Living.* New York: Holt, Rinehart and Winston.

Luomala, K. 1986. *Voices on the Wind: Polynesian Myths and Chants,* rev. ed. (Special Publication 75). Honolulu: Bishop Museum Press.

Mountford, C.P. 1965. *Ayers Rock: Its People, Their Beliefs and Their Art.* Sydney: Angus and Robertson.

Trompf, G.W. 1991. *Melanesian Religion.* Cambridge: Cambridge University Press.

## REFERENCES

Hastings, J., ed. 1908–26. *Encyclopaedia of Religion and Ethics,* 12 vols plus index. Edinburgh: Clark.

Heissig, W. 1980. *The Religions of Mongolia.* London: Routledge and Kegan Paul; Berkeley: University of California Press.

Lawrence, P. 1987. 'Cargo Cults'. In *The Encyclopedia of Religion,* edited by M. Eliade, vol. 3, 74–81. New York: Macmillan.

Chapter Seven

# The Nature of Religion

Willard G. Oxtoby

Suppose someone asks: 'The religions are all pretty much the same, aren't they?' My thoughts are: one might mean the religions are equally deserving of acceptance or status, a point we take up in concluding the treatment of the Western group of religions in another volume. Or the questioner might mean that the religions accomplish some common result in their practice or share some essential core in their teachings.

Let us address the last of these, about a shared central core. Some people maintain such a view casually, others penetratingly. What matters is not to fine-tune a subtle nuance or split hairs over a distinction, but to say yes or no to the view of the big picture. Within the range of diversity we have been surveying in this book, is there a fundamental unity?

## Identifying 'Religion'

One way to approach the unity question is to observe the language we use to talk about the subject. There is, after all, a substantial body of discourse about 'religion'. Bookstores and libraries have sections on religion, schools and universities offer courses and conduct research on it, the Saturday newspaper can devote a page to it, and there are laws that guarantee its freedom.

Yes, people do seem to have an idea of what they mean by 'religion'. Some derive it from historical precedent in the use of the term. Others derive it from the characteristics shared by a 'short list' of what are agreed upon as religions. Still others define the concept by contrasting it with what it does not include, refining it through the discussion of borderline cases. We consider each of these approaches in turn.

## Western Use of the Term 'Religion'

The Euro-American West has generated the concept 'religion' primarily with reference to the West's principal religion, Christianity. During the European Middle Ages, the word *religio* in Latin, and its derivatives in the other languages of Christian Europe, had a meaning internal to Christianity: it meant piety, or the faith and action incumbent on a practising member of the Christian community. Indeed, 'a religious' continues to mean a member of a religious order.

This is not to say that European Christians were unaware of other traditions. Early Christian writers referred to rival teachings. The medieval Christians knew of the Muslims as a major challenge to the south and east of Europe, the Jews as a distinct minority within medieval Christendom, and 'pagans' as rivals in the classical Mediterranean and in pre-Christian northern Europe. However, they did not use the term 'religions', in the plural, for these other traditions until after the fifteenth century.

From the 1490s onward, Europe's horizons were vastly enlarged through voyages of discovery and trade. The information gained was rapidly and widely disseminated in Europe, thanks to the introduction of printing. Before long, volumes catalogued the ceremonies and customs of Asia and the Western hemisphere. Eventually, too, the teachings of China and India were described as models of political and metaphysical wisdom, often with an eye to reforming this or that position in Europe.

When the Christian world of the West viewed other traditions, it sought to define them in terms parallel to the way it understood its own Christianity. The Christian historical self-understanding imposed three of its own predilections on what it described.

Among these was Christianity's emphasis on creeds, its desire to pin things down as affirmations of belief. One identified oneself as a Christian by declaring such-and-such about God, Jesus, or the world. So one expected the adherent of another tradition to have a contrasting set of creedal beliefs, which it would be the observer's task to formulate. Some of Asia's great traditions, such as Buddhism, do present substantial, sophisticated, and challenging doctrines, but in the case of Shinto, for instance, statements of doctrine are more of a collector's item.

To expect every religion necessarily to have a systematic doctrine, then, is arbitrary. It excludes a vast and important range of humankind's religious activity from view. So 'religion' defined as 'belief' is not a descriptive definition of the spectrum of phenomena, but a prescriptive restriction to the narrower band within the spectrum that will fit the observer's stipulations.

A second Christian predilection is to impose on all religion Christianity's centuries-old institutional distinction between the sacred and the secular. Christianity started with three centuries of minority status before receiving state patronage, and consequently grew quite accustomed to the idea that some things belong to God and other things to Caesar. Even the medieval Latin Church, at the height of its influence and in its struggles over authority with princes, took conspicuous note of the principle. One of the principal characteristics of modernity in the Euro-American West is a secularity that puts both intellectual and institutional limits on the sphere allocated to religion.

To identify religion in contrast with what one regards as 'secular' may be useful for understanding classical Christianity, but it has not proven helpful towards understanding classical Islam. Islam did not share Christianity's formative experience of 300 years as a minority. Islam was launched in Arabia as a total value system for society, including its laws and commerce and even warfare. In the Islamic case, virtually any aspect of culture and civilization is relevant to religion.

The sacred-secular contrast is unhelpful, but for quite different reasons, when we consider Chinese thought of 2,500 years ago. The principal contribution of Confucius and his early successors was a humane social ethic: what in the West we might consider moral philosophy. Admittedly, Confucius made rhetorical references to Heaven, but he seems to have been rather agnostic about much of traditional religion and ritual in his day.

Confucius is probably as closely parallel to the Greek philosopher Socrates as to any Western figure we might name. For us in the West, Socrates is part of the Hellenic ('secular'?) heritage of our culture, as distinct from our cultural roots in the religion of the ancient Hebrews. But the tradition stemming from Confucius's teachings became quite unmistakably religious in the course of later centuries, when the Neo-Confucians cultivated an inner personal spirituality and speculated on the ultimate nature of things.

A third Christian expectation concerning 'religion' is the notion of exclusive membership. That God should demand loyalty and tolerate no rivals is part of the faith of Judaism, passed on to Christianity and Islam. Each of these three has been at pains to demarcate the boundaries of its community. However, a notion that if you follow one tradition, you cannot also follow another is not one that has always applied across southern and eastern Asia.

For understanding the Sikh tradition, this matter is doubly relevant. The early Sikhs were disciples of a teacher who saw God as transcending all forms, including the boundaries of human communities of worshippers—limits made prominent by the coming of Islam, a boundaried religion, to India. Four centuries after their founding teacher, however, some Sikh leaders were seeking strenuously to define their community in contrast to a Hindu population with whom they had a great deal in common. And five centuries after that teacher, misery persists as Sikhs contend that full recognition of that identity has been denied them.

Do boundaries help us to understand Japan? Studies report that only a small percentage of its population consider themselves as belonging to any religion, yet when surveys ask whether one follows Buddhist or Shinto or other rituals and practices, the positive responses add up to more people than there are in the country.

## The Roster of Religions

Perhaps we can arrive at a definition or characterization of religion in general by looking at its most commonly cited examples. In our times, the most widespread and widely recognized examples include those we have been surveying in this two-volume series.

As eighteenth- and early nineteenth-century handbooks show, European practice was content for three centuries after the 1490s to retain its fourfold classification of religions into Christianity, Judaism, Islam, and paganism. Over time, the category of 'pagan' expanded vastly, as new discoveries in Asia, Africa, and the Americas were added to the literary record of the ancient Mediterranean world and to folkloric survivals of pre-Christian northern Europe. Moreover, there was a shift from initial description of rituals and ceremonies to the inclusion also of philosophically sophisticated doctrines as some texts in Asian languages came to be known in Europe.

The category of 'pagan' was being stretched to the bursting point. As with stress building up along an earthquake fault, a realignment would have to come sooner or later. Probably the increase of information about doctrines, relying substantially on textual sources, was what precipitated the drawing of a new picture. One of the first books in English to devote a chapter to each of half a dozen major traditions was written in 1846 by a versatile Anglican theological scholar, Frederick Denison Maurice (1805–72).

The idea of the 'great' or 'living' or 'world' religions was launched, an idea that has continued to the present. The consensus has centred on a set of traditions that have been historically influential and that are still alive today. But for the past century-and-a-half, the expectation has also been that the short-listed traditions have a developed body of doctrine or literature.

There have been fluctuations over time, depending on the judgement of authors and editors and on the information accessible to them. As with any canon, there have been clear nominees, and more marginal cases. Consensus always lists the three great missionary religions of Buddhism, Christianity, and Islam. It has often included the national religious heritages of Israel (Judaism), Iran before Islam (Zoroastrianism), India (Hinduism), and Japan (Shinto). It can also include two distinct communities in India (the Sikhs and the Jains) and two distinct teachings in China (the Confucian and the Taoist).

If we are to consider the traditions omitted from that core consensus, we find three kinds. One type is the religious life of tribal populations. Despite some overall resemblances, it is fragmented and diverse, and its traditions are oral rather than textual. A second type includes the traditions that, no matter how sophisticated their doctrine or rich their mythology, have essentially died out. Manichaeism is one such, as are the religions of ancient Greece and Rome, Mesopotamia and Egypt, Mexico and Peru. The third type includes developments too recent for inclusion in the nineteenth century's canon, such as Japan's new religions and the Bahā'ī faith.

In the future, things may well change. As some of the new religions endure, achieving historical and doctrinal depth, the canon will need reassessment. Moreover, it is conceivable that a pan-tribal synthesis of Native American or possibly African religion could take shape and gain recognition as a 'new' religion.

So, what are the shared characteristics of religions? By distilling religions, can we arrive at an essence of religion?

- Belief in a personal god or spirits? Early Buddhist doctrine—as distinct from southern Buddhist folk religion and northern Buddhist doctrine—lacks this. For Hindu Vedānta, ultimate reality is not personal.
- A path to personal experience of altered consciousness? There is little in the classical Zoroastrian tradition that clearly offers this.
- A cohesive worshipping community? Confucianism seems to be deficient in this regard.
- Divinely sanctioned morality? It is hard to attribute much of this to Shinto.
- An offer of life after death? Classical Hebrew religion hardly promised this.

We have a hard time identifying any feature as a common characteristic, a feature absolutely essential for something to be called a religion. On inspection, consensus is more about which traditions are the standard examples than about what possible common essence those examples exhibit.

If we are going to generate a characterization of religion from even a small repertory of examples, we must not expect any single feature of religion to be shared by all. We may profitably adopt a 'syndrome' approach, along lines familiar in clinical medicine. We would identify as a religion whatever displays a majority of the symptomatic features on a list such as the above.

Such a characterization is fuzzy. From a strict logical and philosophical standpoint, it is unsatisfactory. All the same, it seems to be what Western civilization has meant by 'religion' for 500 years now.

## Defining by Exclusion

Another way of demarcating the sphere of religion starts by considering religion-like activities that we commonly agree are not religion. Observing and contrasting these, perhaps we can identify a distinguishing feature or features of religion in respect of which these other candidates fall short.

The modern Protestant theologian Paul Tillich (1886–1965) gained much attention for his characterization of religion as 'ultimate concern', concern for what ultimately matters most in this world, this life, and beyond. His view has sometimes been distorted to mean that one's highest priority—whatever that is, even golf—is religion, but to Tillich some concerns are validly ultimate and are religion, while other more mundane ones are not. Contrasted with golf, religion has more to do with the overall meaning of the universe and of life in it.

For over seventy years after the Russian revolution of 1917, it seemed to many that the communist system, built on the atheistic socialism of Karl Marx (1818–83), posed a worldwide threat to the future of religion. As implemented after mid-century all the way from Czechoslovakia to China, it repressed traditional religious institutions while at the same time bearing some curious resemblances to religion itself. These resemblances are particularly noticeable *vis-à-vis* the three major Western monotheistic religions: Judaism, Christianity, and Islam.

Communism, like the prophets, seeks to liberate the poor from exploitation and injustice. Communism, like the monotheistic religions, finds direction, meaning, and significance in history. Again like them, it idealizes a future moment when evil is to be overthrown and justice is to prevail. A new order will be ushered in, the classless society corresponding to the kingdom of heaven.

Communism, like traditional religions, wants to state an 'is' and derive from it an 'ought'. There is a huge philosophical difference between descriptive laws of nature, which must be modified to suit the behaviour of phenomena, and prescriptive laws of society, which expect the individual to modify or conform in behaviour and which threaten punishment for failure to do so. Both communism and religion seek the benefits of description and prescription simultaneously. Each sees the order of things as a description of the way things necessarily are, and at the same time proposes to derive from that a prescription of the way individuals should voluntarily behave.

Moreover, communist ideologues have resembled missionaries in their zeal to spread their teaching. The community of the committed participates in group rituals that reinforce solidarity. Intense pressure is brought on individuals to confess and publicly disavow their faults and shortcomings. And the cult of the leader, in the case of China's Chairman Mao Zedong (r. 1949–76), featured a scripturelike use of an anthology of his quotations, a pocket-sized book bound in red.

Yet communism has not thought of itself as a religion, and has shown considerable hostility towards it. In some states, freedom of religion, promised formally, has been ignored in practice, and open identification with any religious community has often been a barrier to party membership. Nor, worldwide, have devotees of religion or students of it commonly considered communism a religion. Communism has been a politico-economic ideology, with analogies to religion in both doctrine and practice.

A key difference is whether a power may exist above or beyond humankind. Religion, characteristically, says yes: the way or power of the universe governs us. Communism has said no; history is human history, and controllable by humans. This postulation of a transhuman power is sometimes termed faith in transcendence. When communism is excluded from status as a religion, it is generally because those who exclude it deem its ideals to lack the essential ingredient of such faith.

It remains to consider one further alternative to 'religion'—namely, philosophy. Are there not philosophies that share with religion the contemplation of ultimate reality? Do not both enterprises seek to map out the good that people should seek in their conduct? In particular, when we look at the Chinese moral teachers in their cultural setting, it is not easy to draw a clear line between philosophy and religion.

If I form a view of the universe or a set of prescriptions for thought and action, I may have stated a personal philosophy, but—at least as I use the term—I have not started a religion. If with a circle of friends and disciples I discuss these views, subjecting them to rational criticism and argument, we may have participated in a philosophical movement, but I do not consider that we have formed a religion. If our group meets on a regular basis, repeating similar conduct each time, we may have ritualized our activity, but we still may not have become a religion. Where do we cross the line?

Part of the difference is that philosophy is an intellectual, rational activity, while religion seeks a commitment of the will and the emotions as well. Philosophy's decisions are by nature decisions for an individual mind to make; many of religion's decisions are made by groups. The rituals of philosophers are seldom essential to the force of their arguments, but the rituals of religion are often seen as creating or confirming centrally important states of affairs.

We can now sum up these efforts at characterizing religion. We have looked at the evolution of our vocabulary, at standard religions as examples, and at some key counterinstances. In so doing, we have been circling our prey. No single line of definition seems to be able to trap it, but we can weave a net.

Religion is a sense of power beyond the human, apprehended rationally as well as emotionally, appreciated corporately as well as individually, celebrated ritually and symbolically as well as discursively, transmitted as a tradition in conventionalized forms and formulations that offers people an interpretation of experience, a guide to conduct, and an orientation to meaning and purpose in the world.

## THEORIES OF RELIGION

Lurking in many efforts to define religion is an implicit attempt to explain it. In effect if not in intent, the characteristics one selects as the essential identifying features of religion are often taken as explanations of religion's origins or of its current function.

We should start by remarking what an explanation is. Generally people offer explanations when there is a perceived mismatch between one's expectations and the facts. Why, one wants to know, have things not turned out as we thought they would?

A number of classic theories of religion are attempts to explain why human beings are religious. That is not commonly something that a religious person thinks needs explaining at all. If somebody is offering a general explanation of religion, we should be on the lookout to see how that person is putting some distance between himself or herself and religion.

## Some Ancient Explanations of Religion

In the ancient Greek and Roman world, a tradition of distance from religion can be observed. One element in this was the description of the religion of other peoples by historians and geographers. This inevitably introduced an element of cultural distance.

Among the ancient Greek philosophers, we see theorizing about the religious myths and practices of Greek culture itself. The philosophers were distancing themselves from beliefs popular among the masses. An early example is this critique of religion's anthropomorphism by Xenophanes of Colophon (c. 570–475 BCE):

> If oxen, or lions, or horses had hands like men, they too,
> If they could fashion pictures, or statues they could hew,
> They would shape in their own image each face and form divine—
> Horses' gods like horses, like kine the gods of kine.
> 'Snub-nosed are the Immortals, and black,' the Ethiops say;
> But 'No,' the Thracians answer, 'red-haired, with eyes of grey.'
> (Lucas 1951:257)

Numerous classical writers subsequently interpreted the details of their own culture's myths as allegorical representations of the forces of nature. One of them, Plutarch (46?–120?), compared Egyptian mythology with the Greek and Roman.

Another interpretation of myths was offered by Euhemerus (c. 330–c. 260 BCE). He imaginatively describes finding on an island in the Indian Ocean a column with a long inscription. Purportedly written by the god Zeus himself, the text says that the gods were originally men and women, deified and worshipped during their own lifetimes, with worship continuing after their deaths.

Euhemerism, the idea that the gods are deified humans, has continued to crop up through the centuries.

The ancient world therefore anticipated some of the stances regarding religion that have come to the fore in the modern Western world in the last several centuries, a period of rationalistic thought whose spirit we characterize by referring to it as the Enlightenment.

## Philosophical Speculation on Religion

Edward, Lord Herbert (1583–1648), baron of Cherbury in England, was a forerunner of the philosophical movement known as Deism. The Deists were ready to believe in God as a powerful and intelligent creator, but were disinclined to suppose that after creating the universe, God subsequently intervenes in its operation. In Herbert's view, traditional religious forms and institutions are misleading. However, we are led to revere God and conform to morality because of how human reason is structured; people have what he calls 'common notions'.

> All these considerations depend upon Common Notions. Can anyone, I beg to ask, read the huge mass of books composed with such immense display of learning, without feeling scorn for these age-long impostures and fables, save in so far as they point the way to holiness? What man could yield unquestioning faith to a body which, disguised under the name of the Church, wastes its time over a multitude of rites, ceremonies and vanities, which fights in so many parts of the world under different banners, if he were not led to perceive, by the aid of conscience, some marks of worship, piety, penance, reward and punishment? Who, finally, would attend to the living voice of the preacher if he did not refer all his deeds and words to the Sovereign Deity (*De Veritate*, Carré 1937)?

The German philosopher Immanuel Kant (1724–1804) studied and taught in Königsberg in East Prussia, now Russia's Kaliningrad and separated from Germany by Poland. Historians of philosophy regularly refer to his contribution as a 'watershed'. He demonstrated that one cannot gain knowledge of the transcendent through the operation of reason on the data received through the senses. Hence, by their very nature, religious affirmations are unprovable. Yet in considering moral action, Kant argued, we suppose God to exist if rewards for altruistic action are to make any sense. For Kant, it is not cognitive reason but rather the operation of moral will that makes people religious.

Friedrich Schleiermacher (1768–1834) studied and taught in Germany. The literary and intellectual currents of his day included romanticism, an emphasis on feeling. What Kant had said could not be demonstrated could nonetheless be felt; so intuitive feelings account for why humans are religious. As Schleiermacher put it:

> This idea [the term God], which is nothing more than the expression of the feeling of absolute dependence, is the most direct reflection upon it and the most original idea with which we are here concerned, and is quite independent of that original knowledge (properly so called), and conditioned only by our feeling of absolute dependence (Mackintosh 1928:17).

Prior to the middle of the nineteenth century, in the examples we have been citing, European explanation of human religiousness was devoted largely to considerations of European culture. If one was to show religion to be humanly appropriate, one was generally justifying a form of Christianity known within Europe. Moreover, such efforts were speculative; they were armchair reflections on data in the ambient culture, and did not seek nor give important consideration to the data concerning religion from distant parts of the world.

## Nineteenth-Century Developmental Theories

The modern comparative study of religion reflects a crosscultural perspective. Observations of exotic custom and ritual had been available since the sixteenth century, but by the nineteenth a significant number of Indian and Chinese philosophical and doctrinal texts were being translated into European languages. The German Sanskritist Friedrich Max Müller (1823–1900), who taught in England, was the organizer of an ambitious fifty-volume translation series, the *Sacred Books of the East*.

A pioneer in the study of comparative mythology, Müller located religion's origins in the language of myth. He was persuaded that the *Vedas*, the hymns of the Aryans, are our oldest literature and, as such, closest to the origin of religion.

> How does the fact, that the Aryan languages possess this treasure of ancient names in common, or even the discovery that all these names had originally an expressive and poetical power, explain the phenomenon of mythological language among all the members of this family? How does it render intelligible that phase of the human mind which gave birth to the extraordinary stories of gods and heroes,—of gorgons and chimæras,—of things that no human eye had ever seen, and that no human mind in a healthy state could ever have conceived (Müller 1869–85:ii.53)?

In his view, the imprecision of references to the phenomena of nature traps people into the personification of natural qualities as entities and forces. Names, he said, become deities. Religion, for Müller, is 'a disease of language', but if one is truly modern, one is exempt from it.

Among Müller's contemporaries, there were others who also saw religion as rooted in attempts to explain natural phenomena, and who employed cross-cultural data. Intellectual excitement was generated by the theory of biological evolution (Charles Darwin, 1809–82; *The Origin of Species*, 1859), and some turned their efforts to tracing evolutionary patterns in human culture as well.

The Englishman Edward Burnett Tylor (1832–1917) became fascinated with Native culture while visiting the Caribbean and Central America, and went on to become a pioneer in the emerging field of anthropology. He became convinced that a common denominator among the cultures he observed was belief in spirits, for which he coined the term 'animism'. In writings such as his 1871 book *Primitive Culture*, he elaborated a view of animism as the simple and essential feature of all religion, from which even the most complex forms of religion are developments.

Tylor's theory sees early humans as reasoning about their experience and environment. Observing the difference between a living person and a dead body, or between waking and dream experiences, Tylor argues, people must have identified the soul as something that can inhabit the body but can also act independently of it. Supposing souls also to be present in animals, plants, or natural phenomena, people classify and organize them until arriving at the idea of cosmic spirits and high gods. The importance Tylor attached to observing belief in spirits has remained influential among anthropologists, even when they have not been persuaded of the evolutionary aspects of his theory.

James Frazer (1854–1941), who began as a British classical scholar, was among those who looked elsewhere than to animism for the origin, and therefore presumably the essential nature, of religion. Frazer's assemblage of anthropological and folkloric information, *The Golden Bough*, was first published in 1890 and was expanded to twelve volumes in 1907–15. Frazer spurred an interest in the relationship between myth and ritual, but his principal theoretical position was that magic lies at the root of religion.

Magic is in important ways like modern applied science: its practitioner seeks to control occurrences in the world. It presumes a cause-and-effect relationship between manipulative activity and observed change. The difference between magic and science is that magic is unsophisticated or mistaken in what it understands as the causal factors.

Sometimes, by coincidence, the magical methods appear to work. This is taken as validation of the technique, just as cures 'prove' faith-healing as a technique (but a failure to cure is held only to prove insufficiency of faith). Sometimes magical methods do not work, occasioning an attitude of fear and awe contributing to religion. Religion, for many in Frazer's day, was sustained by the mystery of the unexplained, and as science was continually making new discoveries, religion's sphere could be expected to dwindle. Frazer could be snide and supercilious in his confidence that we moderns know better than to agree with the beliefs of those we study.

The family of Émile Durkheim (1858–1917) had expected him to become a rabbi, but his studies with a prominent classical social historian in Paris confirmed his preference to think sociologically rather than theologically. Indeed, Durkheim became a major pioneer in sociology. In his mature command of the field, he produced an extremely influential work, *The Elementary Forms of the Religious Life* (1912), which locates the origin and the essence of religion in the identity of the social group.

Influenced by the evolutionary thinking of his day, Durkheim chose to describe Australian Aborigines, a population dependent for subsistence on the food they could gather and the quarry they could hunt. Since plants and animals were domesticated in the neolithic era more than 10,000 years ago, presumably these Aborigines were survivors from an early stage of human cultural evolution generally. Might not their religion therefore illustrate what religion was like in prehistory, before civilizations developed?

Central to Australian religion is the concept of clan membership. The key term used in theorizing about it—'totem'—is not of Australian origin, but was picked up from the Ojibway, an Algonkian Indian people in eastern North America, but its denotation, clan membership, is appropriate. A totem is characteristically a plant or animal species with which the clan group is identified. It is often set apart as protected, to be killed or eaten only at particular ritual occasions or by particular ritual specialists. Durkheim sees the totem as the symbolic projection of the clan identity itself:

> The totem is before all a symbol, a material expression of something else ... it is the outward and visible form of what we have called the totemic principle or god. But it is also the symbol of the determined society called the clan ... So if it is at once the symbol of the god and of the society, is that not because the god and the society are only one? ... The god of the clan, the totemic principle, can therefore be nothing else than the clan itself, personified and represented to the imagination under the visible form of the animal or vegetable which serves as totem (Durkheim 1915:206).

One year after Durkheim's *Elementary Forms* came out, the Viennese psychoanalyst Sigmund Freud (1856–1939) published *Totem and Taboo*, a study locating in a prehistoric 'primal horde' the roots of interpersonal conflict that he observed clinically in the case histories of individual patients. Somewhat in the way evolutionary biology had matched the development of the species and the development of the individual organism, Freud was proposing that the early social development of the human community paralleled the childhood struggles of individuals.

Few among Freud's followers, or even Freud throughout his own career, have consistently maintained the primal-horde theory. However, Freud's general view of religion as infantile dependence and wishful thinking has had wide influence. For instance, the American anthropologist Weston La Barre (b. 1911), in his book *The Ghost Dance: Origins of Religion* (1970), points to the prolonged dependency of the newborn upon the parent after birth as a feature of human life different from that of most species. To a Freudian, it is no surprise at all that religious traditions should portray God as a father or that such a portrayal should produce tension and struggle in personal religious lives.

## Some Twentieth-Century Analyses

In the years after Durkheim wrote, social-scientific theory largely turned away from the quest for origins. Many anthropologists and sociologists have been hesitant to view patterns of tribal societies as unchanged survivals from prehistory. Instead, the emphasis has been on analysing the function of religion in our own era. Akin to Durkheim, but without the evolutionary theory, is the 1966 characterization of 'Religion as a Cultural System' by the American anthropologist Clifford Geertz (b. 1926). The often-cited article expands on each clause of this definition:

> A *religion* is: (1) a system of symbols which acts to (2) establish powerful, pervasive and long-lasting moods and motivations in men by (3) formulating conceptions of a general order of existence and (4) clothing these conceptions with such an aura of factuality that (5) the moods and motivations seem uniquely realistic (Geertz 1966:4).

Many have found Geertz's article a useful mainstream representative of twentieth-century social theory of religion. This is so despite the evident elasticity of some of its wording. Just what, for instance, is an 'aura' of factuality? Just how, exactly, do symbols, rather than people, 'act'? But a strength of the definition is its parallel between clause 4 as intensification of clause 3, and clause 5 as intensification of clause 2.

Twentieth-century social scientists, then, have stood back from the theories of religious origins contributed by their nineteenth-century pioneers. Since about the time of the First World War, they have preferred to speak of religion's social function rather than its prehistoric development. But most have shared with their nineteenth-century predecessors the conviction that religion can be treated as a social and psychological phenomenon and analysed by using conceptual tools from outside religion itself.

## The Role of the Participant

After mid-century, anthropologists increasingly questioned the usefulness, if not the validity, of describing cultural structures in alien terms. Sometimes for intellectual reasons, sometimes for political ones, investigators sought to give voice in cultural description to terms or concepts internal to a tradition or community. They were seeking to bridge the classic gulf between participant and observer.

Borrowed from linguistics, the terms '-etic' and '-emic' were applied to this contrast between techniques. In linguistics, a phonetic description is one that records all gradations and differentiations of sound, regardless of whether they make any difference in meaning in a particular language. A phonemic description, on the other hand, is one that concentrates on distinctions of sound that are heard as meaningful differences by the speakers of a particular language or dialect.

Phonemic description implies a segmenting of the spectrum of sound, but claims that that segmenting accurately represents the objective behaviour of the speech community. Similarly, 'emic' description of cultural structures tries to respect as an object of study the dispositions and outlooks of the social community, themselves often subjective or at least not objectively verifiable. It does so by allowing theoretical structures maintained by the people studied, whose status is initially data, to become preferences in the investigator's handling of the material, and thus to obtain status at the level of theory.

But are the participants in a system always consciously aware of what the system relies on? A common-sense answer must be no. In researching many aspects of human affairs, investigators have repeatedly identified instances where the observer can detect patterns, relationships, and similarities of which the participant is unaware. A member of a Siberian tribe, for instance, may know the tribe's own shaman, but not necessarily be aware of shamanism as a crosscultural phenomenon. The '-emic' descriptions of cultures in what are purportedly their own terms are descriptions chosen, even imposed, by outsiders.

## The Perspective of the Observer

From the 1960s through the 1980s in several fields of cultural studies, 'structuralist' approaches were popular. The term 'structuralism' was multifaceted, its specific sense depending on the field in which one was working, whether anthropology, developmental psychology, linguistics, or literary studies. But a recurring feature of efforts termed 'structuralist', such as those of the French anthropologist Claude Lévi-Strauss (b. 1908), was that the structures proposed had validity if they made sense in the mind of the investigator, regardless of whether they were understood in the minds of tribal populations or were the overtly declared intent of literary texts. James Frazer had thought he knew better than his subjects what they were doing. So had Freud. And so did Lévi-Strauss.

The poststructuralist era emerging in the 1980s in a sense took the assumption 'We know better than you what you are doing' and turned it on the stance of the investigator itself. Twentieth-century scholarship has undergone a kind of politicization, in which the motives of the investigator are analysed as socially and economically determined. Intellectuals are seen as slaves to their political, racial, class, and gender preferences. Scholars are portrayed as career-driven rather than thirsting for understanding. Where one might have assumed a kind of free will in the history of ideas, one is now confronted with a kind of determinism in the sociology of knowledge. To overstate the development only slightly: people do not seek truth, but act out of interests.

Recent discussions along these lines may seem new, but the issues are long-standing. In every age, people have striven to comprehend the world. In every age, people have called for fairness in action and fair criteria in judgement. And the determinists are to a considerable extent right: in every age, people have been influenced by the terms of their own class or community to interpret the world with the unexamined and unchallenged assumptions received through that class or community. As debates continue, people will continue to disagree, while seeking (according to different understandings) to do justice to the data. And we must all go on trying to bring our own unexamined presuppositions to greater awareness.

## Religious Theories of Religion

Adherents of religions have long seen their own message as divinely constituted. However, to advance on philosophical grounds a view that treats various religions simultaneously as God-given is a relatively modern phenomenon.

We can view such a religion-in-general stance as in part a reaction to European social-scientific theories that emerged in the late nineteenth century. Theories such as Tylor's animism or, later, Durkheim's totemism attributed religion to human causes. They saw it as the product of cultural circumstances and psychological needs, a product of the human imagination. Religious people were understandably alarmed at such interpretations of religion; for while many may have been willing to dismiss other people's religions, they were alarmed at the thought of explaining away their own.

Theologians have employed a term to describe this explain-it-away spirit: reductionism. Religion is 'reduced' to the factors claimed to cause it. It is explained in terms other than itself. Theologians and many religion scholars speak of reductionistic arguments as a bad thing. However, before writing them off completely, one should consider what other kinds of arguments, if any, could constitute acceptable explanations. Even '-emic' anthropology, according to our critique above, imposes the outsider's categories on the data.

The theological religion-in-general view was a reaction also to the constraints put on certifying anything as knowledge in European philosophy after Kant. As indicated above, Kant showed that the objects of religion are not susceptible to empirical proof. The French philosopher Auguste Comte (1798–1857) went further, elaborating positivism, a view that the only entities that can be declared to exist are those that admit of such proof. His view was compatible with the spirit of much nineteenth-century science, and many concluded science to be at war with religion.

The German philosopher of religion Rudolf Otto (1869–1937) was profoundly disturbed by the turn-of-the-century trend to explain religion as socially conditioned. In 1910, he wrote an article sharply criticizing a culturally evolutionist multivolume work on ethnic psychology by the German Wilhelm Wundt (1832–1920), a work that, interestingly enough, Durkheim admired greatly.

Otto's principal statement was *The Idea of the Holy*, which came out in 1917 and became a theological best-seller. Otto wrote in the tradition of Schleiermacher, who viewed religion as intuitive feeling. In his book Otto gave some structure to that feeling. He characterized human awareness of the divine as that of an overpowering yet fascinating mystery. The term he coined for that, a sense of the 'numinous', continues in use. Otto described the divine power as experienced across various traditions, even if in his own exposition he gave a privileged place to Christian examples of it.

Gerardus van der Leeuw (1890–1950), a theologian and historian of religions who taught in Holland, published a wide-ranging survey in 1933 whose English title is *Religion in Essence and Manifestation*. Like Otto, Van der Leeuw treats religion as response to a divine stimulus; he speaks of it as Power. And as with Otto, Christian examples appear as the definitive ones for Van der Leeuw.

In his treatment, Van der Leeuw classifies the material topically, gathering together material from various religions dealing with the soul, myth, magic, and so on. Collecting and classifying examples across the religions was hardly a novelty with Van der Leeuw. One of his teachers, the Dutchman Pieter Daniel Chantepie de la Saussaye, had carried out a similarly taxonomic project with his *Manual of the Science of Religion* in 1887–9. But for Van der Leeuw's work in the 1930s his German publisher used the title 'Phenomenology of Religion', and the term 'phenomenology' has been applied to this type of enterprise ever since.

This term, 'phenomenology', had already gained a specialized meaning in continental European philosophy. Established by Edmund Husserl (1859–1938), who taught in Germany, the phenomenological movement was primarily concerned with theoretical problems of knowledge. Entities, one says, present themselves to our consciousness; we should suspend critical judgement as to whether they really exist, and treat what presents itself as an overall pattern in its totality.

Philosophical phenomenology, focusing on the cognitive process, thus had a different agenda than the phenomenology of religion, concerned mainly with the information being categorized. But some religion scholars attempted to link the two enterprises, finding in what the philosophers had said about allowing patterns to display themselves a justification for using religion's (or religions') own terms to portray religion. Religion could be analysed, they seemed to say, without being reduced to something else.

Influential along these lines was the Romanian Mircea Eliade (1907–86), who worked after mid-century in Paris and then Chicago. Eliade's extensive output of comparative writing, drawing particularly on Hindu and tribal traditions, is descriptive rather than theoretical. Others termed his work phenomenological, though he chose to call himself a 'historian' of religions. Terminology aside, the lineage in which Eliade can be placed is that of Otto, who had spoken of religiosity as a response to the holy, and Van der Leeuw, who described a response to power. Eliade presents the variety of religions as responses to the sacred—a sacred that he allows the reader to understand like Otto's holy as a transcendent reality, in contrast with the sacred analysed as a human social construct by Durkheim.

Do the religions ultimately say the same thing? In the view of these religious theorists, the answer seems to be yes. The sacred or the holy is what the religions all point to, despite their vast variety.

## Some Prominent Similarities

In discussing the possible unity of religions, another line of investigation is to observe in what kinds of circumstances claims have been made for their fundamental similarity and in what kinds of circumstances people have asserted key differences.

One does not have to look far for situations in which religions are treated as different. Every community that conducts missionary activity is implicitly asserting this. Not only must the difference be perceptible enough that the target audience can be expected to notice it, but it must ultimately be important enough that the missionary's dedicated activity, sometimes in the face of rejection or danger, will have been worth the sacrifice.

Non-proselytizing communities can also assert fundamental differences among religions. This happens, for instance, when religion is closely linked with national identity, as in the case of Shinto. It is not common for a participant in Shinto, subscribing to the characteristically Japanese idea that Japan's heritage is unique, to make the theoretical assertion that all religions are essentially the same. But it is common for Japanese individuals to participate in the rituals of more than one religion at different times, drawing on each tradition for its distinctive benefits.

One approach towards difference among religions that interests philosophers in particular has been to identify opposing claims on particular issues made in different traditions. In cases where religions have become established in geographical areas remote from each other, one might be able to push the problem aside. One could say that any differences between Confucian and Christian notions of duty and morality, for instance, are accidental because of the different cultural vocabularies in which they are expressed. More ambitiously, one could attempt to harmonize Shinto and Hebrew biblical narratives of creation, taking virtually all details as metaphorical.

But sooner or later, one must face up to outright disagreements within a particular time, place, and vocabulary. For example, Hindus assert the reality of the self; even in Vedānta, while individual identity is seen as illusory, it merges with reality in a cosmic self. Early Buddhist doctrine, on the other hand, totally repudiated the human self as a persisting reality. Buddhists and Hindus shared much: monastic asceticism, for instance, and the notion of cyclical rebirth. However, their difference over the self is a stumbling block to any facile equation of religions.

Another unmistakable and comparably central difference exists between Christianity and Islam on the subject of divine incarnation. For Christians, Jesus is the son of God, a manifestation of God's very nature in a human life. For Muslims, the absolute otherness of God forbids the association of any other being with God at God's level. The *Qur'ān* (112:3) explicitly states that God does not beget and is not begotten. There is even a charming passage in the *Qur'ān* (5:116) where God is to ask Jesus at the day of judgement, 'Did you tell them you were to be worshipped as divine?' and Jesus is to reply, 'No; why would I ever tell them such a thing?'

In the face of such differences as this, people still assert religion's fundamental unity. Traditions still assert such things as the Hindu saying, 'Truth is one; the sages call it by different names.' (This, it has been observed, is not necessarily quite as generous as it sounds, for often the subtext is 'We know this better than anyone else.') We need to consider whether the fundamental unity of religions is asserted as a rhetorical or apologetic claim, as this saying could be read. Or is it a matter of revelation, or a moral necessity, both of which are things the Bahā'ī tradition has been interpreted as saying? Is it a conclusion that we might propose could be substantiated from our comparative data?

## A Similarity of 'Ways'

I incline towards claiming one similarity, if not unity, among major religions in terms of the dedication they seek from their adherents.

As late as the 1950s, two things constituted religion in the minds of many active Christians. One of these was termed 'works'—that is, what one did ritually and ethically. The other was termed 'faith', by which many meant what one believed, the doctrine to which one gave assent.

In the 1960s, the consciousness revolution introduced a third term, which for a generation now has stood alongside faith and works. One can term it 'experience'—that is, how one has felt intensely. Some in the sixties sought feeling in religio-chemical ecstasy through experimentation with hallucinogenic substances; more recent decades have looked back on the sixties as both rebellious and naïve in this quest. Others looked to exotic cultures for depths of experience they considered the West to lack: to Zen, for instance, and Sufism, and yoga. By the early seventies, charismatic movements tapping sources of 'feeling' internal to Western Christian tradition were gaining ground in some previously staid denominations. In any event, the third term, experience, has persisted in the way we have thought about religion for a generation now.

We turn for comparison to a development in the Hindu tradition 2,000 years ago. The *Bhagavad Gītā* is a remarkable text not only for its literary beauty and its religious depth but for the skilful synthesis that it advocates among three alternative 'ways' in religion. There is the way of works, *karma mārga*, corresponding in both ethics and ritual to the works expected in my tradition. There is the way of knowledge, *jnana marga*, corresponding to the doctrinal or faith affirmations expected of me and my peers. And then the *Gītā* outlines the way of devotion, *bhakti mārga*, presenting it as the climax and fulfilment of the other two ways. The experiential and devotional aspect of religion has constituted Hinduism's principal appeal over the centuries since.

Similar paths or emphases can be located in Islam, though not grouped in a triad as a formula or slogan. Much of the practice of Islam can be subsumed under the *sharī'ah* or law, which one follows in ritual and conduct; *kalām* or philosophical theology; and Sufism, the mystical tradition, which has had the most popular appeal. Indeed, Ṣūfī devotion provided Islam's entrée to the Hindu and Buddhist culture of Malaysia and Indonesia. Devotional Islam, Sufism, was also a prime basis for understanding and rapport between the Muslim ruling minority and the Hindu majority population of medieval northern India.

If there is a common denominator among the religions, it is humankind. Human action, human thought, and human devotion.

The unity-and-diversity question is not a pseudo-question. Nor, from what we have seen, can it be answered with a simple yes or no. Adding up the comparisons among religions is, in the end, a balance of similarities and differences. While the religions are not in detail the same, they are similar in some important respects. And the unity-diversity question does not boil down to mere wordplay. It is a serious question, of fundamental moral, political, and intellectual significance for the world we live in.

## FURTHER READING

al Fārūqī, I.R., and D.E. Sopher, eds. 1974. *Historical Atlas of the Religions of the World.* New York: Macmillan.

de Vries, J. 1967. *The Study of Religion: A Historical Approach.* New York: Harcourt, Brace & World.

Eliade, M., ed. 1987. *The Encyclopedia of Religion,* 16 vols. New York: Macmillan.

*Le Grand Atlas des Religions.* 1988. Paris: Encyclopaedia Universalis.

Hastings, J., ed. 1908–26. *Encyclopaedia of Religion and Ethics,* 13 vols. Edinburgh: Clark.

Lessa, W.A., and E.Z. Vogt, eds. 1979. *Reader in Comparative Religion: An Anthropological Approach,* 4th ed. New York: Harper & Row.

Philips, C.H., ed. 1963. *Handbook of Oriental History.* London: Royal Historical Society.

Sharpe, E.J. 1975. *Comparative Religion: A History.* London: Duckworth.

## REFERENCES

Carré, M.H., trans. 1937. *Herbert of Cherbury, De Veritate.* Bristol: J.W. Arrowsmith for the University of Bristol.

Durkheim, E. 1915. *The Elementary Forms of the Religious Life.* London: Allen & Unwin.

Geertz, C. 1966. 'Religion as a Cultural System'. In *Anthropological Approaches to the Study of Religion,* edited by M. Banton, 1–46. London: Tavistock.

Lucas, F.L., trans. 1951. *Greek Poetry for Everyman.* London: Dent.

Mackintosh, H.R., trans. 1928. *The Christian Faith* by Friedrich Schleiermacher. Edinburgh: T. & T. Clarke.

Mueller, F.M. 1869–85. *Chips from a German Workshop,* 5 vols. New York: Scribner.

Appendix One

# Transliteration of South Asian Terms

## South Asian Languages

Sanskrit is a classical language of the Hindu, Buddhist, and Jain traditions. Its structure and much of its vocabulary derive from the speech of the people called Aryans (or Indo-Europeans), who invaded the Indian subcontinent from the northwest prior to 1000 BCE. It was used for formal expression and scholarly writing in classical India, but was not widely spoken by the masses. Instead, vernaculars that linguists call 'prakrits' developed, such as Pali, the language of many Buddhist texts.

Hindi, Bengali, Gujarati, Marathi, Punjabi, and other modern vernacular languages of northern India basically owe their origin to prakrits. Tamil and other languages of southern India, however, belong to a quite separate linguistic group, the Dravidian, reflecting a presence in India prior to the Indo-European migration.

### South Asian Terms and Names

With only minor variations, Western students of Asia use a system of diacritical marks to render Sanskrit terms and names in our Latin alphabet. In this text, we employ these diacritics, in order to familiarize the reader with the forms one will encounter when consulting references and reading further. We do not, however, use diacritics for current geographical names or for personal names from the nineteenth and twentieth centuries in India, where spellings have been established through use in English in India.

The vowels of Sanskrit transliteration can be loosely approximated with the vowel sounds of Italian, familiar to many readers through musical terms or through the names of Italian foods.

The chief counterintuitive exception is the distinction between long and short *a*. When marked long, Sanskrit *ā* is pronounced as in 'father'; but the unmarked *a* is like the short neutral sound of various English vowels that lose their flavour when unaccented, such as the *a* in 'soda' or the *e* in 'belong'. This is true even when short *a* carries the stress accent of the word. Thus *candra*, Sanskrit for 'moon', rhymes with the English word 'tundra', and the name of the lawgiver Manu rhymes with a rapid pronunciation of 'the one who'.

Also belonging in the vowel category is *ṛ*, which looks like a consonant to native speakers of English. Perhaps surprisingly, the sounds of English include the same vowel, for instance in 'word' and 'bird'.

Among the consonants, *c* is a surprise; it is pronounced as in 'cello', that is, like 'ch' in the English word 'charm'.

There are two diacritics that occur with the letter 's'; their sounds are distinct, but the distinction is lost on ears attuned to English. For practical purposes, the first sound of the English word 'ship' will serve for both *ś* as in Śiva and *ṣ* as in Kṛṣṇa.

An *ṃ* with a dot beneath it, and either *ṁ* or *ṅ* with dots above, are nasalized, roughly like the *n* in the French expression *en masse*.

The *h* following a consonant represents aspiration, a puff of breath. Thus the sequence *th* is pronounced as in English 'pothole', the sequence *kh* as in English 'blockhead', and *bh* as in 'clubhouse'.

As a general rule, the next-to-last syllable of a word will attract the stress or accent, provided that it contains a long vowel (for example, *saṃsāra*) or could be considered closed with a final consonant (for example, Brahmaputra). If the next-to-last syllable has a short vowel and is not closed with a consonant, the accent is drawn back to the third-to-last syllable (for example, *Rāmāyaṇa* and *Mahābhārata*).

Appendix Two

# East Asian Dynastic Eras and Transliteration of Chinese Terms

## East Asian History

The following partial list of dynastic eras in East Asian history includes those that the reader is likely to encounter most often in the dating of religious and cultural developments.

China

| | |
|---|---|
| Shang | c. 1766–1112 BCE |
| Chou/Zhou | 1122–249 BCE |
| Han | 206 BCE–220 CE |
| T'ang | 618–907 |
| Sung/Song | 960–1269 |
| Ming | 1368–1644 |
| Ch'ing/Qing | 1644–1911 |

Korea

| | |
|---|---|
| Paekche and Koguryo, to 668 | |
| Silla | 668–935 |
| Koryo | 918–1259 |
| Yi | 1392–1910 |

Japan

| | |
|---|---|
| Nara | 730–84 |
| Heian | 794–1160 |
| Kamakura | 1185–1333 |
| Tokugawa | 1600–1867 |
| Meiji | 1868–1912 |

# EAST ASIAN NAMES

In Chinese, Korean, Japanese, and Vietnamese usage, one's family name goes first, before one's personal name. Thus the modern Chinese leader Mao Tse-tung/Mao Zedong would be Chairman Mao in formal usage, Zedong only in intimate (what Westerners would call 'first name') contexts.

# TRANSLITERATION OF CHINESE WORDS AND NAMES

Materials on China in English employ two distinct transliteration systems, known as Wade-Giles and Pinyin.

In this text, the Wade-Giles system is used throughout, with the exception of a few common names of cities and provinces (e.g., Szechwan) whose spellings deviating from technical transliteration have been established through widespread usage. Usually at the first occurrence of a name or term, if the difference between the two systems of transliteration for that term is significant, the Pinyin spelling is also given following a diagonal stroke.

## Wade-Giles

The Wade-Giles system has been in use for much of the twentieth century among scholars of Chinese history, literature, and philosophy writing in the English-speaking world. It is also close to the system currently used in Taiwan's contact with the West for personal names and in commercial and technical as well as cultural fields. Even if the system were given up tomorrow, one would need to deal with it for at least a generation because of the many reference works and library catalogues that have been produced using it.

To speakers of English, the chief counterintuitive feature of the Wade-Giles system is its handling of a series of what linguists call unaspirated consonants. That is, these consonants are pronounced in Chinese without being followed by any release of breath. The distinction between aspirated and unaspirated consonants in Chinese carries a distinction in meaning and therefore needs to be noted, whereas in English it is generally automatic according to adjoining sounds and is not significant for meaning. Consider the 'p' sound in the English word 'pin', for instance, and compare it with the 'p' in 'spin'. The native speaker of English will pronounce the first with a puff of breath, the second without. Wade-Giles uses an apostrophe to indicate aspiration; thus, if the first example were a Chinese word, Wade-Giles would spell it *p'in*. To pronounce the corresponding unaspirated consonants written in Wade-Giles without the apostrophe, English speakers generally use the corresponding English consonant that is 'voiced', that is, where the vocal cords vibrate, for in English these, as it happens, are also unaspirated. Thus the word for 'way', *tao*, is pronounced like the English name Dow. So the aspirated English sounds p–t–k–ts–ch are rendered in Wade-Giles transliteration as *p'–t'–k'–ts'–ch'*, while what is written as *p–t–k–ts–ch* in Wade-Giles transliteration would be pronounced b–d–g–dz–j.

Also, among the consonants, a faintly Parisian-sounding *r* is spelled *j* by Wade-Giles. And the quaint-looking *hs* is a kind of 'sh'.

There are some surprises among the vowels as well: *ou* is pronounced like English 'owe', *ui* is like English 'way', and *iu* is like 'yeo'. Moreover, strange things happen when *e* as a single vowel precedes *n*: it is then pronounced like the 'u' in 'fun'.

## Pinyin

This system was promoted for official and administrative purposes in the People's Republic of China in the 1960s. Attempts to replace with it the characters of the traditional Chinese writing system proved abortive because China's non-phonetic characters more successfully bridged dialect differences. Pinyin began to gain currency in the West with the growth of diplomatic and trade relationships with the PRC in the 1970s. It is now standard in journalistic writing and is gradually becoming established in academic textbooks and reference works, more quickly in the social sciences than in the humanities.

Pinyin's consonants have one or two equivalents that look more like Portuguese than English. That may not be inappropriate, given the fact that the Portuguese were among the first Europeans to initiate contact with China in the sixteenth century. The resource used when Pinyin was developed was the very technical International Phonetic Alphabet, first introduced by European linguists in 1888.

There are four consonantal values in Pinyin that stand out as counterintuitive to speakers of English: *q* is like the *ch* in 'cheese'; *x* is like the *sh* in 'sheep'; *c* is like the *ts* in 'nuts'; and *zh* is like the *j* in 'junk'.

Among the vowels, the full list of surprises given earlier for Wade-Giles also applies to Pinyin. There are two more for Pinyin: *ia* before *n* (but not before *ng*) is pronounced like *ye* in 'yet'; and while *i* is normally like the *i* in 'machine', after *c, ch, r, s, sh, z,* and *zh*, it becomes like the *i* in 'sir'. Here are some examples illustrating the principles:

| *Wade-Giles* | *Pinyin* | *Sound, informally in English* |
|---|---|---|
| jen | ren | run |
| T'ien | Tian | tyenn |
| ch'i-kung | qigong | chee-goong |
| Hsün-tzu | Xunzi | shoon-dzuh |
| Chuang-tzu | Zhuangzi | dzhwang-dzuh |
| Po Chü-i | Bo Juyi | bo dzhoo-yee |

# ACKNOWLEDGEMENTS

W.G. ASTON. Extracts from *Nihongi: Chronicles of Japan from the Earliest Times to A.D. 697*, translated by W.G. Aston (Kegan Paul/Charles E. Tuttle Co., Inc., 1896).

A. BLOOM. Extract from *Shinran's Gospel of Pure Grace* by A. Bloom. Copyright © 1965. Reprinted by permission of University of Arizona Press.

D. BODDE. Extracts from 'Myths of Ancient China' by Derk Bodde in *Mythologies of the Ancient World*, edited by S.N. Kramer. Reprinted by permission of Doubleday, a division of Bantam Doubleday Dell Publishing Group, Inc.

J. CARMAN and V. NARAYANAN. Extract from *The Tamil Veda: Pillan's Interpretation of the Tiruvāymoḷi* translated by John Carman and Vasudha Narayanan (Chicago: University of Chicago Press, 1989). © 1989 by The University of Chicago.

W. CHAN. Extracts from *A Source Book in Chinese Philosophy* by W. Chan (Princeton: Princeton University Press, 1963) © 1963 renewed 1991 by Princeton University Press. Reprinted by permission. Extract from *Instructions for Practical Living* by W. Chan. Copyright © 1967 by Columbia University Press. Reprinted with permission of the publisher.

K.K.S. CH'EN. Extracts from *Buddhism in China* by K.K.S. Ch'en (Princeton: Princeton University Press, 1964). Reprinted by permission of Princeton University Press.

J. CHING. Extract from *To Acquire Wisdom* by J. Ching. Copyright © 1976 by Columbia University Press. Reprinted with permission of the publisher.

W.O. COLE and P.S. SAMBHI. Extract from *The Sikhs: Their Religious Beliefs and Practices* by W.O. Cole and P.S. Sambhi (Routledge and Kegan Paul/Kegan Paul International Ltd, UK, 1978).

W.T. DE BARY. Extracts from *Sources of Indian Tradition*, edited by William Theodore de Bary. Copyright © 1958 by Columbia University Press. Reprinted with permission of the publisher. Extracts from *Sources of Chinese Tradition*, edited by William Theodore de Bary. Copyright © 1960 by Columbia University Press. Reprinted with permission of the publisher.

W. DONIGER with B.K. SMITH. Extracts from *The Laws of Manu*, translated by W. Doniger with B.K. Smith (Penguin Books Ltd, 1981).

W. DONIGER O'FLAHERTY. Extracts from *The Rig Veda: An Anthology*, selected, translated, and annotated by W. Doniger O'Flaherty (Penguin Books Ltd, 1981).

A.J.A. ELLIOTT. Extract from *Chinese Spirit Medium Cults in Singapore* by A.J.A. Elliott (London: Royal Anthropological Society, 1955). Reprinted by permission of the Royal Anthropological Institute of Great Britain and Ireland.

I.R. al FĀRŪQĪ and D.E. SOPHER. 'Indigenous Religions of the Indian Subcontinent: Hinduism, Buddhism, Jainism, Sikhism' map and 'Indigenous Chinese Religions' map from *Historical Atlas of the Religions of the World*, edited by I.R. al Fārūqī and D.E. Sopher (Macmillan Publishing Company, 1974).

T. HA and G.K. MINTZ. Extracts from *Samguk yusa: Legends and Histories of the Three Kingdoms of Ancient Korea* by T. Ha and G.K. Mintz (Seoul: Yonsei University Press, 1972). Reprinted by permission of Yonsei University Press.

Y.S. HAKEDA. Extract from *Kukai: Major Works* by Yoshito S. Hakeda. Copyright © 1972 by Columbia University Press. Reprinted with permission of the publisher.

D. HAWKES. Extracts from *Ch'u Tz'u: The Songs of the South* by D. Hawkes (Oxford University Press, 1959).

J.S. HAWLEY and M. JUERGENSMEYER. From *Songs of the Saints of India* by John Stratton Hawley and Mark Juergensmeyer, copyright © 1988 by Oxford University Press, Inc. Reprinted by permission.

W. HEISSIG. Extracts from *The Religions of Mongolia* by Walther Heissig, trans./ed. by Samuel, Geoffrey. Copyright © 1980 Routledge & Kegan Paul. Reprinted by permission of the University of California Press and Verlag W. Kohlhammer.

I. HORI. Extract from 'Chronicle of Wei' in *Folk Religion in Japan* by I. Hori, edited by J.M. Kitigawa and A.L. Miller (Chicago: University of Chicago Press, 1968). © 1968 by The University of Chicago.

I.B. HORNER. Extract from *Women under Primitive Buddhism* by I.B. Horner (Dutton, 1930).

E.R. HUGHES and K. HUGHES. Extract from *Religion in China* by E.R. Hughes and K. Hughes (Hutchinson/Random House UK Ltd, 1950).

L. HURVITZ. Extracts from *Scripture of the Lotus Blossom of the Fine Dharma*, translated by Leon Hurvitz. Copyright © 1976 by Columbia University Press. Reprinted with permission of the publisher.

W. JACKSON. Extracts from *Tyagaraja: Life and Lyrics* by W. Jackson (Delhi: Oxford University Press, 1991). Reprinted by permission of Oxford University Press, India.

H. JACOBI. Extracts reprinted from *Jaina Sutras*, translated by H. Jacobi, Clarendon Press, 1895, by permission of Oxford University Press.

D.K. JORDAN and D.L. OVERMYER. Extract from *The Flying Phoenix* by D.K. Jordan and D.L. Overmyer (Princeton: Princeton University Press, 1986). Reprinted by permission of Princeton University Press.

D.C. LAU. Extracts from *The Tao Te Ching* by D.C. Lau (Penguin Books Ltd, 1963).

D.C. LAU. Extracts from *Mencius*, translated by D.C. Lau (Penguin Books Ltd, 1970).

P. LAWRENCE. Extract from 'Cargo Cults' by Peter Lawrence. Excerpted with permission of Simon & Schuster Macmillan from *The Encyclopedia of Religion*, Mircea Eliade, Editor in Chief, Vol. 3, pp. 74–81. Copyright © 1987 by Macmillan Publishing Company.

C. LE BLANC. Extract from *Huai Nan Tzu*, translated by C. Le Blanc (Hong Kong University Press, 1985).

J. LEGGE. Extract reprinted from *Li Ki* by J. Legge, Clarendon Press, 1885 by permission of Oxford University Press.

A. LIPSKI. *The Life and Teachings of Sri Anandamayi Ma* by A. Lipski (Motilal Banarsidass Publishers, 1977).

S. LIU. Extract from *How to Be a Good Communist* by S. Liu (Beijing: Foreign Languages Press, 1951). Reprinted by permission of the publisher.

F.L. LUCAS. Extract from *Greek Poetry for Everyman*, translated by F. Lucas, J.M. Dent, 1951, by permission of J.M. Dent.

M.A. MACAULIFFE. Extract from *The Sikh Religion*, Volume 1, by M.A. Macauliffe, Clarendon Press, 1909, by permission of Oxford University Press.

W.H. McLEOD. Extracts from *Textual Sources for the Study of Sikhism* by W.H. McLeod (Manchester: University of Manchester Press, 1984). Reprinted by permission of the author. Extracts reprinted from *Who Is a Sikh? The Problem of Sikh Identity* by W.H. McLeod, Clarendon Press, 1989, by permission of Oxford University Press. Extracts from *The Evolution of the Sikh Community* by W.H. McLeod (Delhi: Oxford University Press, 1975). Reprinted by permission of Oxford University Press, India.

B.S. MILLER. Extracts from 'On the Immortality of the Soul', 'On the Way of Action', 'On the Mystery and Purpose of Incarnation', and 'On the Nature of God and the Way of Devotion'. From *The Bhagavad Gita*, translated by Barbara Stoller Miller. Copyright © 1986 by Columbia University Press. Reprinted with permission of the publisher.

V.S. NAIPAUL. Extract from article by V.S. Naipaul in *The New York Review of Books*, 25 October 1995.

ÑĀṆAMOLI. *The Life of the Buddha* by Ñāṇamoli (Buddhist Publication Society, 1972).

T. NHAT HANH. Extract reprinted from *The Heart of Understanding: Commentaries on the Prajnaparamita Heart Sutra* by Thich Nhat Hanh (1988) with permission of Parallax Press, Berkeley, California.

N.C. NIELSEN et al., eds. 'Hinduism' map and 'Spread of Buddhism' map adapted from *Religions of the World*, 3rd ed., edited by N.C. Nielsen et al. (St Martin's Press, 1993).

D.Y. PAUL. Extract from *Women in Buddhism* by D.Y. Paul (Asian Humanities Press/Jain Publishing Co., 1979).

S. RADHAKRISHNAN. Extracts from *The Principal Upanisads*, edited by S. Radhakrishnan (Harper & Brothers Publishers/George Allen & Unwin, 1953).

C. RHYS DAVIDS. Extract from *Psalms of the Early Buddhists* by C. Rhys Davids (London: Luzac for Pali Text Society, 1964). Reprinted by permission of the Pali Text Society.

T.W. RHYS DAVIDS. Extract reprinted from *The Questions of King Milinda*, translated by T.W. Rhys Davids, Clarendon Press, 1890, by permission of Oxford University Press. Extract from *Buddhist Sutras*, translated by T.W. Rhys Davids, Clarendon Press, 1881, by permission of Oxford University Press.

R.H. ROBINSON. Extract from 'Buddhism in China and Japan' by R.H. Robinson in *The Concise Encyclopedia of Living Faiths*, edited by R.C. Zaehner. (Hutchinson/Random House UK Ltd, 1959).

F. SCHLEIERMACHER. Extract from *The Christian Faith* by Friedrich Schleiermacher, translated by H.R. Macintosh et al. (Edinburgh: T. & T. Clark, 1928). Reprinted by permission of T. & T. Clark Ltd.

N.-G.K. SINGH. Extracts from *The Feminine Principle in the Sikh Vision of the Transcendent* by N.-G.K. Singh (Cambridge: Cambridge University Press, 1993).

© Cambridge University Press 1993. Reprinted with the permission of Cambridge University Press.

R. TAGORE. From Rabindranath Tagore: *Songs of Kabir*. (New York: Macmillan Publishing Company, 1915). Reprinted by permission of Simon & Schuster.

H. THOMSEN. Extracts from *The New Religions of Japan* by H. Thomsen (Charles E. Tuttle Co., Inc., 1963).

R. TSUNODA. Extracts from *Sources of Japanese Tradition*, edited by R. Tsunoda. Copyright © 1958 by Columbia University Press. Reprinted with permission of the publisher.

A. WALEY. Extracts reprinted from *Chinese Poems* by Arthur Waley, from *The Book of Songs* by Arthur Waley, and from *The Analects of Confucius* by Arthur Waley by permission of HarperCollins Publishers Limited.

B. WATSON. Extracts from *Hsün Tzu: Basic Writings*, translated by Burton Watson. Copyright © 1963 by Columbia University Press. Reprinted with permission of the publisher. Extracts from *Mo Tzu: Basic Writings* by Burton Watson. Copyright © 1963 by Columbia University Press. Reprinted with permission of the publisher. Extracts from *The Complete Works of Chuang Tzu*, translated by B. Watson. Copyright © 1968 by Columbia University Press. Reprinted with permission of the publisher.

A.P. WOLF. Extract from 'Gods, Ghosts and Ancestors' reprinted from *Religion and Ritual in Chinese Society*, edited by A.P. Wolf, by permission of Stanford University Press.

P. YAMPOLSKY. Extracts from *Platform Sutra of the Sixth Patriarch*, translated by Philip Yampolsky. Copyright © 1976 by Columbia University Press. Reprinted with permission of the publisher.

W.A. YOUNG. 'Japan and Korea: Major Cities and Religious Sites' map adapted from W.A. Young, *The World's Religions,* © 1995, p. 211. Reprinted by permission of Prentice-Hall, Upper Saddle River, New Jersey.

Every effort has been made to determine and contact copyright owners. In case of any omissions, the publisher will be pleased to make suitable acknowledgement in future editions.

# Index

Page numbers in **boldface** indicate an illustration.
Page numbers in *italics* indicate a map.